PHONEMES OF AMERICAN SPEECH

Vowels

Front vowels		Back vowels	
SYMBOL	**KEY**	**SYMBOL**	**KEY**
[i]	heed [hid]	[u]	who'd [hud]
[ɪ]	hid [hɪd]	[ʊ]	hood [hʊd]
[e]	hayed [hed]	[o]	hoed [hod]
[ɛ]	head [hɛd]	[ɔ]	hawed [hɔd]
[æ]	had [hæd]	[ɑ]	hod [hɑd]

Central vowels		Diphthongs†	
[ɝ-ɜ]*	hurt [hɝt]	[aɪ]	file [faɪl]
[ʌ]	hut [hʌt]	[aʊ]	fowl [faʊl]
[ɚ-ə]*	under [ʌndɚ]	[ɔɪ]	foil [fɔɪl]
[ə]	about [əbaʊt]	[ju]	fuel [fjul]

Consonants

Stops		Fricatives	
[p]	pen [pɛn]	[f]	few [fju]
[b]	Ben [bɛn]	[v]	view [vju]
[t]	ten [tɛn]	[θ]	thigh [θaɪ]
[d]	den [dɛn]	[ð]	thy [ðaɪ]
[k]	Kay [ke]	[h]	hay [he]
[g]	gay [ge]	[s]	say [se]
[tʃ]	chew [tʃu]	[ʃ]	shay [ʃe]
[dʒ]	Jew [dʒu]	[z]	bays [bez]
		[ʒ]	beige [beʒ]

Nasals and lateral		Glides	
[m]	some [sʌm]	[w]	way [we]
[n]	sun [sʌn]	[hw]	whey [hwe]
[ŋ]	sung [sʌŋ]	[j]	yea [je]
[l]	lay [le]	[r]	ray [re]

* [ɝ] and [ɚ] are the "r-colored" vowels. [ɜ] and [ə] are the pronunciations typical of r vowels in Eastern, Southern, and English speech.

† Does not include the "nondistinctive" and centering diphthongs.

PHONETICS: Theory and Application to Speech Improvement

PHONETICS: Theory and
Application to Speech Improvement

JAMES CARRELL, Ph.D.

Professor of Speech
Director, Speech and Hearing Clinic
University of Washington

WILLIAM R. TIFFANY, Ph.D.

Associate Professor of Speech
Director, Phonetics Laboratory
University of Washington

McGRAW-HILL BOOK COMPANY, INC.

1960   New York   Toronto   London

PHONETICS: Theory and Application to Speech Improvement

PREFACE

Although it might prove difficult to find his counterpart in real life Prof. Henry Higgins, the phonetician in Shaw's *Pygmalion*, at least illustrates in dramatic form the simple truth that better speech is beyond no one. We profess no particular desire to emulate the professor by transforming the Eliza Doolittles of the world, and we certainly deny belonging to the "How now brown cow?" school of speech improvement.

We have attempted, however, to offer some assistance to a considerable and varied group of persons who are concerned in one way or another with what may be called the *form* of speech. These include the English-speaking student—in or out of school—who wishes to speak his native language acceptably, and thus effectively. Next are those who are learning English as a new language and need to become familiar with its patterns. We have had in mind also the speech therapist or teacher, for whom a thorough knowledge of the speech sounds and their dynamics is absolutely essential, and any others who may have reason to inquire into the details of English speech. Finally, it would be gratifying to think that there may be some who would like to know about this aspect of their language as a matter of general culture.

The whole premise of this book is that the acquisition of accurate and effective speech—or the teaching thereof—depends first upon understanding certain principles of speech form and next upon applying them intelligently in learning or teaching the oral use of language. The surest road to effective speech lies in this direction, since the acquisition of good speech involves a good deal more than vocal drill and exercise.

A word of caution: throughout the process of speech improvement one must keep a sense of proportion; there is no single standard of correctness that can be applied, as we shall presently explain. Furthermore, good speech is never to be thought of as a kind of superficial gloss, applied to make the surface shine. It cannot make one a different kind of person. Skill in the mechanics of speech can, however, help one avoid mannerisms and inadequacies of pronunciation or articulation which might stand between the true personality and its full expression. Good speech form naturally can never substitute for *content;* it is an elementary principle that form complements content and makes it effective.

More specifically, the application of phonetics to speech improvement involves a careful study of the sounds of English—their production and the ways in which they change in connected speech—and an understanding of the characteristics of speaking—stress, intonation, and other aspects which will be discussed in due course. As a method, phonetics leads the student to a more nearly accurate perception of speech patterns—the speech sounds individually and in context. As he becomes sophisticated phonetically, he will find himself better able to recognize acceptable speech patterns as he hears them. He is then in a better position to become perceptive about his own speech—a basic requirement in the development of expressive skills.

Although the potential value of such an approach to speech improvement seems to be generally accepted, there has not been an entirely satisfactory text or manual to apply phonetic theory and method, at an appropriate level, to speech improvement. Consequently the gap between the academic and the practical has appeared wide. This is not to find fault with the academic phonetician; he may legitimately and profitably be occupied entirely with the scholarly study of spoken language. However, even those who might wish to bridge theory and practice have found no way to do so. In this text we have at least made an earnest attempt to achieve this goal, believing that the effort is thoroughly worthwhile.

Among those persons who have managed only a bowing acquaintance with phonetics there is some complaint that the whole subject has been made much too complicated and needlessly detailed for anyone whose interests lie more in speaking well than in academic matters. The accusation that a study of phonetic theory is an unnecessarily long and difficult route to speech improvement is quite unfounded, as we hope to demonstrate; it is, instead, the most direct and efficient approach. The charge that phonetic theory has been made unduly obscure may have some evidence for its support. In studying what purport to be elementary discussions of phonetics, one often gets the feeling that they have been written with the assumption that the reader already knows a great deal about the subject. This error also we try earnestly to avoid. At the same time, it is our purpose to present what seems to be sound theory and adequate basic information, including even some reference to research findings. Along with this is an introduction to terminology and principles which should prepare the student for further excursions into phonetic literature, if he finds the subject interesting.

It seems obvious that such a book as this will be of greatest use to the student if he also enjoys the guidance of a skilled teacher. No one can describe the sound of speech accurately by writing about it; speech is something that must be heard, so that written descriptions are not fully meaningful unless they can be supplemented by spoken examples provided by an informed and resourceful instructor.

Nevertheless, we have tried, in so far as possible, to make this text a "do it yourself" book. We have hoped to accomplish this by presenting understandable theory along with liberal exercise materials. No apology is made for this attempt, nor does it seem to us that any supposed demands of scholarship make such an apology necessary. We frankly should like to feel that a student who reads this book and follows its counsel can, with no other help, become a better and more effective speaker. Of course we recognize the practical impossibility of completely achieving such a goal, but it seems to us that this is the manner in which any textbook should be written.

A bibliography has been supplied for the more serious student who wishes to pursue the study of phonetics further, because of an interest in such subjects as speech therapy, experimental phonetics, or linguistics. In this connection, a comment should be made on the system used in this text to record speech. There are at present—and doubtless there always will be—differing schools of thought about the best way to make basic linguistic analyses and about the vocabulary and phonetic symbols to employ in facilitating such study. Many of the differences are superficial, to be sure, but there are also some rather fundamental conflicts on theory.

One of two major schools is represented by those who follow the more traditional, or at least older, type of analysis embodied in the alphabet of the International Phonetic Association. The other, a more recent movement, employs a somewhat different system of notation and is based on some divergent ideas about the nature of speech sounds, individually and in context. An excellent reference in this connection is the book by Trager and Smith.[36]* A second is a comprehensive text on descriptive linguistics by Gleason,[10] which contains a convenient comparison of various methods of recording speech in reasonably common use.

An elaborate discussion of these schools of thought would scarcely be germane to the purpose of this text, but we should like the reader to be aware that they exist and that, at least for some purposes, the system of notation used by Trager and Smith and others has certain advantages over the IPA method. We have chosen to retain the general pattern of analysis imposed by the IPA for several reasons. First, it appears to be better adapted for a simplified treatment, particularly for those whose native language is English, or for those who have already learned English in the traditional way. Second, the IPA notation conforms to the usage

* Superior numbers refer to the references at the end of the book.

and to the symbol systems which are most widely used in phonetic literature. Articulatory and acoustic phonetics employ the IPA method almost exclusively. Finally, there is the very important practical advantage growing out of the fact that what is perhaps the best and most authoritative American pronouncing dictionary, that of Kenyon and Knott,[17] is based on the IPA symbols.

The authors wish to express their thanks for help in arranging the use of broadcast speech samples to John King, secretary, Queen City Broadcasting Company, Seattle; Milo Ryan, professor, School of Communications, University of Washington, and the Columbia Broadcasting System. They are grateful also to Mrs. Frances Howard and Miss Ann Cannon for typing the original manuscript of this book.

Finally, we should like to acknowledge the patience and skill of Mrs. Shirley Risser, who prepared the illustrations.

James Carrell
William R. Tiffany

CONTENTS

TABLE 1. PHONEMES OF AMERICAN SPEECH

Vowels

Front vowels		Back vowels	
SYMBOL	KEY	SYMBOL	KEY
[i]	heed [hid]	[u]	who'd [hud]
[ɪ]	hid [hɪd]	[ʊ]	hood [hʊd]
[e]	hayed [hed]	[o]	hoed [hod]
[ɛ]	head [hɛd]	[ɔ]	hawed [hɔd]
[æ]	had [hæd]	[ɑ]	hod [hɑd]

Central vowels		Diphthongs†	
[ɝ-ɜ]*	hurt [hɝt]	[aɪ]	file [faɪl]
[ʌ]	hut [hʌt]	[aʊ]	fowl [faʊl]
[ɚ-ə]*	under [ʌndɚ]	[ɔɪ]	foil [fɔɪl]
[ə]	about [əbaʊt]	[ju]	fuel [fjul]

Consonants

Stops		Fricatives	
[p]	pen [pɛn]	[f]	few [fju]
[b]	Ben [bɛn]	[v]	view [vju]
[t]	ten [tɛn]	[θ]	thigh [θaɪ]
[d]	den [dɛn]	[ð]	thy [ðaɪ]
[k]	Kay [ke]	[h]	hay [he]
[g]	gay [ge]	[s]	say [se]
[tʃ]	chew [tʃu]	[ʃ]	shay [ʃe]
[dʒ]	Jew [dʒu]	[z]	bays [bez]
		[ʒ]	beige [beʒ]

Nasals and lateral		Glides	
[m]	some [sʌm]	[w]	way [we]
[n]	sun [sʌn]	[hw]	whey [hwe]
[ŋ]	sung [sʌŋ]	[j]	yea [je]
[l]	lay [le]	[r]	ray [re]

* [ɝ] and [ɚ] are the "r-colored" vowels. [ɜ] and [ə] are the pronunciations typical of r vowels in Eastern, Southern, and English speech.

† Does not include the "nondistinctive" and centering diphthongs.

TABLE 2. OTHER SYMBOLS OF THE INTERNATIONAL PHONETIC ALPHABET

Vowels

SYMBOL	APPROXIMATE DESCRIPTION	SYMBOL	APPROXIMATE DESCRIPTION
[y]	Lip rounded [i]	[ɒ]	Lip rounded [ɑ]
[Y]	Lip rounded [ɪ]	[ɤ]	Unrounded [o]
[ɨ]	"Dull" centralized [ɪ]	[ɯ]	Unrounded [u]
[φ]	Lip rounded [e]	[ɨ]	High-central, unrounded, between [i] and [u]
[œ]	Lip rounded [ɛ]		
[a]	Unrounded, between [æ] and [ɑ]	[ʉ]	Same, lip rounded

Consonants

Stop consonants

SYMBOL*	APPROXIMATE DESCRIPTION
[q][G]	Postvelar or uvular
[c][ɟ]	Palatal
[ʔ]	Glottal

Intermittent stops (Trills)

[R]	Uvular trill
[ɾ]	Single tap *r*
[ɹ]	Alveolar trill†

Nasals

[ɲ]	Palatal
[N]	Uvular
[ɱ]	Labiodental

Lateral

[ʎ]	Palatal

Fricatives

SYMBOL		APPROXIMATE DESCRIPTION
[ħ]	[ʕ]	Pharyngeal
[χ]	[ʁ]	Postvelar (uvular)
[x]	[ɣ]	Velar
[ç]		Palatal
[ɕ]	[ʑ]	Alveolopalatal (prepalatal)
[ɬ]	[ɮ]	Lateral (lateral lisp)
[ɸ]	[β]	Bilabial
	[ɦ]	Glottal (voiced [h])

Glides

[ʋ]	Labiodental
[ɥ]	Palatal

* First column voiceless, second column voiced.
† IPA symbol is [r], used in this text for the glide rather than for the trilled *r*.

TABLE 3. PROSODIC AND MODIFYING SYMBOLS

Symbols for Prosodic Features

Symbol	Description	Example
[']	Primary stress	['tɛlə¸fon]
[¸]	Secondary stress	['tɛlə¸fon]
[.]	Syllabic consonant	Especially [l̩] [m̩] [n̩]
[¹]	Low pitch level	
[²]	Medium pitch level	[¹ɪts ən ə⁴stɑ³nɪʃɪŋ²θɪŋ]
[³]	High pitch level	
[⁴]	Very high pitch level	
[↗]	Upward inflection	[wɛl↗]
[→]	Level inflection	[wɛl naʊ→]
[↘]	Downward inflection	[go hom↘]
[·]	Half-long	[nɑt bæ·d]
[:]	Long	[o: hi wɑz]
[|]	Short pause	[wɛl | aɪ dont no]
[||]	Long pause	[dont || nɑt hɪr]
[⁺]	Open juncture	[dʒæk⁺kold]

Articulatory Modifiers

Symbol	Description	Example
[~]	Nasal resonance	[sĩŋ θrũ ðõ nõz]
[ᵥ]	Voiced, or weak and unaspirated	[bʌtᵥ ɪz betᵥ]
[₀]	Voiceless (breathed)	[z̥æd̥] is about like [sæt]
[ˤ]	Aspirated (fricative release)	[pˤ ipl]
[ω]	Labialization (lip rounding)	[ræbɪt] is like [wæbɪt]
[ₙ]	Dentalization (linguadental rather than lingua-alveolar)	[t̪im]
[·]	Palatalization (similar to retroflexion)	[z̓u]
[ᶩ]	Retroflexed (palatized)	[ɬ] [ɳ] [ɭ] [ɽ] [ʐ] [ʂ]
[⊥]	Raised tongue	[ɪ⊥] is like [i]
[⊤]	Lowered tongue	[i⊤] is like [ɪ]
[⊣]	Fronted tongue	[a⊣] is like [æ]
[⊢]	Retracted tongue	[æ⊢] is like [a]
[··]	Centralized vowel	[ï] is like [ɨ]
[)]	Lips rounded	[ɑ)] is like [ɒ]
[(]	Lips spread	[ɒ(] is like [ɑ]
[iᴵ]	Example of vowel modifier	[sɪtiᴵ]
[fᵛ]	Example of consonant modifier	[fᵛæn] is like [vᶠæn]
[‿]	Tie mark to indicate diphthong or affricate	[dʒɔɪn]
[⁻]	Unreleased	[hɑt⁻taɪm]

TABLE 4. COMPARATIVE CHART OF PHONETIC ALPHABETS

IPA	Webster's New Collegiate	Webster's New World	American College	NBC Handbook
i	ē	ē	ē	ee
ɪ	ĭ	i	ĭ	i
e	ā	ā	ā	ay
ɛ	ĕ	e	ĕ	ai e
æ	ă	a	ă	a
ɑ	ä	ä o	ä	ah
ɔ	ô	ô	ô	aw
o	ō	ō	ō	oh
ʊ	o͝o	oo	o͝o	oo
u	o͞o	o͞o	o͞o	oo:
ʌ	ŭ	u	ŭ	uh
ɜ˞	ûr	ûr	ûr	er
ə	(italics)	ə	ə	uh
ɚ	ẽr	ẽr	ər	er
aɪ	ī	ī	ī	igh
ɔɪ	oi	oi	oi	oi
ju	ū	ū	ū	yoo:
aʊ	ou	ou	ou	ow
p	p	p	p	p
t	t	t	t	t
b	b	b	b	b
d	d	d	d	d
k	k	k	k	k
g	g	g	g	g
tʃ	ch tü	ch	ch	ch
dʒ	j dü	j	j	j
f	f	f	f	f
v	v	v	v	v
θ	th	th	th	th
ð	th	th	th	th:
s	s	s	s	s
z	z	z	z	z
ʃ	sh	sh	sh	sh
ʒ	zh	zh	zh	zh
h	h	h	h	h
m	m	m	m	m
n	n	n	n	n
ŋ	ng	ŋ	ng	ng
l	l	l	l	l
w	w	w	w	w
hw	hw	hw	hw	hw
j	y	y	y	y
r	r	r	r	r

Note: Because of the different concepts of linguistic structure, dictionary pronunciation systems are not strictly comparable on a phoneme-to-phoneme basis. For this reason not all vowel symbols used by the dictionaries represented here are given—only those which most closely compare with the IPA symbols for the vowels of stressed syllables. For example, even when they are used by the dictionary in question, symbols for "half-long" or "*r*-diphthong" vowels are not included.

1. *Webster's New Collegiate Dictionary* (based on *Webster's New International Dictionary*), 2d ed., Springfield, Mass.: G. & C. Merriam Company, 1956.

2. *Webster's New World Dictionary of the American Language,* college edition, Cleveland: World Publishing Company, 1954.

3. *The American College Dictionary.* C. L. Barnhart (ed.), text edition, New York: Harper & Bros., 1948.

4. *NBC Handbook of Pronunciation,* compiled by J. F. Bender, 2d ed., New York: Thomas Y. Crowell Company, 1951.

1

PHONETICS AND
SPEECH IMPROVEMENT

The ability to speak well is an attribute that has both utility and beauty. To be sure, *what* one says is more important than *how* he says it; yet it is evident that there can be no fully effective communication through spoken language unless the manner of speaking gives force and impact to the thoughts and feelings that are to be conveyed. Good speech is not, then, a cloak for superficiality. It is, instead, the rightful and natural mark of the educated, cultured, and intellectually vigorous person. The acquisition of speaking skills, through whatever study and practice are necessary, therefore merits the careful and conscientious attention of serious students.

A primary objective of this book is to assist such students in developing whatever level of skill they aspire to in the use of speech form. It would be naïve to suppose that good speech can somehow come about without effort or that it can be achieved simply through vocal drill and exercise, necessary as these may be in an incidental way. Rather, the approach must be through a study of the speaking process and the various aspects of speech form, including a consideration of such matters as standards of correctness or acceptability. Once these are fully understood, the student can work intelligently toward the control of his own speech patterns.

The basic information needed for improvement of speech form is contained in the general body of knowledge called *phonetics*. This may be defined as the science of speech sounds as elements of language and the application of this science to the understanding and speaking of languages. Phonetics bears a close relationship to *linguistics*, which embraces the study of language in the broadest sense. *Experimental phonetics* employs objective laboratory techniques in the analysis of spoken language. *Articulatory*, or *physiological*, *phonetics* is concerned particularly with the formation of speech sounds and with the dynamics of speaking. When the

1

products of these specialized fields of study are synthesized in such a way that they can be used in the development of acceptable and effective speech, this area of study is one facet of *applied phonetics*. It is from the point of view of this discipline that the material in this book is selected and organized.

We shall be concerned for the most part with only one aspect of the total speaking process: what has been called the *form* of speech. As contrasted to *content*, the term *form* refers to the sounds of the language and to the phenomena of spoken language which occur when these sounds are combined into meaningful words, phrases, and sentences. The inquiry into the characteristics of connected speech will lead us to a consideration of the mechanics and dynamics of syllable, word, and sentence formation and into such other pertinent matters as stress, intonation, and standards of correctness in pronunciation.

Although anyone who embarks on a speech improvement program—or who wishes to teach others—must have a theoretical knowledge of what he is setting out to do and a clear idea of where he wishes to go, extensive practice of various kinds obviously will be necessary. In some respects, learning to speak well is not unlike learning to play a musical instrument. Anyone who is fortunate enough to possess certain unusual skills and aptitudes may possibly perform creditably without the tedium—if it is tedium—of extensive study of music theory or long hours of exercise. More often, however, the musician must learn the principles of his art and devote himself to intelligent practice.

The same reasoning applies to the learning of language skills. We do not expect to acquire legible handwriting without a study of the way in which letters are formed or a good deal of practice in penmanship. Fortunately, many persons grow up in an environment where good speech is the rule and quite unconsciously follow the patterns set for them. Even so, most of us need to invest some time and interest in the conscious effort to speak well, just as we must learn to use language in reading and writing. One is fortunate if the study of speech was part of his early education, but if it was not, he can take comfort in the fact that it is never too late.

Thus, along with the discussion of *phonetic theory* in relation to the effective use of speech form, great stress will be laid on the importance of the *phonetic method*. It is absolutely essential that one learn to *hear* and *analyze* the full details of spoken language so that he can recognize with certainty the exact characteristics of pronunciation, stress, intonation, and the other attributes of speech. Only on this basis can the speaker actually become aware of speech and learn to control consciously, as he must, his own patterns of speaking. These two aspects of our study —*theory* and *method*—are complementary; each facilitates the other, and together they constitute the foundation for an intelligent and scholarly program of speech improvement.

After one has become sophisticated about the kind of thing for which he should listen, the ability to hear speech analytically calls for no skill or ability which the average person cannot develop. The problem of using the phonetic method is principally one of learning to direct attention perceptively toward the *sound* of speech rather than to focus primarily on word meanings. Practice is necessary, of course, particularly in becoming critically aware of one's own patterns of speech. We shall return to this topic in a later section, with specific suggestions on developing skill in speech analysis, and to an explanation of *phonetic transcription*. Transcribing speech is an excellent way to develop the necessary listening skills, and it has other important uses as well.

CHARACTERISTICS OF GOOD SPEECH FORM

Let us turn now to a question that is basic for any program of speech improvement: What are the characteristics of an acceptable and effective use of speech form? Modern teachers for the most part try to avoid the sort of schoolmastering that prevails when correct speech form is taught on the basis of rigid rules. Instead, the approach is a more reasonable one, based on the idea that speech can be considered good if it communicates fully, which means, among other things, that it must conform to an accepted usage. Since there is no single way of talking that can be considered "correct" in the schoolmaster's sense, we shall often use the term *standard* to describe speech that conforms to an acceptable usage and *substandard* for speech that does not.

From the practical point of view, however, anyone who undertakes to improve his use of spoken language is forced to formulate an operational definition of good speech, no matter how aware he may be of the fact that there are many acceptable standards. If it is true, as Emerson suggests, that every man might well be occupied in writing his own bible, then it is equally true that he should be formulating, in an intelligent way, his own standard of speech. He can do this best if he takes a fairly broad look at some of the linguistic, historical, and phonetic considerations which are involved in speech standards.

Since this text has speech improvement as an ultimate goal, the authors have felt it necessary to make recommendations from time to time about what they consider desirable speech traits. Many points in the later discussion are based frankly on the authors' own ideas about good speech form. At the same time, the intention is to make the student aware of the problems of speech standards, the reasons why these problems have arisen, and the possible ways in which they may be resolved. Nowhere in the discussion of standards of speech or pronunciation is there any effort to enforce a particular set of rules on what is correct and what is not.

Intelligibility. The most elementary requisite of good speech form—and there is little disagreement about this—is *intelligibility*. To be clearly understood, the speaker's *articulation*, or formation of the speech sounds, must be sufficiently accurate to make his words easily distinguishable. If they are not spoken in this way, he simply will not communicate adequately. He may likewise give the impression that he is careless or uneducated or that he possesses some undesirable trait of personality. Judgments about an individual based on the way he speaks may on occasion prove wrong, of course, but this does not alter the fact that they will be made.

Articulation which is adequate for a minimum level of understanding should not be difficult for the native speaker to achieve, since the only requirement is that the movements of the articulators be sufficiently vigorous and precise to give the speech sounds the characteristics they should have. In addition, of course, the individual speech sounds must be properly blended into syllables and meaningful words, which involves an understanding not only of the individual sounds but also of the ways these sounds change when they are placed in the context of speech.

Unfortunately many persons fail at this elementary level. The reasons may be numerous, but they should never prove insurmountable for the physically normal speaker. The student must become aware of the need for distinct articulation, develop the capacity for perceptive listening so that he can recognize correctly articulated speech, make an intelligent comparison of this standard with his own speech form, and be willing to monitor consciously his own articulation. Practice will naturally be needed. Typical errors and the ways in which they can be dealt with are discussed in a later chapter. The help of a speech therapist should be required by only the relatively few persons whose difficulties arise from some motor disability, a defect in mouth structure, or some unusual learning problem.

Pronunciation. A second requisite of good speech form is pronunciation which conforms to an acceptable standard. In a general way, the term *pronunciation* refers to the choice of sounds used in forming words, whereas *articulation* is the process of forming the sounds and syllables. A word is *mispronounced* if it contains one or more wrong sounds or if the correct word pattern is distorted by adding, omitting, or transposing sounds (or by improper use of stress). The word is *misarticulated*, on the other hand, if the sounds it contains are not spoken with sufficient accuracy and precision. These two factors—the choice of sounds and their articulation—can, of course, be interrelated in many ways.

Before attempting to develop his own pronunciation practices, the student should know, first of all, that there are three principal speech regions in the United States. These usually are designated as *Eastern American* (EA), *Southern American* (SA), and *General American* (GA). The geographical boundaries of these areas are not clean-cut, nor have they been exactly located, despite the large number of systematic studies of regional dialect. In general, however, Eastern American is heard in the New England states, New York City, and in those portions of Canada which lie east of the Province of Quebec. Southern American is heard in the states of the old Southern Confederacy, with Kentucky added but with west and central Texas excluded. In the remaining states General American is most commonly heard among the natives. In terms of population GA is used by the largest number of persons in the United States and EA by the fewest.

This general description of the three speech areas is an oversimplification which would be seriously misleading for anyone with an academic interest in American dialects, although it will suffice for our purposes. Not only do the boundaries overlap, but there are numerous interesting subregional dialects; it is therefore impossible to generalize beyond a certain point about the speech traits of any one region. Extensive studies on this subject have been in progress for many years, notably those involved in the compilation of the *Linguistic Atlas of the United States and Canada*, and they have produced a wealth of data. It is not profitable to go into these matters in detail in this text, but anyone interested in exploring this topic further would find Wise's *Applied Phonetics*[39]* an excellent starting point.

Up to this point we have not gone far enough into phonetic notation to make it possible to discuss easily the nature of the typical differences among the three speech regions. There are, however, some common misconceptions about them. Actually, the really conspicuous regional differences among educated speakers from each of these three areas are relatively few; most of the more obvious distinguishing features center around the way the *r* sound is handled and upon the pronunciation of the *a* vowels. Careful analysis, of course, will reveal a number of fine points of difference, but these are not apparent to the average listener. Subtle nuances in stress and intonation also play a role in indicating the speaker's linguistic origins.

In most cases the person who is criticized for dialect speech is either using very narrow localisms or is employing obtrusive pronunciations which might be considered substandard even in his own area. For instance, one who seems to say "cain't" for "can't," "po' boy" for "poor boy," "sho' nuff" for "sure enough," or "pernt" for "point" is certainly not talking in conformity with the usages of educated speakers in any of the

* Superior numbers refer to the references at the end of the book.

American speech regions. The genuine subregional dialects which might be sufficiently conspicuous to attract a great deal of attention, possibly unfavorable, outside their own area are spoken by relatively few persons. Good-quality speech from one linguistic area is rarely unduly conspicuous in another dialect region.

What attitude should the student take toward culturally inherited dialect characteristics in his own speech? If he is from North Carolina and talks as the educated individuals in his area do, need he feel any obligation to eradicate the traces of his speech environment? Will he somehow be thought of as more "cultured" if he conforms to the pronunciations which are standard in Eastern American (or possibly even Southern British), or should he go along with the majority in a democratic fashion and talk General American? The answer in most cases is that it really does not matter, provided that he rids his speech of any substandard usages. Standard, clearly articulated Southern, Eastern, or General American speech is good anywhere, and there is no need to apologize for any of them.

It is naïve and positively foolish to argue that a single standard should be enforced by the schoolmaster or that GA, SA, EA, or some other standard is "best." As Wise sensibly points out, one cannot charge that the mode of pronunciation used by some 90 million people, or even by 30 million, is wrong. It would be equally absurd to take the position that some given standard of speech reflects more culture than another, and it is doubtful that a truly cultured person would make such a judgment. Culture, good taste, and learning are surely centered in no one geographic area, and even if they were, one who sought to draw the cloak of culture around himself by relying on such surface traits as a certain way of talking would be on very unsure ground.

There may be perfectly legitimate reasons for choosing a standard of speech to which one was not born, although, strictly speaking, no reason need be offered for taking such a step. One who finds himself in an area where most persons speak a standard different from his may wish to conform for business or social reasons. If he is employed as an actor or announcer in motion pictures, radio, television, or the legitimate theater, he must necessarily employ usages suitable to his profession. In the case of the first three, this probably would be a stylized form of good-quality General American; the stage actor possibly would be guided into a form of diction derived originally from Southern British. He would need to take care to adopt the new standard thoroughly, and not to mix dialects, lest he run the risk of becoming at least mildly foolish.

At various points in this text it has seemed easiest and simplest to make recommendations about good speech form in terms of a selected standard of speech. This is true, for example, in the exercise materials.

When such a situation arises, the discussion and examples are phrased in terms of General American. This amounts to a tacit endorsement of General American usages in preference to Eastern or Southern American, but the student should understand that he need not follow the implied advice that he adopt General American—provided always that he avoids substandard usages in the dialect he prefers.

Actually, a qualified recommendation of General American conceivably could be supported by what seem to be some common-sense reasons. In the first place, GA comes closest to the common currency of speech in this country. It is accepted anywhere and is spoken far more widely in the United States than are either EA or SA. Furthermore, it seems clear that the processes of growth and change in pronunciation are tending strongly to eradicate geographical differences of usage in favor of a more nearly uniform standard. Although we are admittedly on speculative grounds, it seems reasonable to suppose that, if and when dialect differences largely disappear, General American will have exerted greater and more numerous influences than either Eastern American or Southern American.

Historically, an important factor in maintaining the dialects of spoken English in the British Isles was the relatively great degree of cultural isolation. The dialect differences were very marked during the Old English and Middle English periods. It was not until about the sixteenth century, approximately a hundred years after the Modern English period began, that anything approaching uniformity of usage in spoken English arose. The immigrants to the United States brought with them their native English dialects, and these, in turn, came under the influence of other language imports and cultural forces. Once in the Colonies, the dialects spread out from their original areas in keeping with the migrations of the settlers. Until comparatively recent times cultural and geographic isolation tended to go together, a situation which favored the growth and perpetuation of dialect differences in speech.

From early historical times there has been a tendency toward homogeneity in the language, and everything that is happening now seems to be accelerating the trend toward greater uniformity in the spoken language. Now we move rapidly from place to place for long or short periods of time, so that population shifts are much more rapid than they once were. Permanent dispersions of population from one part of the United States to another were particularly great during World War II and have seemed to continue since that time. Aside from quite limited exceptions, there are no longer any major geographic areas where the bulk of the population has a recent common origin, as was the case in the early history of the United States.

Even those portions of the population who live out their days in some one geographic area no longer are isolated from the speech influences of other dialect regions. Possibly the most significant force which affects the speaking habits of the nation are the media for mass communication, although the widespread compulsory educational system also exerts a strong influence. A surprising portion of the leisure time of the typical American seems to be spent at the motion pictures, listening to the radio, and watching television. Much of the speech heard through these channels has the principal characteristics of General American, and although the final effect of such a wide dispersion of a certain kind of speech cannot yet be measured—or at least has not been—it certainly will be significant.

Assuming that a standard has been selected—General American or some other dialect—the student must next develop a clear idea of what constitutes accepted usage within this standard. This task will require some fairly careful and conscientious study, but the reward can be the security which goes with the knowledge that one's speech conforms to an accepted, and therefore effective, usage.

A good starting point for the discussion of usage is a consideration of the functions and limitations of the dictionary as a guide to pronunciation. The dictionary undertakes to record those usages which may be heard among educated speakers; it does not, of course, make rules for pronunciation, but rather tries to report what the editors believe to be the actual usages of educated persons at the time when the material is prepared. Such judgments are made after considerable study and research, including a great deal of polling of one sort or another.

In general, despite certain reservations which will be pointed out, one can and should turn to any recent standard dictionary for an authoritative statement about the accepted pronunciation or pronunciations of any English word. If its limitations are recognized and taken into account, the dictionary is obviously a most important source of information about accepted usage and should be consulted routinely.

The first limitation arises from the fact that, except for certain *pronouncing dictionaries*, the dictionaries in widest use list only the formal, literary pronunciation, or, more properly, the *lexical* pronunciation. This is the way the word is pronounced when it is spoken carefully by itself, rather than in connected speech. This is useful information, but it is perfectly clear that when words are joined in expressive, communicative utterance they are not necessarily spoken in this way. Speech would indeed sound odd if they were. The whole subject of the ways in which pronunciation may change in contextual speech is discussed in Chapter 12, but the present point is that one must know the laws that govern these changes before he can acquire practiced ease in speaking. Furthermore, lexical dictionaries do not ordinarily list regional differences in pronunciation, although most pronouncing dictionaries take at least some cognizance of such variations.

A second, but possibly somewhat less important, limitation is that the pronunciations listed in most dictionaries may be out of date, at least to some extent. Pronunciations do not change from day to day, of course, but the shifts that do occur may be relatively rapid as the historian measures time. Most of the changes are lawful and can be accounted for by the operation of known phonetic principles, but we are by no means completely free from fashions in speech. When the editors of a dictionary record current usages, they have no wish to "freeze" such pronunciations, even if they were so unrealistic as to believe that they could if they tried. Altered pronunciations in the typical speech of educated persons are listed as soon as they are judged by the dictionary editors to meet the criterion of use. Since dictionaries can be reviewed and printed only at fairly long intervals and since the average person does not buy each new edition as soon as it is issued, a given usage may become very common indeed before it gets dictionary sanction. There is a natural and understandable tendency for the editors of a lexical dictionary to be conservative about adopting changes in the recognized pronunciation.

Examples of this conservatism are easily found. For instance, as this is being written, the most recent edition of *Webster's New Collegiate Dictionary*, an excellent reference, lists the pronunciation of the word "chassis" with *sh* as the first sound; yet *ch* (as in "chair") is certainly more frequent in the authors' own speech area and is probably the most common General American usage. It would seem unreasonable to regard this pronunciation as incorrect. Likewise, the word "just" is always marked so that it rhymes with "must," but in connected speech the vowel is almost always closer to that in either "hit" or "met"—even in the speech of those who consider themselves purists in the use of language.

As a matter of common sense one should recognize that accepted usages do not change so rapidly that the current edition of an authoritative dictionary is likely to be seriously out of date. On the other hand, the dictionary does not have to be followed slavishly, provided that an "unauthorized" pronunciation is unquestionably in wide use among educated speakers. If there is a margin of doubt, it is prudent to stay reasonably close to dictionary pronunciations, with due allowance for the variations which occur naturally in contextual speech. Generally, pronouncing dictionaries, such as that of Kenyon and Knott[17] for American speech, and Jones[14] for British usage, are quicker to recognize changed usages, but even these sources cannot always be completely current.

A second important source of guidance on acceptable speech usages comes from the careful observation of persons whose speech can be considered worthy of emulation. These are the individuals we customarily refer to as the "educated speakers" whose usages form the criteria for accepted pronunciation. We know who these people are as a group, but it is sometimes a bit difficult to identify them as individuals. Nevertheless, everyone has an opportunity to hear good speakers in business and social contacts, in the pulpit, on radio and television, and elsewhere. No one individual will suffice as a model for speech form, nor will educated speakers always talk alike. But from a wealth of observation one will be able to draw useful conclusions. Herein lies the unique value of the phonetic method; one develops a heightened perception of speech form, supported by an understanding of theory. All the material in this text is, in one way or another, directed toward this goal.

Any discussion of pronunciation problems would be incomplete without mention of the complex and vexatious spelling-pronunciation relationships of English. English spelling is notoriously nonphonetic, a fact which is a particular source of grief for the foreigner who is trying to bring order into his study of the language. This characteristic is at least understandable if some of the history of the language is reviewed.

English is classified as one of the languages of the Germanic branch of Indo-European. Originally three general divisions were recognized: (1) East Germanic, represented by the now extinct Gothic; (2) North Germanic, from which Scandinavian arose; and (3) West Germanic, which was the parent of High and Low German, Frisian (spoken by the inhabitants of Friesland, a province of the Netherlands), and English. The ancient origins of English can be traced to three tribes who settled in the British Isles in the fifth century: the Jutes, Saxons, and Angles. Three general periods, or "kinds," of English are recognized:

Old English (OE)   prior to 1100
Middle English (ME)   from 1100 to 1500
Modern English (MnE)   from 1500
    Early Modern   from 1500 to 1700
    Late Modern   from 1700

Many exceedingly complicated and interrelated processes of growth took place during each of these periods in response to numerous influences. Old English, sometimes called Anglo-Saxon, was made up predominantly of native words brought by the migrants from northwestern Europe. After their arrival, complex processes of amalgamation and further growth occurred in the language. From the eighth to the eleventh century the Scandinavian conquests brought many hundreds of new words into England, including many place names. As early as the tenth century, when what was called West Saxon became predominant, a strong tendency for the language to become homogeneous throughout the English-speaking area had become apparent.

A large number of French words came into the language during a period of some 350 years beginning with the Norman Conquest in 1066. The language of the Normans, which was a northern French dialect, was in general use by the higher classes for some time, although it presently was spoken in a modified fashion. French ceased to be the language of court and church after 1350, but the influx of French words continued. By this time, however, Parisian French, rather than the northern dialects, exerted the greater influence, thus complicating the situation still further. Large numbers of words were borrowed from Latin also by the scholars of the Middle English period, and these new imports became a part of the language. It is said that there is no language from which English has not borrowed words at some time or other. One study of contemporary English words classifies their origins as follows: native, 18.4 per cent; French, 32.4 per cent; Latin, 14.4 per cent; Greek, 12.5 per cent; and other, 23.3 per cent. It is easy to imagine that complicated changes occurred in the pronunciation of these words, both when they found a foothold in English and later when they were subjected to modification in pronunciation by English speakers.

Historical phoneticians agree generally that there was no spoken standard until the sixteenth century, when the speech of the upper classes in London and Oxford became the pattern which educated persons throughout the country tended to follow. By 1800, however, usage had undergone great change in London, although the older standard persisted in the North of England. These events are thought to have laid the groundwork for the present differences between Northern and Southern (London) British dialects. The early American settlers brought with them a variety of dialects, but one of the most important was the earlier London and Oxford standard.

During the period when loan words were coming into the language in such great number, English speakers tended to retain some semblance of the original pronunciation, particularly in the case of French derivatives. In due course these pronunciations were altered—by a shift of accent and otherwise—but the original spellings were retained. When French was the fashionable language, even some native English words took on a French flavor in their pronunciation. There still remain many words whose standard pronunciation in English is close to that in the original language, but others have been more or less completely anglicized —with the net result that one cannot safely infer pronunciation of such loan words from their spelling.

Throughout the history of the language, spelling practices have changed relatively little—although there has naturally been change— but pronunciation has been much less stable. Spelling conventions were first fixed by scribal tradition and, after the invention of printing, by published books and manuscripts. However, one of the most noteworthy characteristics of spoken English since the early history of the language has been the numerous and extensive changes in the sounds of the language and in the pronunciation of words. Phonetic change takes place slowly but steadily; it occurs in part because of the assimilative influences of one sound on another, a topic discussed in Chapter 12, and possibly also because of the listener's inability to duplicate exactly what he hears. Whatever the nature of the process may be, it still goes on. Historically, vowels have been particularly unstable. One very marked alteration, sometimes called the *great vowel shift*, took place in the Early Modern period, so that the speech of Shakespeare's time would sound strange in the production of his plays on the modern stage. Without going further into the details of changes in sounds, we can appreciate the statement that today we have modern pronunciations based on medieval spellings.

Other factors have further complicated pronunciation practices. Despite the relative rigidity of spelling, it has been influenced to some degree by pronunciation. There is always a tendency to sound words as they are spelled, as when a speaker replaces the missing *t* in "often." Linguistically unsophisticated teachers commonly ignore the changes in usage that have occurred in the past and attempt to impose spelling pronunciations on the naïve assumption that words should be spoken in the way that seems called for by their spelling. Such schoolmastering has been quite fashionable at certain times in the past. There are also less obvious alterations in pronunciation that have taken place historically, particularly in loan words, because of changes in inflectional endings and in stress.

This discussion of some of the historical aspects of English pronunciation has not been intended to provide any set of rules or principles that the student can put into everyday use in deciding on his own usages; rather, it is offered as a partial explanation of the reasons why spelling-pronunciation relationships often seem so confusing—and for whatever inherent interest the topic may have. It leads us quite naturally to a reaffirmation of the idea that the only sensible way to achieve acceptable speech form is to study English as a spoken language by phonetic methods. Written English and spoken English are truly estranged.

Speech Styles. One final topic remains to be discussed as an important factor which determines what can be considered an appropriate and acceptable speech form. This is the so-called *speech style*. Speech which is fully effective must, of course, be suited to the occasion, whether this is greeting a friend, talking with a group of business associates, or delivering a sermon. The manner of one's utterance will, of course, have a great deal to do with pronunciation. The rate may be relatively slow and the pronunciation quite formal if the occasion is one where this demeanor is in the best taste; in more informal situations the manner of talking may be very comfortable and easygoing, with somewhat different pronunciations.

There have been some attempts to classify styles. Jones,[13] for instance, speaks of a "rapid familiar style," a "slower colloquial style," a "natural style used in addressing a fair-sized audience," an "acquired style of the stage," and the "acquired style of singing." Kenyon[16] is somewhat more lucid on the matter. He describes a "familiar colloquial," a "formal colloquial," and "public speaking" and "public reading" styles. One who is using either of the colloquial styles, he says, employs many contractions, an informal vocabulary, and a conversational manner of utterance. The public speaking style is characterized by a more formal vocabulary and syntax, a slower rate, and more careful pronunciation. These latter qualities are said to grow out of the relatively greater difficulty the speaker may have in making himself understood or in "projecting." Kenyon considers the public reading style appropriate for oral reading of literature, for church services, and for declamation.

Such classifications seem neither very realistic nor particularly helpful to the student who is trying to make his own speech effective. There seems to be little point in trying to adopt a particular style or even in trying to describe the differences which distinguish one style from another. A more intelligent approach is to focus attention on developing a *communicative style*, bearing in mind that the ultimate test of good speech is whether or not it serves as a means of making the listener fully receptive to the ideas and feelings of the speaker. It is our conviction that anyone who has mastered the techniques of speech form need give little conscious attention to style, provided that he has those inner qualities which must always underlie a true communicative relationship between the speaker and his listener.

In most circumstances we want to speak what is sometimes called "easy English"—a direct, conversational style which is unobtrusive and without affectation but which communicates effectively because it is comfortable for both speaker and listener. At the same time we should never be misled into supposing that "easy English" is a careless form of speech; articulation is precise, and the pronunciation standards are always in keeping with an acceptable standard. There are naturally many contractions, such as "doesn't" for "does not" and "won't" for "will not," and the vocabulary and syntax may differ from what might seem suitable to some formal occasions; but the speech is, so to speak, always well-groomed. A desire to communicate and a sensitivity to the audience and occasion should motivate the adaptations in speech style; there need be no studied effort to adopt some preconceived mode of talking.

Actually, we hear very few examples in these days of the classical formal style, at least in the United States. When the occasion demands, the best speakers may talk more formally than they would in an intimate face-to-face situation. Even so, a study of the public utterances of those whom we consider our best contemporary speakers shows the style to be quite conversational and most unlike the layman's concept of the formal public speaking manner. It may be that a familiar style is in keeping with the climate of our modern culture. Certainly one important influence grows out of the fact that so much contemporary speaking is through the mass-communication media, which permit the speaker to "come right into the living room and join the family circle."

There is no more reason to mourn the passing of the supposed elegancies of formal speech than there is to regret that buildings of functional design have largely replaced the more ornate architecture of an earlier day. As with a building of contemporary design, the beauty which good speech possesses—and this may be considerable—comes from the fact that it does so well what it is supposed to do, without obtrusive and useless embellishments.

With this general discussion as a background, we now are ready to turn to those details of phonetics which bear directly on learning or teaching good speech form. The principles conducive to success in this area can be summarized quite simply: make *effective communication* the primary goal in speaking; choose a standard of speech which is in keeping with an accepted usage, and a speech style which is appropriate to the occasion; recognize the importance of good speech form, and devote a scholarly interest to its achievement. This can be done best, as we have said more than once, by applying the *phonetic method:* become familiar with the facts of speaking and speech form; acquire the phonetic skills needed to hear and recognize the characteristics of speech, so that you can become your own teacher and critic—or can help others to evaluate and improve their speech—and, finally, practice faithfully, as you will be directed. The details of all this make up the subject matter of the chapters which follow.

2

GENERAL CONSIDERATIONS

SYLLABLES, PHONEMES, THE ALPHABET OF THE
INTERNATIONAL PHONETIC ASSOCIATION, AND THE
TYPES OF SPEECH SOUNDS

Certain matters which are basic to an understanding of the structure of speech and the process of speaking require discussion at this point. These include (1) the nature of syllables, (2) the phoneme theory, (3) the alphabet of the International Phonetic Association, and (4) the types of speech sounds and the ways in which they are classified and described.

THE SYLLABLE

When speech is analyzed as if it were simply a certain kind of sound, and without reference to meaning, it is found to consist of a series of pulses of sound energy, which are called *syllables*. The syllable is considered the basic physiologic and acoustic unit of *speech*, in contrast to the individual speech sounds, which are the basic units of *language*.

The *meaning* of words is determined by the particular pattern of speech sounds each contains, and when a word is written or printed, conventional letter symbols are used to designate these sounds. When a single word or a series of words is spoken, however, the speech consists not of a succession of speech sounds but of a series of syllabic pulses, each preceded and followed by brief intervals of relative silence. In connected speech the syllables follow one another very rapidly (usually about two to five per second) and are grouped in such a way that they form meaningful words, phrases, and sentences. The syllable, not the individual speech sound, must be considered the irreducible unit in speaking, although a single spoken syllable may contain as many as four or five speech sounds. This concept is of more than theoretical interest, for one key to better speech is to get away from the idea of speaking as a train of individual

15

sounds and to become increasingly aware of syllabic units, as is brought out in greater detail in a later section.

The fact that speech can be divided into syllables is probably perfectly familiar to every student, but some examples of syllabification might prove useful at this point. Words like "me," "I," "show," "take," and "palm" obviously consist of a single pulse, or syllable. The following are two-syllable words: "baseball" (base-ball), "today" (to-day), "showroom" (show-room), "college" (co-llege), and "midway" (midway). Three syllables or pulses can be sensed in "attitude" (att-i-tude), "possible" (poss-i-ble), and "precedent" (prec-e-dent). In words such as "automobile" (aut-o-mo-bile) and "catastrophe" (ca-tas-tro-phe) there are four syllables, and in such a word as "refrigerator" (re-frig-e-ra-tor) there are five. Words of one syllable are *monosyllabic;* those of more than one are *polysyllabic.*

Experimental phoneticians have made careful studies of the acoustic and physiologic nature of the syllable, but many points are still somewhat obscure. In general, each syllable is set off, or separated, from the preceding and following speech flow by a period of silence or by a very brief interval in which the speech flow drops to an appreciably lower level of energy output. When one says such a phrase as "cat nap," there seems to be a complete break between the two syllables, although its duration is very brief. If "you all" is spoken as a two-syllable phrase, the boundary between the syllables is likely to be somewhat less distinct; yet the listener, if he pays careful attention, will clearly hear two syllables. The syllables are the fluctuations, which we have called *pulses,* in the acoustic output.

What causes these syllabic pulses? Articulation movements certainly play a major role. In many phonetic situations there is a complete cessation of breath flow between syllables. This occurs, for instance, when the breath stream is completely stopped, as it is on the *t* of "cat nap." The interruption becomes less marked if the speaking rate is increased. In some cases a syllabic division is not so much a stopping of the breath flow as a fluctuation of breath pressure caused by a distinct change in articulation position. For instance, in the phrase "Hi ya" there is probably no complete cessation of breath flow, but there is nevertheless a readily observed variation in the pressure of the outgoing breath. Some phoneticians (see Stetson, 29) interpret certain experimental findings as showing that syllabic divisions are brought about by arresting movements of the chest muscles, but this explanation is not universally accepted. Those who object to it argue in part that the apparent arresting movements of the chest muscles are the result of syllabic divisions rather than their cause.

Although further discussion of the physiologic and acoustic properties

of the syllable would probably not be profitable at this point, it is essential
to recognize certain phonetic characteristics of the syllable which are
important both theoretically and practically. First, a vowel or some
vowellike sound is a major element of every syllable. A syllable may
consist of a single vowel, as in "ago" (a-go) or "ebbing" (e-bbing), or
of a "vowel blend," or diphthong, as in the first syllable of "eyesore."
A more accurate description of diphthongs is given in a later section.

The nonvowel sounds which can be *syllabic* have some of the important
characteristics of vowels but are not conventionally classified as such.
The characteristics which make these sounds vowellike can be explained
more readily following the discussion of vowels in a later section. Notable
examples of nonvowels which can become syllabic are [m], [n], and [l].
For instance, if the phrase "keep 'em here" is pronounced rapidly, the
second syllable of the phrase may become simply [m]. The same phenomenon can be recognized with [l] in "it'll be" and with [n] in "he 'n
I." When words are transcribed phonetically, a procedure to which the
reader will be introduced presently, a special mark is used to show that a
nonvowel sound has become syllabic in the sample of speech being
recorded.

Syllables may also be made up of a vowel and one or more consonants.
Thus, a syllable may consist of (1) a vowel preceded by one or more
consonants, as in "to" or "try"; (2) a vowel followed by one or more
consonants, as in "at" or "ask"; or (3) a vowel both preceded and followed by one or more consonants, as in "top," "stop," "tops," or "stops."
Phonetically, consonants serve either to *initiate* or *terminate* a syllable,
or to do both. Aside from the exceptions noted, consonant sounds cannot
by themselves form syllables; they must always be combined in some
way with a vowel resonance if a syllable is to be formed. For this reason
some phoneticians call vowels the *syllabic* speech sounds and consonants
the *nonsyllabic* speech sounds, a terminology which is in some ways more
satisfactory than the more familiar vowel-consonant classification.

Earlier the statement was made that the syllable, rather than the
individual speech sound, is the irreducible unit of speech—a remark which
may not have been fully understood. If it was not, the matter can perhaps
be clarified now. Although vowels are syllabic, consonants are not; in
speaking, the consonant is the result of a movement or adjustment of the
articulators which serves to initiate or terminate a vowel sound, or both,
and thus to create a syllable. In contextual speech, a consonant has no
separate identity but is bound to the vowel.

The individual sounds—or, more properly, the *phonemes*—are necessary
parts of any language, and the nature of these sounds is distinctive in
each language. Out of the almost infinite number of ways man could
conceivably adjust his mouth to produce various syllabic sounds (*vowels*)

or to initiate and terminate such sounds (through the *consonant* positions or movements), only a relative few are employed in any given language. Each language has its own standardized assortment of movements or postures which recur again and again in the various patterns that make up the words of that language. The phenomena of syllabification are much the same for all spoken languages, but each language has its own distinctive set of phonemes. The phonemes of English will be discussed in the following section.

Before going on, however, one practical application of all this information about the syllabic nature of speech should be emphasized again. When one wishes to speak a language correctly, it is of course necessary to master the standard sounds. But this is not sufficient; the most careful attention must be given to syllabification, since the syllable is the basic unit of speaking. As a matter of fact, a significant proportion of the inadequacies in speaking arise from faults of syllabification rather than from any difficulty with the individual speech sounds.

THE PHONEME

From the foregoing discussion it should be clear that the individual sounds of a language are *linguistic* units; they determine *meaning*. If the sounds represented in English by the letters *p*, *e*, and *n* are spoken in such a way as to form a syllable, the listener who understands this language will receive the verbal signal "pen," which has meaning for him. Even though the sounds have a primarily linguistic function, the phonetician has a basic interest in them. He wishes at the outset to have answers to such seemingly simple—but actually complex—questions as "How many different vowel and consonant sounds are there in this language?" and "How do we know?"

A literal and perfectly truthful answer to the question "How many?" could be "An infinite number." Philosophers tell us that no two events ever happen twice in exactly the same way. The sound quality of the vowel in "pen" is no more likely to be spoken in precisely the same way twice by a given person, or in precisely the same way by two different speakers, than are two clouds likely to be the same. A common-sense answer is that these minor differences don't matter since "I know what he said" or "I can recognize a cloud when I see one." This is a perfectly reasonable reply, and one which anticipates a problem involved in the analysis of speech: What differences among sounds *do* matter?

First of all, of course, differences which matter are those which change the speech sound to such an extent that meaning is affected. For instance, if a speaker goes too far in altering the vowel in "pen," the word may be heard as "pan" or "pin," in which case the listener thinks of something altogether different from a writing instrument. Differences of this kind, involving a change in meaning, are termed *phonemic* differences. A *phoneme*, then, is a linguistic unit consisting of a group, or family, of sounds which are not identical but which may be used interchangeably within words without affecting their meaning, or linguistic significance.

Meaning is not the only feature that the sounds of a phoneme have in common, of course. In general, they will be produced with largely similar articulation movements, although occasional exceptions to this principle can be cited. An interesting idea offered by some authorities is that the listener's recognition of a sound as belonging to a certain phoneme depends upon his sensing the articulation movements involved in its production. These phoneticians point to the fact that, even where various members of a sound family do not give exactly the same auditory experience, they are nevertheless articulated with the same pattern of muscular movement. Even though members of a phoneme may not always sound alike, it is generally true that they will more often have common acoustic factors; that is, they will be heard as the "same" sound.

In summary, when the linguist seeks to analyze a language, he may describe its distinctive phonemes; the physiological phonetician focuses his analysis primarily upon the articulatory and acoustic similarities and differences among the sounds in each phoneme. In this text the individual speech sounds are treated from this latter point of view, and with the ultimate goal of speech improvement in mind. Some of the sound families that will be discussed may not be considered "pure" by the linguist, but they have been classified in a way which is useful and practical for learning and teaching acceptable speech.

The term *allophones* refers to the sounds which are classified as belonging to a particular phoneme, despite the differences among them that may be heard by the listener. For example, compare the *t* sounds in the words "teem" and "butter." Although both are the "same" sound, acoustically they are quite different. If the *t* from "butter" were to be used in the other word (and vice versa), meaning would not be changed, but the pronunciation would be quite unlike that of the educated speaker. Nevertheless, the two *t* sounds are placed in the same phoneme because they have the same meaning and are made with the same basic articulation pattern. Acoustically they are somewhat dissimilar, largely because of their phonetic context. In order to indicate all these facts, one says that the two *t* sounds are different *allophones* of the *phoneme* [t].

There is no theoretical limit to the number of allophones that may exist within any one phoneme. The number distinguished in any given discussion depends upon the interests of the investigator and upon the refinement of his techniques for detecting differences among sounds. In this text both phonemic and allophonic differences are described; the sounds are classified according to phonemes, and the important allophonic variations are noted for each family of sounds. One might contend that some of the phonemes in this text are actually allophones of a single phoneme, but such an argument would be of more concern to the theoretical phonetician than to the teacher or student. Throughout, an attempt has been made to organize and present the sounds in a way which, without doing serious violence to theory, serves practical purposes best.

Some further examples of allophonic variations within a phoneme may be helpful. If we ask someone to pronounce the words "lit" and "law" (or say them ourselves), we have no difficulty in placing the initial sounds in the [l] phoneme. Yet if the two initial sounds in these words are carefully compared, it becomes obvious that they are not exactly alike. In pronouncing the [l] in "lit," most speakers bring the tongue into contact with the gum ridge behind the upper teeth, whereas the point of contact for "law" is somewhat farther back. Because of this difference in tongue position the two sounds are not quite the same; they are separate allophones in the phoneme. In other words, the movements which initiate each syllable are essentially the same, although not identical, and the sounds mean the same thing. A similar variation can be detected in the initial [k] in such a pair of words as "keep" and "caught," and the student can easily discover additional examples.

Some of the allophonic variations in a phoneme simply reflect individual differences among speakers, often of a dialect nature. Primarily, however, they are the result of the influence of *phonetic context;* that is, the production of the sounds in question is affected by the nature of the sounds which precede or follow. In the illustration of "lit" and "law" the slight difference in tongue position for the two [l] sounds is attributed to the following vowel. The vowel [ɪ] in "lit" is ordinarily made with the front of the tongue raised and forward, whereas the [ɔ] in "law" is produced with the back of the tongue raised and somewhat retracted. This accounts for the more forward position of the [l] in "lit," since the tongue is preparing, so to speak, for the shift to the vowel position. We might remind ourselves, however, that in making such an explanation we are really talking in *linguistic* terms and that in considering the processes of speech it might be more meaningful to revise the explanation in terms of the role of the consonant in the *syllable.* The influence of phonetic context on pronunciation is discussed in Chapter 12, and many of the principles involved have a practical bearing on speech improvement.

THE PHONETIC ALPHABET

Any alphabet is simply an arbitrary system of symbols which can be used to set down speech in printed or written form. A *phonetic alphabet* is one in which each symbol stands invariably for some particular speech sound. By "speech sound" is meant any *distinctive* sound for which a symbol is convenient. This usually means that there should be a different symbol to stand for each phoneme, but in many practical situations it may prove desirable to have a way of noting distinctions within phonemes. If *linguistic function*, or communication of meaning through writing or printing, is the only concern, a nonphonetic set of symbols like the stylized picture ideographs of Chinese might theoretically be satisfactory, no matter how complicated they might become in practical situations. When one wants to record speech and pronunciation, however, a phonetic set of symbols is necessary.

The conventional English alphabet and the spellings derived therefrom are nonphonetic to a serious degree. Some letters are used to indicate several sounds, or several phonemes, such as the varying pronunciations of *a* in "lay," "calm," "hat," "carry," and "father." On the other hand, frequently a given speech sound may be represented by several different letter symbols or combinations of letters, to the vast confusion of the foreign student of the language. Take, for example, the different ways in which the sound [s] is spelled in the words "see," "pass," "circle," "science," and "psychology." Observe that in the word "circle" the letter *c* stands for both [s] and [k]. Since the spellings of English are highly nonphonetic, an awkward situation is created for those who wish to study pronunciation systematically and to record the sound of spoken language. True, most dictionaries make use of a system of *diacritical marks* to show pronunciation, but these identifying marks are cumbersome, confusing, and far less satisfactory in all respects than would be a genuinely phonetic alphabet and spelling.

The alphabet of the International Phonetic Association (IPA), portions of which will be used in this text, has been devised to meet this need. It consists of a large number of symbols which may be employed to represent the sounds of many languages, with modifying marks which are useful for showing several kinds of differences in articulation of sounds in the speech of persons speaking a variety of dialects. Throughout, the basic concept is that each symbol shall, within limits to be mentioned, stand for a given sound and only that sound and that the sound in question shall be represented by only one symbol.

One of the limitations of the IPA alphabet is that it cannot be completely "international" since there are dialect differences in the sound systems of various languages which are too elaborate to be recorded in this way. For instance, the [ɑ] (as in "father") family of sounds is not exactly the same for British and General American English, even though the same phonetic symbol is used to represent that phoneme. At best, of course, there must always be some degree of inadequacy in any attempt to record speech sounds in writing, particularly if there is any effort to note fine distinctions. Despite this limitation and any other shortcomings the phonetic alphabet may have, the symbols can be used so that they have nearly, if not exactly, the same pronunciation value from language to language. Certainly the great usefulness of the IPA alphabet for the student of speech will more than repay him for the time and effort required to become familiar with the phonetic symbols.

A list of the most important symbols needed for recording General American speech is given in the charts in Table 1. The student should begin now to familiarize himself with these symbols, for they will be used from this point forward in the discussion of the English speech sounds. Chapter 4 contains many specific suggestions for learning to work with the sounds of speech in this way.

Phonetic spelling is accomplished simply by setting down in proper order the phonetic symbols representing the sounds of the speech sample being recorded. This is called *phonetic transcription*. In what is called *broad transcription* one uses only the standard symbols to represent the *phonemes*. Little effort is made to recognize phonetic variations within the limits of the phonemes, although marks for stress, pausing, and so on may be used. *Narrow*, or *close*, transcription, which attempts a more nearly exact representation of the speech sample, makes use of additional symbols or modifying marks, such as those in Tables 2 and 3 on pages xii and xiii. Broad transcription usually will serve the beginning student, but narrow transcription is very useful for more careful studies of speech, both good and bad, and for certain kinds of language analyses that may interest the academic phonetician.

The student of speech improvement will use phonetic transcription basically as a way of training himself to be perceptive about the sounds of speech, for this is essential to his purpose. He will make transcriptions of the pronunciation of persons he considers good models and use this material for practice. In addition, he will work from transcriptions prepared by others, such as those included in the Appendix. For comparative purposes he will learn to transcribe his own speech. He is certain to find that exercises in transcribing both the standard and substandard speech of others provide an excellent method for developing the listening skills so necessary for good speech. In later chapters exercises are given for developing skill in hearing and transcribing speech. The following example is a broad transcription of a passage as it might be spoken by a person using General American pronunciation:

[ðɪs ɪz ə sæmpl̩ əv fənɛtɪk trænskrɪpʃən. hwɛn ju gɛt bɛtɚ əkwɛntəd wɪð ɪt, ju wɪl faɪnd ɪt vɛrɪ izɪ tə rid. ɪt meks ðə saʊndz əv spɪtʃ mʌtʃ lɛs kənfjuzɪŋ ðən ðe ɑr hwɛn ju juz ðə kɑmən ælfəbɛt.]

Spelled out in the usual way, these sentences would be:

This is a sample of phonetic transcription. When you get better acquainted with it, you will find it very easy to read. It makes the sounds of speech much less confusing than they are when you use the common alphabet.

The limitations of conventional English spelling are so evident that there has grown up a spelling reform movement of considerable proportions. Very persuasive arguments can be made in favor of changing over to a phonetic spelling that would have an adequate linguistic function and at the same time leave far fewer uncertainties about pronunciation. Written and spoken language would be drawn much closer together, and the increased ease of learning language in all its aspects would doubtless win the gratitude of generations of children yet unborn. Like so many good ideas, however, spelling reform faces the apparently insurmountable obstacle of tradition, and it is most unlikely that spelling practices will change in any other way than by slow growth. In the meantime, the student of speech can best serve his purposes by learning to use the symbols of the IPA, a task which will not prove unduly difficult.

TYPES OF SPEECH SOUNDS

When one listens to speech, what he actually hears is a series of standardized noises or tones; grouped in certain ways, these are recognized as meaningful words. Sounds are made by the speaker when he molds the outgoing breath pulses to create the particular tones or noises needed for the words he wishes to say. The characteristics of the speech sounds obviously merit careful study, since this information is basic to an understanding of what must be done with the articulatory mechanism to produce the sounds of speech acceptably.

Speech sounds may first be divided, as has been explained, into those which are syllabic and those which are nonsyllabic. Within limits this is approximately the same as saying that the speech sounds may be classified as either vowels or consonants, but these terms are less adequate. The *syllabic* sounds include, first, the *vowels* and *diphthongs*. Added to these are the *nasals* and one *lateral* sound, which may be either syllabic or nonsyllabic, depending upon phonetic circumstances to be explained later. Because these sounds are somewhat vowellike they can be referred to as *semivowels*. In addition to the *nasals* and the *lateral*, which are most often nonsyllabic, the sounds which are nearly always nonsyllabic are the *glides*, *stops*, *fricatives*, and *affricates*. The sounds in each of these classes naturally have distinctive acoustic characteristics and thus require certain articulatory adjustments for their production. These are explained in the following sections.

Vowels. The nature of vowels and the process of vowel formation in relation to the syllable will be more easily understood after the detailed discussion of this topic in later chapters. For the moment, however, we may say that each vowel is a sound having a distinctive *quality* which leads to its recognition; it is a unique kind of "musical tone." This tone, incidentally, contains the major energy of the syllable. To understand why the vowel is described in this way, we must first review briefly certain acoustic and physiological factors which influence the way in which a listener perceives sounds.

If the sound waves which reach the ear are comparatively regular in form, the listener will experience a more or less musical *tone;* if the train of waves consists of vibrations occurring irregularly—or if this element is prominent—he may perceive *noise.* The waveforms of the vowels are essentially regular in voiced speech, hence they can be classified as tones; whereas many of the consonants—particularly the stops, fricatives, and affricates—contain prominent noise components.

Voiced speech tones, and hence all normally produced vowel sounds, are called *complex;* that is, the sound, although heard as a single tone, actually is a composite of a number of separate elements, in the same way that a musical chord consists of two or more separate notes blended together. These components are called *partials* or *overtones*, and with proper instrumentation any complex sound can be analyzed (by frequency analysis) into its individual partials in the same way that a musical chord can be taken apart. Various kinds of musical chords sound different to us because of differences in the number, pitch, and relative loudness of the individual notes each contains. In a similar manner each vowel sound gets its distinguishing characteristics primarily from the number, frequency, and relative energy levels of its partial vibrations.

Although there are a number of vowel theories, we can say in general that the total pattern of the partials for any given vowel is determined by the manner in which the mouth, throat, and perhaps other cavities act as resonators. When a speaker produces a vowel sound, he tunes these cavities in certain ways by muscular adjustments, including lip and tongue postures, but the vocal passage still remains relatively open and unobstructed. He creates different vowels by changing the resonance properties of the cavities through various configurations of muscular adjustment. Because of their acoustic properties, vowels are known as *resonance phenomena.*

Diphthongs. Like vowels, diphthongs are always syllabic. Sounds of this class, however, appear to be formed from the blend or fusion of two vowels spoken together in the same syllable. What actually occurs is that the articulators begin the syllable in the position for one vowel then shift with a smooth and continuous transition movement toward the position for some other vowel. One can learn to detect the first and second vowels of the diphthong without too much difficulty; yet the blend in actual speech is so close that the diphthong would lose its essential characteristics if it were to be clearly separated into two vowels. To describe the phenomenon more accurately, the essential quality of the diphthong depends upon *resonance change;* the diphthong owes its individuality to a movement from one tone quality to another within the space of a single syllable. For example, in the word "out," as commonly spoken in the General American dialect, the diphthong involves a shift from [a] (similar to the vowel in "hot") to a sound resembling the vowel in "put" [ʊ]; the combination, however, is something different from the two vowels spoken separately in sequence.

Instead of talking about vowels and diphthongs, many phoneticians speak of syllables as having *simple nuclei* or *complex nuclei:* that is, vowels and diphthongs are termed, respectively, *simple* and *complex syllabics.* In a simple nucleus the vowel can properly be described in terms of a single kind of resonant quality, even though truly pure vowels are not common, as is explained later. In contrast, the complex-syllabic sounds, including those we are describing as diphthongs, involve both a resonance and a significant resonance *change.* Whether one speaks of complex nuclei or of diphthongs, the important fact is that some syllabics are distinguished more by a changing resonance than are others. A more careful description of these changes is given in later sections, particularly in the discussion of individual diphthongs in English.

Semivowels. This term can be used for certain sounds which can, in effect, stand as either vowels or consonants. In some phonetic contexts such sounds are syllabic and therefore act as vowels; in other cases these sounds start or terminate syllables, thus functioning as consonants. This situation was mentioned earlier in the discussion of the syllable, where the syllabic nature of [m], [n], and [l] in "keep 'em," "he 'n I," and "it'll" was shown. Since these sounds, and also [ŋ], can be syllabic, they may be classed as semivowels. When they are syllabic they are designated by the symbols [m̩], [n̩], [l̩], and [ŋ̍]. Acoustically such semivowels resemble true vowels, for their recognition depends on resonance patterns; yet the vocal passage is not open as for vowels, since there is always some contact of the articulators which partially obstructs breath flow.

Some classify [j] as in "yet," [r] as in "rain," and [w] as in "wit" as semivowels because they are *resonant* sounds. This is perfectly legitimate, but it seems more convenient to class them as *glide consonants.* When these sounds are resonant, the vowel symbols [ɝ], [u], and [i] are used in place of [r], [w], and [j], respectively.

Consonants. *Nonsyllabics,* or *consonants,* are characterized physiologically by some kind of obstruction of the vocal passages or contact of an articulator. Acoustically they resemble *noises,* as was explained earlier, or at least contain prominent noise elements. Consonants are traditionally classified according to the degree of closure as they initiate or terminate a syllable. If closure in the mouth or throat is complete, the sound is called a *stop.* If it is incomplete, the consonants thus produced are called fricatives, a name suggested by the friction noise which is the identifying characteristic of the sound. In the *affricates* a complete closure is followed by a relatively gradual and prolonged release of the impounded breath to create a kind of sound which is, loosely, a combination of a stop and a fricative. As with the combination of vowel resonances into diphthongs, however, an affricate depends upon the shift, or change, for its basic nature and is not to be thought of as a simple stop-plus-fricative combination. The semivowels, including the nasals and lateral, were explained in a previous paragraph. The *glides,* including [w], [j], [r], and [hw], initiate (and occasionally terminate) syllables and are, in general, produced by a movement rather than by a static position of the articulators. In the paragraphs which follow, each of these classes of sounds is explained in greater detail.

Stops. In general a *stop* is a speech sound which involves a complete blocking of the breath stream at some point, in contrast to a *fricative,* which is made with a continuously flowing (but constricted) breath stream. If one wishes, all sounds which are not stops can be called *continuants.* Physiologically, the English stop sounds are made by blocking the vocal passage with the lips or by placing the tongue in contact with the roof of the mouth in such a way as to impound the breath stream. English sounds usually classified as stops are [p], [b], [t], [d], [k], and [g].

Under certain conditions a stop is more accurately called a *stop plosive* (usually shortened to *plosive*). Any stop is a plosive if the breath, after being impounded, is subsequently released with a somewhat audible explosive puff. If the audible release does not occur, the sound is of course a stop, but not a plosive. In English speech any of the sounds of this class may be either stops or plosives, depending upon phonetic context and, to some extent, upon the individual practices of the speaker. Since the stops are later described individually in detail, only a brief illustration will be given at this point. In the word "book" the syllable is begun with the lips completely shut, but they then are opened to the vowel position, making the initial sound a plosive, or stop plosive. Notice, however, that the word "grab" can be pronounced in such a way that the syllable is terminated by closing the lips without subsequently opening them to release an audible puff of air. In this case the final sound is a stop, but not a plosive.

What the listener senses when a *plosive* sound is produced is the *cessation* of the flow of sound, followed after a very short interval of silence by an audible release of the voiced or unvoiced breath stream. Actually, as we shall learn later, in this situation the cue unconsciously used to identify the terminating movement, or "sound," is the configuration of the entire syllable.

Affricates. There are two distinctive phonemes in English which we customarily classify as *affricates:* [tʃ] as in *"church"* and [dʒ] as in *"judge."* The affricates are in reality special kinds of stops in which the prominent and distinguishing element is the friction noise caused by the release of breath. In producing [tʃ], for example, the breath is stopped by tongue contact at the approximate position for a somewhat retracted [t], then released as the fricative [ʃ] sound. The other English affricate, [dʒ], is essentially a voiced counterpart for [tʃ]. As stressed in several previous paragraphs, the unique affricate character of these sounds depends upon the total pattern, and it is incorrect to regard such a sound as simply a stop plus a fricative.

Fricatives. These consonants consist acoustically of friction noises. In general, the fricative sounds of English are made by directing the breath stream with adequate pressure against one or more mouth surfaces, principally the hard palate, the gum ridge behind the upper teeth, the teeth, and the lips. (The [h] is a special case which will be explained when the sound is discussed in detail.) Breath so constricted and directed will lead to the hissing or "hishing" noises of the distinctive fricatives of English. The breath is not completely stopped, of course. Sounds usually classified as fricatives in English are [s], [z], [ʃ], [ʒ], [f], [v], [θ], [ð], and [h].

Glides. Sounds classified as *glides* are those which consist primarily of the movement of an articulator, in contrast to sounds produced with the articulators held in a relatively static position. Acoustically a glide is a rapid *change* of resonance which occurs at a syllable boundary, usually without prominent noise elements of the sort heard in stops and fricatives. In English, as mentioned earlier, the glides are [r], [w], and [j]. It has seemed convenient to include [hw] as a glide also, although many writers prefer to consider it a fricative. Strictly speaking, the sound is physiologically a glide but acoustically a fricative.

In addition to serving as the class name for certain sounds, the term *glide* provides a way of designating certain events which take place during articulation. These are the *on-glides*, or *fore-glides*, which are initiating movements of the articulators toward the position for any of the sounds, and the *off-glides*, or *after-glides*, which are movements away from the most prominent adjustment for any of the sounds. Such transition movements toward and away from articulation adjustments always take place when the articulators shift from one sound to another in speech, but they are particularly prominent in certain combinations of sounds.

Nasals. This term is used to designate the semivowels [m], [n], and [ŋ]. The class name is chosen, of course, because of the distinctive nasal resonance which these sounds contain. In English, only these sounds have nasal resonance as a distinctive characteristic, but in some languages many sounds are nasalized. Nasal resonance is imparted to the sounds by adjusting the soft palate and certain muscles of the throat in such a way that an opening is left into the nasal passages.

Lateral. Among the English speech sounds only one, [l], is classified as a *lateral.* The term is not particularly apt, perhaps, but is loosely suggested by the manner in which the voiced breath stream escapes laterally over the sides of the tongue when the sound is made. The name *liquid* is applied to this sound by an occasional writer. Phonetically, [l] is possibly more closely related to the nasals than to any other class of sounds. As with the nasals, the breath stream is stopped at one point but allowed to flow freely at another. In making each of the three nasals, the mouth is blocked in some way, but the breath stream is allowed to flow freely through the nose; for [l] the tongue dams the center of the mouth, but the air stream is permitted to flow around the sides of the tongue. As with other semivowels, [l] has a distinctive resonance and typical "on-off" characteristics. The latter are so prominent, in fact, that an occasional phonetician classifies the sound as a glide.

In summary, this chapter has been devoted to what one might call the elements of speech form—*syllables, phonemes,* and *allophones;* methods of recording sounds through the use of a phonetic alphabet; and the kinds of speech sounds. These are aspects of oral language which can be isolated for study and given attention in a program of speech improvement. Speaking is, however, an ongoing process, and there are many kinds of information about this process with which the student should be familiar. Some of these basic facts about the dynamics of speech are therefore introduced in the next chapter.

3

THE PROCESS OF SPEAKING

The total process of speaking is a very complex matter which cannot be dealt with adequately in any text such as this one, interesting though the subject may be. We must confine ourselves instead to those aspects of voice production and articulation—the end products of the total speech process—which we need to know about in order to understand the sounds of English and to use them correctly in speaking. Specifically, this involves a study of the dynamics of articulation and phonation, or of the manner in which the mechanism of speech functions in producing speech sounds. It will not be necessary for the general student to master anatomical detail, but the teacher or speech therapist will naturally want this information if it is not already at his disposal.

VOICING

The human voice is created by vibration of the vocal folds in the throat structure called the *larynx* (Figure 1). Physiologically, the larynx is part of the respiratory system; it functions as a kind of valve at the upper end of the windpipe (*trachea*) and serves several biological purposes, among them exclusion of foreign objects, food, and liquid. The larynx may be located by referring to the so-called Adam's apple, which is one of the laryngeal cartilages (*thyroid*). In phonation the vocal folds are set in motion by air forced upward through the trachea and past the vocal folds by the muscles of exhalation. During phonation the vocal folds are brought together (*adducted*) to lie approximately parallel; in periods of silence they are open (*abducted*). The opening between the vocal folds is called the *glottis*.

The action of the vocal folds in phonation is not unlike the vibration of a trumpet player's lips when he is sounding a note. The sound produced by vocal-fold vibration is called the *cord tone*. *Pitch* is determined by the frequency of vibration of the folds, and this, in turn, is influenced by the

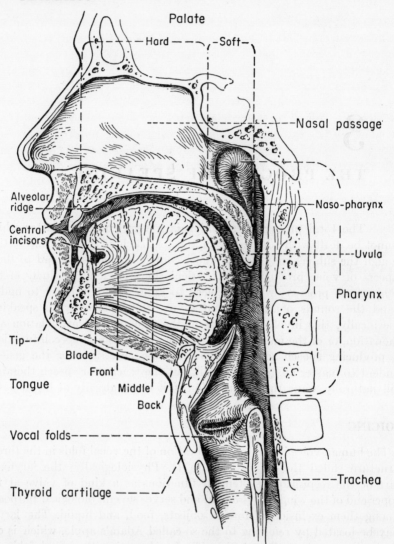

Palate
—Hard— —-Soft-—
—Nasal passage
Alveolar ridge
Central incisors
—Naso-pharynx
—Uvula
Pharynx
Tip
Blade
Front
Tongue
Middle
Back
Vocal folds
Trachea
Thyroid cartilage

Fig. 1. The mechanism of articulation.

tension of the vocal folds, how tightly the glottis is closed, the strength of the air pressure built up in the trachea by the muscles of exhalation, and the inherent mass of the vocal folds. The vocal note is reinforced or resonated in certain throat and head cavities, principally the throat (*pharynx*), mouth, and, in the case of the nasal sounds, the nose cavities. Voice quality depends not only on the way in which the vocal folds vibrate but also on the resonance characteristics of these cavities—their size, shape, and other factors related to the way in which the muscular walls and openings of the cavities are adjusted. Quite technical matters are involved here, but it is sufficient if we understand that voice, as an element of articulate speech, originates in the larynx and is reinforced and given a distinctive tone quality in the cavities of the throat and head.

All speech sounds are either *voiced* (*sonant*) or *voiceless* (*surd, unvoiced, whispered*). The amount of voicing naturally varies. With only a little practice it is usually easy to detect whether or not most speech sounds are made with or without voice simply by listening carefully for the vocal note. Several pairs of English speech sounds, called *homophones*, are made with approximately the same articulation adjustments but differentiated by the fact that one member of each pair is voiced and the other is voiceless. These are [p]–[b], [t]–[d], [k]–[g], [s]–[z], [f]–[v], [θ]–[ð], [ʃ]–[ʒ], and [tʃ]–[dʒ]. The pair [w]–[hw] may also be considered homophones, although strictly speaking this is not quite accurate.

VOWEL FORMATION

The general nature of the vowels has already been indicated in describing them as more or less open sounds, in contrast to the constricted or stopped consonants. Now that the process of phonation has been presented, it is possible to clarify further the manner in which the vowels are formed. For purposes of simplification we may think of the differences among the various vowels as differences in tone quality. Just as an adjustment of the vocal resonators is a major determinant of voice quality, a further alteration in the resonance properties of the cavities creates a vowel quality which is characteristic of each of these speech sounds. The position of the tongue and lips is important in tuning the cavities for the various vowels, but vowel production cannot be described as accurately in terms of position or movement as is possible for the consonant and semivowel sounds.

Each vowel is, of course, a complex sound with a distinctive acoustic spectrum of its own, as was explained in an earlier section. There are usually two or more frequency regions which carry a significant proportion of the total sound energy for each of the vowel phonemes. The reason the pattern of partials varies for different vowels is that the tuning of the cavities acts to reinforce some partials, whereas others are *damped* out or not reinforced. Just how this takes place is a subject of acoustic theory, but these matters—although interesting to the phonetician—can be passed over by the student who is concerned only with some aspect of speech improvement. What is important to understand is that in vowel production the speaker is tuning the resonators to bring about certain characteristic sound patterns. This is done principally by means of tongue and lip positions, but other alterations of the mouth and throat cavities and even, conceivably, different patterns of muscular adjustment within the larynx itself are also involved. Since slight differences in articulation position may significantly alter the sound patterns produced, it is easy to see that there may be a large number of allophonic variations within each of the vowel phonemes. The minor variations in tongue and

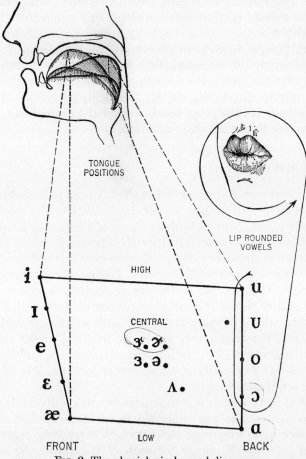

TONGUE
POSITIONS

LIP ROUNDED
VOWELS

HIGH

i   u

I   CENTRAL   U

e   ɝ ɚ   o
                     ɜ ə
ɛ   ʌ   ɔ

æ   ɑ

                     LOW
FRONT   BACK

Fig. 2. The physiological vowel diagram.

lip posture which account for these minimal vowel changes may be very difficult or even impossible to describe physiologically. One can, however, learn to *hear* the differences in the sounds and to monitor his speech by ear to achieve acceptable pronunciation.

Despite what has just been said about the difficulty of describing definite positions for the vowels, there are certain consistent patterns of tongue and lip adjustment for each vowel phoneme. These are presented graphically in the vowel diagram shown in Figure 2. First is the grouping into *front*, *back*, and *central* vowels. These three terms refer in general to the part of the tongue which is critically involved in producing the vowels of that particular kind or to the point in the mouth at which the vocal passage is narrowed. In the series of front vowels the tongue is at its lowest position for [æ], and the front of the tongue rises (but not by equal steps) as one successively speaks [ɛ], [e], [ɪ], and [i]. The back vowels progress in a similar way from [ɑ] through [ɔ], [o], [ʊ], and [u]. The central vowels—[ʌ], [ə], [ɜ], [ɚ], and [ɝ]—all involve mid-mouth adjustment, but the relative positions cannot be described so simply.

Applied to the vowels, the terms *high*, *low*, and *mid* refer to the extent of tongue elevation (or narrowing of the vocal passage). The vowel diagram of Figure 2 can be considered a representation of the mouth cavity. It is not the exact shape of the mouth cavity, to be sure, but the lines do represent schematically the space in which the tongue moves in production of the various vowels. The phonetic symbols are located on this hypothetical mouth-cavity diagram in accordance with the position of the high point of the tongue, or the point of greatest mouth constriction, for each vowel.

The degree of lip *rounding* is usually also included in the vowel descriptions. Normally the lips are not rounded for any of the English front or central vowels, but they are typically rounded for the back-vowel series. The amount of rounding progressively increases from [ɑ], which is the only unrounded back vowel, through [ɔ], [ʊ], [o], and [u], although not by equal stages. Actually, the presence or absence of lip rounding, or its amount, is not a critical matter since any of the so-called round vowels can be produced accurately without rounding, and often is in connected speech. Nevertheless, the rounded vowels are more readily produced with lip rounding.

The attribute of *tenseness* or *laxness* is sometimes mentioned in describing vowels, although these terms may be misleading inasmuch as the difference between a tense and lax vowel primarily involves a change in the position of the articulators rather than an alteration in the strength of the muscular contraction per se. A general understanding of the types of vowels and of the vowel diagram will suffice for the present, but we shall return to these matters later with a more detailed description of each of the vowels commonly used in English speech.

CONSONANT ARTICULATION

The various manipulations which constrict and stop the breath stream to make the consonant sounds are carried out by movements of the *lips*, *tongue*, *lower jaw*, and *velopharyngeal mechanism*. This mechanism consists of the soft palate and certain muscles in the upper part of the throat which, by their combined action, close the opening from the throat and mouth into the nasal passages, thus directing the breath outward through the mouth and preventing its flow through the nose. In addition, consonant articulation may involve directing the breath stream against the palate and teeth, or these latter structures may be points of contact for the tongue or lips. All the parts of the mouth mentioned can be referred to collectively as the *organs of articulation*. The breathing mechanism must be functioning, of course, to provide a stream of air with which to form the voiced or voiceless speech sounds. The general student need not be unduly concerned about anatomical details, but he must be thoroughly familiar with the functioning of the articulators in speech and capable of visualizing clearly their positions or movements for the speech sounds.

A simple phonetic terminology is used to refer to the articulatory structures in relation to their speech function. The term *lingual* refers to the tongue, *velar* to the soft palate, *palatal* to the bony or hard palate, *alveolar* (or *rugal*) to the gum ridge above and behind the upper central teeth, *dental* to the teeth themselves, and *labial* to the lips. In compound words (such as *labiodental*) the terms become *labio-*, *velo-*, and *lingua-*.

By using these terms, and others given in preceding sections, it is possible to describe in a general way the position or movement of the articulators for the speech sounds; this also constitutes a classification of the consonants according to their *place of articulation*. Thus, a sound made by lip movement is referred to as a *labial*. If it is also voiced and a plosive, such as the [b] in "boy," one can classify it as a *voiced labial plosive*, and at the same time give a general indication of the necessary articulatory movements. The [f] in "foot" is made by placing the lower lip against the cutting edge of the upper teeth; breath is forced through this closure to create a distinctive friction noise; although the breath stream is not completely stopped, the sound is without voice. It is, therefore, a *voiceless labiodental fricative*.

All the stop, fricative, affricate, and other consonant sounds can be classified and described in this fashion, although naturally not in complete detail. In connection with this designation of sounds according to their place of articulation, we might remember that the word *articulation* itself comes from a root word meaning "bring together." Thus when one articulates a sound he brings together the articulators—the lips, the lips and teeth, the tongue and teeth, or the tongue and palate. The classification of sounds according to their place of articulation depends upon the fact that two articulators are brought together, or nearly so, to produce the speech sound in question.

Movement of the tongue is an essential element in the articulation of

a significant number of speech sounds. Because of its intricate musculature, the tongue is capable of extremely complicated adjustments. Those
muscles which have their origin and insertion within the tongue itself
(*intrinsic muscles*) function in general to raise the anterior part of the
tongue, curl the tip backward, shorten the tongue, thus arching it toward
the roof of the mouth, and otherwise draw it into a wide variety of
postures and configurations. Muscles having their origin elsewhere but
inserting into the tongue (*extrinsic muscles*) provide for its extension,
retraction, and lateral movement and for the depression and elevation
of the posterior portion.

Certain parts of the tongue are specifically named for purposes of
phonetic description, as shown in Figure 1. These areas are not set off by
distinct anatomic landmarks but are more in the nature of general
designations. The most anterior part of the tongue is the *tip;* the successive
areas behind this are the *blade, front, middle,* and *back.* The outer edge of
the tongue is referred to simply as the *margin.* This terminology can be
used for quite detailed descriptions of the tongue movements or positions
for various speech sounds, namely, the linguavelar, linguapalatal, lingua-
alveolar (or linguarugal), and linguadental sounds.

Like the tongue, the lips and the surrounding facial areas contain
complex groups of muscles, which need not be described in detail. The
principal labial movements in speech are closing, opening, and rounding
to various degrees. Sometimes the lips are rounded and pushed forward
or *everted,* as in the pronunciation of [u] in "shoe"; or the corners may be
drawn back, as in the pronunciation, by some speakers, of the vowel [i]
in "see." The basic classes of English consonant sounds which require
lip adjustment are the *labials* (sometimes called *bilabials*) and the *labiodentals.* The lower jaw also participates in articulation movements,
primarily to maintain appropriate mouth-size-to-tongue relationships.
Movements of the lower jaw serve to increase and decrease the size of
the mouth and mouth opening in a way which is characteristic for each
of the speech sounds. Note, for example, how the jaw tends to drop as
the front vowels of the words "beet," "bit," "bait," "bet," and "bat"
are spoken.

The remaining active articulator is the *velopharyngeal mechanism.* As
mentioned earlier, its action prevents the flow of breath into the nose
passages and directs the breath stream through the mouth, an action
which is necessary on all phonemes except the *nasals.* Closure is effected
by movements of the soft palate and through contraction of certain
muscles which line the throat cavity at the level of the velum. Specifically,
the soft palate is drawn backward and somewhat upward; at the same
time the pharyngeal muscles narrow the diameter of the throat by a

pattern of contraction which draws the lateral walls of the pharynx inward and the posterior wall forward. The velum comes into contact with the pharyngeal walls, or nearly so.

The role of velopharyngeal action in speech is twofold. First, it determines the presence or absence of nasal resonance as a component of the speech sounds. If the voiced breath stream is allowed to enter the part of the pharynx which lies above the soft palate (*nasopharynx*) and the nasal passages themselves, the voice note takes on a distinctive quality which we call *nasality*. In English, it will be recalled, this is normally part of the articulatory pattern for [m], [n], and [ŋ] only. For the remaining sounds velopharyngeal closure occurs, and there is therefore no nasal resonance in the tone quality. Actually, the degree of tightness in velopharyngeal closure on the nonnasal sounds tends to vary among different speakers, and there are consequent differences in voice quality. Some nasal resonance in the voice may be considered pleasing by the listener, but the tone becomes unpleasant if the amount of nasality on the nonnasal sounds exceeds some subjectively determined level. Certain undesirable voice qualities which are sometimes described as "nasal" may be the result of factors other than incomplete velopharyngeal closure.

The second way in which velopharyngeal closure affects speech is through its influence on the level of breath pressure in the mouth. All the stop, fricative, and affricate sounds require a considerable amount of breath pressure for their normal production. In making the plosives, for example, the breath flow is completely stopped, then released with a relatively strong puff, an action which obviously would be impossible if it were not for velopharyngeal closure. Fricatives are made by directing the breath stream against some mouth surface, and pressure is required to create the necessary friction sound. One can get enough breath pressure to articulate these sounds even though velopharyngeal closure is not absolutely tight, but when the force of the breath stream falls below a certain minimum, the sounds become weak, and there may even be an audible escape of breath through the nasal passages. Inadequate intraoral breath pressure is not often a problem for the physically normal speaker, but it is characteristic of the speech of persons with defects of the velopharyngeal mechanism, such as a cleft palate. Inadequate breath pressure may be the result of factors other than faulty velopharyngeal closure, of course.

The hard palate and teeth play an important, although passive, part in articulation. The *bony palate* forms the anterior part of the roof of the mouth. It consists of horizontal processes, or "shelves," which project inward from the upper jaw (*maxilla*), and two palate bones which lie at the back. On some sounds the palate serves as a point of contact for the tongue and on others as a surface against which the breath stream is directed. These are called the *linguapalatal* sounds. In connection with certain sounds it is useful to distinguish *back-*, *mid-*, and *front-palate* areas.

The principal attribute required of the *teeth*, as articulatory structures, is that they provide an adequate surface against which the breath stream can be directed for certain fricatives. They may also prevent the breath stream from escaping in unwanted places during speech. The adult mouth contains 32 teeth, 16 in each jaw, if a full complement is present. Starting at the midline of either jaw, there are two *incisors;* one *canine,* or *cuspid;* two *bicuspids,* or *premolars;* and three *molars.* In general, when the jaws are together, the molars and premolars are in end-to-end *occlusion,* or contact, and the surfaces of the opposed upper and lower teeth fit closely together. This facilitates their grinding and crushing action in chewing. The incisors and cuspids in the upper jaw overlap the corresponding lower teeth slightly, providing a chopping or cutting function.

The teeth serve as a point of contact for the tongue in making the *linguadentals* and for the lower lip on the *labiodentals.* Several other fricatives, notably [s], [z], [ʃ], and [ʒ] get much of their sound from breath friction against the teeth, particularly the upper centrals. The plosives [t] and [d], and perhaps [k] and [g] to some extent, also get part of their noise from the friction of the breath stream against the teeth, as would be true also of the affricates, [tʃ] and [dʒ]. There can be some deviation from the completely normal occlusal relationship without any serious effect on articulation, but the most efficient speech-sound production requires that there be no abnormal openings in the bite, particularly in the anterior central and lateral regions, and that the position of the upper teeth be such that the tongue or lower lip can be readily brought into contact with them.

At this point the general facts about the dynamics of the various classes of consonant sounds should be clear, although the details of the production of each of the sounds have been reserved for a later section. In summary, the fricatives are articulated (1) by constricting the breath stream through tongue or lip contacts and (2) by directing it against one or more mouth surfaces, particularly the palate, alveolar ridge, and teeth. The stops require that the breath be impounded by the tongue or lips and, in the case of plosives, released audibly. Affricates are special kinds of stops, characterized by prominent fricative release. All the sounds may be either voiced or voiceless.

Summarizing further, consonants may be described from three viewpoints: (1) type of articulation (*stop, fricative, glide, nasal, lateral*); (2) presence or absence of *voicing;* and (3) place of articulation (*velar, palatal, dental,* and so on). Figure 3, which presents this information in

Place of articulation	Stops		Fricatives		Nasals		Glides and lateral	
	Voiceless	Voiced	Voiceless	Voiced	Voiceless	Voiced	Voiceless	Voiced
Bilabial	[p]	[b]				[m]	[hw]	[w]
Labiodental			[f]	[v]				
Linguadental			[θ]	[ð]				
Lingua-alveolar	[t]	[d]	[s]	[z]		[n]		[l]
Linguapalatal	[tʃ]	[dʒ]	[ʃ]	[ʒ]				[j] [r]
Linguavelar	[k]	[g]				[ŋ]		
Glottal			[h]					

FIG. 3. The consonant classification chart.

38

tabular form, comprises what is familiar, in one or more of its forms, as the *consonant chart*. The student should familiarize himself thoroughly with this chart, for it summarizes most of the essential features of the consonant sounds in one simple and compact table.

At this point we must refer again to the fact that speech is more than a series of separable speech sounds which are joined end to end in order to form words. The way the articulators move from one sound to the next in contextual speech is just as important as the posture or movement that would be necessary for isolated sounds. Although the dynamics of connected speech cannot be fully explained until the individual speech sounds have been described, certain important general principles should be stated here.

If one keeps in mind the fact that the basic function of a consonant is to start or terminate a syllable, it is easy to understand that there actually is almost nothing in the process of speaking that could be called a "steady state," particularly in consonant articulation. The consonant turns out to be more of a gliding movement or change of the articulators between syllables. The only stability lies in the general position through which the articulators move in the transition from one syllable to the next.

In the articulatory movements which mark the boundaries of the syllable three phases can be distinguished: (1) the movement *away* from whatever position the articulators were in (either the end of a previous syllable or a neutral position of rest); (2) the arrival at, and possible *hold* in, the "point of articulation" (the position of maximum constriction); and (3) the movement away from the point of articulation and toward the position which marks the beginning of the next syllable, or to a neutral rest position. These three phases are not always of equal interest; in some cases a consonant may be primarily an initiating feature of the syllable, in others a terminating feature. In most cases of juncture between two syllables the movements of articulation are so rapid that we can consider consonant articulation only as a position *through which* the articulators move on their way to another syllable. In other cases, however, there is a definite *hold* of the articulators in the consonant position, depending upon the type of juncture and the kind and speed of the articulation involved.

The three stages mentioned can easily be distinguished in the plosives and are important for an understanding of the articulation of phonemes of this class. For example, in pronouncing [k] as in "keep" as an isolated sound, one can note first the upward movement of the tongue until it touches the roof of the mouth, stopping the breath stream; this is the *fore-glide*, or, as it is sometimes called in the case of stops, the *implosion* stage. Next, the breath is momentarily stopped by the linguavelar contact (a *hold*), after which there is a downward and sometimes forward movement of the tongue, which breaks the linguavelar contact and releases the impounded breath. This latter is the *off-glide* (after-glide) or, in the case of plosives, the *explosion* stage of the sound. These three stages in articulation, although perhaps most easily detected in the plosives, may be thought of as a part of the production of all sounds when they are considered physiologically. Plosives which are strongly pronounced are termed *fortis* and, since there is almost certain to be an audible escape of breath on the release, they are also said to be strongly *aspirated*. A *lenis* consonant is one which is weakly articulated and therefore less aspirated. This distinction is important in describing, for example, the difference between the weak and *d*-like [t] typical of the American pronunciation of "butter" and the strong aspirated [t] of "time."

Some additional comment may be needed on the fore-glide, hold, and off-glide for consonants other than stops. In the case of the nasals and lateral the hold may be somewhat more prominent than in the articulation of stops, since more of the resonant energy of the sounds occurs during this interval. The hold may be prominent in the fricatives also, inasmuch as this phase is essential for the production of a suitably long fricative noise. Among the glides, on the other hand, no hold at all is heard; only the gliding movement itself is perceptible. In all consonants, however, the unique characteristic of the phoneme is gained from two attributes: (1) the events which take place during or immediately adjacent to the hold (a pause or either an explosive or fricative noise) and (2) the changes involved in the gliding movement itself. Both factors are important.

There are a number of distinctive characteristics associated with the *juncture* of consonants, not only when stops are involved but also when other types of consonants occur together. When a consonant is doubled, as is the [k] in "black cat" or the [m] in "Sam might," two separate consonants are not pronounced. Instead, there is actually only a fore-glide, a hold, and an off-glide; the hold, however, is much longer than it would be for a single sound. When two different stops occur in sequence, as do the [k] and [t] in "black tomcat," there is a fore-glide to the [k] position, then a hold during which the tongue shifts to the [t] adjustment, followed by an off-glide, whose nature is such that [t] is a plosive. Sounds adjacent to stops may determine whether or not the stop itself becomes a plosive. In the phrases "stop me" or "stop now" the adjustment of the articulators is from [p] to [m] or [n], but no plosive escape of breath is heard in typical speech; on the other hand, there is usually definite aspiration of [p] in such a phrase as "stop and." There are many intricacies in consonant juncture which will become clearer with greater understanding of the individual speech sounds and the dynamics of speech, but these illustrations will suffice to indicate the general principles. Many of the phenomena of juncture may prove of no more than theoretical interest to the student who has always spoken English, but a clear understanding of what takes place in connected speech will be of practical concern to the person with a foreign-language background, inasmuch as some of his foreign-dialect characteristics may involve differences between what he and the native speaker do when they join sounds in running speech. Likewise, the teacher who has taught a pupil individual isolated speech sounds or syllables will need to know these facts when the time comes for the student to incorporate the newly learned sounds into meaningful connected speech.

Before pursuing such matters any further, we shall turn, in the next several chapters, to a study of the individual speech sounds. Chapter 4 contains some important general suggestions for studying the speech sounds and should be read with particular care.

4

STUDYING THE SOUNDS OF SPEECH

In the next several chapters the English speech sounds are treated individually and in detail. Later chapters are concerned with the ways these sounds change when they occur in connected speech and with a consideration of numerous other matters which are important for the understanding and effective use of speech form. The present chapter is intended to prepare the student for this study by giving him a start in the development of certain essential phonetic attitudes and skills.

At this point we can begin to apply phonetic theory to speech improvement. In Chapters 5 to 11 each of the sounds of English is discussed separately. Each section concludes with exercise material which will help the student understand and use the sound that has been described. It is awkward to give complete instructions on speech improvement until phonetic theory has been covered comprehensively; hence the summary of this topic is reserved for Chapter 14, Speech Improvement.

Nevertheless, the student should, after he has mastered the present chapter, give Chapter 14 its first reading. Not everything it contains will be fully understood, but the basic principles set forth should be clear, and the student can begin to apply them in learning to master the individual sounds. Particular attention is called to the section headed "Steps in the Speech Improvement Program."

THE INDIVIDUAL SPEECH SOUNDS

It is necessary to study the speech sounds as isolated phenomena, even though they do change in context. They usually retain their primary acoustic and physiological characteristics no matter where they are found, and these must be fully understood by anyone interested in learning or teaching correct articulation and acceptable pronunciation. In keeping with the concept of *phonemes* and their *allophones*, we should regard the treatment of each of the sounds in the following chapters as a

42

description of a kind of average or standardized sound as it might occur in isolation or in some simple uniform phonetic context.

Strictly speaking, the so-called individual sounds cannot always be produced in isolation, since the syllable, as we have learned, is the irreducible unit of spoken language. If a sound is *syllabic*, it is a separable speech unit and hence can be spoken alone. This applies to the vowels and diphthongs and to those other sounds which on occasion become syllabic. Although nonsyllabic, any continuant consonant can be produced in isolation sufficiently well to permit study and practice. Certain other sounds—the stops, glides, and affricates—cannot become syllabic in themselves; hence they can be produced in "isolation" only if a neutral vowel resembling an "uh" of very short duration is added. This general point is perhaps more important theoretically than practically, since the distinctive features of the nonsyllabics can and should be abstracted for study even though the sound in question is not completely isolated. This analytic method is an important step in developing adequate speech-sound discrimination, although the syllable is the basis for practice in most of the later exercise material.

The first and most important rule in mastering the individual sounds is *learn to listen perceptively*. This is entirely a matter of practice and of adopting certain *listening attitudes*. When we ourselves are talking, or when someone is talking to us, our natural inclination, obviously, is to pay attention to *what* is being said, not to the *how* of it. This behavior is so deeply rooted and so nearly unconscious that the average person without phonetic training makes only the grossest discrimination of sounds, and then only in terms of word meanings. In consequence a speaker may be quite unaware of conspicuous deviations in articulation and pronunciation, particularly in the case of errors he himself may make habitually. He simply has not learned to listen to himself. Errors in the speech of another are somewhat more likely to be noted, but even then the listener rarely takes the trouble to analyze exactly what is wrong. One hears himself much more perceptively when speech is recorded and played back, and this is an excellent technique for practice. Incidentally, one's first experience with a recording of his voice almost invariably draws out the astonished (and sometimes disillusioned) question "Is that me?"

To develop a good phonetic attitude, follow the basic principle of listening to speech as if it were only a certain kind of sound. For purposes of practice ignore the element of meaning; in due course you will be able to perceive both the *form* and *content* of speech. Identifying the individual sounds and syllables which make up words is primarily a matter of listening *set* or attitude. When you begin studying the individual sounds, you should pronounce them aloud again and again, perhaps hundreds of times; listen for them in your own speech and in that of other persons.

Some sounds will be easy to distinguish and you will recognize them at once, although you still will need to learn their fine characteristics. Other sounds, notably certain vowels, may be harder to identify—partly because you have been accustomed to think in terms of the vowel letters *a, e, i, o,* and *u* and may not have fully realized that there are many more than five vowel sounds in English. Vowels are more variable, also. Sounds which you may have accepted as simple vowels, such as the *i* in "time," may actually be complex vowels, or diphthongs. With practice, you will presently be able to isolate, identify, and discriminate the individual speech sounds; this is a basic goal.

For phonetic purposes it is a mistake to think of speech in terms of conventional word spellings, or *orthography.* From the earlier discussion and from your own experience, you know that printed words are regularly not pronounced the way they are spelled. Unfortunately for the phonetic attitude, the typical person is "visual-minded" with respect to language, because in his school experience he has learned words almost exclusively in terms of reading and writing. Now it is essential to learn to hear words in terms of auditory experience.

Therefore, in acquiring this basic phonetic skill, do not be concerned at all with the way words are conventionally spelled; this will tend only to mislead you and to get in the way of phonetic analysis. For example, if you are trying to deal phonetically with the word "palm" and think first in terms of familiar orthography, you may be considerably confused by the *l,* which is almost never pronounced. In short, try for the moment to forget all about spelling; have no preconceived notion of what you *ought* to hear.

Next, do not think of the descriptions of the speech sounds in this text as factual information to be read and remembered by rote. Look on them instead as suggestions about what to listen for as you study each of the speech sounds. Learn the sounds by listening to them, not by reading about them. When some detail about the acoustic characteristics of a sound is raised in the course of a discussion, verify the fact immediately by a sufficient number of listening experiences. If at a later time you need to know this fact, you can refresh your memory by listening to yourself or someone else, and it will be quite needless to make any effort to recall "what the book said."

For example, you will read that [θ] (as in "*th*ink") is voiceless, whereas the [ð] (as in "*th*at") is voiced. If you do not recognize this distinction at once, then immediately try to pronounce these two sounds many times in isolation and in different words and listen specifically for this difference. Pay particular attention to this aspect of these sounds as they are used by speakers around you. Do the same with all details about the sounds, and they will at once become more meaningful. Most of the terminology used in describing and classifying the speech sounds will also be easily mastered if this study procedure is followed.

The extent to which the student must become familiar with the articulation movements or position for each of the distinctive sounds may depend to a degree on his interests, but for almost every purpose this information is desirable. Certainly the teacher who undertakes to help others must be thoroughly familiar with the physiology of sound production. A student who has acquired a trained perception may be able to make correct speech sounds without too much conscious awareness of the exact mechanics of his own speech. Even so, a good knowledge of the *kinesiology* of sounds, or their mode of production in terms of muscle movement, is most helpful for the person with any sort of articulation or pronunciation problem.

The native student should have no trouble with these details if he follows the principle of learning the sounds by observing their production, rather than by reading about them. The written description of the kinesiology of a sound should indicate some of the things to look for when the sound is made. As you study the text discussion of each phoneme, produce the sounds many times, both in isolation and in words, and observe what is happening. Sounds can be sensed in a number of ways, not merely through hearing.

Visual cues often may help. Movements can be observed by watching the lips and, to some extent, the tongue of another person as he speaks. Watch yourself in a mirror. Visible movements or positions are particularly important for the *labial* sounds [p], [b], [w], [hw], and [m]; for the linguadental [θ] and [ð]; for the labiodental [f] and [v]; and for some other sounds, such as the lip-rounded vowels. Even when the movement or adjustment for a sound is not readily seen in actual speech, one can nevertheless get supplemental help from visual stimuli. For instance, one can produce [l] and hold the tongue in position while the mouth is opened wide enough so that the adjustment can be observed. Visual cues are especially important in instructing the deaf and hard-of-hearing.

Touch, or *tactual* cues, may provide a great deal of information about the way sounds are made. Many of the consonants require some contact between the tongue or lower lip and some other structure. Where this is the case, it is possible to sense the position through touch. In making [f], for instance, one can feel that the lower lip is in contact with the cutting edge of the upper teeth. In a similar way he can sense that the tongue is in contact with the roof of the mouth behind the upper front teeth for such sounds as [t] or [l]. A great number of the consonant and semi-vowel sounds offer tactual cues of which one can learn to be aware.

Touch can be used in another way. In many sounds an important factor is the manner in which the breath stream is directed against some mouth surface, and the breath flow can be sensed tactually. The amount of pressure in the breath stream may also be important. In producing [s], for instance, one can get help in learning the physiology of the sound by becoming conscious of the fact that the breath stream is striking the alveolar ridge, and with considerable pressure. The distinct difference between this tactual stimulus and that associated with [ʃ] illustrates the point that tactual cues can be used to discriminate between sounds. As might be supposed, cues of this kind are very useful for individuals who have defective speech arising from deficiencies in other senses, particularly in hearing. The feeling of vibration, which in this context can be thought of as a variety of tactual sensation, can be made the basis for differentiating voiced from voiceless sounds; the speaker can "feel" the presence or absence of phonation.

Kinesthetic cues can be widely used, although they may at first be more difficult to identify than visual, tactual, or auditory sensations. Kinesthetic sensations enable us to judge the position of the tongue, lips, and soft palate and also to recognize the direction and extent of movement. These sensations are the result of impulses carried to sensory areas of the brain by nerves whose endings are in the joints and muscles. The kinesthetic sense enables us to judge, even though our eyes may be closed, the position of our arm, for instance, or the direction and extent of any movement it may be making. We depend to a great extent upon kinesthesis to control posture and movement, including speech movements. In most circumstances we are not consciously aware of such sensations, but we can learn to be. To do so, pronounce the speech sound being learned many times, focusing attention specifically on the position of the articulators or their pattern of movement. Conscious monitoring of speech movements will most certainly be facilitated by a sensitivity to kinesthetic cues.

The easiest part of studying the individual speech sounds can be learning to classify them as linguadentals, labiodentals, and so on. Such terminology simply represents a convenient summary of the production of a sound, and no one who has fixed in his mind the way in which a sound is made should have any difficulty in arriving at the proper classification. Thus, if we discover that a sound is articulated by placing the tongue in contact with the teeth, as with [θ], it obviously is a linguadental (or tongue-teeth) sound. We note whether or not it is voiced and what kind of sound it is—fricative, plosive, glide, or whatever. All these details can be determined by examining the sound and its mode of production. For [θ] we put these facts together and thus classify the sound as a voiceless linguadental fricative. The same procedure can be carried out with any sound, without the necessity of memorizing the classification from the textbook.

We now have reached the point in our study of phonetics where it becomes essential for the student to begin working with *phonetic transcription*. This technique, which is basic to any and all kinds of phonetic study, makes a particularly important contribution to speech improvement. As a general tool, transcription is a means of recording the actual sounds of spoken language with greater fidelity than the conventional alphabet permits. As an aid to speech improvement, transcription is especially important in helping the student analyze the types of speech—good and bad—which he needs to study. The unique value of transcription lies in the fact that such an exercise sharpens one's ability to hear perceptively; there is nothing of greater importance for the mastery of speech form.

A number of points connected with phonetic transcription need fuller explanation. The whole idea of a set of phonetic symbols for the study of speech is made clear in the criteria drawn up originally in 1888 for the construction of the International Phonetic Alphabet:[40]

1. There should be a separate letter for each distinctive sound; that is, for each sound which, being used instead of another, in the same language, can change the meaning of a word.

2. When any sound is found in several languages, the same sign should be used in all. This applies also to very similar shades of sound.

3. The alphabet should consist as much as possible of the ordinary letters of the Roman alphabet, as few new letters as possible being used.

4. In assigning values to Roman letters, international usage should decide. . . .

5. Diacritic marks should be avoided, being trying on the eyes and troublesome to write.

If one grasps the theory which underlies the International Phonetic Alphabet, he will quickly come to the realization that its designers succeeded admirably in their efforts to devise an efficient and relatively simple method to record speech and pronunciation. Remember that the use of phonetic symbols makes good sense, because each symbol stands for only one phoneme. Once learned, this system of notation will prove much easier than confusing respellings, cross references to other words, and the diacritical markings found in most dictionaries.

As guides to pronunciation, the lexical dictionaries are most unsatisfactory. If, for example, one encounters the vowel symbol *a*, he is put to the trouble of investigating further to discover, from the relatively complicated diacritical markings, just which particular *a* this happens to be. Much too often the key word given in the pronunciation chart still leaves room for uncertainty.

Practical necessity will require the student to become familiar with diacritical marks if he is to use most standard dictionaries, but he will soon realize that phonetic symbols are the less complicated of the two systems of marking pronunciation. As a matter of convenience, the common dictionary marks have been translated into the IPA symbols in Table 4. There is reason to believe that at least some of the editors of current English dictionaries would be happy to change over from diacritical marks to phonetic symbols if it were not for the inertia of accepted practice. For our purposes, the advantages of phonetic symbols easily justify the really minor effort of learning to use them.

Any impression that the phonetic alphabet introduces an unconscionable number of new symbols for familiar English sounds will be found in error. There are only nine symbols for consonant sounds which will require new associations; the remainder have the pronunciation value which is most usual for them in conventional orthography. The new consonant symbols are:

[θ]	as in *th*ink
[ð]	as in *th*at
[ʃ]	as in *sh*oe
[ʒ]	as in mea*s*ure
[tʃ]	as in *ch*in
[dʒ]	as in *j*ump
[hw]	as in *wh*at
[ŋ]	as in si*ng*
[j]	as in *y*es

The primary reason for adopting these new symbols is that there were not enough existing symbols to represent all the consonant sounds without doubling up in some way, and the principle was to assign only one sound family (and always the same one) to a given symbol. The use of [j] may prove temporarily confusing, since those whose native language is English have learned to associate the letter with the first sound in such a word as "jug." The alphabet is international, however, and the usage adopted for this symbol is easily justified: English borrowed the letter from another language, but changed its pronunciation, and the [j] of the phonetic alphabet represents the original sound.

There are 9 to 15 vowel sounds in English, depending on how many phonemes are recognized, and therefore the Roman vowel letters *a, e, i, o,* and *u* had to be augmented considerably in the phonetic alphabet. In conventional spelling single vowel letters must often represent diphthongs, which places a further burden on them. It is not necessary to list the symbols for the vowels and diphthongs here, since they are given in Table 1, but if they are examined closely, it will be seen that many of them are simply different forms of familiar letters. Only the [æ], [ɔ], [ʌ], [ɝ], [ə], and [ɚ] are really completely new.

SPECIAL PHONETIC SYMBOLS

There are a number of symbols for such special modifying purposes as noting accent, pausing, and lengthening of sounds. These are explained at appropriate points in later chapters and are listed in summary form in Table 3. Many of them would be used only in a kind of close transcription which cannot be described in detail until we have gone further in our study of phonetic theory. For broad transcription of the sort we are about to undertake the principal marks needed are:

ˈ   to indicate primary or principal stress, as in "duty" [ˈdutɪ].

ˌ   to indicate secondary stress, as in "notebook" [ˈnotˌbʊk]. (Note that stress marks are placed *before* the syllable in question, not after.)

‖   indicates a longer pause; the approximate equivalent of a period or a break between paragraphs.

| indicates a shorter pause; the approximate equivalent of a comma.

Even these simple marks are used sparingly in broad transcriptions of the sort in which we are interested at this time. Accent marks are the most commonly needed. The usual custom is to mark a primary accent only when there may be some question about where the stress should fall. Secondary accents are indicated only when such stressing is critical for correct usage, which is not very often. The marks for pausing may be used, although for ordinary broad transcription conventional punctuation will, for the present at least, usually be sufficient.

The handling of pauses in broad transcription requires some additional explanation. When we speak, there is not always a pause between words which corresponds to the space between them in written or printed language. Thus, the phrase "How are you?" when spoken naturally, is, so to speak, run together in this way: "Howareyou?" The sentences "How are you now? Are you better?" become "Howareyounow areyoubetter?"

Obviously, individual words are linguistic units, not separate phonetic units in spoken language. When some special feature of speaking needs to be pointed out, the phonetic transcription may be written in a way that indicates the phonetic, instead of the linguistic, divisions. This is done by putting the marks for pausing wherever the pauses occur, regardless of whether or not the breaks come between words. For most purposes, however, words are separated in phonetic transcription in the usual way, since we do not wish to lose sight of linguistic considerations entirely.

THE PHONETIC ALPHABET

The first step in learning to use the phonetic alphabet should be to recognize the sound associated with each symbol. This will be easy in the case of the consonant symbols taken over from the Roman alphabet, since in phonetic notation the pronunciation does not change from that which is most familiar. (The minor exceptions will not be confusing.) Associations between the symbol and its sound will be formed quickly by most students, but some suggestions may help.

First, memorize the key words which are given for each sound, although you should be careful to compare your pronunciation of them with that of other American speakers. The key words are carefully chosen so that none of them is likely to be pronounced in such a way that the illustrated sound will represent a different phoneme from the one intended. If you are not a native American you cannot depend upon your own pronunciation, of course, and your learning must be based upon the pronunciation of persons who do use standard English speech.

Following the discussion of each speech sound there are lists of words illustrating the sound and lists of word pairs to assist in discriminating between somewhat similar phonemes. These should be studied carefully, of course, and always read aloud. You should also ask someone else, preferably several persons, to read them for you as you listen carefully. Transcribe these words for practice. You will also find it profitable to browse through the Kenyon and Knott pronouncing dictionary,[17] noting the way in which familiar words are spelled. At the end of the section on each sound there is also a prose passage loaded with the sound being studied. This should be treated in the same way as the individual words. If these suggestions are followed, it should not be long before you can easily identify the pronunciation called for by a phonetic spelling; at this point you will have developed a *recognition* use of the phonetic alphabet.

If you have not yet become acquainted with the dictionary mentioned above—Kenyon and Knott, *A Pronouncing Dictionary of American English*—you certainly should do so at this point. It uses the same symbols as those employed in this text, and the system of phonetic analysis differs only in very minor details. The pronunciation of many hundreds of familiar words is transcribed in this volume, and you can profitably spend a great deal of time browsing through its pages, simply for the purpose of coming to recognize the sounds that go with the various symbols. The words must be spoken aloud, of course, as the phonetic transcription is noted. A good supplementary exercise is to copy the transcription of the words in which you become interested.

It should be understood, of course, that the dictionary uses a very broad phonemic transcription and leaves out many of the more subtle features of pronunciation, so that it records only a kind of "average" usage. For this reason you should be on the lookout for variant pronunciations in your own speech. An important word of warning: when you begin to make your own transcriptions from actual speech samples, it will not be wise to look up the words in the pronouncing dictionary. Your purpose then will be to note how the word actually was pronounced, not the pronunciation it would have been given by the average educated speaker.

It goes without saying, of course, that you should study the symbols of the phonetic alphabet very carefully. Bear in mind, however, that learning the symbols is not an end in itself and that as a matter of common sense there is no reason why you should not keep a copy of the alphabet at your elbow as long as you need to. This period will prove surprisingly short for most persons. The important first step is to reach the point of being able to recognize the sounds of English when you hear them and to associate each with the proper symbol; this should be done through use, not as a feat of memory.

PHONETIC TRANSCRIPTION

As soon as you have made a good start on acquiring recognition use of the phonetic symbols, begin making your own transcriptions. The central principle of phonetic transcription is perfectly simple: words are spelled *according to the sounds they contain*, using the appropriate symbols. Since the exercise material in the remainder of the book will make you thoroughly familiar with transcription, only a few examples will be given here to illustrate the principle. In each case the number of phonetic symbols indicates the number of sounds (but not syllables) the word contains. In the examples chosen, not much variation in pronunciation would be expected among native speakers.

The sounds in the following words, pronounced in a typical General American way, should be readily recognized:

go [go]	glass [glæs]
no [no]	water [wɑtɚ]
do [du]	pencil [pɛnsəl]
to [tu]	justice [dʒʌstəs]
has [hæz]	surgeon [sɝdʒən]
see [si]	protest [protɛst]
shoe [ʃu]	father [fɑðɚ]
baby [bebi]	satisfy [sætəsfaɪ]
comma [kɑmə]	singular [sɪŋgjəlɚ]
watch [wɑtʃ]	theater [θiətɚ]

If the following sentences are read with reasonable care and as unemotional statements of fact, the General American pronunciation might be as indicated.

It's time we quit.
[ɪts taɪm wi kwɪt]

I paid my bill.
[aɪ ped maɪ bɪl]

I won't be home before lunch.
[aɪ wont bi hom bɪfɔr lʌntʃ]

The class meets Thursday.
[ðə klæs mits ðɝzdɪ]

John said yesterday his father plans to buy a car.
[dʒɑn sɛd jɛstɚdɪ hɪz fɑðɚ plænz tə baɪ ə kɑr]

In so far as the principles are concerned, phonetic transcription offers few problems for anyone who recognizes the pronunciation values of the symbols. As a matter of fact, skill in transcribing seems to be surprisingly easy to acquire for many beginning students; sometimes a person who is almost completely untrained can, after a minimum study of the phonetic symbols and a short explanation of the technique, begin at once to make very respectable transcriptions. On the other hand, an occasional person finds the process a source of great distress and discovers that he must work very hard before he can acquire reasonable facility. This is the person who most needs the listening skills involved in transcription.

It is the authors' suspicion that a good share of the trouble such a student may have is based on some fairly obvious psychological factors and that his troubles are needless. Sometimes there is very little motivation to attempt transcriptions, since the student has no clear concept of its purpose. He will do better if he realizes that transcription is an extremely useful and practical way of mastering speech form. Ultimately it will simplify his problems, not complicate them.

Many are confused at first because they misjudge the number of new symbols that must be learned; there really are not many, as we have pointed out. A superficial but probably important mistake is to suppose that the symbols must be memorized before they can be used; as we have explained, they may be memorized by use—first by learning to recognize the sounds as they are spoken and then by making one's own speech analyses. The student may use the printed copy of the alphabet as long as he likes.

If there is such a thing as an inherent lack of aptitude for phonetic transcription, it must arise from the fact that certain persons truly cannot become "sound-minded." Some students seem unable, for example, to recognize that the word "cat" is composed of three distinctive sounds; or if they advance this far, they appear unable to sense differences among sounds well enough to tell which ones go into the word. For such persons, the vowels in "law" and "father" remain forever indistinguishable. It is possible that a few who believe themselves in this category do indeed have such a unique auditory disability, but for the vast majority the cause lies in poor listening attitudes.

If you have inordinate difficulty when it comes to making transcriptions and you have learned to recognize the symbols fairly well, review what has been said about the listening set. As you have been told, this is a matter of *intending to listen to the sound of speech* as *sound* and of learning not to be distracted by word meanings or the conventional mode of spelling. At the outset you will find it easiest to practice the transcription of individual words and short phrases from your own speech. Begin quickly, however, to make similar analyses of the speech of others—both good and bad. Recorded material, which can be played again and again, is excellent for practice. In a formal phonetics class there are certain to be many exercises in transcribing from dictation; otherwise a cooperative friend can be pressed into service. As you gain experience, you will find that your perceptions are sharpened, and you will come naturally and easily to a level of real proficiency in speech analysis.

Here are some additional details of procedure which are sometimes helpful in phonetic transcription:

1. In attacking a sample of speech, try to determine the number of syllables; remember that they will be heard as pulses of sound energy. Since the syllable is the irreducible element of speech, it should be located as the first step in transcription.

2. After the syllabic divisions are determined, ask yourself what is the basic, distinguishing sound quality of each—usually a vowel or diphthong resonance. Now try to select the symbol which most closely corresponds to the sound you have heard. When this choice has been made, set down the key part of each syllable, allowing a suitable amount of space between symbols. The phrase "now let me sleep" might look like this: [aʊ   ɛ   i   i].

3. Next decide how each syllable was started and stopped, and insert the appropriate consonant symbols or combinations of consonant symbols. Even the inexperienced person will find this quite easy, unless he has some trouble distinguishing between voiced and unvoiced consonants. This will not often happen, however, and transcription will become quite easy after you get the knack of recognizing syllables and their basic resonances. Throughout every step just mentioned, check your tentative transcription by pronouncing it aloud. In the example "now let me sleep," you will come up with [naʊ lɛt mi slip].

4. At the beginning you probably will do well to use conventional word divisions and punctuation and to confine your modifying notations to accent marks.

One final reminder bears repeating: analyze and record what you actually hear, not what you think you ought to hear. If you need to say the words or phrases to yourself or aloud syllable by syllable, be sure you do not distort the speech in the process. The tendency is to change many sounds, especially the unstressed vowels, when the normal rate and rhythm of speech are tampered with. In analyzing the speech of another, be certain that you transcribe what he actually says, not what you expected him to say or what you yourself would have said.

Before turning to the description of the individual speech sounds in the next seven chapters, a word should be said about the use of the exercise material which accompanies each sound. The aim has been to provide a wealth of exercises to aid the student in identifying and discriminating each sound and to give him an opportunity to study that sound in the context of a sample of English prose. The Appendix also contains numerous examples of prose which are to be used for study and practice. Although specific instructions are given for each group of exercises when they appear, it may help at this point to indicate the general nature of the material and to explain briefly the criteria which have been used in preparing the drills.

For each distinctive sound there are three types of exercises. First, there is a prose paragraph written by the authors in an attempt to present a speech sample which includes a generous sampling of the sound in a reasonably sensible context. This exercise is to be used in various ways. The student should try to pick out from the passage the sounds which have been discussed in the preceding section. Most of the possible spellings are illustrated. He should, of course, read the passage aloud. Each paragraph is transcribed phonetically at the end of the exercises for the sound, and the student will wish to use the earlier paragraphs to enhance his recognition use of the phonetic symbols. As soon as possible, however, he should try to make his own transcription before comparing it with the authors'.

Certain comments should be made about the pronunciations called for in the transcriptions. All are General American and are approximately those of one of the authors. The transcriptions are necessarily broad, however, and no attempt is made to note any of the fine features of speech, beyond the use of accent marks where they seemed to be helpful. The style is intended to be conversational, but rather frequently the pronunciations given are a shade more careful than they might have been in animated speech. This was deliberate, since it was felt that it would be best to err, if at all, in this direction.

The second type of exercise material consists of word lists illustrating the common appearances of the sound under discussion, with all common spellings represented. Considerable thought and care have gone into the selection of words, particularly those for the vowels, where the problems of analysis and discrimination are most difficult. The words have been drawn mainly from two sources: the list of *The One Thousand Most Frequently Spoken Words*,⁽³⁸⁾ and from the 1,000 most common words in the count of Thorndike and Lorge.⁽³³⁾ The words are, of course, to be used for practice in analysis and pronunciation.

The third type of exercise, and one which should be used to the fullest possible extent, consists of what are sometimes called minimal word pairs. The words in such pairs differ from each other only with respect to a single sound, which is always the sound under study. Practice in hearing the distinction between the words in each pair will be of great benefit in developing perception, particularly in regard to the vowels and diphthongs. These minimal pairs can be used in two ways. Read them aloud yourself many times and test on someone else your ability to produce the appropriate differences in speech quality; have someone else read them for you as you listen and transcribe.

Anyone who practices these exercises carefully and faithfully as he goes along should find himself understanding the English sound system better than he did, and the groundwork will be laid for improvement in his own speech. At no time, however, should he forget that the exercises we have provided are intended only as a starting point; the student is urged to devise his own drill material for each of the points made in the discussions of speech form. He should come to place more and more reliance on phonetic transcription as a basis for practice. Above all, he must develop a thorough *phonetic attitude* toward his own speaking, because herein lies the secret of a truly effective program of speech improvement.

5

THE FRONT VOWELS

[i], [ɪ], [e], [ɛ], [æ]

The vowels in this series are called *front vowels* because their usual pronunciation—and the differentiation of one from another—depends in large part upon the way in which the tongue is adjusted in the front part of the mouth. The various positions are presented graphically in the following portion of the vowel diagram:

[i]   High-front
   [ɪ]   Lower high-front
      [e]   Higher mid-front
         [ɛ]   Lower mid-front
            [æ]   Low-front

The tongue is thus at its lowest relative position for [æ] and rises as one goes through the series to [i], at which point the tongue is at its highest position for the series. An excellent way to study the positions for all the vowels is to whisper them. If this is done with the front-vowel series, we can note a successive elevation of the tongue from [æ] to [i]. It is apparent, however, that the steps are not necessarily equal and that it is not tongue height alone which brings about the differences among these vowels.

The extent of the mouth opening varies somewhat for each of the vowels. The jaw is dropped lowest for [æ], then is raised progressively for [ɛ], [e], [ɪ], and [i]. Actually, the elevation of the tongue and the movement of the jaw go together. Note that the lips are not ordinarily rounded for any of the front vowels. Some speakers draw the corners of the lips slightly outward in progressing through the steps from [æ] to [i]; others do not.

Three of the front vowels—the [ɪ], [ɛ], and [æ]—are often described as *simple nuclei*, or *pure*, vowels, whereas the [i] and [e] are considered more *complex*. This distinction is made because one of the characteristics

56

of [i] and [e] is a kind of vowel change or diphthongization. Tongue tension is also often mentioned in the classification of these vowels, with [i] and [e] being described as *tense* vowels and the others *lax*. All vowels, including those of the front series, are normally made without appreciable nasal resonance.

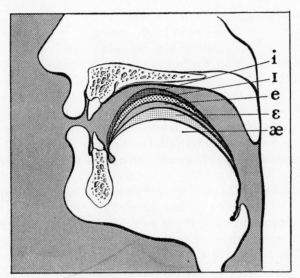

Fɪɢ. 4. Articulation adjustments for the front vowels.

A word of caution should be added about the vowel diagram (page 32). It is correct to think of the vowels in terms of a front-, central-, and back-vowel series and to regard the position of any sound on the chart as representative of the tongue adjustment for that particular vowel phoneme. To this extent the vowel diagram is useful in developing acceptable pronunciations. On the other hand, we must not forget that the acoustic end result of each vowel can be produced with quite different tongue positions and that this regularly happens in the habitual pronunciation of some speakers. Moreover, the phonetic context brings about a large number of variations in the specific sounds within a vowel phoneme as they are used in various words. For these reasons we should not think of the vowel diagram as giving exact and invariable tongue and lip positions for these sounds; it is, instead, more in the nature of a schematic representation of standard vowel positions. Both the height and the degree of fronting of the tongue, in the front and other vowels, are relative, rather than absolute, measures. A vowel is "front" or "high" only in relation to others which are "lower" or "back." The best way to ensure accurate vowel sounds in one's own speech is to develop a trained ear, rather than to rely primarily on tongue and lip positions. Attention to the latter, however, may be very helpful as a supplemental aid.

More detailed descriptions of each of the vowels, together with notes about common spellings and pronunciations, are given below.

[æ] as in cat, man, dash

Common Spellings: *a* as in hat, add
au as in laugh, aunt
Also spelled *ai*, as in plaid.

Production. The [æ] is the lowest of the front-vowel series, in terms of tongue position. The tongue lies on the floor of the mouth, but is advanced toward the front. This can be observed easily by pronouncing [æ] and [ɑ] (as in "father") alternately, since the [ɑ] is a *back* vowel. The mouth opening for [æ] is wider than for any other front vowel but is less than that for the low-back vowel [ɑ]. The lips are not rounded. Ordinarily [æ] is an unnasalized, low, simple (or undiphthongized), and fairly lax vowel.

Pronunciation. In English speech we use [æ] at the beginning of and within words, but rarely as a final sound. This vowel presents a number of problems in pronunciation. It can be produced acceptably with a tongue position somewhat higher than that indicated, but if the height passes a certain maximum and if the sound becomes too tense, it will seem to take on a "flat" quality which is considered typical of the objectionable "twang" sometimes heard in certain dialects of American speech. In addition it may acquire, or appear to acquire, a kind of "brittle" and sometimes unpleasant nasal quality not generally admired. This common fault should be avoided.

In certain Southern dialects a long diphthongized [æʌ] or [æjə] may be heard. For instance "had" sometimes becomes [hæʌd] or [hæjəd]. Speakers with a foreign-language background often have trouble mastering [æ], since English is one of the comparatively few languages in which a distinction is made between [æ] and [ɑ]. Among these individuals the substitution of some sound from the [ɑ] phoneme in place of [æ] is very common. The Frenchman's pronunciation of "sad," for example, may sound much like "sod" [sɑd] to an American ear.

There are many cases in English pronunciation in which either [æ] or some other sound may properly be used. Before *r* in words such as "vary," "carry," and "Harry," the vowel may be heard as [æ] or as [ɛ], depending on the habitual pronunciation of the speaker. In General American, [ɛ] probably predominates. In many words the presence of [æ] is a distinguishing characteristic of General American speech, as compared with other dialect forms.

In this connection an interesting historical change has occurred in a group of about 150 English words. In Southern British these formerly had the [æ] pronunciation but now are given the pronunciation of [ɑ]. Where the [ɑ] or [æ] precedes the [s], [f], [θ], or a nasal, the [æ] of seventeenth-century British has changed to the [ɑ] of modern British. It is this change which has led to the broad *a* of Southern British, which is one of its distinguishing features. The General American (GA) dialect was derived more directly from seventeenth-century British. Therefore, it uses [æ] in these words. On the other hand, Eastern American (EA) speech, with more influences from eighteenth-century British, uses the [ɑ], or something very close to a typical [ɑ]. Such words as "laugh," "mast," and "can't" would be pronounced in England and typically in EA as [lɑf], [mɑst], and [kɑnt], whereas elsewhere in the United States the pronunciations would be [læf], [mæst], and [kænt].

In the EA and British pronunciation of such words a vowel may be heard which is neither exactly [æ] or [ɑ] but appears to be a compromise between them. Such a sound lies on the vowel diagram between [æ] and [ɑ] and may be called the intermediate [a]. It is, ordinarily, only a variety of [ɑ], however, and need not be learned as a distinctive vowel.

Attempts by GA speakers to adopt the broad *a* "out of dialect," so to speak, are to be avoided since they nearly always result in a ridiculous caricature of British or Eastern speech.

Exercises

1. The following paragraph contains about 28 words which are normally pronounced, in the General American dialect, with the [æ] sound. In addition, there are a number which are pronounced with the [æ] when stressed but which may more often be pronounced [ə] when unstressed. For some of the words the so-called broad *a* may be heard in some dialects of English and American speech. See whether you can identify the words in which these various [æ] sounds might appear. Read the paragraph aloud and practice observing in your own pronunciation the formation of the vowels of these words. Listen for this sound in the speech of others. After you have tried to identify the sounds in your own speech, turn to the phonetic transcription of this passage, following these exercises, to observe the author's pronunciation, which is typical of one kind of General American speech.

Good speech habits, in the last analysis, do not demand any special aptitude. Drill must be carried out after the fashion of trial-and-error learning, so that speech has exactly the sound demanded by acceptable standards of pronunciation. It is necessary to give careful attention to the pattern of sound, and to practice until one is satisfied that he has actually mastered an accurate standard. When the capacity to catch fine distinctions between sounds has at last been mastered, there will be ample reward for past effort, and the battle for good speech will have been half won. One must ask, "How should it sound?" Then marry academic theory to practical accomplishment.

2. The following list contains a number of words in which the [æ] sound is commonly heard in English. Note that in some dialects certain of thewords may be pronounced with the [a] or [ɑ] (the broad-a sounds). In some of the words certain other alternative pronunciations may be found. Study these words, observing such differences in the speech of your friends and acquaintances. Which sounds do *you* use in context? In isolated words? List *e* has been included to draw to your attention the special quality [æ] often possesses, or may appear to possess, when it occurs in combination with [ŋ]. Be careful not to make these sounds too flat or nasal.

a. Illustrative words using [æ] in stressed syllables:

accident	camp	hand	practically
act	captain	happen	practice
action	catch	happy	ran
activity	contact	hat	sat
actually	drastic	land	stamp
add	exactly	Latin	stand
animal	examination	man	standard
average	fact	manner	taxation
bad	factory	mathematics	taxes
back	family	matter	traveling
bag	glad	national	understand
balance	graduate	natural	valley
battle	grammar	perhaps	value
began	grass	plan	

b. Illustrative words pronounced [æ] or, in Eastern speech, [a] or [ɑ]:

advance	chance	France	master
advantage	class	glass	past
after	command	grant	pass
afternoon	demand	half	plant
answer	dance	last	rather
ask	drama	laugh	slant
can't	fast		

c. Illustrative [ær] words, in which either [æ] or [ɛ] is commonly heard:

apparently	carry	marry	share
character	care	various	

d. Illustrative unaccented [æ] words, usually pronounced in connected speech with [ə]:

an	at	had	than
and	can	has	that
as	cannot	have	

e. Illustrative [æŋ] words:

bank	language	sank	rang
hang	crank	tank	thank

3. The following list contains pairs of words which differ only with respect to the single sound under study. Practice the pairs, making each word sound distinctively different from the other member of the pair. Can you think of any more such pairs? (For other minimal pairs involving [æ], see Exercise 3 following the discussion of [ɪ].)

[æ]—[ɛ]

bad [bæd]	bed [bɛd]
back [bæk]	beck [bɛk]
bag [bæg]	beg [bɛg]
and [ænd]	end [ɛnd]
man [mæn]	men [mɛn]
pat [pæt]	pet [pɛt]
sad [sæd]	said [sɛd]
sat [sæt]	set [sɛt]
tan [tæn]	ten [tɛn]
land [lænd]	lend [lɛnd]

[æ]—[ɑ]

add [æd]	odd [ɑd]
ax [æks]	ox [ɑks]
bag [bæg]	bog [bɑg]
battle [bætl̩]	bottle [bɑtl̩]
cat [kæt]	cot [kɑt]
lack [læk]	lock [lɑk]
pat [pæt]	pot [pɑt]
hat [hæt]	hot [hɑt]
sap [sæp]	sop [sɑp]
valley [vælɪ]	volley [vɑlɪ]

[æ]—[ɔ]

Al [æl]	all [ɔl]
at [æt]	ought [ɔt]
cast [kæst]	cost [kɔst]
crass [kræs]	cross [krɔs]
lag [læg]	log [lɔg]
lass [læs]	loss [lɔs]
last [læst]	lost [lɔst]
rang [ræŋ]	wrong [rɔŋ]
sang [sæŋ]	song [sɔŋ]
tat [tæt]	taught [tɔt]

Phonetic Transcription. The following is a phonetic transcription of the paragraph given in Exercise 1, as it was spoken in a conversational manner by one of the authors. You should compare this pronunciation with your own, checking on your conclusions with regard to the pronunciations of the [æ] words in particular. It should be emphasized at this point that this is not the only way this paragraph could be correctly

62   PHONETICS

pronounced—or even, possibly, the best way for your own particular
purposes or locality. It is spoken in what we call a General American
dialect—roughly synonymous with that spoken in the West and North,
as opposed to the Eastern and Southern regions.

[gʊd spitʃ hæbəts, ɪn ðə læst ənæləsəs, du nɑt dɪ'mænd ɛnɪ speʃəl 'æptə,-
tud. drɪl mʌst bi 'kɛrɪd aʊt æftɚ ðə fæʃən əv traɪəl ən ɛrɚ 'lɝnɪŋ, so ðət
spitʃ hæz ɛg'zæktlɪ ðə saʊnd dɪ'mændəd baɪ æk'sɛptəbl̩ stændɚdz əv
prə,nʌnsi'eʃən. ɪt ɪz 'nɛsə,sɛrɪ tə gɪv kɛrfəl ətɛnʃən tə ðə pætɚn əv saʊnd,
æn tə præktəs əntɪl wʌn ɪz 'sætəs,faɪd ðət hi əz 'æktʃəwəlɪ mæstɚd ən
ækjərət stændɚd. hwɛn ðə kəpæsətɪ tə kætʃ faɪn dɪ'stɪŋkʃənz bɪ'twin
saʊndz hæz ət læst bɪn mæstɚd, ðer wəl bi æmpl̩ rɪ'wɔrd fɔr pæst ɛfɚt,
ænd ðə bætl̩ fɔr gʊd spitʃ wɪl həv bɪn hæf wʌn. wʌn mʌst æsk, "haʊ ʃʊd
ɪt saʊnd?" ðɛn 'mɛrɪ ,ækə'dɛmɪk 'θɪrɪ tʊ 'præktɪkl̩ ə'kʌmplɪʃmənt.]

[ɛ] as in get, many, head

Common Spellings: e as in bed, best
ea as in bread, lead
Also spelled a, as in many; ai, as in again; ue, as
in guess; u, as in bury; ay, as in says; ei, as in
heifer; oe, as in asafoetida; eo, as in Leonard.

Production. Vowels in the [ɛ] phoneme call for a tongue position somewhat higher than that for [æ] and perhaps slightly farther forward. The
jaw closes slightly from [æ] to [ɛ], but the lip position is otherwise similar.
This vowel is relatively short and ordinarily pure, or undiphthongized,
in comparison with the [e] and [i], and perhaps the [æ]. Nasal resonance
is not ordinarily a part of this vowel, and the tongue tension is described
as lax. The [ɛ] may be classified as a lower mid-front, lax vowel.

Pronunciation. A special comment should be made about the various
spellings which have come to have the pronunciation value of [ɛ]. Most
often the sounds in this phoneme are represented by the letter e in conventional orthography, although it is unfortunate for the beginning
student of English pronunciation that this letter may also designate
several other sounds. Note, for example, variations in the words "fetus,"
"fete," "fern," "Lewis," and "reply."

Although [ɛ] is not the worst offender in this respect, over 10 different
spellings may be found (though not all are common). These variations
in orthography for a single sound have their origin in a number of changes
which took place historically in the development of the English language,
but their effect from a practical point of view has been to create a confusing situation for the speaker who attempts to infer pronunciation
from spelling alone. Only careful listening to standard speech and use
of a dictionary will clear up the difficulties which may arise.

There are a good many variations in the pronunciation of [ɛ] in addition to those which have their basis in spelling practices. The use of [e] for [ɛ]—as in [freʃ] for [frɛʃ] or [eg] for [ɛg]—may be encountered. Although common, this usage probably should be avoided. Some speakers omit [ɛ] where the diphthong [ɛɚ] is ordinarily used in General American speech, which would result in the pronunciation of "there" as [ðɚ] or [ðɝ] rather than [ðɛɚ] ([ðɛr]). In informal pronunciation, however, or when the word which normally uses [ɛɚ] is unstressed, the [ɚ] may be acceptable. For example, [ðɚ ɑrnt ɛnɪ] for "there aren't any" might be all right, whereas [ðɝ ðe ɑr] for "there they are" would not. Failure to sound [ɛ] is usually considered substandard in such pronunciations as [bɝɪ] for "bury" [bɛrɪ] or [baɚ] for "bear" [bɛɚ].

Perhaps particular notice should be taken of the substitution of [ɪ] for [ɛ]. Although the number of words affected by this change may not be so great as it sometimes seems, the frequency of [gɪt] for [gɛt], [pɪn] for [pɛn], and [mɪnɪ] for [mɛnɪ] may make this substitution particularly annoying to the sensitive listener. It should not be inferred that all departures from a General American [ɛ], as used in stressed syllables, are substandard. There are very good reasons for arguing that many common [ɛ] words, and some others as well, are pronounced naturally, and by most people, with a sound approaching the quality of [ɪ]. Nevertheless, when good usage calls for the vowel to be accented, such substitutions or "distortions" of vowel quality may not be the best choice for the person who wishes his speech to be most acceptable to the greatest number of people.

In addition to these variations in pronunciation, some speakers use [ɛ] as an alternative to [æ], particularly in such words as "vary" and "marry." For a discussion of this substitution refer to the section on [æ].

Exercises

1. In the following paragraph about 32 of the words may be pronounced with some sound from the [ɛ] phoneme. See whether you can identify these words. In addition look for those [ɛ] words which might also be pronounced with an [ɪ] and for those words which might be acceptably pronounced with either an [æ] or an [ɛ]. When you have identified them, see what the authors did with the phonetic transcription of this passage.

The discerning student of speech will have many occasions to speculate on the relation between voice and personality. Unless he is completely insensitive to what is said in his presence—and to how it is said—he may note that such things as tension in the voice and certain patterns of inflection may sometimes allow him to make fairly correct guesses about the personality, education, or place of residence of the speaker. This matter of the relation between voice and personality has been studied many times by various investigators, apparently with somewhat disparate results. There is one very important fact that has emerged from all of these attempts to clarify the situation: whether we like it or not, people do get a picture of us from the sound of our voice alone. This picture is not necessarily a true one, but it is very often a reliable one. This means that the effect spread by our voices is one listeners agree upon, even though it may not be the same as the effect spread by other kinds of behavior. We should remember these lessons as we prepare to be better speakers.

2. The following is a list of common [ɛ] words. Do you pronounce any of these with [ɪ]? Should you? Do you use [e] or [æ], in place of [ɛ], in any of these words? Is it common usage? Is it good usage? For further words which may be pronounced with [ɛ] consult list *c* in the exercises for the sound [æ].

again	eleven	intelligent	primarily	step
against	else	itself	process	strength
ahead	energy	kept	protect	success
already	end	left	question	tell
amendment	enter	less	read	ten
America	ever	let	red	test
any	every	letter	remember	their
attempt	evidently	many	represent	them
attention	expression	measure	rest	themselves
benefit	February	men	said	then
best	federal	mental	scarcely	there
better	fair	met	second	twenty
century	fellow	method	self	unless
correct	French	mention	sell	very
death	forget	necessary	sense	wears
December	friend	never	separate	well
debt	general	next	September	went
definite	generation	November	set	when
depend	get	pen	send	Wednesday
develop	hair	percentage	sentence	where
direct	head	personnel	seven	whether
education	heavy	prepare	specialize	yellow
effect	held	present	spend	yes
egg	help	president	spent	yet
element	however			

3. The following minimal pairs differ with respect to the sound [ɛ] only. Practice making the distinctions indicated; then try to find other pairs which will illustrate the same distinctions. (For other minimal pairs involving [ɛ], see [ɝ].)

[ɛ]—[e]		[ɛ]—[æ]	
edge [ɛdʒ]	age [edʒ]	any [ɛnɪ]	Annie [ænɪ]
M [ɛm]	aim [em]	bet [bɛt]	bat [bæt]
best [bɛst]	based [best]	head [hɛd]	had [hæd]
debt [dɛt]	date [det]	left [lɛft]	laughed [læft]
get [gɛt]	gate [get]	less [lɛs]	lass [læs]
let [lɛt]	late [let]	letter [lɛtɚ]	latter [lætɚ]
men [mɛn]	main [men]	met [mɛt]	mat [mæt]
sell [sɛl]	sale [sel]	pen [pɛn]	pan [pæn]
west [wɛst]	waste [west]	sell [sɛl]	Sal [sæl]
wreck [rɛk]	rake [rek]	then [ðɛn]	than [ðæn]

[ɛ]—[ɪ]	
head [hɛd]	hid [hɪd]
letter [lɛtɚ]	litter [lɪtɚ]
met [mɛt]	mitt [mɪt]
pen [pɛn]	pin [pɪn]
red [rɛd]	rid [rɪd]
said [sɛd]	Sid [sɪd]
sell [sɛl]	sill [sɪl]
tell [tɛl]	till [tɪl]
ten [tɛn]	tin [tɪn]
well [wɛl]	will [wɪl]

Phonetic Transcription. In the following phonetic transcription of the paragraph in Exercise 1, most of the [ɛ] words appear in accented syllables, and their pronunciation is fairly uniform. This is not always the case, however. Which of the following [ɛ] sounds might be pronounced with an [ɪ] quality by some speakers? Which might be pronounced with [æ] rather than [ɛ]?

[ðə dɪ'zɝnɪŋ studn̩t əv spitʃ wɪl hæv mɛnɪ əkeʒənz tə 'spɛkjə,let ɔn ðə rɪ'leʃən bɪ'twin vɔɪs ən ,pɝsə'nælətɪ. ʌn'lɛs hi ɪz kəmplitlɪ ɪn'sɛnsətɪv tə hwʌt ɪz sɛd ɪn hɪz prɛzəns—æn tə hau ɪt ɪz sɛd—hi me not ðət sʌtʃ θɪŋz əz tɛnʃən ɪn ðə vɔɪs ən sɝtn̩ pætɚnz əv ɪn'flɛkʃən me 'sʌm'taɪmz əlau hɪm tə mek fɛrlɪ kərɛkt gɛsəz əbaut ðə ,pɝsə'nælətɪ, ,ɛdʒə'keʃən, ɔr ples əv rɛzədəns əv ðə spikɚ. ðɪs mætɚ əv ðə rɪ'leʃən bɪ'twin vɔɪs ən ,pɝsə-'nælətɪ hæz bɪn 'stʌdɪd 'mɛnɪ taɪmz baɪ 'vɛriəs ɪn'vɛstə,getɚz, əpɛrəntlɪ wıθ 'sʌm'hwʌt dɪspərət rɪ'zʌlts. ðɛr ız wʌn vɛrı ım'pɔrtnt fækt ðət hæz ɪ'mɝdʒd frəm əl ə ðiz ətemps tə 'klɛrə,faı ðə ,sıtʃə'weʃən: hwɛðɝ wi laık ıt ɔr nɑt, pipḷ du gɛt ə pıktʃɝ əv ʌs frʌm ðə saund əv aur vɔıs əlon. ðıs pıktʃɝ ız nɑt ,nɛsə'sɛrəlı ə tru wʌn, bʌt ıt ız vɛrı ɔfən ə rɪ'laıəbḷ wʌn. ðıs minz ðət ði əfɛkt sprɛd baı aur vɔısəz ız wʌn lısənɝz əgri əpɔn, ivən ðo ıt me nɑt bi ðə sɛm æz ði əfɛkt sprɛd baı ʌðɝ kaındz əv bɪ'hevjɝ. wi ʃəd rɪ'mɛmbɝ ðiz lɛsənz æz wi prɪ'pɛr tu bi bɛtɝ spikɝz.]

[e] as in late, take, haste

Common Spellings: *a* as in taste, place
  ai as in rain, pain
  ay as in say, play
  ea as in steak, break
  ey as in they, obey
  e as in debris, mesa
  Also spelled *au*, as in gauge; *uet*, as in bouquet; *et*, as in chalet.

Production. As most frequently pronounced in General American speech, the [e] is a step higher than [ɛ] in the front-vowel series. To shift from [ɛ] to [e] one should raise the jaw slightly and bring the front of the tongue somewhat nearer the alveolar ridge, or front of the hard palate. Subjectively there may be an impression that [e] differs from [ɛ] primarily because it is a tense rather than a lax vowel, but there is also a difference in tongue posture.

The vowel [e] is often described as one of the complex nuclei, or diphthongal, vowels. Although the sound can be made without diphthongization (and for this and other reasons is described here as a vowel rather than as a diphthong), it is ordinarily made in such a way that considerable resonance *change* takes place within the syllable. The tongue movement is typically from a position close to [ɛ] toward the position for [i]. Many phoneticians, indeed, would prefer to use such symbols as [eɪ], [ei], or [ɛj] instead of [e] to represent the articulation of this vowel. For [e] the lips are not rounded and there is no nasal resonance as a rule. It is conventionally classified as a higher mid-front, tense vowel.

Pronunciation. The usual confusions which arise from the variable spelling of a sound occur similarly with words containing [e]. There are also sub-standard or dialectal usages which should be avoided, especially in the substitution of [ɛ] for [e] in old-fashioned, or *relic*, pronunciations like [nɛkəd] for "naked" and [ɛt] for "ate," or in the pronunciation of a word such as "great" as [grɛt].

The amount of stress given [e] has a great deal to do with its actual pronunciation in American speech. The diphthongization of [e], like that of other vowels, varies with the length of the sound, which in turn depends upon its stress and upon context. Diphthongization can be noticed particularly when the sound occurs at the end of a word, so that "way" tends to be more clearly [weɪ], or even [wei], than [we]. The sound may also be pronounced in this way when it occurs within a word if the speaker for some reason stresses the vowel, although there is less tendency to diphthongize in this situation. The word "cake," for instance, may be heard as either [keɪk] or [kek], depending partly on the amount of stress given the vowel. Although too much diphthongization may occasionally be heard, the common fault in foreign-dialect speech is too little.

When [e] loses its stress it often becomes [ɪ] or a sound very much like [ɪ]. Note, for example, the pronunciations of the days of the week. The colloquial pronunciation of "Monday" is more often [mʌndɪ] or [mʌndi] than [mʌnde]. Some speakers may wish to avoid the pronunciation [mʌndi], since it may be considered of borderline acceptability.

Exercises

1. In this paragraph about 35 of the sounds are normally pronounced with some variation of the phoneme [e]. See whether you can identify these sounds. In addition, which do you think receive a relatively great amount of diphthongization? Which relatively little? Comment on the pronunciation of the definite article "a." Check your pronunciation with the transcription following these exercises.

Good taste in speech will repay one daily for such small effort as it may entail. Basically, the way in which we talk is taken as a measure of our personality traits, our education and culture. It can be claimed, with considerable persuasive force, that too much stress can be placed on slavish concern for pronunciation rules. The practiced ease of a good speaker, however, is mainly a painstakingly cultivated "feel" for the rhythm and style of spoken language. In the main, he will favor plain and straightforward ways of saying what he has to convey, and will not deign to lay on, like a cape, the presumed elegancies of stage diction or some other strained or ornate manner. He will thus be related to his listener in a communicative way, but ostentation and seeming display will play no part in his speech behavior.

2. Study the following list of [e] words. Note the variations in diphthongization which may result from stress or phonetic context. In which words would the pronunciation [ɪ] be preferable in contextual speech?

able	education	late	pay	station
afraid	eight	lay	phase	stay
age	eighth	made	place	straight
aid	escape	main	play	strange
always	explain	maintain	race	Sunday
away	face	major	radio	taste
baby	famous	make	rain	take
based	Friday	making	raise	taken
basis	gain	may	remain	taxation
bay	game	maybe	safe	Thursday
became	gate	name	same	today
break	gave	nation	sale	Tuesday
came	generation	Monday	Saturday	trade
case	graduate	nature	save	train
change	gray	neighbors	say	wait
contain	great	occasion	shape	wave
create	illustrate	page	space	way
date	labor	paint	stage	Wednesday
day	laid	paid	state	weight
educate	lake	paper		

3. Practice the following list of minimal pairs, attempting to make the words in each pair sound distinctively different from each other. Try to find other pairs of the same nature. (For other minimal pairs, see [aɪ].)

[e]—[ɪ]

ale [el]	ill [ɪl]
break [brek]	brick [brɪk]
case [kes]	kiss [kɪs]
eight [et]	it [ɪt]
gave [gev]	give [gɪv]
laid [led]	lid [lɪd]
lake [led]	lick [lɪk]
pain [pen]	pin [pɪn]
stake [stek]	stick [stɪk]
tape [tep]	tip [tɪp]

[e]—[ɛ]

aid [ed]	Ed [ɛd]
bale [bel]	bell [bɛl]
laid [led]	led [lɛd]
laced [lest]	lest [lɛst]
paced [pest]	pest [pɛst]
paint [pent]	pent [pɛnt]
phase [fez]	fez [fɛz]
taste [test]	test [tɛst]
rain [ren]	wren [rɛn]
wait [wet]	wet [wɛt]

[e]—[i]

great [gret]	greet [grit]
laid [led]	lead [lid]
lake [lek]	leak [lik]
male [mel]	meal [mil]
main [men]	mean [min]
pace [pes]	peace [pis]

shape [ʃep]   sheep [ʃip]
way [we]   we [wi]
wake [wek]   week [wik]
wave [wev]   weave [wiv]

Phonetic Transcription. Study the following phonetic transcription of the paragraph in Exercise 1. Compare your pronunciation with that of the author, keeping in mind that the author's pronunciation illustrates only *one* of many which would have been acceptable. This pronunciation is informal colloquial. What changes would occur in a formal style?

[gʊd test ɪn spitʃ wɪl rɪ'pe wʌn delɪ fɚ sʌtʃ smɔl ɛfɚt əz ɪt me əntel. 'besɪklɪ ðə we ɪn hwɪtʃ wi tɔk ɪz tekən əz ə mɛʒɚ əv aʊr ˌpɚsə'næləti trets, aʊr ˌɛdʒə'keʃən ən kʌltʃɚ. ɪt kən bi klemd, wɪθ kənsɪdərəbḷ pɚ'swesɪv fɔrs, ðət tu mʌtʃ strɛs kən bi plest ɑn 'slevɪʃ kənsɚn fɔr prəˌnʌnsi'eʃən rulz. ðə præktəst ɪz əv ə gʊd spikɚ, haʊ'ɛvɚ, ɪz menlɪ ə 'penzˌtekɪŋlɪ 'kʌltəˌvetəd fiəl fɔr ðə rɪðəm ən staɪəl əv spokən 'læŋgwɪdʒ. ɪn ðə men hi wəl fevɚ plen ən 'stret'fɔrwɚd wez əv seɪŋ hwʌt hi hæz tə kənve, ænd wəl nɑt den tə le ɑn, laɪk ə kep, ðə prɪ'zumd 'ɛləgənsiz əv stedʒ dɪkʃən ɔr sʌm ʌðɚ strend ɚ ɔr'net mænɚ. hi wəl ðʌs bi rɪ'letəd tu ɪz lɪsnɚ ɪn ə kəm'junɚˌketɪv we, bət ˌɑstən'teʃən ən 'simɪŋ dɪs'ple wɪl ple no pɑrt ɪn hɪz spitʃ bɪ'hevjɚ.]

[ɪ] as in hit, listen, sister

Common Spellings: *i* as in sit, thin
y as in duty, hymn
Also spelled *ui*, as in build; *e*, as in here; *u*, as in busy; *ea*, as in dear; *ee*, as in deer; *ie*, as in pierce; *o*, as in women.

Production. The vowel [ɪ] is directly above [e] in the front-vowel series. The front of the tongue is somewhat higher than it is for the standard [e] position, and the jaw is moved slightly upward. The subjective impression given by [ɪ] is that of a lax vowel, particularly when compared with [i], which is the highest of the front vowels. The lips are not rounded. The [ɪ] may be classified as a lower high-front, lax vowel. It is relatively short in length and is simple, or without significant diphthongization.

Pronunciation. The [ɪ] and [i] vowels are often a source of considerable perplexity to students, for a relatively large number of phonetic variations within each of these phonemes can be detected in conversational speech. At times it may be difficult to decide whether a certain vowel one hears belongs in the [i] or [ɪ] phoneme. The classical illustration of this point is the final vowel in the word "city," but the same phonetic conditions exist in other words, such as "very" and "company." "City" may be either [sɪtɪ] or [sɪti], or the final sound may actually be somewhere intermediate between the usual [ɪ] and [i] pronunciations. The [i] usage is possibly more typical of General American speech than of Eastern or Southern. Stress and context determine the precise form of the vowel, of course. For example, even though the General American pronunciation of "beauty" may employ the final [i], the [ɪ], or even [ə], would be more acceptable in the word "beautiful" [bjutəfəl]. Pronunciations like [bjutifəl] are occasionally heard but are mildly substandard.

In most of the foregoing illustrations the vowels in question have not been stressed, but even when the sound is more strongly stressed, there may be variations from [ɪ] to [i] among various speakers. A familiar illustration is the [bin] rather than [bɪn] for "been" in Southern British. When the succeeding sound is spelled with *r*, variations from [ɪ] to [i] may be heard. Thus, "zero" may be either [ziro] or [zɪro]. Here again none of the pronunciations mentioned would usually be considered substandard, although in some regions they may be considered somewhat obtrusive. Only an ear sensitive to the speech of the educated native speakers in your locality will tell you which is preferable. The substitution of [i] for [ɪ] in stressed syllables may be definitely substandard in some words. For example, [miʃiet] for "initiate" and [miʃigən] for "Michigan" are localisms to be avoided by the careful speaker. A far from infrequent substandard usage is the "careless" habit of centralizing the vowel [ɪ], and other vowels as well, so that this sound takes on a dull-[ʌ]-ish quality, as in [aɪwʌʃ i wʌd] for "I wish he would."

Before the consonant [ŋ] in the *ing* words the [ɪ] takes on a somewhat tense, and possibly nasal, quality. If not overdone, this coloring is perfectly natural. The substitution of [i] for [ɪ] in such contexts, however, is usually substandard. Thus, [sɪŋɪŋ əv sprɪŋ] is a more careful pronunciation than [siniŋ əv spriŋ].

For the most part outright unacceptable pronunciations of sounds in the [ɪ] phoneme are heard only among speakers with a foreign-language background. Such persons typically substitute a stressed [i] for [ɪ] in words like "it," "is," and "hit." The vowel in each case is tense rather than lax and may tend to be longer or more diphthongal than the [ɪ] which would be used by the American speaker in these words. The foreigner may make this error because in his own language the two phonemes are not separated. The Italian dialect, for example, may typically lead to confusions between "ship" and "sheep," "slip" and "sleep," and "dip" and "deep." Omission of [ɪ] as in [ɛvɚbadɪ] for [ɛvrɪbadɪ] in the word "everybody" is a noteworthy substandard usage.

Exercises

1. Here is a paragraph which contains a generous sampling of words normally pronounced with some variation of the [ɪ]. See how many you

can identify. Pay special attention to the quality of [ɪ] in the *ing* context and in words receiving relatively little stress. Check the author's transcription following these exercises.

By this time the beginner will find that the seeming intricacies of phonetic transcription should be resolving themselves into certain relatively simple principles which enable him to begin spelling with sounds instead of less meaningful letters. As this ability improves, an important skill will begin developing: the capacity to distinguish the different sounds in the myriad familiar words we hear repeatedly, and to notice what has hitherto been missed. Bit by bit, listening facility is being acquired in easy but effective ways. It is within the realm of possibility for nearly every individual to become so proficient that he can, without seeming design, get a vivid impression of the pronunciation of English. Learning the diction of a language will appear increasingly simple if the novice makes it his business to consider words as sounds fitted together in a close-knit mosaic.

2. Study the following list of [ɪ] words. For which of them do you think acceptable variations in pronunciation exist? Check yourself by looking up the pronunciation of some of these words in a pronouncing dictionary.

a. Illustrative words using [ɪ] in stressed syllables:

ability	different	increase	miniatures	simple
activity	dishes	Indian	Mr.	since
appears	district	individual	Mrs.	situation
been	efficient	industry	miss	six
begin	exist	information	official	still
bill	fifteen	instant	opinion	system
bit	figure	institution	particularly	this
build	fill	isn't	permit	thrift
built	finish	instrument	physical	until
business	give	international	physics	visit
children	given	interpret	picture	which
city	him	introduce	political	will
civilization	his	insurance	position	wind
committee	history	intelligent	possibility	window
composition	illustrate	killed	principle	wish
condition	impossible	liquor	quick	with
consider	imply	little	religion	within
continue	importance	live	river	without
criminal	income	milk	rich	women
did	include	million	ship	written

b. Illustrative words using [ɪ] in unstressed, or relatively unstressed, syllables (pronunciation may vary among [i], [ɪ], [ɛ], and [ə]):

accomplish	begin	design	expression	result
advantage	believe	divide	extent	remain
always	between	economics	furnish	return
article	benefit	enjoy	in	remember
audience	college	enough	if	receive
average	decide	entirely	it	represent
became	degree	employ	is	reserve
because	demand	examination	knowledge	subject
become	department	example	language	the
before	describe	except	percentage	topic
began	drastic	experiment	public	various

c. Illustrative *ing* words:

being	doing	going	resulting	think
bring	during	king	single	training
coming	English	putting	thing	trying

d. Illustrative [ɪr] words:

appears	dear	hear	merely	serious
beard	experience	here	near	spirit
clear	fear	material	period	year

e. Illustrative final-*y* words (pronunciation may vary between [ɪ] and [i], and in general either is correct):

ability	city	fifty	ninety	seventy
activity	community	finally	opportunity	sixty
actually	duty	forty	party	study
apparently	early	Friday	personality	thirty
already	easily	happy	philosophy	Thursday
any	easy	heavy	policy	Tuesday
army	eighty	history	poetry	twenty
body	elementary	immediately	possibility	university
carry	entirely	industry	practically	usually
committee	especially	lady	pretty	variety
company	every	Monday	primarily	very
country	exactly	money	probably	Saturday
century	family	necessary	scarcely	Sunday

3. Practice the following lists of minimal pairs. Learn to discriminate between them and learn to produce them with clarity. Try to expand the lists. (For other minimal pairs, see [e].)

[ɪ]—[i]

bid [bɪd]	bead [bid]
been [bɪn]	bean [bin]
did [dɪd]	deed [did]
dim [dɪm]	deem [dim]
live [lɪv]	leave [liv]
rich [rɪtʃ]	reach [ritʃ]
rill [rɪl]	real [ril]
is [ɪz]	ease [iz]
sin [sɪn]	seen [sin]
ship [ʃɪp]	sheep [ʃip]

[ɪ]—[æ]

bit [bɪt]	bat [bæt]
did [dɪd]	dad [dæd]
fist [fɪst]	fast [fæst]
his [hɪz]	has [hæz]
in [ɪn]	an [æn]
miss [mɪs]	mass [mæs]
mister [mɪstɚ]	master [mæstɚ]
sit [sɪt]	sat [sæt]
begin [bɪgɪn]	began [bɪgæn]
him [hɪm]	ham [hæm]

[ɪ]—[ɛ]

bill [bɪl]	bell [bɛl]
bitter [bɪtɚ]	better [bɛtɚ]
bit [bɪt]	bet [bɛt]
fear [fɪr]	fair [fɛr]
here [hɪr]	hair [hɛr]
lift [lɪft]	left [lɛft]
in [ɪn]	N [ɛn]
wrist [rɪst]	rest [rɛst]
sit [sɪt]	set [sɛt]
knit [nɪt]	net [nɛt]

Phonetic Transcription. Here is a transcription of the material in Exercise 1. Criticize and compare your own pronunciation with that of the author. In which ways do you differ?

[baɪ ðɪs taɪm ðə bɪˈgɪnɚ wɪl faɪnd ðæt ðə ˈsimɪŋ ˈɪntrəkəsɪz əv fəˈnɛtɪk ˌtrænˈskrɪpʃən ʃəd bi rɪˈzɑlvɪŋ ðɛmˈsɛlvz ɪntə sɝtṇ ˈrɛlətɪvlɪ sɪmpḷ prɪnsəpḷz hwɪtʃ ənebḷ hɪm tə bɪˈgɪn ˈspɛlɪŋ wɪθ saʊndz ɪnˈstɛd əv lɛs ˈmɪnɪŋfəl lɛtɚz. æz ðɪs əbɪlətɪ ɪmˈpruvz, æn ɪmˈpɔrtṇt skɪl wɪl bɪˈgɪn dɪˈvɛləpɪŋ: ðə kəpæsətɪ tə dɪsˈtɪŋgwɪʃ ðə dɪfrənt saʊndz ɪn ðə ˈmɪriəd fəmɪljɚ wɝdz wi hɪr rɪˈpitədlɪ, æn tə notəs hwʌt həz ˌhɪðɚˈtu bɪn mɪst. bɪt baɪ bɪt, ˈlɪsənɪŋ fəˈsɪlətɪ ɪz ˈbiɪŋ əkwaɪɚd ɪn ɪzɪ bət ɪˈfɛktɪv wez. ɪt ɪz wɪˈðɪn ðə rɛlm əv ˌpasəˈbɪlətɪ fɔr nɪrlɪ ɛvrɪ ˌɪndəˈvɪdʒəwəl tu bɪˈkʌm so prəfɪʃənt ðət hi kæn, wɪˈðaʊt ˈsimɪŋ dɪˈzaɪn, gɛt ə vɪvəd ɪmˈprɛʃən əv ðə prəˌnʌnsiˈeʃən əv ˈɪŋglɪʃ. ˈlɝnɪŋ ðə dɪkʃən əv ə ˈlæŋgwɪdʒ wɪl əpɪr ɪnˈkrisɪŋlɪ sɪmpḷ ɪf ðə navəs meks ət ɪz bɪznəs tə kənsɪdɚ wɝdz æz saʊndz fɪtəd təgɛðɚ ɪn ə klos nɪt moˈzeɪk.]

[i] as in seem, wheat, fleet

Common Spellings: e as in even, equal
ee as in seen, between

ea as in read, eager

ei as in receipt, deceive

ie as in believe, field

i as in machine, ravine

Also spelled *eo*, as in people; *oe*, as in amoeba; *ae*, as in Caesar; *uay*, as in quay.

Production. The [i] is the final phoneme of the front-vowel series. A shift from [ɪ] to [i] requires some additional elevation of the front of the tongue, but the change in position is comparatively small. For [i] the tongue is higher than for any of the other front vowels. With most speakers the tongue nearly touches the alveolar ridge or anterior part of the hard palate; the approximation is so close that some slight fricative sound is often heard along with the vowel. The lower jaw is raised so that the teeth are nearly in occlusion. The lips are not rounded, and may be noticeably drawn back. The [i] is one of the complex, or diphthongal, vowels. The amount of diphthongization varies, but proceeds from a lower and laxer to a higher and tenser vowel position. Such symbols as [ɪi], [ɪj], or [ij] are sometimes used to illustrate this. The generalized classification for [i] is as a high-front, tense vowel.

Pronunciation. Some of the characteristics of the phoneme [i] in English pronunciation were brought out in connection with the discussion of [ɪ], but a few additional features must be noted. There is a great deal of variation in the length and diphthongization of sounds in the [i] phoneme, depending, of course, upon the amount of stress. In words like "seem," "repeat," and "scream," as commonly pronounced, the stress pattern is actually such that [i] could be quite accurately transcribed as a diphthong [ɪi]. When the vowel is not diphthongized—as in the pronunciation of some foreign speakers—the sound seems vaguely unfamiliar, even though we may not be able to tell exactly why this is so. Diphthongization need not always occur, however, even though the [i] may be quite strongly stressed. For example, words such as "teak," "seat," and "meter" are customarily pronounced with a fairly long [i], but it may be with a relatively pure rather than with a strongly diphthongized vowel. However, this is not ordinarily the case with a stressed [i] in English.

The [i] vowels may retain their distinctive quality even though their duration is short, as in some pronunciations of words like "revise," "preclude," or "economy." In such cases, however, the lessened stress may easily lead to the perfectly acceptable substitution of [ɪ], or perhaps of [ə]. "Revise," for example, might be heard as [rɪivaɪz], [rivaɪz], [rɪvaɪz], or [rəvaɪz]. The student should not be concerned if he cannot at first detect these subtle differences in length and diphthongization, although he should listen carefully for them. The differences are due primarily to the influences of stress and surrounding sounds. These forces operate in such a way that the native speaker is not likely to make grievous mistakes, although he is not entirely safe.

Pronunciation of sounds in the [i] phoneme does not ordinarily pose much of a problem in working toward speech improvement. In general they are rather easy to distinguish, except possibly in occasional instances when the vowel is very lightly stressed. Not many of the phonetic variations brought out in the notes on pronunciation are likely to make one's speech unacceptable, but if they should do so, correction is relatively easy, since [i] is produced with articulators in a limit position (highest front). Speakers who are learning English as a new language will ordinarily have little difficulty acquiring good English [i] vowels, even though there may be some tendency to confuse the [i] and [ɪ] at first.

Exercises

1. The following passage contains a number of words normally pronounced with some variation of the phoneme [i]. See how many you can identify. In some cases either [i] or [ɪ] would be appropriate, depending upon such factors as stress and the dialect of English spoken. Can you identify these? Note the different ways [i] can be spelled. How many different spellings can you identify? Turn to the phonetic transcription for the pronunciation of one of the authors.

There are many reasons why the study of speech sounds would give each of us a keener appreciation of the language we speak. Our information is sometimes really meager. Seemingly the obvious reason is that we deem spelling the most important feature of a word, when this may not be exactly true. Needless to say, there must be no tendency to become too easygoing about orthography. But even the most pedantic teacher would be obliged to agree that ordinary devices of spelling constitute a very ineffective means of recording, with any real accuracy, the precise details of the language we hear when someone is speaking. Editors of dictionaries would be pleased, if it became even remotely feasible, to replace our present inefficient procedure for recording pronunciation. Various schemes have been devised for alleviating some of the agonies created by inconsistencies in spelling, but these ideas, although ingenious and appealing in some respects, are neither practical nor realistic.

2. Study the following list of [i] words, saying each aloud to familiarize yourself with the distinctive features of this vowel sound. For other words which may be pronounced with [i], see list *e* among the [ɪ] words of the preceding section.

be	feel	keep	reach	speak
being	feet	least	realized	speech
believe	field	leave	reason	speed
between	fifteen	machine	receive	street
complete	fourteen	me	sea	teacher
ease	free	mean	seal	these
each	green	meal	seam	thirteen
easily	Greek	meet	season	three
easy	he	need	see	tree
economics	heating	nineteen	seem	we
eighteen	idea	people	seen	week
either	increase	piece	seventeen	weak
evening	indeed	read	sixteen	Z

3. Practice the following minimal pairs and any additional pairs as you can think of. Note particularly the differences between [i] and [ɪ].

[i]—[ɪ]

each [itʃ]	itch [ɪtʃ]
feel [fil]	fill [fɪl]
feet [fit]	fit [fɪt]
green [grin]	grin [grɪn]
lead [lid]	lid [lɪd]
least [list]	list [lɪst]
meal [mil]	mill [mɪl]
meet [mit]	mitt [mɪt]
read [rid]	rid [rɪd]
week [wik]	wick [wɪk]

[i]—[ɛ]

bead [bid]	bed [bɛd]
beast [bist]	best [bɛst]
each [itʃ]	etch [ɛtʃ]
heed [hid]	head [hɛd]
lease [lis]	less [lɛs]
mean [min]	men [mɛn]
read [rid]	red [rɛd]
seed [sid]	said [sɛd]
seal [sil]	sell [sɛl]
seat [sit]	set [sɛt]

[i]—[e]

be [bi]	bay [be]
ease [iz]	A's [ez]
feel [fil]	fail [fel]
feet [fit]	fate [fet]
free [fri]	fray [fre]
he [hi]	hay [he]
least [list]	laced [lest]
me [mi]	may [me]
see [si]	say [se]
we [wi]	way [we]

Phonetic Transcription. Criticize the following version of the paragraph in Exercise 1. A few intentional vowel errors have been included, in addition to any which may have crept in unintentionally. There are supposed to be fewer than 12 but more than 4. How many can you find? Are you sure they are *errors?* Or are they simply acceptable alternatives?

[ðɛr ɑr 'mɛnɪ rizənz hwaɪ ðə 'stʌdi əv spitʃ saundz wud gɪv itʃ əv əs ə kinɚ ə‚priʃɪ'eʃən əv ðə 'lɪŋgwɪdʒ wi spik. ɑr ɪnfɚ'meʃən ɪz 'sʌm‚taɪmz 'rɪli migɚ. 'simɪŋlɪ ðɪ 'ɑbviəs rizən ɪz ðət wi dim spɛlɪŋ ðə most ɪm'pɑtn̩t fitʃɚ əv ə wɝd, hwɛn ðɪs me nɑt bi ɛg'zæktlɪ tru. nɪdləs tə se ðɛr mʌs bi no 'tɛndənsi tə bɪ'kʌm tu izɪgoɪŋ əbaut ɚr'θɑgrəfɪ. bət ivən ðə mos pə'dæntɪk titʃɚ wud be o'blidʒd tu əgri ðət 'ɔrdɪnɛrɪ dɪ'vaɪsəz əv 'spɛlɪŋ 'kɑnstətut ə vɛrɪ ‚ɪnɪ'fɛktɪv minz əv rɪ'kɑrdɪŋ, wɪð ɛnɪ riəl ækjərəsɪ, ðə prɪ'saɪs dɪ'teəlz əv ðə læŋgowɪdʒ wi hir hwɛn sʌmwən əz 'spikɪŋ. ɛdətɚz əv 'dɪkʃə'nɛriz wud bi plizd, ɪf ɪt bɪkem ivən rɪ'motlɪ fizəbl̩, tu rɪples aur prezənt ɪnɪ'fɛktɪv prəsidʒɚ fɚr rɪ'kɔrdɪŋ prə‚nʌnsi'eʃən. 'vɛriəs skimz həv bɪn dɪ'vaɪzd fɚ ə'livi‚etɪŋ sʌm ə ðɪ 'ægəniz kri'etəd baɪ ‚inkən'-sɪstənsiz ɪn 'spɛlɪŋ, bət ðiz aɪ'diəz, ɔl'ðo ɪn'dʒinjəs æn ə'pilɪŋ ɪn sʌm rɪ'spɛkts, ɑr niðɚ 'præktɪkl̩ nɔr ‚riə'lɪstɪk.]

Foreign and Nonphonemic Variants. The preceding list includes a description of the front-vowel phonemes of primary importance to the speaker of American English. This is not to say, however, that it exhausts the list of possible distinctive sounds or even completes the description of the sound system in the best way for all dialects of English. Certainly the list is inadequate for the student interested in a foreign language.

Although it is beyond the scope of this book to make analyses of sound systems other than the American, the student may gain a better perspective if he becomes aware of the major phonemes in other sound systems. The following are some important front vowels which are phonemic in sound systems other than the General American.

The [a] symbol is used by phoneticians to stand for a low-front, unrounded, lax vowel which in quality stands between the [æ] and the [ɑ]. This vowel might well have been included among the five common front vowels of American English on the strength of its occasional use in certain American dialect regions (see [æ]) and its participation in the diphthongs [aɪ] and [au]. However, it is seldom used in General American dialect except self-consciously or "by accident," and even in Eastern dialect, where [paθ] and [laf] may sometimes be heard for "path" and "laugh," [a] is not a strictly phonemic variant.

The [œ], described as a mid-front, rounded, lax vowel, sounds much like the [ɛ], except for the lip rounding. It may be heard in the French word "peur" and in the German "wörter." '

The [φ] is the mid-front, rounded, tense vowel; it is roughly a lip-rounded version of [e], heard in French "peu" and German "hören."

The [Y] is the high-front, rounded, lax vowel; it is roughly a lip-rounded version of [ɪ], as heard in German "Glück."

The [y] is the high-front, rounded, tense vowel; it is related to [Y] in the same way that [ɪ] is related to [i]. It is the vowel sound normally heard in French "ruse" and German "über."

6

THE BACK VOWELS

[u], [ʊ], [o], [ɔ], [ɑ]

The term *back* is applied to this series of vowels because the distinctive feature of their production is the arching or adjustment of the tongue in the back part of the mouth. As in the case of the front vowels, these back vowels can be arranged in a series ranging from *high* to *low* postures of the tongue. The relative positions are:

[u]   High-back
[ʊ]   Lower high-back
[o]   Mid-back
[ɔ]   Higher low-back
[ɑ]   Low-back

Lip rounding plays an important part in producing the back vowels, which is not true of the English front and central vowels. We can form the back vowels without lip rounding, to be sure, but it appears that the necessary resonance characteristics can most easily be created if the lips are rounded—and the typical American speaker habitually does so. The degree of rounding is greatest for [u] and becomes less for [o], [ɔ], and [ʊ]. There is ordinarily no lip rounding for [ɑ], the lowest of the back vowels. In most contexts it is simpler and more efficient to pronounce these vowels, except the [ɑ], with the appropriate amount of lip rounding. One can judge this for himself by observing how seemingly difficult it is to make a good [u] when the lips are not rounded.

As with the front vowels, the back vowels can be described as varying in degree of complexity, or diphthongization. Although all the back vowels are complex, a change of resonance is particularly noticeable on the [u] and [o], whereas the [ɔ], [ɑ], and [ʊ] become relatively simpler and shorter in about that order. Descriptions of each of the back vowels and notes about their pronunciation are provided in the following sections.

78

[u] as in boot, food, moon

Common Spellings: *oo* as in too, boot
                    u as in rule, studious
                    o as in move, tomb
                    ew as in grew, knew
                    ue as in flue, due
                    ou as in troupe, group
                    Also spelled *ui*, as in fruit; *ough*, as in through,
                    ous, as in rendezvous; *wo*, as in two; *oe*, as in shoe.

Production. The [u] is the highest, most tense, and most rounded of the back vowels. In its production the lips are often almost puckered.

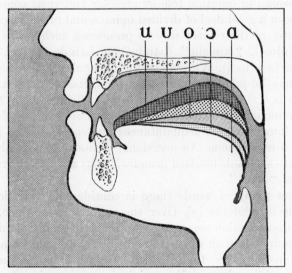

FIG. 5. Articulation adjustments for the back vowels.

The teeth and jaws, although as nearly closed as they are for any other back vowel, are "semilax," or parted about the same amount as for the [e] of the front series. In its normal pronunciation in American English [u] is markedly diphthongal. During production of this sound the tongue ordinarily continues to rise and the lips continue to round.

Pronunciation. With the exception of a few words such as "ooze" and "oolong," [u] is heard only in medial and final positions in English words, and only in accented syllables. In common with other English "long" vowels, [u] often has diphthonglike characteristics, but since these are not distinctive in the same way that they are for true diphthongs, the sound is classified as a vowel. In much the same manner that [i] is often more accurately transcribed [ɪi], so [u] is in reality [ʊu]. Vowel quality and stress are always interrelated, and it is interesting to note how the strength of pronunciation influences the quality of [i] and [u]. As stress is decreased from maximum to minimum, the character of the sound changes from [ii] through [i] to [ɪ] and finally to [ə]. In like manner [u͜u] changes to [u], then to [ʊ] and [ə]. As an illustration of this, carefully compare the pronunciations of the following:

I have *too* much. (Maximum stress: [u͜u].)

The numbers were six, *two*, five. (Secondary stress: [u].)

It was a six-*to*-one chance. (Tertiary stress: [ʊ].)

I don't know what *to* do. (Unstressed: [ə].)

In numerous English words pronunciation varies between the diphthongs [ju] and [ɪu] and the vowels [u] and [u͜u]. This occurs particularly where the sound in question follows alveolar and velar consonants, and there has been a good deal of divided opinion and much schoolmastering on the matter of the correct way to pronounce such words as "news" ([nuz] or [njuz]), "student" ([studn̩t] or [stjudn̩t]), and "attitude" ([ætətud] or [ætətjud]). Without trying particularly to settle any arguments, it may be pointed out that, in the General American dialect at least, there is a strong trend toward [u]—as illustrated by the practice of a radio announcer friend of one of the authors, who comfortably discusses the [nuz] with his acquaintances but speaks of the [njuz] when faced with a microphone. An occasional anxious speaker allows himself to be led into such substandard pronunciations as [njun] instead of [nun] for the word "noon."

In another group of words there is considerable variation in usage between the [u] and the [ʊ]. Over the country as a whole, cultivated colloquial pronunciation seems to be surprisingly evenly divided between these two sounds in such words as "roof," "hoof," and "soot." In most dialect regions, however, the substitution of [ʊ] for [u] in such words as "room," "food," and "noon" certainly is unacceptable on the basis of cultivated usage.

Except for such variations in usage as those mentioned, the [u] ordinarily gives little trouble to the native speaker. It is easily visible on the lips and hence is somewhat more easily taught and learned than any of the front or central vowels. The foreign speaker may have a little difficulty if he fails to diphthongize the sound as a native would, but this is usually a minor problem. Spelling-pronunciation irregularities may plague the foreigner, of course.

Exercises

1. The following paragraph contains between 20 and 30 words which are pronounced with the [u] by most speakers of English. See how many you can identify. Also try to identify the [ju] and [ʊ] sounds, with which

the [u] may sometimes be confused. Check yourself against the phonetic transcription following these exercises.

Anyone who has ever been to school knows all too well of the importance of phonetic rules in learning to read and write. Although schoolteachers who are interested in such rules choose to call their subject *phonics*, the study really uses nothing new to the student of phonetics. Loosely speaking, phonics is the application to the language-learning problem of just such principles as are outlined in this book. This is especially true with regard to the correlation, or lack of it, between audible events (sounds, syllables) and visual cues (letters and letter groups). In its simplest (perhaps too simple) form it involves introducing to the student the root notion that, loosely speaking, it is possible to "sound out" words through the process of associating with each letter, and with some letter groups, a certain kind of sound. Of course it would not only be foolish but also would surely prove to be impossible that this notion could be carried to its logical conclusion. A completely phonetic approach is doomed from the start because English neither looks nor sounds like a phonetic language. Nevertheless, as most would agree, phonetic knowledge is a useful tool in language learning.

2. The following list contains a selection of [u] words for your reference and practice. Even though this list comes close to exhausting those to be found in *The One Thousand Most Frequently Spoken Words*, it should prove easy to make many additions to it. See whether you can do so.

a. Words pronounced [u] by most speakers:

afternoon	fruit	mood	root	soup
blue	grew	moose	route	to
cool	goose	moon	rule	too
choose	group	move	school	two
do	include	movement	soon	who
doing	into	noon	super	whom
doom	loop	prove	through	whose
food	loose	room	tomb	zoo
fool	lose	roost		

b. [u] words which may be heard with [ju] or [ɪu]:

attitude	institution	knew	opportunity	through
consumer	introduce	new	produce	Tuesday
due	June	news	shoe	tune
duty	junior			

3. Practice and, if possible, add to this list of minimal pairs:

[u]—[ju]		[u]—[ʊ]	
boot [but]	butte [bjut]	booer [buɚ]	boor [bʊr]
booty [butɪ]	beauty [bjutɪ]	cooed [kud]	could [kʊd]
coot [kut]	cute [kjut]	fool [ful]	full [fʊl]
food [fud]	feud [fjud]	gooed [gud]	good [gʊd]
fool [ful]	fuel [fjul]	Luke [luk]	look [lʊk]
moos [muz]	muse [mjuz]	pool [pul]	pull [pʊl]
moot [mut]	mute [mjut]	shoed [ʃud]	should [ʃʊd]
ooze [uz]	use [juz]	stewed [stud]	stood [stʊd]
who [hu]	Hugh [hju]	who'd [hud]	hood [hʊd]
whose [huz]	hews [hjuz]	wooed [wud]	would [wʊd]

[u]—[ʌ]	
boost [bust]	bust [bʌst]
doom [dum]	dumb [dʌm]
mood [mud]	mud [mʌd]
moose [mus]	muss [mʌs]
whom [hum]	hum [hʌm]
soon [sun]	sun [sʌn]
soup [sup]	sup [sʌp]
school [skul]	skull [skʌl]
root [rut]	rut [rʌt]
roost [rust]	rust [rʌst]

Phonetic Transcription. The following phonetic transcription of the paragraph in Exercise 1 represents the pronunciation of one of the authors. Compare your pronunciation with his. Does your pronunciation of the [u] words differ? Note the uses of [ju] and [ʊ].

['ɛnɪwʌn hu hæz ɛvɚ bɪn tə skul noz əl tu wɛl əv ðɪ ɪm'pɔrtəns əv fə'nɛtɪk rulz ɪn 'lɜ·nɪŋ tə rid n̩ rait. əlðo skultitʃɚz hu ɑr ɪntərɛstəd ɪn sʌtʃ rulz tʃuz tə kəl ðer 'sʌbdʒɪkt 'fɑnɪks, ðə stʌdɪ rilɪ juzəz nʌθɪŋ nju tə ðə studn̩t əv fə'nɛtɪks. luslɪ 'spikɪŋ, 'fɑnɪks ɪz ðɪ ˌæplɪ'keʃən tə ðə 'læŋgwɪdʒ 'lɜ·nɪŋ prɑbləm əv dʒʌst sʌtʃ prɪnsəpl̩z æz ɑr 'aʊt͵laɪnd ɪn ðɪs bʊk. ðɪs ɪz əspeʃəlɪ tru wɪθ rɪ'gɑrd tə ðə ˌkɔrə'leʃən, ɔr læk əv ət, bɪtwin ədəbl̩ ɪ'vɛnts (saʊndz, sɪləbl̩z) ən 'vɪʒuəl kjuz (lɛtɚz ən lɛtɚ grups). ɪn ɪts sɪmpləst (pɚhæps tu sɪmpl̩) fɔrm ɪt ɪn'vɑlvz ɪntrə'dusɪŋ tə ðə studn̩t ðə rut noʃən ðət, 'luslɪ'spikɪŋ, ɪt ɪz pɑsəbl̩ tə saʊnd aʊt wɜ·dz θru ðə 'prases əv ə'soʃietɪŋ wɪð ɪtʃ lɛtɚ, æn wɪθ sʌm lɛtɚ grups, ə sɜ·tn̩ kaɪnd əv saʊnd. əv kɔrs ɪt wəd nat onlɪ bi 'fulɪʃ bət 'ɔlso wʊd ʃʊrlɪ pruv tə bi ɪm'pɑsəbl̩ ðət ðɪs noʃən kəd bi kɛrid tu ɪts 'lɑdʒɪkəl kən'kluʒən. ə kəm'plitlɪ fə'nɛtɪk əprotʃ ɪz dumd frəm ðə stɑrt bɪkɔz 'ɪŋglɪʃ niðɚ lʊks nɔr saʊndz laɪk ə fə'nɛtɪk 'læŋgwɪdʒ. 'nɛvəðələs, æz most wʊd əgri, fə'nɛtɪk 'nɑlɪdʒ ɪz ə jusfəl tul ɪn 'læŋgwɪdʒ 'lɝnɪŋ.]

[ʊ] as in book, foot, stood

Common Spellings: *oo* as in look, took
                      u as in pull, full
                      Also spelled *oul,* as in could; *o,* as in woman;
                      or, as in worsted.

Production. The vowel [ʊ] stands just below [u] in the vowel diagram and is therefore classified as a lower high-back vowel, produced with lax tongue and only moderate lip rounding. The vowels [ʊ] and [u] are often confused with each other, and the distinction between them is not necessarily great in some respects. However, one important difference is in lip rounding, which is considerably greater for [u] than for [ʊ]. The student can test this for himself by going rapidly from [u] to [ʊ] and noting which adjustments produce the easiest shifts in vowel quality. It is perfectly possible to go from one to the other without moving the lips, but it is certainly much easier to make the shift if there is a difference in lip rounding. The transition from [ʊ] to [u] can probably be made by most speakers with no marked change in tongue position, but on the basis of *average* or *typical* tongue position, [ʊ] must be considered lower.

Unlike [u], the vowel [ʊ] has no significant amount of diphthongization; it is one of the shortest of the accented vowels. Nevertheless, [ʊ] resonance is an important part of several complex vowels and diphthongs, including [aʊ] and [oʊ]. As a simple vowel it does not occur in either an initial or final position in words.

Pronunciation. This vowel seems to present difficulties far out of proportion to its frequency of use, both in attempting to achieve acceptable pronunciation and in learning to listen analytically. It is astonishing how many persons do not recognize that [ʊ] is a vowel distinct from [u], even though they may use it properly in their own speech. This is possibly the result of the fact that [ʊ] appears fewer times than any other stressed vowel in American speech. Linguists would say that the vowel doesn't carry much of a "functional load." Like the letter *q* in spelling, it could probably be dropped without too much damage to the language. Nevertheless, [ʊ] is with us and needs to be learned.

Before *r,* and in unstressed syllables, the historical tendency has been for [u] to change to the [ʊ]. Restoring the [u] in such cases often results in such slightly questionable pronunciations as [pur] instead of [pʊr] for "poor" and [lur] instead of [lʊr] for "lure." The [u] may be occasionally substituted for [ʊ] in other types of words as well, in certain American dialects (see [u]), or a sound close to [ʌ] may be heard, especially in careless or inaccurate articulation, as [wʌd] for [wʊd] and [ʃʌd] for [ʃʊd]. The [ju], which was shown to be an occasional variant pronunciation of [u] words, may also be found as an occasional variant in some [ʊ] words. For example, the word "during" may be heard as [djʊrɪŋ] or [dʊrɪŋ] with equal acceptability.

Foreign speakers often have conspicuous difficulty with [ʊ]. In most foreign languages no phonemic distinction is made between [u] and [ʊ], with the result that [u] is substituted or the two sounds are confused; [puʃəmɑp] instead of [puʃəmʌp] would be a possible dialectal version of "push him up." The substitution of [u] for [ʊ] may also occur in certain regional dialects in America.

The dependence of vowel quality on stress is nowhere more evident than in the pronunciation of the [ʊ] words. A very large proportion of these words, such as those listed in the exercises of this section, may be quite acceptably pronounced [ə] where stress is minimal, as it often is in context. Examples include "would," "should," and "could." Shifts among [u], [ʊ], and [ə] can be heard in such words as "to," "you," and "education." Lowering of [ʊ] to [ə], as in [aɪ ʃər du] for "I sure do," is a common substandard dialect usage.

Exercises

1. This paragraph contains at least 13 words pronounced with the [ʊ]. The precise pronunciation of many of the words, however, depends upon the amount of stress placed upon them. Which words must be [ʊ]? Which may be pronounced with [u] or with [ə]? The author's pronunciation is shown following these exercises.

Sometimes we find that individuals have poor speech and a drab speech manner which could be improved simply by putting more energy into the task. As any good speech book will tell us, successful oral communication requires full participation during the speech act, and this full participation should mean that the man or woman doing the speaking should actually be working harder. Slovenly speech and "butchered" articulation can be cured only by those who would apply this principle to their speech training program. Why should it be assumed that an efficient oral output ought to be easy? It isn't, and the student who is looking for an effective speech education should be prepared to foot the bill.

2. If the following list of [ʊ] words seems short, the reason is that the sound is little used in English. You may observe that even for some of these words alternative pronunciations are often heard. The problem here, however, is to learn the [ʊ] pronunciation. Therefore, you should practice the following words with this vowel.

a. Words nearly always pronounced with the [ʊ]:

book	hood	poor	sugar
bull	insurance	pull	sure
cook	hook	put	took
could	look	putting	woman
full	looking	shook	wood
foot	nook	should	would
good	output	stood	

b. Words in which [ʊ] or some variant may be heard:

actually	education	roof	you
beautiful	Europe	to	yourself
cure	individual	your	situation
during			

3. Practice the following pairs of words. Pay particular attention to the [ʊ]–[u] and the [ʊ]–[ɝ] pairs. Try to add to these lists.

[ʊ]—[ʌ]		[ʊ]—[u]	
book [bʊk]	buck [bʌk]	could [kʊd]	cooed [kud]
could [kʊd]	cud [kʌd]	boor [bʊr]	booer [bur]
look [lʊk]	luck [lʌk]	full [fʊl]	fool [ful]
put [pʊt]	putt [pʌt]	good [gʊd]	gooed [gud]
puts [pʊts]	putts [pʌts]	hood [hʊd]	who'd [hud]
puss [pʊs]	pus [pʌs]	look [lʊk]	Luke [luk]
roof [rʊf]	rough [rʌf]	pull [pʊl]	pool [pul]
shook [ʃʊk]	shuck [ʃʌk]	stood [stʊd]	stewed [stud]
took [tʊk]	tuck [tʌk]	should [ʃʊd]	shoed [ʃud]
stood [stʊd]	stud [stʌd]	wood [wʊd]	wooed [wud]

[ʊ]—[ɝ]	
book [bʊk]	Burke [bɝk]
could [kʊd]	curd [kɝd]
hood [hʊd]	heard [hɝd]
look [lʊk]	lurk [lɝk]
pull [pʊl]	pearl [pɝl]
put [pʊt]	pert [pɝt]
shook [ʃʊk]	shirk [ʃɝk]
stood [stʊd]	stirred [stɝd]
took [tʊk]	Turk [tɝk]
wood [wʊd]	word [wɝd]

Phonetic Transcription. Study the following phonetic transcription, paying particular attention to the pronunciation of [ʊ] words. This transcription shows the way one of the authors read the paragraph in Exercise 1. Compare your own pronunciation.

['sʌmtaɪmz wi faɪnd ðət ɪndɪ'vɪdʒuwəlz hæv pʊr spitʃ ən ə dræb spitʃ 'mænɚ hwɪtʃ kəd bi ɪm'pruvd 'sɪmplɪ baɪ pʊtɪŋ mɔr 'ɛnɚdʒɪ 'ɪntʊ ðə tæsk. æz ɛnɪ gʊd spitʃ bʊk wɪl tɛl əs, sək'sɛsfəl ɔrəl kəmjunə'keʃən rɪ'-kwaɪrz fʊl pɚtɪsə'peʃən dʊrɪŋ ðə spitʃ ækt, ənd ðɪs fʊl pɚtɪsə'peʃən ʃʊd min ðət ðə mæn ɔr wʊmən dʊɪŋ ðə spikɪŋ ʃʊd 'ækʃʊəlɪ bi wɝ·kɪŋ hɑrdɚ. 'slʌvənlɪ spitʃ ən bʊtʃɚd ɑrtɪkju'leʃən kæn bi kjʊrd onlɪ baɪ ðoz hu wʊd ə'plaɪ ðɪs 'prɪnsəpḷ tu ðer spitʃ trenɪŋ 'progræm. hwaɪ ʃʊd ət bi ə'sumd ðət ən ɪ'fɪʃənt ɔrəl aʊtpʊt ɔt tə bi izɪ? ɪt 'ɪznt, ænd ðə 'studənt hu ɪz 'lʊkɪŋ fɔr ən ɪ'fɛktɪv spitʃ ɛdʒə'keʃən ʃʊd bi prɪ'pɛrd tə fʊt ðə bɪl.]

[o] as in note, coat, token

Common Spellings: *o* as in mote, tote

oa as in coat, boat

ow as in tow, blow

oe as in toe, roe

Also spelled *oh*, as in oh; *owe*, as in owe; *ew*, as in sew; *ough*, as in though; *ou*, as in soul; *au*, as in hautboy; *eau*, as in beau; *eo*, as in yeoman; *oo*, as in brooch; *os*, as in apropos.

Production. The [o] is found just below [ʊ] on the vowel diagram and is described as a mid-back vowel. In producing this sound, the tongue is between the positions for [ʊ] and [ɔ] in height, probably somewhat closer to [ʊ]. It is described as a tense vowel and has considerable lip rounding. The [o] is one of the complex vowels and is often diphthongal to the extent that a complex symbol such as [oʊ] is appropriate to indicate the speech movements involved. During the production of [o] the tendency is for the tongue to move to a higher position and the lips to round more markedly.

Pronunciation. When [o] occurs in the final position and when it is prolonged or stressed, the tendency to diphthongize is particularly strong. Failure to give the typical diphthongization to [o] gives the sound a foreign flavor frequently heard in the pronunciation of those whose native language is not English. Thus, words like "so" and "go" may sound odd to the American because of the relative shortness and purity of the vowel. Although the difference between [o] and [oʊ] is easily recognized in American speech, no serious pronunciation problem is likely to arise if the native speaker fails to make this distinction in his own use of the sounds. It will be satisfactory to follow the convention of using only the symbol [o] in ordinary phonemic transcription.

Several minor variants of the [o] or [ou] sound are frequently heard in English and American speech. Before *r* the [o] is often somewhat lowered, sometimes to an [ɔ], so that the student should be very careful that what he expects will be [or] is not actually [ɔr]. For example "horse" is most often heard as [hɔrs], "corn" as [kɔrn]. Even in some cases where the [o]–[ɔ] difference could distinguish between words, such as "hoarse" [hors] and "horse" [hɔrs], the [o] before *r* is slightly lower than usual. Incidently, such distinctions as these appear to be losing ground, at least in the General American dialect, where "horse" and "hoarse" are generally indistinguishable.

There are other variants of, and substitutions for, [o] which would be considered substandard or dialect for the General American speaker. Among these is the [ɔu], as heard in the Southern British pronunciation of such a word as "coat." Another is a variety of short [o] approaching [ʌ], which is sometimes heard in the phrases "go home" [gʌ hʌm] and "so long" [sʌ lɔŋ]. The substitution of [ə] for [o] in *ow* words is often considered substandard except for the most informal usage and in unstressed positions. Compare, for example, [fɑlo] and [fɑlə] as pronunciations of "follow" and [fɛlo] and [fɛlə] as pronunciations of "fellow."

Exercises

1. In the following paragraph there are more than 33 words which usually are pronounced with [o]. Note that some are more diphthongized than others. Note also that in some cases either [or] or [ɔr] would be acceptable. The author's transcription is given at the end of these exercises.

So-called "loaded" passages of prose or poetry, which are supposed to contain heroic doses of a single sound for the neophyte to pore over in his efforts to master pronunciation, have been the favorite device of professors of diction since time immemorial. The composers of this opus are loath to forgo this custom. Because the vowel [o] is noteworthy for the role it plays in English words, the authors are going along with their fellow tutors. There have been, of course, some notable and often quoted examples of such sentences, liberally sprinkled with such old familiar words as "alone," "blow," "gold," "cold," "soul," and so on. Actually, those who will devote a few moments to such material in practice at home can hope before long that their own pronunciation has grown more nearly correct. Fine differences in the sounds must be noted, of course, if the novice is to progress as he is supposed to; he need not be bored with the proposal that he force himself to go through such a procedure.

2. Use the following list of common [o] words for practice and reference:

a. Words employing [o] in a first or intermediate syllable:

almost	control	known	open	smoke
alone	cooperate	lower	over	sold
boat	don't	moment	own	soldier
bonus	goes	most	owned	soul
broke	gold	motor	poetry	spoke
broken	golden	nose	post	stone
chosen	grown	note	prose	suppose
close	hold	notice	program	those
coal	holds	ocean	road	told
coat	hole	old	robe	tones
cold	home	older	role	whole
compose	hope	only	rose	won't

b. Words employing [o] or [ou] in a final stressed syllable:

ago	blow	know	know	so
although	go	low	O	snow
below	grow	Negro	oh	though

c. Words in which pronunciation may vary between [o] or [ə], depending upon stress, dialect, formality, and other factors:

fellow	project (v.)	pronunciation	Chicago	tobacco
follow	protection	provide	so	tomorrow
opinion	potato			

d. [or] words, which are sometimes pronounced with [or] but more often with [ɔr]:

before	chorus	floor	more	store
board	court	force	report	shore
course	door	four	sport	

3. Practice the following contrasts. Try to find additional examples.

[o]—[ɔ]		[o]—[ʌ]	
bole [bol]	ball [bɔl]	boat [bot]	but [bʌt]
coal [kol]	call [kɔl]	bone [bon]	bun [bʌn]
coast [kost]	cost [kɔst]	coal [kol]	cull [kʌl]
goes [goz]	gauze [gɔz]	hole [hol]	hull [hʌl]
know [no]	gnaw [nɔ]	home [hom]	hum [hʌm]
low [lo]	law [lɔ]	known [non]	none [nʌn]
pole [pol]	Paul [pɔl]	note [not]	nut [nʌt]
hole [hol]	hall [hɔl]	robe [rob]	rub [rʌb]
row [ro]	raw [rɔ]	stone [ston]	stun [stʌn]
oh [o]	awe [ɔ]	tones [tonz]	tons [tʌnz]

[o]—[ɑ]

coat [kot]	cot [kɑt]
dole [dol]	doll [dɑl]
hope [hop]	hop [hɑp]
known [non]	non [nɑn]
note [not]	not [nɑt]
own [on]	on [ɑn]
road [rod]	rod [rɑd]
soak [sok]	sock [sɑk]
tome [tom]	Tom [tɑm]
wrote [rot]	rot [rɑt]

Phonetic Transcription. Compare the pronunciation indicated by this transcription of the paragraph in Exercise 1 with your own pronunciation and explain any differences on the basis of the discussions in this chapter.

[so kɔld 'lodəd 'pæsɪdʒəz əv proz ɚ 'poətrɪ, hwɪtʃ ɑr sə'pozd tə kən'ten hɪ'roɪk dosəz əv ə sɪŋgl̩ saund fɚ ðə 'niə,faɪt tə pɔr ovɚ ɪn hɪz ɛfɚts tə mæstɚ prə,nʌnsɪ'eʃən, hæv bɪn ðə fevərət dɪ'vaɪs əv prə'fɛsɚz əv dɪkʃən sɪns taɪm ,ɪmə'mɔrɪəl. ðə kəm'pozɚz əv ðɪs opəs ɑr loθ tə fɔrgo ðɪs kʌstəm. bɪkɔz ðə vaʊl o ɪz 'notwɝ̇ðɪ fɔr ðə rol ɪt plez ɪn 'ɪŋglɪʃ wɝ̇dz, ðɪ əθɚz ɑr goɪŋ əlɔŋ wɪð ðɚ fɛlo tutɚz. ðer həv bɪn, əv kɔrs, səm 'notəbl̩ ən ɔfən kwotəd ɪg'zæmplz̩ əv sʌtʃ sentənsəz, 'lɪbrəlɪ sprɪŋkəld wɪθ sʌtʃ old fə'mɪljɚ wɝ̇dz æz əlon, blo, gold, kold, sol, ænd so ɔn. 'æktʃuəlɪ, ðoz hu wɪl dɪ'vot ə fju 'momənts tə sʌtʃ mə'tɪrɪəl ɪn præktəs ət hom kən hop bɪfɔr lɔŋ ðət ðer on prənənsɪ'eʃən hæz gron mɔr 'nɪrlɪ kə'rɛkt. faɪn 'dɪf-rənsəz ɪn ðə saʊndz məst bi notəd, əv kɔrs, ɪf ðə 'navəs ɪz tə prə'grɛs æz hi ɪz sə'pozd tu; hi nid nɑt bi bɔrd wɪð:ə prə'pozəl ðət hi fɔrs hɪmsɛlf tə go θru sʌtʃ ə prə'sidʒɚ.]

[ɔ] as in law, saw, taught

Common Spellings: *a* as in ball, call
aw as in raw, jaw
au as in fault, vault
o as in soft, lofty
Also spelled *ough*, as in ought; *augh* as in caught; *ah*, as in Utah; *oa*, as in broad; *al*, as in talk.

Production. The [ɔ] is classified as a higher low-back, rounded vowel. It is typically produced with greater lip and tongue tension than characterizes [ɑ], and with a tongue height which is approximately intermediate between the positions for [o] and [ɑ], probably closer to the latter. As [ɔ] is pronounced by the typical American speaker, its most significant feature is possibly lip rounding. Although some speakers may produce the sound with the lips rounded little or not at all, [ɔ] is most readily differentiated from [ɑ], with which it is often confused, if the lips are rounded. A slight degree of diphthongization may be heard in the pronunciation of some [ɔ] words, with the tongue moving toward a more central vowel position which might be represented as [ɔə]. In general, however, [ɔ] is classed as simple or pure.

Pronunciation. The [ɔ] is one of a somewhat varied and complex group of sounds which may be called the *ah* vowels. The two sound families within this group most easily recognized are represented by the symbols [ɔ] and [ɑ], and these are the symbols usually employed in broad phonetic transcription. However, two other sounds commonly heard in certain American and English dialects are important but nonphonemic variations within the general *ah* group. These latter are represented by the symbols [a] and [ɒ].

As a standard vowel, [ɔ] is placed below [o] on the diagram, which implies that the tongue is in a somewhat lower position and that it is somewhat more lax. In the speech of the typical American, the tongue may likewise be slightly more retracted for [ɔ] than for [o], and there is certainly less lip rounding. Lying below [ɔ] is the standard low-back, unrounded [ɑ], for which the key word "father" is usually reasonably satisfactory. There is, however, a series of intermediate *ah* sounds; in broad transcription many of them would be placed in either the [ɑ] or [ɔ] phoneme, but some others have seemed sufficiently distinctive to make it more accurate to classify them in the [ɒ] group. The [ɒ] is, therefore, a lip-rounded back vowel intermediate between [ɑ] and [ɔ]. The student may be able to make a more or less satisfactory [ɒ] if he attempts a somewhat tense [ɑ] with lip rounding.

To identify the [ɔ] sound verbally and by written example is exceedingly difficult because of variations in pronunciation practices. Many General American speakers use [ɔ] in words such as "law," "applaud," and "gnaw"; the Southern British pronunciation would almost certainly be [ɔ], and this pronunciation is also quite likely in Eastern American. On the other hand, many Americans make few or no distinctions among members of the *ah* family. For these speakers there would be no clear difference between the words "cot"–"caught" or "dotter"–"daughter." On a dictionary basis, the first pair would be transcribed [kɑt]–[kɔt], but in the common dialect under discussion the vowel in each of the words would more than likely be [ɒ], although in other kinds of phonetic contexts the vowel playing a comparable role might be closer to either [ɑ] or [ɔ]. This failure to make an [ɑ]–[ɔ] distinction is common in at least some parts of the Western United States, so much so that in these regions this usage cannot be considered substandard. However, the same pronunciation is heard so often in all parts of the country that one suspects the [ɑ]–[ɔ] distinction may be losing ground, at least in General American speech. It is difficult to say how seriously the student should try to maintain a difference between [ɑ] and [ɔ] words; there is little point in being pedantic, but on the other hand the authors' impulse is to pay some attention to the distinction.

The other prominent member of the *ah* family of sounds can be considered intermediate between the low-*back* vowel [ɑ] and the low-*front* vowel [æ]. It is indicated phonetically by the symbol [a]. In physiological terms, [a] could be described as a more "backward" and lax [æ] or as an "advanced" or "fronted" [ɑ]. The [a] is another of the sounds for which there really is no key word that all English or American speakers would pronounce in the same way. General American speakers usually use [a] as the first resonance in the diphthongs [aʊ] and [aɪ], but this is hard for the untrained ear to distinguish. Those who in the main follow General American patterns seldom if ever replace [æ] with [a] except self-consciously, although Eastern American speakers may do so more frequently, particularly in words like "ask," "aunt," and "dance." Those speakers who are said to use a broad *a* on words which in General American are pronounced with [æ] may use the [a] pronunciation for such words as "dance" and "aunt," although they may, of course, go completely to the Southern British [dɑns] and [ɑnt]. Incidentally, the untrained person sometimes gets carried away in his efforts toward Southern British and is heard to give pronunciations such as [dɔns] and [ɔnt].

The rules for pronunciation of [ɔ] and [ɑ], like most other book rules about pronunciation, are not easily listed or followed. One widely used phonetics text devotes four pages to such an enumeration. No attempt will be made here to be so thorough, nor does it seem worthwhile to try to state the circumstances in which each member of the *ah* family is proper. It is highly recommended, however, that the student give careful attention to learning to recognize the different shades of resonance in the various sounds he hears and that he develop a sensitivity to the practices of the cultivated speakers he wishes to emulate.

If the lists of common [ɔ] and [ɑ] words found in the exercises are consulted for examples of *ah*-word pronunciations, certain interesting generalizations can be made. Note, for example, that whenever [ɑ] occurs in a stressed syllable it is spelled with the letter *o*. Note also that all the common stressed [ɑr] pronunciations are spelled *ar* or *ear*. On the other hand, observe that only eight of the words using [ɔ] in a stressed syllable are spelled with an *o*. Note also that the common words pronounced [ɔr] are mostly spelled *o*, *oa*, or *ou*. Finally, note that most of the exceptions to these "rules" occur in words beginning with a [w] sound, which would normally be expected to exert an influence toward lip rounding.

Exercises

1. In the following paragraph there are 20 or more words usually pronounced with the sound [ɔ]. Try to identify these and to compare them with the words pronounced with [ɑ]. In which words may either [ɑ] or [ɔ] be used? Check the author's transcription following these exercises.

If you will think about it a short time you will doubtless recall many instances of what might be called speech snobbery caused by mistaken notions as to what is thought to be correct pronunciation. Many people who would not ordinarily want to be thought of as "culture conscious" often display a kind of self-taught haughtiness in their speech. They nearly always do this when they try to mimic a dialect not their own, for the laudable but wrongly directed purpose of becoming more cultivated and effective in their speech habits. Most experts have taught that although a discussion of pronunciation logically belongs in a speech course it is the clarity and precision of formation of the sounds which is of strongest importance, not the choice of sounds as such. Not only will the adoption of certain foreign or regional pronunciations fail to improve speech but also it will almost always cause the speech to sound tawdry and draw attention to itself.

2. The following list contains a minimum vocabulary of [ɔ] words for study and practice. It may be particularly helpful for you to compare this list with the one given for the sound [ɑ] in Exercise 2 of the next section.

a. Words using [ɔ] in the stressed syllable:

across	brought	long	saw
almost	call	loss	soft
already	cause	lost	tall
although	cost	off	taught
also	daughter	often	thought
always	draw	ought	walk
ball	hall	salt	wall
belong	law		

b. Unaccented [ɔ] words, which are sometimes pronounced with [ɚ]:
for   nor

c. Words pronounced with [ɔr]:

before	force	lord	shore
board	forty	more	short
born	form	morning	storm
course	four	north	sport
court	forth	sort	war
chorus	forward	store	warm
corner	horse	story	George

d. Words varying between [ɔ] and [ɑ]:

along	log	want	long
foreign	song	water	wash
officer	strong	watch	Washington
offer	tomorrow	wrong	

3. Practice and try to add to this list of minimal pairs. (See also [ɔɪ] and [ɑʊ].)

[ɔ]—[ɑ]

aught [ɔt]	Ott [ɑt]
caught [kɔt]	cot [kɑt]
core [kɔr]	car [kɑr]
for [fɔr]	far [fɑr]
law [lɔ]	lah [lɑ]
naught [nɔt]	not [nɑt]
pawed [pɔd]	pod [pɑd]
sought [sɔt]	sot [sɑt]
wrought [rɔt]	rot [rɑt]
taught [tɔt]	tot [tɑt]

[ɔ]—[ʌ]

bawdy [bɔdɪ]	buddy [bʌdɪ]
call [kɔl]	cull [kʌl]
lost [lɔst]	lust [lʌst]
naught [nɔt]	nut [nʌt]
pawn [pɔn]	pun [pʌn]
log [lɔg]	lug [lʌg]
wrought [rɔt]	rut [rʌt]
caught [kɔt]	cut [kʌt]
taught [tɔt]	tut [tʌt]
long [lɔŋ]	lung [lʌŋ]

[ɔ]—[o]

awning [ɔnɪŋ]	owning [onɪŋ]
caught [kɔt]	coat [kot]
called [kɔld]	cold [kold]
clause [klɔz]	close [kloz]
daunt [dɔnt]	don't [dont]
gnaws [nɔz]	nose [noz]
hauled [hɔld]	hold [hold]
lawn [lɔn]	lone [lon]
naught [nɔt]	note [not]
Raleigh [rɔlɪ]	rolly [rolɪ]

Phonetic Transcription. This transcription represents the pronunciation of one of the authors as he read the paragraph in Exercise 1. It may differ considerably from yours, and these variations should be noted. Do you find any unacceptable pronunciations in his reading of the passage or in yours?

[ɪf ju wɪl θɪŋk əbaut ɪt ə ʃɔrt taɪm ju wɪl 'dautləs rɪ'kɔl menɪ 'ɪnstənsəz əv hwʌt maɪt bi kɔld 'spitʃ 'snabərɪ kɔzd baɪ mə'stekən noʃənz æz tə hwʌt ɪz θɔt tə bi kə'rɛkt prənʌnsɪ'eʃən. menɪ pipl̩ hu wud nat ɔrdən'ɛrəlɪ want tə bi θɔt ʌv æz 'kʌltʃɚ 'kantʃəs ɔfən dɪsple ə kaɪnd əv 'sɛlf 'tɔt 'hɔtɪnəs ɪn ðer spitʃ. ðe nɪrlɪ 'ɔlwɪz du ðɪs hwɛn ðe traɪ tə 'mɪmɪk ə 'daɪələkt nat ðer on, fɔr ðə 'lɔdəbl̩ bət rɔŋlɪ də'rɛktəd pɝpəs əv bɪkʌmɪŋ mɔr 'kʌltə,vetəd ænd ɪ'fɛktɪv ɪn ðer spitʃ hæbəts. most 'ɛkspɝts hæv tɔt ðət ɔlðo ə ,dɪs'kʌʃən əv prənʌnsɪ'eʃən 'lad3ɪklɪ bɪ'lɔŋz ɪn ə spitʃ kɔrs ɪt ɪz ðə 'klɛrətɪ ən prɪ'sɪʒən əv ,fɔr'meʃən əv ðə saundz hwɪtʃ ɪz əv ðə 'strɔŋgəst ɪm'pɔrtəns, nat ðə tʃɔɪs əv saundz æz sʌtʃ. nat onlɪ wɪl ðɪ ə'dapʃən əv sɝtn̩ fɔrən ɔr 'rid3ənəl prənʌnsɪ'eʃənz fel tu ɪmpruv spitʃ bət ɔlso ɪt wɪl ɔlmost ɔlwɪz kɔz ðə spitʃ tə saund 'tɔdrɪ ən drɔ ə'tɛnʃən tu ɪtsɛlf.]

[ɑ] as in father, cot, bar

Common Spellings: *o* as in on, doll
   a as in father, are
   ar as in far, as pronounced by those who drop
      their *r*'s
   Also spelled *al*, as in calm; *ah*, as in Utah; *e*, as in sergeant; *ua*, as in guard; *ho*, as in honest; *ea*, as in hearth.

Production. The [ɑ] is the lowest of the back vowels in terms of tongue position and is the only back vowel commonly made without perceptible lip rounding. It is relatively undiphthongized and is produced with "relaxed" tongue and ample mouth opening. The summary description of [ɑ] is a low-back, lax, unrounded vowel.

Pronunciation. After the previous discussion of the similarities and differences among the various members of the *ah* group of vowels, there is little more that need be said about the pronunciation of [ɑ]. Despite the difficulties often encountered in distinguishing among various *ah* sounds, the native American speaker is unlikely to have any difficulty producing some acceptable sound from this group, and the [ɑ]–[ɔ] confusions rarely render speech substandard.

Occasionally, to be sure, substandard dialect usages replace [ɑ]. One instance of this may be heard in the diphthong, or "combination sound," [ɑr] which may frequently, in some regions, be heard as [ɔr], thereby leading to potential confusion between such pairs of words as "card"– "cord" and "barn"–"born." Another instance is the substitution of [æ] for [ɑ], although this is not frequent. "Calm," for example, may become more nearly [kæm]—which was standard in colonial times in America but is no longer acceptable.

The situation with respect to the so-called broad a has been touched upon in the previous section. Since the broad a is such a well-known distinction between American and Standard British speech, it is perhaps desirable to add a few more comments on this sound at this point.

In general, the whole group of ah vowels is pronounced differently in Southern British than in American speech, and the same set of phonetic symbols cannot be used accurately to represent both languages. However, the specific pronunciations which lead to the popular feeling that British and Eastern American speakers use a broad a occur mostly in a limited group of words like "ask" and "aunt." These are pronounced [ɑ] in Southern British and [ɑ] or [a] in Eastern American speech. Most of the more common words in this category, which are pronounced with an [æ] by the majority of American speakers, are included in the exercises of this chapter.

It is not possible or desirable to set down rules for the average student who may wish to learn how to use the broad a. Only a great deal of listening experience will accomplish this. It is respectfully suggested, however, that the student avoid the attempt unless he has some compelling reason for doing so.

Exercises

1. In the following paragraph there are more than 25 words which in the authors' dialect are pronounced with the [ɑ]. See how many you can identify. List separately those which appear in the diphthong [ɑr], those which appear in isolation, and those which may be either [ɑ] or [ə]. After you have picked out the sounds you believe to be [ɑ], turn to the phonetic transcription to find out how one of the authors pronounced this passage.

If the student has followed the text closely and observed its counsel, he should by this time have accomplished at least some modest improvement in his own speech. It is almost never possible, of course, to describe effective speech simply; one must take cognizance of the fact that the whole matter is far too complex. It would also be hard to say what qualities are the best mark of a good speaker. One can be certain that good speech is honest; it follows that the speaker himself must have a sincere interest in the topic or content of his utterance. Good speech is the offspring of honest convictions, a stock of logical ideas, and a genuine desire to communicate them to his auditor. Beyond this, the job of speaking well involves a mastery of the language and a proper respect for its usage. Many of the bars to effective communication lie far below the surface, and one must seek constantly to take stock of himself and his true feelings and beliefs. The gain has been large when even a modicum of self-understanding has been reached. Good speech is an art, but it starts from within.

2. Use the following list of common [ɑ] words for practice and for reference. After studying this list, go back to Exercise 1 and see whether you can identify any [ɑ] sounds you may have missed before.

a. Words using [ɑ] in a stressed syllable:

accomplish	father	October	project (n.)
body	follow	opera	profit
beyond	god	opposite	product
bomb	honor	popular	proper
box	hot	possible	rock
college	job	population	shop
common	John	possibility	shot
doctor	logical	probably	spot
dollar	lot	problem	stock
drop	modern	promise	top
economics	not	process	topic

b. Unaccented [ɑ] words, which may be pronounced with [ə] or, in some cases, with [ɚ]:

of	was	got
on	what	are

c. Words pronounced with [ɑr]:

arm	hard	start	farm
army	heart	art	farmer
artist	mark	Arthur	March
car	part	article	star
far	party	charge	yard

d. Some common words pronounced [ɑ] in British and Eastern American speech and [æ] in General American speech:

(1) Vowels preceding [s]:

ask	disaster	last	past
basket	fast	mast	plaster
blast	fasten	master	rasp
cast	glass	nasty	task
class	grass	pass	

(2) Vowels preceding [f] and [θ]:

after	craft	half	shaft
bath	draft	laugh	staff
calf	graft	raft	path

(3) Vowels preceding [m] and [n]:

advance	branch	demand	glance
advantage	cant	dance	grant
answer	chance	example	plant
aunt	command	France	sample

3. Practice making the following distinctions among vowel sounds. Pay particular attention to the [ɑ]–[ɔ] and the [ɑ]–[ʌ] pairs. For some these may prove particularly difficult. (See also [o], [aɪ], and [au].)

[ɑ]—[ɔ]		[ɑ]—[ʌ]	
body [bɑdɪ]	bawdy [bɔdɪ]	cot [kɑt]	cut [kʌt]
hock [hɑk]	hawk [hɔk]	not [nɑt]	nut [nʌt]
collar [kɑlɚ]	caller [kɔlɚ]	rot [rɑt]	rut [rʌt]
Moll [mɑl]	maul [mɔl]	sock [sɑk]	suck [sʌk]
rah [rɑ]	raw [rɔ]	lock [lɑk]	luck [lʌk]
popper [pɑpɚ]	pauper [pɔpɚ]	hot [hɑt]	hut [hʌt]
are [ɑr]	or [ɔr]	got [gɑt]	gut [gʌt]
car [kɑr]	core [kɔr]	spotter [spɑtɚ]	sputter [spʌtɚ]
farm [fɑrm]	form [fɔrm]	cop [kɑp]	cup [kʌp]
star [stɑr]	store [stɔr]	shot [ʃɑt]	shut [ʃʌt]

[ɑ]—[æ]	
box [bɑks]	backs [bæks]
job [dʒɑb]	jab [dʒæb]
lost [lɑst]	last [læst]
not [nɑt]	gnat [næt]
possible [pɑsəbl]	passible [pæsəbl]
rock [rɑk]	rack [ræk]
spot [spɑt]	spat [spæt]
stock [stɑk]	stack [stæk]
sot [sɑt]	sat [sæt]
top [tɑp]	tap [tæp]

Phonetic Transcription. The following is a transcription of a GA pronunciation of the paragraph in Exercise 1.

[ɪf ðə studṇt həz fɑlod ðə tɛkst 'klosɪ ænd əb'zɜ·vd ɪts kaunsəl, hi ʃud baɪ ðɪs taɪm həv ə'kamplɪʃt ət list sʌm mɑdəst ɪm'pruvmənt ɪn ɪz on spitʃ. ɪt ɪz ɔlmost nɛvɚ pɑsəbḷ, əv kɔrs, tə dɪ'skraɪb ɪ'fɛktɪv spitʃ sɪmplɪ; wʌn məst tek 'kɑgnəzəns əv ðə fækt ðət ðə hol mætɚ ɪz fɑr tu kɑm'plɛks.

ɪt wʊd ɔlso bi hɑrd tə se hwʌt 'kwɑlətɪz ɑr ðə bɛst mɑrk əv ə gʊd spikɚ. wʌn kən bi sɝtn̩ ðət gʊd spitʃ ɪz ənəst; ɪt fɑloz ðət ðə spikɚ hɪm'sɛlf mʌst hæv ə sɪn'sɪr 'ɪntərəst ɪn ðə 'tɑpɪk ɔr 'kɑntɛnt əv ɪz 'ʌtərəns. gʊd spitʃ ɪz ðə 'ɔfsprɪŋ əv 'ɑnəst 'kənvɪkʃənz, ə stɑk əv 'lɑdʒɪk̩l̩ aɪ'dɪəz, ænd ə 'dʒɛnjuən dɪ'zaɪr tu kə'mjunəket ðəm tu hɪz 'ɔdətɚ. biɑnd ðɪs ðə dʒɑb əv spikɪŋ wɛl ɪnvɑlvz ə mæstərɪ əv ðə 'læŋˌgwɪdʒ ənd ə prɑpɚ rɪ'spɛkt fɔr ɪts 'jusɪdʒ. mɛnɪ əv ðə bɑrz tu ɪ'fɛktɪv kəmjunə'keʃən laɪ fɑr bɪlo ðə 'sɝfəs, ænd wʌn məst sik 'kɑnstəntlɪ tʊ tek stɑk əv hɪmsɛlf ənd hɪz tru 'filɪŋz ən bɪ'lifs. ðə gen həz bɪn lɑrdʒ hwɛn ivən ə 'mɑdəkəm əv sɛlf ʌndɚ'stændɪŋ həz bɪn rɪtʃt. gʊd spitʃ ɪz ən ɑrt, bət ɪt stɑrts frəm wɪð'ɪn.]

Foreign and Nonphonemic Variants. The major nonphonemic and foreign back-vowel symbols of use to the average student include the following:

The [ɒ] is a low-back, rounded vowel which has already been discussed (see [ɔ]). It lies roughly between the [ɑ] and the [ɔ]. It is heard in the British pronunciations of "sorry," "not," and "long" and is a not infrequent variant of [ɑ] in a number of American pronunciations. It has been described as equivalent to [ɑ] with some lip rounding.

The [ɣ] is a mid-back, unrounded vowel. It is a kind of unrounded [o], which is said to occur in the Pekin dialect of Chinese and in other exotic contexts.

The [ɯ] is a high-back, unrounded, tense vowel. It approximates an unrounded [u]. Like [ɣ], it is not part of the French, English, or German sound systems and occurs only in more exotic contexts of little interest to the average reader of this book.

7

THE CENTRAL VOWELS

[ɝ], [ɜ], [ɚ], [ə], [ʌ]

The central vowels present a more complex problem for analysis than do either the front- or back-vowel series. In the first place, the central vowels have even less fixed and well-defined tongue positions with which they can be identified. For this reason it is not possible to place them on a vowel diagram with any real accuracy. Nevertheless, it is conventional to assign them a position, and the custom will be followed in this discussion for its schematic value. *Stress* plays a much more important part in differentiating the central vowels than it does in connection with the other English vowels. Instead of placing the central vowels on a vowel diagram, it would be more meaningful in some respects to summarize their characteristics in relation to three factors: (1) tongue position, (2) degree of stress, and (3) the presence or absence of *r* coloring.

In considering tongue position it is scarcely worthwhile to make any effort to designate more than two different tongue heights. It is conventional to classify [ɝ], [ɚ], [ɜ], and [ə] as *mid-central*. This implies that the tongue is at approximately the same height as [o] among the back vowels and [ɛ] in the front-vowel series. Only [ʌ] among the central vowels is customarily termed a *lower mid-central* vowel.

Stress differences clearly divide the central vowels into two groups. Three of the vowels—[ɝ], [ɜ], and [ʌ]—appear only in stressed syllables. The remaining two, [ɚ] and [ə], acquire their principal acoustic characteristics from the fact that they are unstressed; they are short in duration and carry very little force. Two of the central vowels, [ɝ] and [ɚ], are *r*-colored as they occur in General American speech. This simply means that they possess a quality which resembles that of the consonant [r] as it is pronounced by most American speakers. The central vowels without *r* coloring are, of course, [ɜ], [ʌ], and [ə]. The principal difference

99

between the two *r*-colored vowels, as indicated earlier, is in the degree of stress which each receives.

The problem of determining which differences are phonemic and which are not is difficult to solve for the central vowels. The [ɝ] and [ɜ], for example, are never contrasting phonemes in the usual sense of the word. This problem is discussed in the following sections.

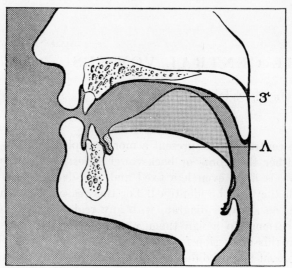

Fɪɢ. 6. Articulation adjustments for the central vowels.

[ɝ] (or [ɜ]) as in burn, urge, fir

Common Spellings: *er* as in term, herd
               ir as in stir, whir
               ur as in hurt, burst
               or as in word, worst
               ear as in learn, earn
               Also spelled *our*, as in courage; *yr*, as in myrtle;
               olo, as in colonel.

Production. The [ɝ] is described as a mid-central, *r*-colored vowel, produced with moderate jaw opening, considerable tongue tension, and no significant lip rounding. Two distinctly different methods of production have been described. Perhaps the easiest to visualize is the *retroflexed-tongue* production, in which the tip of the tongue is curled back, or retroflexed, in the oral cavity. The second method of production, probably of more frequent use, features an arching of the tongue in its mid-portion.

The symbol [ɝ] designates only the *stressed* syllables having a very definite *r* quality and should be reserved to indicate such sounds. A similar, if not identical, resonance appearing as the major syllabic element in *unaccented* syllables occurs in English and is transcribed [ɚ]. It should be emphasized that the symbol [ɝ] designates a vowel and therefore is used only to represent the major resonance of the syllable. The resemblance between [ɝ] and [ɚ]—which are vowels—and the glide [r], which is considered a consonant, will be discussed presently.

The [ɝ] occurs in all three positions in words, is ordinarily not diphthongized, and is used only by those who do not drop their *r*'s. A variation of this sound as it is pronounced by those who do drop their *r*'s is symbolized by the [ɜ]. The production of this sound is roughly the same as for the [ɝ], except that there is no *r* coloring and the tongue is not retroflexed.

Pronunciation. Most native speakers are quite likely to need some instruction and practice before they are able to discriminate accurately among the various *r* sounds and use the appropriate symbols in transcription. In general, pronunciation problems centering around [ɝ] arise first because of the confusion occasioned by the fact that *r* resonance is a feature of three sounds: [ɝ], [ɚ], and [r]; second, because of failure to understand the way in which *stress* (and perhaps only stress) differentiates [ɝ] and [ɚ]; and finally, because of the somewhat marked difference in usage of the *r* sounds in various dialect regions of the United States and England. In this last connection, the difference between the *r*-colored [ɝ] and the [ɜ], which has no *r* coloring, must be understood.

For the most part, it is not difficult to differentiate [ɝ], [ɚ], and [r] as they occur in American speech. As will be brought out in more detail later (see Chapter 11), the glide [r] either initiates or terminates a syllable, as in the words "remark" [rɪmɑrk] and "archive" [ɑrkaɪv]; but it does not make up the major resonance of the syllable to which it belongs. On the other hand, in the words "early" [ɝlɪ] and "burden" [bɝdn̩], the sound [ɝ] clearly makes up the major resonance of the syllable. If "remark" and "archive" were pronounced with [ɝ] or [ɚ] instead of [r], they would have to be spoken as three-syllable words, not as the two-syllable words they actually are. So far as the distinction between [ɝ] and [ɚ] is concerned, the former is never used in unaccented syllables, and the latter is never accented. An example often used to illustrate the distinction between these two sounds is the word "pervert." If it is spoken with the first syllable accented, the pronunciation would correctly be transcribed [pɝvɚt]; if, however, the second syllable receives the stress, the pronunciation is [pɚvɝt]. Once this distinction is clearly understood, one may have less difficulty deciding whether any given syllable has had [ɝ] or [ɚ] as the major resonance.

The way in which the various *r* sounds are used makes up one of the most distinctive differences between dialect regions in the United States and between American and British speech. In ordinary language, we say that certain persons "drop their *r*'s." In general, those who use Eastern or Southern American speech or who follow British usage drop their *r*'s, but the General American speaker pronounces his.

In the speech of about two-thirds or more of all American speakers, the pronunciation symbolized by [ɝ] is used for all syllables which could, because they have an *r* spelling, contain *r* coloring. Geographically, this is the typical speech wherever General American is the standard. In Eastern American, Southern American, and British speech, dropping the *r* consists of replacing the vowel [ɝ] with [ɜ], which is its non-*r*-colored counterpart. To the untrained ear the latter sound seems to resemble a somewhat prolonged [ʌ], although it is not, of course, quite the same sound.

Without going into all the rules for pronouncing *r* sounds at this point, we may note that the speaker who replaces [ɝ] with [ɜ] also uses [ə] instead of [ɚ]. Typical pronunciations of those who drop their *r*'s would be [mɜmə] instead of [mɝmɚ] for "murmur" and [rɪfɜ] instead of [rɪfɝ] for "refer." The [ə] sound and other matters relating to the pronunciation of words with *r* are discussed in later sections.

Persons who are phonetically and linguistically naïve may have a good many mistaken notions about "proper" usage for the various *r* sounds. To be sure, any one of these sounds may be too tense or too nasal or may be pronounced with an exaggerated *r* coloring. This so-called "twang" should be avoided, as should any other bad speech habit. On the other hand, there is positively nothing objectionable about pronouncing one's *r* sounds where this practice is consistent with the general dialect characteristics of his speech, as it is for the General American speaker. Indeed, the most grievous error occurs when the self-conscious person with a false idea of what constitutes cultured speech tries to emulate a supposedly superior Eastern or British dialect. If he wishes to do so, he is entitled to adopt such standards *in toto*, but his speech becomes a caricature if he undertakes only to drop his *r*'s.

The [ɝ] appears to be one of the most easily recognized vowels in the English sound system. Nevertheless it is typically the last to be learned by children and often gives them great difficulty. It is one of the most difficult to teach to those who lack the sound. Children sometimes have the greatest trouble with the consonant [r], and often substitute [w]. However, the characteristic substitution of either [ɜ] or [ə] for [ɝ] or [ɚ] is only a little less common and may even be more so in the North and West. Often children substitute a "labialized," or lip-rounded, vowel, something like a rounded [ʊ] or [ʌ] in their attempts to pronounce [ɝ], and it is likely that most *r* distortions in infantile speech are of this type. Such labialization leads to rounded, nonstandard [ɝ] vowels and consonantal [r] sounds, which are very close to [w]. The *r* dialects are most affected by this kind of distortion, but non-*r* dialects are also disturbed because of the consonant [r] problem.

Another type of *r* distortion often heard in the speech of children, and also of adults, is in the direction of the high-front vowels. The [ɝ] may take on an [i]-ish quality, and the [r] may sound something like [j].

In teaching correct *r* quality to children and adults, *ear training* must be relied upon heavily, and trial-and-error learning plays a major part in drills and exercises. It is helpful sometimes, of course, to draw attention to the lip position, the feel of the border of the tongue along the teeth, and the position of the tonguetip.

The diphthong [ɜɪ] may be heard in [ɝ] words in the Deep South and in New York City areas, but it is considered too much a localism to be accepted as fully standard. It is this diphthong which gives the impression that [ɔɪ] has been "hoid" and provides the stereotype for the Brooklyn dialect. It should be pointed out, of course, that the [ɜɪ] is a variant of [ɜ] rather than of [ɝ] directly.

Sometimes the [ɝ] (or [ɜ]) vowel is confused with a vowel-plus-[r] diphthong—[ɪr], [ɛr], [ær], [ɑr], [ɔr], or [ʊr]. The substitution of [ɝ] for one of these diphthongs is occasionally heard and is often considered substandard; it is involved in such confusing pronunciations as [hɝ] for "here" [hɪr] or [fɝ] for "far" [fɑr]. Unacceptable substitutions of one of the vowel-plus-[r] diphthongs in place of [ɝ] may also be heard, as in [lɑrn] for "learn" [lɜn] and [hɪrd] for "heard" [hɝd]. Such pronunciations, of course, are to be avoided as narrowly dialectal or substandard. On the other hand, in some words, notably in words like "hurry" and "worry," either the diphthong or the *r*-colored vowel may be correct, depending upon the dialect region. Compare [hʌrɪ] with [hɝɪ], [wʌrɪ] with [wɝɪ], and [sɪrəp] with [sɝəp] (in the words "hurry," "worry," and "syrup"). This problem of variation in *r* usage may be better understood after the discussion of the consonant [r] in Chapter 11. The numerous difficulties of the foreign speaker with this sound can also be discussed more conveniently in the section on the consonant [r].

Exercises

1. In the following paragraph identify the words which employ the sound [ɝ] or [ɜ] (depending upon which dialect you speak). In which may a vowel-plus-[r] diphthong be heard with equal acceptability? In which words is the *r*-colored vowel heard only as an unstressed syllable? In the author's speech a count reveals about 22 [ɝ] sounds, 22 [ɚ]'s, 21 vowel-plus-[r] syllables, and 17 [r]-plus-vowel syllables. Try to identify these in your own speech before turning to the phonetic transcription of the paragraph.

Work is variously a curse and a blessing, depending upon the circumstances one is forced to meet. Certainly, a world in which there were no daily tasks to be performed, no new opportunities for the pursuit of truth, or no earth to be turned by the farmer's plow would indeed be a sterile place. Nevertheless, there are times in the life of every person when he dreams of the vast delights that would surely be his if he were a millionaire, freed of the burdens of earning a living or performing any task for which he had no fancy. He is prone, in intervals such as these, to regard himself as a kind of poor serf, forced by an unfriendly world to concern himself with matters for which he has no taste, merely to fatten a lean purse. Yet there are few persons who would not, if brought face to face with stern reality, admit, perhaps grudgingly, that they are happier by virtue of the fact that they have been furnished an opportunity to carry out some productive labor. Man can learn true happiness only if he is creative, whether his achievement is great or small. There is a pride in such accomplishment which goes far beyond any material reward the worker may receive; it is the satisfaction of knowing that to a greater or lesser degree he has served, that he has in at least some small measure made the earth on which he lives a better place.

2. The practice words in this exercise, like others included in this text, are derived primarily from lists of the 1,000 most frequently written and spoken words of American English. However, because of the difficulty many people experience with the [ɝ], the following list has been considerably augmented with other words of common occurrence in the vocabularies of college students.

  a. Words using [ɝ] or [ɜ] in stressed syllables:

bird	dirt	herself	return	Thursday
burn	early	hurt	reserve	turn
clerk	earth	jerk	serve	university
church	earnest	learn	service	verse
circle	furnish	occur	shirk	were
curve	fur	person	skirt	word
certain	further	personnel	squirt	work
certainly	curse	personality	stir	world
concern	German	purpose	term	worth
concerning	heard	purse	third	worst
commercial	her	research	thirty	urge

  b. Words using [ɝ] or a vowel-plus-[r] diphthong:

hurry	syrup	worry	courage

3. Practice making the following distinctions among the [ɝ] and other sounds. Why are no [ɝ]-[ə] pairs listed?

[ɝ]—[ʌ]

bird [bɝd]	bud [bʌd]
burn [bɝn]	bun [bʌn]
circle [sɝkl]	suckle [sʌkl]
hurt [hɝt]	hut [hʌt]
third [θɝd]	thud [θʌd]
turn [tɝn]	ton [tʌn]
pert [pɝt]	putt [pʌt]
stern [stɝn]	stun [stʌn]
girl [gɝl]	gull [gʌl]
earn [ɝn]	un [ʌn]

[ɝ]—[ɔɪ]

early [ɝlɪ]	oily [ɔɪlɪ]
hurt [hɝt]	Hoyt [hɔɪt]
learn [lɝn]	loin [lɔɪn]
burl [bɝl]	boil [bɔɪl]
earl [ɝl]	oil [ɔɪl]
sir [sɝ]	soy [sɔɪ]
verse [vɝs]	voice [vɔɪs]
burrs [bɝz]	boys [bɔɪz]
curl [kɝl]	coil [kɔɪl]
verge [vɝdʒ]	voyage [vɔɪdʒ]

[ɝ]—[ɛr] (or [ær])

burr [bɝ]	bare [bɛr]-[bær]
cur [kɝ]	care [kɛr]-[kær]
fir [fɝ]	fair [fɛr]-[fær]
her [hɝ]	hair [hɛr]-[hær]
hurry [hɝɪ]	Harry [hɛrɪ]-[hærɪ]
purr [pɝ]	pair [pɛr]-[pær]
spur [spɝ]	spare [spɛr]-[spær]
stir [stɝ]	stair [stɛr]-[stær]
were [wɝ]	wear [wɛr]-[wær]
err [ɝ]	air [ɛr]-[ær]

Phonetic Transcription. The following transcription of the paragraph in Exercise 1 represents the General American pronunciation:

[wɝk ɪz 'vɛrɪəs‚lɪ ə kɝs ænd ə 'blɛsɪŋ, dɪ'pɛndɪŋ ə'pɑn ðə 'sɝkəm‚-stænsəz wʌn ɪz fɔrst tə mit. 'sɝtənlɪ, ə wɝld ɪn hwɪtʃ ðer wɝ no delɪ tæsks tə bi ‚pɝ'fɔrmd, no nu apɝ'tunətɪz fɔr ðə pɝsut əv truθ, ɔr no ɝθ tə bi 'tɝnd baɪ ðə 'fɑrmɝz plau wud ɪn'did bi ə 'stɛrəl ples. ‚nɛvɝðə'lɛs ðer ɑr taɪmz ɪn ðə laɪf əv ɛvrɪ pɝsn̩ hwɛn hi drimz əv ðə væst dɪ'laɪts ðət wəd ʃurlɪ bi hɪz ɪf hi wɝ ə 'mɪljənɛr, frid əv ðə bɝdənz əv ɝnɪŋ ə lɪvɪŋ ɔr pɝformɪŋ ɛnɪ tæsk fɝ hwɪtʃ hi hæd no fænsɪ. hi ɪz pron, ɪn ɪntɝvəlz sʌtʃ əz ðɪz, tə rɪ'gɑrd hɪmsɛlf æz ə kaɪnd əv pur sɝf, fɔrst baɪ ən ʌn'frɛndlɪ wɝld tu kən'sɝn hɪmsɛlf wɪð mætɝz fɝ hwɪtʃ hi hæz no test, mɪrlɪ tə fætn̩ ə lin pɝs. jɛt ðer ɑr fju pɝsənz hu wud nɑt, ɪf brɔt fes tə fes wɪθ stɝn ri'ælətɪ, ədmɪt, pɝ'hæps grʌdʒɪŋlɪ, ðət ðe ɑr hæpiɝ baɪ vɝtʃu əv ðə fækt ðət ðe həv bɪn fɝnɪʃt ən apɝ'tunətɪ tə kɛrɪ aut sʌm prə'dʌktɪv lebɝ. mæn kən lɝn tru 'hæpɪnəs onlɪ ɪf hi ɪz kri'etɪv, hwɛðɝ hɪz ətʃivmənt ɪz grɛt ɔr smɔl. ðer ɪz ə praɪd ɪn sʌtʃ ə'kʌmplɪʃ‚mənt hwɪtʃ goz fɑr bɪjɑnd ɛnɪ mə'tɪrɪəl rɪwɝd ðə wɝkɝ me rɪ'siv; ɪt ɪz ðə sætəs'fækʃən əv noɪŋ ðət tu ə gretɚ ɔr lɛsɚ dɪgri hi hæz sɝvd, ðət hi həz ət list ɪn sʌm smɔl mɛʒɚ med ðɪ ɝθ ɔn hwɪtʃ hi lɪvz ə betɚ ples.]

[ɚ] (or [ə]) as in persistent, better

Common Spellings: er as in manner, finer
                     or as in harbor, color
                     ur as in Saturday, murmur
                     ar as in burglar, altar
                     Also spelled *our*, as in labour; *yr*, as in martyr;
                     ir, as in elixir.

Production. The [ɚ] is a short, lax, mid-central, *r*-colored vowel which can be produced by tongue retroflexion (see [ɝ]) and which is to be found only in unaccented syllables. The sound probably has somewhat less *r* coloring typically than does the [ɝ], but it may, in general, be described as the counterpart of an [ɝ] with minimal accent. The [ɚ] occurs most often in the medial and final positions in words.

Pronunciation. As with [ɝ], problems centering around [ɚ] can be separated into those related to the question of when the symbol should be properly used for transcription and to more basic variations in pronunciation practices. The resonance of the sound is not hard to identify, but the discrimination between [ɚ] and other *r* sounds may not be easy for the unsophisticated listener. To understand the distinction between [ɝ] and [ɚ], which is largely a matter of stress, the earlier discussion of this point, in connection with the description of [ɝ], should be reviewed. It was explained then that [ɝ] is always *stressed*, whereas [ɚ] is always unstressed, and this rule can easily be used to select the correct symbol in recording speech samples. An extended discussion of stress is included in Chapter 12, but in nontechnical language the term is used to describe the forcefulness with which a syllable is spoken. Numerous examples of [ɝ] and [ɚ] words are given in the exercises for these sounds.

It is somewhat more difficult, at least in many phonetic contexts, to tell whether the speaker has used an *r*-colored vowel ([ɚ] or [ɝ]) or the consonant [r]. The beginner cannot be blamed for his confusion when [ɚ] follows a vowel, for even experts disagree in many instances about whether the *r* coloring should be considered part of a diphthong, and thus transcribed with the vowel symbol [ɚ], or whether it should be regarded as a glide, which would call for the consonant symbol [r]. For example, in the word "bear," do we hear the pronunciation [bɛɚ] or [bɛr]? The question is even more vexatious in a word such as "terrific," which might be either [tərɪfɪk] or [tɚɪfɪk].

Most of the argument about [r] versus [ɚ] in instances such as those just mentioned can be considered a mere debate over terminology. The difference between [ɚ] and [r] in the above examples is certainly not phonemic in the sense that meaning would be affected by either pronunciation. Practically speaking, the student will not be seriously wrong if he uses either notation in broad transcription. Nevertheless, in many cases the careful and experienced listener can transcribe most accurately if he does make the fine distinction between [ɚ] and [r]. In such a word as "merry," for instance, the pronunciation could be either [mɛɚɪ] or [mɛrɪ], depending upon whether the word was pronounced so that the r coloring initiated the second syllable or terminated the first. Such distinctions are admittedly difficult to make, and the student need not concern himself about them unless he wishes. More information about central diphthongs involving [ɚ] is included in Chapter 8.

There can be no real justification for the transcription practice of using [r] when the r coloring is the major resonance of the syllable, whether the syllable is stressed or unstressed. Nor does the transcription [ər], as occasionally used in such a word as "better" [bɛtər], ordinarily serve as well as [ɚ] ([bɛtɚ]). The transcription [bɛtər] would indicate a neutral vowel followed by a glide, whereas characteristically only a single resonance is present for this syllable. This is not to say, however, that [ər] cannot be heard instead of [ɚ] in some cases where the syllable on which the r coloring rests is in question, for it can. "Mirage," for example, may be heard as [məɚɑʒ] or [mərɑʒ], depending upon very subtle temporal cues. Here again the difference is not distinctive and need not be considered important by the student just beginning his study of speech analysis.

In general, the comments about [ɝ] in connection with dialect differences also apply to [ɚ]. Thus, in words spelled with the letter r, those persons who pronounce their r's will say [ɚ] as the r resonance for unstressed syllables and [ɝ] for the r resonance in stressed syllables. Those who do not pronounce their r's will, of course, substitute [ə] for [ɚ].

Because [ɚ] tends to lose its r coloring more easily than [ɝ], an occasional speaker who habitually uses [ɝ] in the accented position will nonetheless use [ə] in unstressed syllables. In Eastern American, for example, "further" might be heard as [fɝ'ðə], though [fɜ'ðə] would be more frequent.

The problem of handling [ɚ] and other sounds in the r group in one's own speech should not prove too difficult. Much of the discussion has revolved around transcription practices and dialect differences. In acquiring good speech it does not matter, in a sense, whether the student does or does not pronounce his r's. If his over-all speech pattern is General American, he should pronounce his r's in a way which is consistent with General American usages; if his speech is Eastern American, Southern American, or British, he should handle r sounds as do the educated speakers in these groups. The important consideration is whether or not his *r*-sound usages are consistent; Eastern *r* usages in speech which is otherwise General American are at least naïve.

A conspicuous fault of those who pronounce their *r*'s may be a tense, nasalized sound. This is likely to occur when the tongue is unduly retracted, giving the sound an unpleasant resonance. The speaker who pronounces *r* sounds in this way will probably show the same characteristics on many other sounds, particularly such vowels as [æ], [e], and [ɛ]; these are the resonances that make up what is loosely called a "twang." If properly articulated, however, the speech of those who pronounce their *r*'s will be fully as acceptable as that of persons who speak another dialect. Rarely, one may hear speakers who make an effort to be overprecise with words spelled with a final *r*, with resulting pronunciations such as [ʃugɑr] instead [ʃugɚ] for "sugar" and [hɑrbɔr] rather than [hɑrbɚ] for "harbor." Such usages are, of course, awkward and substandard.

The developmental difficulties which children have with other sounds in the *r* group extend as well to words which normally contain [ɚ]. These difficulties are also a problem for foreign speakers, who bring to their English pronunciation a variety of nonstandard sounds. Both children and adults with defects of this kind may find themselves faced with the need for long and careful practice. Additional information about *r*-sound difficulties is included in Chapter 11 in connection with the discussion of the consonant [r].

Exercises

1. The following paragraph includes about 35 words that the authors pronounce with the [ɚ] sound (the *r*-colored vowel in an unaccented syllable). In these words a speaker who drops his *r*'s would ordinarily use the sound [ə]. See how many of these words you can identify. Practice them with both the [ɚ] and [ə]. In which words should the symbol [ɝ] be used? Is the difference between [ɝ] and [ɚ] *phonemic?* Check your pronunciation of this paragraph with the phonetic transcription included at the end of these exercises.

The question as to how one determines whether a pronunciation is standard is rather difficult to answer. It certainly depends on a great number of factors. Among these the speaker should consider the nature of the subject, together with the nature of the occasion and the factors involving the dialect region in which the speaking is done. After all, what is thoroughly acceptable in Denver may be considered entirely substandard in a finishing school in Vermont. On the other hand, grammar and pronunciation which are thoroughly permissible around the family dinner table may not be permissible from the lips of a radio announcer. It is almost certain, however, that if one ceases to worry about what is "proper" or popular and asks himself only what is most efficient and contributes most to better and quicker communication, he will not fail to discover the better answer to the problem in the greater number of cases.

2. Use the following list of [ɚ]-or-[ə] words for practice and reference:

a. Words using [ɚ] in General American and [ə] in Eastern speech:

after	finger	mister	proper
another	figure	modern	rather
answer	flower	nature	remember
better	further	neighbors	river
brother	future	never	Saturday
center	gather	November	shoulder
character	government	number	smaller
color	grammar	October	soldier
consider	greater	offer	speaker
corner	higher	officer	standard
cover	however	older	suffer
daughter	information	opportunity	superintendent
December	international	order	sugar
desire	junior	other	summer
dinner	labor	outer	surprise
discover	later	over	teacher
doctor	letter	paper	together
dollar	liquor	particularly	under
effort	lower	perhaps	understand
either	manner	per cent	weather
energy	major	perform	whether
enter	manufacturer	permit	winter
ever	matter	picture	wonder
farther	measure	pleasure	worker
father	mother	popular	

b. [ɚ] triphthongs, which may be one- or two-syllable sounds:

entire	environment	power
fire	iron	require
hour	our	tire

c. Sometimes pronounced [ɚ], sometimes [ər]:

centering	difference	generation	opera
cooperate	factory	interest	separate
consideration	general	natural	several

d. [ɚ] or [ə] only when unstressed (as is usually the case):

are	her	there	your
for	herself	were	yourself
forget	nor	where	

3. Because the [ə] is not phonemically distinct from [ɝ] in quite the same way as are the other stressed vowels, it is not possible to produce lists of minimal pairs of exactly the same type. The following pairs will, however, indicate the importance of the stress difference between [ɝ] and [ɚ] as a matter of practical pronunciation (or between [ɜ] and [ə], if that is your choice).

[ɝ]—[ɚ]

fed early [fɛdɝlɪ]	Fedderly [fɛdɚlɪ]
man erring [mænɝ·ɪŋ]	Mannering [mænɚɪŋ]
great err [gretɝ·]	greater [gretɚ]
lay burr [lebɝ·]	labor [lebɚ]
neigh burrs [nebɝ·z]	neighbors [nebɚz]
pay purr [pepɝ·]	paper [pepɚ]
some myrrh [sʌmɝ·]	summer [sʌmɚ]
I earn [aɪɝ·n]	iron [aɪɚn]
cub bird [kʌbɝ·d]	cupboard [kʌbɚd]
back word [bækwɝ·d]	backward [bækwɚd]

Phonetic Transcription. Practice the following paragraph, comparing the author's pronunciation with your own. Where you find [ɚ], try substituting [ɝ], [ɜ], and [ə] to observe the effect that this has on the pronunciation and rhythm of the passage.

[ðə kwɛstʃən æz tu hau wʌn dɪ'tɝmənz hwɛðɚ ə prənʌnsɪ'eʃən ɪz stændɚd ɪz ræðɚ 'dɪfə‚kʌlt tu ænsɚ. ɪt sɝtənlɪ dɪ'pɛndz ɑn ə gret nʌmbɚ əv 'fæktɚz. əmʌŋ ðiz ðə spikɚ ʃud kənsɪdɚ ðə netʃɚ əv ðə 'sʌbdʒɪkt tə'gɛðɚ wɪθ ðə netʃɚ əv ðɪ ə'keʒən ænd ðə fæktɚz ɪnvɑlvɪŋ ðə daɪəlɛkt rɪdʒən ɪn hwɪtʃ ðə spikɪŋ ɪz dʌn. æftɚ ɔl, hwʌt ɪz 'θɝəlɪ æk'sɛptəbḷ ɪn dɛnvɚ me bi kənsɪdɚd ɛn'taɪrlɪ 'sʌbstændɚd ɪn ə 'fɪnɪʃɪŋ skul ɪn vɚ'mɑnt. ɑn ðɪ ʌðɚ hænd, græmɚ ən prənʌnsɪ'eʃən hwɪtʃ ɑr θɝəlɪ pɚ'mɪsəbḷ əraund ðə fæmlɪ dɪnɚ tebḷ me nɑt bi pɚ'mɪsəbḷ frəm ðə lɪps əv ə redɪo ə'naunsɚ. ɪt ɪz ɔlmost sɝtən, hauɛvɚ, ðət ɪf wʌn sisəz tə wɝɪ əbaut hwʌt ɪz prɑpɚ or 'pɑpjulɚ ænd æsks hɪmsɛlf onlɪ hwʌt ɪz most ɪ'fɪʃənt ænd ‚kən'trɪbjuts most tə bɛtɚ ən kwɪkɚ kəmjunə'keʃən, hi wɪl nɑt fel tə dɪ'skʌvɚ ðə bɛtɚ ænsɚ tə ðə prɑbləm ɪn ðə gretɚ nʌmbɚ əv kesəz.]

[ə] as in about, serene, drama

Common Spellings: *a* as in alone, soda
e as in system, the

i as in easily, policy

o as in gallop, of

u as in circus, supply

Also spelled *ai*, as in mountain; *ei*, as in mullein; *eo*, as in dungeon, *ia*, as in parliament; *oi*, as in porpoise; *ou*, as in curious; *he*, as in vehement. This sound also may be spelled in any of the ways used to spell [ɚ] for people who drop their *r*'s.

Production. The [ə] is a lax, mid-central vowel, but this designation falls far short of an adequate description of the sound. Its classification is relatively unimportant, compared to its function in the stress pattern of the language. It has been variously called the *neutral, unstressed, indefinite, schwa,* or *obscure* vowel, all these terms suggesting the character of the sound.

The [ə] is *neutral* inasmuch as there is actually no truly standard tongue position typical for it. It is *unstressed* because it is pronounced with the least energy of any of the vowels and tends to be lower in pitch and shorter in duration. It is *indefinite* or *obscure* because it has little in the way of identifiable vowel quality of its own; it is rather a kind of "vocal murmur," a name by which it has sometimes been known.

The lack of distinctness in the quality of [ə] results from what Kenyon has called the *law of obscuration* (Ref. 16, p. 198). This is the tendency for any of the definite vowels of stressed syllables to be leveled out to a common neutral quality when the stress is greatly reduced. This happens often in English speech. Physiologically, the tongue and other articulators do not always reach the height or shape necessary for definite vowel resonances within the brief time interval and lax muscular conditions of an unstressed syllable.

One reason why no tongue position can be described for [ə] is that the adjustment of the articulators is determined to some degree by the position for the vowel of which it is a "reduced" version, as well as by the amount of stress, the nature of the surrounding sounds, the length of the syllable, and other such factors. In some words [ə] may have a quality resembling [ɪ], whereas in others it may be closer to [ʌ], or perhaps to [ʊ]. As commonly pronounced, [ə] is somewhat like [ɪ] in "attitude" [ætətud] and like [ʌ] in "ago" [əgo].

Pronunciation. Problems in the proper use of [ə], and incidental difficulties in phonetic transcription, center to a large extent around a seeming unawareness of the frequency with which the sound occurs in English. So far as transcription is concerned, the commonest mistake is to think that some definite vowel resonance has been heard, usually the one with which the spelling of the word is most often associated. For instance, "system" may be misheard and incorrectly transcribed [sɪstɛm]. It is possible, of course, that the word was spoken with the vowel [ɛ] rather than [ə] in the final syllable, but this is most unlikely even in formal speech. If the student grasps this point, he will soon be able to recognize in the speech around him innumerable instances where [ə] is used instead of the definite vowel suggested by the spelling. One difference between formal pronunciations listed by the average dictionary and the way words are heard in everyday speech grows out of the frequency with which the definite vowels marked in the dictionary are replaced by [ə].

When the student begins to study his own speech and lacks the assurance which comes with a trained ear, he is likely to have the impulse to shun the indefinite vowel in favor of some more definite vowel resonance—again, the sound suggested by spelling or listed by the dictionary as "correct." But it can be shown that it is not at all unusual to obscure more than one-third of the syllables in conversational pronunciation. In one 94-syllable passage from Mark Twain the authors counted 35 syllables which could have been correctly pronounced [ə].

To give an accented, definite pronunciation to vowels in most unaccented syllables in English is to distort the over-all rhythm of the spoken language and to produce a pedantic and unnatural-sounding articulation. This is particularly true in English speech, because of the marked tendency toward alternation of stressed and unstressed syllables that is so typical of its rhythm pattern. Thus, the pronunciation of two definite vowels in words such as "again," "correct," "science," and "given" is certain to result in an unnatural or even an unintelligible pronunciation, particularly if there is any effort to pronounce the word as it is spelled.

The phenomenon of alternation of stress and the replacement of some definite vowel with [ə] is particularly noteworthy in connected speech, as compared with the pronunciation of words in isolation. *Sense stress*, or the emphasis of certain words as a way of making meaning clear, tends to knock out the accentuation of the relatively unimportant "helping" words. For instance, in context words such as "a," "an," "the," "but," "of," and "at" are almost always [ə], [ən], [ðə], [bət], [əv], and [ət]. Any effort to use the appropriate definite vowel which these words would have if they were stressed is quite artificial, unless, of course, the sense of the sentence requires that these words be emphasized. Note how sense stress would change the pronunciation of "should" in the natural expression of the sentence "You should always emphasize the word *should*" [ju ʃəd əlwɪz ɛmfəsaɪz ðə wɝd ʃud].

A somewhat minor, but sometimes substandard, usage grows out of the process known as *restressing*. Here a syllable which has been obscured from a definite (and historically older) vowel pronunciation is restressed and given an [ʌ] pronunciation instead of the resonance from which [ə] developed through unstressing. The central-vowel characteristics of the indefinite vowel are retained. The sentence "I said *a* boy, not *the* boy" would, for purposes of making sense, lead to restressing of the two words "a" and "the." If the speaker restressed a central vowel, he would say [ʌ] for "a" and [ʌ] for "the," but in most cases it would be better to restore the original vowels, [e] and [i]. In a similar way "ascending" is usually pronounced [əsɛndɪŋ], but if the sense of the sentence made it natural to emphasize the initial sound of the word, as in "*a*scending, not *de*scending," it might be pronounced [esɛndɪŋ] rather than [ʌsɛndɪŋ], cultivated usage being the deciding factor, of course.

The examples just given are drawn from changes that take place in connected speech, but in a number of words the process of restressing has been a historical trend. Such pronunciations as [bɪkʌz] for "because" and [hwʌt] for "what" are also examples of restressing. These usages are sometimes regarded as substandard, or at least marginal, and the careful speaker would perhaps do better to select [ə], or a nearby sound in the *a* group, for the first word ([bɪkəz]) and an [ɑ] for the second ([hwɑt]).

In certain words, and when the speech is relatively formal or careful, the sound used in unstressed or relatively unstressed syllables may hover between [ə] and [ɪ] or [ʊ]. For example, "remark" is commonly either [rəmɑrk] or [rɪmɑrk], and "demand" may be either [dəmænd] or [dɪmænd]. In such words either pronunciation is quite acceptable.

As the speech grows more formal, the tendency is naturally to come closer to a full restoration of the vowel quality, and it is difficult to define the point where this tendency should be checked if overprecise and pedantic speech is to be avoided. If the sentence "Just the same, he should go" is spoken as [dʒʌst ðə sem, he ʃud go] instead of [dʒəst ðə sem, hi ʃəd go], the speaker certainly has not been guilty of overpronunciation. On the other hand, the sentence "As he remarked today, the reason is good enough" would probably sound somewhat stilted if restressing led to [æz hi rimɑrkt tude, ði rizən ɪz gud inʌf]. Despite the fact that good speakers quite naturally exhibit the tendency to unstress vowels to [ə] in unstressed syllables, one must remain aware of the fact that the person who yields too readily to this trend may end up with careless and underpronounced speech. Attentive listening will provide many examples of this fault in the speech of the man on the street, so that one illustration will suffice: [sə fjə gənə ənsɪst, əl hæf tə]. ("So if you're going to insist, I'll have to.")

Unstressing has so far reduced the historically older definite vowel in some syllables that the vowel has disappeared altogether, to be replaced by the appropriate semivowel. Thus in a word like "candle" or "button" or in a phrase like "help them" the unstressed syllables may be [l̩], [n̩], and [m̩], respectively. Such pronunciations may be perfectly appropriate in many words, even in the most formal speech, but in other, similar words they may not be sanctioned by general usage and would be judged substandard by careful speakers.

Exercises.

1. Practice pronouncing the following paragraph, first in an informal conversational manner, then in a more formal style without, however, making it seem stilted or unnatural. In which words is the vowel changed to a definite vowel in the more formal reading? In which must it not be changed to a definite vowel? Turn to phonetic transcription at the end of these exercises for the pronunciation of one of the authors.

The principles and facts concerning speech sound production which we learn in a study of phonetics are a great deal more than mere mental exercises. They will be found to be very useful notions, capable of helping us to be better speakers in a more practical way. For example, the seemingly obscure observation that the vowel in an unstressed syllable tends to become indefinite in quality, short in duration, and low in pitch, even in highly cultivated speech, may help us to avoid a number of errors in pronunciation. It may prevent our speech from becoming conspicuous and overpronounced as we work for more precise and acceptable articulation. Finally, if we are foreigners, it may help us to obtain a rhythm pattern more typical of American speech, with its heavy and marked alternation of stressed and unstressed syllables.

2. Use the following lists of [ə] words for practice and for reference. Note that for many of them, [ə] is not the only acceptable pronunciation.

a. Words with [ə] in the initial position:

another	again	allowed	apply	upon
about	ago	among	around	occur
above	against	amount	attempt	occasion
accomplish	ahead	another	attention	enough
across	alone	appear	away	essential
advance	along			

b. Words with [ə] in the initial syllable:

believe	control	compose	today	prepare
before	complete	combine (v.)	together	provide
between	committee	community	produce (v.)	protect
consider	concern	machine	present (v.)	receive
continue	commercial	supply	project (v.)	reserve
correct	consumer	suppose		

c. Words with [ə] in a middle syllable:

activity	difficult	educate	primarily
benefit	illustrate	immediately	policy
company	economics	industry	probably

d. Words with [ə] in the final syllable:

audience	foreign	insurance	movement	purpose
balance	German	interest	Mrs.	reason
basis	government	interpret	nation	science
cases	given	instant	natural	second
children	graduate (n.)	isn't	normal	seven
common	greatest	judges	often	several
dishes	happen	April	open	system
different	human	material	opera	taken
environment	hundred	mention	parents	thousand
even	husband	million	period	Washington
experience	idea	minutes	problem	woman
expression	individual	moment	profit	hundred

e. Words with [ə] in more than one syllable:

ability	condition	evidently	national	possibility
accident	department	essential	occasion	president
amendment	develop	examination	official	principle
American	education	experiment	opposite	protection
beautiful	efficient	instrument	philosophy	production
commercial	element	intelligent	political	requirements
composition	especially	generation	population	

f. Words using [ɚ] in GA and [ə] in EA:
See list a under the sound [ɚ].

g. Words whose weak form uses the vowel [ə] (or drops the vowel entirely):

a	can	is	on	them
am	could	it	shall	to
an	from	its	than	us
and	had	just	that	was
as	has	must	the	what
at	have	my	then	you
but	in	of		

3. Although the same kinds of minimal pairs cannot be listed for the [ə] that were listed for the definite vowels, the pairs given below do indicate the very important and practical kind of distinction which the

[ə] represents. Practice these pairs, noting specifically the part played by stress.

[ə]—[ʌ]

lettuce [lɛtəs]	let us [lɛt ʌs]
mention [mɛnʃən]	men shun [mɛn ʃʌn]
instance [ɪnstənts]	in stunts [ɪn stʌnts]
Washington [waʃɪŋtən]	washing ton [waʃɪŋ tʌn]

[ə]—[ɛ]

greatest [gretəst]	gray test [gre tɛst]
hundred [hʌndrəd]	hun dread [hʌn drɛd]
material [mətɪriəl]	materiel [mətɪriɛl]
shortest [ʃɔrtəst]	shore test [ʃɔr tɛst]

[ə]—[ɚ]

panda [pændə]	pander [pændɚ]
manna [mænə]	manner [mænɚ]
"Hi ya" [haɪə]	higher [haɪɚ]
seven [sɛvən]	Severn [sɛvɚn]

[ə]—[ɪ]

foreign [fɔrən]	four in [fɔr ɪn]
given [gɪvən]	give in [gɪv ɪn]
judges [dʒʌdʒəz]	judge is [dʒʌdʒ ɪz]
license [laɪsəns]	lie since [laɪ sɪns]

[ə]—[ɑ]

produce (v.) [prədjus]	produce (n.) [prɑdjus]
project (v.) [prədʒɛkt]	project (n.) [prɑdʒɛkt]
German [dʒɜ˞mən]	germ on [dʒɜ˞m ɑn]
often [ɔfən]	off on [ɔf ɑn]

[ə]—[æ]

human [hjumən]	hue man [hju mæn]
insurance [ɪnʃurənts]	insure ants [ɪnʃur ænts]
normal [nɔrməl]	Norm, Al [nɔrm æl]
parents [pɛrənts]	pair ants [pɛr ænts]

Phonetic Transcription. Compare the following informal colloquial GA pronunciation of the paragraph from Exercise 1 with your own pronunciation. Try to account for any differences on the basis of the discussion of the sound [ə].

[ðə prɪnsəpḷz ən fækts ˌkən'sɜ˞nɪŋ spitʃ saund prə'dʌkʃən hwɪtʃ wi lɜ˞n ɪn ə stʌdɪ əv fə'nɛtɪks ɑr ə gret dil mɔr ðən mɪr mɛntəl 'ɛksɚsaɪzəz. ðe wɪl bi faund tə bi vɛrɪ jusfəl noʃənz, 'kepəbḷ əv 'hɛlpɪŋ əs tə bi bɛtɚ spikɚz ɪn ə mɔr 'præktəkḷ we. fɚ ɛg'zæmpḷ, ðə 'simɪŋlɪ əb'skjur ˌabzɚ'veʃən ðət ðə vaʊl ɪn ən 'ʌnstrest sɪləbl̩ tendz tə bɪkʌm ɪn'defənət ɪn 'kwɑlətɪ, ʃɔrt ɪn dʊ'reʃən, ən lo ɪn pɪtʃ, ivən ɪn haɪlɪ 'kʌltəvetəd spitʃ, me help əs tu əvɔɪd ə 'nʌmbɚ əv erɚz ɪn prənʌnsɪ'eʃən. ɪt me prə'vent aʊr spitʃ frəm bɪkʌmɪŋ kən'spɪkjuəs ən ˌovɚprə'naʊnst æz wi wɝk fɚ mɔr prɪ'saɪs ən æk'septəbl̩ ɑrtɪkjə'leʃən. 'faɪnəlɪ, ɪf wi ɑr 'fɔrənɚz ɪt me help əs tu əb'ten ə rɪðəm pætɚn mɔr 'tɪpɪkl̩ əv ə'merəkən spitʃ wɪð ɪts hevɪ ən mɑrkt ɔltɚ'neʃən əv strest ən 'ʌnstrest 'sɪləblz̩.]

[ʌ] as in unless, under, come

Common Spellings: *u* as in cup, stuff

o as in some, above

ou as in couple, young

Also spelled *oe*, as in does; *oo*, as in flood.

Production. In the production of [ʌ] in the General American dialect the tongue is typically in the lax, lower mid-central position. The lips are open and unrounded. If sounds can be said to require varying degrees of effortful movement, it is likely that the [ʌ] requires the least of all the definite vowels. It is a short vowel, not only in name but in actual duration, and is relatively simple, or undiphthongized. The precise tongue position for this vowel, however, varies somewhat among dialect regions of English, with the tongue being carried somewhat farther back in certain British dialects and in Eastern American.

Pronunciation. Although the American speaker seldom has difficulty with this sound, the fact that it has few counterparts in other languages leads to frequent mispronunciations by those whose native tongue is not American. For example, one of the characteristics of a British dialect often is a slight [ɑ] coloring to this sound. Among speakers of other languages [u], [ɔ], or [ɑ], or even [o] or [ʊ], may be substituted, because of inadequate auditory discrimination or as a result of spelling-pronunciation mistakes. Many foreigners, for example, appear to say [bɑt], [lɔv], or [dʊn] for [bʌt], [lʌv], or [dʌn]. All such substitutions are, of course, dialectal.

Occasionally [ɛ] or [ɪ] is heard in a dialect pronunciation of words like "such," "just," and "judge." Indeed, the pronunciation of the word "just" as [dʒɪst] or [dʒɛst] is heard so frequently that it almost has the sanction of universal usage. It has not, however, reached the point of schoolbook acceptability, and such usages should probably be avoided. Actually, there is a vowel quality which lies about midway between [ʌ] and [ɪ] and which is frequently heard where we seem to hear the vowel [ɪ]. The phonemic status of this midway vowel is somewhat in doubt among phoneticians, and the question is a rather complex one which need not concern us here.

Acceptable variations in pronunciation may occur in some American dialects in words such as "hurry," "worry," and "surrey," where either [hʌrɪ] or [hɝɪ] is appropriate, depending upon the dialect spoken. In general [hʌrɪ] would be spoken by a person who habitually says [fɑrəst] instead of [fɔrəst] for the word "forest." These pronunciations are encountered in Eastern dialect.

The sound [ʌ] is not to be confused in phonetic transcription with the neutral vowel [ə], whose resonance it resembles very closely. In some ways the [ʌ] is roughly equivalent to a stressed [ə], but a study of the function of [ə] reveals clearly that it is much more than an unstressed [ʌ]. There are, of course, instances where the border line between a definite [ʌ] and an indefinite [ə] is extremely vague, but in most cases the distinction is clear. Because the [ə] sounds so much like a weak [ʌ], words like "because" and "of" may be mispronounced through *restressing*. This problem has been discussed in the section on the [ə].

Exercises

1. In the following paragraph one of the authors counted 28 [ʌ] sounds in his own pronunciation. Make a phonetic transcription of the passage and count the occurrences of [ʌ] in your own speech. Note particularly your pronunciation of the words "some," "somewhat," "us," and "from." Check your pronunciation with the transcription of the author's speech at the end of these exercises.

One exercise the serious student might someday undertake is the study of why it is that some dialects have greater social status than do others. He might try to understand, for example, why the American is more tolerant of Standard British (sometimes with a kind of grudging admiration) than is our English cousin of the American dialects. In a number of words (perhaps hundreds) where no good phonetic reason can be found to favor the pronunciation of one country over another the educated Britisher will have something of a feeling that the American word, no matter how carefully articulated by us, is somehow substandard or undesirable. On the other hand, the equally well educated American will often show a kind of unconscious snobbishness in reverse in his willingness to accept as superior, or just as good, the different British pronunciation. However, the reasons for the muddle are likely to be normal historic-linguistic-phonetic ones. None is likely to stem from any innate perversity, snobbishness, or linguistic superiority for either tongue.

2. Use the following list of [ʌ] words for reference and practice:

a. Words using [ʌ] in stressed syllables:

above	cup	husband	once	such
among	cut	income	other	sudden
another	done	judge	production	suffer
blood	double	lover	public	sun
brother	dull	Monday	result	Sunday
club	enough	money	run	thus
color	front	month	rush	trouble
come	fund	mother	something	trust
coming	government	much	son	uncle
company	gum	none	stuck	under
country	gun	nothing	study	wonderful
cover	hundred	number	subject	young

b. Words in which the [ʌ] syllable is commonly unstressed to a [ə] or some other pronunciation:

anyone	does	must	some	up
but	from	one	unless	us
difficult	just	product		

3. Practice and expand the following lists of minimal pairs. (See also [u] and [ɝ].)

[ʌ]—[ɑ]		[ʌ]—[ʊ]	
color [kʌlɚ]	collar [kɑlɚ]	bucking [bʌkɪŋ]	booking [bʊkɪŋ]
done [dʌn]	Don [dɑn]	crux [krʌks]	crooks [krʊks]
dull [dʌl]	doll [dɑl]	huck [hʌk]	hook [hʊk]
gun [gʌn]	gone [gɑn]	huff [hʌf]	hoof [hʊf]
none [nʌn]	non- [nɑn]	lucky [lʌkɪ]	"looky" [lʊkɪ]
puck [pʌk]	pock [pɑk]	lux [lʌks]	looks [lʊks]
pup [pʌp]	pop [pɑp]	putt [pʌt]	put [pʊt]
sup [sʌp]	sop [sɑp]	rough [rʌf]	roof [rʊf]
stuck [stʌk]	stock [stɑk]	ruck [rʌk]	rook [rʊk]
un- [ʌn]	on [ɑn]	shuck [ʃʌk]	shook [ʃʊk]

[ʌ]—[ɔ]	
but [bʌt]	bought [bɔt]
cussed [kʌst]	cost [kɔst]
cut [kʌt]	caught [kɔt]
done [dʌn]	dawn [dɔn]
fun [fʌn]	fawn [fɔn]
lung [lʌŋ]	long [lɔŋ]
ruckus [rʌkəs]	raucous [rɔkəs]
rung [rʌŋ]	wrong [rɔŋ]
stuck [stʌk]	stalk [stɔk]
sung [sʌŋ]	song [sɔŋ]

Phonetic Transcription. The following is a phonetic transcription of the paragraph in Exercise 1 as it might be spoken in GA. Compare this transcription with your own and comment on the differences.

[wʌn 'ɛksəˌsaɪz ðə 'sɪrɪəs 'stjudn̩t maɪt 'sʌmde ˌʌndəˈtek ɪz ðə stʌdɪ əv hwaɪ ət ɪz ðət sʌm 'daɪələkts hæv gretə 'soʃəl stetəs ðən du ʌðəz. hi maɪt traɪ tu ʌndəstænd, fər ɛgˈzæmpl̩, hwaɪ ðɪ ə'merəkən ɪz mɔr 'tɑlərənt əv 'stændəd 'brɪtɪʃ ('sʌmˌtaɪmz wɪð ə kaɪnd əv 'grʌdʒɪŋ ˌædmə'reʃən) ðən ɪz aʊr 'ɪŋglɪʃ kʌzən əv ðɪ ə'merəkən 'daɪələkts. ɪn ə 'nʌmbə əv wɜ˞dz (pə'hæps 'hʌndrədz) hwɛr no gʊd fə'nɛtɪk rizən kən bi faʊnd tə 'fevə ðə prənʌnsɪ'eʃən əv wʌn kʌntrɪ ovə ə'nʌðə ðɪ 'ɛdʒuketəd 'brɪtɪʃə wɪl hæv 'sʌmθɪŋ əv ə filɪŋ ðət ðɪ ə'merəkən wɜ˞d, no mætə haʊ 'kerfəlɪ ˌɑr'tɪkjuletəd baɪ ʌs, ɪz 'sʌmˌhaʊ 'sʌbstændəd ɔr ˌʌndɪ'zaɪrəbl̩. ɔn ðɪ ʌðə hænd ðɪ 'ikwəlɪ wɛl ɛdʒuketəd ə'merəkən wɪl ɔfn̩ ʃo ə kaɪnd əv ʌnkanʃəs 'snɑbɪʃnəs ɪn rɪ'vɜ˞s ɪn hɪz 'wɪlɪŋnəs tu æk'sɛpt əz sə'pɪrɪə, ɔr dʒʌst əz gʊd, ðə dɪfrənt 'brɪtɪʃ prənʌnsɪ'eʃən. haʊɛvə, ðə rizənz fɔr ðə mʌdl̩ ɑr laɪklɪ tə bi nɔrməl hɪs'tɔrɪk lɪŋ'gwɪstɪk fə'nɛtɪk wʌnz. nʌn ɪz laɪklɪ tə stɛm frəm ɛnɪ ɪnet ˌpə'vɜ˞sətɪ, 'snɑbɪʃnəs, ɔr ˌlɪn'gwɪstɪk səpɪrɪ'ɔrətɪ fər 'iðə tʌŋ.]

Foreign and Nonphonemic Variants. Many varieties of centralized vowels in addition to those covered in this chapter have been distinguished by phoneticians, but it is difficult, if not impossible, to describe them to a native American speaker. Two symbols appearing on the standard vowel charts of the IPA are the high-central vowels [i] and [ʉ], which represent Russian and Swedish sounds. These are located between [i] and [u] at the top of the vowel diagram. The student may also find use for the symbol [ɨ] to represent the dull [ɪ], a sound midway between [ɪ] and [ʌ], often heard in American pronunciations of the word "just."

8

THE DIPHTHONGS

[aɪ], [aʊ], [ɔɪ], [ju], AND THE NONDISTINCTIVE DIPHTHONGS

As a preface to the description of the common diphthongs of American speech, certain general facts about this class of sounds should be reviewed. A diphthong was defined earlier as a syllabic in which *two* vowel resonances can be identified, with a *change* of resonance as an essential attribute of this kind of speech sound.

A diphthong is said to be *distinctive* if it is phonemic in the sense that meaning would be changed if another sound were substituted. Phoneticians do not agree completely, however, on which English diphthongs are distinctive, nor do they concur in their choice of symbols. All symbol systems have their inadequacies, but we have chosen that of the International Phonetic Alphabet as used in the *Pronouncing Dictionary of American English*[17] as best for our purposes. In this scheme the distinctive diphthongs are [aɪ] as in "high," [aʊ] as in "how," [ɔɪ] as in "boy," and [ju] as in "few."

One cannot get an accurate idea of English pronunciation, however, if he supposes that there are only four diphthongs. In the first place, nearly all the vowels are diphthongized to some extent, and these resonance changes are necessary for accurate pronunciation. Second, there are numerous differences within each of the so-called distinctive diphthongs—differences that can be recorded by variations in the choice of symbols. If a highly detailed analysis were to be made, a really large number of diphthongs could be listed. Not all, however, would be *distinctive*.

Before going any further, the dynamics of diphthongization should be explained. These are centered around the change of resonance and involve a *glide*, which brings them, in this respect, very close to the *glide consonants*. The change of resonance within the syllable may be in the nature of an *on-glide* or an *off-glide*. An *on-glide* is one in which the

121

relatively more stable, stressed, or prominent resonance *follows* the movement or shift. Thus the diphthong [ju] as in "use" is made as an on-glide because there is a shift from the relatively unstressed [j] resonance to the more strongly stressed [u]. The reverse is true of an *off-glide;* this is a syllabic in which the major resonance comes *before* the shift. The diphthong [ɔɪ] is made as an off-glide because the principal stress is on [ɔ]. With the exception of [ju] all the syllabics customarily classed as diphthongs are characterized by off-glide changes in resonance.

The on-glides in English are usually classified, not as diphthongs, but as *glide consonants.* These include (1) [j], where the movement is begun from a high-front-vowel position resembling that for [i] or [ɪ], as in "you" [ju]; (2) [w], where the movement is begun from a high-back-vowel position resembling that for [u] or [ʊ], as in "we" [wi]; and (3) [r], which is begun from a central-vowel position resembling that for [ɝ] or [ɚ], as in "row" [ro]. No further explanation of the glide consonants is needed at this point, but they will be treated fully in Chapter 11.

Like the on-glides, the off-glides in English fall into three types: syllable resonance can glide off to the quality of (1) a high-front vowel such as [i] or [ɪ], (2) a high-back vowel such as [u] or [ʊ], or (3) a central vowel such as [ʌ], [ɝ], [ɚ], or [ə]. The resonance quality to which the shift is made in each case is the one ascribed to that sound in the chapters on the vowels. Theoretically, any vowel resonance could be combined with any one of the three off-glide qualities and thus produce a complex syllabic which could be classified as either a diphthong or as a vowel–glide consonant combination.

With this information as a background, some of the diphthongal characteristics of English speech should be easier to understand. Vowels are rarely "pure"; more often there is a perceptible shift of resonance. The [e] and [o] are excellent examples. On [e] there typically is a gliding off toward [i] or [ɪ] (or even [j], which has approximately the same articulation position as these vowels). One way to hear this phenomenon is to compare a word like "debris" [de'bri], where in this pronunciation [e] is present but not stressed, with "lay" ['le] where the actual pronunciation, because of stress, is usually [leɪ]. Stressed and unstressed [o] sounds follow the same pattern, with the shift moving toward [ʊ] in most cases. A detailed pronunciation analysis of such a word as "team" might yield [tim], [tijm], [tɪjm], or conceivably some other pattern. How far one goes in trying to record such details depends upon his purpose.

Variations in transcription practices were mentioned earlier. In the convention adopted for this text the on-glides are generally indicated by the appropriate consonant symbol—[j], [w], or [r]—and the off-glides by a vowel symbol—[ɪ], [ʊ], or [ɚ] or [ə]. Thus the general rule would be "on-glide, consonant symbol; off-glide, vowel symbol." There is one important exception, which follows for the most part the convention adopted by Kenyon and Knott.[17] Unless there is a special reason to do otherwise, the symbol for the glide consonant [r] is used in recording the central off-glide pronunciations of speakers in the *r*-pronouncing dialects. Examples of the *r* diphthongs are "beard" and "board," which we would ordinarily transcribe as [bɪrd] and [bɔrd] rather than [bɪɚd] and [bɔɚd].

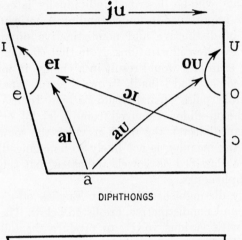

DIPHTHONGS

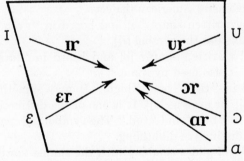

CENTERING DIPHTHONGS

Fig. 7. Articulation movements for the diphthongs.

In addition to these common conventions in transcribing are the necessary variations that must be introduced when one undertakes to record fine details of pronunciation. For instance, possible variations of [aɪ] might be [ai], [ɑi], and even [aj] or [ɑj]. It takes a very sophisticated listener to catch these distinctions, to be sure, but it can be done. Some authors go into this kind of detail, and a few prefer one of our variant forms as the principal marking. To give other examples, [o] might be [oʊ], [ou], or [ow]; and [ɔɪ] might be [ɔi].

All this detail has been introduced in the hope that it will help the student to hear and become familiar with the diphthongal characteristics which are so typical of the syllabics of English speech. Only [aɪ], [aʊ], [ɔɪ], and [ju] are *distinctive*, in keeping with the earlier definition. A good case might be made for including the central or *centering* diphthongs as distinctive phonemes, but we shall not do so for reasons which seem too complicated to outline here. Nevertheless, [ɪr], [ɛr], [ɑr], [ɔr], and [ʊr] and their variants will be described individually later in the chapter because of their importance in understanding American pronunciation.

The concept of distinctive and nondistinctive diphthongs may be clarified further by a few illustrations. Note that elimination of the glide in the following examples would result in a change in meaning: "hide" [haɪd] would become "hod" [had], "gown" [gaʊn] would approximate "gone" [gan], and "poise" [pɔɪz] would become "pause" [pɔz]. On the other hand, if the off-glide is removed from [ɪ], [e], [o], or [ʊ] (as it sometimes is in foreign dialects), the word in which the sound appears may sound odd, but the meaning is not likely to be changed. The fact that these sounds are classified as vowels indicates that they are regularly nondistinctive diphthongs.

The commonly distinguished American English off-glide diphthongs, both distinctive and nondistinctive, are listed below. The high-front off-glide combines with various vowels to produce the following complex syllables in the General American dialect:

[ii], commonly written simply [i] and heard in "even" and "team." Some phoneticians use the symbol [ɪj].

[eɪ], commonly written simply [e] and heard in "fate" and "day." The symbol [ɛj] is also used by some.

[aɪ], as heard in "tight" and "high." It may sometimes be written [ɑɪ], as [ɑi] or [ai], or even as [aj]. It is one of the distinctive diphthongs.

[ɔɪ], as heard in "boy" and "toil." The symbol [ɔj] may also be used. This is another distinctive diphthong.

The high-back off-glides combine with the simple vowels to make the following complex syllabics:

[ʊu], commonly written simple [u] and heard in "boot" and "too." The symbol [ʊw] may also be encountered.

[oʊ], commonly written simply [o] and heard in "tone" and "go." Some phoneticians prefer the symbol [ow].

[aʊ], as heard in "house" and "town." A variant usage is [aw]. An [ɑ] may also be employed as the first element of this distinctive diphthong.

[ɪu], for which a more common pronunciation is [ju]. This is an exception to the *off*-glide principle. This distinctive diphthong may be heard in "music" and "view."

The central off-glides, either *r*-colored or non-*r*-colored, combine with simple vowels to give the following:

[ɪr] or [ɪə], as heard in "fear" and "steer." A variation of this sound sometimes, but not always, heard as distinct from [ɪr] is [ir]. The symbol [ɪɚ] may also be used.

[ɛr] or [ɛə], as heard in "wear" and "air." Variations of this sound which may or may not be distinctive are [er] and [ær]. The symbol [ɛɚ] may also be used.

[ɑr] or [ɑə], as heard in "car" and "dark." May also be written [ɑɚ].

[ɔr] or [ɔə], as heard in "horse" and "core." The sound [or] is a diphthong which may or may not be distinctive, depending upon the dialect spoken. May also be written [ɔɚ].

[ur] or [uə], as heard in "your" and "poor." It may also be written [uɚ]. The sound [ur] may be heard but is rare.

We turn now to a detailed consideration of each of the distinctive and central diphthongs.

[aɪ] as in hide, ice, my

Common Spellings: *i* as in find, I
  ie as in pie, cried
  y as in by, fly
  igh as in high, light
  Also spelled *ai*, as in aisle; *aye*, as in *aye*; *eye*, as in eye; *uy*, as in buy; *ye*, as in lye; *ui*, as in guide; *ei*, as in height; *is*, as in island.

Production. The diphthongal movement of [aɪ] proceeds from a position near that for the [ɑ] to a position near [ɪ] or [i]. In the usual General American production of the sound the tongue may be somewhat farther forward than for the vowel [ɑ] of "hot." This has influenced the choice of symbol, so that [a] is probably more commonly used to represent the initial resonance, as it is in this text, than the [ɑɪ], which is occasionally seen. In gliding toward the high-front position, the tongue probably never reaches a point quite as high as it does for [i]. Beyond mention of this fact, however, no exact statement can be made about the final resonance of this off-glide. It is variable, although it is always in the direction of [i]. The symbol [ɪ] has been chosen as the best representation of this resonance.

In the production of the [aɪ], the gliding toward [ɪ] is rapid and smooth, occurring in the space of a single syllable. The first element of the diphthong is given more prominence, with the energy diminishing as the resonance proceeds to the [ɪ]. The essential inseparable nature of this glide-plus-vowel combination can be demonstrated by trying to sustain the sound as a sung tone. When this is attempted it will become apparent that in order to produce [aɪ] rather than some other distinctively different sound ([a] or [ɪ]) a resonance *change* must occur.

Pronunciation. In the pronunciation of [aɪ], like that of most diphthongs, the direction and rate of movement are much more stable properties of the phoneme than are the precise locations of the terminating and initiating resonances. The exact quality of the first element of this sound is variable. Although [a] is generally considered the best approximation of the initiating resonance, the [ɑɪ] is a common and perfectly acceptable variant in some areas, perhaps more often in the South. Another version, also frequently heard in the South, may be represented by the symbol [a:], where the [:] indicates increased length. Thus, in this pronunciation a drawn-out, or "drawled," vowel replaces the diphthong. A Southern pronunciation of "nice smile" might be transcribed [na:s sma:l]. This usage would be considered dialectal in most places. Still other dialectal pronunciations may be encountered for this diphthong, including versions tending toward the quality of [ɔɪ], [ʌɪ], or [eɪ].

When words with [aɪ] receive a minimum amount of stress, the diphthong may be replaced by the neutral vowel [ə]. This often occurs, for example, in the pronunciation of "I" or "I'm." In rapid colloquial speech "I don't know what I'm going to do" might be heard [ə dont no hwʌt əm goɪŋ tə du]. This is not necessarily substandard. On the other hand, an overprecise pronunciation of [aɪ] may result in a two-syllable sound. In this case [taɪm] would become [ta·im]. This would, of course, be considered substandard.

Exercises

1. In reading the paragraph below, the author used the [aɪ] sound 37 times. Identify and transcribe the words in which these sounds appear. Then turn to the phonetic transcription to see what differences you find.

After we had climbed about a mile in the rising sunshine of that bright July day, we turned to look at the sky line as it lay far away over our right shoulders. As far as the eye could see, the horizon was afire with the glow of the morning. We stood there, our eyes glued to the sight, while we rested, tired and quite out of breath. Finally our guide surprised us by inviting us to untie our lines and to lay our packs on the white snow. I have since decided, in the light of later events, that he decided at that time to take the entire party over the ice field and to fight on to the summit before we realized that danger as well as beauty was in the climb; and that we would try it right after this last respite.

2. Use the following list of [aɪ] words for reference and practice:

a. Words in which [aɪ] appears in the initial or medial position:

arrive	fight	iron	outside	surprise
behind	finally	island	price	time
beside	find	kind	provide	tried
bright	fine	knight	primarily	tire
child	fire	life	require	type
combine	five	light	ride	while
crime	Friday	like	realize	white
decide	guide	line	right	wife
design	high	live	rise	wide
define	higher	might	side	wild
desire	height	mile	sight	united
describe	ice	mind	sign	wind (v.)
divide	idea	mine	size	wise
drive	idle	nice	smile	write
entire	I'll	night	society	variety
environment	I've	mite	specialize	

b. Words in which [aɪ] appears in the final position:

buy	die	I	my	tie
by	eye	July	imply	try
cry	fly	lie	sky	why

3. Practice making the discriminations indicated for the following pairs of words:

[aɪ]—[ɔɪ]

buy [baɪ]	boy [bɔɪ]
fire [faɪr]	foyer [fɔɪr]
fried [fraɪd]	Freud [frɔɪd]
imply [ɪmplaɪ]	employ [ɪmplɔɪ]
ire [aɪr]	oyer [ɔɪr]
rye [raɪ]	Roy [rɔɪ]
sigh [saɪ]	soy [sɔɪ]
tie [taɪ]	toy [tɔɪ]
tile [taɪl]	toil [tɔɪl]
try [traɪ]	Troy [trɔɪ]

[aɪ]—[ɑ]

fire [faɪr]	far [fɑr]
guide [gaɪd]	God [gɑd]
high [haɪ]	hah [hɑ]
light [laɪt]	lot [lɑt]
like [laɪk]	lock [lɑk]
mile [maɪl]	moll [mɑl]
night [naɪt]	not [nɑt]
ride [raɪd]	rod [rɑd]
side [saɪd]	sod [sɑd]
time [taɪm]	Tom [tɑm]

[aɪ]—[e]

fight [faɪt]	fate [fet]
high [haɪ]	hay [he]
ice [aɪs]	ace [es]
I'll [aɪl]	ale [el]
light [laɪt]	late [let]
like [laɪk]	lake [lek]

mine [maɪn]   mane [men]
ride [raɪd]   raid [red]
time [taɪm]   tame [tem]
wise [waɪz]   ways [wez]

Phonetic Transcription. Count the [aɪ] diphthongs in the following transcription of the paragraph in Exercise 1; then read the passage aloud and note the variations that may occur within the phoneme.

[æftɚ wi həd klaɪmd ə'baʊt ə maɪl ɪn ðə 'raɪzɪŋ 'sʌn‚ʃaɪn əv ðæt braɪt dʒulaɪ de, wi tɝnd tə lʊk ət ðə 'skaɪ‚laɪn æz ɪt le fɑr əwe ovɚ aʊr raɪt 'ʃoldɚz. əz fɑr əz ði aɪ kəd si, ðə hə'raɪzən wəz ə'faɪr wɪð:ə glo əv ðə 'mɔrnɪŋ. wi stʊd ðer, aʊr aɪz glud tə ðə saɪt, hwaɪl wi restəd, taɪrd ən kwaɪt aʊt əv brɛθ. 'faɪnlɪ aʊr gaɪd sɚ'praɪzd əs baɪ ɪn'vaɪtɪŋ ʌs tu ʌntaɪ aʊr laɪnz æn tə le aʊr pæks ɔn ðə hwaɪt sno. aɪ həv sɪns dɪ'saɪdəd, ɪn ðə laɪt əv 'letɚ ɪvents, ðət hi dɪ'saɪdəd ət ðæt taɪm tə tek ði ɛn'taɪr pɑrtɪ ovɚ ði aɪs fild æn tə faɪt ɔn tə ðə sʌmət bɪ'fɔr wi 'riəlaɪzd ðət dendʒɚ əz wel əz bjutɪ wəz ɪn ðə klaɪm; ænd ðət wi wʊd traɪ ɪt raɪt æftɚ ðɪs læst 'respət.]

[ɔɪ] as in oyster, join, boy

Common Spellings: *oy* as in toy, enjoy
                       oi as in oil, coin
                       Also spelled *eu*, as in Freud.

Production. The change which produces the diphthong [ɔɪ] is from a low-back vowel [ɔ] to a high-front vowel near [i] or [ɪ]. Since the extent of the off-glide in [ɔɪ] is perhaps greater than for any other diphthong, the second half of this sound is somewhat more prominent than the corresponding resonance in other diphthongs; hence the [ɔɪ] rather easily breaks into two separate vowels. Thus, there seems to be less difference between [ɔɪ] and [ɔ·ɪ] than between, for example, [aʊ] and [a·ʊ]. Nevertheless, the sound is ordinarily classified and pronounced as an off-glide diphthong.

Pronunciation. In native American speech there do not appear to be many difficulties with this sound. The pronunciation may vary normally somewhat toward the [oɪ] or [oi], but unless the variation is marked, this is not necessarily substandard. In some dialects, [aɪ] may be substituted for [ɔɪ] in such words as "hoist" and "boil," so that they are pronounced [haɪst] and [baɪl]. These usages are historically logical but are usually considered substandard or old-fashioned today.

In some subregional dialects in New York the substitution [ɝɪ] may be heard. This fact, together with the use of [ɝɪ] for [ɝ] in these areas, makes for confusion between [ɝ] and [ɔɪ] and leads to the impression that [ɔɪ] has been substituted for [ɝ] and vice versa. "He heard the pot boil" may sound like [hi hɔɪd ðə pɑt bɝl], although this is not, as was noted, an exact representation of the pronunciation usually given in the so-called "Brooklynese." Such substitutions are considered substandard by most speakers. The diphthong [ɔɪ] is notable for having a highly consistent spelling.

Exercises

1. Practice reading the following [ɔɪ] paragraph. There are about 15 [ɔɪ] words in the General American pronunciation. The author's transcription follows these exercises.

Although it is true that voice quality may vary within widely acceptable limits without annoyance, most people would join me in expressing a dislike for the quality known as nasality, at least in its more unalloyed forms. Why it is that by choice most of us avoid the voice with strong nasal resonance is not clear. The fact which should be pointed out, however, is that we do. The employment of excessive nasality has often spoiled what would otherwise be an enjoyable and effective speech quality. The correction of the annoying quality involves the avoidance of certain faults of palate movement and the direction of the tone through the mouth instead of the nose. To coin a phrase, we might enjoin the speaker to use his head and not to get nosey.

2. The following list of [ɔɪ] words is for reference and practice:

annoy	coin	join	pointing	spoil
alloy	convoy	joy	poison	toil
boy	destroy	noise	Roy	toy
boil	employ	oil	soil	voice
choice	enjoy	point	soy	void

3. Practice the following sound discriminations:

[ɔɪ]—[aɪ]		[ɔɪ]—[ɝ]	
voice [vɔɪs]	vice [vaɪs]	boy [bɔɪ]	burr [bɝ]
boil [bɔɪl]	bile [baɪl]	Boyd [bɔɪd]	bird [bɝd]
coin [kɔɪn]	kine [kaɪn]	avoid [əvɔɪd]	averred [əvɝd]
foil [fɔɪl]	file [faɪl]	coy [kɔɪ]	cur [kɝ]
loin [lɔɪn]	line [laɪn]	foil [fɔɪl]	furl [fɝl]
point [pɔɪnt]	pint [paɪnt]	foist [fɔɪst]	first [fɝst]
poi [pɔɪ]	pie [paɪ]	hoist [hɔɪst]	Hurst [hɝst]
Lloyd [lɔɪd]	lied [laɪd]	noil [nɔɪl]	knurl [nɝl]
lawyer [lɔɪɚ]	liar [laɪɚ]	poi [pɔɪ]	purr [pɝ]
oil [ɔɪl]	isle [aɪl]	voiced [vɔɪst]	versed [vɝst]

[ɔɪ]— [ɔ]

boil [bɔɪl]	ball [bɔl]
coil [kɔɪl]	call [kɔl]
joy [dʒɔɪ]	jaw [dʒɔ]
oil [ɔɪl]	awl [ɔl]
poi [pɔɪ]	paw [pɔ]
noise [nɔɪz]	gnaws [nɔz]
Roy [rɔɪ]	raw [rɔ]
soy [sɔɪ]	saw [sɔ]
toil [tɔɪl]	tall [tɔl]
loin [lɔɪn]	lawn [lɔn]

Phonetic Transcription. The following is a phonetic transcription of the paragraph in Exercise 1:

[ɔlðo ɪt ɪz tru ðət vɔɪs 'kwɑlətɪ me vɛrɪ wɪðɪn 'waɪdlɪ æk'sɛptəbl̩ lɪməts wɪðaut ə'nɔɪəns, most pipl̩ wʊd dʒɔɪn mi ɪn ɛks'prɛsɪŋ ə 'dɪs,laɪk fɔr ðə 'kwɑlətɪ non æz ne'zælətɪ, ət lɪst ɪn ɪts mɔr ˌʌn'əlɔɪd fɔrmz. hwaɪ ɪt ɪz ðət baɪ tʃɔɪs most əv əs ə'vɔɪd ðə vɔɪs wɪθ strɔŋ nezəl 'rɛzənəns ɪz nɑt klɪr. ðə fækt hwɪtʃ ʃʊd bi pɔɪntəd aut, hauɛvɚ, ɪz ðət wi du. ðɪ ɛm'plɔɪmənt əv ɛk'sɛsɪv ne'zælətɪ həz ɔfən spɔɪld hwʌt wʊd 'ʌðɚˌwaɪz bi ən ɛn'dʒɔɪəbl̩ ænd ɪ'fɛktɪv spitʃ 'kwɑlətɪ. ðə kə'rɛkʃən əv ðɪ ə'nɔɪɪŋ 'kwɑlətɪ ɪn'vɑlvz ðɪ ə'vɔɪdəns əv sɝtn̩ fɔlts əv 'pælət muvmənt ænd ðə də'rɛkʃən əv ðə ton θru ðə mauθ ɪnstɛd əv ðə noz. tə kɔɪn ə frez, wi maɪt ɛn'dʒɔɪn ðə spikɚ tə juz hɪz hɛd ənd nɑt tə gɛt nozɪ.]

[aʊ] **as in out, brown, cow**

Common Spellings: *ow* as in how, owl
ou as in loud, ouch
Also spelled *au*, as in kraut; *ough*, as in bough; *hou*, as in hour.

Production. The [aʊ] is an off-glide diphthong which proceeds from the relatively more stable resonance of the [a] or [ɑ] and glides off toward the vowel quality of [ʊ], though perhaps not always reaching that point. The amount of resonance change is often very small, perhaps less than occurs in any other distinctive diphthong discussed in this chapter.

Pronunciation. The precise quality represented by the first element of the digraph [aʊ] may vary considerably from one English dialect region to another. Probably the most frequent pronunciation in the General American dialect is [a]—a vowel quality between the [ɑ] and [æ]. In many regions the more retracted vowel quality of the [ɑ] in "father" is frequently heard and, unless exaggerated, is not considered unusual or substandard.

In addition to [aʊ] and [ɑʊ], both of which are widely accepted, the pronunciation [æʊ] may be heard in parts of the East and South, but this usage has less general acceptance and is usually considered substandard by speakers of General American. In parts of the East and Canada several other variations are heard for this diphthong in some contexts. The most frequent is [ɛʊ], although [ʌʊ], and even [oʊ] and [ʊʊ], may be substituted in some localities and contexts.

In American speech there seems to be a distinct tendency to neglect the second element of this diphthong, so that words like "house" and "cloud" come to sound like [hɑs] and [klɑd]. Although it is normal for this diphthong to have a weaker glide than the [aɪ], [ɔɪ], or [ju], for example, such a tendency may often reach the point of being substandard.

Exercises

1. Practice the following paragraph, with particular attention to the pronunciation of words containing the [aʊ]. Try to avoid both an overtense [æʊ] and an underdiphthongized [ɑ]. The author's transcription follows these exercises.

It is possible to analyze vowel production much more exhaustively than we have found it desirable to do in this text. Some authors list more than forty sounds of the vowel category, without counting those listed as semivowels or diphthongs. We may, of course, break down vowel quality however we wish, the only real limitation being the usefulness of the breakdown. Now it goes without saying that the student should be aware of many degrees of difference among vowels. There are thousands, almost countless, distinctions which could be made. But it is doubtful whether any very powerful arguments can be found for applying phonetic labels to all of these unless some specific interest calls for such labeling. The important thing for the student of speech is that he have as good a grounding as possible in the functionally important differences among sounds in his language and an understanding of how those sounds vary and influence one another.

2. Use the following list of [aʊ] words for reference and practice:

about	count	how	outer	sound
account	doubt	however	output	south
allowed	down	mount	outside	thou
amount	found	mountain	pound	thousand
around	flower	mouth	power	throughout
brown	ground	now	round	town
crowd	hour	our	shout	without
cloud	house	out		

3. Practice pronouncing and discriminating among the following pairs of words:

[aʊ]—[ɑ]		[aʊ]—[ɔ]	
cloud [klaʊd]	clod [klɑd]	brown [braʊn]	brawn [brɔn]
doubt [daʊt]	dot [dɑt]	cloud [klaʊd]	clawed [klɔd]
down [daʊn]	don [dɑn]	down [daʊn]	dawn [dɔn]
hour [aʊr]	are [ɑr]	found [faʊnd]	fawned [fɔnd]
how [haʊ]	hah [hɑ]	howl [haʊl]	haul [hɔl]
lout [laʊt]	lot [lɑt]	now [naʊ]	gnaw [nɔ]
our [aʊr]	are [ɑr]	out [aʊt]	ought [ɔt]
outer [aʊtɚ]	otter [ɑtɚ]	town [taʊn]	tawn [tɔn]
pound [paʊnd]	pond [pɑnd]	louse [laʊs]	loss [lɔs]
shout [ʃaʊt]	shot [ʃɑt]	owl [aʊl]	awl [ɔl]

[aʊ]—[o]	
about [əbaʊt]	a boat [əbot]
couch [kaʊtʃ]	coach [kotʃ]
crowd [kraʊd]	crowed [krod]
ground [graʊnd]	groaned [grond]
how [haʊ]	hoe [ho]
now [naʊ]	know [no]
shout [ʃaʊt]	shoat [ʃot]
thou [ðaʊ]	though [ðo]
town [taʊn]	tone [ton]
noun [naʊn]	known [non]

Phonetic Transcription. The following transcription represents the pronunciation of one of the authors as he read the paragraph in Exercise 1:

[ɪt ɪz 'pasəbl̩ tu 'ænəlaɪz vaʊl prə'dʌkʃən mʌtʃ mɔr ɛg'zɔstɪvlɪ ðen wi həv faʊnd ɪt dɪ'zaɪrəbl̩ tə du ɪn ðɪs tɛkst. sʌm əθɚz lɪst mɔr ðen 'fɔrtɪ saʊndz əv ðə vaʊl 'kætəgɔrɪ wɪðaʊt 'kaʊntɪŋ ðoz lɪstəd æz 'semaɪ, vaʊlz ɔr 'dɪfθɔŋz. wi me, əv kɔrs, brek daʊn vaʊl 'kwɑlətɪ haʊevɚ wi wɪʃ, ðɪ onlɪ rɪl lɪmə'teʃən bɪŋ ðə 'jusfəlnəs əv ðə 'brek,daʊn. naʊ ɪt goz wɪðaʊt seɪŋ ðət ðə studənt ʃʊd bi əwer əv menɪ dɪ'griz əv 'dɪfrəns əmʌŋ vaʊlz. ðer ɑr 'θaʊzəndz, ɔlmost 'kaʊntləs, dɪ'stɪŋkʃənz hwɪtʃ kʊd bi med. bʌt ɪt ɪz 'daʊtfəl hweðɚ ɛnɪ verɪ paʊrfəl 'ɑrgju,mənts kən bi faʊnd fɔr ə'plaɪɪŋ fo'netɪk 'lebəlz tu ɔl əv ðiz ənles sʌm spə'sɪfɪk 'ɪntərəst kɔlz fɔr sʌtʃ 'lebəlɪŋ. ðɪ ɪm'pɔrtənt θɪŋ fɔr ðə studənt əv spitʃ ɪz ðət hi hæv æz gʊd ə 'graʊndɪŋ əz 'pasəbl̩ ɪn ðə 'fʌŋkʃənəlɪ ɪm'pɔrtənt 'dɪfrənsəz əmʌŋ saʊndz ɪn hɪz 'læŋgwɪdʒ ænd ən ʌndɚ'stændɪŋ əv haʊ ðoz saʊndz verɪ ænd 'ɪnfluəns wʌn ənʌðɚ.]

[ju] as in united, cute, view

Common Spellings: u as in mule, unit
   ew as in few, hew

ue as in cue, hue
you as in you, youth
iew as in view, review
Also spelled *eu*, as in feud; *eau*, as in beauty;
yu, as in yule; *yew*, as in yew; *ieu*, as in adieu;
ugh, as in Hugh; *eue*, as in queue.

Production. The [ju] is the only distinctive diphthong which may be produced with an *on-glide* rather than an off-glide change of resonance. For this reason we often call [ju] a *rising*, as distinguished from a *diminishing*, diphthong. The syllabic energy rises rapidly to a more stable resonance in this diphthong. In [aɪ], [ɔɪ], and [aʊ], on the other hand, the energy falls off *from* a more stable resonance. Although the starting point for this glide is approximately the tongue position of the [i] or [ɪ], the consonant symbol [j] is used to draw attention to the on-glide function of the initial resonance. Phonetically the glide performs the same function it does with many consonant-vowel combinations, like "yet" [jɛt] and "yawn" [jɔn]. It might make good sense, in fact, to treat [ju] as merely a syllable or "compound" sound rather than as a diphthong, but we have preferred the conventional usage.

A common variant of this diphthong within and at the end of words can be transcribed [ɪu], as in "ridicule" [rɪdəkɪul] or "askew" [əskɪu]. This symbol indicates a pronunciation in which the first sound has relatively more stress or prominence than it does in the [ju]. Such a diphthong is diminishing, but not usually to the degree that characterizes other diphthongs. The tongue position for the [u] of this diphthong is often influenced in such a way that the vowel is farther forward than the [u] of such a word as "fool." The vowel quality of the [u] probably lies somewhere midway between the typical [i] and [u] of stressed syllables. This distinction can be made in phonetic transcription, if necessary, with the symbol [ʉ].

Pronunciation. For the most part, the [ju] sound heard in American speech is that of the rising diphthong.

The off-glide variety symbolized by [ɪu] is, however, neither infrequent nor, in most cases, substandard. This pronunciation may be heard in words such as "museum" [mɪuzɪəm] (or [mɪuziəm]) and "confuse" [kənfɪuz]. It is interesting to note that [ɪu] is probably the historically older pronunciation, which later developed into the [ju] and [ɪu] varieties (Ref. 31, pp. 210–218).

The question arises as to the use of [u] versus [ju] in some words like "news" and "tune." Where the diphthong in question follows a lingua-alveolar or linguadental, usage varies. In Southern British and Eastern American, [njuz] and [tjun] would be heard most often. In General American the practice is less uniform; although [njuz] and [tjun] are very common, so also are [nuz] and [tun], which must be regarded as perfectly acceptable, provided that the vowel is not lowered excessively to [ʊ]. The [u] pronunciation, in fact, is probably growing more widespread.

In positions of less than maximum stress the [ju] may frequently weaken to [jʊ] or even [jə]. This may not be objectionable in some cases. For example, "immunize" may be heard correctly as [ɪmjunaɪz], [ɪmjʊnaɪz], or [ɪmjənaɪz]. In other cases, however, such a substitution could be substandard. For example, [kəntɪnjə] and [mɛnjə] for "continue" and "menu" would be close to the border line of acceptability.

Exercises

1. Read the following paragraphs aloud, taking careful note of words using the diphthongs [ju], [jʊ], and [jə]. For which are alternative pronunciations acceptable? Turn to the phonetic transcription of this passage for the pronunciation of one of the authors.

It is interesting to speculate on what will happen to the dialects of the United States in the future. Will there continue to be the same kinds of change we have seen in the past? Will the new patterns used by the youth of today prevail to become the accepted standards utilized by adults and taught in your schools tomorrow? If we could review the future dialects from some fourth-dimensional vantage point, would we view the new as more or less beautiful than the old? Will speech become more or less efficient from the viewpoint of communication? We can't say, but as sure as we are human beings our speech will continue to change in the future. It will continue to improve so long as those who use it are not more interested in speech for its own sake than as a tool to be used toward the end of more useful and effective social cooperation.

2. Use the following list of [ju] words for reference and practice:

a. amuse	cute	mule	used	usually
beautiful	few	music	uses	utilize
beauty	fuse	musical	union	value
community	future	refuse	unit	view
continue	huge	review	united	you
cube	human	use	university	youth

b. For words pronounced with [u] by some speakers, [ju] by others, see list *b* under sound [u].

3. Practice the following sound discriminations:

[ju]—[u]

Butte [bjut]   boot [but]

beauty [bjutɪ]   booty [butɪ]

cute [kjut]	coot [kut]
feud [fjud]	food [fud]
fuel [fjul]	fool [ful]
muse [mjuz]	moos [muz]
mute [mjut]	moot [mut]
use [juz]	ooze [uz]
Hugh [hju]	who [hu]
hews [hjuz]	whose [huz]

Phonetic Transcription. The following phonetic transcription of the paragraph in Exercise 1 represents the pronunciation of one of the authors:

[ɪt ɪz 'ɪntərestɪŋ tə 'spɛkjələt ɔn hwʌt wɪl hæpən tu ðə 'daɪəlɛkts əv ðə ju'naɪtəd stets ɪn ðə 'fjutʃɚ. wɪl ðɛr kən'tɪnju tə bi ðə sem kaɪndz əv tʃendʒ əz wi həv sin ɪn ðə pæst? wɪl ðə nu 'pætənz juzd baɪ ðə juθ əv tə'de prə'vel tə bɪkʌm ðɪ æk'septəd 'stændɚdz 'jutə,laɪzd baɪ ə'dʌlts ənd tɔt ɪn jɔr skulz tə'maro? ɪf wi kʊd rɪ'vju ðə 'fjutʃɚ 'daɪəlɛkts frəm sʌm 'fɔrθ dɪ'menʃənəl 'væntɪdʒ pɔɪnt, wʊd wi vju ðə nu æz 'mɔr ɔr 'lɛs 'bjutəfəl ðæn ðɪ old? wɪl spɪtʃ bɪkʌm 'mɔr ɔr 'lɛs ɪ'fɪʃənt frəm ðə 'vjupɔɪnt əv kəmjunə'keʃən? wi kænt se, bət əz ʃur əz wi ɑr hjumən biɪŋz aʊr spɪtʃ wɪl kən'tɪnju tə tʃendʒ ɪn ðə 'fjutʃɚ. ɪt wɪl kən'tɪnju tu ɪm'pruv so lɔŋ æz ðoz hu juz ɪt ɑr nɑt mɔr 'ɪntərestəd ɪn spɪtʃ fɔr ɪts on sek ðæn æz ə tul tə bi juzd tɔrd ðɪ ɛnd əv mɔr 'jusfəl ənd ɪ'fɛktɪv 'soʃəl koɑpə'reʃən.]

[ɪr] (or [ɪɚ]) and [ɪə] as in steer, hear, here

Common Spellings: *ear* as in dear, hear
                ere as in we're, here
                er as in material, period
                Also spelled *eir*, as in weir; *eer*, as in queer; *ier*, as in pier; *ir* as in spirit.

Production. This diphthong combines an off-glide with a relatively stable vowel near [ɪ]. The off-glide may be toward the resonance of [ɚ] or, in some Eastern and Southern dialects, toward the resonance of [ə]. The accepted phonetic symbol for the former is [ɪr] or [ɪɚ]. In the latter case the accepted symbol is [ɪə].

Pronunciation. There is some variation in the resonance of the stable portion of this diphthong. Ordinarily the tongue glides from the lower high-front position, but the rare pronunciation of [ir] may be heard, and this difference may constitute a significant change in some regions. If one distinguishes in pronunciation between "we're" and "weir," without making a two-syllable word of "we're," he may have both [ir] and [ɪr] diphthongs in his phonetic vocabulary. This is not likely, however. In any event, the differences are not very important for the average native speaker.

Whether one says [ɪr] or [ɪə] is generally determined by his dialect region. If the *r*-colored vowels are used habitually, the pronunciation is likely to be [ɪr]. If not, [ɪə] is a more natural choice. Either is "correct," of course, so long as it is consistent with the rest of the speaker's dialect pattern.

With the [ɪr] or [ɪə], as well as with the other central diphthongs, the pronunciation may be slightly different when the sound is followed by a vowel rather than by a consonant. When [ɪr] is followed by a consonant (as in "beard" [bɪrd]), there is little question that the sound should be classified as a diphthong, which may be transcribed equally well as [ɪr] or [ɪɚ]. When [ɪr] is followed by a vowel, however (as in "leering" [lɪrɪŋ]), there is a strong tendency for the off-glide to become an on-glide for the next syllable, so that it can best be classified as a consonant. Thus [lɪ·rɪŋ] may be a somewhat more appropriate phonetic transcription than [lɪɚɪŋ]. For the most part, of course, this is a hairsplitting argument. The glide separates two syllables, with an off-glide from one and an on-glide to the other. In the *r*-less dialects [ɪə] changes to [ɪr] when followed by a vowel. To give an example of this, the Easterner who normally says [hɪə] for "hear" will nevertheless say [hɪrɪŋ] for "hearing." For further information on this point turn to Chapter 11.

Exercises

1. Identify the [ɪr] (or [ɪə]) sounds in the paragraph below. In an *r*-pronouncing dialect there should be about nine [ɪr]'s. In an *r*-less dialect there may be a distribution of both [ɪə] and [ɪr] sounds. See how many you can identify before you turn to the word lists and the phonetic transcription.

The job of classifying speech sounds appears to be nearly impossible unless we clearly specify the type of speech to be analyzed, the audience for whom we're writing, and the purpose of the classification. If we are to steer clear of serious errors here, we must realize that none of these factors is irrelevant.

2. Use the following list of [ɪr] words for reference and practice:

a. Words with [ɪr] in a final position or followed by a consonant:

appears	dear	here	nearly
beard	fear	mere	steer
beer	gear	merely	year
cheer	hear	near	we're
clear			

b. Words with [ɪr] followed by a vowel:

appearing	material	period	spirit
fearing	miracle	serious	steering

3. Practice making the discriminations indicated for the following pairs of words:

[ɪr]—[er]   [ɪr]—[ɪ]

[ɪə]—[ɛə]   [ɪə]—[ɪ]

cheer [tʒɪr]   chair [tʃer]   beard [bɪrd]   bid [bɪd]

dear [dɪr]   dare [der]   leered [lɪrd]   lid [lɪd]

fear [fɪr]   fair [fer]   reared [rɪrd]   rid [rɪd]

here [hɪr]   hair [her]   seared [sɪrd]   Sid [sɪd]

steer [stɪr]   stair [ster]   tears [tɪrz]   'tis [tɪz]

Phonetic Transcription. The following is a phonetic transcription of the author's pronunciation of the paragraph in Exercise 1. The alternative transcriptions shown in parentheses are possibilities for a hypothetical Eastern dialect. These have been given only for [ɪr] diphthongs.

[ðə dʒɑb əv 'klæsəfaɪɪŋ spitʃ saundz ə'pɪrz (ə'pɪəz) tə bi' nɪrlɪ ('nɪəlɪ) ɪm'pɑsəbl ənlɛs wi 'klɪrlɪ ('klɪəlɪ) 'spɛsə,faɪ ðə taɪp əv spitʃ tə bi 'ænəlaɪzd, ðɪ 'ədiəns fər (fɔə) hum wɪr (wɪə) 'raɪtɪŋ, ænd ðə 'pɝ·pəs əv ðə klæsəfə'- keʃən. ɪf wi ɑr tə stɪr (stɪə) klɪr (klɪə) əv 'sɪriəs 'ɛrərz hɪr (hɪə), wi məst 'rɪəlaɪz ðət nʌn əv ðiz 'fæktɝz ɪz ɪ'rɛləvənt.]

[ɛr] (or [ɛɚ]) and [ɛə] as in pair, wear, there

Common Spellings: *er* as in very, heron

err as in merry, berry

ar as in character, canary

arr as in carry, marry

are as in care, spare

air as in chair, pair

Also spelled *eir*, as in their.

Production. The sounds of this class are centering diphthongs, where the glide moves from a relatively stable resonance near [ɛ] or [æ] toward a central-vowel position resembling [ɝ] for those who pronounce *r* and toward [ə] for those who do not pronounce *r*. Diphthongs starting with an [æ] rather than an [ɛ] resonance are not considered separately, for in General American speech there are few words, if any, whose meaning would be affected by such a difference. In actual speech one may hear a whole range of slightly different resonances from [ɛ] to [æ] for the start of these diphthongs, but there is no practical reason for listing them.

Pronunciation. The distinctions among these diphthongs are so fine and the usage so varied that it seems impossible to formulate any rule about when each is (or should be) used. The usual practice in General American is to employ [ɛr] or its approximate equivalent, regardless of spelling. In other dialects, perhaps most commonly in Eastern American, a distinction may be made between *e* and *a* words—although not necessarily with any consistency. Where this practice is followed, one may hear such distinctions as [vɛrɪ]–[værɪ] for "*very*"–"*vary*," [kɛrɪ]–[kærɪ] for "*Kerry*"–"*carry*," and [mɛrɪ]–[mærɪ] for "*merry*"–"*marry*." Since any attempted generalization is subject to many exceptions, the student may as well plan to establish his own practice after due observation. It is not likely that he will fall into substandard usages, since the distinctions among these diphthongs are slight and unobtrusive.

Another infrequent variation from [ɛr] is the use of [er]. For instance, the phrase "they are" when contracted to "they're" becomes [ðer]. Not many Americans make such a distinction. Pronunciations such as [wer] for "*wear*" and [ker] for "*care*" are dialectal, but not necessarily objectionable. In words like "they're" the [er] diphthong tends to break down into two syllables, becoming [ðe ɝ].

Exercises

1. In the following paragraph the author uses only the [ɛr] pronunciation for both the *er* and the *ar* words of the type mentioned in the preceding section. There are about 12 of them. Compare your pronunciation with the phonetic transcription following these exercises.

It may interest you to discover whether or not all of these *ar* and *er* words in the following nonsense sentence share the same pronunciation in your vocabulary: "One very merry Christmas evening Mary narrowly escaped being married to a fair-haired boy named Jerry, a librarian who had come there from Gary."

2. The following [ɛr] or [ær] words are for reference and for practice:

air	dare	narrow	share	vary
care	fair	necessary	stare	wear
carry	hair	pair	spare	where
character	marry	prepare	square	very
bare	merry	primarily	their	wear
chair	Mary	scarcely	there	where

—and other words with stressed *-ery* or *-ary* syllables.

3. Distinguish among the following pairs of words:

[ɛr]—[ɝ]

carry [kɛrɪ]   curry [kɝɪ]

air [ɛr]   err [ɝ]

fair [fɛr]	fir [fɜ˞]
pair [pɛr]	purr [pɜ˞]
bare [bɛr]	burr [bɜ˞]
merry [mɛrɪ]	Murray [mɜ˞ɪ]
spare [spɛr]	spur [spɜ˞]
stare [stɛr]	stir [stɜ˞]
wear [wɛr]	were [wɜ˞]

Phonetic Transcription. The following is a phonetic transcription of the paragraph in Exercise 1. The pronunciation recorded represents a Western dialect. Compare this pronunciation with your own.

[ɪt ˌme 'ɪntərest ju tə dɪs'kʌvɚ 'hwɛðɚ ˌɔr ˌnɑt ˌɔl əv ðiz 'eˌɑr ən 'iˌɑr ˌwɜ˞dz ɪn ðə 'fɑloɪŋ 'nanˌsɛns 'sɛntəns ʃɛr ðə sem prəˌnʌnsɪ'eʃən ɪn jɔr vo'kæbjulɛrɪ: 'wʌn 'vɛrɪ 'mɛrɪ 'krɪsməs 'ivnɪŋ 'mɛrɪ 'nɛrolɪ əs'kept ˌbiɪŋ 'mɛrɪd tʊ ə 'fɛr 'hɛrd ˌbɔɪ nemd 'dʒɛrɪ ə ˌlaɪ'brɛriən hu həd ˌkʌm ˌðɛr frəm 'gɛrɪ.]

[ɑr] (or [ɑɚ]) and [ɑə] as in car, start, army

Common Spellings: *ar* as in art, star

Also spelled *ear*, as in heart; *er*, as in sergeant; *uar*, as in guard; *or*, as in some pronunciations of forest.

Production. The [ɑr] diphthong features an off-glide from the relatively stable low-back [ɑ] to the central-vowel position for [ɜ˞] or [ɜ]. Among those who do not pronounce their *r*'s the glide is either toward [ə] or virtually absent. In the latter case the *monophthong* [ɑ] is increased in length and would be distinguished from the [ɑ] of "father" in this way. The symbol for this long monophthong is [ɑ:].

Pronunciation. The historical development of the [ɑr] pronunciation has led to some interesting dialect differences and spelling inconsistencies. A detailed discussion of these points would, however, be beyond the scope of this book, although the student might enjoy reading more about these and other historical changes in the works of Kenyon,[16] Krapp,[18] Bloomfield,[4] Sweet,[30,31] and others. Attention is drawn to the British pronunciations of "clerk" and "derby" as [klɑrk] and [dɑrbɪ] and to the dialect pronunciations of a few words like "certain" and "learning" as [sɑrtn̩] and [lɑrnən]. Such pronunciations as these are substandard or dialectal in General American speech.

Occasionally substitutions of [ɔr] for [ɑr] are found among native speakers and may be substandard. Some variation within the range [a]–[ɑ]–[ɔ]–[o] is, of course, to be expected. For example, one hears either [hɔrs] or [hɑrs] for "horse." Occasionally, however, a speaker may take undue liberties with the latitude allowed him and be guilty of such breaches as [hɑrs] for "horse," [fɔrmɚ] for "farmer," and [dɔrk] for "dark."

Among Eastern and Southern speakers a common variant of [ɑr] is a prolonged [ɑ], transcribed [ɑ:], as in "car" [kɑ:] and "bar" [bɑ:]. In these dialects "pot" [pɑt] and "part" [pɑ:t] are distinguished largely by the lengthening of the vowel in the latter word. This is definitely a dialectal characteristic, but is not considered substandard. The diphthong [ɑə] instead of [ɑr] is, of course, regularly heard among EA and SA speakers, since they may not pronounce r.

There are some interesting variations in pronunciation between [ɑ] and [ɔ] in what are sometimes called the *for* words. Examples of words which might contain either sound are "forest," "forehead," and "foreign." Either pronunciation must be considered acceptable, with [ɔr] tending to predominate in General American. (You will recall the same variation between the vowels [ɑ] and [ɔ] in words such as "cot.") In the words listed in part *b* of Exercise 2, usage seems to be quite equally divided between [ɑr] and [ɔr] pronunciations.

Exercises

1. In the following paragraph there may be as many as 10 examples of [ɑr] or as few as 7, depending upon the dialect spoken and upon the stress of certain monosyllables. Count the number of [ɑr] sounds in your pronunciation of this passage before you check the phonetic transcription.

It is never very hard to start an argument about pronunciation. It is far more difficult to win. Take a word like "forest" for example. Part of the population may insist on rhyming the first syllable with "far," while others will insist on rhyming it with "four." Both groups are partly right and partly wrong. They are right in their pronunciations but wrong in their insistence.

2. Use the following list of [ɑr] words for reference and practice:

a. Words nearly always pronounced with [ɑr] rather than [ɔr]:

army	bargain	farther	hard	start
are	card	farm	large	star
artist	article	farmer	heart	market
bar	dark	guard	part	department
bark	far			

b. Words which may be pronounced with [ɑr] or [ɔr]:

forehead	foreign	forest	moral	tomorrow
sorrow	borrow	warrant	Warren	torrid

3. Distinguish among the following pairs of words:

[ɑr]—[ɑ]		[ɑr]—[ɔr]	
card [kɑrd]	cod [kɑd]	lard [lɑrd]	lord [lɔrd]
lark [lɑrk]	lock [lɑk]	card [kɑrd]	cord [kɔrd]
shark [ʃɑrk]	shock [ʃɑk]	far [fɑr]	four [fɔr]
far [fɑr]	fah [fɑ]	part [pɑrt]	port [pɔrt]
part [pɑrt]	pot [pɑt]	star [stɑr]	store [stɔr]
farther [fɑrðɚ]	father [fɑðɚ]	bar [bɑr]	bore [bɔr]
dark [dɑrk]	dock [dɑk]	mar [mɑr]	more [mɔr]

Phonetic Transcription. The following is a phonetic transcription of the paragraph in Exercise 1. It is in the General American dialect of one of the authors. What changes would be made in the [ɑr] sounds in Eastern or Southern dialect?

[ɪt ɪz 'nevɚ ˌverɪ 'hɑrd tə 'stɑrt ən 'ɑrgjəmənt əˌbaʊt prəˌnʌnsi'eʃən. ɪt ɪz 'fɑr ˌmɔr 'dɪfəkəlt tə 'wɪn. ˌtek ə ˌwɝd ˌlaɪk 'fɔrəst fɔr ɪg'zæmpl̩. 'pɑrt əv ðə ˌpapjə'leʃən me ɪn'sɪst ən ˌraɪmɪŋ ðə ˌfɝst 'sɪləbl̩ wɪð 'fɑr, hwaɪl 'ʌðɚz wɪl ɪn'sɪst ən ˌraɪmɪŋ ət wɪð 'fɔr. 'boθ ˌgrups ɑr 'pɑrtlɪ 'raɪt ən 'pɑrtlɪ 'rɔŋ. ˌðe ɑr 'raɪt ɪn ðɛr prəˌnʌnsi'eʃənz bət 'rɔŋ ɪn ˌðɛr ɪn'sɪstəns.]

[ɔr] (or [ɔɚ]) and [ɔə] as in horse, order, more

Common Spellings: or as in form, short
   our as in course, court
   ar as in warm, ward
   oar as in hoarse, oar
   Also spelled eor, as in George.

Production. In this diphthong the gliding is from the more stable resonance of a back vowel near [ɔ] or [o] toward the position of the central vowel [ɚ] or [ə].

Pronunciation. It is a very real question whether the [or] and [ɔr] should be considered distinctive diphthongs or simply important variations of a single phoneme. Here [or] and [ɔr] are treated as variations of a single sound, since this seems the best way to describe the usage of most speakers of General American. For a significant number of people, however, the difference between [ɔr] and [or] does serve to differentiate some words. Common examples are such pairs of words as "mourning" and "morning," "hoarse" and "horse," "oar" and "or." Those distinguishing between these pairs must use both sets of symbols. Those who do not differentiate these pairs will find that one symbol will suffice for phonetic transcriptions of their own speech. The serious student will, of course, wish to develop a sensitivity to the distinction between such usages as [hɔrs] and [hors].

The substitution of the sound [ɑr] for [ɔr] or [or] is often encountered. In most words this pronunciation becomes somewhat conspicuous and would be considered substandard in the General American dialect region. This would hold particularly for those words where the [ɔr]–[ɑr] distinction is important to the meaning. Thus "born in a barn" should not sound like [bɑrn ɪn ə bɑrn] or [bɑrn ɪn ə bɔrn]. The picture is somewhat complicated by that group of words in which usage varies *normally* between [ɑr] and [ɔr], as in the pronunciation of "foreign," "forest," and other words in which the diphthong [ɔr] or [ɑr] is followed directly by an unstressed vowel.

In Eastern and Southern speech, of course, the [oə] and [ɔə] replace the [ɔr] and [or]. In some Southern dialects a long monophthongal [o:] is used in place of the diphthong. The phrase "board up the door," for example, might be heard [bo:d ʌp ðə do:]. This usage is distinctly substandard.

Exercises

1. In reading the following paragraph, the author used the diphthong [ɔr] 18 times. However, in one word either [ɔr] or [ɚ] would be acceptable; in at least six words either [or] or [ɔr] would be acceptable; and in at least three words either [ɔr] or [ɑr] could be used. Compare your pronunciations with those of the author, as indicated by the phonetic transcription following these exercises.

In the morning we boarded the foreign ship from the wharf at the foot of Fourth Street. Going forward toward what we supposed was our cabin, I was thrown into a mortal panic to discover that my passport and tickets were not in the portfolio or the pocket where I was certain I had placed them before the quarrel with Horace. After a few moments of mental torture, and a show of concern I would normally abhor, I was fortunate to find the missing documents.

2. The following [ɔr] and [or] words are for reference and practice:

a. Words ordinarily pronounced only with [ɔr] in most dialects:

born	form	lord	order	sort
cord	forward	morning	ordinary	storm
corner	George	normal	organized	warm
course	horse	north	perform	war
for	important	or	short	

b. Words for which both [or] and [ɔr] pronunciations are acceptable (according to Kenyon and Knott[17]):

before	court	forty	port	tore
board	force	fourth	sport	torn
chorus	ford	hoarse	store	toward
course	forth	more	story	

c. Words for which either [ɔr] or [ɑr] may be acceptable (according to Kenyon and Knott):

borrow	foreign	quarrel	torrid	Warren
forehead	Horace	tomorrow	sorrow	
forest	moral	torrent	warrent	

d. Words for which either [ɔr] or [ɚ] may be correct, depending upon stress:

for   nor   or

3. Distinguish among the following sets of minimal pairs:

[ɔr]—[o]

board [bɔrd]	bowed [bod]
court [kɔrt]	coat [kot]
more [mɔr]	mow [mo]
store [stɔr]	stow [sto]
toward [tɔrd]	toad [tod]

[ɔr]—[ɔ]

board [bɔrd]	bawd [bɔd]
court [kɔrt]	caught [kɔt]
lord [lɔrd]	laud [lɔd]
more [mɔr]	maw [mɔ]
tore [tɔr]	taw [tɔ]

[ɔr]—[ɑr]

tore [tɔr]	tar [tɑr]
core [kɔr]	car [kɑr]
board [bɔrd]	bard [bɑrd]
pour [pɔr]	par [pɑr]
shored [ʃɔrd]	shard [ʃɑrd]

Phonetic Transcription. The following is a phonetic transcription of the paragraph in Exercise 1. The words "boarded," "Fourth," "toward," "passport," "portfolio," and "before" could also be pronounced with [or]. The use of [ɑr] would be equally acceptable for the words "foreign," "Horace," and "quarrel." The word "or" could be pronounced with [ɚ]:

[ɪn ðə ˈmɔrnɪŋ wi ˈbɔrdəd ðə ˈfɔrən ˈʃɪp frəm ðə ˌwɔrf ət ðə ˌfut ə ˈfɔrθ ˌstrit. ˌgoɪŋ ˌfɔrwɚd ˌtɔrd hwʌt wi səˈpozd wəz aur ˈkæbən, aɪ wəz ˌðrɔn ɪntu ə ˈmɔrtəl ˈpænɪk tu dɪsˈkʌvɚ ðət ma ɪˈpæsˌpɔrt æn ˈtɪkəts wɚ ˈnɑt ɪn ðə pɔrtˈfolio ɔr ðə ˈpɑkət hwɛr aɪ wəz ˈsɚtən aɪ həd ˌplest ðəm bɪˈfɔr ðə ˈkwɔrəl wɪθ ˈhɔrəs. ˌæftɚ ə ˌfju ˈmomənts əv ˈmɛntəl ˈtɔrtʃɚ, ænd ə ˌʃo əv kənˈsɚn aɪ wud ˈnɔrməlɪ əbˈhɔr, aɪ wəz ˈfɔrtʃənət tə ˌfaɪnd ðə ˌmɪsɪŋ ˈdɑkjəmənts.]

[ur] (or [uɚ]) and [uə] as in poor, your, tour

Common Spellings: *our* as in you're, tour
                       oor as poor, moor
                       ure as in sure, cure

Production. The more stable portion of this diphthong is usually produced as a lower high-back vowel near [u], although it may vary in some pronunciations toward the [u] or the [o] position. As in the other central diphthongs, the off-glide is toward the [ɝ] or [ə], depending upon the dialect spoken.

Pronunciation. Although [ur] may occasionally be substituted for [ʊr], as in [pur] for "poor," this pronunciation is common only in some subregional dialects. When this usage does occur, the tendency is for the diphthong to break down into two syllables so that [ur] becomes [u·ɚ]. A more frequent variation in the pronunciation of [ʊr] involves a lowering of the tongue to the point where the pronunciation becomes [or], or perhaps even [ɔr], so that "poor" [pʊr] becomes more like "pour" [pɔr]. Such a distortion would generally be considered substandard in General American, although in some regional dialects and in some words it is common. Only careful listening and a sensitive ear will guide you.

One rather prominent characteristic of some Southern speech is the substitution of [oə] for the Northern [ʊr] or [ʊə]. For example, in the sentence "He sure was a poor man," we may hear [hi ʃoə wʌz ə poə mæn]. Although this is dialectal, it may not be noticeable in some regions. The substitution of a long monophthong [o:] may also be heard in the South, as in [hi ʃo: wʌz po:]. This is considered substandard in almost any case.

In a few words [ɚ] or [ɝ] may be substituted for [ʊr], as in [ʃɝ] instead of [ʃʊr] for "sure." With the possible exception of [jɚ] for "your," which is acceptable where the word is not stressed, this usage is not sanctioned in cultivated speech. Pronunciations such as [ʃɝ] and [kjɝ] for "sure" and "cure" are best avoided.

Exercises

1. Identify the [ʊr] sounds in the following paragraph and practice their pronunciation. In reading this passage, one of the authors used the sound 10 times. His pronunciation is shown in the transcription following these exercises.

One sure way to do poorly in phonetic transcription is to write furiously without listening carefully. During the period when your mastery of the symbols is so limited that you do not feel secure, permit nothing to lure your attention from the sounds the speaker makes. It is a curious fact that it may go against your nature to ignore his meaning, but the skills of listening will endure, once they are mastered, and will be a form of real insurance against bad speech form.

2. Use the following [ʊr] words for reference and practice:

a. Words using [ʊr] in the final position or preceding a consonant:

cure	boor	moor	sure
poor	lure	spoor	tour
allure			

b. Words using [ʊr] followed by a vowel:

Europe	during	curious	fury
insurance	rural	mural	bureau

3. Practice the following pairs:

[ʊr]—[ɔr]		[ʊr]—[o]	
lure [lʊr]	lore [lɔr]	lure [lʊr]	low [lo]
moor [mʊr]	more [mɔr]	poor [pʊr]	Poe [po]
poor [pʊr]	pour [pɔr]	sure [ʃʊr]	show [ʃo]
your [jʊr]	yore [jɔr]	tour [tʊr]	tow [to]

[ʊr]—[uɚ]	
cure [kjʊr]	cue'er [kjuɚ]
poor [pʊr]	"pooer" [puɚ]
moor [mʊr]	mooer [muɚ]
sure [ʃʊr]	shoer [ʃuɚ]

Phonetic Transcription. Compare the following phonetic transcription of the paragraph in Exercise 1 with your own pronunciation. Do any of the differences indicate substandard usages in your speech?

['wʌn 'ʃʊr ˌwe tə du 'pʊrlɪ ɪn fə'nɛtɪk træns'krɪpʃən ɪz tə ˌraɪt 'fjʊriəslɪ wɪð͵aʊt 'lɪsənɪŋ ˌkɛrfəlɪ. 'dʊrɪŋ ðə 'pɪriəd hwɛn jʊr 'mæstrɪ ə ðə 'sɪmbəlz ɪz so 'lɪmətəd ðət ju du 'nɑt 'fil sɪ'kjʊr, pɚˌmɪt 'nʌθɪŋ tə lʊr jɚ ə'tɛnʃən frəm ðə 'saʊndz ðə ˌspikɚ 'meks. ɪt ɪz ə 'kjʊriəs 'fækt ðət ɪt ˌme ˌgo ə'gɛnst jʊr 'nɛtʃɚ tʊ ɪg'nɔr hɪz 'minɪŋ, bət ðə ˌskɪlz əv 'lɪsənɪŋ wɪl ɛn'dʊr, 'wʌns ðe ɑr 'mæstəd, ænd wɪl ˌbi ə ˌfɔrm əv 'riəl ɪn'ʃʊrəns ə'gɛnst ˌbæd ˌspitʃ ˌfɔrm.]

9
THE STOPS AND AFFRICATES

[p], [b], [t], [d], [k], [g], [tʃ], [dʒ]

[p] as in paper, apply, stop

Common Spellings: *p* as in pay, top
                      pp as in apple, tapping
                      Also spelled *ph*, as in shepherd; *gh*, as in hiccough.

Production. The [p] is classified as an unvoiced labial (or bilabial) stop (or stop-plosive). To produce this sound the unvoiced breath stream is impounded by closing the lips; pressure is built up behind this closure during a *hold*, or short period of silence, and is then released by opening the lips to the position for the following sound, or to a neutral position if [p] occurs as a final sound. Velopharyngeal closure is complete, or nearly so. If [p] is a plosive, the sound heard is the noise created as the released breath stream passes across the lips.

Pronunciation. Like all other sounds of this class in English, [p] may be either a stop or a plosive. When it occurs as a final sound in words such as "lap" and "hope," there is commonly little or no plosive element. In these cases most of the energy has been expended on the vowel, and [p] serves primarily as a terminating movement for the syllable, or as an off-glide. Similarly, when [p] is followed by [t] or [k], as in "slapped" [slæpt] or "upkeep" [ʌpkip], there is almost no plosion on [p]. Such pronunciations are, of course, perfectly acceptable and, indeed, excessive aspiration of a final unvoiced stop may be undesirably obtrusive.

On the other hand, English speakers usually aspirate [p] quite strongly when it is an initial sound, as in "paper" [pepɚ], "put" [pʊt], and "patron" [petrən], or when it is a medial sound which begins an accented syllable, as in "suppose" [sə'poz], "apparel" [ə'pɛrəl], and "appendix" [ə'pɛndɪks]. In phonetic transcription the following form can be used to call attention to strong aspiration wherever it may occur: [əpʻɛrəl], [əpʻɛndɪks]. The plosive escape is less marked when [p] is followed by

146

another consonant, as in "plate" [plet], "provide" [provaɪd], and "please" [pliz]. Too strong an aspiration of the stop in these cases is part of a phonetic process which may lead to an outright substandard usage, such as the overemphatic "puh-leeze" [pʌliz] for "please."

In medial positions the aspiration of [p] is also usually minimal when the sound introduces an unstressed, rather than a stressed, syllable. Examples of this can be found in the conversational pronunciation of

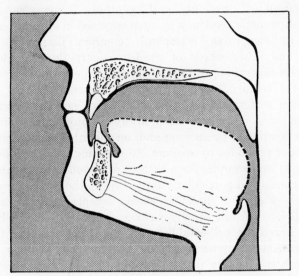

FIG. 8. Articulation adjustment for [p] and [b].

words such as "apparatus" [æpəretəs] and "appetite" [æpətaɪt]. As a rule all unvoiced plosives are more strongly pronounced than their voiced counterparts, and aspiration is not a prominent feature of the voiced stops. Interesting variations in the breath escape caused by the nature of the following sound are found in the [pm] combination, which leads to a nasal plosion, and in [pl] combinations, where the plosion is partly lateral, that is, over the sides of the tongue. Examples would be "help-mate" [hɛlpmet] and "apple" [æpl].

For the most part, persons whose native language is other than English aspirate sounds in the [p] phoneme less strongly than is common in English speech. This difference may be so marked that it imparts a subtle but perceptible dialect characteristic to their English pronunciation. It is most marked when [p] is followed by a vowel in a stressed syllable. What happens is that voicing of the vowel begins immediately with the opening of the lips, or even before, and in consequence [p] comes to resemble [b]. The result is an apparent substitution of [b] for [p] in words like "pay," "pat," and "pocket." If the speaker makes this typical error, he should, of course, study carefully the finer characteristics of the English [p] and practice these patterns.

Several other facets of the articulation of [p] should also be noted. When [m] is followed by certain other sounds, particularly by [t], [k], [f], [θ], [s], or [ʃ], a [p] may easily occur when the lips open from the [m] position to the following unvoiced sound. Historically this has led to the adoption of the letter *p* as a spelling convention in words such as "pre-empt," "bumpkin," "exempt," and "glimpse." In many cases, however, this natural phonetic tendency is not recognized in spelling. A [p] is usually heard in "something" [sʌmpθɪŋ], "comfort" [kʌmpfɚt], "warmth" [wɔrmpθ], and other words of similar construction. Incidentally, an occasional speaker will omit the [p] when it is spelled, as in [ɛmtɪ] instead of [ɛmptɪ] for "empty," which is perfectly allowable.

A question sometimes raised is whether or not the careful speaker should take pains, on the one hand, always to pronounce [p] in situations where it is sanctioned by spelling and, on the other, not to let it intrude where it is not called for by spelling. "Something" [sʌmpθɪŋ] or [sʌmθɪŋ] may serve as an example. As a matter of common sense, the question cannot be considered particularly important in the typical pronunciation of those whose general speech is within acceptable limits, since under these conditions [p] will be very weak and scarcely audible. Since insertion of the sound is a well-established phonetic phenomenon, there seems to be no reason to oppose it. It must be conceded, however, that those whose speech is generally poor often allow [p] in these cases to become quite conspicuous and hence, to a degree, substandard. Sometimes [m] tends to be assimilated into adjacent sounds so that such a word as "warmth" becomes [wɔrpθ], which certainly is substandard.

In an earlier section the general characteristics of doubled stops were discussed in some detail, and these remarks of course apply to [p]. Note, for example, that in the typical pronunciation of such a word as "lamp-post" only one stop-plosive occurs. There is, however, a perceptible hold between the stop at the end of the syllable "lamp" and the plosive release which initiates the syllable "post." This pronunciation can be transcribed [læmp:ost], with the symbol [:] designating the distinctive hold.* Very few difficulties in pronunciation arise in this connection, although failure to make a sufficient hold may occasionally impair clarity of articulation. On the other hand, the person who consciously tries to pronounce two contiguous identical stops may be guilty of conspicuous overpronunciation. For further discussion of this problem of joining

---

* The symbol [:] actually is meant to designate a sound of longer than normal duration. When this mark is used with the stop consonants, however, the duration is not so much of the sound as a whole as it is of the hold phase of that sound.

sounds in adjacent syllables or words, you may consult the section on juncture in Chapter 12.

In English the sound [p] is quite regularly spelled either *p* or *pp*. There are, however, a number of words in which *p* is regularly silent, including those beginning with *pt* or *pn* and the larger group beginning with *ps*. Examples are "ptomaine" [tomen], "Ptolemy" [tɑləmɪ], "ptosis" [tosəs], "pneumonia" [numonjə], "pneumatic" [numætɪk] or [njumætɪk], "psychology" [saɪkɑlədʒɪ], "pseudo" [sudo], "psalm" [sɑm], and "psi" [saɪ]. The instances where *p* is pronounced but not spelled have been discussed previously.

The [p] is one of the sounds which may be underpronounced, since it requires a relatively precise and firm articulatory adjustment and often a distinct plosive release. The speaker must be sure to develop sufficient breath pressure, which calls for firm lip closure; otherwise the result may be an indistinct sound of the sort said to be characteristic of the "lip-lazy." It requires only a little care and extra energy to correct this error. In some speech disorders, particularly those associated with disease of, or injury to, the central nervous system, there may be actual weakness in the labial musculature or difficulty with its control. For these cases the speech therapist must employ special procedures. Certain dental malocclusions, which fortunately are not common, involve abnormal relationships between the upper and lower teeth which are so marked that it is difficult or impossible for the speaker to bring his lips together. In this case he will often make [p] as a labiodental by bringing the lower lip into contact with the upper teeth, or the reverse—a practice which may have the unfortunate effect of aggravating the dental deformity.

Despite the necessity for this somewhat extended discussion of [p], it is, after all, a relatively easy sound to learn and teach and one which is less often defective than are many other sounds. It is one of the earliest consonant sounds acquired by the infant and is not often troublesome for physically normal children. The errors of the foreign speaker usually prove quite easy to correct.

Exercises

1. Identify the [p] sounds in the following paragraph. Practice transcribing your pronunciation of this paragraph for comparison with that of one the authors, shown in the transcription at the end of these exercises. Find examples of strongly and weakly aspirated [p], [pθ] combinations, and doubled or abutting [p].

Perhaps one of the most remarkable examples of animal performance is to be found in the perfectly trained sheep dogs who help the shepherd tend his flock. The sheep dog apparently has bred into him an aptitude for his work and an understanding of sheep psychology which far surpasses that of the people who are supposed to be his superiors. The mountain traveler will sometimes come upon a sheepherder, camped in some alpine meadow and presumably guarding the flock. More probably he will be found perched on a convenient rock, sopping up the warmth of the sun, and peering at something just beyond the empty horizon. His dog, however, poised and vigilant, allows nothing to escape him. If a sheep strays too far, he leaps and plunges into instant motion. The sheep dog is happy only when he is working; he is not to be pampered or petted. He and others of his corps are indeed the philosophers and psychologists of the sheep raising industry.

2. The following [p] words are representative examples of various allophones of [p] in different contexts and consonant combinations. Practice these and find other examples of each type illustrated.

Initiating consonant: pat, pay, pie, pill
Terminating consonant: ape, rope, up, weep
Initiating and terminating: pep, pipe, pop, Pope
Strong consonant: apart, appeal, comply, repair
Weak consonant: copper, happen, open, stopping
Initial blends: [sp] space, speech; [pr] pray, prize; [pl] place, plead; [spr] spring, spry; [spl] splash, splay
Final blends: [ps] rips, tops; [pt] kept, wrapped; [mp] damp, stump; [mps] bumps, lamps; [mpt] prompt, stamped

3. Practice and try to add to the following lists of minimal pairs:

[p]—[b]		[p]—[t]	
cop [kɑp]	cob [kɑb]	flap [flæp]	flat [flæt]
pat [pæt]	bat [bæt]	flapper [flæpɚ]	flatter [flætɚ]
pay [pe]	bay [be]	grape [grep]	great [gret]
pie [paɪ]	by [baɪ]	hip [hɪp]	hit [hɪt]
pill [pɪl]	bill [bɪl]	P [pi]	T [ti]
pin [pɪn]	been [bɪn]	pen [pɛn]	ten [tɛn]
rip [rɪp]	rib [rɪb]	pile [paɪl]	tile [taɪl]
ripping [rɪpɪŋ]	ribbing [rɪbɪŋ]	pipe [paɪp]	type [taɪp]
rope [rop]	robe [rob]	pun [pʌn]	ton [tʌn]
staple [stepl̩]	stable [stebl̩]	top [tɑp]	tot [tɑt]

[p]—[k]	
supper [sʌpɚ]	sucker [sʌkɚ]
lip [lɪp]	lick [lɪk]
open [opən]	oaken [okən]
P [pi]	key [ki]

past [pæst]	cast [kæst]
pay [pe]	K [ke]
play [ple]	clay [kle]
purr [pɝ]	cur [kɝ]
stop [stɑp]	stock [stɑk]
ape [ep]	ache [ek]

Phonetic Transcription. The following is a transcription in GA of the paragraph in Exercise 1:

[pɚhæps wʌn əv ðə most rɪ'mɑrkəbl̩ ɛg'zæmpl̩z əv ænəməl pɚ'fɔrməns ɪz tə bi faund ɪn ðə 'pɝfɪktlɪ trend ʃip dɔgz hu help ðə ʃepɚd tɛnd ɪz flɑk. ðə ʃip dɔg ə'pɛrəntlɪ hæz brɛd 'ɪntu hɪm ən 'æptə,tud fɔr hɪz wɝk ænd ən ˌʌndɚ'stændɪŋ əv ʃip saɪ'kɑlədʒi hwɪtʃ fɑr sɚ'pæsəz ðæt əv ðə pipl̩ hu ɑr sə'pozd tə bi hɪz sə'pɪriɚz. ðə mauntən trævələ wɪl 'sʌm'taɪmz kʌm əpɔn ə 'ʃip,hɝdɚ, kæmpt ɪn sʌm 'ælpaɪn mɛdo ən prɪ'zuməblɪ 'gɑrdɪŋ ðə flɑk. mɔr prɑbəblɪ hi wɪl bi faund pɝtʃt ɔn ə kən'vinjənt rɑk, 'sɑpɪŋ ʌp ðə wɔrmpθ əv ðə sʌn, ən 'pɪrɪŋ ət sʌmpθɪŋ dʒʌst bi'ɑnd ði ɛmptɪ hə'raɪzən. hɪz dɔg, hauɛvɚ, pɔɪzd ən 'vɪdʒələnt, əlauz 'nʌθɪŋ tu əskep hɪm. ɪf ə ʃip strez tu fɑr, hi lips ən plʌndʒəz ɪntu 'ɪnstənt 'moʃən. ðə ʃip dɔg ɪz hæpɪ onlɪ hwɛn hi əz 'wɝkɪŋ; hi əz nɑt tə bi pæmpɚd ɚ pɛtəd. hi ən ʌðɚz əv ɪz kɔr ɑr ɪn'did ðə fə'lɑsəfɚz ən ˌsaɪ'kɑlədʒəsts əv ðə ʃip 'rezɪŋ ɪndəstrɪ.]

[b] as in boy, baby, rob

Common Spellings: b as in bring, bet
      bb as in bubble, robber

Production. The [b] is classified as a voiced labial (or bilabial) stop (or stop-plosive). The articulation movements involved are essentially the same as for [p], except that voice is added. It is generally held that [b] is made with somewhat more lax lip closure and a lesser degree of breath pressure than [p].

Pronunciation. Although much of the discussion concerning the pronunciation of [p] is applicable to [b], certain additional considerations should be mentioned. Since [b] is voiced, there is ordinarily no aspiration on the plosive form of the sound. The characteristic weakening from [p] to [b], which may cause "paper" to resemble "baber" in careless speech, is consistent with what happens in the case of other pairs of unvoiced-voiced stops. As with [p], nasal plosion of [b] may be heard when the sound is followed by [m], as in the phrase "rob 'em" [rɑbm̩]. What occurs is simply that the soft palate lowers while the lips remain closed in the position for [m]. When [b] is followed by [l], as in "trouble" [trʌbl̩], the familiar lateral plosion is heard.

In spelling, [b] is the customary sound for either b or bb. There are numerous words, however, where *b* is silent, such as "lamb," "comb," and "dumb." Dropping of the final [b] sound is one of the historical changes that have occurred in pronunciation. Kenyon[16] notes, however, that certain words derived from Old English, such as "limb" and "numb," never had a [b] sound and were spelled "lim" and "num." After [b] was dropped from words such as "climb" and "lamb," however, the *b* was added to the spelling of "limb" and "numb" by a process which sometimes is called *reverse* or *inverse* spelling. Note that the letter *b* which follows *m* in medial positions is usually pronounced if it introduces a syllable—as it typically does in this spelling situation. Examples are "December" [disɛmbɚ] and "number" [nʌmbɚ]. The *b* remains silent in a number of words where it is followed by *t*, as in "subtle" [sʌtl̩], "doubt" [daʊt], and "debt" [dɛt].

Among those who have a non-English native language, notably German, sounds in the [b] phoneme may lose so much of their voicing that they approach a weakened form of [p] in such typical words as "about" [əbaʊt] and "better" [bɛtɚ]. These pronunciations may be transcribed [b̥ɛtɚ] and [əb̥aʊt]. In other cases, including Spanish, the speaker is likely to produce the sound with an incomplete lip closure, so that it becomes a labial fricative, indicated by the symbol [β]. This is heard most prominently when [b] occurs in a medial position, as in "labor" [lebɚ] and "robber" [rabɚ].

Many difficulties that the native English speaker may have with [b] correspond to those mentioned for [p], and it is customary to teach and learn the two sounds together. In keeping with the tendency to weaken [b], it may rather easily become underpronounced in conversational speech. The difficulty does not often occur on initial sounds, but in words like "neighbor" [nebɚ] or "rob" [rab], where it is medial or final, there may be incomplete voicing or lax lip closure. There are cases where a distinction in meaning may thus be obscured, as in the pairs "rip"–"rib" [rɪp–rɪb], "cap"–"cab" [kæp–kæb], and "sop"–"sob" [sɑp–sɑb]. The vowel before [p] usually is slightly shorter than before [b], and this is sometimes the principal cue in discriminating the two sounds. Naturally any tendency for the learner to go too far in the direction of forceful articulation of [b], particularly in the final position, should stop short of such pronunciations as [stæbə] for "stab" or ['rʌbə] for "rub." Mistakes of this sort, however, are not particularly troublesome, except in some foreign dialects.

Exercises

1. Analyze the following [b] paragraph for the special cases discussed in the preceding section. Practice reading this passage aloud, paying particular attention to sufficient forcefulness of articulation, and compare

your pronunciation with the phonetic transcription following these exercises.

There is sometimes a curious snobbery about good speech. Many who write ably and who would doubtless be greatly troubled by shabby writing seem to be quite oblivious to the basic need to make themselves understood. There seems to be a subtle belief that the habits of good writing and good speaking bear no resemblance, and in consequence unnumbered good and useful thoughts lie as buried as in the tomb. Such a basically false concept of speech will rob both the speaker and the listener of any benefits which might be theirs. These observations are no invitation for anyone to clamber onto a platform, bent on rabble-rousing, but thrice-blest will be he who obeys our plea that he content himself neither with dumb show nor unrecognizable babbling.

2. The following [b] words are representative examples of various allophones of [b] in different contexts and consonant combinations. Practice these and find other examples of each type illustrated:

Initiating consonant: bay, bee, bow, boy
Terminating consonant: Abe, rob, rub, web
Initiating and terminating: babe, bib, bob, boob
Strong consonant: above, about, rebuff, imbibe
Weak consonant: habit, robber, rubbing, stubborn
Initial blends: [br] break, brown; [bl] black, blue
Final blends: [bz] clubs, rubs; [bd] clubbed, stubbed

3. Practice and try to add to the following lists of minimal pairs:

[b]—[p]		[b]—[d]	
Abe [eb]	ape [ep]	Abe [eb]	aid [ed]
about [əbaʊt]	a pout [əpaʊt]	about [əbaʊt]	a doubt [ədaʊt]
ball [bɔl]	pall [pɔl]	B [bi]	D [di]
bee [bi]	P [pi]	ball [bɔl]	doll [dɔl]
bet [bɛt]	pet [pɛt]	bet [bɛt]	debt [dɛt]
bill [bɪl]	pill [pɪl]	bill [bɪl]	dill [dɪl]
lab [læb]	lap [læp]	buy [baɪ]	die [daɪ]
rib [rɪb]	rip [rɪp]	lab [læb]	lad [læd]
sob [sab]	sop [sap]	rib [rɪb]	rid [rɪd]
sobbing [sabɪŋ]	sopping [sapɪŋ]	sob [sab]	sod [sad]

[b]—[m]	
bat [bæt]	mat [mæt]
bay [be]	may [me]
bee [bi]	me [mi]

bet [bɛt]   met [mɛt]
bill [bɪl]   mill [mɪl]
bob [bɑb]   bomb [bɑm]
buy [baɪ]   my [maɪ]
cob [kɑb]   calm [kɑm]
lab [læb]   lamb [læm]
rib [rɪb]   rim [rɪm]

Phonetic Transcription. The following is a transcription in GA of the paragraph in Exercise 1:

[ðɛr ɪz 'sʌm,taɪmz ə 'kjʊriəs snɑbəri əbaʊt gʊd spitʃ. mɛni hu raɪt ɛblɪ ən hu wʊd daʊtləs bi gretlɪ trʌbḷd baɪ ʃæbɪ raɪtɪŋ sim tə bi kwaɪt ə'blɪviəs tə ðə 'bɛsɪk nid tə mek ðəmsɛlvz ʌndɚ'stʊd. ðɛr simz tə bi ə sʌtḷ bɪ'lif ðət ðə hæbəts əv gʊd 'raɪtɪŋ ən gʊd 'spikɪŋ bɛr no rɪ'zɛmbləns, ænd ɪn 'kɑnsə,kwɛns ,ʌn'nʌmbɚd gʊd ṇ jusfəl θɔts laɪ əz bɛrɪd əz ɪn ðə tum. sʌtʃ ə besɪklɪ fɔls 'kɑnsept əv spitʃ wɪl rɑb boθ ðə spikɚ ən ðə 'lɪsənɚ əv ɛni 'bɛnəfɪts hwɪtʃ maɪt bi ðɛrz. ðiz ,abzɚ'veʃənz ɑr no ,ɪnvə'-teʃən fɔr 'ɛni ,wʌn tə klæmɚ ɔntu ə 'plætfɔrm, bɛnt ən 'ræbl̩,rauzɪŋ, bət θraɪs blɛst wɪl bi hi hu əbez aʊr pli ðət hi kəntɛnt ɪmsɛlf niðɚ wɪθ dʌm ʃo nɔr ʌn'rɛkəg,naɪzəbḷ 'bæblɪŋ.]

[t] as in *to, into, at*

Common Spellings: *t* as in tell, hat
tt as in attend, attempt
d as in talked, asked
Also spelled *ct*, as in indict; *ght*, as in brought; *th*, as in thyme; and *phth*, as in phthisic.

Production. The [t] is classified as an unvoiced lingua-alveolar, or lingua-rugal, stop (or stop-plosive). In articulating this sound the tonguetip is placed on the alveolar ridge behind the upper central teeth, and the lateral margins of the tongue are in contact with the teeth and gums in such a way as to form an airtight closure. Breath pressure is built up behind this closure, then released as the tongue moves either to the position for the next sound or, if there is no sound immediately following, to a neutral position. On the plosive [t], the sound heard is the noise produced as the breath, under pressure, strikes the hard and soft surfaces at the front of the mouth. Velopharyngeal closure is complete, or nearly so.

Pronunciation. The sounds within the [t] phoneme vary considerably, and there are, as a result, some interesting pronunciation problems. These variations include (1) allowable differences dictated by phonetic influences, (2) substandard usages, and (3) foreign-dialect characteristics.

Several phonetic differences occur in standard speech. Like other stops, the [t] tends to be much more strongly aspirated in initial and medial positions than in the final position. Compare the usual pronuncia-tion of such words as "took" [tʊk] and "attack" [ətæk] with "get" [gɛt] and "past" [pæst]. In the latter two cases the sound takes on the usual characteristics of a terminating stop, although a final [t] is more likely to be audibly aspirated than are some other final stops.

In some circumstances the influence of a following sound reduces the extent to which [t] is aspirated or affects the manner in which the aspira-tion takes place. Thus, in conversational speech the phrase "last night" [læst naɪt] would probably be spoken with no release of breath on [t];

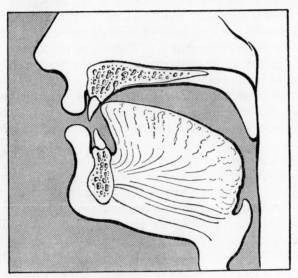

Fig. 9. Articulation adjustment for [t] and [d].

the result would be a kind of initial plosive [n], or the [t] might be elimi-nated ([læs naɪt]). The reason is, of course, that the tongue already is in the position for the following [n]; hence it is natural to make the shift by lowering the soft palate while the tongue is in the [t] position (or the [n] position, if you like). Much the same phenomenon can be found in such a phrase as "past me" [pæs mi], where the lips are closed for [m] before the breath is released. The plosion is likely to be nasal, rather than through the mouth. The doubled [t] has the same characteristics as other doubled stops. When [t] is followed by a different stop, as in "that dog" [ðæt dɔg], "that cat" [ðæt kæt], or "that paper" [ðæt pepɚ], the phonetic situation is much the same. The articulators move to the position for [t], and there is a perceptible hold followed by a release—but in this case the releasing movement is from the position of the second sound, since the articulators have moved to the new position during the hold.

Poorly articulated speech is a danger in phonetic situations such as these. Most often the unconscious inclination is to drop the [t] and move instead to the position for the succeeding sound. The movements necessary to avoid this require some precision. Examples of the elisions of [t] in careless speech may be heard in such changes as "sit down" from [sɪt daʊn] to [sɪdaʊn], "that dog" [ðæt dɔg] to [ðædɔg], "that cat" [ðæt kæt] to [ðækæt], and "that paper" [ðæt pepɚ] to [ðæpepɚ]. If one listens carefully, he can usually sense a short hold before the plosive, which actually is a brief glottal stop followed by the plosive in question. In other instances, there is a simple elision of [t], as when "last night" [læst naɪt] becomes [læsnaɪt] and "past me" [pæst mi] degenerates into [pæsmi]. As a matter of fact, some of these elisions—such as the last two examples—are so common that it is difficult to condemn them as substandard in conversational speech; nevertheless, the good speaker will usually wish to retain both sounds in the form described for consecutive stops and will learn the proper transition movements. This problem may become clearer after the discussion of juncture in Chapter 12.

When [t] comes at the end of a word, particularly after a consonant, it differs appreciably from the initial sound, and there is the familiar tendency toward underpronunciation of any terminal stop. If an error occurs, it is particularly noteworthy when the preceding sound is also a stop. The [kt] and [st], along with the [kts] and [sts] are among the most troublesome combinations, for the articulation movements needed to differentiate these sounds require considerable agility. Thus, "act" [ækt] is likely to approach [æk], and such a word as "ghosts" [gosts] may be heard as [gos]. Even if the [t] is not completely eliminated, it may be weakened to the extent that the speech is deprived of its desired degree of clarity. Combinations of this sort occur frequently in English, and the speaker must take care that the allowable weakening and assimilation of [t] are not exceeded.

One variation of [t] found principally in a medial position calls for discussion. This sound can be heard in such typical words as "butter" [bʌtɚ], "water" [watɚ], and "matter" [mætɚ]. If the pronunciation of these words is compared with that of "top" [tɑp] or "tell" [tɛl], the medial [t] will probably be heard as a weaker and more diffuse sound than the initial [t]. Note, however, that this does not ordinarily occur when a medial [t] begins an accented syllable, as in "attend" [ətɛnd] or "return" [rɪtɝn]. In such a word as "water" the typical American speaker, and to a lesser extent the British, articulates [t] with a very light lingua-alveolar contact, minimal breath pressure, and very little hold before the plosion. When the force of articulation is relatively light, the sound is described as a *lenis* consonant, as opposed to a strongly articulated, or *fortis*, consonant. There is also a tendency to voice the lenis [t] when it occurs medially, so that "water" and "battle" [bætl] may closely resemble [wɑdɚ] and [bædl̩], although one who listens carefully will hear a voiced [t], marked phonetically [ṭ], rather than a true [d]. The fact that such a large proportion of educated speakers have come to use this general variety of medial [t] makes it, within limits, a correct pronunciation. At the same time, one should exercise some caution in weakening the sound.

Other variations in [t] grow out of differences in the exact point of tongue contact, as influenced by phonetic context. Sometimes, but not often among native English speakers, [t] is made as a linguadental sound, with the tonguetip in contact with the teeth rather than with the alveolar ridge. Such a dental sound may be heard in the usual pronunciation of the word "eighth" [et̪θ] or in a phrase such as "at them" [æt̪ð̩əm]. In these cases [ṭ] has obviously been influenced by the fact that the following sound is a linguadental. Where [t] is followed by a front vowel, as in "Tim" [tɪm] and "tea" [ti], the tonguetip may be placed very nearly at the point where the teeth and gums meet, in which case the sound is sometimes referred to as *gingival*. If a gingival [t] does not occur in these circumstances, the point of articulation is at least very definitely forward, whereas the contact is much farther back on words such as "Tom" [tɔm], "top" [tɑp], and "tussle" [tʌsl̩]. In these words the influence of a following back vowel is, of course, responsible for the more posterior contact. As with other stops, a nasal after [t] leads to nasal plosion, whereas the [t] in [tl] combinations tends to have lateral plosion.

Compared with many other letters, the *t* in English spelling has a fairly consistent pronunciation value. The usual sound for the letter or for the doubled *tt* is one of the varieties of [t]. The spelling *ed* calls for the pronunciation [t] in the past tenses and past participles of words which end in voiceless consonants. Examples include "risked" [rɪskt], "pushed" [puʃt], "slapped" [slæpt], and "mashed" [mæʃt]. Note that if such verb forms end in a voiced consonant the pronunciation is [d], as in "sagged" [sægd] and "robbed" [rɑbd]. The letter *t* is silent in words ending in *sten* and *stle*, such as "fasten" [fæsn̩], "chasten" [tʃesn̩], "bustle" [bʌsl̩], "castle" [kæsl̩], and "whistle" [hwɪsl̩].

Because of certain historical and phonetic influences the *t* is not pronounced [t] in the combinations *-tion*, *-tial*, *-tient*, and *-tious*. The usual shift is to [ʃ] as in "rational" [ræʃənəl], "partial" [pɑrʃəl], "patient" [peʃənt], and "cautious" [kɔʃəs], but [tʃ] is heard in "bestial" [bestʃəl], and there are other occasional exceptions. In a few words [t] is spelled *th*, such as "thyme" [taɪm], "Thames" [temz], and "Thomas" [tɔməs], but these are not so common as to cause much confusion, and the pronunciation for *th* remains quite reliably either [θ] or [ð].

Americans, and to a lesser degree Englishmen, tend to insert a [t] between [n] and either [s] or [θ] where the sound is not indicated by the spelling. This is illustrated by the common pronunciations of "dance" [dænts], "tense" [tɛnts], "prance" [prænts], "pence" [pɛns], "tenth" [tɛntθ], and "labyrinth" [læbərɪntθ]. This is comparable to the addition of [p] between [m] and [θ] in "warmth" [wɔrmpθ], which was described in an earlier section. In the present instance the [t] occurs with the breath release from [n] because of the similarity of the tongue positions between [n] and [t]. Such an incidental [t] cannot be considered substandard, since it is heard so frequently among educated speakers, but a pronunciation without the sound is sometimes taught.

There are a number of foreign-dialect peculiarities which result when lingua-alveolar sounds from another language are carried over into English pronunciation. One of the most common is the dental [t], which, as pointed out earlier, is only rarely heard in standard English speech. If a dental [t] is used consistently in most phonetic contexts, it sounds very unfamiliar to the native speaker of English and should, of course, be avoided. Because the dental [t] is likely to have very little aspiration, it may be heard as a [d] by the listener who is phonetically unsophisticated. A number of Oriental languages, as well as Italian and French, contain [t] sounds which have many or all the principal characteristics of the typical dental [t̪]. Excessive aspiration of [t] may also occur in the speech of persons with a foreign dialect.

Among native speakers imprecise articulation of [t] is one of the commonest characteristics of substandard speech, along with omissions of the sound or use of one of its nonstandard variations. These errors were noted in the earlier portions of this discussion. Another and perhaps even more conspicuous defect is substitution of the glottal stop [ʔ] for [t]. A glottal stop is a speech sound produced by a momentary hold of the breath effected by closure of the glottis, the opening between the vocal folds. It may be classified as unvoiced, and there are no necessary articulation movements of either the tongue or lips. The objectionable substitution of [ʔ] for [t] is heard principally on medial sounds; the words "water" [wɑtɚ], "gentlemen" [dʒɛntəlmən], "matter" [mætɚ], and "dental" [dɛntəl], for example, may become [wɑʔɚ], [dʒɛnʔlmən], [mæʔɚ], and [dɛnʔl]. Words such as "gentlemen" and "dental" may even become [dʒɛʔlmən] and [dɛʔl]. Pronunciations of this sort are largely substandard dialect variations and are very commonly heard in several areas. Among those who have physical defects affecting speech the person with cleft palate is particularly prone to the use of the glottal stop, often as a substitute for the standard stops, which are difficult for him to produce.

Exercises

1. Identify and practice the [t] sounds in the following paragraph, paying particular attention to your pronunciation of weak and abutting [t] sounds. Do you have any spelling mispronunciations? Compare your

pronunciation with that of one of the authors, indicated by the transcription following these exercises.

Good taste in speech, as in all one's habits, will truly stand each of us in good stead. Training in natural, communicative diction should, it seems apparent, be a part of everyone's education. There is certainly no truth to the notion that such an attitude as we have expressed will result in superficiality. Good speech provides the best possible guarantee of sympathetic attention to one's thoughts. The best time to learn is while one still thinks of himself as a student. Ofttimes the question is asked, "Why can't everyone be taught to speak clearly and effectively?" The answer is, of course, that teaching these skills is not too difficult a process; it wants only better acceptance as an important part of the educational process.

2. The following [t] words are representative examples of various allophones of [t] in different contexts and consonant combinations. Practice these and find other examples of each type illustrated.

Initiating consonant: tea, tie, two, toe
Terminating consonant: eat, ought, ate, at
Initiating and terminating: taught, Tate, tight, toot
Strong consonant: attach, atone, between, esteem
Weak consonant: better, bottle, bottom, butter
Initial blends: [st] stand, stay; [tr] train, try; [str] straight, string; [tw] twelve, twin
Final blends: [ts] lets, puts; [st] lost, past; [pt] kept, stopped; [ft] laughed, sift; [nt] rent, want; [nts] pants, tents; [ʃt] cashed, pushed; [mpt] lumped, stamped; [ŋkt] honked, ranked; [rt] part, start; [ntʃt] pinched, wrenched; [rts] parts, carts; [nst] fenced, glanced

3. Practice and try to add to the following lists of minimal pairs:

[t]—[d]		[t]—[k]	
at [æt]	add [æd]	ate [et]	ache [ek]
ate [et]	aid [ed]	batter [bætɚ]	backer [bækɚ]
boat [bot]	bowed [bod]	late [let]	lake [lek]
cart [kɑrt]	card [kɑrd]	lot [lɑt]	lock [lɑk]
matter [mætɚ]	madder [mædɚ]	mate [met]	make [mek]
patter [pætɚ]	padder [pædɚ]	rater [retɚ]	raker [rekɚ]
T [ti]	D [di]	tall [tɔl]	call [kɔl]
ten [tɛn]	den [dɛn]	tame [tem]	came [kem]
tick [tɪk]	Dick [dɪk]	tea [ti]	key [ki]
two [tu]	do [du]	toy [tɔɪ]	coy [kɔɪ]

[t]—[p]		[t]—[θ]	
ate [et]	ape [ep]	Bert [bɜt]	birth [bɜθ]
cotter [kɑtɚ]	copper [kɑpɚ]	boat [bot]	both [boθ]
Kate [ket]	cape [kep]	pat [pæt]	path [pæθ]
matter [mætɚ]	mapper [mæpɚ]	rat [ræt]	wrath [ræθ]
sheet [ʃit]	sheep [ʃip]	sheet [ʃit]	sheath [ʃiθ]
tack [tæk]	pack [pæk]	team [tim]	theme [θim]
tea [ti]	P [pi]	tick [tɪk]	thick [θɪk]
tie [taɪ]	pie [paɪ]	tie [taɪ]	thigh [θaɪ]
toe [to]	Poe [po]	tread [trɛd]	thread [θrɛd]
ton [tʌn]	pun [pʌn]	tree [tri]	three [θri]

Phonetic Transcription. The following is a transcription in GA of the paragraph in Exercise 1:

[gud test ɪn spɪtʃ, æz ɪn əl wʌnz hæbəts, wɪl trulɪ stænd ɪtʃ əv əs ɪn gud stɛd. 'trenɪŋ ɪn 'nætʃərəl, kə'mjunə,ketɪv dɪkʃən ʃud, ɪt sɪmz ə'pɛrənt, bi ə pɑrt əv 'ɛvrɪ,wʌn ,ɛdʒə'keʃən. ðɛr ɪz 'sɜtənlɪ no truθ tə ðə noʃən ðət sʌtʃ ən 'ætətud əz wi həv ɛk'sprɛst wɪl rɪ'zʌlt ɪn ,supɚ,fɪʃɪ'ælətɪ. gud spɪtʃ prəvaɪdz ðə bɛst pɑsəbl̩ ,gɛrən'ti əv ,sɪmpə'θɛtɪk ə'tɛnʃən tə wʌnz θɔts. ðə bɛs taɪm tə lɜn ɪz hwaɪl wʌn stɪl θɪŋks əv ɪmsɛlf əz ə studn̩t. 'ɔf'taɪmz ðə 'kwɛstʃən ɪz æskt, hwaɪ kænt 'ɛvrɪ,wʌn bi tɔt tə spik klɪrlɪ ənd ɪ'fɛktɪvlɪ? ðɪ ænsɚ ɪz, əv kɔrs, ðət titʃɪŋ ðiz skɪlz ɪz nat tu 'dɪfɚ,kʌlt ə prɑsɛs; ɪt wɔnts onlɪ bɛtɚ ək'sɛptəns æz ən ɪm'pɔrtənt pɑrt əv ðɪ ,ɛdʒə'keʃənəl 'prɑsɛs.]

[d] as in do, body, had

Common Spellings: d as in dish, bed
                                 dd as in sadder, add

Production. The [d] is classified as a voiced lingua-alveolar, or lingua-rugal, stop (or stop-plosive) and is made in essentially the same way as [t], except that voice is added for [d]. The usual differences between the unvoiced stops and their voiced counterparts obtain, which means that [d] is ordinarily articulated with somewhat less force than [t] and has little or no aspiration.

Pronunciation. The varieties of sounds within the [d] phoneme are to some extent comparable to those described in the discussion of [t]. This certainly applies to the exact point of tongue contact, which may range from a dental to a nearly palatal placement. As usual, these variations are mainly the result of phonetic context, so that the point of contact tends to be forward in such words as "width" [wɪdθ], "deem" [dim], and "dip" [dɪp] and much farther back in such words as "dog" [dɔg] and "doctor" [dɑktɚ], where [d] is followed by a back vowel.

The spelling of the sound [d] is fairly regular—usually either *d* or *dd*—but there are some spelling-pronunciation variants which should be noted. Of particular interest is the pronunciation of the final *-ed* in the past tense and past participle of verbs. As mentioned in the discussion of [t], these forms are pronounced with a [d] when the verb ends with a voiced consonant. Examples are "bragged" [brægd], "tugged" [tʌgd], "sobbed" [sɑbd], "moved" [muvd], and "inscribed" [ɪnskraɪbd].

Questionable pronunciations of [d] are fairly common. Possibly the most frequent difficulty in native colloquial substandard speech is the undue weakening or omission of the sound. Although there are normally some phonetic contexts in which the educated speaker may weaken a sound by unvoicing, the student must be perceptive about the allowable limits, lest he fall into such careless pronunciations as [wʊtn̩t] instead of [wʊdn̩t] for "wouldn't" or [ʃʊtnɑt] instead of [ʃʊdnɑt] for "should not." The sound [d] is often omitted in cases like these, which would lead to the definitely substandard [wʊnt] and [ʃʊnt] for "wouldn't" and "shouldn't." In a similar way the [d] may be missing, or almost so, in any situation where either the preceding or following sound has a similar articulation position. Examples include [stæn ʌp] for "stand up" [stænd ʌp], [hi hæ sʌm] for "he had some" [hi hæd sʌm], and [ol bɔɪ] for "old boy" [old bɔɪ]. The medial [d] gives the same sort of trouble in such typical words as "handle," which becomes [hæn̩l] rather than [hænd̩l]; "friendly," which changes from [frɛndlɪ] to [frɛnlɪ]; or "sounds," which becomes [saʊnz] rather than the more precise [saʊndz].

Despite the fact that all the weakened [d] pronunciations in the examples just given represent something less than the best speech, no infallible generalizations can be made, since there are other, comparable words in which [d] has been dropped by the most careful speakers. Examples are "grandfather," "handsome," and "handful," which are almost universally pronounced [grænfɑðɚ], [hænsəm], and [hænfʊl]. Since there is no fully satisfactory rule to cover the situations where [d] may be omitted, the only safe procedure is to listen carefully to the models one has chosen from among educated speakers and to consult a good pronouncing dictionary when a question arises. It is interesting to note in passing that a number of words which now contain the letter *d* once were spelled without it, so that "thunder" and "sound," for example, have developed from "thunor" and "soun" (see Kenyon, Ref. 16, p. 124). The dialect addition of [d] in "drown," so that it becomes [draʊnd], and in the past tense [draʊndəd], is quite common.

Foreign-dialect pronunciations of sounds in the [d] phoneme generally parallel those for [t]. Possibly the most common is a dental [d], employed by the same speaker who has a dental [t]. In some languages, particularly those in the Romance group, the approximate counterpart of the English

[d] is made with the blade of the tongue flattened against the teeth, resulting in what might be thought of as an extreme form of dental [d]. The sound thus produced takes on some of the attributes of a fricative, since the tongue contact is relatively short and lax, and as a consequence what might have been [d] becomes much like [ð]. A typical Spanish pronunciation of the word "padre" illustrates this pronunciation. Foreign speakers also may show a tendency to unvoice [d] very perceptibly, giving the impression that a [t] has been substituted. It goes without saying that overpronunciation of [d] will lead to artificiality in speech.

Exercises

1. Analyze the following paragraph and practice reading it aloud. Look especially for strong and weak forms, *d*'s which are pronounced as [t], *d*'s which may not be pronounced, and abutting *d*'s. The pronunciation of one of the authors is shown following these exercises.

You should now and then seek out individuals who can serve as models for your own diction, for speech is a living thing, better to be heard than read about. Those individuals whom we encounter in daily life who speak the language of the educated man can provide us with the needed examples. Of course a good deal of bad diction and decidedly careless articulation is certain to be heard, for many of us have become addicted to a mode of speech which is far below what a modern standard should be. Radio diction is not too reliable a guide, since the speech is often too studied and thus robbed of its naturalness. Formal public addresses, likewise, often produce a tendency toward formal usage. Speech of cultured persons in animated conversation affords a good opportunity for study since the odds are great that none of the speakers will use stilted pronunciations—but at the same time, bad usages will not be condoned.

2. The following [d] words are representative examples of various allophones of [d] in different contexts and consonant combinations. Practice these and find other examples of each type.

Initiating consonant: day, die, do, dough
Terminating consonant: add, aid, eyed, odd
Initiating and terminating: dad, dead, deed, did
Stronger consonant: condone, produce, reduce, today
Weaker consonant: indicate, model, modern, study
Initial blends: [dr] draw, dress
Final blends: [nd] end, round; [ld] called, cold; [dz] beads, loads; [rd] card, ford; [md] calmed, tamed; [gd] bagged, rigged; [zd] pleased, raised; [bd] robbed, stabbed; [vd] behaved,

starved; [dʒd] caged, judged; [gd] hanged, wronged; [rdz] birds, boards; [ndʒd] hinged, impinged; [ðd] bathed, soothed

3. Practice and try to add to the following lists of minimal pairs:

[d]—[t]

bad [bæd]	bat [bæt]
bed [bɛd]	bet [bɛt]
bedding [bɛdɪŋ]	betting [bɛtɪŋ]
died [daɪd]	tied [taɪd]
do [du]	too [tu]
dough [do]	toe [to]
had [hæd]	hat [hæt]
leader [lidɚ]	liter [litɚ]
made [med]	mate [met]
wader [wedɚ]	waiter [wetɚ]

[d]—[b]

cad [kæd]	cab [kæb]
dad [dæd]	dab [dæb]
Dan [dæn]	ban [bæn]
darn [dɑrn]	barn [bɑrn]
dead [dɛd]	bed [bɛd]
deed [did]	bead [bid]
died [daɪd]	bide [baɪd]
did [dɪd]	bid [bɪd]
din [dɪn]	bin [bɪn]
dressed [drɛst]	breast [brɛst]

[d]—[n]

bead [bid]	bean [bin]
bed [bɛd]	Ben [bɛn]
cad [kæd]	can [kæn]
D [di]	knee [ni]
deed [did]	need [nid]
debt [dɛt]	net [nɛt]
dot [dɑt]	not [nɑt]
dough [do]	no [no]
made [med]	main [men]
leader [lidɚ]	leaner [linɚ]

[d]—[ð]

breeding [bridɪŋ]	breathing [briðɪŋ]
D [di]	thee [ði]
Dan [dæn]	than [ðæn]
die [daɪ]	thy [ðaɪ]
dine [daɪn]	thine [ðaɪn]
dare [dɛr]	there [ðɛr]
dough [do]	though [ðo]
fodder [fɑdɚ]	father [fɑðɚ]
read [rid]	wreathe [rið]
ride [raɪd]	writhe [raɪð]

Phonetic Transcription. The following is a transcription in GA of the paragraph in Exercise 1:

[ju ʃud nau ənd ðən sik aut ɪndə'vɪdʒuwəlz hu kən sɝv əz mɑdl̩z fɔr jɔr dɪkʃn̩, fɔr spitʃ ɪz ə 'lɪvɪŋ θɪŋ, betɚ tə bi hɝd ðən rɛd əbaut. ðoz ɪndə' vɪdʒəwəlz hum wi ɛn'kauntɚ ɪn delɪ laɪf hu spik ðə 'læŋgwɪdʒ əv ði 'ɛdʒə‚ketəd mæn kən prə'vaɪd ʌs wɪð ðə nidəd ɛg'zæmpl̩z. əv kɔrs ə gud diəl əv 'bæd 'dɪkʃən ən dɪ'saɪdədlɪ kɛrləs ɑrtɪkjə'leʃən ɪz sɝtən tə bi hɝd, fɔr mɛnɪ əv əs hæv bɪ'kʌm ə'dɪktəd tu ə mod əv spitʃ hwɪtʃ ɪz fɑr bilo hwʌt ə mɑdən stændɚd ʃud bi. 'redɪo dɪkʃən ɪz nɑt tu rɪ'laɪəbl̩ ə gaɪd, sɪns ðə spitʃ ɪz ɔfən tu 'stʌdɪd ən ðʌs rɑbd əv ɪts 'nætʃərəlnəs. fɔrməl pʌblɪk ə'drɛsəz 'laɪk‚waɪz ɔfən prə'dus ə 'tɛndənsɪ tɔrd fɔrməl 'jusɪdʒ. spitʃ əv 'kʌltʃɚd pɝsənz ɪn 'ænəmetəd kɑnvɚ'seʃən əfɔrdz ə gud apɚ'tunətɪ fɔr stʌdɪ sɪns ðɪ ɑdz ɚ gret ðət nʌn əv ðə spikɚz wɪl juz stɪltəd prə‚nʌnsɪ'eʃənz—bʌt ət ðə sem taɪm, bæd 'jusɪdʒəz wɪl nɑt bi kən'dɑnd.]

[k] as in keep, actor, back

Common Spellings: *k* as in kill, king
c as in cat, cab
ch as in character, echo
ck as in luck, pick
cc as in account, accurate
kh as in khaki
The combination [ks] is commonly spelled *x*, as in extra, box; the combination [kw] is commonly spelled *q*, as in quick, quit, or *cq*, as in acquire, acquaint.

Production. The [k] is classified as an unvoiced linguavelar stop (or stop-plosive). To make this sound the middle of the tongue is placed in

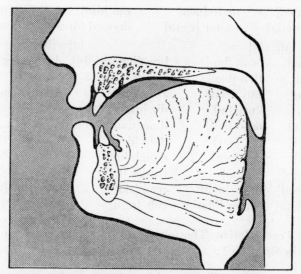

Fig. 10. Articulation adjustment for [k] and [g].

contact with the anterior part of the soft palate; breath pressure is built up behind this closure, then released as the tongue is moved to the position for the following sound, or to a neutral position if there is no sound immediately following and [k] is a plosive. Velopharyngeal closure is complete, or nearly so. When [k] is made as a plosive, what is heard is the friction noise as the breath, under pressure, strikes the hard and soft surfaces in the front of the mouth.

Pronunciation. The [k] is one of the phonemes which contain a relatively large number of sounds, principally because the exact point of articulation is so often strongly influenced by the character of the sounds which precede and follow. For instance, if [k] is followed by a front vowel, as in "keep" [kip], "keen" [kin], or "kitten" [kɪtn̩], the contact which stops the breath is quite far forward, perhaps even on the hard palate, rather than on the velum. On the other hand, when words like "car" [kɑr], "cook" [kʊk], or "caught" [kɔt] are pronounced in the usual way, the contact is much farther back, since in each case the sound following [k] is from the back-vowel series. The assimilation of [k] with the following sound takes place naturally in connected speech and does not ordinarily lead to substandard pronunciations. A lip-rounded [k] occurs in the [kw] combination, and the familiar nasal or lateral plosion is heard when [k] is affected by adjoining nasals or an [l].

There is considerable variation in the amount of aspiration given [k] in English speech, as is true of the other unvoiced plosives. A final [k] is likely to carry a minimal amount of aspiration, but the completely stopped final sound is not commonly heard. When compared with a typical final [p], for instance, the final [k] ordinarily has perceptibly greater plosion. Where [k] is the initial sound in a stressed syllable, there is almost always considerable aspiration, as in "keep" [kip], "cup" [kʌp], and "cotton" [kɑtn̩]. The [k] in unstressed syllables is aspirated, but less strongly, as can be observed from the ordinary pronunciation of such words as "broker" [brokɚ], "liquor" [lɪkɚ], and "taking" [tekɪŋ].

Irregularities in spelling conventions for [k] may prove a source of considerable confusion to both the native and the foreign speaker. The [k] regularly occurs where an initial *k* is followed by a vowel, as in "kick" [kɪk] or "keep" [kip], or where the letter is between vowels within a word, as in "broken" [brokən] or "taken" [tekən]. In such spelling situations *ck* or *cn* is also pronounced [k], as in "luck" [lʌk], "back" [bæk], "packer" [pækɚ], and "acne" [æknɪ]. Note, however, that the *k* is silent in *kn* combinations such as "knee" [ni], "knuckle" [nʌkl̩], and "know" [no].

The letter *c* may call for either [k] or [s], but the rule which generally holds is that *c* is pronounced [k] when it occurs at the end of a word or when it is followed by a consonant letter or by *a, o,* or *u*. Thus, "climactic" and "Arctic" are [klaɪmæktɪk] and [ɑrktɪk]. The rule applies well for the initial *c*, as illustrated by "cling" [klɪŋ], "cringe" [krɪndʒ], "candy" [kændɪ], "cot" [kɑt], and "curse" [kɝ·s]. Otherwise an initial *c* carries the sound [s]. It is scarcely worthwhile to frame a rule for the medial *c* since practice is so variable, and the dictionary should be considered the only safe guide. A *cc* is either [k], as in "account" [əkaʊnt], or [ks], as in "accept" [æksɛpt]. The rule pertaining to *c* followed by *a, o,* or *u* holds true for the medial *c* in many cases, but not in all.

The spelling pronunciation problems presented by the digraph *ch* are even more complicated. Any rule would need to take cognizance of word origin, which is in itself a complex matter, so that the common-sense solution is to consult the dictionary when there is any question about the pronunciation of *ch*. In general, however, an initial *ch* in English is more often [tʃ] or [ʃ] than [k], although it may be any one of these three. Those words in which *ch* is sounded [k] are predominantly of Greek origin, such as "character" [kɛrɪktɚ], "chemistry" [kɛməstrɪ], "chimera" [kəmɪrə], "Christian" [krɪstʃən], and "alchemy" [ælkəmɪ].

If the *ch* word has come into English from French, an approximation of the original pronunciation may remain, as in "chagrin" [ʃəgrɪn], "chalet" [ʃæle], "champagne" [ʃæmpen], "chemise" [ʃəmiz], and "cha-peau" [ʃæpo]. Where such original pronunciations are not retained, the sound is [tʃ], as in "chap" [tʃæp], "chain" [tʃen], and "chalk" [tʃɔk]— either because the word has been anglicized or for other reasons. For the most part *x* is pronounced [ks] as in "except" [ɛksɛpt] or "exercise" [ɛksɚsaɪz], but there are occasional exceptions, such as "exaggerate" [ɛgzædʒɚet] and "example" [ɛgzæmpl̩], where [ks] is replaced by [gz]. In a few words either sound may be heard for *x*, as in "exit" [ɛksət] or [ɛgzət].

The phenomenon associated with doubled stops occurs with [k], of course. In such a phrase as "black cat" the usual pronunciation is [blæk:æt], with the characteristic prolongation of the hold. A certain amount of care needs to be taken with expressions of this sort since there is always the possibility that such a phrase as "like king" might become "liking" [laɪkɪŋ] or that "black cat" might be heard as "black hat" [blæk hæt]. This is obviously a matter of relatively minor importance since such phrases are in fact almost always pronounced in nearly identical manner and the meaning is usually inferred from context.

Even if one avoids errors arising from the variable spelling of [k], he may encounter problems. Certain combinations of sounds are incon-venient, particularly [sk] and [ks]. In the case of "ask" [æsk], for example, the pronunciation [æst] is very often heard in substandard speech. Care-less articulation of a word such as "accept" [æksɛpt] may lead to [əsɛpt], and [k] may be underpronounced or omitted in various other situations. Sounds in the [k] phoneme are involved in certain foreign-dialect errors. Some German speakers may conspicuously overaspirate the sound, whereas others may substitute a palatal or velar which loosely resembles [k]. Both French and Scandinavian speakers may give [k] somewhat less aspiration than would be normal for the English speaker; Scandinavians may produce a lax sound, but this is not true of the French.

For reasons that are not entirely clear, [k] seems to be among the English sounds that are relatively difficult. Many children are quite late in learning this sound, and the substitution of [t] for [k] is very frequently heard in infantile speech. Any kind of [k] also typically presents marked difficulties for the cleft-palate speaker or for the individual who has inadequate velopharyngeal closure for some other reason. In these cases [k] may be weak and distorted by perceptible nasal plosion or may be replaced by some nonstandard glottal or pharyngeal sound.

Exercises

1. In the following paragraph there are about 47 [k]'s. Try to identify these and to observe your pronunciation of them. How many are spelled with *k*? With *c*? With *q*? Check your pronunciation with the phonetic transcription at the end of these exercises.

A pleasant vocal quality is an aspect of cultured speech which ranks high in importance, although necessary facts about voice production cannot be included in this text. Voice and personality are connected in a unique way, and the key to an accurate appraisal of what most persons are really like can often be found in voice cues. Strength of character will be reflected by a manner of talking which is honest and forthright. If the voice is timid and weak, we account it no accident that a lack of courage lies back of this manner of talking. If one's thinking is chaotic and unclear, this laxity is certain to become known through vocal inflections; think clearly, and the groundwork has been laid for effective communication. There is little extra difficulty required in taking care that one's vocal skills are adequate to his needs and that his voice does not weaken his chances of success.

2. The following [k] words include representative examples of various allophones of [k] in different contexts and consonant combinations. Practice these and find other examples of each type.

Initiating consonant: coo, cur, Kay, key
Terminating consonant: ache, irk, oak, Ike
Initiating and terminating: cake, coke, cook, kick
Stronger consonant: become, income, recount, request
Weaker consonant: backer, bucket, taken, vacant
Initial blends: [sk] school, sky; [kr] crown, cry; [kl] clay, clip; [kw] queen, quite;[skr] scratch, screen; [skw] squash, squire
Final blends: [ks] backs, six; [kt] looked, parked; [ŋk] sank, think; [ŋks] thanks, honks; [ŋkt] linked, thanked; [sk] ask, risk; [rk] fork, park

3. Practice and try to add to the following lists of minimal pairs:

[k]—[g]		[k]—[t]	
came [kem]	game [gem]	back [bæk]	bat [bæt]
back [bæk]	bag [bæg]	backer [bækɚ]	batter [bætɚ]
backer [bækɚ]	bagger [bægɚ]	cone [kon]	tone [ton]
come [kʌm]	gum [gʌm]	cool [kul]	tool [tul]
could [kʊd]	good [gʊd]	lick [lɪk]	lit [lɪt]
Kay [ke]	gay [ge]	neck [nɛk]	net [nɛt]
lock [lɑk]	log [lɑg]	knock [nɑk]	not [nɑt]
locker [lɑkɚ]	logger [lɑgɚ]	pack [pæk]	pat [pæt]
pick [pɪk]	pig [pɪg]	pick [pɪk]	pit [pɪt]
racks [ræks]	rags [rægz]	racks [ræks]	rats [ræts]

[k]—[tʃ]	
ache [ek]	H [etʃ]
back [bæk]	batch [bætʃ]
cat [kæt]	chat [tʃæt]
Dick [dɪk]	ditch [dɪtʃ]
kill [kɪl]	chill [tʃɪl]
knock [nɑk]	notch [nɑtʃ]
pack [pæk]	patch [pætʃ]
pick [pɪk]	pitch [pɪtʃ]
racket [rækət]	ratchet [rætʃət]
suck [sʌk]	such [sʌtʃ]

Phonetic Transcription. The following is a transcription in GA of the paragraph in Exercise 1:

[ə plɛzənt vokəl 'kwɑlətɪ ɪz ən 'æspɛkt əv 'kʌltʃɚd spitʃ hwitʃ ræŋks haɪ ɪn ɪm'pɔrtəns, ɔlðo 'nɛsəserɪ fækts əbaʊt vɔɪs prə'dʌkʃən kə'nɑt bi ɪn'kludəd ɪn ðɪs tɛkst. vɔɪs ən ˌpɝsə'nælətɪ ɑr kənɛktəd ɪn ə junik we, ænd ðə ki tu ən 'ækjurət ə'prezəl əv hwʌt most pɝsənz ɑr rili laɪk kən ofən bi faʊnd ɪn vɔɪs kjuz. strɛŋθ əv 'kerɪktɚ wɪl bi rɪ'flɛktəd baɪ ə mænɚ əv təkɪŋ hwitʃ əz 'ɑnəst ən 'forθˌraɪt. ɪf ðə vɔɪs ɪz tɪməd ən wik, wi əkaʊnt ət no 'æksədɛnt ðət ə læk əv 'kɝrɪdʒ laɪz bæk əv ðɪs mænɚ əv təkɪŋ. ɪf wʌnz 'θɪŋkɪŋ ɪz ke'ɑtɪk ænd ˌʌn'klɪr, ðɪs læksətɪ ɪz sɝtən tə bɪ'kʌm non θru vokəl ɪn'flɛkʃənz; 'θɪŋk 'klɪrlɪ, æn ðə graʊnd wɝk həz bɪn led fɔr ɪ'fɛktɪv kəˌmjunə'keʃən. ðɛr ɪz lɪtḷ ɛkstrə ˌdɪfə'kʌltɪ rɪ'kwaɪrd ɪn tekɪŋ ker ðət wʌnz vokəl skɪlz ɑr 'ædəkwət tu ɪz nidʒ æn ðət ɪz vɔɪs dəz nɑt wikən hɪz tʃænsəz əv sək'sɛs.]

[g] as in go, again, beg

Common Spellings: g as in get, game
gg as in beggar, trigger
Also spelled *gh*, as in ghetto.

Production. The [g] is classified as a voiced linguavelar stop (or stop-plosive). It is produced like [k] so far as place of articulation is concerned, but it is voiced. Like other voiced stops, [g] tends to have less force of articulation than its unvoiced counterpart [k], and the sound ordinarily has no perceptible aspiration.

Pronunciation. Notes on the pronunciation of [g] parallel those for [k], but there are some additional considerations. As one might expect, the exact place of articulation may vary from a distinctly forward position to one well back on the soft palate. These extremes are approximated in the words "geese" [gis], where the front vowel leads to a forward position, and "gone" [gɔn], in which [g] is followed by the back vowel [ɔ]. Where the word contains the combination [gw], as in "language" [læŋgwɪdʒ], the [g] is made with lip rounding. A [g] followed by [l] results in lateral plosion, as in words such as "struggle" [strʌgl̩], "haggle" [hægl̩], and "wiggle" [wɪgl̩]; and a [g] before a nasal, of course, produces a nasal plosion, as in "stagnate" [stægnet].

Pronunciation rules for the letter *g* based on spelling are not too satisfactory because of the exceptions that must be made to any general principle. A final *g* is pronounced [g], although there are allowable differences in the extent of voicing in various words. A *gg*, as in "trigger" [trɪgɚ], also is normally [g], although in some words this spelling indicates a sound with some of the characteristics of a doubled stop. When an initial *g* is followed by a consonant letter or by *a, o,* or *u*, the pronunciation is quite reliably [g], since such exceptions as "gaol" [dʒel]—which once was [gel]—are exceedingly rare. This rule also holds generally true for the medial *g*, except where the *gh* combination is found. With respect to this digraph, an initial *gh* is always [g], as in "ghastly" [gæstlɪ] or "ghost" [gost], but is [f] in either medial or final positions, as in "laughter" [læftɚ] and "enough" [inʌf]. This rule is not entirely reliable, however, since a number of words which superficially appear comparable to "laughter" are not pronounced in a similar way. Examples that might be cited are "daughter" [dɔtɚ], "fought" [fɔt], and "fraught" [frɔt]. Note, too, the illogical spelling-pronunciation relationship in "hiccough" [hɪkʌp], but as far as the authors know, this is the only instance in English where *gh* is pronounced [p].

When an initial *g* is followed by the letters *i* or *e*, the pronunciation may be either [g] or [dʒ]. It is [g] in "get" [gɛt], "geese" [gis], "give" [gɪv], and "giddy" [gɪdɪ], but [dʒ] in such representative words as "gem" [dʒɛm], "gesture" [dʒɛstʃɚ], and "gin" [dʒɪn]. A medial *g* followed by *i* or *e* is usually pronounced [dʒ], as in "regent" [ridʒənt], "digest" [daɪdʒɛst], and "register" [rɛdʒəstɚ].

A final *ge* is usually [dʒ], as in "marriage" and "carriage." The pronunciation of many such words, which were originally borrowed from

French, has come to be quite thoroughly anglicized, but for numerous others the accepted pronunciation is still an approximation of the original French. Among them are "beige" [beʒ], "rouge" [ruʒ], and "mirage" [mɪrɑʒ]. In these cases a final [dʒ] usually would be considered substandard.

In the discussion of [k] we noted that the letter *x* usually calls for [ks], as in "six" [sɪks]. An exception must be made in many cases where *ex* is used as a prefix, since here the pronunciation is predominantly [gz]. Examples are "examine" [ɛgzæmən] or [ɪgzæmən], "exact" [ɪgzækt], and "exasperate" [ɪgzæspəret]. In what may seem to be comparable words, however, the pronunciation is more nearly [ks], as in "excite" [ɪksaɪt] and "except" [ɛksɛpt], in which a following unvoiced sound has exerted an influence.

When the combination *gn* occurs in an initial position, the *g* is silent, although it was pronounced at one time during the history of the language. There are a fair number of words with this spelling, such as "gnu" [nu], "gnaw" [nɔ], "gnarled" [nɑrld], and "gnome" [nom]. The *g* is also silent in a final *gn* or *gne* combination, as in "campaign" [kæmpen] or "champagne" [ʃæmpen]. One may find an occasional word where a medial *gn* is [n], as in "peignor" [penwɑr] or "seigneur" [sinjɝ]; but most often *g* and *n* are in different syllables when they occur medially, and each letter receives its conventional pronunciation, as in "stagnate" [stægnet] and "ignite" [ɪgnaɪt].

Except in dialect speech, the final letter *g* is never pronounced in an *ng* sequence; hence words such as "sing," "bring," and "wrong" are pronounced [sɪŋ], [brɪŋ], and [rɔŋ] in conformity with the rule that the final *ng* is to be pronounced [ŋ]. This convention has changed historically, since both [ŋ] and [g] were pronounced at one time, as in [sɪŋg]. A medial *ng* is usually [ŋg], as in "linger" [lɪŋgɚ], "finger" [fɪŋgɚ], or "stronger" [strɔŋgɚ], but there are some exceptions, such as "stranger" [strendʒɚ] and "ranger" [rendʒɚ].

If the preceding discussion of the pronunciation value of the letter *g*, alone and in various combinations, has seemed complicated and confusing, such a reaction is certainly understandable. The rules cited hold true in general and are hence of some value, but they scarcely provide a safe guide to usage, because of the many exceptions. Obviously this situation serves as a warning that one must be alert to exceptions and points to the necessity for intelligent use of a dictionary, combined with careful attention to the pronunciation of educated speakers.

In addition to the spelling-pronunciation pitfalls, difficulties with [g] parallel those noted for [k]. Both sounds in this pair frequently are involved in infantile speech errors, and the typical substitution of [d] for [g] is usually heard among children who also substitute [t] for [k]. Native English speakers may, of course, either underpronounce or over-pronounce the sound, but this is not a particularly common or con-spicuous fault. The dialect addition of [g] in such a word as "sing," so that it becomes [sɪŋg], is quite obtrusive. Some speakers with a non-English native language, such as German, sometimes unvoice [g] to the point where it is heard as [k], whereas others may weaken the sound to a fricative, as in the Spanish linguavelar [ɣ].

Exercises

1. Practice this [g] paragraph, making special note of the *g* problems discussed in the preceding section. Compare your pronunciation of the [g] words with the transcription following these exercises.

The emergence of speech in an infant is a great and wonderful thing. Psychologists recognize its beginning in what is sometimes called the prelinguistic period of growth. In the early months of growth adults should make a big game of the gurglings and cooings which are actually the genesis of articulation. The little beggar will then acquire agility in tongue and lip movements which later will be guided into recognizable words. The sounds he exhibits at this period beggar description, and the attempt to make an exact catalogue has exhausted observers who have made this attempt. Much early com-munication is by gesture, but as time goes by one must expect to get from the child stronger efforts to show true linguistic behavior in the form of recognizable words. One cannot exaggerate the great importance of motivation, for the biggest gains are made by the child who is in a stimulating world.

2. The following [g] words are representative examples of various allophones of [g] in different contexts and consonant combinations. Practice these and find other examples of each type.

Initiating consonant: gay, go, goo, guy
Terminating consonant: egg, erg, ugh, hog
Initiating and terminating: gag, gig, Greg, Grieg
Stronger consonant: ago, began, forget, regret
Weaker consonant: bargain, begger, biggest, struggle
Initial blends: [gr] green, grow; [gl] glass, glue
Final blends: [gz] bags, digs; [gd] bagged, logged

3. Practice and try to add to the following lists of minimal pairs:

[g]—[k]		[g]—[dʒ]	
bagging [bægɪŋ]	backing [bækɪŋ]	bag [bæg]	badge [bædʒ]
gall [gɔl]	call [kɔl]	bagger [bægɚ]	badger [bædʒɚ]
gap [gæp]	cap [kæp]	egg [ɛg]	edge [ɛdʒ]
gate [get]	Kate [ket]	gain [gen]	Jane [dʒen]
gauge [gedʒ]	cage [kedʒ]	gig [gɪg]	jig [dʒɪg]
ghost [gost]	coast [kost]	go [go]	Joe [dʒo]
guild [gɪld]	killed [kɪld]	goon [gun]	June [dʒun]
lag [læg]	lack [læk]	gust [gʌst]	just [dʒʌst]
rig [rɪg]	rick [rɪk]	log [lɑg]	lodge [lɑdʒ]
gum [gʌm]	come [kʌm]	slug [slʌg]	sludge [slʌdʒ]

[g]—[ŋ]		[g]—[d]	
bag [bæg]	bang [bæŋ]	gad [gæd]	dad [dæd]
bagging [bægɪŋ]	banging [bæŋɪŋ]	God [gɑd]	Dodd [dɑd]
big [bɪg]	Bing [bɪŋ]	gain [gen]	deign [den]
hug [hʌg]	hung [hʌŋ]	go [go]	dough [do]
log [lɑg]	long [lɑŋ]	grain [gren]	drain [dren]
rig [rɪg]	ring [rɪŋ]	goal [gol]	dole [dol]
rigger [rɪgɚ]	ringer [rɪŋɚ]	tag [tæg]	tad [tæd]
rug [rʌg]	rung [rʌŋ]	lag [læg]	lad [læd]
sag [sæg]	sang [sæŋ]	beg [bɛg]	bed [bɛd]
slug [slʌg]	slung [slʌŋ]	big [bɪg]	bid [bɪd]

Phonetic Transcription. The following is a transcription in GA of the paragraph in Exercise 1:

[ðɪ ə'mɝdʒəns əv spitʃ ɪn ən ɪnfənt ɪz ə 'gret ænd 'wʌndɚfəl θɪŋ. ˌsaɪ-kalədʒəsts 'rɛkəgˌnaɪz ɪts bɪ'gɪnɪŋ ɪn hwʌt ɪz 'sʌmˌtaɪmz kɔld ðə 'priˌ-lɪn'gwɪstɪk 'pɪrɪəd əv groθ. ɪn ðɪ ɝlɪ mʌnθs əv groθ ədʌlts ʃud mek ə 'bɪg 'gem əv ðə 'gɝglɪŋz ənd kuwɪŋz hwɪtʃ ar 'ækʃuəlɪ ðə 'dʒɛnəsəs əv artɪkju'leʃən. ðə lɪtl̩ begɚ wɪl ðɛn ə'kwaɪr ə'dʒɪləti ɪn tʌŋ ənd lɪp ˌmuvˌ-mənts hwɪtʃ letɚ wɪl bi gaɪdəd ɪntu 'rɛkəgnaɪzəbl̩ wɝdz. ðə saundz hi ɛg'zɪbəts æt ðɪs 'pɪrɪəd begɚ dɪ'skrɪpʃən, ənd ðɪ ətɛmpt tə mek ən ɛg'zækt 'kætəlɔg həz ɛg'zɔstəd əb'zɝvɚz hu həv med ðɪs ətɛmpt. mʌtʃ ɝlɪ kəˌ-mjunə'keʃən ɪz baɪ 'dʒɛstʃɚ, bət əz taɪm goz baɪ wʌn məst ɛk'spɛkt tə get frəm ðə tʃaɪld strɔŋgɚ ɛfɚts tə ʃo tru ˌlɪn'gwɪstɪk bɪ'hevjɚ ɪn ðə fɔrm əv 'rɛkəgnaɪzəbl̩ wɝdz. wʌn 'kænat ɛg'zædʒəret ðə gret ɪm'pɔrtəns əv motə'veʃən, fɔr ðə bɪgəst genz ar med baɪ ðə tʃaɪld hu ɪz ɪn ə 'stɪmjuletɪŋ wɝld.]

Before going on to a detailed description of [tʃ] and [dʒ], a few general facts about *affricates* should be brought out. First, do not be misled by the digraph nature of the symbols into supposing that [tʃ] and [dʒ] are combinations of sounds. Linguistically and physiologically these affricates are distinctive and phonemic, not blends of other sounds. In line with this fact, some phoneticians have chosen single symbols, often [č] and [ǰ], for the unvoiced and voiced affricates. Others, including the present authors, have preferred the IPA usage. Although it is not a major consideration, the digraph may possibly have some value in calling specific attention to the fricative breath release which is an essential feature of both [tʃ] and [dʒ].

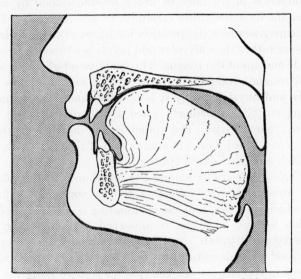

FIG. 11. Articulation adjustment for [tʃ] and [dʒ].

These sounds have several distinctive acoustic and articulation characteristics. An affricate may generally be thought of as a stop, but one with a special kind of plosion or breath release. Articulation of the sound is in the nature of an off-glide movement, with a prominent fricative element as an essential feature. The point of contact and the position during release resemble [t]–[d] and [ʃ]–[ʒ] only in a general way.

[tʃ] as in change, watch, patch

Common Spellings: ch as in chair, chicken
                              tch as in match, catch
                              t as in question, nature
                              Also spelled c, as in cello.

Production. The [tʃ] may be classified as an unvoiced lingua-palatal (or lingua-palato-alveolar) affricate. The sound is started by placing the tip and blade of the tongue in broad, firm contact with the front of the palate and, not infrequently, the alveolar ridge of the palate; the margins of the tongue are in contact with the teeth and gums laterally. The breath stream thus impounded is released in such a way as to create a distinct fricative sound, with the blade and tip of the tongue flattened and near the anterior palate and alveolar ridge. Velopharyngeal closure is complete, or nearly so. What is heard is the unique plosive-friction noise created in the front part of the mouth by the relatively forceful and, in comparison with a typical plosive, somewhat prolonged fricative breath release.

The production of [tʃ] may be much misunderstood by anyone who fails to examine its articulation carefully. In general outline, the starting tongue posture resembles the position for [t], except that it is palatal or palatoalveolar rather than alveolar and involves a broader area of contact by the blade and tip of the tongue. The fricative off-glide has a [ʃ] quality because the tongue contact is in the same area as it is for this sound, but acoustically and physiologically it is not the same. There may be some lip rounding on [tʃ], particularly when a lip-rounded vowel follows, as in the word "chew" [tʃu]. The sound is not doubled as are the non-affricate plosives, since there are always two affricates (illustrated by the phrase "catch children" [kætʃ tʃɪldrən]).

Pronunciation. Variations among the allophones in this phoneme are somewhat prominent. The initiating tongue contact is influenced by the sound which precedes, and the terminating position is affected by the sound which follows. This can be observed by contrasting the words "witch" [wɪtʃ] and "watch" [wɑtʃ]. In the former word the presence of the front vowel [ɪ] leads naturally to a somewhat advanced tongue contact, whereas in the latter word the contact is more posterior because of the adjacent back vowel [ɑ]. The exact fricative release posture reflects similar influences.

Note that the tongue position on the terminal portion of [tʃ] may be very much like that for [j]. Kenyon[16] points out that during the Early Modern period [tʃ] evolved from [tj] in a number of words. Without going into the details of these changes, the results can be indicated by the following alterations: "question" [kwɛstjən] has become [kwɛstʃən], "adventure" [ædvɛntjur] has become [ædvɛntʃɚ], and "literature" [lɪtərətjur] has become [lɪtərətʃur], or even [lɪtrətʃɚ]. It is reasoned that, when a linguapalatal glide such as [j] follows [t], a [tʃ] may emerge.

A comparable phenomenon occurs often when a word which would end with [t] if pronounced alone is followed by another which in isolation would begin with [j]. For instance, the words "that" [ðæt] and "young" [jʌŋ] quite naturally become [ðætʃʌŋ] in the phrase "that young man." Other expressions where this occurs are "that you" [ðætʃu], "what you" [hwɑtʃu], "hit your" [hɪtʃɚ], "can't you" [kæntʃu], and so on.

These pronunciations are entirely within the limits of acceptable speech and, indeed, efforts to retain a separate identity for [t] and [j] in such combinations might result in stilted, unnatural pronunciation. In the same way one generally need not try to retain [tj] in words such as "nature," "posture," and "Christian," since this pronunciation is not standard even in formal speech. The [tj], however, is still heard in a few words, such as "bestial," "overture," "literature," and "armature," which can without too much difficulty be pronounced [bɛstjəl], [ovɚtjʊr], [lɪtrətjʊr], and [ɑrmətjʊr], although "bestial" is possibly the only one of these which receives such a pronunciation with any frequency.

Through a curious combination of circumstances a number of words formerly pronounced with a [tʃ] now have a [ti] sound. "Beauteous," "piteous," and "bounteous," for example, are pronounced [bjutiəs], [pɪtiəs], and [bauntiəs] despite the fact that they were once [bjutʃəs], [pɪtʃəs], and [bauntʃəs]. The latter pronunciations may still be heard from time to time, but they are now substandard. It is presumed that the spelling eous was a factor in restoring a still older pronunciation, but the [tʃ] has been retained in "righteous" [raɪtʃəs] and in several other words of this sort.

Generally speaking, the combination tch is safely [tʃ]. The spelling ch may be [k], as in "ache" [ek], but is more often either [tʃ] or [ʃ]. A ture is usually [tʃ]. Words spelled tion are typically [tʃ], but there are some with [ʃ], such as "nation" [neʃən] and "ration" [reʃən]. For Americans nch is almost always [ntʃ], as in "inch" [ɪntʃ] and "wrench" [rɛntʃ], but the British may often pronounce these words [ɪnʃ] and [rɛnʃ].

Words where ch is pronounced [ʃ] are primarily those of French origin which have not become thoroughly anglicized, such as "chic" [ʃik], "chateau" [ʃæto], and "charade" [ʃəred]. These irregularities in usage lead to many errors in unfamiliar words. Examples include [tʃɪk] for "chic" and [tʃæle] or [tʃælɛt] for "chalet." The process of anglicizing still goes on, of course, and there seem to be at least a few common words where everyday usage has outstripped many standard dictionaries. A case in point is "chassis," which is almost always [tʃæsɪ] in American speech. Perhaps through mistaken spelling-pronunciation analogy the word "Chicago" [ʃəkɔgo] is sometimes heard as [tʃəkɔgo], and there are a few others like it.

The commonest difficulties involving the [tʃ] sounds come from variations in the spelling-pronunciation relationship. Sounds within this phoneme do not appear to be particularly hard for the foreign speaker to master, but he is frequently misled by spelling. This may trouble the Frenchman particularly, since the digraph ch is uniformly [ʃ] in his language.

It is possible, if one is too easygoing in his speech, to pass allowable limits in combining [t] and [j] into [tʃ], particularly when the following vowel is too markedly unstressed. For example, the phrase "aren't you" is legitimately [ɑrntʃu] in conversational speech, but there are at least some circumstances in which [ɑrntʃə] would not be in good taste. If [tʃ] is underpronounced, on the other hand, such a phrase as "wouldn't you," which is properly [wʊdn̩tʃu], might become indistinguishable from "wooden shoe" [wʊdn̩ʃu], or it might even degenerate into [wʊnʃə].

Errors associated with failure to learn [tʃ] are heard quite often in children with developmental speech delay. They usually take the form of substitution of [ʃ] and occasionally [ts]. When this happens, such a word as "chicken" [tʃɪkən] becomes [ʃɪkən] and "church" [tʃɝtʃ] may approximate [tsɝts]. The latter substitution is not unlike a foreign-dialect trait which is sometimes heard.

Before going on to [dʒ], we should note that, although [tʃ] and [dʒ] are the only English sounds classified as affricates, there are other sound combinations which may have affricate characteristics. One is the [tθ] combination, as in "eighth." Here the glide from a stop to a fricative is acoustically like an affricate, although the phonetician would say that this combination is not phonemic. Similar affricatelike pronunciations are heard in [ts] as in "outside" [aʊtsaɪd], "curtsey" [kɝtsɪ], and particularly in the rare words where [ts] is initial, such as "tsetse" [tsitsi]. Other examples of the tendency toward "affrication" are provided by the [dz] in "adds" [ædz], [tr] in "entrance" [ɛntrəns] or [ɛntrənts], and [dr] in "drag" [dræg]. These phenomena create no particular pronunciation problem.

Exercises

1. Identify the [tʃ] sounds in the following paragraph. Make special note of those instances where the [tʃ] may result from the influence of consonants on one another in adjacent words. The transcription following these exercises records 25 [tʃ] sounds. How does this compare with your pronunciation? How do you explain the differences?

Choices of all sorts face you as a college student, and you are indeed fortunate if you reach a wise decision half the time. To mention a few: you must first learn to choose the kind of work into which you propose to put your energies and talents for, perhaps, the remainder of your life. The amount of attention given to vocational counseling has not shown much change for a long time, which is most unfortunate. All too often, students make a selection without a chance to ask the kind of questions that should be answered before a decision is reached. You bet your life, so to speak, without watching the odds. The chap with an itch for learning has an enchanting vista before him, and a challenge to achieve. He cheats himself, really, if he does not range widely in the field of knowledge—not so much in search of "culture," but because time so spent will purchase something of lasting value.

2. The following [tʃ] words are representative examples of various allophones of [tʃ] in different contexts and consonant combinations. Find other examples of each type.

Initiating consonant: chair, chill, chore, chow
Terminating consonant: each, etch, itch, ouch
Initiating and terminating: church
Stronger consonant: perchance, recharge, unchecked, unchanged
Weaker consonant: picture, pitcher, purchase, urchin
Final blends: [ntʃ] bench, ranch; [ntʃt] punched, launched

3. Practice and try to add to the following lists of minimal pairs:

[tʃ]—[dʒ]

beseech [bɪsitʃ]	beseige [bɪsidʒ]
char [tʃɑr]	jar [dʒɑr]
chain [tʃen]	Jane [dʒen]
chin [tʃɪn]	gin [dʒɪn]
chive [tʃaɪv]	jive [dʒaɪv]
chumps [tʃʌmps]	jumps [dʒʌmps]
chunk [tʃʌŋk]	junk [dʒʌŋk]
match [mætʃ]	Madge [mædʒ]
search [sɝtʃ]	serge [sɝdʒ]
perch [pɝtʃ]	purge [pɝdʒ]

[tʃ]—[ʃ]

batch [bætʃ]	bash [bæʃ]
cheap [tʃip]	sheep [ʃip]
catch [kætʃ]	cash [kæʃ]
cheer [tʃɪr]	sheer [ʃɪr]
chin [tʃɪn]	shin [ʃɪn]
choose [tʃuz]	shoes [ʃuz]
ditch [dɪtʃ]	dish [dɪʃ]
match [mætʃ]	mash [mæʃ]
matching [mætʃɪŋ]	mashing [mæʃɪŋ]
watching [wɑtʃɪŋ]	washing [wɑʃɪŋ]

[tʃ]—[t]

batch [bætʃ]	bat [bæt]
catch [kætʃ]	cat [kæt]
cheer [tʃɪr]	tear [tɪr]
chew [tʃu]	too [tu]
chick [tʃɪk]	tick [tɪk]
chin [tʃɪn]	tin [tɪn]

match [mætʃ]   mat [mæt]
matching [mætʃɪŋ]   matting [mætɪŋ]
patch [pætʃ]   pat [pæt]
patcher [pætʃɚ]   patter [pætɚ]

[tʃ]—[k]

chain [tʃen]   cane [ken]
char [tʃɑr]   car [kɑr]
cheap [tʃip]   keep [kip]
chick [tʃɪk]   kick [kɪk]
chin [tʃɪn]   kin [kɪn]
ditch [dɪtʃ]   Dick [dɪk]
latch [lætʃ]   lack [læk]
patch [pætʃ]   pack [pæk]
patcher [pætʃɚ]   packer [pækɚ]
watching [watʃɪŋ]   walking [wakɪŋ]

Phonetic Transcription. The following is a transcription in GA of the paragraph in Exercise 1:

[tʃɔɪsəz əv ɔl sɔrts fes ju æz ə kɑlɪdʒ studn̩t, ənd ju ɚ ɪn'did fɔrtʃənət ɪf ju ritʃ ə waɪz dɪ'sɪʒən hæf ðə taɪm. tə mentʃən ə fju: ju məst fɝst lɝn tə tʃuz ðə kaɪnd əv wɝ·k ɪntə hwɪtʃ ju prə'poz tu pʌt jɔr 'enɚdʒɪz ən tælənts fɔr, pɚhæps, ðə rɪ'mendɚ əv jɔr laɪf. ði əmaunt əv ə'tenʃən gɪvən tu vo'keʃənəl 'kaunsəlɪŋ həz nat ʃon mʌtʃ tʃendʒ fɔr ə lɔŋ taɪm, hwɪtʃ ɪz most ʌn'fɔrtʃənət. ɔl tu ɔfən, studənts mek ə sə'lekʃən wɪ'ðaut ə tʃænts tə æsk ðə kaɪnd əv 'kwestʃənz ðət ʃud bi ænsɚd bɪ'fɔr ə dɪ'sɪʒən ɪz ritʃt. ju betʃɔr laɪf, so tə spik, wɪ'ðaut watʃɪŋ ði adz. ðə tʃæp wɪð ən ɪtʃ fɚ 'lɝnɪŋ hæz ən ˌen'tʃæntɪŋ vɪstə bɪ'fɔr ɪm, ənd ə 'tʃæləndʒ tu ə'tʃiv. hi tʃits hɪmself, riəlɪ, ɪf hi dəz nat rendʒ waɪdlɪ ɪn ðə fild əv 'nɑlɪdʒ—nat so mʌtʃ ɪn sɝtʃ əv 'kʌltʃɚ, bət bɪ'kɔz taɪm so spent wɪl pɝtʃəs 'sʌmpθɪŋ əv læstɪŋ vælju.]

[dʒ] as in June, age, edge

Common Spellings: *j* as in June, jump
g as in agitate, gem
dg as in edge, budge
Also spelled *dj*, as in adjust; *gg*, as in exaggerate;
d, as in soldier.

Production. The [dʒ] is classified as a voiced lingua-palatal (or lingua-palato-alveolar) affricate. The details of its articulation can be considered the same as for [tʃ], except that [dʒ] is voiced, and the earlier comments concerning the articulation features of [tʃ] also apply to [dʒ].

Pronunciation. As with the pairs of unvoiced-voiced stops, the voiced [dʒ] usually is articulated with less force than the voiceless [tʃ]. The [dʒ], however, shows the same characteristic variation of sounds within the phoneme and has all the other attributes of [tʃ] discussed in the preceding section.

The spelling-pronunciation relationships, and their historical development, follow much the same pattern for the two sounds. Uniform rules are difficult to frame. Except for an occasional proper noun, such as Jung [juŋ], and the rare final *j*, as in "Taj Mahal" [tɑʒ məhɑl], every letter *j*—between vowels or with *d*—is safely pronounced [dʒ]. Many of the possible [g] or [dʒ] pronunciations for *g* were treated in the section on [g], and these remarks should be reviewed; but some additional points can be mentioned here. An initial *gy* is always [dʒ], except for an occasional word such as "gynecology," which may be either [dʒaɪnəkɑlədʒɪ] or [gaɪnəkɑlədʒɪ]. Most final *gy* spellings call for [dʒɪ], although [gɪ] occurs in some words, such as "buggy" [bʌgɪ], and in the rare adjectival forms, such as "piggy" [pɪgɪ]. The [gɪ] does not invariably occur in adjectives, however; "edgy," for example, remains [ɛdʒɪ].

Although a final *ge* is usually [dʒ], it is practically impossible to infer the proper choice between [g] and [dʒ] for either an initial or medial *ge* spelling by reference to any rule. The [dʒ] sound for *gi* holds for all cases among reasonably common words, except:

gibbon	gilt	girl
Gibson	gimmick	girt
gift	gimp	girth
gig	gink	Gissing
giggle	Ginn	give
Gilbert	gird	gizzard
gild	girdle	begin
gill (of a fish)		

The *dg* is always [dʒ], except when [d] and [g] are found in separate syllables, as in "headgear" [hɛdgɪr]. The *dj* spelling is safely [dʒ].

The problems of the native speaker in pronouncing [dʒ] resemble those he encounters with [tʃ]. Thus, words which might have been spoken with [dj] or [dɪ] have quite generally acquired [dʒ], but this is not always the case, as illustrated by the substandard pronunciation of "Indian" [ɪndɪən] as [ɪndʒən] and of India [ɪndɪə] as [ɪndʒə]. Even though the shift of [dj] to [dʒ] in connected speech is perfectly natural in such instances as "did you" [dɪdʒu] and "would you" [wʊdʒu]—and any other pronunciation would incur the risk of becoming pedantic—too much unstressing of the following vowel in these circumstances can lead to somewhat objectionable pronunciations, such as [dɪdʒə] and [wʊdʒə]. It must be conceded, however, that these pronunciations are very common in conversational speech of all kinds. Among children those who have not learned [tʃ] usually cannot say [dʒ] either and may substitute [z] or an affricate [dz].

Although the foreign speaker may not find [dʒ] a difficult sound to make, he may commit pronunciation errors of a dialect nature. One whose native language is German may unvoice [dʒ] so extensively that such a word as "job" [dʒɑb] may be heard as [tʃɑp]—the [b] also becoming voiceless. More often the pronunciation problems of the foreign speaker arise from English spelling practices. As is well known, the letter *j* has the pronunciation value [j] in some languages, and for this reason the Swede, for instance, may give words such as "jump," "just," and "joke" an initial [j]. The French native who is learning English is likely to retain [ʒ] in places where the customary English pronunciation demands [dʒ]. Examples are the pronunciations [ʒʌst] for "just" [dʒʌst] or [ʒɑk] for "Jack" [dʒæk].

Exercises

1. Practice the following paragraph, paying special attention to the production and identification of the [dʒ] sound. The author's pronunciation is given at the end of these exercises.

The importance of regional speech usages in the United States has probably been exaggerated, if one can judge from the amount of heat generated by arguments on the subject. Generally speaking, genuine and major deviations from region to region are, at least to some degree, more imaginary than real. It seems to us poor pedagogy to badger students with suggestions that they reject what are, at the worst, only marginal usages. The average person is not unfavorably judged if he adjusts his speech reasonably well to the pronunciations he hears most often around him. To be practical, we must budge just a bit from the rigid positions we sometimes take. It is almost always safe to urge that the student be intelligible, but the barrage of criticisms sometimes laid down quite often verges on the ridiculous.

2. The following [dʒ] words are representative examples of various allophones of the [dʒ] in different contexts and consonant combinations. Practice these and find other examples of each type.

Initiating consonant: jay, jaw, Joe, joy
Terminating consonant: age, edge, ridge, urge
Initiating and terminating: George, judge
Stronger consonant: adjust, adjudicate, adjunct, rejuvenate
Weaker consonant: major, paging, region, Roger
Final blends: [dʒd] judged, raged; [ndʒ] orange, range; [ndʒd] ranged, tinged

3. Practice and try to add to the following lists of minimal pairs:

[dʒ]—[tʃ]

age [edʒ]	H [etʃ]
badge [bædʒ]	batch [bætʃ]
edge [ɛdʒ]	etch [ɛtʃ]
jeep [dʒip]	cheep [tʃip]
jeer [dʒɪr]	cheer [tʃɪr]
Jews [dʒuz]	choose [tʃuz]
Jill [dʒɪl]	chill [tʃɪl]
joke [dʒok]	choke [tʃok]
ridge [rɪdʒ]	rich [rɪtʃ]
surge [sɝdʒ]	search [sɝtʃ]

[dʒ]—[d] and [dz]

age [edʒ]	aid [ed]
badge [bædʒ]	bad [bæd]
jeep [dʒip]	deep [dip]
jeer [dʒɪr]	dear [dɪr]
ridge [rɪdʒ]	rid [rɪd]
age [edʒ]	aids [edz]
budge [bʌdʒ]	buds [bʌdz]
edge [ɛdʒ]	Ed's [ɛdz]
hedge [hɛdʒ]	heads [hɛdz]
ledge [lɛdʒ]	leads [lɛdz]

[dʒ]—[g]

badge [bædʒ]	bag [bæg]
budge [bʌdʒ]	bug [bʌg]
edge [ɛdʒ]	egg [ɛg]
jail [dʒel]	gale [gel]
James [dʒemz]	games [gemz]
jeer [dʒɪr]	gear [gɪr]
jet [dʒɛt]	get [gɛt]
Joe [dʒo]	go [go]
ledge [lɛdʒ]	leg [lɛg]
ridge [rɪdʒ]	rig [rɪg]

Phonetic Transcription. The following is a transcription in GA of the paragraph in Exercise 1.

[ðɪ ɪm'pɔrtəns əv 'rɪdʒənəl spitʃ 'jusɪdʒəz ɪn ðɪ ju'naɪtəd stets hæz 'prɑbəblɪ bɪn ɛg'zædʒəretəd, ɪf wʌn kən dʒʌdʒ frəm ðɪ əmaunt əv hit 'dʒenə,retəd baɪ 'ɑrgjumənts ɔn ðə 'sʌbdʒɪkt. 'dʒɛnrəlɪ 'spikɪŋ, 'dʒɛn-jəwən ənd 'medʒɚ ,dɪvɪ'eʃənz frəm rɪdʒən tə rɪdʒən ɑr, ət list tə sʌm dɪ'gri, mɔr ə'mædʒənɛrɪ ðən riḷ. ɪt simz tə ʌs 'pur 'pɛdəgodʒɪ tə bædʒɚ studənts wɪθ sə'dʒɛstʃənz ðət ðe ri'dʒɛkt hwʌt ɑr, æt ðə wɝst, onlɪ 'mɑrdʒənəl 'jusɪdʒəz. ðɪ 'ævrɪdʒ pɝsən ɪz nɑt ʌn'fevərəblɪ dʒʌdʒd ɪf hi ə'dʒʌsts ɪz spitʃ 'rizənəblɪ wɛl tə ðə prə,nʌnsɪ'eʃənz hi hɪrz most ɔfən əraund hɪm. tə bi 'præktɪkḷ, wi mʌst bʌdʒ dʒʌst ə bɪt frəm ðə rɪdʒəd pə'zɪʃənz wi 'sʌm,taɪmz tek. ɪt ɪz 'ɔlmost 'ɔlwez sef tə ɝdʒ ðət ðə studṇt bi ɪn'tɛlədʒəbḷ, bət ðə bə'rɑʒ əv 'krɪtə,sɪzəmz 'sʌm,taɪmz led daun kwaɪt ɔfən vɝdʒəz ɔn ðə ri'dɪkjuləs.]

10

THE FRICATIVES

[f], [v], [θ], [ð], [s], [z], [ʃ], [ʒ], [h]

[f] as in for, after, half

Common Spellings: *f* as in fly, after
ff as in affair, staff
ph as in phone, photograph
gh as in tough, laugh

Production. The [f] is classified as an unvoiced labiodental fricative. In its articulation the lower lip is raised into light contact with the cutting edge of the upper central teeth; an unvoiced breath stream is forced through this light contact, creating the friction noise which is the principal characteristic of sounds in the [f] phoneme. Velopharyngeal closure is complete, or nearly so.

Pronunciation. There is little phonetic variation within the [f] phoneme. When the sound is pronounced in isolation, the teeth usually are in contact with a point fairly well out on the carmine border of the lip, and it is convenient to teach and learn this standard position. In connected speech, however, the teeth more often touch the upper part of the inner surface of the lower lip, presumably because this involves less contrast with the positions of the articulators for preceding and following sounds. Although the tongue lies on the floor of the mouth when [f] is pronounced in isolation, it tends to assume the position of adjacent sounds when [f] is in context. To some extent, the lips may approximate the position for the following vowel during the production of [f], as in the word "fool" [ful]. When [f] follows a bilabial sound, there is some tendency for [f] to become a labial fricative, with the lips forming a slit and no true labiodental contact. This is illustrated by such words as "comfort" [kʌmfɚt], "cupful" [kʌpful], and "cab fare" [kæbfɛr]. These changes of the sound do not ordinarily lead to conspicuous deviations in pronunciation, however.

182

In contrast to many other sounds, the spellings which call for [f] are fairly regular. Both *f* and *ff* are uniformly pronounced [f], and the letters are never silent. Likewise, a *ph* at the beginning or end of a word calls for [f], except in the uncommon *phth* of "phthisic" [tɪzɪk] and a few other words. A medial *ph* is also [f], except in such words as "shepherd" [ʃepɚd] and in the occasional words where the digraph is given a [v] sound, as in some pronunciations of "Stephen" [stivən] or the British pronunciation of "nephew" [nɛvju]. Although an initial *gh* is never [f], this

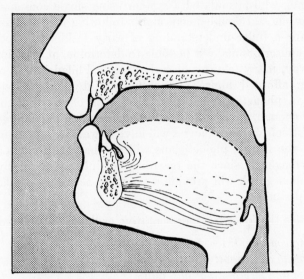

FIG. 12. Articulation adjustment for [f] and [v].

combination is usually pronounced [f] when it occurs in a medial or final position, with some exceptions in the case of words such as "neigh" [ne] and "weigh" [we], where the *gh* is silent, and in a few other circumstances.

Sounds in the [f] phoneme are among the easier ones to deal with in any kind of speech improvement program. Native speakers rarely have any conspicuous errors of pronunciation or articulation involving [f], presumably because the articulatory pattern for the sound is relatively simple. The speech therapist may occasionally encounter an individual who finds it difficult to make the necessary labiodental contact because of a dental malocclusion, but children are more likely to choose [f] as a substitute for another sound, as in the interchange of [f] and [θ], than they are to omit or substitute for it. Among foreign speakers failure to produce an acceptable [f] is not common, although a bilabial fricative, sometimes called the "candle-blowing" sound, may occasionally be heard in place of the more usual pronunciation.

Exercises

1. Find and practice the more than 40 [f] sounds in the following paragraph. How many are spelled *gh* or *ph*? Comment on the pronunciation of "have." Check the phonetic transcription following these exercises.

The idea of a phonetic alphabet to facilitate the recording of pronunciation with the greatest possible fidelity occurred to orthographers as early as the eleventh or twelfth century. One of the first was Orme, who formulated a system using single consonants after short vowels and doubled consonants following long vowels. Fortunately for a fuller understanding of early fashions in speech, his early manuscripts make it possible to determine, at least in a fairly rough way, many features of early speech. Philadelphia's own Ben Franklin afforded himself an excursion into spelling reform by offering a phonetic alphabet in 1768. His efforts did not weigh heavily enough, however, to affect the established philosophy of spelling. Such spelling changes will have to wait for a more favorable day. In the future, phoneticians will not have to rely as fully on written language, since the recordings of human speech by means of the phonograph will provide a far more accurate foundation for historical studies.

2. Practice the following representative examples of [f] words:

Initiating consonant: fee, fir, few, Fay
Terminating consonant: if, off, oaf, wife
Initiating and terminating: fife, fluff
Stronger consonant: affirm, conform, perform, refuse (v.)
Weaker consonant: laughing, offer, suffer, taffy
Initial blends: [fl] fly, flap; [fr] front, free
Final blends: [ft] laughed, left; [fs] laughs, stuffs

3. Practice the following minimal pairs:

[f]—[v]		[f]—[θ]	
face [fes]	vase [ves]	deaf [dɛf]	death [dɛθ]
fast [fæst]	vast [væst]	first [fɝst]	thirst [θɝst]
few [fju]	view [vju]	fought [fɔt]	thought [θɔt]
feel [fiəl]	veal [viəl]	fin [fɪn]	thin [θɪn]
fine [faɪn]	vine [vaɪn]	free [fri]	three [θri]
half [hæf]	have [hæv]	fret [frɛt]	threat [θrɛt]
proof [pruf]	prove [pruv]	Goff [gɑf]	Goth [gɑθ]
safe [sef]	save [sev]	half [hæf]	hath [hæθ]
serf [sɝf]	serve [sɝv]	miff [mɪf]	myth [mɪθ]
thief [θif]	thieve [θiv]	offer [ɔfɚ]	author [ɔθɚ]

[f]—[p]		[f]—[s]	
fast [fæst]	past [pæst]	after [æftɚ]	aster [æstɚ]
face [fes]	pace [pes]	fame [fem]	same [sem]
fact [fækt]	pact [pækt]	fed [fɛd]	said [sɛd]
fair [fer]	pair [per]	feel [fiəl]	seal [siəl]
far [far]	par [par]	feet [fit]	seat [sit]
feet [fit]	peat [pit]	fought [fɔt]	sought [sɔt]
feel [fiəl]	peal [piəl]	fun [fʌn]	son [sʌn]
fine [faɪn]	pine [paɪn]	fine [faɪn]	sign [saɪn]
laugh [læf]	lap [læp]	gaff [gæf]	gas [gæs]
suffer [sʌfɚ]	supper [sʌpɚ]	laugh [læf]	lass [læs]

Phonetic Transcription. The following is a transcription in GA of the paragraph in Exercise 1:

[ðɪ aɪdɪə əv ə fə'nɛtɪk 'ælfəbɛt tə fə'sɪlətet ðə rɪ'kɔrdɪŋ əv prə,nʌnsɪ-
eʃən wɪð ðə gretəst pɑsəbḷ fə'dɛlətɪ əkɜˑd tu ɔr'θɑgrəfɚz əz ɜˑlɪ əz ðɪ
ɪ'lɛvənθ ɔr twɛlfθ 'sɛntʃɚɪ. wʌn əv ðɪ fɜˑst wəz ɔrm, hu 'fɔrmjə,letəd ə
sɪstəm juzɪŋ sɪŋgḷ kɑnsənənts æftɚ ʃɔrt vaʊlz ən dʌbḷd kɑnsənənts
'falowɪŋ lɔŋ vaʊlz. 'fɔrtʃənətlɪ fɔr ə fulɚ ʌndɚ'stændɪŋ əv ɜˑlɪ fæʃənz ɪn
spɪtʃ, hɪz ɜˑlɪ 'mænjuskrɪpts mek ət 'pɑsəbḷ tə dɪ'tɜˑmən, æt lɪst ɪn ə
ferlɪ rʌf we, mɛnɪ fɪtʃɚz əv ɜˑlɪ spɪtʃ. fɪlə'dɛlfɪəz on bɛn fræŋklən əfɔrdəd
hɪmself ən ɛk'skɜˑʒən ɪntə spelɪŋ rɪ'fɔrm baɪ əfərɪŋ ə fə'nɛtɪk 'ælfəbɛt
ɪn sevəntin sɪkstɪ et. hɪz ɛfɚts dɪd nɑt we hɛvəlɪ ənʌf, haʊevɚ, tu əfɛkt
ðɪ ə'stæblɪʃt fələsəfɪ əv 'spelɪŋ. sʌtʃ 'spelɪŋ tʃendʒəz wɪl hæf tə wet fɔr ə
mɔr 'fevərəbḷ de. ɪn ðə fjutʃɚ, fonə'tɪʃənz wɪl nɑt hæf tə rɪ'laɪ əz fulɪ
ɑn rɪtṇ 'læŋgwɪdʒ, sɪns ðə rɪ'kɔrdɪŋz əv hjumən spɪtʃ baɪ minz əv ðə
fonəgræf wɪl prəvaɪd ə far mɔr ækjərət faʊn'deʃən fɔr hɪ'stɔrɪkḷ 'stʌdɪz.]

[v] as in very, over, move

Common Spellings: *v* as in victim, aver

Also spelled *f*, as in of; *vv*, as in flivver; *ph*, as in Stephen.

Production. The [v] is classified as a voiced labiodental fricative. It is made in essentially the same manner as [f], except for the addition of voicing. As with all pairs of unvoiced-voiced homorganic fricatives, [v] is articulated less forcibly than [f], and hence has a less marked friction noise. The general remarks made about variations in the production of [f] also hold true for [v]. Thus, there may be some deviations from what one might describe as a "standard" position of articulation because the tongue and lips tend to assume the position for the succeeding sound.

Pronunciation. Spellings of [v] are relatively consistent and uncomplicated. This sound is regularly required by the letter *v*, which is by far the most frequent spelling. The *vv* is also always [v], but this spelling is found in only a limited number of words, such as "flivver" [flɪvɚ] and "navvy" [nævɪ]. Also uncommon are those words where f and ph must be given the pronunciation [v].

One interesting peculiarity in the pronunciation of [v] is the rather extensive unvoicing which occurs naturally, and quite acceptably, when [v] is found in a final position or when it is followed by an unvoiced sound, as in "I have to go" [aɪ hæf tə go]. Where the [v] is in a relatively weak position (as an initiating consonant for an unstressed syllable), friction noise may be minimal. Compare, for example, the fricative "hiss" of [v] in "view" [vju] with the [v] sound in "lover" [lʌvɚ].

Foreigners may fairly frequently display dialect characteristics in their pronunciation of the English [v]. These are generally identified by the listener as a substitution of [f] for [v], so that "have you ever" [hæv ju ɛvɚ] is heard as [hæf ju ɛfɚ]. In many instances the error arises from the use of a fricative peculiar to the native language, such as the bilabial [Φ], rather than the [f]. Not uncommonly, dialect mistakes involve words in which f should be given a [v] sound but which are pronounced with [f] because of the misleading spelling. Since [v] is relatively easy to produce, it should not be troublesome for foreign speakers to learn. Native speakers usually pronounce [v] satisfactorily, except for the occasional person who unduly unvoices the sound or who slights it in careless speech.

Exercises

1. Practice the following paragraph, paying particular attention to [v]. Make a mental note of the relative amounts of friction and voice in the various examples of [v]. Comment on your pronunciation of "of." The author's transcription follows these exercises.

The vast majority of Americans have never viewed spoken language with the same concern they have shown for writing and reading. Nevertheless, if the modern vogue in education continues, it is very likely that the language arts curriculum will stress spoken communication to a greater degree. It has always been a matter of grave concern that, save in a few schools, so little time has been devoted to speech. The more obvious deviations have been given over to the speech therapist, but the average child has never enjoyed the advantages that training in speech could give. The inevitable consequence, which could have been predicted by anyone with vision, has been that the greatest poverty in the use of language has been in its everyday use in speaking. If we should sever our ties with tradition and revive an interest in our native tongue, there would be much that would prove of value to the child which would result from such a revision of the language arts curriculum.

2. Practice the following representative examples of [v] words:

Initiating consonant: V, vow, vie, view
Terminating consonant: eve, Irv, I've, you've
Initiating and terminating: verve, valve
Stronger consonant: convex, convey, review, revolt
Weaker consonant: braver, given, having, river
Final blends: [vd] starved, waved; [vz] saves, stoves

3. Practice making the required distinctions among the following minimal pairs:

[v]—[f]

believe [bɪliv]	belief [bɪlif]
five [faɪv]	fife [faɪf]
leave [liv]	leaf [lif]
live [laɪv]	life [laɪf]
save [sev]	safe [sef]
vault [vɔlt]	fault [fɔlt]
versed [vɝst]	first [fɝst]
very [vɛrɪ]	fairy [fɛrɪ]
vile [vaɪl]	file [faɪl]
vine [vaɪn]	fine [faɪn]

[v]—[ð]

breve [briv]	breathe [brið]
clove [klov]	clothe [kloð]
lave [lev]	lathe [leð]
loaves [lovz]	loathes [loðz]
V [vi]	thee [ði]
van [væn]	than [ðæn]
vat [væt]	that [ðæt]
vie [vaɪ]	thy [ðaɪ]
vine [vaɪn]	thine [ðaɪn]
vow [vau]	thou [ðau]

[v]—[b]

rove [rov]	robe [rob]
thieves [θivz]	Thebes [θibz]
V [vi]	B [bi]
vase [ves]	base [bes]
vat [væt]	bat [bæt]
versed [vɝst]	burst [bɝst]
very [vɛrɪ]	berry [bɛrɪ]
vet [vɛt]	bet [bɛt]
vie [vaɪ]	buy [baɪ]
vile [vaɪl]	bile [baɪl]

[v]—[z]

brave [brev]	braize [brez]
clove [klov]	close [kloz]
grave [grev]	graze [grez]
have [hæv]	has [hæz]
live [laɪv]	lies [laɪz]
pave [pev]	pays [pez]
rove [rov]	rose [roz]
V [vi]	Z [zi]
veal [vil]	zeal [zil]
wave [wev]	ways [wez]

Phonetic Transcription. The following is a transcription in GA of the paragraph in Exercise 1.

[ðə væst məˈdʒɔrətɪ əv əˈmɛrəkənz həv nɛvɚ vjud spokən ˈlæŋgwɪdʒ wɪθ ðə sem kənsɝn ðe həv ʃon fɚ raɪtɪŋ ən ˈridɪŋ. ˌnɛvɚðəˈlɛs, ɪf ðə madən vog ɪn ɛdʒuˈkeʃən kənˈtɪnjuz, ɪt əz vɛrɪ laɪklɪ ðət ðə ˈlæŋgwɪdʒ ɑrts kərɪkjələm wɪl strɛs spokən kəmjunəˈkeʃən tu ə gretɚ dɪˈgri. ɪt həz ˈɔlwɪz bɪn ə mætɚ əv grev kənsɝn ðæt, sev ɪn ə fju skulz, so lɪtḷ taɪm həz bɪn dɪˈvotəd tə spitʃ. ðə mɔr ˈɑbvɪəs divɪˈeʃənz həv bɪn gɪvən ovɚ tu ðə spitʃ θɛrəpəst, bət ðɪ ˈævrɪdʒ tʃaɪld həz nɛvɚ ənˈdʒɔɪd ðɪ ədˈvæntɪdʒəz ðət 'trenɪŋ ɪn spitʃ kʊd giv. ðɪ ɪnevətəbḷ 'kɑnsɪkwɛns, hwɪtʃ kʊd əv bɪn prɪ'dɪktəd baɪ 'ɛnɪwʌn wɪð vɪʒən, həz bɪn ðət ðə gretəst pavətɪ ɪn ðə jus əv 'læŋgwɪdʒ həz bɪn ɪn ɪts 'ɛvrɪde jus ɪn 'spikɪŋ. ɪf wi ʃʊd sɛvə aur taɪz wɪθ trədɪʃən ænd rɪ'vaɪv ən ɪntrəst ɪn aur 'netɪv tʌŋ, ðɛr wʊd bi mʌtʃ ðət wʊd pruv əv 'vælju tʊ ðə tʃaɪld hwɪtʃ wəd rɪ'zʌlt frəm sʌtʃ ə rɪ'vɪʒən əv ðə 'læŋgwɪdʒ ɑrts kərɪkjələm.]

[θ] as in think, pathway, myth

Common Spelling: th as in thick, bath

Production. The [θ] is classified as an unvoiced linguadental fricative. The sound is made by placing the flattened tip of the tongue on, or very

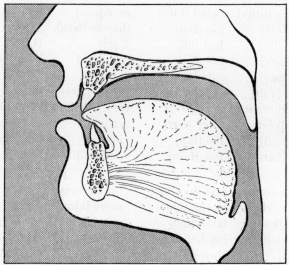

FIG. 13. Articulation adjustment for [θ] and [ð].

close to, the cutting edge of the upper central teeth and by directing an unvoiced breath stream through this light "closure." The lower teeth usually touch the undersurface of the tonguetip. Velopharyngeal closure is complete, or nearly so. What is heard is the friction sound created by passage of the breath stream between the tongue and the upper teeth.

In so far as acoustic characteristics are concerned, there are scarcely any perceptible differences among the various [θ] sounds used by native English speakers. There are, however, some slight differences in the exact place of articulation, and these should be noted. The [θ] can be described as an interdental sound, with the tonguetip between the teeth, and it is convenient to use this position when it becomes necessary to demonstrate an articulation position for the sound. Although [θ] can be produced this way in connected speech by some persons, the tongue-teeth contact is very often on the lower portion of the back surface of the teeth, just behind and above the cutting edge. This adjustment creates acoustic conditions which, for practical purposes, are equivalent to those for the interdental [θ]; hence there is no perceptible acoustic difference. One who is taught the interdental position may have some slight difficulty in incorporating such an articulation position into connected speech, but this problem usually solves itself without conscious attention.

Pronunciation. The spelling of [θ] is quite uncomplicated in the sense that it is represented only by the letters *th*. The situation is made complex, however, by the fact that these same letters are used for [ð]; furthermore, in a relatively small number of words *th* is pronounced [t]. Certain rules hold for most cases. An initial *th* calls for [θ] in nearly all words except pronouns and words related to them, such as "their" [ðɛr], "thy" [ðaɪ], "those" [ðoz], and "than" [ðæn]. A medial *th* is usually [ð] in words of Germanic or Anglo-Saxon origin, as in "mother" [mʌðɚ] and "lather" [læðɚ], but is [θ] in other cases. In a final position [θ] is the pronunciation for *th* in most words, except those with the spelling *the*, as in "writhe" [raɪð], "tithe" [taɪð], and "bathe" [beð]. There are a few additional exceptions to this rule, as illustrated by the word "smooth" [smuð], the verb "mouth" [mauð], and, in many phonetic contexts, "with" [wɪð].

In forming plurals [θ] changes to [ð] in many cases when [z] is added, although the pronunciation [θs] tends to remain if the sound is preceded by a consonant or by [ɪ], [ɛ], [ɔ], [ə], or an *r*-colored vowel. Compare the examples [pæðz], [tɛnθs], and [mɪθs]. As a matter of common sense, one must conclude that such rules—although valid in the main—become very laborious to apply.

It is perhaps futile to enumerate the rules governing a choice between [θ] and [ð] in standard speech, for the differences between these sounds are often minimal, and distinctions in meaning do not often depend upon whether one says [θ] or [ð]. There are such wide variations in the amount of voicing on these sounds that in conversational speech it often becomes really impossible to say whether a given sound should be considered a voiced [θ] or a voiceless [ð]. Phonetic context naturally has a great effect. Take, for example, the word "with," which would almost certainly be [wɪð] in the phrase "with many" but would be [θ] where a voiceless sound follows, as in "with Sam" [wɪθ sæm]. Acoustically [θ] is the weakest sound in the language, in the sense that it is produced with the least amount of physical energy and is therefore among the most difficult to hear. In learning the sounds of the language, the typical student has more difficulty with the reliable discrimination of [θ] and [ð] than with any other pair of unvoiced-voiced homophones.

The [θ] sound is often involved in articulation errors. One of the commonest defects in infantile speech is some sort of substitution for [θ], very frequently [f], as in [fɪŋk] for "think" [θɪŋk]. Presumably the relative difficulty in hearing the sound accounts for the fact that it is so often missing from the child's repertoire of sounds. Fortunately, once recognized, the [θ] usually proves relatively easy to learn. Substitution of [t] for [θ] is heard in some kinds of dialect speech, so that "with him" [wɪθ hɪm] becomes something like [wɪt ɪm]. Foreign speakers often have difficulty acquiring an English [θ], largely because there are many languages which have no comparable phoneme. Such persons may substitute [s], so that "think" [θɪŋk] becomes [sɪŋk]; less often, [f] may be used in place of [θ]. Another common substitution in foreign dialect is a dental [t̪] for [θ].

Exercises

1. In the following paragraph take care to distinguish [θ] and [ð]. Incidentally, note that words using the combination *nth* may be pronounced [nθ] or [ntθ]. Transcribe your own pronunciation of this paragraph before turning to the transcription following these exercises.

The earliest months of a child's life are rather important for his later growth in speech and language. One can think of the infant's birth cry, sounded as he draws his first breath, as the first thing he has done to prepare for speaking. By the third month, he will have begun to express many kinds of information through sound, although only Mother is likely to understand that one means that he is thirsty, another that he thinks the time has come for a change. Without conscious tutoring, he will learn the sounds of speech, and the pathways thus formed will be with him always. Later, by perhaps between the ninth or tenth and the twelfth month, he may have spoken his first word—an indescribably thrilling thing for both Father and Mother. Though the way will not always be smooth, through patience and understanding the child can be set upon the path which will lead to a full realization of his capabilities.

2. Practice the following representative examples of [θ] words:

Initiating consonant: thaw, thigh, thing, threw
Terminating consonant: earth, oath, wrath, youth
Stronger consonant: cathedral, unthinkable, pathetic, unthankful
Weaker consonant: author, birthday, healthy, nothing
Initial blends: [θr] thread, through
Final blends: [θs] births, youth's

3. Practice the following minimal pairs:

[θ]—[ð]

ether [iθɚ]	either [iðɚ]
loath [loθ]	loathe [loð]
mouth (n.) [mauθ]	mouth (v.) [mauð]
sooth [suθ]	soothe [suð]
sheath [ʃiθ]	sheathe [ʃið]
teeth [tiθ]	teethe [tið]
thigh [θaɪ]	thy [ðaɪ]
wreath [riθ]	wreathe [rið]

[θ]—[f]

author [ɔθɚ]	offer [ɔfɚ]
death [dɛθ]	deaf [dɛf]
three [θri]	free [fri]
oath [oθ]	oaf [of]
sheaths [ʃiθs]	sheafs [ʃifs]
thigh [θaɪ]	fie [faɪ]
thin [θɪn]	fin [fɪn]
thread [θrɛd]	Fred [frɛd]
threat [θrɛt]	fret [frɛt]
wreath [riθ]	reef [rif]

[θ]—[t]

death [dɛθ]	debt [dɛt]
hath [hæθ]	hat [hæt]
myth [mɪθ]	mitt [mɪt]
themes [θimz]	teams [timz]
thin [θɪn]	tin [tɪn]
thigh [θaɪ]	tie [taɪ]
thread [θrɛd]	tread [trɛd]
three [θri]	tree [tri]
thought [θɔt]	taught [tɔt]
through [θru]	true [tru]

[θ]—[s]

mouth (n.) [mauθ]	mouse [maus]
myth [mɪθ]	miss [mɪs]
themes [θimz]	seems [simz]
thigh [θaɪ]	sigh [saɪ]
thin [θɪn]	sin [sɪn]
thing [θɪŋ]	sing [sɪŋ]
think [θɪŋk]	sink [sɪŋk]
thong [θɔŋ]	song [sɔŋ]
thought [θɔt]	sought [sɔt]
thumb [θʌm]	some [sʌm]

Phonetic Transcription. The following is a transcription in GA of the paragraph in Exercise 1:

[ðɪ ɝlɪəst mʌnθs əv ə tʃaɪldz laɪf ɑr ræðɚ ɪm'pɔrtənt fɔr hɪz letɚ groθ ɪn spɪtʃ ən 'læŋgwɪdʒ. wʌn kən θɪŋk əv ðɪ ɪnfənts bɝθ kraɪ, saundəd əz hi drɔz hɪz fɝst brɛθ, æz ðə fɝst θɪŋ hi həz dʌn tə prɪ'pɛr fɚ spikɪŋ. baɪ ðə θɝd mʌnθ hi wɪl həv bɪ'gʌn tu ɛk'sprɛs mɛnɪ kaɪndz əv ɪnfɚ'meʃən θru saund, ɔlðo onlɪ mʌðɚ ɪz laɪklɪ tu ʌndɚ'stænd ðət 'wʌn mɪnz ðət hi ɪz θɝstɪ, ənʌðɚ ðət hi θɪŋks ðə taɪm həz kʌm fɚ ə tʃɛndʒ. wɪ'ðaut kʌnʃəs 'tutərɪŋ, hi wɪl lɝn ðə saundz əv spɪtʃ, ænd ðə 'pæθwez ðʌs fɔrmd wɪl bi wɪθ hɪm 'ɔlwez. letɚ, baɪ pɚhæps bɪ'twin ðə naɪnθ ɚ tɛnθ ænd ðə twɛlfθ mʌnθ, hi me həv spokən hɪz fɝst wɝd—æn ɪndə'skraɪbəblɪ 'θrɪlɪŋ θɪŋ fɔr boθ fɑðɚ ən mʌðɚ. ðo ðə we wɪl nat 'ɔlwɪz bi smuð, θru peʃəns ən ʌndɚ'stændɪŋ ðə tʃaɪld kən bi sɛt əpɑn ðə pæθ hwɪtʃ wəl lid tu ə ful rɪələ'- zeʃən əv hɪz kepə'bɪlətɪz.]

[ð] as in that, other, bathe

Common Spellings: *th* as in them, breathe

Production. The [ð] is classified as a voiced linguadental fricative. It is made in essentially the same way as [θ], with, of course, the addition of voicing and a lessening of fricative force.

Pronunciation. Most of the general considerations affecting the pronunciation of [ð] can be inferred from the discussion of [θ] and need not be repeated in detail. The variations in place of articulation are similar for the two sounds, but in neither case do they produce any prominent acoustic differences. Perhaps the greatest changes that take place in sounds within the [ð] phoneme are those which come from a tendency to unvoice the initial and final sounds to varying degrees in conversational speech. The spelling-pronunciation relationships also were covered in the notes on [θ]. The sound [ð] is always spelled *th*, but of course this digraph is commonly pronounced [θ] and [t] also.

The errors involving [ð] are, in general, counterparts of those encountered with sounds in the [θ] phoneme. Children who do not master [θ] usually fail also in learning [ð] and commonly substitute [v], with resulting pronunciations such as [væt] for "that" [ðæt] or [mʌvɚ] for "mother" [mʌðɚ]. The [diz] and [doz] of dialect speech (for "these" and "those") are very familiar. Foreign speakers face the same kinds of difficulty with [ð] as they do with [θ]. They may also unvoice [ð] to the point of substituting [θ], an error which is quite common among persons with a German- or Scandinavian-language background.

Exercises

1. In the following paragraph there is a generous sampling of [ð] and a sprinkling of [θ]. As you practice the selection, make sure to distinguish between them. Comment on the pronunciation of "with" and its compounds. The author's transcription follows these exercises.

Those of us who are fast oxidizing, as some heathen has scathingly put it, look back on the healthy days of our childhood growth as without a doubt the most glorious period in American history. Life did not always go smoothly to be sure, and there were many tribulations that faced the youths of this bygone day. I think they must have been made of sterner stuff, for instance, to have withstood the medication that was the order of the day. It bothered my brother not at all, but as I watched my father measure out a generous spoonful of thick and loathsome castor oil, knowing that another would be mine, I remember I would literally writhe in expectant agony, and perspiration would bathe my brow. On these occasions my thoughtful mother was quick to show the white feather; she could not watch in comfort, so prudently withdrew. Later she would soothe me as best she could. I do not know whether this nostrum is

still being ladled out or not, but if it is, then all the orchids that
have been thrust at the feet of medical scientists should have been
left to wither on their vines.

2. Practice the following representative examples of [ð] words:

Initiating consonant: thee, they, thou, though
Terminating consonant: bathe, clothe, smooth, soothe
Stronger consonant: although, to these, to them, without
Weaker consonant: bother, breathing, other, rather
Final blends: [ðz] bathes, breathes; [ðd] clothed, soothed

3. Practice the following minimal pairs:

[ð]—[d]		[ð]—[z]	
bathe [beð]	bayed [bed]	breathe [brið]	breeze [briz]
breathe [brið]	breed [brid]	bathe [beð]	bays [bez]
father [fɑðɚ]	fodder [fɑdɚ]	clothe [kloð]	close [kloz]
loathe [loð]	load [lod]	lathe [leð]	lays [lez]
their [ðɛr]	dare [dɛr]	seethe [sið]	sees [siz]
they [ðe]	day [de]	sheathe [ʃið]	she's [ʃiz]
thy [ðaɪ]	die [daɪ]	teethe [tið]	tease [tiz]
thine [ðaɪn]	dine [daɪn]	thee [ði]	Z [zi]
lathe [leð]	laid [led]	tithe [taɪð]	ties [taɪz]
wreathe [rið]	read [rid]	writhe [raɪð]	rise [raɪz]

[ð]—[θ]
See [θ]–[ð].

[ð]—[v]
See [v]–[ð].

Phonetic Transcription. The following is a transcription in GA of the
paragraph in Exercise 1:

[ðoz əv ʌs hu ar fæst 'aksə,daɪzɪŋ, æz sʌm hɪðən həz 'skeðɪŋlɪ pʌt ɪt,
lʊk bæk ɔn ðə hɛlθɪ dez əv aʊr 'tʃaɪld,hʊd groθ æz wɪ'ðaʊt ə daʊt ðə most
'glɔrɪəs 'pɪrɪəd ɪn ə'mɛrəkən hɪstərɪ. laɪf dɪd nɑt 'ɔlwɪz go so 'smuðlɪ tə
bi ʃʊr, æn ðer wɚ mɛnɪ ,trɪbju'leʃənz ðət fest ðə juðz əv ðɪs 'baɪgɔn de.
aɪ θɪŋk ðe mʌst əv bɪn med əv stɚnɚ stʌf, fɔr ɪnstəns, tə həv wɪθ'stud
ðə mɛdə'keʃən ðət wəz ðə ɔrdɚ əv ðə de. ɪt bɑðɚd maɪ brʌðɚ nɑt ə tɔl,
bət æz aɪ watʃt maɪ fɑðɚ mɛʒɚ aʊt ə dʒenərəs 'spunful əv ðə θɪk ən loðsəm
kæstɚ ɔɪl, noɪŋ ðət ənʌðɚ wəd bi maɪn, aɪ rɪ'mɛmbɚ aɪ wəd 'lɪtərəlɪ raɪð
ɪn ɛk'spɛktənt 'ægənɪ, æn pɚspə'reʃən wʊd beð maɪ braʊ. ɔn ðiz əkeʒənz
maɪ θɔtfəl mʌðɚ wəz kwɪk tə ʃo ðə hwaɪt fɛðɚ; ʃi kəd nɑt watʃ ɪn kʌmfɚt,
so prudəntlɪ wɪθ'dru. letɚ ʃi wəd suð mi əz best ʃi kʊd. aɪ du nɑt no hwɛðɚ
ðɪs nɑstrəm ɪz stɪl bɪŋ ledld aʊt ɚ nɑt, bət ɪf ɪt ɪz, ðɛn ɔl ðə ɔrkədz ðət
həv bɪn θrʌst ət ðə fit əv 'mɛdɪkl̩ 'saɪəntəsts ʃud həv bɪn left tə wɪðɚ ɔn
ðer vaɪnz.]

[s] **as in see, aside, class**

> *Common Spellings:*   s as in sea, ask
> ss as in class, pass
> sc as in science, scene
> c as in circle, cycle
> Also spelled *sch*, as in schizm; *ps*, as in psychology.

Production. The [s] is classified as an unvoiced lingua-alveolar fricative. Along with [z], [ʃ], and [ʒ], it is also frequently referred to as a sibilant. In producing this sound, the margin of the tongue is typically in contact

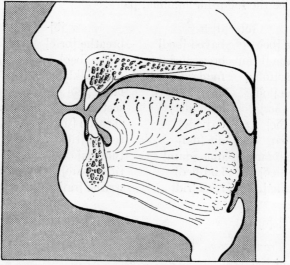

FIG. 14. Articulation adjustment for [s] and [z].

with the teeth and gums laterally, with the blade of the tongue near, but not touching, the alveolar ridge. This position forms a narrow breath channel at the midline of the tongue between the tongue and the anterior part of the hard palate, the alveolar ridge, and the teeth. Velopharyngeal closure is complete, or nearly so. The sound is made as the unvoiced breath stream is forced through the narrow channel between the blade of the tongue and the roof of the mouth. What is heard is the friction noise created as the breath stream strikes the alveolar ridge and then passes downward over the back surface of the upper teeth and outward across the cutting edges of the upper and lower teeth, which usually are almost together.

Among native speakers there is perhaps more variability in the manner of producing [s] than there is for any other sound. As a consequence, there are numerous acoustically different sounds within the phoneme.

The differences in mode of articulation involve principally the posture of the tonguetip and blade. Some individuals make [s] with the tonguetip behind the lower teeth, and others pronounce the sound with the tonguetip at various levels between this placement and a point behind the alveolar ridge. In any case, however, the sounds in this phoneme consist of a friction noise created by directing a concentrated jet of air against a hard surface, and the different tongue positions may not change significantly the acoustic conditions for [s]. Lip positions for [s] may also vary considerably, because of phonetic context, but these do not change the sound acoustically to any important degree. Entirely acceptable sounds can be made with the high, lower, or some intermediate position of the tonguetip, since the breath stream strikes approximately the same surfaces in any case and the acoustic conditions are nearly identical, provided that appropriate channeling is accomplished. In teaching or learning [s] by phonetic placement methods, the low position of the tongue is often preferred, as it seems easier to obtain adequate grooving from this position.

In summary, the essential articulation adjustments for [s] are as follows: (1) the margins of the tongue must be in contact with the teeth and gums so that all lateral escape of breath is prevented, (2) the channel between the tongue and roof of the mouth must be sufficiently narrow to concentrate the breath stream, and (3) the jet of air must be directed against the surfaces at the front of the mouth with enough force to produce an acoustically acceptable friction noise, but not with excessive pressure.

Pronunciation. The spelling-pronunciation rules governing [s] are entirely too complex and too subject to exception to be of much practical use in determining accepted pronunciations. In general, an initial *s* is always [s], but in a medial or final position the letter may be either [s] or [z]. There is really no easy rule for a medial *s*, but examples of the two pronunciations are found in "useful" [jusfəl], "resolve" [rɪzɑlv], "casing" [kesɪŋ], and "reserve" [rɪzɝv]. A final *s* remains [s] when it follows a voiceless consonant to form the plural of nouns, as in "hats" [hæts], "caps" [kæps], "cuffs" [kʌfs], and so on. It is usually voiced, however, if the preceding consonant is voiced, as in "beds" [bɛdz], "legs" [lɛgz], "cabs" [kæbz], and the like. When the plural is spelled *es*, the pronunciation is most often [z], as in "classes" [klæsəz], "horses" [hɔrsəz], "mashes" [mæʃəz], or "masses" [mæsəz]. The third person singular of verbs is also [s] if the preceding consonant is voiceless, as in "slaps" [slæps], "takes" [teks], or "cuts" [kʌts], but it becomes [z] if the preceding sound is voiced, as in "rubs" [rʌbz], "shows" [ʃoz], and "carves" [kɑrvz].

Unless it is mute, as in "debris" [debri], a final *s* which follows *a, i, o,* or *u* is generally pronounced [s]. Examples are "canvas" [kænvəs], "this" [ðɪs], "pathos" [peθɑs], and "bus" [bʌs]. An exception must be made for the inflected forms of nouns and verbs, such as "was" [wɑz] or [wʌz] and "has" [hæz], and for a few other words, including "his" [hɪz] and "whereas" [hweræz].

In the case of final se there is no reliable rule to govern the choice of [s] or [z]. The endings -rse, -lse, -nse, and -pse are pronounced [s] with few exceptions. In a number of cases where noun and verb forms have the same spelling, the final s is [s] for the noun and [z] for the verb. Examples are "close" [klos] (n.)–[kloz] (v.) and "use" [jus] (n.)–[juz] (v.). Unfortunately this convention does not always hold. Silent s letters are fairly common, as in "island" [aɪlənd], "chassis" [tʃæsɪ], and "corps" [kɔr], but again there is no reliable rule which can be easily applied.

The ss is not much easier to deal with. It never occurs as an initial spelling, of course, but at the end of a word the pronunciation [s] is always heard. In some cases a medial ss has the pronunciation [s]—for example, in words derived from others ending in ss, such as "massive" [mæsɪv] (derived from [mæs]) and "classify" [klæsəfaɪ] (from [klæs]); in others ss is [ʃ], as in "emission" [ɪmɪʃən]. The prefixes dis-, diss-, mis-, and miss- are nearly always [s], with a few exceptions pronounced [z].

The initial ps, which is not a particularly common spelling, is always [s], as in "psychic" [saɪkɪk] or "psalm" [sɑm]. When followed by e, i, or y, the initial letters sc are [s], as in "scene" [sin], "scion" [saɪən], and "scythe" [saɪð]. The same holds for any word in common use beginning with ce, ci, or cy, as in "cease" [sis], "circle" [sɝkl̩], and "cycle" [saɪkl̩]. Exceptions must be made for "sceptic" [skɛptɪk] and "cello" [tʃɛlo].

Perhaps special attention should be called to the way in which an [sj] combination, when it occurs in connected speech, may bring about a change in what would otherwise be [s]. Thus, although "kiss" [kɪs] ends in [s] when it is spoken alone and in most contexts, the phrase "kiss you" in conversational speech is usually [kɪʃu]; it is quite unnatural, in fact, for the speaker to make any effort to retain [s] and to strive for [kɪs ju]. The phrase "pass you" [pæʃu] illustrates the same principle. A parallel to the kind of phonetic force that is operating here has brought about a comparable change with [sj] and [sɪ] combinations within words, so that "associate" is almost universally [əsoʃiet], "appreciate" is [əpriʃiet], and "vicious" is [vɪʃəs]; other pronunciations would at least be pedantic. The assimilative changes in connected speech are sometimes less marked than in the examples given.

Articulation difficulties other than those arising from spelling irregularities are numerous. The rather wide variation in [s] among persons with acceptable speech has already been mentioned, but sounds outside any allowable limits are common. The underpronounced [s], which is weak or "fuzzy," may be heard, but the strident and "hissy" sound is much more obtrusive. In most cases this rather unpleasant effect is the result of excessive breath pressure or too narrow a constriction of the breath channel. In some cases an objectionable whistle may be heard.

Perhaps the most conspicuous nonstandard [s], when it is heard in English, is the lateral lisp. Here the sound is made with the tonguetip in contact with the alveolar ridge, much as for [l], so that the breath stream is forced laterally over the sides of the tongue and against the teeth and cheeks. Such a sound is particularly conspicuous when the articulation is forceful. This kind of misarticulation is often extended to all the other sibilant sounds and the affricates as well.

In the field of speech disorders, defective articulation of [s] is quite frequently associated with a dental malocclusion. Since the fricative noise for [s] depends in part on directing the breath stream against the upper central teeth, any deformity which disturbs the occlusion may make it difficult for the speaker to produce the sound. An underbite, overbite, or an abnormal opening in the bite may affect articulation of the sibilants. Sounds in the [s] phoneme are among the last to be learned by many children; hence omissions of, and substitutions for, the sound are very common in infantile speech. The pronunciation of "see" as [θi] instead of [si] is typical, but other voiceless sounds, such as [h], [f], or even [t], may be used. There are doubtless some reasonably complex factors which account for the frequency with which [s], and to a lesser extent other sibilants, present learning difficulties for children. It may be that the grooving of the tongue required for this sound simply demands muscular coordinations too precise for young children.

For the proper articulation of [s] and other sibilants, not only must tooth and jaw alignment be satisfactory and tongue coordination be well learned but also the hearing of the speaker must be sufficiently acute, especially in the high frequencies. Because of the importance of very high frequencies to the recognition of the sibilants and because of the frequency with which high-tone hearing losses are encountered in both children and adults, hearing loss and defective [s] often go together.

Foreign speakers also have difficulty with [s]. A strongly aspirated [s] is likely to color the English pronunciation of those whose native language is German. This is also true of the French, but to a less marked degree. Still other languages have varieties of [s] which sound somewhat strange when transferred to English diction. Voicing of the sound so that it approximates [z] is also a dialect error.

Exercises

1. In pronouncing the following paragraph, one of the authors used [s] 43 times. Compare this figure with one you obtain for your own pronunciation. Beware of confusions arising from non-*s* spellings and from

[z] sounds which are spelled with the letter *s*. The author's transcription is given at the end of these exercises.

It is interesting how certainly a listener can sense the emotional reactions of a speaker through the nuances of his vocal quality and inflection. No trained psychologist is necessary to advise us that someone we chance to meet is passionately opposed to an idea that may come under discussion. Nor are we likely to miss the fact that his feelings have been hurt by a fancied snub or slight, no matter how earnestly he may seek to dissemble. There is perhaps no better or more scientific way to assess emotions than through voice, for the speaker quite unconsciously reveals his true feelings in this way. Most psychiatrists would tell us that they can fix with considerable accuracy the intensity of a neurosis by observing the patient's voice.

2. Practice the following representative examples of [s] words:

Initiating consonant: see, say, saw, sir
Terminating consonant: ace, ice, us, use
Initiating and terminating: cease, sass, source, souse
Stronger consonant: concern, consist, instead, restore
Weaker consonant: fasten, lesson, passing, possible
Initial blends: [sk] scare, sky; [skr] scream, screw; [skw] square, squeak; [sl] slant, slip; [sm] smoke, smooth; [sn] snake, snow; [sp] spare, spoil; [spl] splash, split; [spr] sprain, spring; [st] stay, stop; [str] straight, street; [sw] sway, swell
Final blends: [fs] cuffs, staffs; [ks] lacks, talks; [lts] belts, wilts; [mps] bumps, stamps; [nts] once, plants; [ŋks] tanks, thinks; [ps] lips, tops; [rs] force, farce; [rts] arts, forts; [st] first, past; [sts] lasts, posts; [ts] hits, lets; [θs] deaths, growths; [ntst] fenced, bounced; [sk] bask, mask

3. Practice the following minimal pairs:

[s]—[z]		[s]—[ʃ]	
base [bes]	bays [bez]	class [klæs]	clash [klæʃ]
close (adj.) [klos]	close (v.) [kloz]	close (adj.) [klos]	cloche [kloʃ]
lace [les]	lays [lez]	lass [læs]	lash [læʃ]
lice [laɪs]	lies [laɪz]	mass [mæs]	mash [mæʃ]
race [res]	rays [rez]	same [sem]	shame [ʃem]
rice [raɪs]	rise [raɪz]	see [si]	she [ʃi]
seal [sil]	zeal [zil]	sin [sɪn]	shin [ʃɪn]
see [si]	Z [zi]	so [so]	show [ʃo]
sink [sɪŋk]	zinc [zɪŋk]	son [sʌn]	shun [ʃʌn]
use (n.) [jus]	use (v.) [juz]	sore [sor]	shore [ʃor]

[s]—[t]		[s]—[θ]	
base [bes]	bait [bet]	Goss [gɑs]	Goth [gɑθ]
lice [laɪs]	light [laɪt]	lass [læs]	lath [læθ]
mass [mæs]	mat [mæt]	mass [mæs]	math [mæθ]
pass [pæs]	pat [pæt]	moss [mɑs]	moth [mɑθ]
race [res]	rate [ret]	pass [pæs]	path [pæθ]
rice [raɪs]	right [raɪt]	race [res]	wraithe [reθ]
same [sem]	tame [tem]	sick [sɪk]	thick [θɪk]
see [si]	T [ti]	sinking [sɪŋkɪŋ]	thinking [θɪŋkɪŋ]
sick [sɪk]	tick [tɪk]	souse [saʊs]	south [saʊθ]
so [so]	toe [to]	use (n.) [jus]	youth [juθ]

Phonetic Transcription. The following is a transcription in GA of the paragraph in Exercise 1:

[ɪt ɪz ɪntərɛstɪŋ haʊ sɝtənlɪ ə lɪsənɚ kən sɛns ðɪ imoʃənəl ri'ækʃənz əv ə spikɚ θru ðə 'nuɑnsəz əv ɪz vokəl 'kwɑlətɪ ən ɪn'flɛkʃən. no trend ˌsaɪ'kɑlədʒəst ɪz 'nɛsəsɛrɪ tu ədvaɪz ʌs ðət 'sʌmˌwʌn wi tʃæns tə mit ɪz 'pæʃənətlɪ əpozd tu ən aɪ'dɪə ðət me kʌm ʌndɚ dɪs'kʌʃən. nɔr ɑr wi laɪklɪ tə mɪs ðə fækt ðət ɪz filɪŋz həv bɪn hɝt baɪ ə 'fænsɪd snʌb ɔr slaɪt, no mætɚ haʊ ɝnəstlɪ hi me sik tʊ dɪ'sɛmbl̩. ðɛr ɪz pɚhæps no bɛtɚ ɔr mɔr saɪən'tɪfɪk we tu əsɛs i'moʃənz ðæn θru vɔɪs, fɔr ðə spikɚ kwaɪt ʌn'kɑnʃəslɪ rɪ'vilz hɪz tru 'filɪŋz ɪn ðɪs we. most səkaɪətrəsts wʊd tɛl əs ðət ðe kən fɪks wɪð kən'sɪdərəbl̩ ækjərəsɪ ðɪ ɪn'tɛnsətɪ əv ə nurosəs baɪ əb'zɝvɪŋ ðə peʃənts vɔɪs.]

[z] as in zero, plaza, jazz

Common Spellings: *z* as in zero, fez

                    s as in has, his

                    zz as in buzz, razz

                    Also spelled *sc,* as in discern; *x,* as in xylophone

Production. The [z] is classified as a voiced lingua-alveolar fricative. The details of articulation described for [s] also apply to [z], except for the addition of voicing and the slightly less forceful articulation.

Pronunciation. After the rather extended treatment of [s], the discussion of [z] can be relatively short. All the preceding remarks on the variability of tongue and lip positions are equally pertinent for both [s] and [z], or nearly so. Perhaps the somewhat less forceable articulation of [z] makes its limits of acceptable pronunciation somewhat broader than for [s]. The tongue posture any given speaker employs for [s] is likely to be duplicated for his [z] sounds, although this is not always the case.

Special note should be taken of the tendency to unvoice [z], particularly in initial and final positions. For example, when a typical English speaker says "zebra," the initial sound is much less distinctly voiced than is the medial [z] in "plaza" [plæzə]. A similar tendency to lighten voicing exists with final sounds, as in "keys" and "please." If one listens attentively, he may even hear speakers who completely unvoice these final [z] sounds. Such variations need not be thought of as errors unless unvoicing is extreme, but attention to voicing is an aspect of reasonably careful articulation.

With respect to spelling, [z] is the sound for the letter z and for zz. Under certain conditions, discussed in connection with [s], the letter s represents [z]. The words in which [z] is spelled sc, ss, or x are relatively few, although all words beginning with x should be pronounced with an initial [z] sound, except in the special case of "X ray" and its derivatives.

Pronunciation problems with [z] are comparable to those noted for [s], although ordinarily somewhat less marked. With many words which might be pronounced with either [s] or [z]—or an unvoiced [z]—the distinction is not critical for good pronunciation. It does not matter, for instance, whether one pronounces the word "discern" as [dɪzɜ·n] or [dɪsɜ·n], or whether "disdain" is spoken [dɪzden] or [dɪsden]. Similar examples could be cited almost endlessly. Unvoicing of [z] may reach the point of substandard dialect, however, and in the absence of rules which can easily be applied, the student should be alert to the necessity for paying careful attention to the usages of good speakers with whom he associates and to the recommendations of his dictionary. The assimilative changes characteristic of [sj] and [sɪ] combinations have a counterpart in those for [zj] and [zɪ]. Thus, "as you" always approximates [æʒu] in conversational speech, and although the extent of the change from [z] to [ʒ] may be greater in some cases than in others, most efforts to retain [zj] bring about overprecise pronunciation.

The defects of speech which affect [z] are much the same as those mentioned in the notes on [s], and the person who has difficulty with one of these sounds is likely to make similar errors in articulating the other. In some foreign dialects the [z] sounds may differ somewhat from those commonly heard in English, particularly in being more strongly articulated or more extensively devoiced.

Exercises

1. Practice the following selection, which has about 30 [z] sounds. The author's transcription follows these exercises.

Modern jazz music has both its devotees and its detractors. Where it originated is not certain, although many think its characteristic syncopated rhythms arose in the alleys and byways of New Orleans as a cousin to folk melodies. Chicago and its environs became the jazz capital of the world in the 1920s, an age which was in all ways an amazing period in contemporary American history. The argument as to whether such music is a kind of disease or a genuine art form still rages, and the strains of swing or the exaggerated beat of "rock and roll" continue to dismay or please the listener, depending on his fancies.

2. Practice the following representative examples of [z] words:

Initiating consonant: zee, Zoe, zoo, xi
Terminating consonant: as, ease, eyes, is
Initiating and terminating: Czars, Z's, Zoe's, zoos
Stronger consonant: deserve, disaster, nasality, resign
Weaker consonant: dozen, easy, pleasant, using
Final blends: [bz] jobs, rubs; [dz] beds, fords; [gz] bags, digs; [lz] bells, fills; [mz] comes, swims; [nz] or [ndz] hands, winds; [ŋz] brings, sings; [rz] hears, wears; [rdz] boards, beards; [ðz] bathes, breathes; [vz] saves, stoves; [zd] caused, used

3. Practice the following minimal pairs:

[z]—[s]		[z]—[d]	
his [hɪz]	hiss [hɪs]	has [hæz]	had [hæd]
braize [brez]	brace [bres]	his [hɪz]	hid [hɪd]
curs [kɝz]	curse [kɝs]	lays [lez]	laid [led]
hers [hɝz]	hearse [hɝs]	pays [pez]	paid [ped]
maize [mez]	mace [mes]	phase [fez]	fade [fed]
Jews [dʒuz]	juice [dʒus]	rays [rez]	raid [red]
pays [pez]	pace [pes]	rise [raɪz]	ride [raɪd]
trays [trez]	trace [tres]	ways [wez]	wade [wed]
zoot [zut]	suit [sut]	Z [zi]	D [di]
rays [rez]	race [res]	zoo [zu]	do [du]

[z]—[v]	
arise [əraɪz]	arrive [əraɪv]
close (v.) [kloz]	clove [klov]
dies [daɪz]	dive [daɪv]
does [dʌz]	dove [duv]
has [hæz]	have [hæv]
highs [haɪz]	hive [haɪv]
lays [lez]	lave [lev]
pays [pez]	pave [pev]
rays [rez]	rave [rev]
ways [wez]	wave [wev]

[z]—[ʒ]

bays [bez]	beige [beʒ]
composer [kəmpozɚ]	composure [kəmpoʒɚ]
incloser [ɪnklozɚ]	inclosure [ɪnkloʒɚ]
ruse [ruz]	rouge [ruʒ]
Caesar [sizɚ]	seizure [siʒɚ]

Phonetic Transcription. The following is a transcription in GA of the paragraph in Exercise 1:

[madən 'dʒæz 'mjuzɪk hæz boθ ɪts dɛvə'tiz ænd ɪts dɪ'træktɚz. hwɛr ɪt ə'rɪdʒənetəd ɪz nat sɚtṇ, ɔlðo mɛnɪ θɪŋk ɪts ˌkɛrɪktɚ'ɪstɪk 'sɪŋkəˌpetəd rɪðəmz əroz ɪn ðɪ 'æliz ən 'baɪˌwez əv ˌnu'ɔrlɪənz æz ə kʌzən tə fok 'mɛlodɪz. ʃə'kɔgo ən ɪts ɛn'vaɪrənz bɪkem ðə dʒæz kæpətḷ əv ðə wɚld ɪn ðə 'naɪn'tin 'twɛntɪz, ən edʒ hwɪtʃ wəz ɪn ɔl wez ən ə'mezɪŋ 'pɪrɪəd ɪn kən'tɛmpərɛrɪ ə'mɛrəkən hɪstərɪ. ðɪ 'argjəmənt æz tə hwɛðɚ sʌtʃ 'mjuzɪk ɪz ə kaɪnd əv dɪ'ziz ɔr ə dʒɛnjəwən art fɔrm stɪl redʒəz, ænd ðə strɛnz əv swɪŋ ænd ðɪ ɛg'zædʒəretəd bit əv rak ṇ rol kən'tɪnju tu dɪs'me ɔr pliz ðə lɪsənɚ, dɪ'pɛndɪŋ ɔn hɪz 'fænsɪz.]

[ʃ] as in shoe, fashion, push

Common Spellings: *sh* as in shake, shoe

ss as in passion, fission

ti as in mention, vacation

c as in associate, appreciate

Also spelled *ch*, as in Chicago; *s*, as in sugar; *sc*, as in conscious; *psh*, as in pshaw.

Production. The [ʃ] may be classified as an unvoiced linguapalatal fricative or sibilant. It is also sometimes referred to as a palatoalveolar fricative. A standard [ʃ] is typically produced with the sides of the tongue in contact with the teeth and gums in such a way that lateral escape of breath is prevented; the tip and blade of the tongue are raised toward, but do not touch, the alveolar ridge or front part of the palate; with the tongue held in this position, an unvoiced breath stream is directed against the front part of the palate, alveolar ridge, and teeth. The tongue is adjusted in such a way that a relatively broad breath channel is formed between the tongue and the roof of the mouth. The lips may be rounded and pushed forward, or everted, although this is not always done. The bite is almost closed. Velopharyngeal closure is complete, or nearly so.

In some respects [ʃ] bears a strong resemblance to [s], and a comparison of these sounds will help to identify the unique nature of each. The basic tongue position is much the same for both sounds, in that the adjustment facilitates creation of a friction noise by directing the breath stream against the alveolar ridge and teeth. For [ʃ], however, the tip and blade of the tongue are always somewhat elevated and retracted, and the tonguetip is never low behind the lower teeth. The [s] sound results from a *concentrated* breath stream which produces a "hissing" noise. In contrast, [ʃ] may be thought of as a *diffuse* sound of the sort that would result from a relatively broader breath channel and that might be described as a "hishing" noise. This change from [s] to [ʃ] is accomplished by slightly flattening the tongue front, so that the breath strikes a somewhat wider area in the front part of the mouth. A distinct [ʃ] can be produced somewhat more easily if the lips are rounded, but a perfectly acceptable pronunciation can be achieved without this rounding. In connected speech the typical speaker uses minimal lip rounding in producing [ʃ].

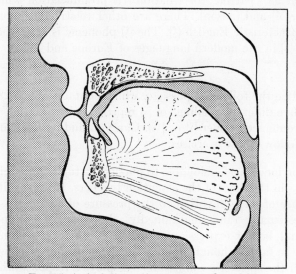

Fig. 15. Articulation adjustment for [ʃ] and [ʒ].

Pronunciation. The various spellings which call for [ʃ] present a somewhat complex picture. The letters *sh*—unless they appear in separate syllables, as in "crosshatch" [krɒshætʃ]—always call for [ʃ]. A rule often given is that [ʃ] is required where *si, ci, sci,* or *ti* is followed by an unstressed vowel or syllabic consonant. Examples include "pension" [pɛnʃən], "vicious" [vɪʃəs], "social" [soʃəl], and "patient" [peʃnt]. As noted in the section on [tʃ], *ch* often is pronounced [ʃ] in words of French origin, such as "chateau" [ʃæto]. The spelling *sc* for [ʃ], though not particularly common, is found in such words as "conscious" [kɑnʃəs] and "luscious" [lʌʃəs]. The [ʃ] is also spelled *ss* in numerous words, such as "mission" [mɪʃən], "passion" [pæʃən], and "omission" [omɪʃən]. The spelling *psh* in "pshaw" [ʃɔ] is the only instance of its kind of which the authors are aware.

The sound [ʃ] is not often involved in substandard dialect errors of native speakers. It may be underpronounced, of course, but even this is not a particularly common fault. The sound is, however, subject to many of the same kinds of defects that are associated with [s], although the [ʃ] errors occur less frequently. It may be distorted by those with dental malocclusions, and it is also typically misarticulated by the lisper who produces his sibilants with a lateral escape of breath.

Foreign speakers may mispronounce [ʃ] in their English speech, but the sound does not usually prove difficult to learn. Undue voicing may occur in the speech of those with a German-language background, particularly where [ʃ] appears between two voiced sounds. This gives words such as "partial" or "nation" a pronunciation which approximates [pɑrʒəl] and [neʒən]. There are other relatively minor deviations from a characteristic English [ʃ]. The [ʃ] phoneme is somewhat less common than [s] in the modern languages of Europe and Asia.

Exercises

1. Practice the following passage, which contains about 28 [ʃ] sounds. Note the five different spellings of [ʃ] represented. Note that at least one may be pronounced either [ʃ] or [tʃ]. Can you find it? The author's transcription follows these exercises.

It is no longer as fashionable to pursue the topic of speech gestures as it was in the days of the elocution teachers. However, it is surely not a case of mere devotion to the pressure of custom to point out that we usually (and unashamedly) show some emotion both by facial and bodily expression as part of the total communication process. In fact, although we may not be conscious of it, we are disturbed if the speaker's countenance displays a response which is out of keeping with his professions. Harsh words with a bashful expression, expressions of shyness with a grimace of grim determination, or words of high resolve issuing from a face showing only a "deadpan" are a shock to the audience. The reaction is likely to be rejection of the speaker's efforts as mere sham and show, no matter how passionately he has argued.

2. Practice and study the following representative [ʃ] words:

Initiating consonant: she, shoe, show, shy
Terminating consonant: ash, rash, wash, wish
Stronger consonant: ashamed, cashier, insure, machine
Weaker consonant: fashion, motion, washer, wishing
Initial blends: [ʃr] shrewd, shrink
Final blends: [ʃt] pushed, rushed

3. Practice and study the following minimal pairs:

[ʃ]—[tʃ]		[ʃ]—[s]	
cashing [kæʃɪŋ]	catching [kætʃɪŋ]	leash [liʃ]	lease [lis]
lash [læʃ]	latch [lætʃ]	push [puʃ]	puss [pus]
mash [mæʃ]	match [mætʃ]	shall [ʃæl]	Sal [sæl]
shin [ʃɪn]	chin [tʃɪn]	sheen [ʃin]	seen [sin]
ship [ʃɪp]	chip [tʃɪp]	shell [ʃɛl]	sell [sɛl]
shoe [ʃu]	chew [tʃu]	shelf [ʃɛlf]	self [sɛlf]
shore [ʃɔr]	chore [tʃɔr]	ship [ʃɪp]	sip [sɪp]
wash [waʃ]	watch [watʃ]	shoe [ʃu]	sue [su]
washer [waʃɚ]	watcher [watʃɚ]	short [ʃɔrt]	sort [sɔrt]
wish [wɪʃ]	witch [wɪtʃ]	sash [sæʃ]	sass [sæs]

[ʃ]—[θ]	
hash [hæʃ]	hath [hæθ]
rash [ræʃ]	wrath [ræθ]
shank [ʃæŋk]	thank [θæŋk]
sheaf [ʃif]	thief [θif]
shin [ʃɪn]	thin [θɪn]
shore [ʃɔr]	Thor [θɔr]
shorn [ʃɔrn]	thorn [θɔrn]
shrew [ʃru]	through [θru]
shrift [ʃrɪft]	thrift [θrɪft]
shy [ʃaɪ]	thigh [θaɪ]

[ʃ]—[ʒ]	
Aleutian [əluʃən]	allusion [əluʒən]
Asher [æʃɚ]	azure [æʒɚ]
Confucian [kənfjuʃən]	confusion [kənfjuʒən]
glacier [gleʃɚ]	glazier [gleʒɚ]
mesher [mɛʃɚ]	measure [mɛʒɚ]
ruche [ruʃ]	rouge [ruʒ]

Phonetic Transcription. The following is a transcription in GA of the paragraph in Exercise 1:

[ɪt ɪz no lɔŋgɚ 'fæʃənəbl̩ tə pɚ'su ðə 'tapɪk əv spitʃ dʒɛstʃɚz æz ɪt wʌz ɪn ðə dez əv ðə ˌɛlə'kjuʃən titʃɚz. haʊɛvɚ, ɪt ɪz 'ʃurlɪ nat ə kes əv mɪr dɪ'voʃən tə ðə preʃɚ əv kʌstəm tə pɔɪnt aut ðət wi 'juʒuəlɪ ænd ʌnə'ʃemədlɪ ʃo sʌm i'moʃən boθ baɪ feʃəl æn 'badəlɪ ɛk'spreʃən æz part əv ðə totl̩ kəˌmjunə'keʃən 'prasɛs. ɪn fækt, əl'ðo wi me nat be kanʃəs əv ət, wi ar dɪ'stɚbd ɪf ðə 'spikɚz 'kauntənəns dɪ'splez ə rɪ'spans hwɪtʃ ɪz aut əv 'kipɪŋ wɪθ hɪz prə'feʃənz. harʃ wɚdz wɪð ə bæʃfəl ɛk'spreʃən, ɛk'spreʃənz əv ʃaɪnəs wɪð ə grɪ'mes əv grɪm dɪˌtɚmən'eʃən, ɔr wɚdz əv haɪ rɪ'zalv 'ıʃuɪŋ frəm ə fes 'ʃowɪŋ 'onlɪ ə dɛdpæn ɑr ə ʃɑk tə ðə 'ɔdıəns. ðə riˈækʃən ɪz laɪklɪ tə bi rɪˈdʒɛkʃən əv ðə spikəz ɛfəts æz mɪr ʃæm ən ʃo, no mætə haʊ 'pæʃənətlɪ hi hæz 'ɑrgjud.]

[ʒ] as in measure, rouge

Common Spellings: s as in measure, leisure

z as in azure, glazier

g as in rouge, regime

Production. The [ʒ] is classified as a voiced linguapalatal fricative or sibilant. It may also be considered a palatoalveolar fricative. The description of the articulatory position for [ʃ] also applies to [ʒ], except, of course, that [ʒ] is voiced. As might be anticipated, many of the earlier comments on the production of [ʃ] pertain to [ʒ] as well. It is generally stated that [ʒ] is articulated with less breath pressure than [ʃ], but in other respects the patterns of production are quite similar. This means that the two sounds show the same variability in place of articulation and that variations within the phoneme are about the same in number and extent. The degree of voicing on [ʒ] is quite variable, and there is a tendency toward unvoicing in those relatively few words which are terminated by [ʒ] alone rather than by the affricate [dʒ]. This tendency is evident in typical pronunciations of words such as "rouge" [ruʒ] and "garage" [gərɑʒ]. The [ʒ] does not occur at the beginning of any English word if it is spoken alone.

Pronunciation. The spelling-pronunciation relationships for [ʒ] do not lend themselves readily to systematic rules. There has never been any spelling which always designated [ʒ]—as *f*, for example, invariably calls for [f]—largely because the [ʒ] sound did not come into English until quite recently. In many words of French origin the sound [ʒ] is represented by *ge* or *gi*, as in "ménage" [mɛnɑʒ], "regime" [rɪʒim], "barrage" [bərɑʒ], and "prestige" [prɛstiʒ]. In all these examples an approximation of the French pronunciation has been retained, but, as mentioned in an earlier section, the sound in a number of comparable words has become the affricate [dʒ]. For instance, "garage" is commonly heard as [gərɑdʒ] and "camouflage" as [kæməflɑdʒ], although many dictionaries do not record these pronunciations. Some persons object to the substitution of [dʒ] for [ʒ] in words like "garage," and the careful speaker may wish to avoid such pronunciations.

The letter *s* or *z* has come to indicate [ʒ] in words where [zɪ] or [zj] has been converted into [ʒ], as in "vision" [vɪʒən], "decision" [dɪsɪʒən], and "seizure" [siʒɚ]. This is the same process by which [sj] becomes [ʒ] in connected speech in such a phrase as "as you" [æʒu]. When a word contains *su* or *zu* pronounced as [ʒ], the spelling has obscured the fact that the sound combination once was actually [zj]. This applies to "pleasure" [plɛʒɚ], "azure" [æʒɚ], "closure" [kloʒɚ], and other, similar words. Some careful speakers may make an effort to retain a diphthongized [jʊ] or [ju] after [ʒ], which would result in pronunciations such as [æʒjʊr] for "azure" or [kloʒjʊr] for "closure." Such pronunciations may sound somewhat pedantic.

Sounds in the [ʒ] phoneme are not often produced incorrectly by the native speaker, although they may occasionally be underpronounced or unvoiced to a somewhat undesirable degree. The [ʒ] shares with [ʃ] the difficulties resulting from malocclusions and the lateral lisp. The child who has not learned [ʃ] usually fails to acquire [ʒ] as well and is likely to substitute another fricative, frequently [z]. Foreign-dialect characteristics are comparable to those mentioned in the notes on [ʃ], with excessive unvoicing of [ʒ] as an additional dialect peculiarity.

Exercises

1. Practice the following short passage, which contains 17 words using the sound [ʒ]. Do any of these sound better with [dʒ]? The author's transcription follows these exercises.

Intrusions into our privacy through the usual hidden persuaders in television and radio and other advertising media are held to be an enemy invasion of one of our most basic human dignities. These seizures of our sacred privacy and leisure time are camouflaged as pleasurable visual and auditory illusions. The resulting lesions in character and erosion of the will are passed off with persiflage and evasion by the huckster who envisions the treasure and prestige resulting from the rape of the public mind.

2. Practice the following representative examples of [ʒ] words:

Terminating consonant: beige, garage, mirage, prestige, corsage, rouge
Stronger consonant: negligee, regime, Roget
Weaker consonant: casual, pleasure, usual, vision
Final blends: [ʒd] camouflaged, rouged

3. Minimal pairs featuring [ʒ] are not easy to find. The common ones are given in the list for [ʃ]–[ʒ] in the exercises for [ʃ] and in the list for [z]–[ʒ] in the exercises for [z]. Practice also the distinctions involved in:

[ʒ]—[dʒ]

lesion [liʒən]	legion [lidʒən]
version [vɝʒən]	virgin [vɝdʒən]
pleasure [plɛʒɚ]	pledger [plɛdʒɚ]

Phonetic Transcription. The following is a transcription in GA of the paragraph in Exercise 1:

[ɪn'truʒənz ɪntu aur praɪvəsɪ θru ði 'juʒuwəl hɪdn̩ pɚ'swedɚz ɪn 'tɛlə-
vɪʒən ən 'redɪo ənd ʌðɚ 'ædvɚ͵taɪzɪŋ mɪdɪə ɑr hɛld tə bi ən 'ɛnəmɪ
ɪn've ʒən əv wʌn əv aur most 'besɪk hjumən 'dɪgnətɪz. ðiz siʒɚz əv aur
'sekrəd 'praɪvəsɪ ən liʒɚ taɪm ɑr 'kæmə͵flɑʒd əz 'plɛʒərəbl̩ 'vɪʒəwəl ənd
'ɔdətɔrɪ ɪ'luʒənz. ði rɪ'zʌltɪŋ liʒənz ɪn 'kɛrɪktɚ ænd ɪ'roʒən əv ðə wɪl ɑr
pæst əf wɪθ 'pɚ·sə͵flɑʒ ənd i'veʒən baɪ ðə hʌkstɚ hu ɛn'vɪʒənz ðə treʒɚ ən
pre'stiʒ rɪ'zʌltɪŋ frəm ðə rep əv ðə pʌblɪk maɪnd.]

[h] as in hat, ahead

Common Spellings: *h* as in head, him
Also spelled *wh*, as in who.

Production. The [h] is classified as an unvoiced glottal fricative. Acoustically [h] is a soft, diffuse friction sound created as the breath is expelled
with the vocal passage only slightly constricted. It is termed a glottal
fricative because some of the sound is presumably created when the
breath passes across the edges of the vocal folds while the glottis, or
opening between the folds, is partly closed. Friction noise also is created
when the breath strikes the hard and soft surfaces of the throat and
mouth. Velopharyngeal closure is complete, or nearly so, although this
is not an important factor in the production of [h]. There is no given
tongue and lip posture which is critical for the sound, but these articulators tend to be in the position for an adjacent sound when [h] is spoken
in context.

Pronunciation. Although [h] seemingly is one of the simpler sounds
of the language, it has many interesting characteristics. Physiologically
it is more a distinctive manner of initiating a vowel, or any other sound
whose distinctive feature is resonance, than it is a fricative or plosive
sound. To illustrate: If the name of the letter *e* is pronounced, the vowel
is initiated from a closed position of the glottis, with the vocal folds
closed quickly and without any perceptible aspiration. In articulating
the pronoun "he" [hi], however, the vocal folds are open to begin with,
then are partially adducted as the tongue and lips move to the position
for the vowel [i]; this combined action constricts the vocal passage to the
point where a perceptible friction noise is created before the vowel is
voiced.

The same phenomenon can easily be observed if one pronounces [h]
before any of the vowels or diphthongs, as in the words "hah" [hɑ],
"ho" [ho], "who" [hu], "high" [haɪ], "hat" [hæt], and so on. In each
case the [h] is made with the tongue and lips in the position for the fol-

lowing sound. The sound we conventionally represent with the symbol [h] could, therefore, be regarded as an unvoiced [ɑ̥], [o̥], [u̥], or whatever the case may be. A related fact is that [h] occurs only at the beginning of syllables. Because of the dynamics of its production, there are a large number of sounds within the [h] phoneme. Furthermore, each is somewhat distinctive acoustically, although the differences in sound pass unnoticed unless one listens for them specifically. In Old English, [h] was sometimes pronounced before [r] and [l], and we now regularly use [h] before [w] and [j] in words such as "which" [hwɪtʃ], "when" [hwɛn], "human" [hjumən], and "huge" [hjudʒ], although in [hw] the [h] is not considered a separate sound. In the speculative "hum" or the questioning "hun?" we have a nasal [h] which is approximately [m̥m] or [n̥n].

Despite the way it is related physiologically to other sounds, linguistically [h] may be considered phonemic, since it distinguishes meanings between many pairs of words, such as "owe"–"hoe" [o]–[ho]. If a speaker has difficulty with [h], as might be the case if he has a foreign-dialect problem, he may sometimes find it helpful to regard each particular [h] as merely a way of starting the sound which follows and be guided by the articulation position of that sound.

Pronunciation practices and spelling relationships involve a number of variable factors. A [h] is the regular sound of the letter *h*. In phonetic transcription it is conventional to denote aspiration of other sounds with a [h] symbol, usually of small size, but this sound is acoustically unlike [h]. The letter *h* has also come into frequent use in digraphs where there is no semblance of a [h] sound. For example, in spelling convention the addition of *h* to *g*, as in "cough," is employed to represent [f], and *h* has been added to *p* in "physics" to designate the same sound. All things considered, it is frequently difficult to infer the pronunciation of modern English words containing the letter *h*.

Although the question of whether or not to pronounce an initial letter *h* is often discussed, the correct answer is really not particularly complex. Among common words, the following are regularly pronounced with a "silent" *h*: "heir" [ɛr], "hombre" [ɔmbre], "honor" [ɑnɚ], "hour" [auɚ], "herb" [ɝb], "homage" [ɑmɪdʒ], and derivatives of these. Many of the words beginning with *h* found their way into English by way of Old French. There the usage was to drop the [h], although the letter was retained from Latin originals, where [h] was sounded. In many cases restoration of [h] has come about because of the spelling and, historically, is a relatively late pronunciation change. Further changes may conceivably occur; they are now in progress with "herb" [ɝb] or [hɝb] and "vehicle" [viɪkl̩] or [vihɪkl̩].

The [h] sound may be considerably weakened or even lost in connected speech. Initial sounds are quite commonly obliterated in conversational speech when they occur in unstressed positions in words and phrases, as in "Hello," which is often [ɛlo], or "How are you?" which may be heard as [aʊ ɑr ju]. This is not necessarily substandard. Within words h frequently becomes silent in unstressed positions, as in "shepherd" [ʃɛpɚd], "forehead" [fɔrəd] or [fɔrhɛd], or "vehement" [viəmənt]. The same kind of change takes place with great regularity in connected speech, particularly with the "h pronouns." In the following examples, which represent perfectly acceptable colloquial pronunciation, a clear [h] would risk becoming overprecise: "it's to his credit" [ɪts tʊ ɪz krɛdət], "if he will" [ɪf i wɪl]. Pronunciation, of course, differs under the influence of stress. The sentence "I have none," if spoken as a simple declarative statement, will probably be [aɪ əv nʌn]; if, however, the meaning is "I had, but no longer have," the pronunciation is likely to be [aɪ hæv nʌn]. Note that [h] tends to remain in stressed positions, as in the words "enhance" [ɛnhæns] and "inhibit" [ɪnhɪbət].

Kenyon[16] makes some interesting comments about the supposed tendency of those who speak certain English dialects to drop [h] from words where it should appear, as in [ɪr naʊ] for "here now," and add the sound where it should not be, as in [haɪ se] for "I say." This is not, he believes, a uniform practice, but a change which takes place haphazardly as a result of the fact that [h] is no longer a speech sound in these dialects. The tendency is to use [h] on strongly emphatic words, although this is not always done. He also notes that the common [hɪt] for [ɪt] in some Southern American speech corresponds to the pronunciation of this pronoun in earlier English.

Aside from dialect errors or failure to deal with [h] in conformity with the principles mentioned in earlier paragraphs, there are not likely to be any difficulties arising from misarticulation of the sound by native speakers. In foreign dialect the errors are somewhat more numerous. The [h] may be omitted, as in typical French dialect, or a non-English variant may be substituted, such as the velar fricative [x] or the [ç] of German. The latter is not too dissimilar to an English [h], closely resembling the initial sound in the English pronunciation of such words as "huge." Still other foreign speakers may simply underpronounce [h].

Exercises

1. The following paragraph is for practice and identification of the [h] sound. Note the highly consistent spelling, but don't fail to identify those inconsistencies which are represented. Identify silent h's and decide which others may be safely dropped. The author's transcription follows these exercises.

How can the English alphabet be overhauled so as to hold a more highly consistent relationship to the speech it is somehow supposed to represent? He who has hitherto had hardly any experience with phonetics will perhaps have held no honest convictions on the subject. But even half-taught phoneticians will usually be happy to help you out by having you hear their well-rehearsed plans for an over-all overhaul of an alphabet which they consider wholly outmoded and in general behind the times. The public, however, is highly successful in hiding its zeal for committing any hasty mayhem on its ABC's and generally behaves with habitual indifference toward its academic hecklers, no matter how high their scholarly honors.

2. Practice the following representative [h] words:

Initiating consonant: half, hay, heard, he, him, horse, hoe, who
Stronger consonant: ahead, ahoy, behave, behind, enhance, perhaps, rehearse, unhook
Weak or lost consonant: forehead, mayhem, vehicle, vehement

3. Practice and study the following minimal pairs:

[h]—without [h]		[h]—[f]	
had [hæd]	add [æd]	had [hæd]	fad [fæd]
hair [hɛr]	air [ɛr]	hair [hɛr]	fair [fɛr]
hand [hænd]	and [ænd]	head [hɛd]	fed [fɛd]
has [hæz]	as [æz]	he [hi]	fee [fi]
hat [hæt]	at [æt]	her [hɝ]	fur [fɝ]
her [hɝ]	err [ɝ]	here [hɪr]	fear [fɪr]
his [hɪz]	is [ɪz]	hill [hɪl]	fill [fɪl]
high [haɪ]	eye [aɪ]	hit [hɪt]	fit [fɪt]
hold [hold]	old [old]	hold [hold]	fold [fold]
here [hɪr]	ear [ɪr]	hat [hæt]	fat [fæt]

[h]—[s]		[h]—[θ]	
had [hæd]	sad [sæd]	Hank [hæŋk]	thank [θæŋk]
hand [hænd]	sand [sænd]	hatch [hætʃ]	thatch [θætʃ]
hat [hæt]	sat [sæt]	heard [hɝd]	third [θɝd]
he [hi]	see [si]	hermit [hɝmət]	Thermit [θɝmət]
head [hɛd]	said [sɛd]	hick [hɪk]	thick [θɪk]
halt [hɔlt]	salt [sɔlt]	high [haɪ]	thigh [θaɪ]
hold [hold]	sold [sold]	hill [hɪl]	thill [θɪl]
hope [hop]	soap [sop]	Hong [hɔŋ]	thong [θɔŋ]
high [haɪ]	sigh [saɪ]	horn [hɔrn]	thorn [θɔrn]
her [hɝ]	sir [sɝ]	hump [hʌmp]	thump [θʌmp]

Phonetic Transcription. The following is a transcription in GA of the paragraph in Exercise 1:

[haʊ kən ðɪ 'ɪŋglɪʃ 'ælfəbet bi ˌovɚ'hold so æz tə hold ə mɔr haɪlɪ kənsɪstənt rɪ'leʃənʃɪp tə ðə spitʃ ɪt ɪz 'sʌmˌhaʊ səpozd tə ˌreprɪ'zent? hi hu həz 'hɪðɚtu hæd hɑrdlɪ ɛnɪ ɛk'spɪrɪəns wɪθ fə'netɪks wɪl pɚhæps həv held no ɑnəst kən'vɪkʃənz ɑn ðə sʌbdʒɪkt. bʌt ivən hæf tɔt ˌfonə'tɪʃənz wɪl 'juʒuəlɪ bi hæpɪ tə help ju aʊt baɪ hævɪŋ ju hɪr ðɚ wel rɪ'hɝst plænz fɔr ən 'ovɚol 'ovɚˌhol əv ən 'ælfəbet hwɪtʃ ðe kənsɪdɚ holɪ ˌaʊt'modəd ænd ɪn dʒenərəl bɪ'haɪnd ðə taɪmz. ðə 'pʌblɪk, haʊevɚ, ɪz haɪlɪ sək'sesfəl ɪn 'haɪdɪŋ ɪts zil fɔr kə'mɪtɪŋ ɛnɪ hestɪ 'mehem ɑn ɪts 'e'bi'siz æn dʒenərəlɪ bihevz wɪθ hə'bɪtʃuwəl ɪn'dɪfrəns tɔrd ɪts ˌækə'demɪk heklɚz, no mætɚ haʊ haɪ ðer 'skɑləlɪ ɑnɚz.]

11

THE GLIDES, NASALS, AND LATERAL

[r], [j], [w], [hw], [m], [n], [ŋ], [l]

[r] as in run, around

Common Spellings: r as in red, ran

rr as in hurry, carrot

Also spelled *rh*, as in rhyme; *wr*, as in write.

Production. The [r] is classified as a voiced linguapalatal glide. Like all other glide sounds, it is characterized by a rapid change of resonance produced by a gliding movement of the organs of articulation involved in its production. To start the glide, the tongue front is raised toward, but does not touch, the anterior part of the hard palate. This closely resembles the adjustment for [ɝ].

When [r] is an *on-glide*, and thus initiates a syllable, the tongue moves from the position mentioned to that for the following vowel. If [r] terminates a syllable, as an *off-glide*, the tongue moves from the vowel adjustment to the approximate [ɝ] position. Possible variations in tongue position were discussed in some detail in connection with [ɝ] and also in connection with the *r* diphthongs in Chapter 8. Because [r] is a glide, the sound is made as a movement, with no static position. Velopharyngeal closure is complete, or nearly so, and the teeth are nearly together.

Pronunciation. The greatest source of confusion surrounding the various *r* sounds is the distinction between the glide [r] and the *r*-colored vowels [ɝ] and [ɚ]. This was touched on briefly in the treatment of the two vowels, but it is now possible to explain the matter more fully. Those who hitherto have thought in terms of the conventional alphabet may wonder why, for instance, the word "here" is not transcribed [hɪɚ], since the final sound resembles that of "father" [fɑðɚ]. Actually the word could be transcribed this way with no serious error, since the use of [r]

213

in such a phonetic situation is, within limits, a matter of convention. This aspect of transcription practice was first discussed in connection with [ɚ].

In order to understand the basic reason why there are circumstances (such as in the word [hɪr]) where [r] is sometimes more accurate, one should recall the way in which a glide consonant is related to its associated vowel. The [r] stands in relation to [ɝ] and [ɚ] in almost exactly the same way that [w] is related to [u] or that [j] is related to [i]. In all these cases the glide consonant is created by a rapid *change* in resonance from [u], [i], or [ɝ] to the resonance of the following vowel. The difference between [uɪn] and [wɪn] is largely one of timing and of whether there are two syllables [uɪn] or one [wɪn]. To distinguish [r] from [ɚ], remember that the latter is syllabic (although unstressed) and the former is not. Thus if "here" is monosyllabic, the preferable transcription is [hɪr]. This general rule can be applied to comparable words in which it is desirable to distinguish between [r] as an off-glide and [ɚ].

It is well known that the *r* sounds pose more pronunciation problems than any other group for anyone trying to master good American speech. Within the phoneme there is a rather wide range of perfectly acceptable sounds, depending upon such factors as stress and context. A large number of substandard pronunciations are also heard with great frequency.

One of these substandard sounds is the retracted [r] (and these comments apply equally well to [ɝ] and [ɚ]), made with the tongue too far back and usually with the back of the tongue, rather than the front, raised. This leads to a tense, unduly prominent sound, containing some resonance that may be identified as nasality and that strikes the ear of the more sensitive listener as unpleasant. If there is a "twang" to the speech of some American dialects, it arises in part from this source. The notion that dropping the *r* somehow gives more agreeable-sounding speech is false, since there is nothing inherently unpleasant about *r* coloring. An unduly retracted [r], [ɝ], or [ɚ] is, however, definitely substandard, and this error is particularly unfortunate because of the fact that *r* coloring happens to be one of the more conspicuous resonances.

Foreign speakers have a multitude of problems with the *r* group of sounds. A principal reason is that many modern languages have *r* sounds that differ conspicuously from the English [r], [ɝ], or [ɚ]. When the native sound is carried into English, as it typically is, the result is a very perceptible dialect characteristic. The fact that the foreigner's native sound bears some general resemblance to the English sound makes learning the [r] all the more difficult.

One of the greatest difficulties seems to be teaching the foreigner to treat [r] as a glide, rather than as a fricative, "tap," or "trill." He must remember also that the tongue should not touch the roof of the mouth. The American [r] and [ɝ] represent an evolutionary weakening of a strong trilled sound believed to be the forerunner of the present glide. The historically older sound, still retained in many languages and dialects, has weakened to a single "tap" in certain British dialects and to no "tap" at all in American English.

The dialect differences in r usage in the United States are discussed in detail in Chapter 14 and have already been touched on in the chapters on the central vowels and diphthongs. Briefly, dropping the r is characteristic of Eastern New England, some Southern American dialects, and Southern British. Thomas[32] estimates that three-fourths of all Americans, including most GA speakers, pronounce r in all its positions and wherever it is spelled. Those who drop the r may substitute a non-r-colored vowel in some positions.

Special note should be taken of the *linking* and *intrusive* [r] sounds. One who does not generally pronounce a final r will nevertheless do so in connected speech when the following word begins with a vowel. Thus, when spoken alone, "father" might be [faðə], but "father and I" would be [faðɚ ənd aɪ]. The sound heard in these circumstances is called the *linking*, or *intervocalic*, [r].

An *intrusive* [r] is one which creeps in where it does not belong. This is considered an undesirable trait by the careful speaker, despite the rather widespread occurrence of this phenomenon among persons who usually drop the r. These speakers are accustomed to using the linking r and unconsciously extend this practice to link words even where the first of the pair does not terminate with r. Thus the sentence "The idea is good" becomes [ðɪ aɪdɪr ɪz gʊd]. The [r] in [aɪdɪr] is intrusive. This tendency may degenerate to the point where words which normally would end in [ə] commonly come to have pronunciations such as [kɑmɚ] for "comma." This is clearly substandard.

For reasons that are not entirely clear, [r] and the r-colored vowels appear to be among the most difficult sounds for children to learn. Sounds within these phonemes are typically the last to be acquired during the developmental period, and one of the most common characteristics of infantile speech is the use of [w] for [r]. (This substitution may also be spoken of as *labialization* of [r] and written [r̨]). In speech of this sort the sentence "First read the story about Peter Rabbit" might be spoken [fəst wid ə stɔwɪ baʊt pitə wæbət]. Children can usually overcome this fault most readily if they are first taught the r-colored vowels, then introduced to [r] as a sound that begins with the adjustment learned for the vowels.

Exercises

1. The following passage contains all kinds of *r* sounds in all sorts of phonetic situations. Transcribe your own reading of the paragraph; then make a comparison with the author's conversational pronunciation, which is shown following these exercises. In this transcription an off-glide [r] is often employed where [ɚ] could have been used. Note these instances.

The birth cry marks the origin of speech, we are told. Here for the first time the nerve pathways necessary for articulation are brought into play. Presently the rapidly growing baby will arrive at a period when true rehearsal for speech begins. This is described as vocal play, when a remarkable and varied repertoire of random sounds emerges. Baby and parent both appear to derive great gratification. Whereas early screams and cries reflect primary responses to body states, later use of sounds is aroused by the presence of others, and a true but primitive interaction with persons in the surrounding environment has been brought about. Various curious sounds he may apparently have borrowed from another world now rapidly drop out; he begins to prefer sounds he hears. Random babbling becomes more nearly purposive. Increasing use is made of sound in the second and third three-month periods. As he draws nearer and nearer to the first birthday the first word will probably be heard, and greeted, you may be sure, with praise and approval. The preparatory period is now largely over; crowing and gurgling are replaced by true verbalization.

2. Practice the following representative [r] words. Note that examples of the terminating [r] may be variously pronounced, depending upon the dialect of English spoken. Recall that the final off-glide may be considered a consonant [r] or part of a diphthong with [ɚ].

Initiating consonant: raw, ray, row, rye
Terminating consonant: air, are, ire, oar
Initiating and terminating: rare, rear, roar, Ruhr
Stronger consonant: arrive, arouse, bereave, caress
Weaker consonant: bearing, borrow, hearing, wearing
Initial blends: [kr] crack, cry; [br] breathe, brown; [gr] group, grow; [tr] train, try; [dr] draw, drive; [pr] pray, press; [fr] friend, fry; [str] strain, street; [skr] scream, screw; [θr] threw, thrust
Final blends: [rz] fears, wears; [rd] beard, board; [rt] cart, court; [rts] hearts, parts; [rdz] boards, cards; [rn] barn, horn; [rk] bark, cork; [rks] corks, marks

3. Practice the following minimal pairs:

[r]—[w]		[r]—[j]	
array [əre]	away [əwe]	a cruise [əkruz]	accuse [əkjuz]
crack [kræk]	quack [kwæk]	crew [kru]	cue [kju]
rain [ren]	Wayne [wen]	ram [ræm]	yam [jæm]
rate [ret]	wait [wet]	raw [rɔ]	yaw [jɔ]
read [rid]	weed [wid]	rear [rɪr]	year [jɪr]
red [rɛd]	wed [wɛd]	roar [rɔr]	yore [jɔr]
rent [rɛnt]	went [wɛnt]	rue [ru]	you [ju]
rest [rɛst]	west [wɛst]	rung [rʌŋ]	young [jʌŋ]
run [rʌn]	one [wʌn]	Ruth [ruθ]	youth [juθ]
train [tren]	twain [twen]	rot [rɑt]	yacht [jɑt]

[r]—[l]		[r]—without [r]	
array [əre]	allay [əle]	far [fɑr]	fah [fɑ]
bear [ber]	bell [bɛl]	lore [lɔr]	law [lɔ]
correct [kərɛkt]	collect [kəlɛkt]	rat [ræt]	at [æt]
hear [hɪr]	hill [hɪl]	rate [ret]	ate [et]
rain [ren]	lain [len]	reach [ritʃ]	each [itʃ]
rate [ret]	late [let]	red [rɛd]	Ed [ɛd]
raw [rɔ]	law [lɔ]	real [ril]	eel [il]
read [rid]	lead [lid]	rich [rɪtʃ]	itch [ɪtʃ]
rot [rɑt]	lot [lɑt]	spar [spɑr]	spa [spɑ]
ram [ræm]	lamb [læm]	wrought [rɔt]	ought [ɔt]

Phonetic Transcription. The following is a transcription in GA of the paragraph in Exercise 1:

[ðə bɜ˞θ kraɪ mɑrks ðə 'ɔrədʒən əv spitʃ, wi ɚ told. hɪr fɚ ðə fɜ˞st taɪm ðə nɜ˞v pæθwez 'nɛsəsɛrɪ fər ɑrtɪkjə'leʃən ɑr brɔt ɪntə ple. 'prɛzəntlɪ ðə 'ræpədlɪ 'growɪŋ 'bebɪ wɪl əraɪv ət ə 'pɪrɪəd hwən tru rɪ'hɜ˞səl fər spitʃ bɪ'gɪnz. ðɪs əz dɪ'skraɪbd əz vokl ple, hwən ə rɪ'mɑrkəbl ən 'vɛrɪd 'rɛpə,- twɔr əv rændəm saʊndz i'mɜ˞dʒəz. 'bebɪ n̩ pɛrənt boθ əpɪr tə dɪ'raɪv gret sætəs'fækʃən. 'hwɛræz ɜ˞lɪ skrɪmz ən kraɪz rɪ'flɛkt 'praɪmɛrɪ rɪ'spɑnsəz tə bɑdɪ stɛts, letɚ jus əv saʊndz ɪz ə'raʊzd baɪ ðə 'prɛzəns əv ʌðɚz, ənd ə tru bət 'prɪmətɪv ɪntɚ'ækʃən wɪθ pɜ˞sənz ɪn ðə sə'raʊndɪŋ ɛn'vaɪrnmənt həz bɪn brɔt əbaʊt. vɛrɪəs 'kjurɪəs saʊndz hi me ə'pɛrəntlɪ həv 'bɑrod frəm ənʌðɚ wɜ˞ld naʊ 'ræpədlɪ drɑp aʊt; hi bɪ'gɪnz tə prɪ'fɜ˞ saʊndz i hɪrz. 'rændəm 'bæblɪŋ bɪ'kʌmz mɔr 'nɪrlɪ 'pɜ˞pəsɪv. ɪn'krisɪŋ jus ɪz med əv saʊnd ɪn ðə sɛkənd ən θɜ˞d θri mʌnθ 'pɪrɪədz. æz i drɔz nɪrɚ ən nɪrɚ tə ðə fɜ˞st 'bɜ˞θ,de ðə fɜ˞st wɜ˞d wɪl 'prɑbəblɪ bi hɜ˞d, ən gritəd, ju me bi ʃur, wɪθ prez ən ə'pruvl. ðə prə'pɛrətɛrɪ 'pɪrɪəd ɪz naʊ 'lɑrdʒlɪ ovɚ; 'krowɪŋ ən 'gɜ˞glɪŋ ɑr ri'plest baɪ tru vɜ˞bələ'zeʃən.]

[j] as in yes, beyond

Common Spellings: *y* as in yet, yesterday
i as in million, union
u as in the diphthongs [ju] of use, union
Also spelled *j*, as in hallelujah.

Production. The [j] is classified as a voiced linguapalatal glide. The sound is started with the front of the tongue raised toward, but not touching, the anterior part of the hard palate in the approximate position for [ɪ] or [i]. The glide is made as the tongue moves to the position for the following sound. A resonance *change* is, of course, a distinctive feature of this sound. Velopharyngeal closure is complete, or nearly so, and the teeth are almost together.

If one has become familiar with [i] and [ɪ], the glide [j] will be readily identified, since the starting position of the tongue is, for all practical purposes, the same as for these vowels. This can easily be demonstrated by first pronouncing [ɪ] and [aʊl] as two syllables, then blending them closely. A good approximation of [jaʊl] "yowl" will be the result.

Pronunciation. The [j] is ordinarily thought of as a glide which initiates, but never terminates, a syllable, and this is generally true. If one wishes to be technical, however, there are exceptions, for in ongoing speech the movements of this *high-front glide* may be toward, as well as away from, the [i] position. This leads to an off-glide [j] as well as an on-glide. Such off-glide [j] sounds are, however, distributed primarily among the diphthongs [aɪ], [ɔɪ], [eɪ], and [ɪj].

Accurate production of [j] does not ordinarily offer much of a problem in any kind of speech improvement work. It is very common among the major modern-language sound systems. Foreign speakers may often mistakenly pronounce the letter *j* of English words as [j] (thus [jʊmp] for "jump"), but this arises because the symbol has this pronunciation value in the native alphabet. Children learn the sound readily, although they may omit it in words like "yes" and "you," so that "Oh, yes you are" may be [o ɛs u ɑr] in infantile speech.

Exercises

1. The following passage is loaded with possible [j] glides to a far greater extent than would be found in a representative speech sample. Several words can properly be pronounced either [ju] or [u] (or a nearby vowel); identify these. In transcribing the passage, you should be aware that there is some effort to trick you into use of [j]. The pronunciation

of the author, though not always consistent, is faithfully recorded in the transcription following these exercises.

We have always been fascinated by yogi, although we have yet to accumulate any ability to use this unique art. How useful, though, to a tutor of youth would be the curious power to keep the young pupils in view through a new but hidden eye. Meanwhile, we could with impunity pursue our fancies or commune with beautiful nature, yet be ready for the usual moment of punitive retribution. Millions of other valuable uses could be found. The power to transmute the body to another place without the nuisance of actual travel would be nice. But there are drawbacks; few of us could endure the singularly uncomfortable posture which seems a purely preliminary measure for communicants, although we might eventually become inured to it. Certainly we would be accused of behavior unsuited to a mature man and there might be considerable furious abuse of a secular nature.

2. Practice and study the following representative [j] words. Recall that when [j] is used as an off-glide one of the diphthongs [aɪ], [ɔɪ], [eɪ], or [ɪj] is produced.

Initiating consonant: year, yore, you, your
Terminating "consonant": A, I, Ray, Roy
Stronger consonant: accuse, beyond, yesterday, yanking
Weaker consonant: accurate, argument, familiar, volume
Initial blends: [kj] cute, cure; [pj] puny, pure; [hj] hew, human; [fj] few, fuse; [mj] mew, mule; [vj] view, viewed

3. Practice the following minimal pairs:

[j]—[r]		[j]—[dʒ]	
use [juz]	ruse [ruz]	use (v.) [juz]	Jews [dʒuz]
Yale [jel]	rail [rel]	use (n.) [jus]	juice [dʒus]
yak [jæk]	rack [ræk]	yak [jæk]	Jack [dʒæk]
yen [jɛn]	wren [rɛn]	Yale [jel]	jail [dʒel]
yip [jɪp]	rip [rɪp]	yaw [jɔ]	jaw [dʒɔ]
yo [jo]	row [ro]	yell [jɛl]	jell [dʒɛl]
you'd [jud]	rude [rud]	yo [jo]	Joe [dʒo]
you'll [jul]	rule [rul]	yolk [jok]	joke [dʒok]
your [jʊr]	Ruhr [rʊr]	yessed [jɛst]	jest [dʒɛst]
"yum" [jʌm]	rum [rʌm]	you'll [juəl]	jewel [dʒuəl]

[j]—without [j]		[j]—[l]	
use [juz]	ooze [uz]	few [fju]	flew [flu]
Yale [jel]	ale [el]	use [jus]	loose [lus]
yawl [jɔl]	awl [ɔl]	yacht [jɑt]	lot [lɑt]
yea [je]	A [e]	yaw [jɔ]	law [lɔ]
yearn [jɝn]	earn [ɝn]	yea [je]	lay [le]
year [jɪr]	ear [ɪr]	year [jɪr]	leer [lɪr]
yegg [jɛg]	egg [ɛg]	yegg [jɛg]	leg [lɛg]
yell [jɛl]	L [ɛl]	yip [jɪp]	lip [lɪp]
yo [jo]	owe [o]	yo [jo]	low [lo]
yolk [jok]	oak [ok]	your [jʊr]	lure [lʊr]

Phonetic Transcription. The following is a transcription in GA of the paragraph in Exercise 1:

[wi həv 'ɔlwɪz bɪn 'fæsənetəd baɪ 'jogɪ, əl'ðo wi həv jɛt tu ə'kjumjəlet ɛnɪ ə'bɪlətɪ tə juz ðɪs ju'nik ɑrt. haʊ jusfəl, ðo, tu ə tutɚ əv juθ wəd bi ðə kjʊrɪəs paʊr tə kip ðə jʌŋ pjupəlz ɪn vju θru ə nu bət hɪdn̩ aɪ. 'min,- hwaɪl, wi kʊd wɪθ ɪm'pjunətɪ pɚsu aʊr 'fænsɪz ɔr kə'mjunəket wɪð 'bjutəfəl netʃɚ, jɛt bi rɛdɪ fɚ ðə 'juʒjəwəl momənt əv 'pjunətɪv ,rɛtrə'- bjuʃən. 'mɪljənz əv ʌðɚ 'væljəbl̩ jusəz kəd bi faʊnd. ðə paʊr tə trænz'mjut ðə bɑdɪ tu ənʌðɚ ples wɪθ'aʊt ðə 'nusəns əv 'æktʃuwəl trævl̩ wəd bi naɪs. bət ðɛr ɑr 'drɔ,bæks; fju əv əs kəd ɪn'djʊr ðə 'sɪŋgjələlɪ ʌn'kʌmftɚbl̩ pɑstʃɚ hwɪtʃ simz ə 'pjʊrlɪ pri'lɪmənɛrɪ mɛʒɚ fɚ kə'mjunəkənts, əl'ðo wi maɪt i'ventʃuwəlɪ bɪ'kʌm ɪ'njʊrd tu ət. 'sɝtənlɪ wi wəd bi əkjuzd əv bɪ'hevjɚ ʌn'sutəd tu ə mə'tjur mæn ən ðɛr maɪt bi kən'sɪdərəbl̩ fjʊrɪəs əbjus əv ə 'sɛkjələ netʃɚ.]

[w] as in we, away

Common Spellings: *w* as in wet, swing

                 u as in quite and other *qu* words

                 o as in once, choir

Production. The [w] may be classified as a voiced labial (or bilabial) glide. It is articulated by rounding the lips, then moving them to the position for the following vowel while emitting a voiced stream of breath. Velopharyngeal closure is complete, or nearly so. In a sense this sound could also be classified as a linguapalatal glide, for it is made by moving from the approximate position of the *high-back, lip-rounded* [ʊ] or [u] to the adjustment for the following vowel within the space of a single syllable. Both lip and tongue movements occur.

The lip movement for this glide is certainly more prominent than tongue movement, however, and the [w] derives the name *bilabial* from the rapid unrounding of the lips which takes place during its production. The [w] is related to [u] in the same way that [j] is related to [i] and that [r] is related to [ɝ]. To verify this, note that the word "way" [we] can be closely approximated by blending [u] and [e] rapidly.

Pronunciation. Although the pronunciation [w] is usually consistent with the spelling where the letter *w* is found, there are a few interesting variations of this reliable spelling-pronunciation relationship. At the beginning of a word, *w* calls for the on-glide [w] except for initial combinations of *wr* and *wh*. The *w* is silent in *wr*, as in "wreck" [rɛk], "write" [raɪt], and so on; and the *wh* is [hw], although [w] is commonly closer to the actual pronunciation heard ("which" [hwɪtʃ] or [wɪtʃ], and so on). When an initial or medial *w* occurs before a [ʊ] or [u] sound, it is sometimes silent, as in "two" [tu] and "who" [hu] and their derivatives. It is silent also in some unaccented syllables, as in "answer" [ænsɚ]. There is a tendency for the sound to be dropped in "toward" [tɔrd]. Finally, the word "one," along with its derivatives, is an interesting and special case of a *w* sounded but not spelled.

Although [w] may seem to be a relatively stable glide sound with little or no variation, this actually is not the case. A number of slightly varying sounds within the phoneme can be heard if one examines pronunciations carefully. In words like "woo" and "woe," for example, there is relatively little lip unrounding because both [u] and [o] are lip-rounded vowels. In these circumstances [w] may take on a fricative quality, imparted by raising the middle of the tongue very near the roof of the mouth as the lips are closely rounded. This [w] is quite different from the [w] in such a word as "we" [wi].

Like [j] and [r], the sound [w] is primarily an on-glide, but occasionally there is at least a semblance of an off-glide, involving a movement toward a [u] position. This occurs principally on the diphthongs [aʊ], [oʊ], [ju], and [ɪu]. Although some phoneticians go so far as to use the [w] symbol to represent off-glides in certain circumstances, it seems simpler to reserve this mark for the on-glide and to employ the appropriate vowel symbol for the high-back off-glides. Conventional spelling often uses a final *w*, of course, and in most such words ("cow," "flow," and so on) there actually is a high-back off-glide.

In contextual speech there are many instances of [w] off-glides, some of them verging on the substandard. In these cases the blending of sounds is so close that the high-back off-glide becomes in essence the on-glide for the following syllable. For example, "going" may be either [goɪŋ] or something closer to [gowɪŋ], depending partly on the speed of utterance. Again, "how often" may be [haʊ ɔfən] or [haʊwɔfən] and "how awful" either [haʊ ɔfəl] or [haʊwɔfəl]. This is the same kind of change that occurs with [j] when "I am" becomes [aɪjæm] instead of [aɪ æm]. It is possibly too demanding to ask that such off-glide [w] usages be avoided, although the careful speaker tends not to use them prominently.

On the whole, however, one need not be seriously worried about the effect on his speech of the fairly large variety of [w] sounds that arise from differences of the sort we have been discussing; most of these are of more theoretical than practical interest. An accurate [w] is not hard to produce. The foreign speaker may carry over into English the practice of pronouncing the letter *w* as [v], but even he should quickly learn an entirely acceptable sound and will need only to remember when it should be used.

Exercises

1. The following passage contains many [w] sounds. Transcribe your pronunciation, then compare it with the transcription at the end of these exercises.

How language began will always remain a qualified mystery. One theory is that words were first acquired by imitation of sounds made by birds and animals or fashioned after the noises in nature. We sometimes call this the onomatopoetic theory. Words like "swish" and "buzz" would possibly have begun this way; however, this theory is quite inadequate, for it in nowise accounts for the complexities of language, and there must have been subsequent influences. Language grew as words were acquired by subsequent use. We do not know what was the first language. The first evidences with which scholars are acquainted date back only to about 4000 B.C. There is no question but that newer language grew out of older, but the situation is that no records of these exist. Fewer than six languages can be followed back as far as 1800 B.C. Few are aware of the large number of languages that have existed; American Indians alone had more than 350, which were grouped into 25 families. The consequence of communication problems in our multilingual world has been to point up the need for one tongue.

2. Practice the following representative [w] words. Recall that when [w] is used as an off-glide it produces one of the diphthongs [aʊ], [oʊ], or [ʊw]. Comment on the examples of weaker consonants.

Initiating consonant: way, we, woe, Y
Terminating "consonant": cow, low, new, owe
Stronger consonant: away, bewail, request, reward
Weaker consonant: cower, going, Howard, lower
Initial blends: [sw] sway, swing; [kw] question, quick; [skw] squeak, squelch; [tw] twenty, twin; [dw] Duane, dwell

3. Study the following minimal pairs:

[w]—[r]		[w]—[hw]	
quack [kwæk]	crack [kræk]	way [we]	whey [hwe]
quest [kwɛst]	crest [krɛst]	wear [wɛr]	where [hwɛr]
twill [twɪl]	trill [trɪl]	wen [wɛn]	when [hwɛn]
wave [wev]	rave [rev]	were [wɝ]	whirr [hwɝ]
way [we]	ray [re]	wet [wɛt]	whet [hwɛt]
ways [wez]	raise [rez]	wile [waɪl]	while [hwaɪl]
week [wik]	reek [rik]	wine [waɪn]	whine [hwaɪn]
went [wɛnt]	rent [rɛnt]	witch [wɪtʃ]	which [hwɪtʃ]
wife [waɪf]	rife [raɪf]	world [wɝld]	whirled [hwɝld]
will [wɪl]	rill [rɪl]	Y [waɪ]	why [hwaɪ]

[w]—[v]		[w]—[f]	
wane [wen]	vane [ven]	way [we]	fey [fe]
want [wɔnt]	vaunt [vɔnt]	wear [wɛr]	fair [fɛr]
weep [wip]	"veep" [vip]	were [wɝ]	fir [fɝ]
went [wɛnt]	vent [vɛnt]	wife [waɪf]	fife [faɪf]
west [wɛst]	vest [vɛst]	wile [waɪl]	file [faɪl]
wet [wɛt]	vet [vɛt]	will [wɪl]	fill [fɪl]
wine [waɪn]	vine [vaɪn]	wine [waɪn]	fine [faɪn]
worse [wɝs]	verse [vɝs]	witch [wɪtʃ]	Fitch [fɪtʃ]
wow [waʊ]	vow [vaʊ]	world [wɝld]	furled [fɝld]
Y [waɪ]	vie [vaɪ]	Y [waɪ]	fie [faɪ]

Phonetic Transcription. The following is a transcription in GA of the paragraph in Exercise 1:

[haʊ 'læŋgwɪdʒ bɪ'gæn wɪl 'ɔlwɪz rɪ'men ə 'kwɑləfaɪd 'mɪstrɪ. wʌn 'θiərɪ ɪz ðət wɝdz wɝ fɝst ə'kwaɪrd baɪ ɪmə'teʃən əv saʊndz med baɪ bɝdz ən ænəməlz ɔr fæʃnd æftɝ ðə nɔɪzəz ɪn netʃɝ. wi 'sʌm,taɪmz kɔl ðɪs ðə ˌɑnəmɑtəpo'wetɪk 'θiərɪ. wɝdz laɪk swɪʃ ən bʌz wəd 'pɑsəblɪ həv bɪ'gʌn ðɪs we; haʊ'ɛvɝ, ðɪs 'θiərɪ ɪz kwaɪt ˌɪn'ædəkwət, fɔr ɪt ən 'no,waɪz əkaʊnts fɝ ðə kəm'plɛksətɪz əv 'læŋgwɪdʒ, ənd ðɛr mʌst əv bɪn 'sʌbsəkwənt 'ɪnfluwənsəz. 'læŋgwɪdʒ gru æz wɝdz wɝ ə'kwaɪrd baɪ 'sʌbsəkwənt jus. wi du nɑt no hwʌt wəz ðə fɝst 'læŋgwɪdʒ. ðə fɝst 'ɛvədəns əz wɪð hwɪtʃ skɑlɝz ɑr ə'kwɛntəd det bæk onlɪ tu əbaʊt fɝ 'θaʊzənd bi si. ðɛr ɪz no 'kwɛstʃən bət ðət nuwɝ 'læŋgwɪdʒ gru aʊt əv oldɝ, bət ðə sɪtʃjə'weʃən ɪz ðət no rɛkɝdz əv ðiz ɛg'zɪst. fjuwɝ ðən sɪks 'læŋgwɪdʒəz kən bi 'fɑlod bæk əz fɑr əz e'tin hʌndrəd bi si. fju ɑr əwɛr əv ðə lɑrdʒ nʌmbɝ əv 'læŋgwɪdʒəz ðət əv ɛg'zɪstəd; ə'mɛrəkən ɪndɪjənz əlon hæd mɔr ðən θri hʌndrəd ən fɪftɪ, hwɪtʃ wɝ grupt ɪntu 'twɛntɪ faɪv 'fæmlɪz. ðə 'kɑnsəkwɛns əv kə'mjunəkeʃən prɑbləmz ɪn aʊr 'mʌltə,lɪŋgwəl wɝld həz bɪn tə pɔɪnt ʌp ðə nid fɝ wʌn tʌŋ.]

[hw] as in while, anywhere

Common Spelling: wh as in which, awhile

Production. The [hw] may be classified as an unvoiced labial (or bilabial) glide, as it is in this text, or as an unvoiced labial fricative. To articulate the sound, the lips are rounded, then moved to the position for the following sound as an unvoiced breath stream is emitted. Usually the back part of the tongue is raised toward the soft palate. Velopharyngeal closure is complete, or nearly so.

Acoustically the initial portion of [hw] is usually a very brief fricative sound resembling [h]; this is followed by a smooth transition movement through the lip position for [w] and on to the following vowel. The fricative element may come from passage of the breath through the lip opening or may be made within the mouth. When the sound is made with lip friction, it often is classified as a voiceless fricative, which can be transcribed, if one wishes, by use of the symbol [ʍ]. It may help the student to think of [hw] as an unvoiced [w], even though this is not, strictly speaking, a complete description from the phonetic point of view. Here the sound is classified as a glide, since this seems best for purposes of emphasizing the articulation movements of the sound. Incidentally, although the fricative noise may resemble [h], it is quite dissimilar to the initial sound in words such as "how" and "hen," and hence the [h] symbol in the digraph [hw] may be misleading. The symbol [ʍ] has some advantages, but it seems to be falling into disuse.

Pronunciation. The [hw] is one of the relatively few sounds in English that has a virtually consistent spelling; hence there are not often spelling-pronunciation errors. A cursory search of the dictionaries in common use turned up only the following list of words where an initial wh calls for [h] rather than [hw] (derivatives should be included): "who," "whole," "whore," and "whoop." The word "whoa" is sometimes [ho].

A good deal of energy seems to have been expended uselessly on the matter of [hw] versus [w] in words such as "when," "where," and "what." Although these words are marked [hw] in most dictionaries, the aspirate quality may be sharply reduced, or entirely absent, in contextual speech. If so, the sound becomes a voiceless [w], or it may even be voiced; when analyzed, "wear" and "where" may have become indistinguishable.

Great stress is sometimes laid on the desirability of making certain that this does not happen, but in most phonetic situations [hw] can move toward [w] without rendering the pronunciation seriously substandard. To be sure, such phrases as "which witch?" "what watt?" and "weigh whey" would need to be judiciously spoken, and it must be granted that the more careful speakers generally tend to preserve the aspirate quality of [hw]. In the main, the sound does not prove too troublesome.

Exercises

1. The following passage is loaded with [hw] sounds. Transcribe your pronunciation and compare it in the usual way with the transcription at the end of these exercises. Not many unusual features will be found in this sample because of the regularity of spelling for the sound. However, note the numerous shadings in actual speech.

Phonetic transcription can be practiced anywhere with whatever samples of speech come along. When we first became intrigued with phonetics we whiled away a good deal of time which probably should have been spent otherwise recording the professor, who candidly was not the best speaker we have heard. After a while it was possible to turn out what proved very readable notes, although whenever a classmate observed the hen scratches he either became over-whelmed by curiosity or dismissed us as a whimsical fellow. "Odd ball" was the way he often put it in a whispered aside. Whetted by these small successes, we were wholly delighted to discover the amazing variety of dialects that could be heard on the elevated train. Somewhat later in what is sometimes called a whistle-stop town we tried to help with a dialect study, which was made by recording samples of the speech of persons who came into the white-washed office of the county clerk. If you are seriously interested, do the same kind of thing; transcribe whenever and wherever you can.

2. Practice the following representative [hw] words:

Initiating consonant: what, when, where, whey, which, whirr, why, whoa

Stronger consonant: awhirl, awhile, anywhere, somewhere

3. Practice the following minimal pairs:

[hw]—[w]		[hw]—[v]	
whacks [hwæks]	wax [wæks]	whale [hwel]	vale [vel]
whale [hwel]	wale [wel]	whee [hwi]	V [vi]
whee [hwi]	we [wi]	wheeze [hwiz]	V's [viz]
wheel [hwil]	weal [wil]	whet [hwɛt]	vet [vɛt]
wheyed [hwed]	weighed [wed]	wherry [hwɛrɪ]	very [vɛrɪ]
while [hwaɪl]	wile [waɪl]	whew [hwju]	view [vju]
whig [hwɪg]	wig [wɪg]	while [hwaɪl]	vile [vaɪl]
whist [hwɪst]	wist [wɪst]	whine [hwaɪn]	vine [vaɪn]
white [hwaɪt]	wight [waɪt]	why [hwaɪ]	vie [vaɪ]
whys [hwaɪz]	wise [waɪz]	whys [hwaɪz]	vies [vaɪz]

[hw]—[f]

whale [hwel]	fail [fel]
whee [hwi]	fee [fi]
wheel [hwil]	feel [fil]
wherry [hwɛrɪ]	ferry [fɛrɪ]
whig [hwɪg]	fig [fɪg]
while [hwaɪl]	file [faɪl]
whine [hwaɪn]	fine [faɪn]
whist [hwɪst]	fist [fɪst]
white [hwaɪt]	fight [faɪt]
why [hwaɪ]	fie [faɪ]

Phonetic Transcription. The following is a transcription in GA of the paragraph in Exercise 1:

[fə'nɛtɪk træn'skrɪpʃən kən bi 'præktəst 'ɛnɪhwer wɪð hwʌt'ɛvɚ sæmplz əv spitʃ kʌm ələŋ. hwɛn wi fɚst bɪ'kem ɪn'trigd wɪθ fə'nɛtɪks wi hwaɪld əwe ə gud dil əv taɪm hwɪtʃ 'prabəblɪ ʃud əv bɪn spɛnt 'ʌðɚwaɪz rɪ'kɔrdɪŋ ðə prə'fɛsɚ, hu 'kændədlɪ wəz nat ðə bɛst spikɚ wi həv hɚd. æftɚ ə hwaɪl ɪt wəz pasəbḷ tə tɚn aut hwʌt pruvd tə bi vɛrɪ ridəbḷ nots, 'ɔlðo hwən'ɛvɚ ə 'klæs,mɛt əb'zɚvd ðə 'hɛn ,skrætʃəz hi iðɚ bɪ'kem ovɚ'hwɛlmd baɪ ,kjʊrɪ'asətɪ ɔr dɪs'mɪst ʌs æz ə 'hwɪmzɪkḷ fɛlo. ad bəl wəz ðə we hi əfən put ət ɪn ə 'hwɪspɚd əsaɪd. hwɛtəd baɪ ðiz smɔl sək'sɛsəz, wi wɚ holɪ di'laɪtəd tə dɪ'skʌvɚ ðɪ ə'mezɪŋ və'raɪətɪ əv 'daɪəlɛkts ðət kəd bi hɚd ɔn ðɪ 'ɛləvetəd trɛn. 'sʌmhwʌt letɚ ɪn hwʌt ɪz 'sʌm,taɪmz kɔld ə hwɪsḷ stap taun wi traɪd tə hɛlp wɪð ə 'daɪəlɛkt stʌdɪ, hwɪtʃ wəz med baɪ rɪ'kɔrdɪŋ sæmplz əv ðə spitʃ əv pɚsənz hu kem ɪntə ðə 'hwaɪtwɔʃt əfəs əv ðə 'kaunti klɚk. ɪf ju ɚ 'sɪrɪəslɪ 'ɪntərɛstəd, du ðə sem kaɪnd əv θɪŋ: træn'skraɪb hwɛnɛvɚ ən hwɛrɛvɚ jə kæn.]

[m] as in me, amount, some

Common Spellings: *m* as in met

mm as in comment

Also spelled *lm*, as in calm; *mb*, as in limb; *gm*, as in phlegm; and *mn*, as in hymn.

Production. The [m] is classed as a voiced labial (or bilabial) nasal. In making a standard [m], the lips are closed and a voiced breath stream is emitted through the nasal passages. The tongue position has no significant effect on the [m] resonance, but it is usually at or near the position for any following sound if [m] is initial or medial; otherwise it rests in a neutral position on the floor of the mouth.

The [m] is one of the three English nasal sounds, the others being [n] and [ŋ]. The nasal quality is imparted to the tone because the soft palate is relaxed in such a way that the cavity above the soft palate (*nasopharynx*) and the nasal passages themselves serve as resonators.

On all English sounds except the three nasals velopharyngeal closure is complete, or nearly so; if it is not, an unwanted nasality is given voiced sounds, particularly vowels.

Pronunciation. Like [l], the [m] may be syllabic, in which case the symbol [m̩] is used in transcription. A ready example is the common conversational pronunciation of the phrase "keep them" as [kipm̩]. This use of the syllabic sound, however, is not commended, although it may not be clearly substandard. Note the syllabic [m] in [opm̩d] for "opened" and [kæpm̩] for "captain," which are substandard.

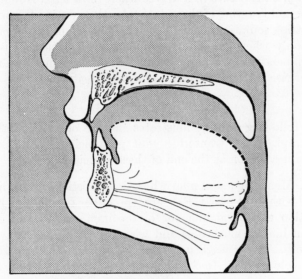

Fig. 16. Articulation adjustment for [m].

Pronounciation problems with [m] are not numerous. The spellings *m* or *mm* are in the majority and always call for [m]. Silent letters adjacent to *m* may be misleading, as in the *lm* and *mn* combinations, but this is scarcely a difficulty involving [m]. There is very little variation among the sounds in this phoneme, except possibly in length. Rarely do children fail to learn and use [m], perhaps because of the relative simplicity of the articulatory adjustment. Persons with a foreign-language background likewise experience little trouble with the sound.

Underpronunciation of [m] deprives speech of a certain sonority, but this does not reach a critical point in the speech of most physically normal persons. If there should be any pathological condition which tends to block the opening into the nasal passages (hypertrophied tonsils or adenoids, for instance) *denasality*, or a lack of adequate nasal resonance, may be a consequence. A full-blown head cold gives the same results. All three nasal sounds are naturally affected.

Although denasality is a kind of voice or resonance defect, an articulation defect is also present. Its outstanding feature is substitution of the appropriate homorganic plosive for the nasal, that is, [b] for [m], [d] for [n], and [g] for [ŋ]. The sentence "Some men make new songs for a living" would be transmuted into [sʌb bɛd bek du sɔgz fɔr ə lɪvɪg]. A student with this defect once temporarily baffled one of the authors who sought to enter her address on the records; he finally was made to understand that [æbɑb led] meant "Ambaum Lane." When resonance from one of the nasals spreads to adjacent sounds, the phenomenon is called *assimilation nasality*. This occurs to a degree wherever a nasal is found, because the raising and lowering of the palate take place during the brief interval when abutting sounds are being "blended." Assimilation nasality is substandard only when present to an unpleasantly conspicuous extent. If underpronunciation of a nasal is functional, the remedy is articulation drill; otherwise the only recourse is medical treatment.

Exercises

1. The following passage illustrates the use of [m]. Practice reading the paragraph aloud, transcribe your pronunciation, then compare it with the transcription at the end of these exercises.

H. L. Mencken was a man whose journalistic writings never are damned with faint praise. Readers tend either to sing high hymns of admiration and deem him one of the immortal wits or else they condemn him as monstrous and wish the Lord would have struck him dumb. Among English scholars he commands immense respect for his volume *The American Language*, which is really a monumental commentary on American usage. For many years a newspaper reporter in a clamorous political age, he maintained a keen interest in oratory. He had great admiration for William Jennings Bryan, in a sort of reverse English manner, and took delight in the Great Commoner's "immortal declaration that man is not a mammal." He has this to say of him: "The average impromptu speech, taken down by a stenographer, is found to be a bedlam of puerile cliches, thumping non-sequiturs and limping, unfinished sentences. But Jennings emitted English that was clear, flowing and sometimes not a little elegant, in the best sense of the word. Every sentence had a beginning, a middle and an end. The argument, three times out of four, was idiotic, but at least it hung together."

2. Practice the following representative [m] words:

Initiating consonant: may, me, moo, my
Terminating consonant: aim, am, arm, him

Initiating and terminating: maim, mam, Maugham, mom
Stronger consonant: admire, amass, commence, remit
Weaker consonant: coming, hamlet, rumor, stammer
Initial blends: [sm] smell, smoke
Final blends: [mz] comes, tombs; [md] blamed, bombed; [mp] lump,
   stamp; [mps] stamps, thumps; [mpt] stamped, clamped;
   [rm] arm, storm

3. Study the following minimal pairs:

[m]—[b]

bombing [bɑmɪŋ]	bobbing [bɑbɪŋ]
mat [mæt]	bat [bæt]
may [me]	bay [be]
meet [mit]	beat [bit]
met [mɛt]	bet [bɛt]
might [maɪt]	bight [baɪt]
moss [mɔs]	boss [bɔs]
must [mʌst]	bust [bʌst]
rum [rʌm]	rub [rʌb]
some [sʌm]	sub [sʌb]

[m]—[n]

a mass [əmæs]	an ass [ənæs]
coming [kʌmɪŋ]	cunning [kʌnɪŋ]
foamy [fomɪ]	phony [fonɪ]
home [hom]	hone [hon]
meal [mil]	kneel [nil]
meat [mit]	neat [nit]
met [mɛt]	net [nɛt]
might [maɪt]	night [naɪt]
ram [ræm]	ran [ræn]
some [sʌm]	sun [sʌn]

[m]—[ŋ]

bombing [bɑmɪŋ]	bonging [bɑŋɪŋ]
dim [dɪm]	ding [dɪŋ]
gum [gʌm]	gung [gʌŋ]
hum [hʌm]	hung [hʌŋ]
rim [rɪm]	ring [rɪŋ]
rum [rʌm]	rung [rʌŋ]
ram [ræm]	rang [ræŋ]
Sam [sæm]	sang [sæŋ]
slam [slæm]	slang [slæŋ]
some [sʌm]	sung [sʌŋ]

Phonetic Transcription. The following is a transcription in GA of the paragraph in Exercise 1:

[etʃ ɛl mɛŋkən wəz ə mæn huz ˌdʒɝnəˈlɪstɪk ˈraɪtɪŋz nevɚ ɑr dæmd wɪð fent prez. ridɚz tɛnd iðɚ tə sɪŋ haɪ hɪmz əv ˌædməˈreʃən n̩ dim ɪm wʌn əv ðɪ ɪˈmɔrtəl wɪts ɔr ɛls ðe kənˈdɛm ɪm əz ˈmʌnstrəs ən wɪʃ ðə lɔrd wud əv strʌk ɪm dʌm. əmʌŋ ˈɪŋgliʃ skɑlɚz hi kəˈmændz əmɛns rɪˈspɛkt fɚ ɪz vʌljəm, ðɪ əˈmɛrəkən ˈlæŋgwɪdʒ, hwɪtʃ ɪz rɪlɪ ə ˈmʌnjəˌmɛntl̩ ˈkɑməntɛrɪ ɔn əˈmɛrəkən ˈjusɪdʒ. fɔr mɛnɪ jɪrz ə ˈnuzpepɚ rɪˈpɔrtɚ ɪn ə ˈklæmərəs ˈpəlɪtɪkl̩ edʒ, hi ˈmentend ə kin ɪntrəst ɪn ˈɔrətɔrɪ. hi hæd ə gret ædməˈreʃən fɚ ˈwɪljəm ˈdʒɛnɪŋz braɪən, ɪn ə sɔrt əv rɪˈvɝs ˈɪŋgliʃ mænɚ, ən tuk dɪˈlaɪt ɪn ðə gret ˈkɑmənɚz ˈɪmɔrtl̩ dɛkləˈreʃən ðət mæn ɪz nɑt ə ˈmæməl. hi həz ðɪs tə se əv ɪm: ðɪ ˈævrɪdʒ ˌɪmˈprɑmtu spitʃ, tekən daʊn baɪ ə stəˈnɑgrəfɚ, əz faʊnd tə bi ə ˈbɛdləm əv pjurəl kliˈʃez, θʌmpɪŋ nɑn ˈsɛkwətɚz ən ˈlɪmpɪŋ ˈʌnˌfɪnɪʃt ˈsɛntn̩səz. bət ˈdʒɛnɪŋz iˈmɪtəd ˈɪŋgliʃ ðət wəz klɪr, ˈflowɪŋ ən ˈsʌmˌtaɪmz nɑt ə lɪtl̩ ˈɛləgənt, ɪn ðə bɛst sɛns əv ðə wɝd. ɛvrɪ ˈsɛntn̩s hæd ə bɪˈgɪnɪŋ, ə mɪdl̩ ænd ən ɛnd. ðɪ ˈɑrgjəmənt, θri taɪmz aʊt əv fɔr, wəz ɪdɪˈatɪk, bət ət list ɪt hʌŋ təˈgɛðɚ.]

[n] as in no, and

Common Spellings: n as in never, can
nn as in annoy, cannot
Also spelled *gn,* as in gnat; *kn,* as in know; *pn,* as in pneumonia; and *mn,* as in mnemonic.

Production. The [n] is classified as a voiced lingua-alveolar nasal. To make this sound, the tonguetip is placed on the alveolar ridge, with the sides of the tongue in contact with the teeth and gums. The soft palate is relaxed. With the tongue and palate in this position, the voiced breath stream is directed through the nose. The lips are opened slightly. The basic tongue adjustment corresponds to that for the plosives [t] and [d].

Pronunciation. The [n] is another of the consonants which can become syllabic, and does so more often than either [m] or [l]. The syllabic sound is transcribed [n̩]. Examples are the usual pronunciations of such words as "fasten" [fæsn̩], "cotton" [kɑtn̩], and "written" [rɪtn̩]. These pronunciations are standard, of course. As a matter of fact, where [n] follows the alveolar plosive [t], the use of [ən] rather than [n̩] would have an overcareful, pedantic flavor in some dialects. (To observe this, pronounce "written" [rɪtən] with [t] initiating the second syllable instead of terminating the first as in [rɪtn̩]).

Although the syllabic [n] is regularly standard, as in the examples given, this is not always so. For instance, the usage [ju n̩ aɪ] for "you and I" (and this can easily degenerate into [junaɪ]) verges on the substandard in any but the most informal speech; [ju ən aɪ] or even [ju ənd aɪ] is certainly better. On the other hand, a syllabic [n] pronunciation for the word "and" is fully standard in contexts where "and" follows an alveolar sound in conversational speech. The phrases "pot and pan" [pɑt n̩ pæn] and "Pat and Mike" [pæt n̩ maɪk] illustrate the point.

The sound is spelled quite consistently, although it is often associated with silent letters which confuse the foreign speaker. A general rule to which there are few exceptions is that *kn*, *pn*, and *gn* are simply [n]; a final *mn* is [m], whereas an initial *mn* is [n]. Final *mn* is common, as in "column," "solemn," and the like; initial *mn*, as in "mnemonic," is a rarity.

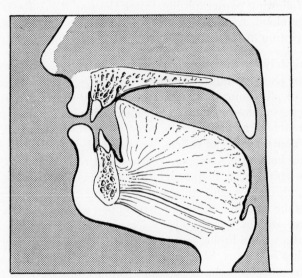

Fɪɢ. 17. Articulation adjustment for [n].

There is some variation among sounds in the [n] phoneme. For instance, the [n] in "knee" is more forward than the sound in "gnaw," once more because of the influence of adjacent vowels. The same holds true for "keen" [kin] and "on" [ɔn]. Changes of this sort can be ignored in practicing pronunciation, since in most instances they are scarcely perceptible even to the phonetically sophisticated listener.

One problem centered around *assimilation* merits a word of comment. When followed by a velar sound ([k] or [g]), the [n] may be replaced by [ŋ] in a way that sometimes is and sometimes is not standard. Assimilations of this sort which are now sanctioned include "conquer" [kɑŋkɚ], "ink" [ɪŋk], and many other words containing *ink*. On the other hand, serious doubts would have to be raised about [ɪŋkʌm] for "income," [bæŋkwət] for "banquet," [ɪŋ kipɪŋ] for "in keeping," [ɪŋkwɛst] for "inquest," and the like.

Notice also the curious phenomenon which occurs when [n] precedes or follows a bilabial [p] or [b]. A phrase such as "on purpose" may come close to [ɔm pɘpɘs], "open" may be heard as [opm̩], "grandpa" as [græmpɘ], "captain" as [kæpm̩], and so on. This change from [n] to [m] is substandard, at least in theory, but it happens so regularly that some of these usages must be accepted. The characteristics of underpronounced [n] with inadequate resonance are comparable to those described for [m].

Exercises

1. The following paragraph illustrates the use of [n]. Practice reading the passage aloud, transcribe your pronunciation, then compare it with the transcription of the author's speech at the end of these exercises.

Fortunately for the peace of mind of many of us, current fads and fancies in teen-age talk are certain to change eventually, after the manner of all fashions. Since time has kindly drawn a mantle over our own postadolescent diction, our inclination is to maintain it could never have held a candle to the zany slang, for instance, of the hot rodder. This machine, of course, is a stripped-down car. An innocent appearing hot rod is a sleeper. White-wall tires are snowballs. Hubcaps are spinners, a double ignition system is known as a flame thrower, chrome ornaments are goodies, and the engine is the mill. Should some mechanical breakdown happen which the genius behind the wheel cannot identify, he solemnly and knowingly explains, "The Johnson rod broke," and all other informed passengers understand what he means. Should they chance to stop for a snack, pancakes are collision mats. A profound thinker has static in his attic, while a maiden who is chronically dizzy is a mixed chick. A dance is a drag, but this also is the name for a kind of nonsensical and insane race. And so on, ad infinitum. We are inclined to say, "Twenty-three skiddoo!"

2. Practice the following representative examples of [n] words. Recall that the "syllabic consonants" are actually vowels from the point of view of their articulation:

Initiating consonant: gnaw, knee, nay, no
Terminating consonant: an, earn, in, on
Initiating and terminating: known, nine, non-, none
Stronger consonant: annoy, canoe, enough, renew
Weaker consonant: any, banner, earning, many
Syllabic consonant: hat 'n coat, cotton, button, fatten
Initial blends: [sn] sneeze, snow

Final blends: [nz] bones, hens; [nd] burned, ground; [nt] bent, count; [nts] or [ns] once, rents; [ntʃ] bunch, ranch; [ntʃt] or [nʃt] benched, wrenched; [ndʒ] mange, orange; [rn] barn, torn; [ndʒd] or [nʒd] hinged, ranged; [nst] or [ntst] bounced, fenced

3. Study and add to the following list of minimal pairs:

[n]—[d]		[n]—[m]	
can [kæn]	cad [kæd]	can [kæn]	cam [kæm]
kneel [nil]	deal [dil]	gain [gen]	game [gem]
man [mæn]	mad [mæd]	gun [gʌn]	gum [gʌm]
near [nɪr]	dear [dɪr]	near [nɪr]	mere [mɪr]
nearly [nɪrlɪ]	dearly [dɪrlɪ]	neigh [ne]	may [me]
neigh [ne]	day [de]	nice [naɪs]	mice [maɪs]
net [nɛt]	debt [dɛt]	nicks [nɪks]	mix [mɪks]
nice [naɪs]	dice [daɪs]	no [no]	mow [mo]
no [no]	dough [do]	Norman [nɔrmən]	Morman [mɔrmən]
pan [pæn]	pad [pæd]	sane [sen]	same [sem]

[n]—[ŋ]	
ban [bæn]	bang [bæŋ]
bun [bʌn]	bung [bʌŋ]
pan [pæn]	pang [pæŋ]
ran [ræn]	rang [ræŋ]
run [rʌn]	rung [rʌŋ]
tan [tæn]	tang [tæŋ]
thin [θɪn]	thing [θɪŋ]
ton [tʌn]	tongue [tʌŋ]
sinner [sɪnɚ]	singer [sɪŋɚ]
win [wɪn]	wing [wɪŋ]

Phonetic Transcription. The following is a transcription in GA of the paragraph in Exercise 1:

['fɔrtʃənətlɪ fɚ ðə pis əv maɪnd əv mɛnɪ əv əs, 'kʌrənt fædz ən 'fænsɪz ɪn tin edʒ tɔk ar sɝtn̩ tə tʃendʒ i'vɛntʃuəlɪ, æftɚ ðə mænɚ əv əl fæʃənz. sɪns taɪm həz kaɪndlɪ drɒn ə mæntl̩ ovɚ aʊr ɒn postædə'lɛsənt 'dɪkʃən, aʊr ɪnklən'eʃən ɪz tə ˌmen'ten ɪt kəd nɛvɚ həv hɛld ə kændl̩ tə ðə 'zenɪ slæŋ, fɚ 'ɪnstəns, əv ðə hat radɚ. ðɪs mə'ʃin, əv kɔrs, ɪz ə strɪpt daʊn kar. ən 'ɪnəsənt ə'pɪrɪŋ hat rad ɪz ə slɪpɚ. hwaɪt wəl taɪrz ar 'snoˌbɔlz. hʌbkæps ar spɪnɚz; ə dʌbl̩ ɪg'nɪʃən sɪstəm əz nɒn əz ɚ flem θroɚ; krɒm 'ɔrnəmənts ar 'gʊdɪz, ən ðɪ ɛndʒən əz ðə mɪl. ʃʊd sʌm mə'kænɪkl̩ 'brekˌ-daʊn hæpn̩ hwɪtʃ ðə 'dʒɪnjəs bɪ'haɪnd ðə hwil kə'nɒt aɪ'dɛntəfaɪ, hi 'saləmlɪ ən 'nowɪŋlɪ ɪk'splenz, ðə 'dʒʌnsən rad brok, ənd əl ʌðɚ ɪn'-

fɔrmd 'pæsəndʒɚz ʌndɚ'stænd hwʌt i minz. ʃʊd ðe tʃænts tə stɑp fɚ ə snæk, 'pænkeks ɑr kə'lɪʒən mæts. ə prə'faʊnd θɪŋkɚ hæz 'stætɪk ɪn ɪz 'ætɪk, hwaɪl ə medn̥ hu əz 'krɑnɪklɪ 'dɪzɪ ɪz ə mɪkst tʃɪk. ə dæns ɪz ə dræg, bət ðɪs ɔlso əz ðə nem fɚ ə kaɪnd əv ˌnɑn'sɛnsɪkḷ ənd ɪn'sen res. ən sowɔn, æd ˌɪnfən'aɪtəm. wi ɑr ɪn'klaɪnd tə se, 'twɛntɪ θri ˌskɪ'du!]

[ŋ] as in think, bring

Common Spellings: *ng,* as in singer, long

                      n, as in sink, anxious

Production. The [ŋ] is classified as a voiced linguavelar nasal. To make this sound, the middle of the tongue is brought into contact with the soft palate, which is relaxed. With the tongue held in this position, the voiced

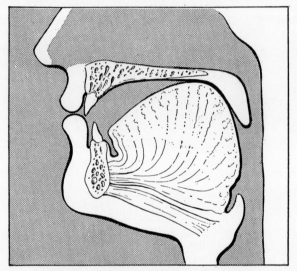

FIG. 18. Articulation adjustment for [ŋ].

breath stream is emitted through the nose. The tongue position resembles that for the plosives [k] and [g].

Pronunciation. The existence of the [ŋ] sound is curiously unrecognized by most persons who speak English, even though they may use it countless times each day. For this reason the beginning student may have some initial difficulty in identifying [ŋ], but this problem should be a minor one. Remember always that the letters *ng* often represent a single nasal sound of the same general type as *m* and *n,* not a combination sound.

Spelling-pronunciation inconsistencies of the digraph *ng* sometimes cause confusion. The historically older [ŋg] pronunciation has been retained in some words, such as "finger" [fɪŋgɚ] and "jungle" [dʒʌŋgəl], but it has been dropped at the end of most words (and within some). This has led to [rɪŋ] for "ring," [hæŋ] for "hang," [sɪŋɚ] for "singer," [sɪŋɪŋ] for "singing," and so on. When followed by [k] or [g], the letter *n* is more often than not [ŋ], because of the influence of the velar plosive. This accounts for such cases as "think" [θɪŋk], "finger" [fɪŋgɚ], and "congress" [kɑŋgrəs]. More literal spelling pronunciations, such as [θɪnk] for "think" and [fɪngɚ] for "finger," tend to sound stilted and pedantic on the very rare occasions when they are heard. There is unfortunately no useful rule of spelling for the student to apply in determining when he should choose any one of the three possible pronunciations—[ŋ], [ng], or [ŋg]—for the *ng* letter combination.

Most of the substandard speech practices involving [ŋ] arise from situations of the sort that have just been discussed. Specific foreign-dialect errors are not frequent, although they are noted occasionally. Persons whose language has been influenced by Yiddish sometimes add [g] or [k] to [ŋ], as with [goɪŋk] for "going" and [sɪŋg] for "sing." Nasals resembling [ŋ] are sometimes carried into English from another language, but this is not really common. The previous discussion of inadequate nasal resonance applies to [ŋ] as well as to [m] and [n].

Exercises

1. The following short passage illustrates numerous [ŋ] usages. Read it aloud, transcribe your pronunciation, then make a comparison with the transcription following these exercises. Be alert for possible sub-standard usages.

Thanks to an astonishing brain mechanism, talking is a singularly unconscious form of behavior. We can keep on expressing ideas without much searching for words; they spring forth with surprisingly little conscious thought. Incoming words are understood, although fleetingly heard. Had not speech increased in keeping with other forms of behavior the brain would look much different, for man's imposing frontal development serves the language function. In contrast, the sloping forehead of the ape is that of a species without linguistic capacity. Brain injury carries a danger to speech, and there is distinct reason to be anxious in such a situation. As the understanding of brain function increases, added knowledge may bring hope for those with such defects.

2. Study and practice the following representative [ŋ] words:

Terminating consonant: rang, ring, long, wrong
Weaker consonant: hanger, longing, ringing, singer

[ŋg] *words:* English, finger, longer, single
[ŋk] *words:* blanket, conquer, sink, thank
[nk] *and* [ng] *words:* ingrate, income, inquest, vanguard
Other blends: [ŋks] honks, thinks; [ŋz] things, wrongs; [ŋkt] junked,
thanked; [ŋd] hanged, wronged

3. Study the following lists of minimal pairs:

[ŋ]—[g]		[ŋ]—[n]	
banger [bæŋɚ]	bagger [bægɚ]	banger [bæŋɚ]	banner [bænɚ]
ding [dɪŋ]	dig [dɪg]	clang [klæŋ]	clan [klæn]
dung [dʌŋ]	dug [dʌg]	ding [dɪŋ]	din [dɪn]
Hong [hɔŋ]	hog [hɔg]	gong [gɔŋ]	gone [gɔn]
hung [hʌŋ]	hug [hʌg]	gung [gʌŋ]	gun [gʌn]
long [lɔŋ]	log [lɔg]	hung [hʌŋ]	Hun [hʌn]
ping [pɪŋ]	pig [pɪg]	king [kɪŋ]	kin [kɪn]
ring [rɪŋ]	rig [rɪg]	ping [pɪŋ]	pin [pɪn]
tongue [tʌŋ]	tug [tʌg]	sing [sɪŋ]	sin [sɪn]
wringing [rɪŋɪŋ]	rigging [rɪgɪŋ]	sung [sʌŋ]	sun [sʌn]

[ŋ]—[ŋk]	
clang [klæŋ]	clank [klæŋk]
dingy [dɪŋɪ]	dinky [dɪŋkɪ]
dung [dʌŋ]	dunk [dʌŋk]
Hong [hɔŋ]	honk [hɔŋk]
hung [hʌŋ]	hunk [hʌŋk]
ring [rɪŋ]	rink [rɪŋk]
sing [sɪŋ]	sink [sɪŋk]
singer [sɪŋɚ]	sinker [sɪŋkɚ]
slung [slʌŋ]	slunk [slʌŋk]
sung [sʌŋ]	sunk [sʌŋk]

Phonetic Transcription. The following is a transcription in GA of the
paragraph in Exercise 1:

[ðæŋks tu ən ə'stɑnɪʃɪŋ bren 'mɛkənɪzm̩, 'tɔkɪŋ ɪz ə 'sɪŋgjʊləlɪ, ʌn'-
kɑntʃəs fɔrm əv bɪ'hevjɚ. wi kən kip ən ɛk'sprɛsɪŋ aɪ'dɪəz wɪ'ðaut mʌtʃ
'sɝ·tʃɪŋ fɚ wɝ·dz; ðe sprɪŋ fɔrθ wɪθ sə'praɪzɪŋlɪ lɪtl̩ kɑnʃəs θɔt. 'ɪn,kʌmɪŋ
wɝ·dz ɑr ʌndɚ'stud, 'ɔlðo 'flitɪŋlɪ hɝ·d. hæd nɑt spɪtʃ ɪn'krist ɪn 'kipɪŋ
wɪθ ʌðɚ fɔrmz əv bɪ'hevjɚ ðə bren wəd luk mʌtʃ dɪfrənt, fɔr mænz ɪm'-
pozɪŋ frʌntl̩ dɪ'vɛləpmənt sɝ·vz ðə 'læŋgwɪdʒ 'fʌŋkʃən. ɪn 'kɑntræst,
ðə 'slopɪŋ fɔrəd əv ðɪ ep ɪz ðæt əv ə 'spiʃɪz wɪ'ðaut ,lɪŋ'gwɪstɪk kə'pæsətɪ.
bren 'ɪndʒərɪ 'kɛrɪz ə dendʒɚ tə spɪtʃ, ənd ðɛr əz dɪ'stɪŋkt rizən tə bi
'æŋkʃəs ɪn sʌtʃ ə ,sɪtʃə'weʃən. æz ðɪ ʌndɚ'stændɪŋ əv bren 'fʌŋkʃən ɪn'-
krisəz, ædəd 'nɑlɪdʒ me brɪŋ hop fɚ ðoz wɪθ sʌtʃ dɪ'fɛkts.]

[l] as in look, alive, ball

Common Spellings: *l* as in look
                        ll as in will

Production. The [l] is classified as a voiced lingua-alveolar lateral. The standard sound is made with the tonguetip against the alveolar ridge, but with the tongue adjusted in such a manner that its margins do not touch the teeth and gums at the sides. With the tongue held in this position, the voiced breath stream is emitted, flowing laterally on either side of the lingua-alveolar contact. Velopharyngeal closure is complete, or nearly so. The teeth are slightly apart.

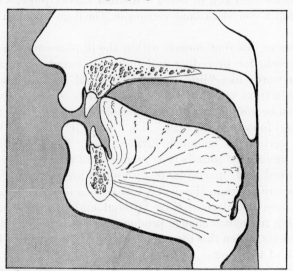

FIG. 19. Articulation adjustment for [l].

The resonance phenomena of its production give [l] a certain glide quality, and a limited number of phoneticians place the sound in this class. This seems defensible in some respects, since as an on-glide or off-glide feature of articulation in words such as "lead" and "ball," [l] is physiologically much like the glide [r] in "reed" and "bore." Nevertheless, the fact that [l] can become syllabic, which means that it can be produced accurately in a static position, and other considerations argue against putting it into the same category with the glides.

Pronunciation. The [l] is another of the sounds which are spelled quite consistently; hence spelling-pronunciation errors are relatively infrequent. There are, however, some instances of a silent *l*, and these may provoke substandard usages, particularly on the part of speakers who are meticulous in a naïve way. Examples are [pɑlm] for "palm," [sælmən] for "salmon," and [bɑlm] for "balm."

Although [l] usually fulfills the function of a consonant by initiating or terminating vowels (and in this role is a *nonsyllabic*), there are phonetic circumstances in which it serves as a separate syllable, and hence becomes *syllabic*. When this occurs, the proper symbol is [l̩]. Examples include "wrestle" [rɛsl̩], "castle" [kæsl̩], and "throttle" [θrɑtl̩]. Such words need not be spoken with a syllabic [l], but in common patterns of speech they are. If one pronounces them aloud in a conversational manner, it is possible, by careful listening, to distinguish the separate energy pulse for [l̩], or at least to achieve a pronunciation in which the sound is syllabic. If the phrase "he will go" is spoken in a "careless" manner, it may become [hi l̩ go], [l̩] being a distinct energy pulse. Compare this with [hil go], a conversational version of "he'll go" spoken with a non-syllabic [l].

A number of different sounds within the [l] phoneme can be heard in English speech, for preceding and following sounds exert a strong influence. In words like "lip" [lɪp], "lead" [lid], and others where [l] is followed by a front vowel, the tonguetip usually is on the alveolar ridge. It may even be *gingival*, or at the junction of the gums and teeth. When a back vowel follows, as in "law" [lɔ], "look" [lʊk], or "lock" [lɑk], the contact is certain to be much farther back. There are fine acoustic differences among the sounds thus produced, of course.

Substandard and unacceptable [l] sounds are common. In the first place, there are limits to the distance that tongue contact can be moved backward from the alveolar ridge without unduly "darkening" the [l]. The resulting resonance change produces a sound which is unacceptable in most dialects. Often this tongue retraction is accompanied by elevation of the back of the tongue, which tends to give an [ʊ]-ish quality to the [l]. This fault is most common on final sounds, though it is not confined to these.

Another common substandard usage, occurring in medial positions, is sometimes called the *palatal* [l], although it actually is an elision of the sound. Familiar examples are found in pronunciations such as [mɪjən] for "million," [wɪjəm] for "William," and [wɪ ju] for "will you." This clearly objectionable habit presumably arises because of the difficulty of shifting from [l] to [j].

Still another undesirable sound is the *labial* [l], a sound which comes close to being in the [w] phoneme. In this error there is usually some lip adjustment resembling that for [w], and the tongue does not take a standard [l] posture. The result is that such a word as "yellow" [jɛlo] becomes something very like [jɛwo].

This labial [l] is very close to the clean-cut substitution of [w] for [l] in infantile speech, where pronunciations such as [wʊk] for "look" and [wɪtl̩] for "little" are common. Incidentally, the substitution of [j] for

[l] is also a familiar infantilism. The [l] sound is often missing from the speech of children, and they may also say [ɪtl] and [aɪk] for "little" and "like" instead of employing substitutes for the unlearned sound. Various vowels, principally [ʊ], [ʌ], [ɜ], or [ə], and occasionally even [o], may be substituted for a final [l] by such children; [jɪtʌ] for "little" would be reasonably typical. The general term *lalling* is sometimes applied to failure to make a standard [l].

Some of the difficulty the adult American speaker has with [l] is on the syllabic sound. This is possibly because the [l̩], since it functions as a vowel, may be replaced by another vowel requiring an easier adjustment. Although the explanation may lie elsewhere, the error is common and gives usages such as [bætʌ], [bætə], or even an approximation of [bæto] for [bætl̩]. It does not differ in any essential respect from the comparable mistake in infantile speech. The correction, of course, is a distinct movement which brings the tongue into proper contact with the alveolar ridge.

Foreign-dialect mispronunciations of [l] are heard frequently. They arise largely from the transfer into English of somewhat similar sounds from the native language (this, of course, is a basic characteristic of foreign dialect). In Japanese, for instance, there is a palatal continuant made with the tongue in a position roughly intermediate between [l] and [r]. To the English-speaking person the Japanese who substitutes this sound for [l] seems to be substituting [r], as in [aɪ raɪk ɪt] for "I like it." Another example is the Spanish *l*, which resembles [lj].

Exercises

1. The following passage contains numerous examples of [l] in contexts of all kinds. Transcribe your own speech; then compare your pronunciation with the transcription at the end of these exercises.

One of the lesser and more useless literary diversions to while away a dull hour is compiling a list of the most beautiful words in the English language. This was popular as a pastime several years ago, culminating in a poll of a number of leading authors. Although our own favorite all-time choice is Camay, words with a liberal sprinkling of *l* sounds walked off with the honors. Among the nominations were such mellifluous sound melodies as "Lillian," "Laura," "lingering," "yellow," "mellow," "low," "ulnar," and even "tintinnabulation," the latter doubtless brought to mind by Edgar Allen Poe's "tintinnabulation of the bells, bells, bells." It is hard to say why these liquid notes are so pleasing to the sensibilities of these literary folk; the gentle murmur of *m* sends us much faster. We recall also that Sinclair Lewis described the mock melodiousness of one of his female characters with something like "her *l*'s were like the trilling of thrushes."

2. Practice the following representative examples of [l] words. Pay particular attention to the pronunciation of terminating and syllabic [l].

Initiating consonant: lay, lee, lie, low
Terminating consonant: ale, awl, earl, eel
Initiating and terminating: Lill, loll, Lowell, lull
Stronger consonant: alarm, asleep, hello, rely
Weaker consonant: ability, careless, pulling, solid
Syllabic consonant: battle, bottle, gable, saddle
Initial blends: [kl] claim, cloth; [sl] slick, slow; [fl] flower, fly; [bl] black, blue; [pl] plan, play; [gl] gleam, glue
Final blends: [lz] fills, holes; [ld] called, pulled; [lt] belt, wilt; [lts] colts, halts; [ldz] holds, molds; [lk] hulk, milk; [lp] help, kelp; [lm] film, helm

3. Practice the following minimal pairs:

[l]—[r]		[l]—[j]	
later [letɚ]	rater [retɚ]	clue [klu]	cue [kju]
law [lɔ]	raw [rɔ]	lack [læk]	yak [jæk]
lay [le]	ray [re]	lamb [læm]	yam [jæm]
lie [laɪ]	rye [raɪ]	lay [le]	yea [je]
light [laɪt]	right [raɪt]	let [lɛt]	yet [jɛt]
line [laɪn]	Rhine [raɪn]	local [lokəl]	yokel [jokəl]
long [lɔŋ]	wrong [rɔŋ]	long [lɔŋ]	Yong [jɔŋ]
lower [loɚ]	rower [roɚ]	loose [lus]	use [jus]
mill [mɪl]	mere [mɪr]	lung [lʌŋ]	young [jʌŋ]
pull [pʊl]	poor [pʊr]	lore [lɔr]	yore [jɔr]

[l]—[w]	
lake [lek]	wake [wek]
later [letɚ]	waiter [wetɚ]
lay [le]	way [we]
led [lɛd]	wed [wɛd]
let [lɛt]	wet [wɛt]
lie [laɪ]	Y [waɪ]
line [laɪn]	wine [waɪn]
long [lɔŋ]	Wong [wɔŋ]
lore [lɔr]	wore [wɔr]
low [lo]	woe [wo]

Phonetic Transcription. The following is a transcription in GA of the paragraph in Exercise 1:

[wʌn əv ðə lɛsɚ ən mɔr 'jusləs 'lɪtə‚rɛri dɪ'vɜ˞ʒənz tə hwaɪl əwe ə dʌl aʊr ɪz kəm'paɪlɪŋ ə lɪst əv ðə most 'bjutəfəl wɜ˞dz ɪn ðə 'ɪŋglɪʃ 'læŋgwɪdʒ. ðɪs wəz 'pɑpjəlɚ əz ə 'pæs‚taɪm 'sɛvrəl jɪrz əgo, 'kʌlmənetɪŋ ɪn ə pol əv ə nʌmbɚ əv 'lidɪŋ ɔθɚz. ɔlðo aur on fevrət əl taɪm tʃɔɪs ɪz 'kæ‚me, wɝdz wɪð ə lɪbrəl 'sprɪŋklɪŋ əv ɛl saundz wɔkt əf wɪθ ðɪ ɑnɚz. əmʌŋ ðə ‚nɑmə'-neʃənz wɝ sʌtʃ ‚mə'lɪfluwəs saund 'mɛlədɪz əz 'lɪlɪən, 'lɔrʌ, 'lɪŋgɚɪŋ, 'jɛlo, 'mɛlo, lo, 'ʌlnɑr, ænd ivən ‚tɪntɪnæbju'leʃən, ðə lætɚ dautləs brɔt tə maɪnd baɪ ɛdgɚ ælən poz ‚tɪntɪnæbju'leʃən əv ðə 'bɛlz, 'bɛlz, 'bɛlz. ɪt əz hɑrd tə se hwaɪ ðiz lɪkwəd nots ɑr so 'plizɪŋ tə ðə ‚sɛnsə'bɪlətɪz əv ðiz 'lɪtə‚rɛrɪ fok; ðə 'dʒɛntl̩ 'mɝ‚mɝ əv ɛm sɛndz ʌs mʌtʃ fæstɚ. wi rɪ'kɔl ɔlso ðət 'sɪn‚klɛr luəs dɪ'skraɪbd ðə mɑk mə'lodɪəsnəs əv wʌn əv ɪz 'fimel 'kɛrɪktəz wɪð sʌmpθɪŋ laɪk "hɚ ɛlz wɝ laɪk ðə 'trɪlɪŋ əv θrʌʃəz."]

Foreign and Nonphonemic Sounds. Because r-like sounds are so common among modern languages and because several varieties may be heard within a given language, many symbols are necessary for these sounds in any device such as an International Phonetic Alphabet. The explanation of even the major sounds of other languages that would roughly fall into an r class would be impossible in this book. A few of the symbols for such sounds and for certain other nasals should, however, be introduced.

The [r] as it ordinarily appears in lower-case form is actually the symbol originally chosen by the IPA to stand for the rolled or trilled r, made with the tip and blade of the tongue trilling against the alveolar ridge. The obvious reason for this choice was that the European scholars who compiled the phonetic alphabet were more familiar with this pronunciation. In American and British treatises on speech sounds, however, it has become conventional to employ [r]—the most familiar form of the letter—to designate the common glide in English. When this is done the symbol [ɹ] is assigned to the trilled r, a practice which is the reverse of the original IPA usage. Some additional symbols are listed below:

[ɾ] is the flapped or one-tap r. It is heard in Spanish and in British English.

[R] is the uvular rolled r. It is the common sound heard in French and German.

[ʁ] is the uvular fricative heard in some French dialects.

[ɱ] is the labiodental nasal of Italian and Spanish.

[ɲ] is the palatal nasal of French and Italian.

[ʋ] is the labiodental glide heard as the Dutch w (and in Hindi).

[ɥ] is the palatal glide of French. It is a glide from a lip-rounded position, much as an English [j] glides from the unrounded [i] position.

[ʎ] is the palatal lateral of Italian, Spanish, and Greek.

[ɬ] is the lateral voiceless fricative, a kind of voiceless [l] heard in the Welsh pronunciation of ll.

12

THE DYNAMICS OF
SOUNDS IN CONTEXT

Up to this point we have discussed the sounds of American speech as though they were much like a collection of individual alphabet blocks which could be placed alongside one another to spell words, without undergoing any changes in their individual forms. This approach was necessarily adopted in an attempt to familiarize students with the essential characteristics of each of the sound families. Having completed this analytic study, we now are ready to pass on to another phase of phonetics: the examination of connected speech, or the sounds in context.

One should start with the realization that connected speech is not a series of individual sounds joined together, like letters in a printed sentence. Instead, the sounds in context are altered in various ways because of their influence on one another and because certain important elements of speech form do not emerge until there is an ongoing flow of meaningful utterance. Speech as we hear it is much more than the sum of its individual sounds. This can be demonstrated in an interesting way in the laboratory. If one were to make separate tape recordings of a sound from each of the phonemes listed in this book, then splice these small lengths of tape together so that they would form meaningful words and sentences, not only would the resulting recording sound most unlike actual speech, but some of it might even be impossible to understand.

In this chapter and the one that follows we shall examine, first, the principles which explain the changes that occur in individual sounds when they are put together into meaningful connected communication and, next, the unique characteristics found only in connected speech. These matters are of great interest to the phonetician in his investigation of speech, but the information is of practical as well as theoretical importance. The closely related phenomena we need to understand first are (1) the role of *movement* in determining the nature of speech sounds;

242

(2) the *influence* of consonants on vowels; (3) *assimilation*, or the inter-action of adjacent sounds on one another; (4) *blending* and *juncture*, or the movement from word to word and syllable to syllable; and (5) *stress*, or the effect of the intensity or force of utterance on the nature of speech sounds.

MOVEMENT

For most phonemes, except the glides and the affricates, there is a single position of the articulators which can be thought of as standard for the sound. This is how the sound might be produced if it were spoken alone. When most sounds appear in contextual speech, however, the *movements* of the tongue, lips, and jaw toward and away from the standard position seem to be important in making the sounds "natural" and in giving each the distinctive characteristics which lead to its recognition by the listener. The speed and extent, or *timing*, of these movements seem to be important in the same way. Specifically, these temporal factors are the length of time taken to approach the standard position, the duration of the hold in this position, and the time involved in moving away from the hold. In some cases, as we shall learn, there may be no actual hold, as such. This is true, you will recall, in the case of the glides.

Although there is still much to be discovered about the timing and movement of the individual sound, recent advances in speech science have clarified many points about the dynamic nature of speech. Techniques have been devised to turn speech sound waves into visual graphic records in such a way that changes in the speech sounds are represented by shift-ing bars or lines on graph paper. Experimental phoneticians have also been able to take X-ray motion pictures of the tongue, jaw, lips, and soft palate during speech, thus making it possible not only to discover the positions typical of isolated speech sounds but also to observe how such positions change in time.

One factor which stands out in all these studies is the constant, rapid change that occurs in the sound patterns and tongue movements. The speech act is not a series of tongue "postures" in sequence but, rather, a complex, smoothly flowing pattern of movement. There actually appears to be very little in the way of a hold in the standard position for any of the sounds; instead the tongue and lips are in a fluid state of constant movement. It may well be that in teaching and learning the speech sounds we should place more emphasis on movement and less on position.

The concept of *movement* as a fundamental characteristic of speech sounds in context, contrasted to the idea of ongoing speech as a sequence of individual "blocks," can be illustrated graphically. In the view of speech as discrete sounds we might imagine the tongue movements in a nonsense word (say, for instance, [ruliælə]) as having this form:

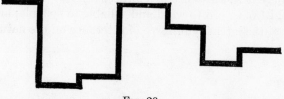

Fig. 20.

A more accurate picture of what actually happens in tongue movements, based on analysis of the sound waves of speech, is represented by the following pattern of flowing movement:

Fig. 21.

INFLUENCE AND ASSIMILATION

If a laboratory analysis is made of speech as just another kind of sound or physical energy, certain curious conclusions can be reached. From the physical standpoint, speech consists of a series of rapidly and constantly changing resonant tones interspersed with very short bursts of noise and brief intervals of silence. Loosely speaking, the tones are the syllabics (vowels and vowellike sounds), and the noises and silences are the consonants. In some circumstances what one thinks of as a consonant sound is only inferred from the timing, rather than actually heard. We know, for example, that one would ordinarily say that there is a final [p] in "cap" and a final [k] in "back," even though in actual running speech there may be no explosion of breath or similar distinctive sound which reaches the ear. The consonant in these instances is simply a way of terminating a vowel utterance.

Why is it possible to "hear" a plosive consonant when no explosion exists? The explanation lies in the *influence* of the consonant articulation on vowel quality. Thus, the reason a listener may have no difficulty in discriminating between the words "hat" and "hack"—words which are phonetically the same except for the "noiseless" terminating sounds—is that distinctively different concluding movements are involved in [t] and [k]. These movements affect the quality of the sound pattern which precedes them. Put in another way, one important factor in consonant recognition is the characteristic way that each consonant terminates a vowel—by a certain alteration of vowel quality brought about as the mouth position is quickly changed to assume the position of the consonant in question.

The influence of the consonant on the vowel is only one example of the way in which speech sounds interact in their complex forward flow. The unique acoustic or physiological pattern of any sound is determined by the phonetic environment in which it occurs. An example which has already been given is that of [t]. When [t] is followed by a high-front vowel, it may have a sound quite different from that of the [t] followed by a low-back vowel; nevertheless, we readily identify both as belonging in the same phoneme. The vowel [ɪ] between [t] and [n] in the word [tɪn] may have a characteristically different resonance from the [ɪ] between [r] and [k] in the word [rɪk]. Thus we are not surprised to find that the final element in the diphthong [aɪ] is not precisely the same as the sound [ɪ] in isolation or as a "pure" vowel. For that matter, it is easy to understand that there really is no such thing as a pure vowel in contextual speech, since we expect always a continuing process of change during the vowel utterance as the articulators move from a consonant position, through the vowel, and on to the position for the following consonant.

Aside from its academic interest to the phonetician, the foregoing discussion may help the student of speech improvement conceive of his problem as involving more than mastery of a set of individual sounds. He must, in addition, realize that speech is a fluid, ongoing pattern of movement. To develop his speech skills fully, he must hold this fact in mind and become sensitive to the "feel" of these movements and to the delicate nuances of sound in connected speech.

The phonetic term *assimilation* is used to designate the phenomena of change which occur in speech sounds when they are spoken in context. The various kinds of assimilation result from the operation of the principle of *influence*, which was discussed in the preceding paragraphs.

An important fact about assimilation is that it is a lawful and orderly process which can usually be quite easily understood on the basis of certain principles. To begin with, assimilation is simply the phonetic process whereby continuous speech is made easier and more efficient to produce through the alteration of the movements involved. It is the way in which standard articulatory adjustments for one or more sounds are modified or altered in order that the speaker can move from one sound to another more quickly and with a minimum of effort. For a simple illustration of this idea, we can refer back to an earlier example of changes in the speech sounds. Because of assimilation the tongue contact in [ki] is more forward than in [kɔ], since [i] is a front vowel and [ɔ] is a back vowel.

If one examines English pronunciation with the factor of assimilation in mind, he will note that there are certain combinations of sounds which are very difficult to pronounce in sequence, because of the articulation adjustments involved, and which are therefore customarily avoided. For instance, it is very hard to make the tongue move rapidly from [n] to [k], because the first sound is produced with the front of the tongue and the second with the back of the tongue. It is much easier to go from [ŋ] to [k], so that we naturally say [mɪŋk] and [ɪŋk] rather than [ɪnk]. The necessities of assimilation explain why these pronunciations have developed and have become the accepted standard. Thus, if a particular combination of sounds is difficult to produce because of the extent or rapidity of the tongue, lip, or palate movements involved, one of the sounds is likely to influence the other in such a way as to make the combination more efficient to produce, even if this means adding, changing, or eliminating a sound.

We do not always seem to make things as easy for ourselves as we might, however, and the tendency toward convenience in talking involves some pitfalls which the student should avoid. For instance, the sequence [sts] is rather awkward to produce, in this case possibly because there is not enough variation in tongue movement to make the differentiation of the three sounds easy. The impulse is to slight the [t] and pronounce a single somewhat prolonged [s]. If we yield too readily to this tendency, "ghosts" may become [gos], which is substandard speech. In a similar way the question "Did you eat?" can degenerate into [dʒit?], to which the answer is often [nodʒu?]. Carried to its ultimate and absurd conclusion, assimilation could make all speech sounds identical.

On the other hand, one cannot resist assimilation too assiduously, or his speech will come to sound stilted and pedantic. Assimilation makes the pronunciation of "tissue" quite naturally take the form [tɪʃu], and [tɪsju] is certainly a conspicuous and pedantic overpronunciation. There is really no universal rule for determining the proper degree of assimilation. It may be that in the course of time our pronunciation practices will change to the point where we never require that sounds be joined in a difficult way, but in the meantime the student must depend for guidance upon what his ear and his dictionary tell him about the practices of educated speakers.

Progressive assimilation takes place when the first sound retains its identity and influences the following sound. Examples are the pronunciation [kipm̩] for "keep them" and the pronunciation [pɪrst] for "pierced," rather than [pɪrsəd] as it was in Chaucer's day. Where it is the first sound which is changed by the influence of the second, the process is known as *regressive assimilation*. Pronouncing the word "congress" as [kɑŋgrəs] rather than [kɑngrəs] is an illustration, as are the instances of [mɪŋk] and [ɪŋk] mentioned in an earlier paragraph. When the sounds interact in such a way that they are combined in a single compromise sound, the phonetic phenomenon is called *reciprocal assimilation*. The choice of [greʃəs] rather than [gresjəs] for the word "gracious" illustrates a compromise of this kind. Assimilations may be defined as *partial* or *complete*, depending upon whether the altered sound has simply been distorted or has actually shifted to a different phoneme. They may also be described as *consonant* or *vowel* assimilations. Ordinarily the consonant has a greater influence on the adjacent vowel than vice versa, because of the less variable, and hence stronger, movement pattern of the consonant, but this does not hold true in all cases.

BLENDING AND JUNCTURE

All these principles of influence and assimilation can be extended to the phonetic situation which arises when words are spoken in sequence. The term *blending* is used to refer to the way speech flows along from word to word within the phrase. We say "phrase" rather than "sentence" in this definition because there is ordinarily sufficient pause between successive phrases to eliminate any particular need for blending.

From a phonetic point of view speech is seldom divided into "words." When we say "Come on out" in a natural manner there is no break whatsoever between the words; for all phonetic purposes the entire phrase is a single word, since the sounds follow each other without interruption. There is nothing of an acoustic or physiologic nature in uttering this phrase which corresponds to the white space we see between the words as they are printed on this page. We speak in "separate words" only in special circumstances—for example, when a statement calls for great emphasis; if we did so in conversational speech, the result would be quite unnatural. Words, as such, are important linguistically and semantically, but they are usually of little concern phonetically.

The foregoing description ignores one very important matter: the way in which *syllables* are blended together—either in a single word *or* in a phrase. This leads us to a consideration of what phoneticians call *juncture*, or the manner in which syllables join one another in contextual speech.

In order to explain juncture we must review some facts about the basic nature of consonants, discussed in Chapter 2. It was explained that consonants are articulatory movements which act to *initiate* or *terminate* a syllable. Spoken in isolation, the syllable may begin with a consonant and end with a consonant; it may begin with a vowel and end with a consonant (in which case we speak of the beginning of the syllable as *open*); it may begin with a consonant and end with a vowel; or it may be only a vowel, that is, open at both ends.

Let us illustrate these types of syllables. The consonant-vowel-consonant (C-V-C) syllable is illustrated by the words "top" [tɑp] and "list" [lɪst]. (Note that a consonant *combination* rather than a single sound can be used to initiate or terminate a syllable.) Typical consonant-vowel-open (C-V-O) syllables are "raw" [rɔ], "burr" [bɝ], and possibly such a combination as "jay" [dʒe]. Examples of O-V-C syllables are "at" [æt], "ace" [es], and "etch" [etʃ]. Syllables such as "awe" [ɔ] and "owe" [o] are O-V-O syllables.

Of these various types of syllables, those with the vowel (open) arrest are by far the least common in isolated syllables. Even words which seem to end with what we normally term "vowels" most frequently end with a kind of off-glide consonant; thus, "how" has, in effect, a [w] off-glide [haw] and "be" has a [j] off-glide [bɪj]. (The final glide is not ordinarily noted in broad transcription.) Observe, if you will, how few words are ended by the simple, lax vowels. Can you, for example, think of a word which ends with [ɛ], [ʌ], or [ʊ]?

Now, although a consonant movement of some kind usually terminates a syllable *in isolation* (where there is no immediately following syllable), this is a rare situation within the phrases of contextual speech, where syllables must be joined together. In speech one syllable is usually followed immediately by another, and in this situation a different relationship between syllabic and nonsyllabic may exist. In blended syllables the terminating consonant for the preceding syllable tends to become an initiating consonant for the following syllable.

We need not concern ourselves extensively here with the reasons why vowel-consonant syllables become consonant-vowel syllables when blended. Apparently ease of movement or linguistic habit leads to a situation in which, at syllabic rates in excess of about 2.5 to 4 per second, the terminating consonants tend to become initiating consonants for the next syllable, or at least tend to be placed between the syllables in such a way that they share the duty of terminating one syllable and simultaneously initiating the next.*

The process whereby terminating consonants become initiating consonants in contextual speech may be easily demonstrated. Say the word "eat" at a rate of about two words per second. Then gradually increase the rate to about four or five per second. If you do this, you will notice that at a certain rate in your speech the "eat-eat-eat" changes, first to "eateateat," then to "tea-tea-tea." This process can be delayed through the exercise of greater than average articulatory care, but at the higher rates of repetition "eat" becomes "tea" regardless of the effort taken to prevent this change.

This change in the function of the consonant as an initiating or terminating element of a syllable constitutes probably the most important aspect of blending in speech. In rapid speech the syllables are joined

---

* This is something of an oversimplification of a rather complex process. The interested student should turn for amplification to Stetson.[29]

together in a normal manner when the bridge between syllables is from vowel to consonant and the syllable itself is of the C-V type. This occurrence has been termed a *normal transition*, or a *closed juncture*. Where successive syllables are not joined in this manner—where an effort has been made to retain the terminal consonant of a syllable—we may say the juncture is *open* or that the transition has been *interrupted*.

Often the nature of the transition between syllables is truly important to the sense of what is being said. The difference between a closed and an open juncture is "a difference which makes a difference," as you may readily observe by comparing "I scream" with "ice cream" or "use park" with "you spark." We should therefore think of juncture as another distinctive feature of speech and one which should be described in any thoroughgoing speech analysis. Although it may be an over-simplification to treat junctures as consisting of two kinds, open and closed, it is convenient to do so at this stage in speech learning. In phonetic transcriptions we shall use no symbol between syllables to stand for a normal contextual consonant-vowel to consonant-vowel type of juncture, but we shall adopt the symbol [+] where it seems necessary to indicate an open juncture. The [+] will mean simply that the normal transition has been interrupted, although it will not explain how the interruption has occurred.*

Let us now observe some examples of the types of juncture. In the first two examples which follow, an effort has been made to transcribe a short excerpt from Shakespeare's *Hamlet* so that each syllable is written as though it were isolated from its neighbor and so that each consonant or consonant blend is transcribed with the syllable to which it seems most clearly to belong. This is not a normal way to transcribe, but it will enable us to observe the shifts of consonants from terminating to initiating positions. The first transcription indicates the way the passage might sound if rendered slowly and with great care. The second represents a rapid, conversational delivery:

[spik+ ðə spitʃ,+ aɪ pre ju,+ æz+ aɪ prə naʊnst+
1. "Speak the speech, I pray you, as I pronounced

ɪt+ tu ju,—trɪ pɪŋ lɪ+ ɑn ðə tʌŋ]
it to you,—trippingly on the tongue. . . . "

[spi kθə spi tʃaɪ pre ju, ʔæ zaɪ prə naʊn stɪ
2. "Speak the speech, I pray you, as I pronounced

tu ju,—trɪ pɪŋ lɪ jɑn ðə tʌŋ]
it to you,—trippingly on the tongue. . . . "

* For more information concerning the [+] as a *phoneme*, the student is referred to Trager.[36]

Example 2 may possibly show more marked blending than would occur in careful, cultivated diction, but on the whole such a reading would not be abnormal for a conversational speech rate. Observe that the only exceptions to the consonant-vowel succession within the syllable occur with the [n] and [ŋ], both *semivowels*. Note also that at phrase endings, where pauses normally occur, the juncture is typically open. This can usually be taken for granted at the end of sentences and need not be marked in phonetic transcription.

Let us now consider some more examples of blending, transcribed in the manner of the two previous examples:

[aɪ θɪŋ kaɪ bɛ tɚ go tə klæs.⁺ ʃʊ dwɪ ji tæ ftɚ
3. "I think I better go to class. Should we eat after

ðə mi tɪ ŋɚ ʃʊ dwi go tə lʌn tʃæ ftɚ klæs?]
the meeting or should we go to lunch after class?"

[a jəm go wɪ ŋə we⁺ i stɚ tə kə lɛ ksəm de tə ʔə baʊ
4. "I am going away Easter to collect some data about

ʔma juθ. aɪ pɪ ktʃʊɚ taʊn tə staɚ tɪn.]
my youth. I picked your town to start in."

[hi wə stæ bdʊ rɪ ŋə faɪ ʔlæ snaɪt.   tɑm⁺
5. "He was stabbed during a fight last night. Tom

med de zi⁺ i vən mɔ ræŋ grɪ hwɛn hæl⁺ left. ha we vɚ
made Daisy even more angry when Hal left. However,

tɑmz⁺ hæ pɪ naʊ tə ki ʔm̩ mə thom.]
Tom's happy now to keep them at home."

In these examples several different facts about blending are brought out. The point is illustrated, for instance, that blending of adjacent syllables may cause a change or omission of sounds through assimilation in the same way that this phenomenon can occur within the syllables of a single word. In Example 4 the [t] of "picked" and the [j] of "your" combine to produce the sound [tʃ], in the same way that this probably happened in the word "picture." Thus, in assimilated, blended speech "picture" and "picked your" can be (and in informal speech usually would be) easily confused. Notice also, in Example 5, that the somewhat awkward consonant combination [stn] of "last night" has, in the informal blended version, become [sn]. Note finally, in this same example, that the somewhat complex syllable [pðəm] of "keep them" has, through assimilation, become [ʔm̩]. Though highly informal, the speech represented here is not at all uncommon, even among cultivated speakers.

Another interesting kind of problem in blending occurs when identical or very similar sounds follow one another in adjacent words. Such a blending might take place, for example, when a [t]-plus-vowel syllable follows a vowel-plus-[t] syllable. In such cases the normal tendency is for the two syllables to share a single consonant, but this may easily result in misunderstanding. "Neat trick" or "neat Rick" become identical with "knee trick." Such an eventuality may be, and often is, prevented by avoiding the normal tendency, that is, by replacing the typical closed juncture with an open juncture.

Between two identical or highly similar sounds an open juncture may be achieved by making a complete pause between the two words. In the case of "neat trick" two distinct [t]'s would be heard, each with its own plosive phrase. Another way to produce the requisite separation is simply to pause between the stop phase of the final [t] of "neat" and the plosive phase of the initial [t] of "trick." This is the usual method of retaining the independence of identical abutting consonants. When this is done, the two syllables still share the [t], but the stop phase clearly belongs to the first and the plosive phase to the second. The shared consonant is, in a sense, stretched or elongated to produce this particular form of open juncture.

When other kinds of identical abutting consonants occur, a similar method of producing an open juncture may be employed. To prevent any possibility of confusion between "case said" and "Kay said" or "case Ed," for example, the normal vowel-to-consonant juncture must be avoided. Here the speaker might use a complete pause between the two [s]'s, but he would be more likely to prolong a single shared [s]. This prolongation may be somewhat complex, but we have no need of elaborating the point in this text.

Junctures of the types we have discussed can occur not only with identical consonants but also with *homorganic* abutting consonants. These are consonants which are made with the same articulatory movements and which therefore present a similar kind of blending problem. Examples of homorganic pairs are [t]–[d], [p]–[b], and [s]–[z].

Several abutting consonant blends occur in Example 5. "Was stabbed," "Tom made," and "Hal left" are examples. Although the blend "Tom's happy" does not involve homorganic or identical abutting consonants, it must be pronounced with extraordinary care to prevent the unfortunate blend "Tom's sappy."

Where vowel sounds join in adjacent words some interesting problems and blends may be encountered. For example, in the words "who under," "saw often," and "weigh even" one would have to handle blending with considerable care to avoid the pronunciation "who wonder," "soften," and "wavin'." To prevent such confusion, the juncture between adjacent vowels may be opened by lengthening the vowel; by inserting an intrusive consonant, usually [ʔ], [j], [w], or [r]; by actually pausing; or by making a sudden change in stress. In the foregoing transcriptions this problem is illustrated by "we eat" in Example 3; by "I am," "away Easter," and "data about" in Example 4; and by "Daisy even" in Example 5.

In summary, blending is simply a tendency in connected speech for the arresting consonants of one syllable to become the releasing consonants of the next. The degree to which this actually takes place in any given sample of speech is determined by the phonetic similarity of the abutting elements, the number and complexity of the articulatory movements involved, the speed of utterance, the stress, and a reaction to the possibilities for misunderstanding. A *closed juncture* indicates a normal consonant-vowel to consonant-vowel sequence among the syllables. An *open juncture* avoids this by means of a pause, a lengthened sound, a sudden change in stress, or an articulatory signal (aspiration, weakening, voicing, etc.). The necessity of such a juncture may be avoided phonetically by eliminating or changing certain sounds or by inserting certain sounds.

Another problem in recording contextual speech can sometimes be handled by using a diacritical mark or symbol to indicate that a consonant is not released as it normally would be in initial, isolated, or some stressed positions. The symbol suggested is [⁻]. Thus, "pick two" might be transcribed [pɪk tu] if each consonant had both stop and plosive phases but [pɪk⁻tu] if the consonant combination between [ɪ] and [u] was stopped and exploded only once.

The problems one faces in attempting to blend sounds in a way that results in good speech, without being either unduly careful or too careless, are about the same as those involved in steering a safe middle course with respect to assimilation. The student should recognize the necessity for blending and the phonetic laws which govern this process. He should become familiar with normal juncture and blending in order to avoid stilted, unnatural word separation; as with assimilation, however, he should not abuse the principle to the extent that his speech lapses to the substandard level. Here, as always, a good ear for the speech of educated persons is the final guide.

Since there really are no phonetic "words," or at least none that correspond to linguistic words, something of a mechanical problem arises when one attempts to record speech as accurately as possible by means of phonetic transcription. Should we observe word boundaries or shouldn't we? The answer must be somewhat arbitrary. Strictly speaking, if one wishes to represent spoken language closely, gaps should come only where the pauses actually occurred in the speech being transcribed. Thus, an informal question such as "How would you like to go, say, Thursday night?" might be recorded [haʊwʊdʒulaɪktəgo seθɝ·zdɪnaɪt?], with a space only between "go" and "say," since this is undoubtedly the way the sentence would be spoken. Anyone who has a wish or a reason to transcribe in this way should feel free to do so. However, the conventional practice is to make the same word divisions in phonetic transcription as in conventional orthography, except occasionally in narrow transcription. This custom is followed because we have carried over habit patterns acquired from reading and writing and because linguistic considerations cannot be ignored. The established convention is often altered temporarily in specific cases to record the pronunciations of nonstandard assimilations, blendings, and junctures.

STRESS

Stress is another factor that must be considered in explaining the changes that speech sounds undergo in connected speech. In general, the term *stress* refers to the amount of force with which the sound is articulated, or the strength of the movements. This is approximately what we mean when we speak of accenting a sound, so that if "the accent is on the first syllable" it is here that the stress is placed. Stress plays an important role in blending, in determining syllables, and in imparting meaning, or shades of meaning, to what one says. The principles of stress are not unduly complicated, but there is more to the matter than the simple question of "accent" in the ordinary sense.

The aspect of stress which is perhaps easiest to grasp is *phrasal stress*, or *sense stress*. Obviously the command "Give me the book" can have at least two somewhat different meanings, depending upon whether the speaker emphasizes "me" or "book." If he stresses the first of these words, he means "Give it to *me*, not someone else"; if he stresses the other word, he means "Give me the *book*, not something else." Other meanings are possible if one chooses a still different stress pattern. In more complex ways, then, there is a constant rise and fall of phrasal stress during ongoing speech, in a pattern which is determined by meaning. The effect of stress is to alter the total acoustic pattern of the word, depending upon the amount of emphasis it receives. If one wishes to express the idea that a certain automobile is best of all he may say it is "*the* car" [ði kɑr], in which case "the" is much different from what it would be if the word were spoken with less force, [ðə kɑr]. In this way we establish meaningful relationships among the words of a phrase, giving prominence to some by stressing and subordinating others by unstressing. Phrases within a sentence are, of course, treated in the same way.

Syllabic stress is essentially the same phenomenon, except that it involves gradations of force within the word. Syllabic stress, incidentally, is superimposed on phrasal stress somewhat as small hillocks or buttes might change the outline of a mountain slope. Both phrasal and syllabic stress require careful listening to be identified. Both have an extensive effect on pronunciation and also play a very important part in determining the over-all rhythm of American speech. An unfamiliar stress pattern, such as is often heard in the speech of a person with a foreign-language background, will make the speech seem unnatural and conspicuous. Even a native American may find that his speech loses effectiveness if he is not sensitive to the distinctive stress patterns of his language.

This whole matter was touched on briefly in connection with the description of the neutral vowel [ə]. American speech is characterized by a strong rhythm pattern in which stressed syllables alternate more or less regularly with unstressed syllables. The relative difference in force between stressed and unstressed syllables is considerably greater in English than in other languages. This means that in order to speak English naturally, one's unstressed sounds must have very little stress indeed. In typical American speech, therefore, the vowel in unstressed syllables is often reduced to a kind of "murmur," or minimal sound pulse. This is called the *neutral* or *indefinite* vowel, and, by some writers, the *schwa* vowel. The stress aspect of speech cannot be entirely separated from the factor of vowel resonance. For practical purposes we may do so, however, and it is important to the communication of meaning that we be able to vary the amount of stress placed on syllables in connected speech.

The exact physical or acoustic nature of stress has not yet been explained. When a word or sound is stressed, its acoustic energy is increased so that it "stands out." The factors which contribute to the prominence of a syllable are to be found among the variables of pitch, quality, loudness, and duration. The characteristics of these speech variables and their contribution to stress are discussed in the following chapter, but it is possible to describe stress without such an analysis.

Because stress is so important in determining both the meaning and the naturalness of what is spoken, it is necessary not only that we have symbols to indicate stress in phonetic transcription but that we have some kind of phonemic classification for describing *degrees* of stress. Without making any attempt to parcel out the various factors which contribute to stress, the IPA and some other phonetic alphabets use a system which may be employed to indicate four different degrees of stress, a number which seems adequate for indicating all but the most subtle variations in sense stress. These four degrees of stress, which have been found to be in a sense distinctive, are the *primary*, *secondary*, *tertiary*, and *weak* stresses:

Primary stress, which is the heaviest, is employed for a monosyllabic word spoken in isolation or for the most important syllable of an important word in context. In the sentence *"Answer the telephone"* the first and fourth syllables have primary stress. In common dictionary usage this degree of stress is noted with the mark ['] following the syllable as in "debris'." In the alphabet of the International Phonetics Association the symbol ['] is used, *before* the syllable, as in [də'bri].

Secondary stress is of a distinctly lesser degree but is still great enough to constitute stressing. Take the example "telephone." Both [tɛl] and [fon] are stressed and thus are strong syllables, but the [fon] is distinctly subordinated to the [tɛl]. The common dictionary custom uses a lighter ['] following the syllable receiving secondary stress: "tel' e phone'." The IPA symbol is [ˌ] *below* the line and *preceding* the syllable as in ['tɛlə,fon] or ['hɝ⋅ə,ken].

Tertiary stress is a little difficult to define briefly because we are getting here into subtle distinctions. It is, however, the third meaningful degree of stress. The following simplified definition may help: tertiary stress is the amount of emphasis necessary to preserve the normal vowel quality without giving it the attention-getting emphasis of a primary or secondary stress.   In general, it is the stress given "unstressed" syllables which are not weakened to the point where the vowel becomes a murmur, or schwa. In the usual pronunciation of the word "failing" ['felɪŋ], for example, the final syllable received tertiary stress; this pronunciation might be contrasted with such pronunciations as [ˌfe'lɪŋ], ['fe,lɪŋ], and the careless ['felən]. All differ to some degree.

There is no special mark for tertiary stress in most systems for indicating pronunciation. The dictionary does not find one necessary for the requirements of lexical pronunciation, nor is there any such symbol in the IPA notation, possibly because any syllable which is not primary, secondary, or weak customarily receives tertiary stress; so long as this fact is understood, no mark is needed.

For a further illustration of tertiary stress, compare "syntax" with "sin tax": ['sɪntæks]–['sɪn ,tæks]. The second syllable of "syntax" has tertiary stress. The same distinction exists between "potash" ['pɑtæʃ] and "pot ash" ['pɑt ,æʃ] and between "hardware" ['hɑrdwɛr] and "hard wear" ['hɑrd ,wɛr]. The final syllables in "hardware" and "potash" certainly do not receive secondary stress as they are usually spoken; yet these syllables are not weak, or else the words would be heard as ['hɑrdwɝ] and ['pɑtəʃ].

In keeping with this last comment, *weak*, or unstressed, syllables can be identified quite easily in most cases through the effect on vowel quality, length, and pitch. The weak syllables are short, often low in pitch, and indefinite in quality. The absence of stress usually leads to a low-central, lax vowel. Thus, almost by definition, the weak syllable is [ə], although [ɝ] and the syllabic consonants [m̩], [n̩], and [l̩] also ordinarily appear only in weak syllables.

It must be admitted that there are some deficiencies in this system of stress notation, primarily because of the lack of special symbols for tertiary and weak syllables. The more advanced student may detect the fact that the schwa, [ə], is not always perfectly synonymous with a weak, or unstressed, vowel. Some syllables may indeed have a definite quality which would seem to disqualify them as schwas but may still lack sufficient stress to be qualified as tertiary. The symbol [ˇ] over a vowel may be used to indicate a weak syllable, although this practice is not followed in the examples given in this text. This procedure might have particular value in indicating weak syllables with an [ɪ] or [ʊ] coloring. It can also be used in differentiating weak from stressed syllabic consonants.

In summary, the simplified system of stress notation suggested for the student at this point recognizes four degrees of stress but employs only two special symbols:

1. Primary: heavily stressed, using the symbol ['] as in "go!" ['go]

2. Secondary: stressed but subordinate to the primary stress, using the symbol [ˌ] as in "telephone" ['tɛləˌfon]

3. Tertiary: definite but unstressed using no special symbol, as in "making" ['mekɪŋ]

4. Weak: minimal stress and indefinite quality, represented by the symbols [ə] and [ɚ], and sometimes by the symbols [m̩], [n̩], and [l̩] (and possibly on occasion [ɪ̆] or [ʊ̆])

Exercises

1. The following two-syllable words and phrases are generally pronounced with one strong and one weaker syllable. The strong syllable usually has primary stress, although this would depend upon sentence context. The weak syllable is ordinarily [ə], [ɚ], [m̩], [n̩], or [l̩], but this also could vary in connected speech. Which syllable is strong when the words are spoken in isolation? Transcribe the words, using stress marks, and practice saying them in such a way that each word has a primary and a weak syllable. Then check yourself with a pronouncing dictionary.

able	causes	enter	notice	service
about	certain	father	people	standard
a boy	colors	fired	profit	suppose
alone	chorus	German	promote	woman
a man	correct	human	pupil	women
better	cotton	idle	return	per cent
business	dollar	mental	science	the boy
button	doctor	nation	second	the man

2. The following three-syllable words and phrases are ordinarily pronounced with two degrees of stress. Most of these pronunciations, if

not all, require one stressed and two weak (or a weak and a tertiary) syllables. Transcribe these words with stress marks. Turn to a pronouncing dictionary for confirmation if you are unsure in any case.

a camper	connection	mineral	stamina
a sadness	delicate	mistaken	the circus
camera	delicious	poisonous	the saddle
caresses	feminine	potato	together
companion	intimate	optimum	palaces
condition	Iowa	remover	

3. The following three-syllable words and phrases usually require three different degrees of stress. In most examples there is a primary stress, a secondary stress, and a weak stress. In some cases, however, two primary (or two secondary) stresses and one weak or tertiary stress might be satisfactory. Transcribe these words with stress marks. When in doubt, consult the dictionary.

abdicate	exercise	medicate	persevere
Birmingham	harmonize	memorize	put it here
cavalier	holiday	now complain	operate
civilize	introduce	overlook	some ice cream
carpetbag	lemonade	pearly gate	telephone
elevate	magazine	penalize	

4. In the following four- and five-syllable words two, three, or four degrees of stress may be employed. Transcribe them phonetically with stress marks, then check a pronouncing dictionary for verification.

additional	especially	intelligence	qualitatively
anniversary	examination	mechanical	requirements
civilization	apparently	manufacturer	situation
consideration	environment	nationally	superintendents
cooperation	experiment	necessarily	university
composition	generation	opportunity	syllabication
educational	immediately	particularly	curriculum
elementary	individual	personality	specialization
elimination	international	possibility	indoctrination

5. Practice assigning the appropriate degrees of stress to the syllables of the following sentence: "John told Jim that Mary could not go." Stress this sentence in three different ways, so that it says these three different things:

  a. *John* and *Jim* are the principals involved, not Dick and Harry.

  b. He said that *Mary* couldn't. He didn't mean Sally or Jo.

c. He *didn't* say she *could* go, but that she could *not*. Furthermore, he *told* her quite clearly.

Show how the sentence "Bob almost wrecked the car" might be spoken with emphasis on the first word, then with emphasis on the second word, and so on (five different sense stresses are possible).

The following are phonetic transcriptions of the above sentences. After you have done the exercises, compare the author's stressing with your own.

a. 'dʒɑn told 'dʒɪm ðət ˌmɛrɪ kən ˌnɑt ˌgo.

b. ˌdʒɑn told ˌdʒɪm ðət 'mɛrɪ kəd ˌnɑt ˌgo.

c. ˌdʒɑn 'told ˌdʒɪm ðət ˌmɛrɪ kəd 'nɑt ˌgo.

d. 'bab alˌmost ˌrekt ðə ˌkɑr.

e. ˌbab al'most ˌrekt ðə ˌkɑr.

f. ˌbab alˌmost 'rekt ðə ˌkɑr.

g. ˌbab alˌmost ˌrekt 'ði ˌkɑr.

h. ˌbab alˌmost ˌrekt ðə 'kɑr.

13

THE ACOUSTIC VARIABLES
OF SPEECH: PITCH, QUALITY,
LOUDNESS, AND DURATION

As we listen to people talk, we acquire two kinds of information. First, if the words are properly chosen and reasonably well arranged, we apprehend the strictly intellectual content—the "logical" meaning—of what is being said. In addition, however, we can perceive what the speaker thinks and feels about what he is saying. This familiar idea is expressed by the remark: "It wasn't so much what he said as the way he said it!"

From the standpoint of communication, the purely intellectual content of speech could be transmitted with entire adequacy without any variation in the fundamental pitch level of the voice; by keeping the speech signals at a constant loudness level; by maintaining a vocal cord tone of unvarying quality; and, at least to some extent, by shortening, "compressing," or otherwise changing the information supplied by the variable duration of sounds and syllables. This, to be sure, would produce only a mechanical type of speech, but the words spoken would still be recognizable as long as vowel resonance and articulation were kept within certain limits. Artificial speech of this type has actually been produced in the laboratory and has proved readily understandable, despite the fact that it sounds peculiar. In certain circumstances such suppression of variation has important applications for the communications engineer, for he may wish to transmit basic minimum information with the least possible power (and as rapidly as possible), and it takes power to vary the speech signal in pitch, quality, strength, and duration.

Most of us, however, want something quite different in the speech situations we are constantly facing. Our conscious or unconscious aim is to communicate a great deal more than the bare meaning of words; we wish to convey fine shades of meaning, to reveal convictions, to express feelings, and to move our listeners to react in various ways. Possibly the

259

best way to ensure speech of this kind is to mean what we say, in the fullest sense; but it is also useful to understand those aspects of speech form which carry meanings over and above the bare intellectual content and to make certain that our speech manner is fully responsive to them. The variables which add the "plus" values to communication are termed the *prosodic* elements of speech: (1) pitch, (2) quality, (3) strength, and (4) duration.

These "plus" values are not at all vague and nebulous; some of the more important can be set down as follows:

1. *Vocal modulations*—variations in pitch, quality, strength, and duration—contribute to meaning by functioning as tools of stress, or emphasis. They may serve somewhat the same purpose in speech as do the punctuation marks of written language.

2. Vocal modulations acting as prosodic speech features go even further and enable the speaker to give much more precise "punctuation" to his speech than would be possible with the limited number of marks available to the writer. Fine shades of meaning can be nicely made.

3. Complex emotional meanings and evaluations are revealed in subtle ways by prosodic variations.

4. It is well known, but sometimes not fully appreciated, that vocal modulations, being governed by one's habitual modes of reaction, may reveal telling information about the speaker's personality traits—traits of which he may be quite unaware.

R-M. S. Heffner, a noted linguist, made this observation in the course of some comments on pitch variation: "What one says in English is probably never contingent upon the melody of one's utterance, but what one thinks about what one says is often implicit in the tune to which one says it, and frequently this, rather than the literal sense of the speech form, is the real gist of an utterance."[11]

The matters we have been discussing are altogether too complex and have too many ramifications for exhaustive explanation here. Nevertheless, it is important to cover certain essential facts about the acoustic variables of speech in relation to meaning.

PITCH

One of the familiar dimensions of sound is its pitch. We do not have a wholly satisfactory way of putting the concept into words, but we may say that the pitch of a note is its "high" or "low" attribute. The pitch of a sound is in the mind of the listener, so to speak, since it is a perception based on sensation. Sound waves differ in *frequency*, which is the number of individual waves per second, and it is primarily the frequency of the sound which determines pitch. Low-pitched sounds have a relatively low frequency, and as the number of waves per second increases, the subjective experience, pitch, rises.

Each of us has a characteristic pitch range for his voice. As we speak, the changes in pitch that occur within this range are designated by the general term *intonation*. Intonation is, in a way, not unlike a musical melody that is spoken, not sung. Where the pitch changes are continuous or without "breaks," they are termed *inflections*.

When the voice goes from one definite pitch to another, without sliding upward or downward, the change is called a *step*. The pitch variations involved in intonation may be either rapid or slow. Inflections are classified as *rising*, *falling*, and *circumflex*. The circumflex inflection is a combination of rising-falling or falling-rising pattern.

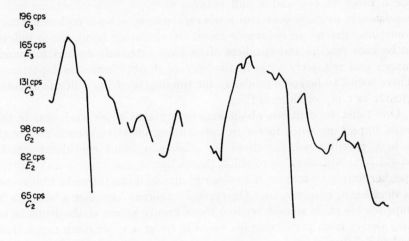

There is   according to   legend   a boiling pot of   gold   at one end

FIG. 22. The melody curve.

A good deal of research, both scientific and artistic, has been devoted to pitch changes during speech. Studies have been made, for example, of graphic records showing the pitch changes which ordinarily take place during reading and speaking. The "melody curve" of Figure 22 is one such graph. This figure shows the many rapid changes in fundamental voice frequency that occurred as one of the authors read the sentence "There is, according to legend, a boiling pot of gold at one end." The peaks and dips in the graph reflect rising and falling pitches. The gaps in the line indicate *breaks*, or *steps*, where the voice changed from one pitch level to another. From objective investigations, employing data such as these, and from sensitive listening to artistic speech, a great many ideas about effective pitch usage have been formulated. We should never want to imply that artificial control of one's pitch patterns is the secret of skillful use of this voice variable; yet the information gained by analyses of these patterns can help one make his speaking manner responsive to intellectual and emotional meanings. Some of the major conclusions from recent research are described in the following paragraphs.

Pitch Range. In general, good male speakers use an average pitch corresponding to a note about one octave below middle C on the piano. Superior female voices are usually pitched about four tones higher. Various studies[20,22,24,35] seem to show, however, that the average pitch level of one's voice is less important in determining the effectiveness of his speech than are *variations* in pitch. In reading an ordinary descriptive prose passage, persons judged to be good speakers have been found to use a range of one and a half octaves or more, with inflections which consistently average over two tones on the musical scale and which may sometimes extend an octave or more. On the other hand, those judged to be poor readers and speakers often have extremely constricted voice ranges and relatively little in the way of flexible inflectional patterns. There seems to be some tendency for the degree of flexibility to become greater as one's pitch level rises.

One must be cautious about concluding that pitch variation is the most important voice factor in determining effective speech (although it may possibly be), for there are other significant considerations. It would certainly be naïve to think that a person can become an effective speaker simply by making his voice run up and down the scale a bit more. It does seem, however, that the typical "average" speaker who seeks to improve his skills should become more keenly aware of the benefits he may derive from permitting his voice to cover a wider pitch range than he has habitually used.

A "Good" Pitch. Most listeners, it is commonly believed, prefer low-pitched voices to those of higher register, at least among male speakers. Other aspects of voice are of such great importance, however, that the male speaker need not be concerned about creating an unfavorable impression simply because his voice tends to be high, provided that he does not go above the normal limit for his sex. If his pitch is abnormally high, he should investigate the possibility of voice training. Critical listeners show some preference for the lower-pitched female voices, unless the pitch is substantially below the average.

A number of studies disclose that in voices given superior ratings the average pitch level used in speech is about one-fourth of the way up from the bottom of the pitch range the speaker possesses (including falsetto). One investigation of this point[27] among a small group of superior speakers showed them to have a singing range of about 13 tones (a little more than two octaves), a range including the falsetto of about 20 tones, and a median speaking level about 5 tones above the lowest note in the range. The consistency with which the subjects of this study clustered about this point would seem to bear out the idea that there is an optimum pitch level for each speaker.

Age and Sex Factors. Change of voice in boys at the time of puberty is a very familiar part of growing up, and the same phenomenon occurs in girls, but less obviously. Between age seven and adulthood, the male voice shifts downward about one octave to a final average level about an octave below middle C on the musical scale. The female voice moves downward only a few tones, reaching an average level about four to six tones above the male average. The amount of pitch variation tends to increase with age, at least up to young adulthood, but the processes of aging may cause a loss of pitch flexibility as well as a change in quality during the presenile and senile decades of life. While a boy's voice is in the process of changing, he temporarily loses control of it, so that his speech, to his great discomfiture, is marked by wide pitch changes and breaks.

On the whole, women may have somewhat less variable voices than do men; at least this has been found true in one comparison of superior male and female speakers.[28] Although the women in this study had as great a total pitch range as the men, they did not appear to use their potential as fully as the male speakers; instead, they confined themselves more closely to a level near the bottom of their range. There probably are distinctive differences in the types of inflection that characterize male and female speech, a fact which has been verified both by casual observation and through some phonetic study, but a discussion of the tentative conclusions would not be of interest here.

Inflection Patterns. It is not possible to be specific about the pitch characteristics of inflections, since there are so many nuances of meaning that the precise patterns are exceedingly varied. Furthermore, there have been relatively few careful descriptive studies of inflection patterns in American speech. Nevertheless, phoneticians agree that certain inflectional configurations are highly typical of the language. These are deep-seated, well-learned patterns which pervade the entire speech structure, contributing as much to the characteristic flavor of the dialect as do the actual sounds used.

The customary pattern of American speech seems to include a tendency to introduce a phrase or idea with a rising pitch attack and to conclude it with a falling pitch release. Frequently, questions and incomplete thoughts end on rising intonations, whereas statements of fact and commands are completed with falling vocal pitches. It would be easy, however, to generalize too freely from this kind of information. As one writer has pointed out, the problem is oversimplified if there is any expectation that a pitch-contour type can be based upon a "grammatical rule of thumb."[26] Pitch contours, if they are definable at all, are probably to be identified with attitudes and emotions rather than with grammatical functions.

Certain patterns of pitch level and pitch change have been found by some researchers to be associated with certain stereotypes of emotional expression. There is evidence to show, for example, that *anger* is associated with wide inflections and a rapid rate of pitch change. *Fear* is characterized by a high pitch level and wide total range. *Indifference* seems to produce a low pitch level and a narrow pitch range. Although these conclusions, based on analysis of the delivery of trained actors, must be looked upon as tentative, emotional states obviously have a critical effect on pitch patterns.

Pitch change appears to be second only to duration change as a significant factor in determining the stress of a word or syllable. Most often the tendency is to give the emphasized syllable a wider pitch inflection and a higher pitch level. It probably is not the higher level that provides the stress, however, but rather the fact that the pitch has *changed*.

Pitch Symbols. For most purposes, phonetic transcription does not include any marking to indicate intonation, despite the importance of pitch modulation to meaning. In English, changes in pitch do not cause any sound to shift from one phoneme to another (although this may occur in some languages); hence the English phonetician faces no complications in this direction. Pitch variations do make some contribution to the over-all stress placed on a word or syllable, but this factor is taken care of by the use of conventional stress marks. Intonation is so complex and personal that, in the opinion of some phoneticians, any system of marking which made any pretense at really accurate notation would need to be so elaborate that its practical value would be questionable.

Despite the practical difficulties in the way of transcribing pitch phonetically, this kind of variation is so important that some system of notation seems desirable. This would be particularly helpful for the student learning English as a foreign language, for the inflectional patterns of a language are essential to its proper pronunciation. To transcribe "He did it!" and "He did it?" in the same way [hi dɪd ɪt] is to miss the really important point of difference between these two utterances. Of course, those of us who habitually speak English correctly would normally infer from the punctuation that the inflection is downward in the first example and is upward in the second. Such inflections, however, are merely a characteristic of our own language; they are not a universal law of speech.

The question that arises at this point is just how much detail—how many shades of pitch variation and inflection—must be indicated in order to express the American English intonation patterns with a reasonable degree of completeness; that is, how much detail is necessary to show appropriate emphasis, emotional appeal, dialect pattern, interrogation, and other aspects of communication. For an exact phonetic analysis a pitch contour such as that of Figure 22 would be ideal. Failing this, the notes of the musical scale could be—and have been—used to indicate speech melody. But such systems are unwieldy and too detailed. More practical analyses could be centered on those differences "which make a difference." This problem may seem a virtually insoluble one, for by definition we are interested here in subtle shades of meaning which are highly personal and variable. Nevertheless, even though we cannot express symbolically all the nuances of meaning indicated by pitch change, we can determine how many different *levels* of pitch are required to produce these subtle variations.

By determining *pitch phonemes*, at least approximately, a system of notation has been devised based upon four degrees of pitch level and three kinds of inflection at *clause terminals*. This system has proved workable and reasonably satisfactory in teaching intonation patterns to foreigners.

At this stage it is suggested that the student use the following form of pitch notation: the average voice level may be symbolized by [2], a low pitch level by [1], a high level by [3], and an extra-high level by [4]. In this system "He *did* it!" might be [²hi ⁴dɪd ¹ɪt]; "He did it?" might be transcribed [¹hi ²dɪd ³ɪt]; "He did it." might be [²hi dɪd ¹ɪt]. The symbols need be used only where a change in pitch takes place.

The pitches designated [1,2,3,4] should not be thought of as absolute levels, capable of expression in terms of cycles per second or notes on the piano keyboard. They are, rather, relative levels; their exact height depends upon the average pitch for the particular utterance and upon such factors as the speaker's pitch level, range, and variability.

It is important to consider not only the pitch level of each syllable but also the inflection, particularly at *clause terminals*. Inflection may be indicated by the symbol [↗], [↘], or [→], depending upon whether the voice at the end of the clause rises in pitch, falls off in pitch, or remains level. Thus, [mi↗] contrasts with [mi↘], the first being a question, the second being an answer. Compare [wɛl→ aɪ dont no↗] (a statement marked by contemplation, incompleteness, or possibly a lack of assurance) with [wɛl↘ aɪ nɛvɚ↘] (a statement of disgusted surprise).

The definition of what constitutes a phonetic clause involves complexities which cannot be discussed fully here. It is sufficient for our purposes to state that a phonetic clause is similar to a grammatical clause, which the student has been taught is a *thought unit*, or to an oral phrase.

The two may be, but often are not, identical. The phonetic clause, in any event, can be illustrated by pronunciation and example more easily than it can be described.

It is, of course, not often that both pitch-level and pitch-inflection symbols are required in the same transcription. Ordinarily the symbols for level are quite sufficient for indicating pitch changes for native speakers. In certain instances, however, both types of symbols, or even the inflection symbols alone, may be more useful.

Here is an example of pitch notation which employs symbols for both pitch level and inflection:

[³hwʌt dɪd ju se↗ ²aɪ ²dɪdnt ³hɪr ¹ju↘
³o ³kʌm ɔn ²nau↘ ¹ju ³rɪlɪ ²dɪdnt du ³ð̃æt²↘
²ju↘ ³tʃɑrlɪ↘ ³gɛt ⁴aut ²əv ¹hɪr↘]

QUALITY

The attribute, or dimension, of voice and speech that is most difficult to describe and discuss is *quality*. A rather unsatisfactory way to define quality is to say that it is an aspect of tone which is independent of pitch, loudness, and duration; it is the remaining cue which enables us to differentiate between two tones if the other three variables are the same in both. We have no difficulty, for instance, in distinguishing between a violin and a clarinet, even though they sound notes of the same pitch, loudness, and duration; for the *quality* is different. The quality of a tone is its distinctive *color* or *timbre*.

Quality is a subjective experience, as is pitch. From the physical point of view, quality is determined by the presence of what are termed *overtones*. Most sounds we hear, and certainly speech sounds, are *complex* (rather than *simple*); that is, they consist of a number of simple tones of different pitches blended together. The reason for this is that, except under laboratory conditions, all sound-producing mechanisms vibrate in a complex way. Instead of having a single, simple back-and-forth motion, they tend to vibrate segmentally at many different rates at once, with a very complex motion. As a result, any sound we are likely to hear consists of a number of sound waves of different frequencies, blended together into a single complex sound. The lowest of these frequencies we call the *fundamental frequency*, and it determines the pitch of the tone. The other frequencies in the complex tone are termed *overtones*, and it is these frequencies (and their particular arrangement) which produce the sensation of tone quality.

A full discussion of the physiological factors involved in speech and voice quality would take us too far afield from our present interests, but the general principles should be understood. First, the sound produced by the vibrating vocal folds is complex, containing a number of overtones. Second, the resonance cavities of the head—the throat, mouth, and nose—act on the vocal-fold tone in a way that *reinforces* some overtones and *damps* out others. The final voice quality, therefore, is a product of the vocal-fold tone as modified by the resonators. We achieve various kinds of voice quality—pleasant and unpleasant—by conscious and unconscious adjustments of the mechanisms of phonation and resonance.

Although voice quality and its improvement are primarily the concern of the speech therapist or voice teacher, the phonetician is interested in some aspects of speech quality. As brought out earlier, variations in quality are the distinctive factors which determine the classification of vowels into different phonemes and allophones. Voice quality and vowel quality are independent to some extent, however, since the former may be determined by changes in overtones above and beyond those required for identification of the vowel. A somewhat similar situation exists when the intricacies of a musical composition are over and above the notes needed for the theme melody. To some extent voice-quality changes are more likely to result from variations in the way the vocal cords vibrate, whereas vowel quality is more dependent upon the vocal resonance produced by tuning of the resonators. It would be a mistake to carry this generalization too far, however.

There is no satisfactory terminology for describing different qualities of voice. A multitude of terms have been used, among them such rather imprecise and subjective designations as "guttural," "pectoral," "metallic," "strident," "harsh," "husky," "hoarse," "thin," "heavy," "light," and "thick." Some of these terms probably are prompted by aspects of voice which are not, strictly speaking, matters of quality alone. Recent research offers some hope that eventually order can be brought into our thinking about voice quality. For the moment we can set down three general variables involved in voice quality:

First, tone quality may be affected by unevenness and irregular movement of the vocal folds (*aperiodic vibration*) and, in addition, by undesired breaks and changes in pitch and rapid fluctuations in intensity. Phenomena of this sort are often the result of some organic malformation, although this is not always the case. The quality which results from such irregular vibrations is often described as "harsh" or "hoarse."

Second, there may be present in the vocal tone a simultaneously produced noise which can add a more or less unpleasant component to the total effect. One of the commonest noises of this sort is a kind of "hishing," such as might be caused when air flows rapidly through a constricted opening. This is probably what happens if the quality is "breathy" as a consequence of the friction noise created when more breath passes between the vocal folds than is needed to set them into vibration or when the folds are not brought sufficiently close together. Unwanted noises may also result from the irregular vibrations of the vocal folds mentioned in the previous paragraph.

Third, the voice quality may seem to be characterized by unusual or unexpected resonances, like those in the tone of an unfamiliar musical instrument. Some of these undesirable resonances, such as those which give the various kinds of nasality, are reasonably well understood; others are not. Among the latter are the distortions described as "throaty," "hollow," and "thin," as well as other conspicuous deviations from what pleases us in the quality of a voice.

In the last analysis, a good voice quality is a matter of the listener's taste, and the concept of "normal" is hard to define. In general, however, a voice is normal if it is sufficiently lacking in one of the foregoing sources of abnormality and is of appropriate pitch and loudness. Certainly the limits of acceptability are very wide, and many different voice qualities may seem pleasing, just as we may listen with equal pleasure to the music of a violin and that of a flute, even though they are not at all the same.

If the student is interested in doing so, he may find it instructive to experiment with producing some of the undesirable voice qualities. To get a rough or harsh quality, tense the muscles of the throat to an abnormal degree and squeeze out the tone. Try a simultaneous whisper and vocal tone to simulate a breathy quality. Duck the chin and pull the larynx downward for an odd sort of "throaty" voice. A certain kind of nasality results if the soft palate is relaxed, as it would be for [m], during phonation; another kind can be produced by tightening the muscles in the upper part of the throat and drawing the tongue backward. The latter method is likely to give the so-called "twang."

Because voice-quality variations do not create shifts from one phoneme to another in English, and possibly also because the whole problem is extremely complex and full of unanswered questions, no symbol system has been devised for showing voice quality in phonetic transcription. The only exception is the use of [~] to designate nasalization and [̥] to indicate unvoicing. These are employed only for particular sounds, not as a way of recording voice quality as such.

LOUDNESS

In phonetics, the term *loudness* has its ordinary meaning, that is, the strength of the auditory experience. In colloquial language we mean much the same thing when we speak of force, volume, or intensity. As a sensation, loudness is related to the amount of energy or power the sound has, although this relationship can become quite technical if one inquires into the details, which we shall not do.

Speech power can be measured by a number of units, among them the watt, although for our purposes the microwatt (one-millionth of a watt) is more convenient, because of the minute amount of physical energy involved in conversational speech. In terms of power there are astonishing variations in speech. A loud voice may have 100 times the power of an average conversational voice, which, in turn, may have 100 times as much power as a soft voice. Within any sample of speech some sounds may have many thousands of times more power than other sounds. The ear is able to respond to a very wide range of powers, so that at some frequencies the ratio between a just audible sound and one which is painfully loud may be 1 to 100,000,000,000,000. If our range of vision were as great, we should have very little need for either microscopes or field glasses.

The loudness factor in speech involves several considerations which are of both theoretical and practical importance. One of them is the effect on intelligibility of the consonant-to-vowel loudness ratio. If this becomes too great, as it sometimes does in shouting, where the vowels are likely to be strongly emphasized, understandability may suffer. In increasing loudness, there is often a tendency to neglect consonant articulation, and it is important that we recognize and guard against this danger.

Most of the important factors involving loudness center around the question of stress, but in considering this matter, we must not forget that stress is dependent also on pitch variation and duration and that these elements are possibly of greater significance than loudness alone. This was borne out by a study of emphasis in which stressed and unstressed versions of the same words were compared.[35] The following conclusions were reached: (1) in 98 per cent of the cases, stressed words were longer; (2) in 84 per cent, stressed words were more highly inflected; (3) in 75 per cent, they reached a higher pitch; (4) in 74 per cent, they were more intense; and (5) in 71 per cent, they reached a lower pitch. The order in which these factors are listed can probably be taken also as the order of their relative importance in determining emphasis, although emphasis must always be thought of as dependent on a combination of influences.

A rather marked variation in intensity has been found to be characteristic of "superior" speech, as judged by critical listeners. In one analysis of the basic aspects of effective speech[24] "good" voices had 21 per cent greater variation in intensity than did "poor" voices. In another study[20] it was found that speakers who received low ratings by listeners were those who used relatively less intensity contrast between articles and prepositions, on the one hand, and the more important sense-carrying words, such as nouns and verbs, on the other. Certainly appropriate stress patterns are necessary, not only for speech intelligibility and conformity to conventional dialect patterns, but also as a means of making clear what one thinks about what he is saying.

Only some common-sense remarks can be offered about the over-all loudness of speech in relation to effectiveness. One should speak loudly enough to press home his ideas, but not so loudly that he becomes offensive. The public speaker needs to be audible to the person in the back row without deafening the front-row listeners. The term *projection* is used to express the idea of establishing communicative contact with the listener through the use of appropriate force combined with other factors. Adequate vocal intensity is probably the most important element in projection, but it is not the only one. Articulation must consciously be made more precise in difficult situations. One should not allow the basic voice pitch to rise unduly as a result of the increased effort involved in using more force, nor should the voice quality become distorted.

No phonetic notation has been devised to record the loudness changes among syllables independently of the factors of pitch and length. Loudness is, of course, an extremely important factor in stress, which can be indicated phonetically, as was discussed in Chapter 12.

DURATION AND TIMING

The term *duration* applies to three variables involved in the rate, or timing, of speech: (1) the length of sounds or syllables, (2) the length of the pauses between phrases, and (3) the over-all rate of speech. Phoneticians have always recognized that the timing of one's speech is important in communicating intellectual and emotional meanings, but they now are beginning to realize even more strongly that durational cues play an important part in the identification of individual speech sounds and in stress patterns.

The length of a given sound may be one of the distinctive characteristics that enable us to recognize it. One phonetician has reported significant differences in the natural duration of the vowel sounds.[3] Measurement of vowel lengths from tape recordings of representative speech showed that they varied from 0.209 to 0.135 second. The stressed vowels decreased in length in the order [ɔ, æ, u, o, ɑ, e, i, ʌ, ɛ, ʊ, ɪ]. In addition, one of the present authors[34] has some evidence to show that listeners unconsciously depend in part on these differences in length for vowel recognition. He found that it became more difficult to identify certain vowels when they were increased or decreased in length beyond their natural limits.

As mentioned previously, the length of sounds or syllables is one of the most critical factors in determining stress. In the study cited in the earlier section[35] stressed words were increased in duration in 98 per cent of the samples of speech analyzed. In this sense duration appeared to be the most important single variable. The degree of difference in length may be considerable. For instance, two investigators who measured the length of certain sounds in the speech of a General American speaker found that stressed vowels averaged 0.154 second and unstressed vowels averaged only 0.059 second.[25]

Common sense tells us that the length of one's pauses has a great effect on meaning, and this principle has always been taught in connection with speech improvement. We pause for emphasis, to indicate the beginning of a new idea, to "punctuate" orally, and for other reasons. Pauses vary in frequency and length in response to changing ideas, ranging from a small fraction of a second to several seconds. Obviously some of the variation must be related to the necessity for taking in fresh breath to speak with. Also, we pause to think; hence the complexity of the ideas which are to follow exerts an influence. It would be a mistake to try to set down a list of arbitrary rules, but the speaker must handle pauses with skill.

There have been a number of interesting studies of pausing. Phoneticians have found, for instance, that trained readers tend to use longer and more varied pauses than do untrained readers.[22,24] Others have found that recordings of the better or more highly trained readers tend to show a greater total speech time, with more and longer pauses as well as longer vowel sounds.[5,22,24]

A final consideration involved in duration is the *rate* of speech. A great deal of attention has been given to the question of how fast a good speaker should talk, probably because of the mistaken notion that "talking too fast" is often the principal reason for inaccurate, badly articulated speech. Parents frequently complain to the speech therapist that their youngster could speak clearly "if he would only slow down." This is by no means always true. There certainly are practical limits to an effective speaking rate; but no one is prepared to say how rapidly one should talk. This must be determined by meaning—intellectual and emotional— and by the exigencies of the situation. Some speakers may find that a slower rate or better pausing facilitates clear articulation, but this is certainly no cure-all for speech faults.

The studies that have been made show a surprising degree of variation in the rate of acceptable speech. It seems to vary from 100 to 200 words per minute, sometimes slower, but seldom faster. One group of 200 college freshmen was found to read easy descriptive prose at an average rate of 167 words per minute.[7] In contrast, a study conducted among a group of oratorical contest winners showed that the fastest spoke at an average rate of 154 words per minute, the slowest at 83.[5] These findings merely point up the fact that the kind of speaking naturally influences rate. In another study 84 students were asked to read at what they believed to be a rapid, a medium, and a slow rate. The rates at which they read were, for the men, 224, 176, and 153 words per minute, respectively. For women the corresponding figures were 211, 170, and 151.[12] A study of the speech rate in actors' portrayals of fear, anger, indifference, and contempt[8] has given us some insight into the effect of emotion on rate. Significant differences were found; for example, indifference elicited the most rapid rate, contempt the slowest.

Not much is known about what we may call the internal variation in speech rate, that is, the manner in which we speed up and slow down our rate within phrases, sentences, and oral paragraphs in response to meanings. We make such changes, of course, in very subtle and complex ways. Some phoneticians have discussed this problem,[6,15] but we do not have many objective descriptive data at present. When the traits which characterize the good speaker become fully understood, we shall almost certainly find that this internal flexibility and various kinds of pausing are much more important than the word-per-minute rate. Incidentally, the problem of the person who "talks too fast" usually is not that he says too many words in a given period but rather that he times them poorly and tends to leave out syllables.

The phonetic notations used for indicating the length of sounds or pauses are fairly uniform. A sound of slightly greater than average length is followed by a single dot [·], sometimes called the *half-length* notation. A sound which is pronounced with considerably more than average length is followed by two dots [:], sometimes called the *full-length* notation. Contrast, for example, the EA pronunciations of "hod" and "hard": [hɑd], [hɑ:d].

For indicating pauses between words, phrases, and sentences many phoneticians rely on conventional English punctuation marks, such as commas, semicolons, and periods, just as they would if the speech were written in conventional orthography. For the most part, this practice is convenient, but when the durational characteristics of speech and the rules of punctuation do not agree, we are forced to the realization that punctuation marks are linguistic, not phonetic, devices. If one tried to designate actual pauses by ordinary punctuation marks, he might have to scatter them about in a bizarre fashion. For example:

[ðə jus əv, stændəd pʌŋtʃueʃən mɑrks ɪn ðə,
ʌ: , kes əv ən, ʌnʃur spikɚ, maɪt lʊk;
laɪk; ðɪs. si?]

This type of notation can be avoided by using a single vertical bar [|], instead of a comma, to mark a shorter pause and a double vertical bar [||], instead of a semicolon or period, to show a longer pause. The sample transcription just given would then appear in this more reasonable form:

[ðə jus əv | stændəd pʌŋtʃueʃən mɑrks ɪn
ðə | ʌː ‖ kes əv ən | ʌnʃʊr spikə | maɪt lʊk ‖ laɪk ‖
ðɪs ‖ si?]

Even with all the devices given in this and the preceding chapter for indicating the variations of speech in context, we cannot expect to transcribe faithfully *all* the phonetic events of the original speech. The notations for pitch, stress, pauses, and so on can only jog the memory regarding the broad aspects of the more important changes that took place. In deciding whether to use conventional punctuation or special marks in transcribing, the student should be guided by his purpose. Since this is very frequently to train his ear to recognize the finer nuances of good speech, he is likely to find a good deal of use for the special marks.

14

SPEECH IMPROVEMENT

This chapter offers a final summary of the principles and procedures through which facts about speech—phonetic theory—can be applied to speech improvement. Most of the important information has been presented in earlier sections, but an effort is made here to clarify, if this is necessary, the specific way in which the student should go about reaching whatever level of speech proficiency he is willing to work for.

It will never be possible to devise a set of ready-made lessons in speech improvement, but we have compiled a substantial amount of supplementary exercise material which should prove useful (see Appendix). Incidentally, the reader who plans to become a speech teacher or a speech and hearing therapist will do well to practice these materials even though his speech may now be good, for in this way he can enhance his mastery of phonetic skills.

The specific topics covered in this chapter are (1) regional-dialect differences, (2) sources of substandard speech, and (3) steps in the speech improvement program. The information on regional dialects is included because the student must be familiar with the kind of speech standard he wishes to adopt. The material on the sources of substandard speech should assist him in seeking out any speech faults he may have. The more detailed description of the steps in the speech improvement process is intended, of course, as a guide in planning and carrying out the necessary drills and exercises.

REGIONAL-DIALECT DIFFERENCES

The whole question of correctness in relation to regional dialect was adequately covered in Chapter 1, and there is no need to repeat this discussion. The conclusion to which we came was that General American, Eastern American, or Southern American speech is entirely acceptable, provided that substandard usages are avoided. The educated speaker may choose his own standard on the basis of personal considerations.

Since most of our discussions, including the exercise materials, have been couched in terms of GA, those who consider either EA or SA more suitable for themselves must be familiar with the major differences in these speech standards. For purposes of comparison, the Appendix contains several passages transcribed in these dialects; the remaining practice materials should be altered as necessary by those who wish to adapt them to speech other than General American.

It is beyond the purpose of a text such as this to describe in great detail the distinguishing differences among the major speech regions of the United States, but the student interested in such matters will find the book by Wise[39] an excellent source of information. Any student of phonetics, however, should have a knowledge of at least the broader features which characterize the speech of the larger dialect regions, even though he may not wish to delve deeply into this special branch of linguistics. To this end the following summary is offered.

Regional variations in stress, pitch patterns, and inflection, as well as in other aspects of intonation, involve far too many complexities to be considered here. We can merely note that many of the seemingly conspicuous speech traits of the various dialect regions may depend upon these factors rather than upon the pronunciation of sounds. There are, however, some outstanding differences which arise from the way in which individual phonemes are handled. Our discussion is limited to the major distinctive pronunciations, but the student will learn to hear some of the more subtle features of regional dialect if he develops phonetic skills.

Syllabic r. In the South and certain parts of the East an outstanding characteristic is the way words spelled with *r* are pronounced when the sound in question is syllabic. In GA, of course, the *r* is pronounced, either as the stressed *r*-colored vowel [ɝ] or as its unstressed counterpart [ɚ]. In SA and in many EA dialects, however, the *r* coloring is largely lost; hence the *r*-colored vowels are replaced by either [ɜ] or [ə]. This is what is meant by the colloquial description "dropping the *r*." Verbal descriptions of these vowels in SA and EA speech are not very satisfactory for the person whose ear is tuned only to GA usages. The best solution is to listen carefully to examples given by an instructor or to study the pronunciation of speakers from these dialect regions. The following are a few representative pronunciations:

	GA	EA or SA
sir	[sɝ] or [sɚ]	[sɜ] or [sə]
bird	[bɝd]	[bɜd]
further	[fɝðɚ]	[fɜðə]
person	[pɝsən]	[pɜsən]
word	[wɝd]	[wɜd]
certain	[sɝtən]	[sɜtən]
mother	[mʌðɚ]	[mʌðə]
pursue	[pɚsu]	[pəsu]

Nonsyllabic r. When the consonant [r] plays the role of an on-glide, as in "run" or "red," there is of course no distinguishing difference among the dialect regions. There are, however, many phonetic situations where the GA speaker uses [r] as an off-glide but where the typical EA or SA speaker drops the sound entirely. The word "car," for instance, would be [kɑr] in GA but [kɑ:] in EA or SA. Note that the vowel in EA or SA is characteristically lengthened. Other examples are [pɑrdən]–[pɑ:dən] and [wɔr]–[wɔ:]. Where r follows a vowel other than [ɔ] or [ɑ], however, the EA or SA speaker usually glides off to the non-r-colored neutral vowel. For example, the "beer" [bɪr] and "care" [kɛr] of the Middle Westerner or Westerner are typically replaced by [bɪə] and [kɛə]. Other comparisons of GA with EA and SA include "fear" [fɪr]–[fɪə], "tire" [taɪr]–[taɪə], and "fireman" [faɪrmən]–[faɪəmən].

An important exception to the foregoing statements is the EA and SA treatment of the *linking r.* In words where r is followed by a vowel, the sound [r] is restored in EA and SA as an on-glide or releasing consonant for the following syllable. For example, although the word "mar" is pronounced [mɑ:], "marring" is heard as [mɑrɪŋ]. As another example, the New Englander who habitually says [hɪə] and [fɑ:] when these words come at the end of a phrase or are followed by a word beginning with a consonant restores the [r] when a vowel follows, as in the phrase "here I am" [hɪr aɪ æm] or "far away" [fɑr əwe]. Note the EA "over and over" [ovər ənd ovə], which has first a linking r and then a final [ə]. In many cases the linking r is more closely attached to the following syllable as a releasing consonant than to the word in which it is spelled; thus such a phrase as "far away" could be transcribed [fɑ rəwe]. For most purposes, however, this violation of linguistic word boundaries would be pointless.

The reader may recall from previous notes that the *intrusive r,* which is heard particularly in EA, creeps in because of a tendency to supply a "linking" [r] after vowels where, strictly speaking, it is not needed. This is a kind of phonetic analogy. A typical example is the pronunciation [ðɪ aɪdɪr əv ɪt] for "the idea of it." In such cases the intrusive r is not particularly conspicuous and hence may be forgiven. When the analogy is carried to the point where "idea" always becomes [aɪdɪr]—as in [ðæts ən aɪdɪr]—then the usage must for the present be considered substandard even in EA, no matter how commonly it may be heard.

Occasionally students with GA origins who undertake to drop their r sounds as a means of achieving EA, Southern British, or perhaps classical stage diction find themselves in an awkward situation when they mistakenly try to drop the r in those phonetic circumstances where a linking r would normally occur. To say "over and over" as [ovə ənd ovə] in conversational speech is unnatural.

Vowels before r. One of the distinctive differences in pronunciation among the dialect regions of the United States is the way in which certain

SPEECH IMPROVEMENT 277

vowels are spoken before *r*. The full details of these variations are too
complex to be discussed here, but a few examples will be given to show
the kinds of pronunciations which may be heard. Many of the distinctive
usages will be overlooked by the average listener and in this sense are
not conspicuous dialect traits. One of the common differences involves
the pronunciation of *a* or *o* before *r*. Compare, for instance, the typical
EA and SA pronunciation of the words "forest," "horrid," and "por-
ridge," which may be broadly transcribed [fɑrəst], [hɑrəd], and [pɑrɪdʒ],
with the GA pronunciations [fɔrəst], [hɔrəd], and [pɔrɪdʒ].

A similar kind of dialect difference may be observed where the vowel
[ɝ] is followed by [i] or [ɪ]. The words "hurry" and "worry," for example,
are pronounced [hɝɪ] and [wɝɪ] in GA but usually [hʌrɪ] and [wʌrɪ] in
the East and South. In still another group of words such typical General
American pronunciations as [kɛrət] for "carrot" and [bɛrən] for "barren"
become [kærət] and [bærən] in Eastern and Southern American.

Broad *a*. One of the most widely recognized characteristics which differentiates many Eastern speakers and most Southern British speakers
from those who use General American is the pronunciation given the
ah group of vowels. What most phonetically naïve persons do not seem
to know is that the dialect differences are very complex and certainly
involve a great deal more than the substitution of [ɑ] for a General
American [æ]. There are, however, about 150 words in which the choice
of [ɑ] or [a] rather than [æ] is a characteristic of EA speech. Common
examples of such pronunciations are [drɑft], [pɑs], [dɑns], and [tɑsk]
for the words "draft," "pass," "dance," and "task," which are [dræft],
[pæs], [dæns], and [tæsk] in General American.

It may interest the student to learn in passing that Southern British,
usually held as the model for the broad *a*, employs many more [æ] than
[ɑ] sounds. Furthermore, as Kenyon[16] points out, " . . . GA has more
[ɑ] sounds than Southern British, owing to the prevalence in GA of the
[ɑ] sounds in words that have the 'short o' in British."

[ɑ] versus [ɔ]. There are few distinctive pronunciations for the broad
speech regions based on choices between sounds in the [ɑ] and [ɔ] phonemes, but when it comes to defining local variations in these usages,
the problems get almost hopelessly complex. It may be possible, however,
to give some illustrations of the extent of variation encountered. Note, for
example, the variant pronunciations, as given in Kenyon and Knott,[17]
of the *o* spelling in the following common words.

log	[lɔg]	[lɑg]	[lɒg]
hog	[hɑg]	[hɔg]	[hɒg]
(Southern)	[hɔg]	[hɑg]	[hɒg]
dog	[dɔg]	[dɒg]	[dɑg]
cog	[kɑg]	[kɒg]	[kɔg]
flog	[flɑg]	[flɒg]	[flɔg]

The use of the low-back, rounded [ɒ] would seem to be a kind of compromise, normally used only by those who do not distinguish between [ɑ] and [ɔ]. Judging from the authors' experience it seems that this compromise sound is growing in frequency of use. This certainly seems to be the case in the Northwest area. However, according to Thomas, except for the Western Pennsylvania and Eastern New England dialect regions, ". . . the distinction is normally kept: *caught, bought, lawn,* and *law* normally have [ɔ], rarely [ɒ]; *broth, soft,* and *cost* probably have [ɔ] more frequently than [ɒ]; *cot, odd, stop,* and *rock* normally have [ɑ]." (Ref. 32, p. 206)

Diphthongs. The pronunciation of various diphthongs is one of the conspicuous differences between Southern American and General or Eastern American. One of the most obvious regional usages is the [aː] or [ɑː] which is heard in SA speech where the diphthong [aɪ] would be used in GA or EA speech. The Southern speaker, in other words, substitutes a long monophthong for the diphthong. Contrast the following:

SA	*GA or EA (except for EA final [ə])*
fire [fɑː] or [faː]	[faɪr]
smile [smɑːl] or [smaːl]	[smaɪl]
tired [taːd]	[taɪrd] or in EA [taɪəd]
hire [hɑː] or [haː]	[haɪr]
admire [ədmɑː] or [ədmaː]	[ədmaɪr]

Another but somewhat less consistent characteristic of some Southern speech is the substitution of what would broadly be marked [æʊ] for the GA and EA [aʊ] in such words as "house," "pound," and "down."

SUBSTANDARD SPEECH CHARACTERISTICS

The concept of substandard speech has been touched on at various points, and many of the substandard pronunciations of individual speech sounds have been mentioned in the descriptions of these sounds. The student, however, should systematically review some of the major characteristics of substandard speech in preparation for a realistic and objective evaluation of the faults he may need to deal with in his own speech. Only those substandard usages which tend to be common to all dialect regions of the United States are covered here.

It might not be impossible to enumerate the myriad typical errors of substandard speech (although the list would be long), but it is certainly difficult to classify them for systematic discussion. We shall do this the best we can, but the student will find that in many cases what seem to be similar errors arise from quite different sources and that there often are complex interrelationships between substandard usages. To give only one example, what might loosely be called "lazy articulation" can lead to errors in stress, sound or syllable elision, changes in phonemes, and other complex effects.

It should prove interesting to the student to become more fully acquainted with some of the phenomena involved in common speech faults, although in the final analysis the most important goal for one whose interests are wholly practical may be simply to recognize and avoid substandard usages, without necessarily becoming familiar with the details which concern the phonetician. Although it may be impossible within the confines of a discussion of reasonable length to present a consistent set of laws or principles explaining when and why substandard usages occur, this fact is not necessarily a great disadvantage for the student of speech improvement. The most fruitful method for his purposes lies in what might be called the *positive approach*, in which attention is focused on correct usage; any deviations can then be perceived and avoided.

One group of substandard usages can be classified loosely as arising from *incorrect sounds*. The words in this category are pronounced in such a way that they contain one or more sounds other than those that would be called for by standard usage. Many of these errors arise simply from the speaker's unfamiliarity with standard pronunciation. He is confronted with a new word, often one that he heretofore has seen only in print, and—lacking the information the dictionary could have given him—he mistakenly uses one or more incorrect sounds. (There are often additional related errors in stress.)

Many such blunders can be considered *spelling-pronunciation* errors. Words are pronounced in the way that seems indicated by the spelling. For example, "chic" is heard as [tʃɪk] rather than [ʃik], "hover" as [hovɚ] rather than [hʌvɚ], "filial" as [filɪəl] rather than [fɪlɪəl], and "ouzel" as [auzəl] instead of [uzəl]. Such errors are naturally very common. The tendency to pronounce words as they are spelled can also lead to the addition of unnecessary sounds, as we shall see later.

A good many substandard usages of this sort can be classified as arising from *analogy*, although this term is used by some phoneticians to include slightly different types of errors as well. In the illustrations given below, the speaker has pronounced words in a way which seems analogous to other words, spelled the same way in part, with which he is familiar.

Familiar word	Analogy (substandard)
earth [ɝθ]	hearth [hɝθ]
January [dʒænjuɛrɪ]	February [fɛbjuɛrɪ]
zoo [zu]	zoology [zuɑlədʒɪ]
volume [vɑljəm]	column [kɑljəm]

Relic pronunciations and *folk etymology* may also lead to substandard pronunciations, particularly among the untutored. At one time such mistakes were thought of as especially common in rural or isolated areas, but this probably is not so true today as it may once have been. The following can be considered "old-fashioned," or relic, pronunciations: "eat" [ɛt], "deaf" [dif], and "certain" [sɑrtən]. Still other unacceptable pronunciations can be heard among the linguistically naïve when a word new to the speaker is confused with a similar familiar word to which it is thought to be related; this process is called folk etymology. Examples are "cold slaw" [kol slɔ], "mattocks" [mætæks], "caulks" [kɔrks], "asparagrass" [əspɛrəgræs], and "skid row" [skɪd ro] (for "skid road").

Persons preoccupied with correctness but lacking sufficient information about usage often mispronounce words because of a tendency to be overprecise. Substandard speech of this sort is sometimes termed a *pseudocultured* or *hyperurban* style. The spelling-pronunciation relationship is often involved. For instance, "salmon" sometimes becomes [sælmən] rather than [sæmən], "forehead" becomes [fɔrhɛd] instead of [fɔrəd], and "hasten" becomes [hestən] rather than [hesn̩]. Overmeticulous vowel pronunciation, which comes from stressing a vowel more strongly than would be consistent with good usage, leads to such stilted pronunciations as [ætɪtjud] for "attitude," [pɑsɪbəl] for "possible," and [ɛlimɛntərɪ] for "elementary." The frequency of such pronunciations among foreign speakers is understandable.

Still other examples of unnatural pronunciations of an "elegant" nature are [tɪsju] for "tissue," [əprɪsɪet] for "appreciate," and [netjʊr] for "nature." A somewhat more obscure example is [mauntɪŋ] for "mountain," where there is a kind of analogy to a word such as "going," which, of course, is properly [goɪŋ] rather than [goən]. Admittedly it is occasionally hard to draw a clear line between a good familiar style, laxity, and overprecision, but here as always we must depend upon perceptive listening to the patterns set by those who speak with practiced ease.

Numerous undesirable speech characteristics may arise from what we have chosen to call *underpronunciation*, that is, failure to give the speech sounds within words an adequate pronunciation value. Among the syllabics either the distinctive resonance for the sound may be insufficient or else a nonstandard resonance may be introduced. Consider, for instance, what may happen to diphthongs when they are underpronounced (or unstressed) to the point where they lose their diphthongal quality: "house" becomes [hɑs] instead of [haus], "flowers" is [flɑrz] instead of [flaurz], "outside" is [ɑtsaɪd] rather than [autsaɪd], and "fireman" is [fɑrmən] instead of [faɪrmən]. Similarly, any vowel that should normally be given perceptible stress in good-quality speech may become unstressed to such a degree that the pronunciation is inaccurate. Although the dividing line between acceptable informal speech and substandard usage may be difficult to define, underpronunciation of the diphthongs and vowels is one of the most pervasive of speech faults.

Underpronunciation of the consonants leads to what is conventionally described as "lazy speech" or "poor articulation." It goes without saying that the movements which initiate and terminate syllables must be made with precision and vigor—but without becoming obtrusive. Naturally the plosive sounds, particularly in final positions, must be made with adequate force, and the same holds true for all the nonsyllabics. A number of exercises are suggested below for the development of good articulation of the consonant sounds. The term *oral inaccuracy* is sometimes applied to the various kinds of inadequate articulation which comprise underpronunciation. The same forces which lead to underpronunciation of the speech sounds may also cause both sound and syllable elision and excessive assimilation; these faults are discussed in a later section.

Associated with underpronunciation are certain typical changes in sounds, particularly in the vowels, which cause speech to become substandard. One of these changes is termed *fronting*. This occurs when the tongue is advanced beyond its standard position to a degree that imparts an unacceptable change in the resonance of the vowel. Often this affects the vowel [ʌ], usually (but not always) in words where this sound is followed by a consonant which calls for the tongue to be raised and fronted. In the following substandard pronunciations note that [ʌ] is replaced by a front vowel: [rɛʃən] for "Russian," [hɛʃ] for "hush," [kɪvɚ] for "cover," [dʒɛdʒ] for "judge," and [ʃɛt] for "shut." A similar phenomenon is the raising of [ɪ], [ɛ], and [æ] when these sounds occur before front consonants. This results in such pronunciations as [frɛʃ] for "fresh," [kɛtʃ] for "catch," [kɪn] for "can," [mɪnɪ] for "many," [fiʃ] for "fish," and [egz] for "eggs."

Lowering of vowels is also fairly common, often becoming quite conspicuous when it causes deviations from a standard [i] or [ɪ]. Examples are the following questionable pronunciations: [krɛp] "creep," [lɪgəl] "legal," [nɪgrə] "Negro," [wɪkɚ] "weaker," and [lɛpt] "leaped."

One of the most pervasive of substandard speech traits is the tendency to *centralize* vowels. This robs the vowel sound of its distinctive resonance or pronunciation value; the proper vowel quality is replaced by one of the central vowels, quite often the indefinite and lightly stressed [ə]. What is referred to here is, in a sense, an aggravation of the tendency of any vowel to move toward [ə] when there is any unstressing. This is an entirely normal change in speech sounds, particularly in informal conversational speech. Carried too far, however, the consequence is inaccurate, substandard speech. Take, for example, the sentence "You can if you want to." In rapid conversational speech certain of the vowels would not be strongly stressed; yet good usage would sound something like [ju kæn ɪf ju wɔnt tu]. Notice what happens, however, when some of the major vowel resonances are reduced to the indefinite vowel (along with some additional changes that go along with this kind of careless speech): [jə kən əf jə wənə].

Sound changes which are phonetically similar may lead to somewhat different substandard usages. The word "because" [bikɔz] changes to [bikʌz]; "widow" may be pronounced [wɪdə], or it may become [wɪdɚ], with a central, unstressed r-colored vowel. Analogous pronunciations are [wɪndə] or [wɪndɚ] for "window" and [ʃædə] or [ʃædɚ] for "shadow."

In a number of loan words from other languages a final [ɪ] commonly becomes [ə] in a manner which cannot be considered correct. Examples are "Missouri" [mɪzʊrə], Cincinnati [sɪnsənætə], "Miami" [maɪæmə], and "macaroni" [mækərɑnə]. In still another group of words [ʌ] often replaces [ɛ], [æ], or [ɪ], as in the following pronunciations: [hwʌp] for "whip," [rʌðɚ] for "rather," and [əmʌrəkə] for "America." Centralization may also lead to substitution of [ʌ] for [ʊ] or [u], as in [tʌk] for "took," [pʌt] for "put," [kʌd] for "could," [rʌm] for "room," and [wʌd] for "would." All of these represent something less than careful usage.

Still another kind of sound change which leads to substandard usage is sometimes called *palatization*. For instance, words in which either [k] or [g] (which are palatal consonants) is followed by [æ] or [aʊ] may be pronounced in such a way that [j] seems to follow the linguapalatal sound. Examples are "good" [gjʊd], "card" [kjɑrd], "cow" [kjaʊ], and "catch" [kjɛtʃ]. When [d] is palatalized, as it sometimes is, one hears such substandard pronunciations as [dʒutɪ] for "duty," [dʒu] for "due," [dʒuk] for "duke," and [trɪmɛndʒəs] for "tremendous." The vowel [u] is replaced by [ju] quite often, a practice that could be called palatization if one wished, but this error is possibly caused more by psuedo elegance than anything else. A characteristic example is [njun] for "noon."

Certain other errors can be grouped loosely as cases in which sounds are omitted, transposed, or added. Omission of medial vowels, a phonetic process called *syncope*, gives rise to pronunciations such as [pɑsbəl] for "possible," [ækət] for "accurate," [rɪlɪ] for "really," and [mɪstrɪ] for "mystery." Elision of consonant sounds is very common, particularly in the case of certain consonant clusters which seem difficult for the English speaker. Common examples are the following:

Omission of final [t] in such words as "didn't" [dɪdn̩] (listen also for [dɪnt] or [dɪn]), "wouldn't" [wʊdn̩] (or [wʊnt]), "shouldn't" [ʃʊdn̩], "last" [læs], "crept" [krɛp], and "wept" [wɛp].

Omission of [d], as in "and" [æn], "wind" [wɪn], "hands" [hænz], "window" [wɪno], "old" [ol], "wild" [waɪl], "pounds" [paʊnz], and so on.

Omission of either [k] or [t] in words such as "masked" [mæst] or

[mæsk], "asked" [æst] or [æs], and "basked" [bæst]; omission of [k] in
words such as "husks" [hʌs]; omission of [s] or [ps] in words such as
"wasps" [wɔs].

Numerous other elisions are characteristic of substandard speech,
and this matter will come up once more in connection with excessive
assimilation. Among characteristic errors are omission of [l], as in [vɑjəm]
for "volume" and [mɪjən] for "million"; elision of [h], as in [jumən] for
"human" and [jumɚ] for "humor"; elimination of [ð], as in [gɪv m̩] for
"give them"; and so on.

Supernumerary, or needless, sounds or syllables are also quite common.
An added syllable, which is a phonetic change called *anaptyxis*, is heard
in such pronunciations as [æθəlɛtɪk] for "athletic," [pəliz] for "please,"
[fɪləm] for "film," and [kərɑɪ] for "cry." Intrusive sounds were mentioned
at various points in the treatment of individual phonemes. Although not
always substandard, they are not acceptable in the following typical
pronunciations: [wɔrʃ] for "wash," [purʃ] for "push," [ɑɪdɪr] for "idea,"
[əkrɔst] for "across," [ɛnɪhwɛrz] for "anywhere," and [ətæktəd] for
"attacked."

Sounds may be interchanged in various ways. One common form of
this error is the confusion of voiced and voiceless sounds. This is illustrated by the following pronunciations, which must be considered substandard, or at least questionable: [holt] for "hold," [kɪlt] for "killed,"
[mɛtəsən] for "medicine," [wɑdɚ] for "water," [kædəl] for "cattle,"
[smɛlt] for "smelled," and [hɑsbɪdəl] for "hospital." The interchange of
voiced and unvoiced sounds may be very frequent in foreign dialect.

In what is termed *metathesis* sounds are transposed. This fairly common fault is illustrated by [æks] for "ask," [hʌnɚt] for "hundred,"
[epɚn] for "apron," [prifɔrm] for "perform," and [pɚskrɑɪb] for "pre-
scribe." *Replacement* of sounds, beyond the kind of error heard in children's immature speech, may bring about substandard usage. Substitution of [n] for [ŋ] (erroneously called dropping the *g*) gives [goən]
for "going," [duən] for "doing," [wɛrən] for "wearing," and so on. Note
also [strɛnθ] for "strength" and [lɛnθ] for "length." The opposite substitution of [ŋ] for [n] leads to such undesirable usages as [ɪŋkʌm] for
"income." All sorts of other sound substitutions may be detected in
careless speech.

Incorrect Stress. Failure to impart correct stress may cause errors
in pronunciation. As we have learned, the English language spoken by
Americans displays characteristic stress patterns and stress differences
which distinguish it from other languages. In addition, stress differences
among the syllables of a single word are sometimes as important for
naturalness and intelligibility as are the sounds themselves.

Some of the typical errors in stressing reflect nothing more than ignorance of the accepted standards. For instance, "exquisite" is more correctly spoken with the primary stress on the first syllable: ['ɛkskwɪzət], not [ɛks'kwɪzət], which is often heard. The same is true of "comparable," which is better as ['kɑmpərəbəl] than as [kəm'pɛrəbəl], and a number of similar words which are commonly mispronounced. In the case of a large group of two-syllable words, such as "research" and "detail," many dictionaries sanction stress on either the first or the second syllable, although stress on the second syllable is possibly preferable in the examples given.

To complicate the situation, another group of two-syllable words can be used as either nouns or verbs, with the stress pattern depending upon the part of speech. The tendency is to accent nouns on the first syllable and verbs on the second. This rule seems to hold for "pervert," which is ['pɝvət] as a noun and [pɚ'vɝt] as a verb, as well as for such words as "increase" and "confines." It certainly breaks down in terms of current usage on "research" (which is about equally ['risɚtʃ] or [ri'sɝtʃ] for either form), and also in the case of "contract" and many other words in this category.

Remember that sounds may change as a result of the amount of stress they receive; "detail," for example, is either ['ditel] or [dɪ'tel]. Certain shifts of stress are unquestionably substandard, as in ['ditrɔɪt] for "Detroit" and ['diklaɪn] for "decline." Throughout, we have called attention to the fact that errors in stressing are an integral aspect of substandard speech of many descriptions. The student must learn to listen carefully for stressing and to consult the dictionary whenever he has any doubt about the standard.

Mention should be made again of substandard usages arising from *restressing*. It is a familiar fact that in conversational speech unstressing takes place. Errors of restressing occur when the speaker is called on to use a stressed form of the word but retains the resonance of the unstressed form. The *stress-unstress-restress* patterns of the following words illustrate the phenomenon of substandard restressing: "for" [fɔr]–[fɚ]–[fɝ]; "of" [ɑv]–[əv]–[ʌv]; and "have" [hæv]–[əv]–[ʌv]—as in "you should have," which thus becomes "you should of" [ju ʃʊd ʌv].

Excessive Assimilation. Many of the speech faults previously discussed are actually examples of excessive and improper assimilation, but this most pervasive of substandard speech characteristics involves some important factors which merit special attention. Assimilation of sounds in connected speech is, of course, a normal phonetic process, as was explained fully in an earlier chapter. Only when assimilation goes beyond certain allowable limits does it become objectionable, but this boundary is passed with astonishing consistency by practicioners of substandard speech.

To begin with, if the principle of assimilation were fully and consistently applied, all speech sounds would be virtually alike, an absurdity that is surprisingly close to realization in some speakers. The point at which assimilation goes beyond allowable limits can be determined only by each individual's judgment, based on his appraisal of whether or not he is intelligible and is conforming to the standards of the educated speaker.

Excessive assimilation is easy to illustrate. For what it is worth, the following transcription records the entirely plausible assimilations that might be imparted to this fictional speech sample:

"Say, what's the time?"
[se, wəsə taɪm?]

"How would I know? I haven't a watch."
[haʊdaɪ no? aɪvənə wɑtʃ.]

"Did you eat yet?"
[dʒitʃet?]

"No, did you?"
[no, dʒu?]

"Why don't you eat with us?"
[waɪn tʃitə θʌs?]

"It's O.K. with me if you'll let me have some money."
[sokeθ mi fjə lɛmɪ æv smʌnɪ.]

"Suits me. Here's your hat. Let's go."
[sus mi. hɪrʒə ræt. ɛs go.]

It is true, of course, that conversational speech patterns are not always assimilated to this extent; yet this example can scarcely be called an improbable exaggeration, for its counterpart can be heard daily by anyone who cares to listen with a perceptive ear. For the kind of speaking most of us are called on to do in the course of our daily lives, there can be no doubt that the goal we wish to achieve is speech with cultivated ease. Assimilations are perfectly commonplace phenomena in "easy English." But these are not wholesale truncations of words, with sounds that are missing, underpronounced, or transmuted into completely different phonemes by reason of overassimilation. It would be impossible to catalogue all the errors of excessive assimilation, but if the student does nothing else, he should surely be alert to this major and primary speech fault.

Syllable Elision. Particular attention should be given to the unacceptable assimilations which result from the complete elision of syllables.

The elimination of syllables is an extremely common characteristic of substandard American speech and goes along with the cluttered, rapid utterance of those who lack a sense of speech rhythm. Perhaps the psychological basis is the lack of a truly communicative attitude.

At various points we have stressed the importance of understanding the syllable as the basic unit of speaking. It follows that attention to syllabification is one of the secrets of developing facility in good speech form. In the imaginary conversation transcribed earlier, there were several examples of syllable elision. Consider the following transcriptions, which represent a correct and a substandard version of the same sentence. There are 25 syllables in the sentence if it is pronounced as it might be by an educated speaker; there are only 15 in the substandard version:

"It is a privilege to be with such an intellectual person as he apparently is."

(Standard)	[ɪt ɪz ə prɪvəlɪdʒ tə bi	8 syllables
(Substandard)	[sprɪvlɪdʒ tə	3 syllables
	wɪθ sʌtʃ ən ɪntəlɛktʃuəl	8 syllables
	biθ sʌtʃ nɪnəlɛkʃəl	6 syllables
	pɝ·sən əz hi əperəntlɪ ɪz]	9 syllables
	pɝ·sən zi pernlɪ ɪz]	6 syllables

Foreign Dialect. No effort will be made here to describe specifically the typical errors of speakers with a non-English-language background. Even if we confined such a discussion to the commonest languages, a long section would be necessary. Anyone interested in such matters will find Wise[39] very helpful. The foreign student using this text may wish to do supplementary reading about his own language.

The foreign speaker faces a real difficulty in mastering standard American speech—particularly if he begins this task as a mature person— and he deserves all the help, support, and encouragement that can be given. At the outset, his English vocabulary may be limited. Even if it is not, it is likely to be a "book" vocabulary, with pronunciations learned from someone who himself has a dialect. Anyone who has tried to use his school French to talk with a Frenchman will be entirely aware of the problem thus created. The idioms of everyday speech may prove tremendously confusing. The intricacies and irregularities of English grammar impose an additional burden. Complicating the situation further is the necessity, at least at first, of "thinking" in the native language, then translating concepts into English words.

The strongly nonphonetic spelling will probably lead to numerous *spelling-pronunciation* errors. Again, the foreign speaker may encounter difficulty with the English sound system. Sounds which are completely new because they are not among those of his native language may prove comparatively easy, for in this case there are no established patterns of sound formation to interfere. But naturally he will not always know when to use them, because of variant spellings, and incorrect sounds will thus be a prominent feature of his English speech.

The English sounds which give the most difficulty will probably be those that resemble a native sound but which still are perceptibly different in the American sound system. Perhaps the commonest example is the *r* group, although there are numerous other phonemes that may prove hard to master. Many of the principal modern languages have sounds which would be placed in a broad [r] phoneme, and the foreign speaker naturally tends to bring his native *r* into English speech. Vowel errors are also very characteristic.

Proper stressing, accent, and melody are perhaps the most vexatious of all English speech characteristics for the foreign speaker to master, since they require a very keen ear to distinguish. Realistically, a person whose native speech habits are firmly entrenched through years of use may have to content himself with something less than perfection in his English speech. This is not too serious a concession, provided that he gets to the point where his speech is readily understood and is free of unduly distracting dialect peculiarities.

The phonetic method of studying English pronunciation and diction offers the most hope for a foreign speaker. He should work seriously to acquire transcription skills, developing his analytic abilities to the point where he can record stress and melody in considerable detail by the use of appropriate phonetic symbols. In this way he will become intimately aware of English pronunciations and cadences and may ultimately get a genuine feeling for the new language.

The foregoing remarks fall far short of a comprehensive treatment of the errors of substandard speech. This general summary, however, should serve to alert the student to many of the questionable usages which are commonly heard. By this time he should understand many of the reasons why they occur and thus should be better able to deal with any of these faults that he detects in his own speech. At all times in his study of speech form he must be engaged in making a compilation of his own errors.

STEPS IN THE SPEECH IMPROVEMENT PROGRAM

The basic assumption of this book, and one which must be thoroughly understood, is that the acquisition of good speech form depends first upon learning about speech through a study of phonetic theory. The important topics in this connection have been treated in the earlier chapters. Next, the student must develop phonetic skills—particularly those which will help him to hear his own speech and that of others analytically and accurately. Finally, he must formulate in an educated way his own speech goals and carry out the necessary practice in the articulation and pronunciation of individual speech sounds, words, and connected speech.

There is one fundamental idea that must be fully accepted by anyone who hopes to improve his speech: *speaking must become a conscious, voluntary process;* it must be controlled and monitored at all times, so that the speaker is always aware of the form as well as the content of what he is saying. In due course he may reach the point where good speech habits become firmly fixed, but the time will never come when conscious self-monitoring can be completely dropped. If this formula seems mechanistic to an unwholesome degree, this is not intended. Remember always the basic truth that truly communicative attitudes and purposes are indispensable attributes of good speaking.

The specific steps in applying phonetic theory to speech improvement can be summarized as follows:

1. Formulate specific goals for your own speech form.

2. Develop phonetic skills which will enable you to hear speech in an accurate and discriminative way.

3. Learn to produce the sounds of speech correctly in isolation and in simple phonetic contexts.

4. Carry out the drill necessary to develop practiced ease in speaking individual words and contextual speech in conformity with the goals that have been formulated.

1. Formulation of Specific Goals. This first important step involves two considerations: (*a*) a general understanding of the characteristics of acceptable speech form and (*b*) an analytic study of the ways in which one's own habitual speech patterns deviate from accepted form, or from the goals that have been set up.

So far as the first consideration is concerned, the whole question of standards of speech and speech styles was covered fully in Chapter 1 and need not be elaborated further at this point, although a review of the earlier discussion might be helpful. Regional speech standards were treated in the first part of the present chapter. What the student must now do, as a practical step in speech improvement, is to clarify for himself exactly how he wishes to talk. He certainly should be ready to do this, provided that he has mastered the various facts that have been presented, for he should be able to understand and recognize the elements of good speech form.

Self-diagnosis is the second consideration. The principle involved is clear and simple, but its application requires meticulous care and competence in phonetic techniques. The most common characteristics of substandard speech were discussed both in connection with the individual speech sounds and, in summary form, in this chapter. The student must now search out in his own speech those inadequacies and habitual substandard usages of which he is guilty. These must be specifically located and recognized, since they will become the focus of his own specially tailored speech improvement lessons.

Even when the student knows in theory what to listen for, locating his own faults in speech form will still require considerable time and effort. Certain common-sense suggestions can be offered. Obviously a competent teacher can prove of the utmost help in directing one's attention to speech errors, and the student will do well to place himself in the hands of such a person if this is at all possible.

With or without a teacher, one of the best ways to study speech objectively is through the use of some kind of recording. It is easy to understand that one can usually recognize errors more readily in someone else's speech than in his own; listening to recorded speech is like hearing another person. Speech samples can be played back again and again for thorough study. In most teaching situations tape recorders or some other type of recording apparatus will be available; if necessary, however, the student will do well to make every possible effort to acquire some kind of recording instrument for his own use.

We can recommend no particular techniques for the use of recordings which would not occur to the student himself. He should choose suitable speech samples, then read or speak into the microphone in such a way as to get the best possible recording. The recorded samples should be played back repeatedly until they have been thoroughly studied. The material should be frequently re-recorded, with, of course, an effort to eradicate any deficiencies that may have been noted. It may be possible to induce someone with good standard speech to record the samples for comparative study; if not, suitable recorded models can be found. Early samples can be preserved for comparison with later recordings as a way of measuring progress. In making the analyses it is very helpful to transcribe the material in phonetic symbols, and this is strongly recommended. The student should conscientiously write down all his errors in a notebook.

2. **Phonetic Skills for Speech Improvement.** The absolutely basic importance of perceptive listening has been stressed many times in the preceding pages; this is a skill which is indispensable to speech improvement. In Chapter 4, as we were preparing to study the individual speech sounds, a great deal was said about learning to recognize the sounds of speech through hearing and other sensory cues. In connection with each of the phonemes various drills and exercises were presented in an attempt

to guide the student in perceptive analysis. It is to be hoped and expected that by this time the student has acquired sound habits of phonetic analysis which he can apply to the improvement of his own speech.

The whole matter of what is sometimes called *ear training* is so important, however, that even at the risk of some repetition the principles should be restated here. Basically, one must learn to *identify* the speech sounds individually and in connected speech; he must also develop the ability to *discriminate* among sounds, particularly those that are acoustically similar. Ultimately this skill in discrimination must extend to very small differences. In addition, he must come to have a keen ear for stress, rhythm, and melody in speech. None of this requires any unusual talent or acuity of hearing, but it does demand a great deal of educated practice.

So far as a review of specific suggestions is concerned, the first is to carry out extensive practice specifically directed toward the goal of analytic listening. Recognize the importance of the *listening set.* Grasp clearly the idea that you will listen to speech only as a certain kind of sound. Ordinarily we attend to speech in somewhat the manner of a person listening to a symphony. In a large orchestra the notes of a score or more instruments blend into a total complex melody, each contributing a share but losing its separate identity. In listening for pleasure one does not usually try to distinguish individual instruments. Not so with the orchestra conductor, however; his is the skilled ear which can sense the slightest off-key playing of a single musician. He is aware of the total configuration of the music; yet his listening is highly analytic. Listening to speech is a comparable skill, and a most important element is *intending* to identify and discriminate the sounds.

Next, *listen to the sounds in isolation.* This is a basic kind of practice that should have been carried out extensively as each of the individual phonemes was studied. You were advised to take each of the speech sounds in turn and pronounce it aloud, continuing this exercise until you become thoroughly familiar with the sound under study. The purpose of such practice is to identify both in broad outline and in detail the characteristics of each phoneme. This may require scores, even hundreds, of repetitions. Remember to listen for the individual sounds in the speech of those around you.

Practice discrimination of similar sounds. This type of practice also was a regular part of the exercises following the discussion of each of the individual sounds, particularly those exercises involving minimal word pairs. If you have studied the earlier chapters carefully and followed instructions faithfully, your ability to discriminate speech sounds should by now be fairly well developed. The lists of phonemic oppositions are by no means complete, and you should prepare additional lists of this sort, laying emphasis on any sounds you find particularly hard to discriminate. All this material should be used for extensive oral practice, supplemented by recording whenever possible.

Listening to the pronunciation of others is naturally very important. It will be excellent practice if you can persuade someone to read lists of phonemic oppositions for you. In addition, plan to pay particular attention to discriminating similar sounds in the speech of those around you. Choose persons with all kinds of speaking habits: those who seem to speak poorly and others whom you believe to have the diction of educated persons, for it is important to be able to distinguish the good from the bad.

Attend carefully to *syllabification* also. In Chapter 2, as you will recall, the syllable was described as the basic unit of spoken language—each syllable consisting of a separate energy pulse, with its own vowel or vowellike resonance. In addition, each has a given degree of stress. Learn to identify the number of syllables in words and phrases and to distinguish syllables with little or no stress, those with average stress, and those with heavy stress. Listen for examples of the kind of substandard syllable elision mentioned earlier in this chapter, both in your own speech and in that of others. Remember that proper attention to the syllable is an important aid in analyzing speech and in developing good articulation and pronunciation.

From the outset we have stressed the usefulness of phonetic transcription. Because it is a basic tool in speech analysis, practice in transcribing is one of the best ways to develop the listening skills upon which we place such a high premium. The suggestions given in Chapter 4 are quite detailed, and there is no need to repeat them here. If you have done the transcribing suggested in connection with the earlier practice material, you should now be able to transcribe speech with relative ease and to make the widest possible use of this technique.

3. Practice the Sounds of Speech in Isolation and in Simple Phonetic Contexts. You can get a good start on the practice needed to acquire good habits of articulation and pronunciation by carrying out the activities described in the preceding section. The difference between these drills and those to be recommended here is largely a question of where the emphasis is placed. A great deal of talking aloud is involved in the process of developing analytic listening, but during this phase the primary focus must be on the listening itself. A greater or lesser amount of careful drill will be necessary to develop articulation and pronunciation skills, which can later be incorporated into meaningful and effective connected utterance. Specifically, this means practicing individual speech sounds, first in isolation and then in various kinds of phonetic contexts.

Obviously precision in the formation of the speech sounds and accurate pronunciation should always be basic goals. In working toward these objectives, you may have to practice each of the speech sounds in isolation many hundreds of times in a careful, *purposive* way, but you will realize at once that such drill is of great value. Now the closest attention should be paid to articulation movements as well as to the sound. There is no more need to feel self-conscious about drills of this sort than there is for the musician to feel so about the scales and finger exercises he must practice so faithfully to develop his technique.

Let us suppose, for instance, that you are working to improve your articulation of [t]. You will first pronounce the sound aloud many times, with definite objectives in mind. Pay the strictest attention to the way it sounds: is it cleanly and distinctly articulated, or is it, perhaps, somewhat indistinct? If it does not seem to be articulated well (it helps to have a critic), continue your practice until you can make the sound accurately and precisely.

Several things can be done to enhance the effectiveness of this practice. It is important to monitor the articulation movements with the greatest degree of care, using every possible sensory cue. Let us suppose that you have reviewed the description of the dynamics of the sound and have thus refreshed your memory on the details of its production and its acoustic characteristics. As you practice, listen carefully; try to get the "feel" of the articulation movements. You may even wish to observe yourself in a mirror. By carrying out such drill patiently and purposively, you can perfect your articulation and learn to produce the sound with practiced ease.

The principles and procedures just outlined should, of course, be applied to the sounds in each of the phonemes. Your understanding of the nature of each class of speech sounds will indicate the critical articulation characteristics. On the vowels, work for a firm position of the articulators which will give the distinctive resonance quality for which you have learned to listen. The same holds true for the vowellike sounds where the articulators are held in a static position.

You should also feel a definite articulation adjustment in producing the fricatives, and the friction sound should be distinct (but not, of course, unduly obtrusive). Plosives need to be made with a sufficiently strong closing contact. Where the sounds involve movements, as with the glides (and also the stops), work for accuracy and vigor of tongue and lip activity. At no time should there be a sense of strain, and there will not be if the basic articulation skills are perfected. When the sounds are put into context, new problems will arise, but you will be able to handle them if you have learned the individual sounds well.

As quickly as possible—but not so soon as to neglect adequate drill in the individual sounds—you should practice each sound in combination with all other sounds with which it is likely to be coupled in conversational speech. One of the best ways to do this is to work with *nonsense syllables*. This provides a very logical way to develop the more complicated articulation skills, since, as you have learned, the syllable is the basic unit of speech.

Nonsense-syllable lists can be made up very easily in the following way: (1) combine each of the vowels and diphthongs in turn with each of the consonants (including now the glides) in consonant-vowel, vowel-consonant, vowel-consonant-vowel, and consonant-vowel-consonant combinations (add more complex patterns if you wish); (2) combine each consonant with each of the vowels in a consonant-vowel, vowel-consonant, and consonant-vowel-consonant cluster. Actually the two lists will duplicate each other, but this is immaterial since the suggested procedure will make it more convenient to select material when you wish to practice a particular sound. It has not seemed worthwhile to prepare and print these lists for the student since he can make them himself so easily. A sample set of nonsense syllables for the consonant [t] and the vowel [ɑ] is shown in Table 5.

The manner in which these lists can be used should need no explanation. Say the nonsense syllables aloud and, as usual, listen carefully for purposes of self-monitoring. Make certain that the articulation is precise and accurate. Once again, recording will help. As with all drill, it is important that the practice be carried out purposefully.

4. Practice Words and Contextual Speech. This is the final step, in which you must bring together all the information and skill which you have been undertaking to build up through the study of phonetics. In a sense you never will be finished with this part of the speech improvement program, for the most important place in which to make effective use of the principles you have learned is in your actual day-to-day speaking. You have presumably become your own teacher and critic.

Drill will be centered first on words and then, of course, on contextual speech of increasing complexity. Extensive practice with word lists of one sort and another, again done purposefully and faithfully, should come first. As you know, illustrative word lists are appended to the discussions of each of the individual sounds in earlier chapters, but you should build up additional lists for your notebook. This may be done easily by combing through appropriate material, such as newspapers, magazines, books, or the dictionary. The words you add should, of course, be written in phonetic script.

In working on a particular phoneme, make certain that you include words to illustrate the sound in every position—initial, medial, and final—in which it appears in English. Read the words aloud in the usual way, but at this point the use of recording apparatus will be especially valuable. It will be wise to check the dictionary (Kenyon and Knott is recommended) for any pronunciation about which you have the slightest doubt.

Words should next be incorporated in practice sentences of your own composition. This will permit you to give special attention to the changes which may take place in word pronunciation in connected speech. Both

TABLE 5. EXAMPLES OF NONSENSE SYLLABLES FOR PRACTICE

Vowels

[it]	[ti]	[iti]	[ʌt]	[tʌ]	[ʌtʌ]
[ɪt]	[tɪ]	[ɪtɪ]	[ət]	[tə]	[ətə]
[et]	[te]	[ete]	[ot]	[to]	[oto]
[ɛt]	[tɛ]	[ɛtɛ]	[ʊt]	[tʊ]	[ʊtʊ]
[æt]	[tæ]	[ætæ]	[ut]	[tu]	[utu]
[ɑt]	[tɑ]	[ɑtɑ]	[ɝt]	[tɝ]	[ɝtɝ]

Diphthongs

| [aɪt] | [taɪ] | [aɪtaɪ] | [ɔɪt] | [tɔɪ] | [ɔɪtɔɪ] |
| [aʊt] | [taʊ] | [aʊtaʊ] | [jut] | [tju] | [jutju] |

Consonants

[pɑ]	[ɑp]	[ɑpɑ]	[ʃɑ]	[ɑʃ]	[ɑʃɑ]
[bɑ]	[ɑb]	[ɑbɑ]	[ʒɑ]	[ɑʒ]	[ɑʒɑ]
[tɑ]	[ɑt]	[ɑtɑ]	[hɑ]		[ɑhɑ]
[dɑ]	[ɑd]	[ɑdɑ]	[tʃɑ]	[ɑtʃ]	[ɑtʃɑ]
[kɑ]	[ɑk]	[ɑkɑ]	[dʒɑ]	[ɑdʒ]	[ɑdʒɑ]
[gɑ]	[ɑg]	[ɑgɑ]	[mɑ]	[ɑm]	[ɑmɑ]
[fɑ]	[ɑf]	[ɑfɑ]	[nɑ]	[ɑn]	[ɑnɑ]
[vɑ]	[ɑv]	[ɑvɑ]		[ɑŋ]	[ɑŋɑ]
[θɑ]	[ɑθ]	[ɑθɑ]	[lɑ]	[ɑl]	[ɑlɑ]
[ðɑ]	[ɑð]	[ɑðɑ]	[wɑ]		[ɑwɑ]
[sɑ]	[ɑs]	[ɑsɑ]	[hwɑ]		[ɑhwɑ]
[zɑ]	[ɑz]	[ɑzɑ]	[jɑ]		[ɑjɑ]
			[rɑ]	[ɑr]	[ɑrɑ]

in the work on isolated words and in sentence practice great care should be taken with problems of syllabification and stressing. If necessary, reread the earlier discussions of these points. Transcribe the sentences phonetically, of course, using the modifying marks for primary and secondary stress. In a liberal amount of this practice material, take the trouble to analyze specifically the syllabification, particularly if you suspect you may be guilty of syllable elision. The foreign speaker should place a great deal of emphasis on stressing and syllabification drill.

Finally, select longer speech samples and practice all the aspects and elements of speech form. There are really no new principles for this kind of drill, but all the suggestions given earlier should be applied. You may, if you wish, hunt for or invent "loaded" passages like those included in the exercises for each of the individual speech sounds. Even the "round the rugged rock" type of sentence may have some temporary usefulness. For the most part, however, the greatest reliance should be placed on sensible samples of communicative speech in the form of prose or poetry.

There is little to add by way of final advice that has not been said at least once before somewhere in these pages. Practice must continue until you have reached the goals of effective speech you have set for yourself. Barring some significant physical defect, there is no theoretical limit to your achievement. The rewards will be great and the task interesting. If you have mastered the theory and will follow the advice that has been given, you will have the requisites for truly effective use of speech form: sound phonetic information, valuable phonetic skills, and an understanding of how to bridge the gap between theory and its application.

REFERENCES

1. Aiken, J. R. *Why English Sounds Change*. New York: The Ronald Press Company, 1929.
2. Aiken, J. R. *English Present and Past*. New York: The Ronald Press Company, 1930.
3. Black, J. W. "Natural Frequency, Duration, and Intensity of Vowels in Reading." *Journal of Speech and Hearing Disorders*, 14:216–221, 1949.
4. Bloomfield, Leonard. *Language*. New York: Henry Holt and Company, Inc., 1933.
5. Brigance, W. N. "How Fast Do We Talk?" *Quarterly Journal of Speech*, 12:337–342, 1926.
6. Cotton, J. C. "Syllable Rate: A New Concept in the Study of Speech Rate Variation." *Speech Monographs*, 3:112–117, 1936.
7. Darley, F. L. "A Normative Study of Oral Reading Rate." Master's thesis, State University of Iowa, 1940.
8. Fairbanks, G., and L. W. Hoaglin. "An Experimental Study of the Durational Characteristics of the Voice during the Expression of Emotion." *Speech Monographs*, 8:85–90, 1941.
9. Fairbanks, G. *Voice and Articulation Drillbook*. New York: Harper & Brothers, 1940.
10. Gleason, H. G. *An Introduction to Descriptive Linguistics*. New York: Henry Holt and Company, Inc., 1955.
11. Heffner, R-M. S. *General Phonetics*. Madison, Wis.: University of Wisconsin Press, 1952.
12. Johnson, D. L. "Voice and Articulation Abilities of Students Registered in a Course in Speech." Master's thesis, State University of Iowa, 1938.
13. Jones, Daniel. *An Outline of English Phonetics*. New York: E. P. Dutton & Co., Inc., 1940.
14. Jones, Daniel. *An English Pronouncing Dictionary*. New York: E. P. Dutton & Co., Inc., 1956.
15. Kelley, J. C., and M. B. Steer. "Revised Concept of Rate." *Journal of Speech and Hearing Disorders*, 14:222–226, 1949.
16. Kenyon, John S. *American Pronunciation*, 9th ed. Ann Arbor, Mich.: George Wahr Publishing Co., 1946.
17. Kenyon, John S., and Thomas A. Knott. *A Pronouncing Dictionary of American English*. Springfield, Mass.: G. & C. Merriam Company, 1944.
18. Krapp, G. P. *Modern English, Its Growth and Present Use*. New York: Charles Scribner's Sons, 1909.

19. Kurath, Hans. *Handbook of the Linguistic Geography of New England*. Providence: Brown University, 1939.
20. Lewis, D., and J. Tiffin. "A Psychophysical Study of Individual Differences in Speaking Ability." *Archives of Speech*, 1:43–60, 1934.
21. Liberman, A. M., P. C. Delattre, L. J. Gerstman, and F. S. Cooper. "Tempo of Frequency Change as a Cue for Distinguishing Classes of Speech Sounds." *American Journal of Psychology*, 52:127–137, 1956.
22. Lynch, G. "A Phonophotographic Study of Trained and Untrained Voices Reading Factual and Dramatic Material." *Archives of Speech*, 1:9–25, 1934.
23. Moser, Henry, John Dreher, and Herbert Oyer. *One Syllable Words*. Technical Report no. 41, Contract no. AF 19(604)–1577. Columbus, Ohio: The Ohio State University Research Foundation, 1957.
24. Murray, E., and J. Tiffin. "An Analysis of Some Basic Aspects of Effective Speech." *Archives of Speech*, 1:61–83, 1934.
25. Parmenter, C. E., and W. N. Trevino. "The Length of the Sounds of a Middle Westerner." *American Speech*, 10:129–133, 1935.
26. Pike, Kenneth. *The Intonation of American English*. Ann Arbor, Mich.: University of Michigan Press, 1945.
27. Pronovost, W. L. "An Experimental Study of Methods for Determining Natural and Habitual Pitch." *Speech Monographs*, 9:111–123, 1942.
28. Snidecor, J. "The Pitch and Duration Characteristics of Superior Female Speakers during Oral Reading." *Journal of Speech and Hearing Disorders*, 16:44–52, 1951.
29. Stetson, R. H. *Motor Phonetics*, 2d ed. Oberlin, Ohio: Oberlin College, 1951.
30. Sweet, Henry. *A Primer of Phonetics*, 2d ed. Oxford: Clarendon Press, 1902.
31. Sweet, Henry. *A History of English Sounds*. Oxford: Clarendon Press, 1888.
32. Thomas, C. K. *The Phonetics of American English*, 2d ed. New York: The Ronald Press Company, 1958.
33. Thorndike, E. L., and Irving Lorge. *The Teacher's Wordbook of 30,000 Words*. New York: Bureau of Publications, Teachers College, Columbia University, 1944.
34. Tiffany, W. R. "Vowel Recognition as a Function of Duration, Frequency Modulation and Phonetic Context." *Journal of Speech and Hearing Disorders*, 18:289–301, 1953.
35. Tiffin, J., and M. D. Steer. "An Experimental Analysis of Emphasis." *Speech Monographs*, 4:69–74, 1937.
36. Trager, G. L., and H. L. Smith, Jr. *An Outline of English Structure*. Washington: American Council of Learned Societies, 1957.
37. Van Riper, Charles, and John Irwin. *Voice and Articulation*. Englewood Cliffs, N.J.: Prentice-Hall, Inc., 1958.
38. Voelker, C. H. "The One Thousand Most Frequently Spoken Words." *Quarterly Journal of Speech*, 28:189–197, 1942.
39. Wise, C. M. *Applied Phonetics*. Englewood Cliffs, N.J.: Prentice-Hall, Inc., 1957.
40. *The Principles of the International Phonetic Association*. London: Department of Phonetics, University College, 1949.

APPENDIX A

This section contains what may be called generalized phonetic transcriptions illustrating an acceptable pronunciation of the speech samples in a General American dialect. These transcriptions may serve several purposes. First of all, they can help the student become familiar with the pronunciation value of the IPA symbols. As his learning progresses, he may use them as a model for transcriptions of the sort which he himself should prepare as part of the technique for analyzing speech. Finally, the samples can serve as a basic set of transcriptions which can be used for articulation and pronunciation practice. The student will need to develop his own transcriptions for practice, of course, and should not be content with those provided by the authors.

A word should be added about the form of these generalized transcriptions. They are quite broad, and no special notations are used, except for the accent markings that seemed necessary. There are, of course, many other modifying marks that could have been inserted to bring out some of the finer features of speech. The student may wish to add some of these notations at various points, and certainly he must learn to use such marks when they are helpful in his own transcriptions. Again, the pronunciations are those that might be heard in General American speech of reasonably good quality. In view of all that has been said about speech standards in earlier parts of the book, the student surely will not get the mistaken notion that these are examples of "perfect" speech which everyone ought to imitate. The pronunciations indicated inevitably tend to be those of the author who prepared the transcriptions (or at least the pronunciations he believes he uses), and his speech is not necessarily free of individual peculiarities. The particular prose and poetry chosen for this purpose seemed to the authors to be suitable for reading aloud and to call for representative degrees of informality and formality in pronunciation.

[ɪn ə lɪst əv ðə most ɪmˈpɔrtənt θɪŋz hi lɜnd ɪn ˈkɑlɪdʒ, ðə lɛt rabɚt ˈbɛntʃlɪ ɪnˈkludəd ðə fækt ðət ɪf ju pʊt wʌn pepɚ bæg ɪnˈsaɪd ənʌðɚ, ju kən ˈkɛrɪ ə ˈmɪlkʃek, ən ðət əf ju tɜn ə sak ˈɪnsaɪd aʊt ðə hol əpɪrz ɪn ə dɪfrənt ples.

299

ðə 'bentʃlɪ lɪst kəd bi mætʃt baɪ 'mɛnɪ bɔɪz ən gɝlz ɪn 'kɑlɪdʒ təde. ðə madən studənt həz dɪ'skʌvəd ðət ɪf ju sɪt ɪn ə lɛktʃɚ rum wɪð ə θauzənd ʌðɚ studənts θri taɪmz ə wik fɚ ə 'kɑlɪdʒ jɪr, ju kən raɪt lɛtɚz hom, kætʃ əkeʒənəl snætʃəz əv tɔk frəm ðə prɔfesɚ ænd, ɪf jə sɪt lɔŋ ɪ'nʌf, ju kən 'grædʒu,wet.

nau kəlidʒət laɪf ɪn ðɪs 'kʌntrɪ həz 'ɔlwɪz hæd ə sɝtən dɪ'tætʃmənt frəm ðɪ 'ɪntə,lɛkt. ðə wɝd kəlidʒət ɪt'sɛlf 'kɛrɪz 'mɛmrɪz əv 'rækun kots, hɪp flæsks, ən 'præktɪkəl dʒoks. bət təde əmɛrəkə həz ritʃt ðə pɔɪnt ɪn wɝld 'hɪstrɪ hwən wi 'kænat əfɔrd tə bi əmjuzd baɪ aur ,junə'vɝsəti 'ɛdʒə'keʃən.

wi ɪg'zɪst ɪn ə wɝld ful əv tɛnʃənz, 'kanflɪkts, dendʒɚz ən 'ægənɪz. tu 'mɛnɪ əv aur juðz ar ,ʌn'ɛdʒəketəd; tu fju əv aur ədʌlts kən hɛlp ðəm. ɪt ɪz nau kruʃəl ðət wi tʃendʒ aur ,ɛdʒə'keʃən ænd, ɪn so 'duwɪŋ, tʃendʒ aur wɝld.]

From an article in Coronet Magazine
By Harold Taylor

Reprinted from Coronet, February, 1949.

[ðer ɪz ən ɪ'mɛns ən 'dʒʌstə,faɪd praɪd ɪn hwʌt aur 'kɑlɪdʒəz həv dʌn. æt ðə sem taɪm ðer ɪz ə 'growɪŋ ,ʌn'izɪnəs əbaut ðer 'pradʌkt. ðɪ jʌŋ men ən wɪmən hu 'kɛrɪ əwe aur dɪ'griz ar ə vɛrɪ ə'træktɪv lat—ɪn luks, ɪn 'badəlɪ fɪtnəs, ɪn 'kaɪndlɪnəs, 'ɛnɚdʒɪ, 'kʌrɪdʒ, ənd 'bujənsɪ. bət hwʌt əv ðer ,ɪntə'lɛktʃul ɪ'kwɪpmənt? ðæt tu ɪz ɪn sʌm wez 'ædmərəbəl; fər ɪn spaɪt əv 'prezədənt 'lowəlz rɪ'mark ðət ðə ,junə'vɝsəti ʃud bi ə rɪ'pazətərɪ əv gret 'lɝnɪŋ sɪnts freʃmən brɪŋ ə stak wɪð:əm ənd ðə sinjɚz tek lɪtḷ əwe, ðə fækt ɪz ðət aur 'grædʒəwəts hæv ɛvrɪ tʃænts tə bi wel ɪn'fɔrmd, ənd 'juʒuwəlɪ ar so. jet ðɪ ,ʌn'izɪnəs pərzɪsts. hwen ɪt bɪ'kʌmz ar'tɪkjələt, ɪt teks ðə fɔrm əv wɪʃəz ðət ðiz ə'træktɪv jʌŋ 'pradʌkts əv aurz hæd mər ,ɪntə'lɛktʃuwəl depθ ən fɔrs, mər ət-homnəs ɪn ðə wɝld əv aɪ'dɪəz, mər əv ðə fɝm, klɪr, kwaɪət θɔtfəlnəs ðət ɪz so nidəd ə gard əgenst bɪ'setɪŋ 'hʌm,bʌg ən kwækərɪ]

From an address by Brand Blanshard
Printed in the Swarthmore College Bulletin

Reprinted by permission of the author.

[maɪ haus stændz ɪn lo lænd, wɪð lɪmətəd 'autluk, ənd ɔn ðə skɝt əv ðə 'vɪlɪdʒ. bət aɪ go wɪð maɪ frend tə ðə ʃɔr əv aur lɪtḷ rɪvɚ, ənd wɪð wʌn strok əv ðə pædḷ aɪ liv ðə 'vɪlɪdʒ 'palətɪks ən pɝsən'ælətɪz, jes, ən ðə wɝld əv 'vɪlɪdʒəz ən pɝsən'ælətɪz, bɪ'haɪnd, ən pæs 'ɪntu ə deləkət relm əv 'sʌnset n̩ 'munlaɪt, tu braɪt əl'most fɚ spatəd mæn tu ɛntɚ wɪð'aut ,no'vɪʃɪet ən pro'beʃən. wi 'penətret 'badəlɪ ðɪs ɪn'kredəbəl 'bjutɪ; wi dıp aʊr hændz ın ðɪs pentəd ɛləmənt; aʊr aız ɑr beðd ın ðiz laıts ən fɔrmz . . . e rɔɪəl rɛvəl, ðə praʊdəst, most hɑrt-rɪ'dʒɔɪsɪŋ fɛstəvəl ðət vælɚ ən 'bjutɪ, paʊɚ ən test, ɛvɚ dɛkt ən ɛn'dʒɔɪd, ə'stæblɪʃəz ɪt'sɛlf ən ðɪ ɪnstənt. ðiz 'sʌnset klaʊdz, ðiz 'dɛləkətlɪ ɪ'mɝdʒɪŋ stɑrz, wɪð ðɛr praɪvət ən ɪn'ɛfəbəl glænsəz, 'sɪgnəfaɪ ət ən prɔfɚ ɪt. aɪ əm tɔt ðə pʊrnəs əv aʊr ɪn'vɛnʃən, ðɪ 'ʌglɪnəs əv taʊnz ən pæləsəz. ɑrt ən 'lʌkʃərɪ həv 'ɝlɪ lɝnd ðət ðe məst wɝk æz ɛn'hænsmənt ən sikwəl tu ðɪs o'rɪdʒənəl 'bjutɪ.]

From the essay "Nature"
By Ralph Waldo Emerson

[bivɚz kən bɪld dæmz: biz kən kənstrʌkt ɪ'frɪʃənt 'dwelɪŋz: ðə minəst bɝd hæz stɪl ə ʃʊrɚ 'mɛkən,ɪzəm fɚ 'flaɪɪŋ ənd 'lændɪŋ ðən mæn həz jet ətʃivd. bət no ʌðɚ kritʃɚ həz kʌm wɪ'ðɪn saɪt əv mæn ın ðɪ ɑrts əv ‚sɪm'bɑlɪk kə,mjunə'keʃən. 'menlɪ θru 'læŋgwɪdʒ mæn həz kri'etəd ə sɛkənd wɝld, mɔr dʊrəbəl ənd vaɪəbəl ðən ðɪ ɪ'midɪət flʌks əv ɪk'spɪrɪəns, mɔr rɪtʃ ın ‚pasə'bɪlətɪz ðən ðə pjʊrlɪ mə'tɪrɪəl 'hæbətæt əv ɛnɪ ʌðɚ kritʃɚ. baɪ ðə sem edʒənt, hi həz rɪ'dust ðə væstnəs ənd 'ovɚ,paʊrɪŋ ‚mʌltə'plɪsətɪ əv hɪz ən'vaɪrənmənt tu hjumən dɪ'mɛnʃənz: ‚æb'stræktɪŋ frəm ɪts ‚to'tælətɪ dʒʌst so mʌtʃ əz hi kən hændəl ən kəntrol.]

From *The Conduct of Life*
By Lewis Mumford

Reprinted by permission of Harcourt, Brace and Company, Inc.

[saɪəns ın ɪts bɪ'gɪnɪŋz wəz du tə mɛn hu wɚ ın lʌv wɪð:ə wɝld. ðe pɚsivd ðə 'bjutɪ əv ðə stɑrz ənd ðə si, əv ðə wɪndz ən ðə maʊntənz. bi'kɔz ðe lʌvd ðɛm ðɛr θɔts dwɛlt əpɔn ðəm, ənd ðe wɪʃt tə ‚ʌndɚ'stænd ðəm mɔr 'ɪntəmətlɪ ðən ə mɪr aʊtwɚd ‚kʌntəm'pleʃən med pasəbl̩. "ðə wɝld," sɛd ‚hɛrə'klaɪtəs, "ɪz ən 'ɛvɚ-'lɪvɪŋ faɪr, wɪθ mɛʒɚz 'kɪndlɪŋ ən mɛʒɚz 'goɪŋ aʊt." ‚hɛrə'klaɪtəs ənd ðɪ ‚aɪ'onɪən fələsəfɚz, frəm hum kem ðə fɝst 'ɪmpʌls tu 'saɪən‚tɪfɪk 'nɑlɪdʒ, fɛlt ðə strɛndʒ 'bjutɪ əv ðə wɝld 'ɔlmost laɪk ə mædnəs ın ðə blʌd. ðe wɚ mɛn əv ‚taɪ'tænɪk pæʃənət 'ɪntə‚lɛkt, ənd frəm ðɪ ‚ɪn'tɛnsətɪ əv ðɛr ‚ɪntə'lɛktʃuwəl pæʃən ðə hol muvmənt əv ðə madən wɝld həz sprʌŋ. bət stɛp baɪ stɛp, æz saɪəns həz dɪ'veləpt, ðɪ 'ɪmpʌls əv lʌv hwɪtʃ gev ət bɝθ həz bɪn ‚ɪn'krisɪŋlɪ θwɔrtəd, hwaɪl ðɪ 'ɪmpʌls əv paʊr, hwɪtʃ wəz ət fɝst ə mɪr kæmp 'fɑlowɚ, hæz 'grædʒuəlɪ ju'sɝpt kəmænd ın 'vɝtʃu əv ɪts 'ʌnfɔr‚sin səkses.]

From *Scientific Outlook*
By Bertrand Russell

Reprinted by permission of W. W. Norton & Company, Inc.

[wi 'sʌmtaɪmz dɪ'spjutəd, ən 'vɛrɪ fɑnd wi wɜ˞ əv 'ɑrgjumənt ən 'vɛrɪ
dɪ'zaɪrəs əv kən'fjutɪŋ wʌn ənʌðɚ; hwɪtʃ ˌdɪspju'teʃəs tɜ˞n, baɪ ðə we,
ɪz æpt tə bɪ'kʌm ə 'vɛrɪ bæd hæbət, 'mekɪŋ pipḷ ɔfən ɪk'strɪmlɪ ˌdɪsə'-
griəbəl ɪn 'kʌmpənɪ baɪ ðə kɑntrə'dɪkʃən ðət ɪz 'nɛsəserɪ tə brɪŋ ət ɪntə
præktəs; ænd ðɛnts, bɪ'saɪdz 'saurɪŋ ən 'spɔɪlɪŋ ðə ˌkɑnvɚ'seʃən, ɪt əz
prə'dʌktɪv əv dɪs'gʌsts, ən pɚhæps 'ɛnmə,tɪz, wɪð:oz hu me hæv əkeʒən
fɔr 'frɛndʃɪp. aɪ həd kɔt ðɪs baɪ 'rɪdɪŋ maɪ fɑðɚz buks əv dɪ'spjut ɔn
rɪ'lɪdʒən. pɜ˞sənz əv gud sɛnts, aɪ həv sɪnts əbzɜ˞vd, sɛldəm fɔl ɪntu ət,
ɛk'sɛpt lɔjɚz, ˌjunə'vɜ˞sətɪ mɛn, ən 'dʒɛnrəlɪ mɛn əv ɔl sɔrts hu həv bɪn
brɛd æt 'ɛdənbɜ˞g.]

From the Autobiography
By Benjamin Franklin

[ænd nau aɪ spik əv 'θæŋkɪŋ gɑd, aɪ dɪ'zaɪr wɪð əl ˌhju'mɪlətɪ tu æk'-
nɑlɪdʒ ðət aɪ ə'trɪbjut ðə mɛntʃənd 'hæpɪnəs əv maɪ pæst laɪf tu hɪz
dɪ'vaɪn pravədəns, hwɪtʃ lɛd mi tu ðə minz aɪ juzd ənd gev ðə səksɛs.
maɪ bɪ'lif əv ðɪs ɪn'dusəz mi tə hop, ðo aɪ məst nɑt prɪ'zum, ðət ðə sem
gudnəs wɪl stɪl bi 'ɛksəsaɪzd tərd mi ɪn kən'tɪnjuɪŋ ðæt 'hæpɪnəs ɔr ən'-
ɛblɪŋ mi tu ber ə fetḷ rɪ'vers, hwɪtʃ aɪ me ɪk'spɪrɪəns æz ʌðɚz həv dʌn;
ðə kəmplɛkʃən əv maɪ fjutʃɚ fɔrtʃən 'biŋ non tu hɪm 'onlɪ ɪn huz paur
ɪt ɪz tu blɛs ʌs, ivən ɪn aur əflɪkʃənz.]

From the Autobiography
By Benjamin Franklin

[so fɑr aɪ mʌst dɪ'fend 'pleto, æz tə plid ðət hɪz vju əv ˌɛdʒu'keʃən ən
'stʌdɪz ɪz ɪn ðə 'dʒɛnrəl, æz ɪt simz tə mi, saund ənʌf, ənd fɪtəd fɔr ɔl
sɔrts ən kən'dɪʃənz əv mɛn, hwʌt'ɛvɚ ðer pɚsuts me bi. "æn ɪn'tɛlədʒənt
mæn," sɛz 'pleto, "wɪl praɪz ðoz 'stʌdɪz hwɪtʃ rɪ'zʌlt ɪn hɪz sol 'getɪŋ
'sobɚnəs, 'raɪtʃəsnəs, ənd wɪzdəm, ənd wɪl lɛs 'vælju ðɪ ʌðɚz." aɪ 'kænɑt
kənsɪdɚ ðæt ə bæd dɪ'skrɪpʃən əv ðɪ em əv ɛdʒu'keʃən, ænd əv ðə 'motɪvz
hwɪtʃ gʌvən ʌs ɪn ðə tʃɔɪs əv 'stʌdɪz, hwɛðɚ wi ɚ prɪ'perɪŋ aur'sɛlvz fɔr
ə hə'rɛdət,ɛrɪ sit ɪn ðɪ 'ɪŋglɪʃ haus əv lɔrdz ɔr fɔr ðə pɔrk trɛd ɪn ʃə'kɑgo.]

From the essay "Literature and Science"
By Matthew Arnold

[. . . wʌn de aur bərd əv ˌɛdʒə'keʃən tuk ə de əf tə θɪŋk ðɪŋz ovɚ
'kwaɪətlɪ ənd æftɚ sevən aurz əv 'stɛdɪ 'θɪŋkɪŋ dɪ'saɪdəd tə put 'ɛvrɪ
'pʌblɪk skul pjupəl θru ə 'θɜ˞o 'fɪzɪkəl ɪg,zæmə'neʃən tə sɑlv, ɪf pɑsəbəl,
ðə 'mɪstrɪ əv hɛlθ ɪn ðə jʌŋ ɪn'hæbətənts əv ðə slʌmz.

ə'kɔrdɪŋ tə ˌdɑkjə'mɛntərɪ pruf, 'pʌblɪʃt ən 'tæbjələtəd, ɔl ðɪ ɪn'-
hæbətənts əv maɪ 'nebɚhud ʃud əv hæd 'bædlɪ ʃept hɛdz, sʌŋkən tʃɛsts,

'fɔltɪ bon strʌktʃɚ, 'halo vɔɪsəz, no 'ɛnɚdʒɪ, dɪs'tɛmpɚ, ən sɪks ɚ sɛvən ʌðɚ maɪnɚ ɔr'gænɪk dɪ'fɛkts.

ə'kɔrdɪŋ tə ðɪ ɛvədəns bɪ'fɔr itʃ 'pʌblɪk skul titʃɚ, 'hauɛvɚ, ðiz 'rʌfɪənz frəm ðə slʌmz hæd wɛl-ʃept hɛdz, saund tʃɛsts, hændsəm fɪgjɚz, laud vɔɪsəz, tu mʌtʃ 'ɛnɚdʒɪ, ənd ə kən'tɪnjuəs kəmpʌlʃən tə bɪ'hev 'mɪstʃəvəslɪ.

'sʌmθɪŋ wəz rɔŋ 'sʌmhwɛr.

aur bɔrd əv 'ɛdʒə'keʃən dɪ'saɪdəd tə faɪnd aut hwʌt.

ðe dɪd faɪnd aut.

ðe faund aut ðət ðə 'pʌblɪʃt ən 'tæbjəletəd ,dakjə'mɛntərɪ pruf wəz rɔŋ.

ɪt wəz ət ðɪs taɪm ðət aɪ fɝst lɝnd wɪð dʒɔɪ ən 'fjurɪ ðət aɪ wəz ə powət. aɪ rɪ'mɛmbɚ 'biɪŋ ɪn ðə 'sɪvɪk ,odə'tɔrɪəm əv maɪ hom taun ət haɪ nun wɪð sɪks hʌndrəd ʌðɚ fjutʃɚ stetsmən, ən aɪ rɪ'mɛmbɚ 'hɪrɪŋ maɪ nem sʌŋ aut baɪ old mɪs 'ogəlvɪ ɪn ə klɪr hɪs'tɛrəkəl sə'præno.

ðə taɪm həd əraɪvd fɚ mi tə klaɪm ðə 'sɛvəntin stɛps tə ðə stedʒ, wɔk tə ðə sɛntɚ əv ðə stedʒ, strɪp tə ðə west, 'ɪnhel, 'ɛkshel, ən bi mɛʒɚd ɔl ovɚ.

ðer wəz ə momənt əv kənfjuʒən ənd ,ɪndɪ'sɪʒən, 'falod 'kwɪklɪ baɪ ə supɚ'hjumən 'ɪmpʌls tə bɪ'hev wɪð staɪl, hwɪtʃ aɪ dɪd, tə ðə horɚ ən bɪ'wɪldəmənt əv ðə hol bɔrd əv ,ɛdʒə'keʃən, θri 'ɛldəlɪ daktɚz, ə 'hæf-dʌzən 'redʒəstəd nɝsəz, ən sɪks hʌndrəd fjutʃɚ kæptənz əv 'ɪndəstrɪ.

ɪn'sted əv 'klaɪmɪŋ ðə 'sɛvəntin stɛps tə ðə stedʒ, aɪ lɪpt.

aɪ rɪ'mɛmbɚ old mɪs 'ogəlvɪ 'tɝnɪŋ tə mɪstɚ 'rɪkənbækɚ, suprən'tɛndənt əv skulz, ən 'hwɪspərɪŋ 'fɪrfəlɪ: ðɪs ɪz ,garog'lenɪən—wʌn əv aur fjutʃɚ powəts, aɪ maɪt se.

mɪstɚ 'rɪkənbækɚ tuk wʌn kwɪk luk ət mi ən sed: o, aɪ si. huz i sɔr æt?

sə'saɪətɪ, old mɪs 'ogəlvɪ sed.

o, aɪ si, mɪstɚ 'rɪkenbækɚ sed. so əm aɪ, bət aɪl bi dæmd əf aɪ kən dʒʌmp laɪk ðæt. lɛts se no mɔr əbaut ət.

aɪ flʌŋ əf maɪ ʃɝt ən stud strɪpt tə ðə west, ə gud:il əv hɛr 'brɪslɪŋ ən maɪ tʃɛst.

ju si? mɪs 'ogəlvɪ sed. ə raɪtɚ.]

From "One Of Our Future Poets"
By William Saroyan

[ənʌðɚ klæs ðət aɪ dɪdn̩t laɪk, bət 'sʌmhau 'mænɪdʒd tə pæs wəz ,ikə'namɪks. aɪ wɛnt tə ðæt klæs stret frəm ðə 'batənɪ klæs, hwɪtʃ dɪdn̩t help mɪ ɛnɪ ɪn ,ʌndɚ'stændɪŋ iðɚ klæs. aɪ just tə gɛt ðəm mɪkst ʌp. bət nat əz mɪkst ʌp əz ənʌðɚ studənt ɪn maɪ ,ikə'namɪks klæs. . . . hi wəz ə tækəl ɔn ðə 'futbɔl tim, nemd ˌbo'lɛŋkəwɪts. . . . ɪn ɔrdɚ tə bi 'ɛləd-ʒəbəl tə ple ɪt wəz 'nesəseri fɚ ɪm tə kip ʌp ɪn ɪz 'stʌdiz, ə 'veri dɪfəkəlt mætɚ, fɚ hwaɪl i wəz nɑt dʌmɚ ðən ən ɑks hi wəz nɑt ɛni smɑrtɚ. most əv ɪz prəfesɚz wɚ 'liniənt n̩ hɛlpt ɪm ələŋ. nʌn gev ɪm mɔr hɪnts, ɪn 'æskɪŋ kwestʃənz, ɚ æskt ɪm sɪmplɚ wʌnz ðən ði ˌikə'nɑmɪks prəfesɚ, ə θɪn, tɪməd mæn nemd bæsəm. wʌn de hwən wi wɚ ɔn ðə 'sʌbdʒɪkt əv ˌtrænspɚ'teʃən, ɪt kem bə'lɛŋkəwɪts tɝn tə ænsɚ ə kwestʃən. "nem wʌn minz əv ˌtrænspɚ'teʃən," ðə prəfesɚ sed tu ɪm. no laɪt kem ɪntə ðə bɪg tækl̩z aɪz. "dʒʌst ɛni minz əv ˌtrænspɚ'teʃən," sed ðə prəfesɚ. bə'lɛŋkə- wɪts sæt 'stɛrɪŋ æt ɪm. "ðæt ɪz," pɚsud ðə prəfesɚ, "ɛni 'midiəm, 'edʒənsi ɔr meθəd əv 'goɪŋ frəm wʌn ples tu ənʌðɚ." bə'lɛŋkəwɪts hæd ðə luk əv ə mæn hu əz 'biːŋ lɛd 'ɪntu ə træp. "ju me tʃuz əmʌŋ stim, 'hɔrs-ˌdrɔn, ɚ ə'lektrɪkli prəpɛld 'vihɪklz," sed ði ɪn'strʌktɚ. "aɪ maɪt səgdʒest ðə wʌn wi tek ɪn 'mekɪŋ lɔŋ 'dʒɝnɪz əkrɔs lænd." ðer wəz ə prəfaund saɪləns ɪn hwɪtʃ ɛvriwən stɝd ˌʌn'izəli, ˌɪn'kludɪŋ bə'lɛŋkəwɪts ən mɪstɚ bæsəm. mɪstɚ bæsəm ə'brʌptli brok ɪz saɪləns ɪn ən ə'mezɪŋ mænɚ. "tʃu-tʃu-tʃu," hi sed ɪn ə lo vɔɪs, ənd 'ɪnstəntli tɝnd skɑrlət. hi glænst ə'pilɪŋli əraund ðə rum. ɔl əv əs, əv kɔrs, ʃerd mɪstɚ bæsəmz dɪ'zaɪr ðət bə'lɛŋkəwɪts ʃəd ste əbrest əv ðə klæs ɪn ˌikə'nɑmɪks, fɚ ðə ɪlə'nɔɪ gem, wʌn əv ðə hɑrdəst n̩ most ɪm'pɔrtənt əv ðə sizən, wəz 'onli ə wik ɔf. "tut, tut, tu-tuːt!" sʌm studənt wɪð ə dip vɔɪs mɔnd, ənd wi ɔl lukt ən'kɝɪdʒɪŋli ət bə'lɛŋkəwɪts. sʌmwən ɛls gev ə faɪn ɪmə'teʃən əv ə ˌlokə'- motɪv 'letɪŋ ɔf stim. mɪstɚ bæsəm ɪm'sɛlf raundəd ɔf ðə lɪtl̩ ʃo. "dɪŋ, dɔŋ, dɪŋ, dɔŋ," hi sed 'hopfəli. bə'lɛŋkəwɪts wəz 'stɛrɪŋ ət ðə flɔr nau, 'traɪɪŋ tə θɪŋk, hɪz gret brau 'fɝod, hɪz hjudʒ hændz 'rʌbɪŋ təgeðɚ, hɪz fes red.

"hau dədʒu kʌm tə 'kɑlɪdʒ ðɪs jɪr, mɪstɚ bəlɛŋkəwɪts," æskt ðə prəfesɚ. "tʃʌfə, tʃʌfə, tʃʌfə, tʃʌfə."

"mə faðɚ sent mɪ," sed ðə 'futbɔl pleɚ.

"hwʌt ɔn," æskt bæsəm.

"aɪ gɪt n̩ əlauwəns," sed ðə tækl̩ ɪn ə lo 'hʌski vɔɪs, 'ɑbviəsli ɪm'berəst.

"no, no," sed bæsəm. "nem ə minz əv ˌtrænspɚ'teʃən. hwʌt dədʒu raɪd hɪr ɔn?"

"tren," sed bə'lɛŋkəwɪts.

"kwaɪt raɪt," sed ðə prəfesɚ. "nau, mɪstɚ nudʒənt, wɪl ju tɛl əs. . . . "]

From *My Life and Hard Times*
By James Thurber

Reprinted by permission of the author.

[jə si, fɚ ə hwaɪl hi wəz ðə bɪgəst mæn ɪn ðə 'kʌntri. hi nevɚ gɑt tə bi prezədənt, bət hi wəz ðə bɪgəst mæn. ðer wɚ θauzəndz ðət trʌstəd

ɪn ɪm raɪt nɛkst tə gɑd ɔlˈmaɪtɪ, ənd ðe told ˈstɔrɪz əbaut ɪm ðət wɚ laɪk
ðə ˈstɔrɪz əv ˈpɛtrɪɑrks ṇ sʌtʃ. ðe sɛd, hwən i stʊd ʌp tə tɔk, stɑrz ən
straɪps kem raɪt aut ṇ ðə skaɪ, ən wʌns i spok əgɛnst ə rɪvɚ ən med ət
sɪŋk raɪt ɪntə ðə graund. ðe sɛd, hwən i wɔkt ɪn ðə wʊdz wɪð ɪz ˈfɪʃɪŋ rɑd,
ˈkɪl͵ɔl, ðə traut wəd dʒʌmp aut əv ðə strimz raɪt ɪntʊ ɪz pɑkəts, fɚ ðe
nu ət wəz no jus ˈpʊtɪŋ ʌp ə faɪt əgɛnst ɪm; ænd, hwɛn i ˈɑrgjud ə kes,
hi kəd tɚn ɔn ðə hɑrps əv ðə blɛsəd ənd ðə ˈʃɛkɪŋ əv ðə ɚ͵θ ͵ʌndɚˈgraund.
ðæt wəz ðə kaɪnd əv mæn hi wʌz, ənd ɪz bɪg fɑrm ʌp ət ˈmɑrʃfild wəz
sutəbḷ tu ɪm. ðə tʃɪkənz hi rezd wɚ ɔl hwaɪt mɪt daun θru ðə ˈdrʌmstɪks,
ðə kauz wɚ tɛndəd laɪk tʃɪldrən, ənd ðə bɪg ræm hi kɔld gəlaɪəθ hæd
hɔrnz wɪð ə kɚl laɪk ə ˈmɔrnɪŋ-ˈglɔrɪ vaɪn ən kəd bʌt θru ən aɪrn dɔr.
bət dænəl wʌzṇt wʌn əv jɚ ˈdʒɛntḷmən fɑrmɚz; hi nu ɔl ðə wez əv ðə
lænd, ənd hid bi ʌp baɪ ˈkændḷaɪt tə si ðət ðə tʃɔrz gɑt dʌn. ə mæn wɪð ə
mauθ laɪk ə mæstəf, ə brau laɪk ə mauntṇ ənd aɪz laɪk ˈbɚnɪŋ ˈænθrə͵-
saɪt—ðæt wəz dænəl wɛbstɚ ɪn ɪz praɪm.]

From The Devil and Daniel Webster
By Stephen Vincent Benét

[maɪ brʌðɚ ˈtʃɑrlɪ ənd aɪ, ɪn ðə dez əv aʊr ˈnɑnɪdʒ, wɚ əlaud əˈfɪʃəlɪ tə
it ɔl ðət wi kəd hold bət twaɪs ə jɪr. ðə fɚst əv aʊr tu dɪˈbɔtʃəz kem ən
ðɪ ɚlɪ sprɪŋ, ðɪ əkeʒən ˈbiɪŋ ðɪ ˈænjuəl ˈpɪknɪk əv ɛf næps ˈɪnstə͵tut . . . ;
ðə sɛkənd wəz ət krɪsməs, bɪˈgɪnɪŋ fɚ ðə sem ən ðə ˈmɔrnɪŋ əv ðə gret de
ɪtˈsɛlf ən kənˈtɪnjuɪŋ ˈdɔgədlɪ əntɪl aʊr gɪzɚdz gev aut ət læst, ən dɑktɚ
zi ke ˈwaɪlɪ, ðə ˈfæməlɪ dɑktɚ, əraɪvd tə lʊk ət aʊr tʌŋz ən plaɪ əs wɪð
olɪəm riˈsini.

aʊr ˈrʌnɪŋ taɪm, ɪn ðɪ ˈævrɪdʒ jɪr, wəz əbaut ˈθɚtɪ-sɪks aʊrz, wɪð ɛt
aʊrz aut fɚ ʌnˈizɪ slip, ˈmekɪŋ ə nɛt əv ˈtwɛnti-et. hwən wi kem ˈlɪpɪŋ
͵daunˈstɛrz ɪn aʊr flænəl ˈnaɪt-͵drɔrz ɔn krɪsməs ˈmɔrnɪŋ ðer wəz nɑt
ˈonlɪ ə ˈblezɪŋ tri tə dæzḷ əs, ənd ə paɪl əv gɪfts tə səpraɪz əs (əv kɔrs
ˈonlɪ ɪn ˈθiərɪ, fɚ wi nu ðə kʌbɚd hwer sʌtʃ θɪŋz wɚ kept, ənd ɔlwɪz ɪnˈ-
vɛstəgetəd ət ɪn ədvæns ənd ət gret lɛŋθ), bət ɔlso ə tebḷ lodəd wɪð
ˈkændɪz, keks, rezənz, sɪtrənz ənd ʌðɚ rɪˈfrɛʃmənts əv ðə sizən, ɔn ɔl
əv hwɪtʃ, ənd tu ɛnɪ əmaunt wi kəd əndur, wi wɚ fri tə wɚk aʊr wɪkəd
wɪl.

æt ʌðɚ taɪmz θɪŋz əv ðæt sɔrt wɚ dold aut tu əs ɪn ə ˈvɛrɪ kɔʃəs ən
ˈɔlmost ˈnɪgɚdlɪ we, fɚ ðə ˈmɛdɪkəl saɪəns əv ðɪ ɪrə tɔt ðət ən ˈɛksɛs əv
swɪts wəd ruən ðə tiθ. bət ət krɪsməs, ʌndɚ ðɪ prɪˈvelɪŋ ˈbuzɪnəs ənd
ˈgʊd͵wɪl tə men, ðɪs dendʒɚ wəz ɪgˈnɔrd, ənd wi wɚ pəmɪtəd tə proˈsid
ædˈlɪbɪtəm, nɑt ˈonlɪ ət hom, bət ɔlso ɔn aʊr ˈmɔrnɪŋ vɪzət tə ˈgrænfɑðɚ
ˈmɛŋkənz haʊs ɪn feˈjɛt strit. ðʌs wi wɚkt əwe ɔl əv krɪsməs de, ˈkipɪŋ

aʊr pakəts fʊl ən 'græbɪŋ ənʌðɚ lod 'ɛvrɪ taɪm wi kem wɪ'ðɪn ɑrmz-ritʃ
əv ðɪ rɪ'zɝvz. hwən wi wɚ ɔrdəd tə bed ət læst, fɚ ə naɪt əv ˌpæθə'lɑdʒɪkəl
drimz, wi went 'onlɪ rɪ'lʌktəntlɪ, ənd ə'mɪdɪətlɪ æftɚ brɛkfəst ɔn krɪsməs
'mʌndɪ wi rɪ'zumd ˌapə'reʃənz. ɪt wəz ɪn ðɪ ɝ˞lɪ 'ivnɪŋ əv ðæt de ðət daktɚ
'waɪlɪ drov ʌp ɪn ɪz 'bʌgɪ, hɪtʃt ɪz hɔrs tə ðə rɪŋ ən ðə mɑrbəl hɔrs-blɑk
aʊt frʌnt, ən kem ɪn tə du ɪz 'dutɪ.

. . . ðə daktɚ wəz ə hju'men ənd 'ʌndɚˌstændɪŋ mæn, ən so i nevɚ
ɪntrə'dust ðə 'sʌbdʒɪkt əv 'sʌkərɪŋ maɪ brʌðɚ ən mi əntɪl wi hæd ə dʌzən
ɚ mɔr læst hwæks ət ðə stʌf ɔn ðə tebl̩. ðen i wəd 'sʌdənlɪ fɪks əs wɪð ɪz
kold gre aɪ, kɔl fɚ ə 'tebl̩spun, ən prəsid tə vju aʊr tʌŋz. hɪz 'vɝ˞dɪkt,
əv kɔrs, wəz 'ɔlwɪz ðə sem. ɪn'did, maɪ mʌðɚ ˌɪn'vɛrɪəblɪ ˌæn'tɪsəpetəd ɪt
baɪ 'fetʃɪŋ ðə ˌkæstɚ-'ɔɪl batl̩ hwaɪl i pandəd ət. tu hɔrəbəl dosəz frəm
ðə sem spun, ənd wi wɚ pækt əf tə bed. krɪsməs wəz ovɚ, ðo ðə tri stɪl
stʊd, ənd sʌm əv ðə tɔɪz wɚ stɪl ˌʌn'brokən. wi nevɚ hæd mʌtʃ 'æpəˌtaɪt
ðə de 'fɑlowɪŋ.]

From *Happy Days*
By H. L. Mencken

Reprinted by permission of Alfred A. Knopf, Inc.

[ənʌðɚ 'fɔrtest əv 'sʌndɪ kem, ɪn aʊr lɑrdʒ 'fæmlɪ, ə'mɪdɪətlɪ æftɚ
dɪnɚ wəz klɪrd əwe. baɪ tu əklɑk ðə 'wiklɪ 'beðɪŋ bɪ'gæn. bɪ'fɔr ðə tɝn əv
ðə 'sentʃərɪ no haʊs ɪn blu hɪl pəzɛst ə 'bæθrum. . . .

ðə 'wiklɪ bæθ, 'ðɛrfɔr, wəz frət wəθ ɪnkən'vinjəns ən 'dɪfəkʌltɪ; 'nevɚðəˌ-
les, ɪn ɔl wel-'regjəletəd 'fæmlɪz, ðɪ əmɪʃən əv ət wəz 'ɪnkənˌsivəbl̩. ɔlðo
ɪn ðə wɔrməst weðɚ ðə si pruvd hɛlpfəl, ə sɔlt watɚ bæθ baɪ tæsət kənsent
əv ɔl ðə best pipl̩ wəz lʊkt əpɔn wɪð səspɪʃən əz nat ˌfʊl'fɪlɪŋ ðə rɪ'kwaɪr-
mənts ɪðɚ əv 'klɛnlɪnəs ɚ əv mɔrəl ən rɪ'lɪdʒəs 'dutɪ. kʌstəm ən taɪm
ə'laɪk həd prəskraɪbd ə 'wɔʃtʌb baɪ ðə kɪtʃən stov; ən taɪm ən kʌstəm
ɪn ðə 'naɪntɪz wɚ nat 'laɪtlɪ set əsaɪd.

wʌn baɪ wʌn wi skrʌbd aʊr'sɛlvz ənd wɚ skrʌbd, ðɪ odɚ əv ðə wɔrm
'sop-sʌdz 'mɪŋglɪŋ wɪðː ə smel əv ðə binz ɪn ðɪ ʌvən. wʌn baɪ wʌn wi
əred aʊr'sɛlvz ɔr wɚ əred ɪn klin 'ʌndɚwer ən freʃ, wel-mendəd 'stakɪŋz.
ɪf wi 'fɪnɪʃt ɝ˞lɪ, wi wɚ ənkʌrɪdʒd tə ple ət tɛmpərət gemz, tə spend ən
aʊr ət ə nebɚz haʊs, ɔr tə rid 'kwaɪətlɪ ɪn ðə kɔrnɚz əv ðə 'laɪbrɛrɪ.
raɪətəsnəs ɔn let 'sætɚdɪ æftɚ'nun wəz fraʊnd əpɔn; ɪt wəz tu mʌtʃ laɪk
ˌdʒakjə'lɛrətɪ æftɚ ðə pɚforməns əv ə sekrəd raɪt. ɔn sætɚdɪ 'ivnɪŋz ɪt
wəz wɪθ ə sents əv kɔrpərət 'dɪsənsɪ ðət wi gæðɚd əraʊnd ðə sʌpɚ tebl̩—ə
sents hwɪtʃ madɚn 'plʌmɪŋ wɪð ɔl ɪts kʌmfɚts kənat prədus.]

From *A Goodly Heritage*
By Mary Ellen Chase

Reprinted by permission of Henry Holt and Company, Inc.

[læftɚ ɪz 'prɪtɪ old stʌf. . . . stivən 'likɑk, ɪn ɪz 'ɛse ɔn ðə 'sʌbdʒɪkt, sɛz ðə lowɚ rendʒ əv ðə skel əv hjumɚ ɪz 'ɪləstretəd bɛst baɪ ðə pʌn. ðə besəs əv ðə pʌn "ɪz ðə ˌdɪs'kʌmfətʃɚ əv 'læŋgwɪdʒ ɪt'sɛlf, ə sɔrt əv ˌɛgzəl'- teʃən ovɚ ðə 'daʊnfəl əv ðə prɪ'tɛntʃəs sə'lemnətɪ əv wɝˑdz." æz ən ɛg'- zæmpəl hi rɪ'kɔlz ðə 'dʒɪŋglɪŋ raɪmz əv tɔm hʊd ('etɪn ˌθɝˑtɪ-'faɪv tu 'etɪn ˌsɛvəntɪ-'fɔr), ðə most femɚs pʌnstɚ əv ðə edʒəz. (hi lɪvd ə ʃɔrt laɪf tu əv bɪ'kʌm so femɚs.) hi rot:

ben bætl̩ wʌz ə soldʒɚ bold
ən just tə wɔrz əlɑrmz.
ə kænən bɔl tʊk ɔf ɪz legz
so hi led daʊn ɪz ɑrmz.

'likɑk sez ðɪs ɪz ə ple ɔn wɝˑdz ən 'nʌθɪŋ ɛls. "bət ə pʌn kəntenz ə haɪɚ 'ɛləmənt əv hjumɚ hwɛn ðə ˌkɑntrə'dɪkʃən ɪn vɝˑbəl fɔrmz 'kɛrɪz wɪð ɪt ɔlso ə ˌkɑntrə'dɪkʃən ɪn ðə sɛnts," æz, fɚ ɪg'zæmpəl:

ə drʌŋkən mæn ɪn ə 'bɑrːum pɪkt ʌp ə 'sændwɪtʃ ən θru ət əgenst ə mɪrɚd wɔl. "ðerz fʊd fɚ rɪ'flekʃən," sed ə 'baɪstændɚ.]

From "Trade Winds" in
The Saturday Review of Literature

Reprinted by permission.

[ðə taʊrz əv zinəθ əspaɪrd əbʌv ðə 'mɔrnɪŋ mɪst; 'ɔstɪr taʊrz əv stil ən səmənt ən 'laɪmston, 'stɝˑdɪ əz klɪfs ən dəlɛkət əz sɪlvɚ rɑdz. ðe wɚ nɪðɚ 'sɪtəˌdelz nɔr tʃɝˑtʃəz bət 'fræŋklɪ ən 'bjutəflɪ ɔfəs 'bɪldɪŋz.

ðə mɪst tʊk 'pɪtɪ ɔn ðə fretəd strʌktʃɚz əv ɝˑlɪɚ ˌdʒenə'reʃənz: ðə post ɔfəs wɪð ɪts sɪŋgl̩ tɔrtʃɚd mænsɚd, ðə red brɪk ˌmɪnə'rets əv 'hʌlkɪŋ old haʊzəz, 'fæktrɪz wɪð 'stɪndʒɪ ən sutəd 'wɪndoz, wʊdn̩ tenəmənts kʌlɚd laɪk mʌd. ðə 'sɪtɪ wəz fʊl əv sʌtʃ ˌgro'teskərɪz, bət ðə klin taʊrz wɚ 'θrʌstɪŋ ðem frəm ðə bɪznəs sentɚ, ənd ɔn ðə farðɚ hɪlz wɚ 'ʃaɪnɪŋ nu haʊzəz, homz—ðe simd—fɚ læftɚ ən ˌtræn'kwɪlətɪ.

ovɚ ə 'kɑnkrit brɪdʒ fled ə 'lɪməˌzin əv lɔŋ slik hʊd ən nɔɪzləs endʒən. ðiz pipl̩ ɪn 'ivnɪŋ kloz wɚ rɪ'tɝˑnɪŋ frəm ən ɔl-naɪt rɪ'hɝˑsəl əv ə lɪtl̩ θiətɚ ple, ən ar'tɪstɪk ədventʃɚ kən'sɪdərəblɪ ə'lumənetəd baɪ ʃæm'pen. bɪ'lo ðə brɪdʒ kɝˑvd ə 'relrod, ə mez əv grin ən krɪmzən laɪts. ðə nu jɔrk flaɪɚ bumd pæst, ən 'twentɪ laɪnz əv 'palɪʃt stil lipt ɪntə ðə gler.

ɪn wʌn əv ðə 'skaɪˌskrepɚz ðə waɪrz əv ði ə'soʃɪˌetəd pres wɚ 'klozɪŋ daʊn. ðə 'teləˌgræf 'apəretɚz 'wɪrəlɪ rezd ðer 'seljeˌlɔɪd aɪ-ʃedz æftɚ ə naɪt əv 'tokɪŋ wɪθ perəs ən 'pikɪŋ. θru ðə 'bɪldɪŋ krɑld ðə skrʌb-wɪmən, 'jɑnɪŋ, ðer old ʃuz 'slæpɪŋ. ðə dɔn mɪst spʌn əwe. kjuz əv men wɪð lʌntʃ- baksəz klʌmpt tɔrd ði ə'mensəti əv nu 'fæktərɪz, ʃits əv glæs ən 'halo taɪl, 'glɪtərɪŋ ʃaps hwer faɪv θaʊzənd men wɝˑkt bɪ'niθ wʌn ruf, 'pɔrɪŋ aʊt anəst werz ðət wəd bi sold ʌp ði ˌju'fretɪz ənd əkrɔs ðə velt. ðə hwɪslz̩

rold aʊt ɪn ˈgritɪŋ, ə kɔrəs tʃɪrfəl əz eprəl dɔn; ðə sɔŋ əv lebɚ ɪn ə sɪti
bɪlt—ɪt simd—fɔr dʒaɪənts.]

From *Babbitt*
By Sinclair Lewis

Reprinted by permission of Harcourt, Brace and Company, Inc.

(Manson has just been asked, "Now! Tell me about your church."
He replies:)

[aɪ əm əfred ju me nɑt kənsɪdɚ ɪt ən ɔltəˈgeðɚ ˈgroɪŋ kənsɚn. ɪt hæs
tə bi sin ɪn ə sɚtn̩ we, ʌndɚ sɚtn̩ kəndɪʃənz. sʌm pipḷ nɛvɚ si ɪt ətɔl. ju
məst ʌndɚˈstænd, ðɪs ɪz no paɪl əv dɛd stonz ən ˈʌnˌminɪŋ tɪmbɚ. ɪt ɪz ə
ˈlɪvɪŋ θɪŋ. hwɛn ju ɛntɚ ɪt ju hɪr ə saʊnd æz əv sʌm ˈmaɪti poəm tʃæntəd.
lɪsən lɔŋ ənʌf ənd ju wɪl lɚn ðət ɪt ɪz med ʌp əv ðə ˈbɪtɪŋ əv hjumən
hɑrts, əv ðə nemləs ˈmjuzɪk əv mɛnz solz—ðæt ɪz, ɪf ju hæv ɪrz. ɪf ju
hæv aɪz, ju wɪl ˈprɛzəntlɪ si ðə tʃɚtʃ ɪtˈsɛlf—ə ˈlumɪŋ ˈmɪstəri əv mɛni
ʃeps ən ˈʃædoz, ˈlipɪŋ ʃɪr frəm flɔr tə dom. ðə wɚk əv no ˈɔrdənˌɛri bɪldɚ.

ðə pɪlɚz ʌv ɪt go ʌp laɪk ðə ˈbrɔni trʌŋks əv ˈhiroz: ðə swit hjumən
fleʃ əv mɛn ən wɪmən ɪz moldəd əbaʊt ɪts ˈbʌlwɚks, strɔŋ, ˌɪmˈprɛgnəbḷ:
ðə fesəz əv lɪtḷ tʃɪldrən læf aʊt frəm ˈɛvəri kɔrnɚ ston: ðə tɛrəbəl spænz
ən artʃəz əv ɪt ɑr ðə dʒɔɪnd hændz əv kamrədz; ənd ʌp ɪn ðə haɪts ən
spesəz ðɛr ɑr ɪnˈskraɪbd ðə nʌmbɚləs ˈmjuzɪŋz əv ɔl ðə drimɚz əv ðə
wɚld. ɪt ɪz jet ˈbɪldɪŋ—ˈbɪldɪŋ ən bɪlt əpɔn. ˈsʌmˌtaɪmz ðə wɚk goz
fɔrwɚd ɪn dip dɑrknəs: ˈsʌmˌtaɪmz ɪn ˈblaɪndɪŋ laɪt: naʊ bɪˈniθ ðə bɚdn̩
əv ˌʌnˈʌtərəbḷ ˈæŋgwɪʃ: naʊ tə ðə tun əv gret læftɚ ənd hɪˈroɪk ˈʃaʊtɪŋz
laɪk ðə kraɪ əv θʌndɚ.

ˈsʌmˌtaɪmz, ɪn ðə saɪləns əv ðə ˈnaɪtːaɪm, wʌn me hɪr ðə ˈtaɪni ˈhæmər-
ɪŋz əv ðə ˈkamˌrædz ət wɚk ʌp ən ðə dom—ðə ˈkamˌrædz hu həv klaɪmd
əhɛd.]

From *The Servant in the House*
By Charles Rann Kennedy

[wʌn naɪt hwaɪl wi wɚ ɪn ðiz ˈtrɑpɪks aɪ wɛnt aʊt tə ðɪ ɛnd əv ðə ˈflaɪɪŋ
dʒɪb-bum, əpɔn sʌm dutɪ, ænd, ˈhævɪŋ ˈfɪnɪʃt ət, tɚnd əraʊnd, ənd le
ovɚ ðə bum fɚ ə lɔŋ taɪm, ədˈmaɪrɪŋ ðə ˈbjutɪ əv ðə saɪt bɪˈfɔr mi. ˈbiɪŋ
so fɑr aʊt frəm ðə dɛk, aɪ kəd luk ət ðə ʃɪp, æz ət ə sepərət vɛsəl;—ən
ðɛr roz ʌp frəm ðə wɑtɚ, səpɔrtəd ˈonlɪ baɪ ðə smɔl hʌl, ə ˈpɪrəmɪd əv
kænvəs, ˈsprɛdɪŋ aʊt fɑr bɪˈjand ðə hʌl, ən ˈtaʊrɪŋ ʌp ɔlmost, æz ət simd
ɪn ðɪ ˈɪndɪˌstɪŋkt naɪt ɛr, tə ðə klaʊdz. ðə si wəz əz stɪl əz ən ɪnlənd lek;
ðə laɪt tred wɪnd wəz stʌdəd wɪðːə ˈtrɑpɪkəl stɑrz; ðɛr wəz no saʊnd bət

ðə 'rɪplɪŋ əv ðə watə ʌndə ðə stɜ·n: ənd ðə selz wə spred aut, waɪd ən
haɪ. . . . so kwaɪət, tu, wəz ðə si, ən so stɛdɪ ðə briz, ðət əf ðoz selz həd
bɪn skʌlptʃəd marbəl, ðe kəd nat əv bɪn mɔr moʃənləs.]

From *Two Years Before The Mast*
By Richard Henry Dana, Jr.

[maɪ frɛndz: no wʌn, nat ɪn maɪ ˌsɪtʃu'eʃən, kæn ə'priʃɪˌet maɪ 'filɪŋ
əv sædnəs ət ðɪs 'partɪŋ. tu ðɪs ples, ən tu ðiz pipḷ, aɪ o 'ɛvrɪθɪŋ. hɪr aɪ
həv lɪvd ə kwɔrtə əv ə 'sɛntʃərɪ, ənd həv pæst frʌm ə jʌŋ mæn tu ən old
mæn. hɪr maɪ tʃɪldrən həv bɪn bɔrn, ənd wʌn laɪz 'bɛrɪd. aɪ nau liv, nat
'noɪŋ hwɛn ɔr ɛvə aɪ me rɪ'tɜ·n, wɪð ə tæsk bɪ'fɔr mi gretə ðən ðæt hwɪtʃ
rɛstəd ɑn 'wɔʃɪŋtən. wɪ'ðaut ðɪ əsɪstəns əv ðæt dɪ'vaɪn 'biɪŋ hu ɛvə
ətɛndəd hɪm, aɪ 'kænɑt səksid. wɪð:æt əsɪstəns, aɪ 'kænɑt fel. 'trʌstɪŋ
ɪn hɪm hu kən go wɪð mi, ənd rɪ'men wɪð ju, ənd bi 'ɛvrɪˌhwer fɔr gud,
let əs 'kʌnfədəntlɪ hop ðət ɔl wɪl jet bi wel. tu hɪz kɛr kə'mɛndɪŋ ju, æz
aɪ hop ɪn jɔr prɛrz ju wɪl kəmɛnd mi, aɪ bɪd ju æn əfɛkʃənət 'fɛr'wɛl.]

Abraham Lincoln's Farewell Address
to the People of Springfield, Illinois, February 11, 1861

[wi mit tʊ 'sɛləbret flæg de bɪ'kɔz ðɪs flæg hwɪtʃ wi anə ənd ʌndə hwɪtʃ
wi sɜ·v ɪz ðɪ ɛmbləm əv aur 'junətɪ, aur paur, aur θɑt ənd pɜ·pəs æz ə
neʃən. ɪt hæz no ʌðə 'kɛrɪktə ðən ðæt hwɪtʃ wi gɪv ɪt frəm ˌdʒɛnə'reʃən
tu ˌdʒɛnə'reʃən. ðə tʃɔɪsəz ar aurz. ɪt flots ɪn mə'dʒɛstɪk saɪləns əbʌv ðə
hosts ðət 'ɛksəˌkjut ðoz tʃɔɪsəz, hwɛðə ɪn pis ɔr ɪn wɔr. ənd jet, ðo saɪlənt,
ɪt spiks tu əs,—spiks əv ðə pæst, əv ðə mɛn ənd wɪmən hu wɛnt bɪ'fɔr
ʌs ənd əv ðə rɛkədz ðe rot əpɑn ɪt. wi 'sɛləˌbret ðə de əv ɪts bɜ·θ; ənd frəm
ɪts bɜ·θ əntɪl nau ɪt həz wɪtnəst ə gret 'hɪstərɪ, həz flotəd ɑn haɪ ðə sɪmbəl
əv gret ɪ'vɛnts, əv ə gret plæn əv laɪf wɜ·kt aut baɪ ə gret pipḷ.]

From Woodrow Wilson's Flag Day
Address, June 14, 1917

[ðə lɔrd ɪz maɪ ʃepəd; aɪ ʃæl nat wɔnt.
hi mékəθ mi tə laɪ daun ɪn grin pæstʃəz;
hi lidəθ mi bɪ'saɪd ðə stɪl wɔtəz.
hi rɪ'stɔrəθ maɪ sol;
hi lidəθ mi ɪn ðə pæðz əv raɪtʃəsnəs fɔr hɪz nemz sek.
je, ðo aɪ wɔk θru ðə 'vælɪ əv ðə 'ʃædo əv dɛθ,
aɪ wɪl fɪr no ivəl: fɔr ðau art wɪð mi;
ðaɪ rad ənd ðaɪ stæf ðe kʌmfət mi.

ðau prɪ'pɛrəst ə tebəl bɪ'fɔr mi ɪn ðə prɛzəns əv maɪn 'ɛnəmɪz:
ðau ənɔɪntəst maɪ hɛd wɪð ɔɪl; maɪ kʌp rʌnəθ ovɚ.
'ʃʊrlɪ gudnəs ənd 'mɝsɪ ʃæl 'falo mi ɔl ðə dez əv maɪ laɪf,
ənd aɪ wəl dwɛl ɪn ðə haus əv ðə lɔrd fɔr ɛvɚ.]

Twenty-third Psalm from *The Bible*
as arranged and edited by Ernest Sutherland Bates

['sʌnset ənd 'ivnɪŋ star,
  ænd wʌn klɪr kɔl fɔr mi!
ənd me ðer bi no 'monɪŋ əv ðə bar
  hwɛn aɪ put aut tu si,

bət sʌtʃ ə taɪd æz 'muvɪŋ simz əslip,
  tu ful fɔr saund ən fom,
hwɛn ðæt hwɪtʃ dru frəm aut ðə 'baundləs dip
  tɝnz əgen hom.

'twaɪlaɪt ənd 'ivnɪŋ bɛl,
  ənd æftɚ ðæt ðə dark!
ænd me ðer bi no sædnəs əv fer'wel,
  hwɛn aɪ ɛm'bark;

fɔr ðo frʌm aut aur bɔrn əv taɪm ən ples
  ðə flʌd me ber mi far,
aɪ hop tu si maɪ paɪlət fes tu fes
  hwɛn aɪ həv krɔst ðə bar.]

"Crossing The Bar"
By Alfred, Lord Tennyson

[hwɛn aɪ kənsɪdɚ hau maɪ laɪt ɪz spɛnt
ɛr hæf maɪ dez, ɪn ðɪs dark wɝld ən waɪd,
ænd ðæt wʌn tælənt hwɪtʃ ɪz dɛθ tu haɪd
lɑdʒd wɪð mi jusləs, ðo maɪ sol mɔr bɛnt
tu sɝv 'ðɛrwɪð maɪ mekɚ, æn prɪ'zɛnt
maɪ tru əkaunt, lɛst hi rɪ'tɝnɪŋ tʃaɪd;
"dʌθ gad ɛg'zækt 'de-ˌlebɚ, laɪt dɪ'naɪd?"
aɪ 'fandlɪ æsk. bʌt peʃəns, tu prɪ'vɛnt
ðæt mɝmɚ, sun rɪ'plaɪz, "gad dʌθ nat nid

ɪðɚ mænz wɝ·k ɔr hɪz on gɪfts. hu best
bɛr hɪz maɪld jok, ðe sɝ·v hɪm best. hɪz stet
ɪz 'kɪŋlɪ: θauzəndz æt hɪz 'bɪdɪŋ spid,
æn post ɔr lænd ənd oʃən 'wɪðaut rɛst;
ðe 'ɔlso sɝ·v hu 'onlɪ stænd ænd wet.]

"On His Blindness"
By John Milton

APPENDIX B

In this section are samples of the speech of a number of public figures, presented in broad transcription. Conventional punctuation is used instead of pause marks, and stress marks are employed sparingly. Non-phonemic and modifying symbols are used only to point out some interesting dialectal features. No attempt is made to have strict uniformity.

Some samples were taken from broadcasts, most of which originated with the Columbia Broadcasting System and were heard in the Seattle, Washington, area over KIRO; others originated with KIRO. Electrical transcriptions of the broadcasts were presented to the University of Washington by KIRO for whatever scholarly use might be made of them, and they constitute a historical collection with the School of Communications.

Section I--American Dialects

DAVE BECK, former labor leader:

[jɛs, wɪ əv hæd ɑr dɪfrənsəz wɪθ ɪmplɔɪəz ɪn ɑr ˈɪndəstrɪ. wi hæv fɔt itʃ ʌðə pɜ·tɪ hɑrd ət taɪmz. raɪt naʊ, haʊɛvə, wɪ ɑr faɪtɪŋ tʊgeðə tu kip ɑr trʌks ɒn ðə rod, hɔlɪŋ ðə gʊdz ðæt ɜ· nidəd tə wɪn ðɪs wɔr. aɪ spik tənaɪt ˌreprəˈzɛntɪŋ mɔr ðən sɪks hʌndəd θaʊzən mɛmbɜ·z əv ðɪ ˌɪntɜ·ˈnæʃənəl ˈbrʌðə₁hʊd əv timstɜ·z hwɛn aɪ ɪnˈdɔrs ðə ˈprogræm hwɪtʃ mɪstɜ· ɪsmən æn mɪstɜ· baɪjɜ· həv prɪˈzɛntəd. ɑr ˈmɛmbɜ·ʃɪp ɪz ˈdiplɪ kənsɜ·nd wɪð:ə prabləm əv kənˈsɜ·vɪŋ taɪəz ən ðə trʌks wi naʊ hæv. aʊr dʒab ən ðə fjutʃɜ· əv ɑr ˈɪndəstrɪz ɑr ɪnˈvalvd. mɔr ðən ðæt, ɑr ˈkʌntrɪ ɪz dəˈpɛndɪŋ an ʌs tə kip ðoz trʌks ˈrolɪŋ....]

FRANCIS BIDDLE, former attorney general:

[tənaɪt aɪ prəpoz tə spik ˈbriflɪ əv sʌm ˈæ₁spɛkts əv θri pətɪkjələ məˈnɒrətɪz huz rɪˈleʃən tə ðə gretə badɪ əv aʊə neʃən

312

hæz bɪn brɔt ɪntu ʃaːp fokəs baɪ tu jɪəz əv wɔə. aɪ rɪ'fɜ tə
ðə 'dʒæpəˌnis, tə ðə dʒɪʊz ænd tə ðə 'nigroz. ɪt ɪz ə 'kjʊrɪəs
'pærəˌdɔks ðət 'ɔlˌðo 'djʊrɪŋ ðɪs wɔə sɜtn sɪvəl 'lɪbətɪz hæv
safəd lɛs ðən ɪn ðə fɜst wɜld wɔə, ðə tɛnʃənz ə'raɪzɪŋ frəm ðə
ples əv ðiz θri reʃəl məˈnarətɪz ɪn ðə næʃnəl laɪf hæv 'gretlɪ
ɪnkrɪst. ɪn ðə læst wɔə ðə raɪts əv eljən 'ɛnəmiz, pə'tɪkjəlɪ
əv dʒɜmənz hu wə 'lɪvɪŋ ɪn a 'kʌntri, ænd əv ðoz 'rædɪkəlz hu
əpozd ðə wɔə ænd aə 'ɛntri ɪntʊwɪt, wə lɪtl̩ rɪ'spɛktɪd. næʃnəl
'predʒʊdɪs ðɛn ræn əgɛnst 'ɛnɪwʌn əv dʒɜmən 'ænsɛstri no mætə
haʊ lɔŋ hi həd lɪvd hɪə ɔə haʊ lɔɪl i wɔz tə ʌs. fridəm əv spitʃ
wəz lɛs 'taləretəd ænd mɔː 'njuzpepəz wɜ səprɛst ɔn ðɪ graʊnd
ðət ðe wɜ sədɪʃəs. ðɛ wə 'mɛnɪ ˌprasə'kjuʃənz boθ stet ən fɛdrəl
ɔfən ɔn ɪl-kən'sɪdɜd ænd pɛtɪ graʊnz. ðiz ətæks hɛv nɒt rɪ'kɜd
ɪn ðɪs wɔə--ɔr ət list tu ə faː lɛs dɪ'gri....]

    RICHARD KLEBERG, former congressman from Texas:
[aɪ səpɔrtəd ði ænti-sʌbsədi bɪl fɔr tu rizəns ɪn vɔɪsɪŋ
maɪ apə'zɪʃən tu ə waɪd opən 'sʌbsədi progrəm fɚ ðə pipl̩ əv ðɪ
ju'naɪtəd stets. aɪ 'kænɒt æn nɛvɚ wɪl bɪ'liv ðæt əmərəkən bɪznəs
æn ði əmərəkən pipl̩ ar ˌɪks'klusɪvlɪ dɪ'pɛndəndənt ʌpɔn ðə fɛdrəl
gʌvəmənt fɔr ðɛr sæl'veʃən. ɪf ðɪs ʃəd hæpən--gad fəbɪd ðɪs ʃəd
evɚ bəkʌm tru--ɪt wɪl onlɪ bi bikɔz ænd hwɛn ar gʌvmənt ɪz no
lɔŋgɚ ʌ gʌvmənt hwɪtʃ əraɪzəz aʊt əv ðə pipl̩ bʌt onlɪ hwɪn ɪt
bɪ'kʌmz ə gʌvmənt ovə ðə pipl̩. ðə vɛrɪ aɪdɪə ʌv dɪ'pɛndəns ɪz
ʌtɚlɪ rɪ'pʌlsɪv tu maɪ we əv ðɪŋkɪŋ bikɔz dɪ'pɛndənsɪ bi'gɛts
səb'sɜvjəns æn ðə mɛn æn wɪmən ðət aɪ no ænd lʌv ðæt 'kanstətjut
ðə pipl̩ ʌv ðɪ ju'naɪtəd stets əv əmərəkə wɪl hæf tʊ tʃɛndʒ ɪ'mɛʒɚ-
əblɪ ɪn fɔrm æn 'stætʃur tu bɪ'kʌm ðə 'krɔlɪŋ sɜvjɪl kritʃəz əv
sʌtʃ ə manstɚ....]

    ELMER DAVIS, Columbia Broadcasting System news commentator:
['sɪrɪəs raɪəts ɚ 'gɔɪŋ ɔn ɪn mɪ'læn ænd 'ɛls'hwɛr ɪn norðən
'ɪtəlɪ ə'kɔrdɪŋ tʊ ˌɪnfɚ'meʃən 'ritʃɪŋ 'dɪpləˌmæts ɪn ˌjugo'slavɪə
ænd rɪ'pɔrtəd baɪ ar ˌkɔrə'spandənt ɪn ˌbɛl'grad, wɪnstən bədet.
ðɛr simz tu həv bɪn sʌm sɔrt əv 'mɪlə'tɛrɪ 'raɪzɪŋ iðɚ əgɛnst ðə
fæʃəst partɪ ɔr əgɛnst ðə dʒɜmən trups hu ar rɪ'pɔrtəd əz numərəs
ɪn norðən ɪtəlɪ, fɚ θri haɪ ɪ'tæljən afəsɚz ɚ sɛd tu həv bɪn
kɪld baɪ dʒɜmənz hu ˌɪntɚ'vind æn blæk ʃɜt junəts ar ə'sɪstɪŋ ðə
dʒɜmənz ɪn rɪ'presɪŋ ðə ˌdɪs'ɔrdɚz. dʒɜmən soldʒɚz ɚ sɛd tu həv

ˈɑkjəˈpɑɪd ðə məlæn ˈrelˌrod steʃən ən ˈtɛləˌfon, ˈtɛləˌgræf
ænd ˈredɪo ɔfəsəz ænd ˈɔlso tə bi ˈgɑrdɪŋ ðə prɪnsəpəl ˈfæktərɪz.
tuˈrɪn ən ˈverɪəs ʌðɚ plesəz ɪn ðə po ˈvælɪ ɑr ˈɔlso ðə sin əv
ˈrɑɪətɪŋ. ðə ˈkæʒuəltɪz ɑr sɛd tə rʌn ʌp ɪntə ðə hʌndrədz. ðɪs
ɪnfɚˈmeʃən ɪz nɑt jet kɔˈrɑbəetəd frəm ʌðɚ sɔrsəz bət mɪstɚ bədet
ɪz ðə kɔrəˈspɑndənt hu gɑt ðə fɚst njuz əv ði ərɑɪvəl əv dʒɚmən
trups æn plenz ɪn ˈɪtəlɪ ænd ɑr ˌkɔrəˈspɑndənt herɪ ˈflænərɪ rɪ-
ˈpɔrtəd frʌm bɚlɪn tənɑɪt ðət pepɚz ðer spik əv ɛndləs trenlodz
əv ðə dʒɚmən ɛr fɔrs æz goɪŋ θru ðə brenɚ pæs tɔrd ɪˈtæljən
sɔɪl....]

JOHN FOSTER DULLES, former secretary of state:

[læst ə frɑɪdi ˈivnɪŋ ɑɪ rɪˈtɚnd tu ˈwɔʃɪŋtən æftɚ fɔr wiks
əv ˈdeli ˌdɪsˈkʌʃən æt bɚlɪn wɪðːi fɑrən mɪnəstɚz əf frænts, gret
brɪtn̩ ænd ðə sovˈjɛt junjən--mɪzɚ biˈdo, mɪstɚ idn̩ æn mɪstɚ mɑlə-
tɔf. ˈɔlso ɔn ðə we bæk ɑɪ mɛt wɪθ tʃænslɚ ˈædnaur ə dʒɚmənɪ. ɑɪ
fɑɪnd ɔn mɑɪ rɪˈtɚn ət ðerz sʌm kənfjuʒən æz tə hwʌt rilɪ hæpənd.
ðæts nɑt səˈprɑɪzɪŋ. ɪts ˈdɪfəkult tə græsp ˈkwɪklɪ ði rɪˈzʌlts
əv fɔr wiks əv dəbet ɔn ˈmɛnɪ dɪfɚnt mætɚz æn ɪnˈdid ðə ful rɪˈ-
zʌlts kænɑt bi ˈklɪrli sin fɚ mɛnɪ mʌns. ɑɪ kæn havɛvɚ se ðət ðɪs
ˈmitɪŋ hæd tu rɪˈzʌlts hwɪtʃ wɪl pɚˈfaundli ˈɪnfluwəns ðə fjutʃɚ.
fɚst, æz fɑr əz jɚəp wəz kənsɚnd, wi brɔt mɪstɚ ˈmɑlətɔf tə ʃo
rʌʃəz hænd ænd ɪt wəz sin əz ə hænd ðə? hɛl fæst tə ˈevrɪθɪŋ ɪt
hæd, ɪnˈkludɪŋ ist ˈdʒɚmənɪ ænd ist ɔstrɪə ænd ɪt ɔlso sɔt tə
græb səm mɔr. æn ˈsɛkəndlɪ ɪz fɑr əz kəriə ænd ɪndotʃɑɪnə wɚ kən-
ˈsɚnd wi brɔt mɪstɚ ˈmɑlətɔf tu ɛkˈsept ə rezəˈluʃən hwɪtʃ speld
aut ði juˈnɑɪtəd stets pəzɪʃən ðæt red tʃɑɪnə mɪɑt ɪn ðiz tu ɪn-
sənsəz bi dɛlt wɪθ hwer ˈnɛsəsɛrɪ, bət nɑt æz ə gʌvəmənt ˈrɛkɪg-
nɑɪzd bɑɪ ðə jənɑɪtəd stets....]

SENATOR GUY GILLETTE, of Iowa:

[ðə wɚd ˈsʌbsədi ɪz diˈfɑɪnd æz piˈkjunɪɛri ed dəˈrɛklɪ
græntəd bɑɪ ə gʌvəmənt tu ən ˌɪndɪˈvɪdʒuwəl ɔr tu ə kəmɚʃəl
ˈɛntəprɑɪz ɪn ðə pʌblɪk ˈwɛlfɚr. ˈsʌbsədɪz ɔr ˈbauntɪz əv ðə kɑɪnd
so dɪˈfɑɪnd ɑr nɑt nu æn hæv bɪn juzd ˌθruˈaut riˈkɔrdəd hɪstrɪ

ænd ar stɪl biɪŋ ɪk'stensɪvlɪ juzd ɪn ar neʃən. wi hæv numərəs
'ɪnstənsɪz ɪn ar on i'kanəmi. wi əv ped 'sʌbsədɪz də'rɛklɪ tə
'pʌblɪk 'kerɪjəz fɚ ʈræns'pɔrtɪŋ meɪ. wi hæv ped 'sʌbsədɪz tə bɪld,
menten æn 'apəret ə mɚtʃənt mərin. wi hev ped 'sʌbsədɪz fɚ ðə
kənstrʌkʃən ən apə'reʃən əv 'reɪrodz ən ʌðɚ taɪps ʌy pʌblɪk ˌju-
'tɪlətɪz. ðiz dərek 'sʌbsədɪz hæv bɪn 'dʒʌstəfaɪd ɔn ðə preməs
ðət pʌblɪk wɪl dɪ'mænz 'sɚtn̩ fə'sɪlətɪz fɚ ðə neʃənz jus hwen
ðə predʌkʃən ɔr ˌmen'tenəns əv ðiz fə'sɪlətɪz dʌz nat əv ɪt'sɛlf
gɪv əʃurəns əv səfɪʃənt 'ɪnkʌm tə 'dʒʌstəfaɪ praɪvet kæpətəl ɪn
'mekɪŋ ðɪ əsenʃəl ɪn'vesmənts for iðɚ ðer kri'eʃən ɔr ˌmen'tenəns.
ðə sem 'ladʒik əz bɪn ðə səport əv 'menɪ paləsɪz ʌv ɪndə'vɪdʒuwəl
sʌbsədɪ sʌtʃ əz aʊr 'sentʃerɪ old 'paləsɪ əv prə'tɛktɪv terəf for
ɪnfənt ˌmænjə'fæktʃərɪŋ 'ɪndəstrɪz....]

HERBERT HOOVER, former president of the United States:
['vɪktərɪ ɪz naʊ ɪn'evətebəl. ðer wəl bi menɪ mɔr hard mʌns,
bət 'evrɪ mʌnθ brɪŋz ʌs nɪrɚ tu ðə prabləmz ʌv pis. ðɪ əmerəkən
pipḷ ɚ əlaɪv tu ðə nid ænd ar dɪ'tɚmənd ðæt wi mʌst hæv ə 'læstɪŋ
pis ðɪs taɪm. frəm kost tə kost ju ɚ 'θɪŋkɪŋ ən dɪs'kʌsɪŋ ðə wez
əv pis. ju wʌnt jur sʌnz ən hʌzbəndz ən faðɚz hom. ju wɔntə mek
jur laɪvz əgen fri frʌm ðə 'hardʃɪps əv wɔr. bət ðə meθəd əv mekɪŋ
pis'ɪz ɔlso 'biɪŋ 'aʊrlɪ dɪs'kʌst ɪn ðə buks ənd ɪn ðə pres ən
ovɚ ðə 'redɪə. kəngreʃnəl rezə'luʃənz ən pə'lɪtɪkəl ə'fensɪvz ar
ɪn moʃn̩ ɔl əlɔŋ ðə pis frʌnt. æn ɪn ðɪs wi hæv tuˈskulz əv dɪ-
'skʌʃən. ɪn ðə fɚst skul ar ðoz pipəl hu ar 'straɪvɪŋ tu dɪ'strɪl
frʌm ðə wɚldz̩ ɪk'spɪrjəns 'sʌmpθɪŋ defənet æn 'pastɪv æn ðer hæv
bɪn ə nʌmbɚ əv 'notəbḷ ˌkantrə'bjuʃənz put fɔrwəd hwɪtʃ mert gret
kən'sɪdəreʃən. ðə sekənt skul ar ðoz hu lɪv ɪn ðɪ ɪn'defnet ænd
ɪn ðɪ ɪnfənet. ðer emz ar mæg'nɪfəsent, ðer frezəz ar sənɔrəs ənd
ðer slogənz ar ɪm'pelɪŋ. bət hwɪn wi sɪft ðem ɔl daʊn ðe ɚ 'mostlɪ
nebjələɚ wɚdz tə ðɪ əfekt ðət wi məst ko'apəret ɔr kə'læbæet wɪð:ə
wɚld tu prɪ'zɚv pis ænd rɪ'stɔr pras'perətɪ. ðer ə lɔŋ wez frəm
haʊ tə du ət....]

H. V. KALTENBORN, radio news commentator:

[gud 'ivnɪŋ 'ɛvrɪbʌdɪ. fɔr mʌnθs pæst ðɛr əz bɪn ə 'kantest əv wɪts bətwin ðə prezədənt əv ðɪ juʼnaɪtəd stets ænd ðə 'wɔʃɪŋtən rɪʼpɔrtəz. ðe hæv sɔt:u mek hɪm tɛl wʌt hi ɪnʼtɛndz tə du əbaʊt ə θɜdʼtɜm. hi hæz sɔt baɪ bæntə, 'pɜsɪ,flaʒ, klɛvə ænsə, smaɪlz ənd əkeʒənəl saɪləns nat tə tɛl hɪm. haʊ lɔŋ kæn ðæt bætl əv wɪts go ɔn wɪðaʊt 'sʌmbʌdi luzɪŋ hɪz tɛmpə? ðə prezədənt ðʌs far æz bɪn ʌnʼjuːʒuəlɪ peʃənt wɪð rɪʼspɛkt tʊ ðɪz pəsɪstənt ,ɪnʼkwaɪrɪz. pəhæps hi filz ðæt ðe ar ,dʒʌstəfaɪd baɪ ðə 'pʌbɪk kjurijasəti ænd pʌblɪk 'ɪntərəst, bət əv kɔrs æz 'prezədənt ɪf hi wɔntəd tu hi kʊd hæv stiv ɜʼli tɛl ðə,bɔɪz. "naʊ ʃi hɪə, no mɔr kwɛstʃənz əbaʊt ðə θɜd tɜm ɔr aɪ wɪl kʌt aʊt ðə prɛs kanfərənsəz....]

CHARLES A. LINDBERGH:

[ɪn taɪmz əv gret iʼmɜdʒənsɪ mɛn ʌv ðə sem bəlif mʌst gæðə təgɛðə fɔr 'mjutʃuəl kaʊnsəl ænd ækʃn. ɪf ðe fel tə du ðɪs ɔl ðət ðe stænd fɔr wɪl bi lɔst ai spik tənʌɪt tʊ ðoz pipəl ɪn ðɪ juʼnaɪtəd stets əv əmerəkə hu fil ðət ðə 'dɛstənɪ ʌv ðɪs 'kʌntrɪ dʌz nat kɔl fɔr aʊr ɪnʼvɔlvmənt ɪn ,jurəʼpiən wɔrz. wi mʌst bænd təgɛðə tu prɪʼvɛnt ðə lɔs ʌv mɔr əʼmerəkən laɪvz ɪn ðɪz ɪnʼtɜnəl strʌgəlz ʌv jurəp. wi məst kip fɔrən ,prapəʼgændə frəm puʃɪŋ aʊr 'kʌntrɪ 'blaɪndlɪ 'ɪntu ənʌðə wɔr. madən wɔr wɪθ ɔl ɪts 'kansɪ,kwɛnsəz ɪz tuʼ.ʼtrædʒɪk æn tu 'dɛvəs,tetɪŋ tə bi əprotʃt frʌm 'ɛnɪθɪŋ bʌt ə 'pjurli əmerəkən 'stændpɔɪnt. wi ʃʊd nɛvə ɛntə ə wɔr ʌnʼlɛs ət ɪz 'æbsəʼlutlɪ əsɛntʃəl tə ðə fjutʃə 'wɛlfər ʌv ar neʃən. ðɪs 'kʌntrɪ wəz 'kalənaɪzd baɪ mɛn ən wɪmən frəm jurəp. ðə hetrədz, ðə ,pɜsɪʼkjuʃənz, ði 'ɪn,trigz ðe lɛft bɪʼhaɪnd gev ðɛm 'kɜɪdʒ tə krɔs ðɪ ætʼlæntɪk oʃən tu ə nu lænd. ðe prəfɜd ðə wɪldənəs ænd ðɪ 'ɪndɪjənz tə ðə prabləmz əv jurəp. ðe wed ðə kɔst əv fridəm frəm ðoz prabləmz ænd ðe ped ðə praɪs....]

ADLAI STEVENSON, former governor of Illinois:

[....ɔlmost 'θɜ˞tɪ jɪrz əgo æn ɪn'kwɪzətɪv jʌŋ mæn trævəld əkrɔst jurəp, ʌp ðə blæk si ænd əkrɔs westən rʌʃə æn wɛn hi gat hʒʊm 'bɜ˞stɪŋ wɪð hɪz traɪəlz ənd əd'vɛntʃɚz, 'sʌmpθɪŋ hæd gɔn rɔŋ. ðɛr wəz no bænd ænd no 'wɛlkəmɪŋ kə'mɪtɪ tʊ mit hɪm ɔn ðə steʃən ɪn 'blumɪŋtən ˌɪlə'nɔɪ. ɪn sæd fæk ðɛr wʌz no wʌn ət ɔl ɛk'sɛpt æn old 'bægɪdʒ mæn ænd hɪz 'gritɪŋ wəz, "haɪ, ædlɪ! ju bɪn əwe?" wɛl, aɪv bɪn 'trævlɪŋ əgɛn æn aɪ mʌs se ðət ðɪs wɛlkəm kəmpɛrz kwaɪt 'fevərəblɪ wɪð:æt. aɪ əm tʌtʃt ən gritlɪ--æn diplɪ 'gretfʊl tu ðə kə'mɪtɪ...ænd tu ɪɔl əv ju hu həv kʌm hɪr tə ðə 'sɪvɪk ʊprə ðɪs 'ivnɪŋ. ju du mi gret anɚ. bət ðə trɪp ɪt'sɛlf wəz ə rɪ'wɔːd æn aɪ wɪʃ ðət 'ɛvrɪwʌn kənsɛnd əbaʊt hɪz 'kʌntrɪz ples ɪn ðə wɜ˞ld kʊd æv hæd ðɪ ˌɑpɚ'tunətɪ aɪv hæd tu hɪr ænd tə si, ə'spɛʃəlɪ 'ɛnɪwʌn hu dʌznt no haʊ lʌkɪ hi ɪz tu bi æn əmerəkən....]

HARRY S. TRUMAN, former president of the United States:

[maɪ fɛlə 'sɪtəzənz. aɪ əm hɪr tənaɪt tə sɛt ðə rɛkɚd stret. aɪ əm glæd ðæt aɪ æm ebl̩ tə du ðɪs an mə'zɜ˞ɪ sɔɪl baɪ dərɛkt kəmˌjunəkeʃən wɪθ so mɛnɪ ʌv maɪ 'fɛlo əmerəkənz. məzɜ˞ɪ ɪz ðə ʃo mi stet. wɛl, al ʃo ju ðə truθ. ɒn no'vɛmbɚ ðə sɪks ðə nju əd'mɪnəˌstreʃən θru hɚbət ˌbraʊnɛl dʒunjɚ, e formɚ tʃɛrmən əv ðə rɪ'pʌblɪkən næʃnəl kə'mɪtɪ naʊ 'sɜ˞vɪŋ əz ə'tɜ˞nɪ dʒɛnrəl, med ə pɚsnəl ətæk ɔn mi. ˌbraʊ'nɛl med ðɪs ətæk ɪn ðə kɔrs ʌv ə po'lɪtɪkəl spitʃ bi'for ə lʌntʃən klʌb ɪn ʃə'kɔgo. ðɪs ətæk ɪz wɪðaʊt 'pɛrəlɛl aɪ bɪ'liv ɪn ðə 'hɪstrɪ əv ar 'kʌntrɪ. aɪ hæv bɪn əkjuzd ɪn əfɛkt əv 'nowɪŋ lɪ bɪ'treɪŋ ðɪ sɪ'kjurətɪ əv ðɪ ju'naɪtəd stets. ðɪs tʃardʒ ɪz əv kɔrs ə 'fɒlshʊd æn ðə mæn hu med ɪt hæd ɛvrɪ rizən tu no ɪt ɪz ə 'fɒlshʊd. an 'tuzdɪ no'vɛmbɚ ðə tɛnθ æz ə dɪ'rɛkt rɪ'zʌlt əv ðɪs tʃardʒ aɪ wəz sɜ˞vd wɪð ə səpinə əv ðə haʊs kə'mɪtɪ ɒn 'ʌnəˌmerəkən æk'tɪvətɪz hwɪtʃ kʊld an mi tʊ əpɪr bɪˌfor ɪt tə bi kwɛstʃənd əbaʊt maɪ 'kanˌdʌkt ʌv ðɪ afəs ʌv prezədənt əv ðɪ ju'naɪtəd stets. fɜ˞st aɪ wəd laɪk tə tɛl ju ðə pipəl əv əmerəkə hwaɪ aɪ dɪ'klaɪnd tʊ əpɪr bɪˌfor ðæt kə'mɪtɪ. ɔn ðə sɝfəs ɪt maɪt sim tə bi æn 'izɪ θɪŋ tə du, æn smart 'palətiks fɚ 'hɛrɪ trumən, ə praɪvət sɪtəzən ʌv ˌɪndɪ'pɛndəns mɪ'zʊrɪ, tʊ juz ðɪ kə'mɪtɪ æz ə fɔrəm tə 'ænsɚ ðə skɝələs tʃardʒəz hwɪtʃ həv bɪn med əgɛnst mɪ. 'mɛnɪ pipəl ɝdʒd mi tə du ðæt. ɪt wəz ən ə'træktɪv səg'dʒɛstʃən æn əpild tə mi. bʌt əf aɪ hæd dʌn ət aɪ wʊd əv bɪn ə 'partɪ ˌwɪð ðə kə'mɪtɪ tu ən ækʃən hwɪtʃ wʊd hæv 'ʌndɚˌmaɪnd ðə ˌkanstə'tuʃnəl pəzɪʃən əv ðə əfəs əv ðə prɛzdənt əv ðɪ ju'naɪtəd stɛts....]

A Western college professor:

[aʊr pipl ɪn ðə stet əv 'wɔɪʃɪŋdən ar 'maɪtɪ praʊd foks ðiz dez æn wi hæv 'ɛvrɪ rizən tə bi. wihæv æn stɪl ar prə'vaɪdɪŋ aʊr fʊl kwotə ʌv mɛn ən wɪmən fɚ ðɪ arm sɝvəsəz ən 'mɛnɪ əv ʊɛm hæv ɔl'rɛdɪ med 'ɛnvɪəbəl rɛkɚdz ɔn ðə wɝldz 'bætlfilᴅz. wi hæv æn stɪl ar prəvaɪdɪŋ sʌm əv ðə most əsɛntʃəl ɪmpləmənts əv wɔr...bət 'ikwəli æz ɪm'pɔrtənt əz ɛnɪ ˌkantrə'bjuʃən wi ar 'mekɪŋ ɪz ðə fud hwɪtʃ 'wɔɪʃɪŋtən stet farmɚz ar 'growɪŋ ən 'harvstɪŋ tə fid ar faɪtɚz, wi səvɪljənz æn ar 'ælaɪz....]

HENRY WALLACE, Iowa editor and former vice-president of the United States:

[ɪn 'tɔkɪŋ tu ðə 'rɛdɪo 'brɔdˌkæstɚz aɪ wɪʃ fɝst tu ɪk'sprɛs maɪ haɪ əˌprɪʃɪ'eʃən ʌv ɔl ðət ju hu wɝk ɪn 'rɛdɪo hæv dʌn. ju hæv 'kɛrɪd ðə lʌv əv gʊd 'mjuzɪk tə 'mɪljənz. ðə 'lonɪɪ ən sɪk ju həv brɔt 'mɛsɪdʒəz əv gʊd wɪl ænd əv med ɪt 'pasɪbəl fɚ ðɛm tu ɛn'dʒɔɪ tʃɝtʃ sɝvəsəz ɔn 'sʌndeɪ. tede ju ar 'brɪldɪŋ ˌhɛməs'fɪrɪk gʊd wɪl baɪ minz ʌy e 'tu'we 'rɛdɪo brɪdʒ 'kɛrɪɪŋ əkrɔs ðə 'skaɪˌwez 'progræmz hwɪtʃ wɪl betɚ ɛn'ebl ʌs tu ə'prɪʃiet ðə kʌltʃɚ æn 'mjuzɪk əv lætn əmɛrəkə, hwaɪl ət ðə sem taɪm ar gʊd nebɚz ar 'lɝnɪŋ θru ðə 'rɛdɪo tʊ no 'ʌs betɚ. ju ar 'pruvɪŋ ðət ðə lætn kʌltʃɚ əv ðə saʊθ æn ðɪ 'ænglo'sæksən kʌltʃɚ əv ðə nɔrθ ar 'fʌndəˌmɛntəlɪ əlaɪk bi'kɔz boθ ar faʊndəd ɔn bəlif ɪn də'makrəsi æn fridəm....]

WILLIAM ALLEN WHITE, Kansas editor:

[evərɪj sæmpəlɪŋ ʌv əmerəkən pʌblɪk əpɪnjən rəvilz æn ovə‐
ˈhwelmɪŋ dɪˈzaɪr ɔn ðə part əv ðə pipḷ əv ðɪ juˈnaɪtəd stets tu
kip aut əv wɔr; ˈɛnɪ wɔr‐‐ðə diˈklɛrd wɔr ɪn jʊrəp ɔr ðɪ ˈʌndɪ‐
ˌklɛrd wɔr ɪn eʒə ɔr ivən ðə pasəbəl wɔr bətwin. rʌʃə æn ðə ˈskæn‐
dəˌnevɪjən dəˈmakrəsɪz. ɔlso, oˈpɪnjən ɪn ðɪ juˈnaɪtəd stets æz
rɪˈvild baɪ ˈɛvrɪ ˈsæmplɪŋ ʃoz frʌm ˈsɪkstɪ tu ˈnaɪntɪ pəsent ʌv
ðə pipḷ hop ðə ˌdeməˈkrætɪk ˈælaɪz wɪl wɪn ɪn westən jʊrəp. haʊ‐
ˈevə e klɪr dɛfənət məˈdʒɔrəti əv ar pipḷ bəliv ðæt wi kæn bes
kip aut əv wɔr baɪ ˈgɪvɪŋ hwʌtevə ˌɛkəˈnamɪk ed wi kæn gɪv tu
gret brɪtn̩ ən fræns ɪn ðer ˈkantest wɪð ˈdʒɜmənɪ. æn əmerəkən
lidʒən pol læst wik ˈkɛrfəlɪ med æt ðə rɪsənt kənvenʃən əv ðə
lidʒən ˈɪndɪˌketəd ðæt ˈsɪkstɪ pəsent ʌv ðə ˈlidʒəners ðer dɪ‐
ˈzaɪr e tʃendʒ ɪn ðə prezənt ˌnuˈtrælətɪ lɔ. ðə lidʒən ˌreprɪ‐
ˈzents æn anəst krɔs sekʃən əv ðɪ əmerəkən pipḷ. ðɪ ˈnanˈpartə‐
sən kəˈmɪtɪ fɔr pis θru ðə rɪˈvɪʒən ʌv ðɪ ˌnuˈtrælətɪ lɔ hæz ɪn‐
ˈrold æn ˈovəˌhwelmɪŋ sentəmənt ʌv ðɪ ˈkalɪdʒ prezədənts əv ðɪs
ˈkʌntrɪ æz səpɔrtəz əv ðə kæʃ ən ˈkɛrɪ prɪnsəpəl....]

MAURY MAVERICK, former congressman from Texas:

[frenz ən fɛlə əmerəkənz. ðɪs spitʃ ɪz biɪŋ med frəm ðə
pəˈsɪfɪk kost ət ˈhalɪwud, raɪt ɪn ðə mɪdḷ əv ðə gret ˈmuvɪ
ˈɪndəstrɪ. flaɪɪŋ hɪr əkrɔs ðə kɒntənənt, siɪŋ ɑː əmerəkən plenz
ən dezəts ən ˈvælɪz ən maʊntənz meks wʌn ˈtrulɪ ˈriəlaɪz ði
əˈmensəti əv ɑə ˈkʌntrɪ; ænd tə trævəl ət naɪt, tə si ðə mɪljənz
əv braɪt ˈʃanɪŋ laɪts, gɪvz wʌn ə ˈfilɪŋ əv gret saləm ˈhæpɪnəs
ðət aʊ ˈkʌntrɪ ɪz nat ɪn ðə ˈblækaut, ðət aʊə pipəl ɚ nat lɪvɪŋ
ɪn ðə hɔrə ən fɪr əv dɛθ frəm ðə skaɪz. ɪts faɪn æftər lɔ tə bi
ən əmerəkən. naʊ ðɪs ɪz ðə fɜst taɪm aɪ əv tɔkt ɔn ə næʃnəl
ˈbrɔdkæst wɪð:i ɪkˈsepʃən əv ˌɪnfəˈmeʃən plɪz sɪns aɪ wəz dɪˈfit‐
əd fɔr ˈriəˈlekʃən tə kɒngrəs ən wʌn əv ðə men rizənz ðət a spik
tənaɪt ɪz tə θæŋk ðə ˈθaʊzəndz əv pipḷ hu əv rɪtn̩ mi kandlɪ letəz,
ˈmenɪ əv hwɪtʃ a əv faʊnd ət ˈɪmpasəbḷ tʊ ænsə. wel, rat sun æftə
a wəz əˈlektɪd mejɚ əv sæn əntonjə hewud brun, me gad rest hɪz sol

ɪn pis, tol mi ðət ˈɛnɪ nɒkt aʊt ˈpraɪzˈfaɪtə hæd tə gɪt bæk
ɪn ðə rɪŋ ət wʌnts ə hi wʊd nɛvə mek ə ˈkʊmˌbæk; so a gɑt bæk
ɪn ðə rɪŋ, nɒkt aʊt ðɪ old pəˈlɪtɪkəl məʃin æn kem bæk....]

HAROLD E. STASSEN, former governor of Minnesota:
[....aɪ brɪŋ ju kɔrdʒəl ˈgritɪŋz æz ju əsɛmbl̩ fɚ ðɪs faɪnl̩
seʃən əy ðə ˈfɔrtɪˈfɔrθ ænjəl kənvɛntʃən əv ði ɛn-e-e-si-pi. ən
aɪ brɪŋ ju əʃʊrəns ət ɪʳ ˈvɛri ˈopənɪŋ ə maɪ rɪˈmɑrks ðət aɪ ʃəl
nɑt spik tu lɔŋ bɪkʌz aɪ ˈɔlso wʌnt ə hɪr ðə mɛrənɚz bɪfɔr aɪ
mʌs go ən kɛtʃ maɪ plen, ən bɪkʌz ɔlso ðə ˈmɛsɪdʒ ðət aɪ brɪŋ
kən bi ɪkˈsprɛst tə ju ˈvɛrɪ kənˈsaɪslɪ ən ˌwɪˈðaʊt ˈtekɪŋ tu
mɛnɪ mɪnəts ɪn ðɪs gret ˈklozɪŋ seʃən əv jɚ kənvɛntʃən. me aɪ
se tə ju ˈvɛrɪ dəˈrɛktlɪ æz aɪ opm̩ maɪ æˈdrɛs ðɪs sɪmpl̩ bət ˌɪm-
ˈpɔrtn̩t stetmənt: ðɪ ɛn-e-e-si-pi ɪz ɪnˈgedʒd ɪn e wɝk əv gret
ˈvæju tu aʊr əmɛrəkə ænd tu ɔl ˈmænˈkaɪnd. æz prɛzədən ˈaɪzənhaʊr
ˈrisəntlɪ rot--æn aɪ kwot hɪm--aɪ ʃæl kənˈtɪnju tɪ diˈvot maɪ
ɝnəst ɛfɚts tu ədvæns boθ ðə spɪrət æz wɛl æz ðə fækt ʌv iˈkwɑl-
ətɪ....]

ROBERT LAFOLLETTE JR., former senator from Wisconsin:
[felə ˈsɪtəzənz. wʌn rizən aɪ fil so ˈstrɔŋli əbaʊt ðə kɔrs
ən hwɪtʃ ar ˈkʌntrɪ hæz ɪmˈbɑrkt ɪz ðət aɪ æv sin ðɪs ˈtrædʒədi
ˈbifɔr. aɪ fil əz ðo aɪ əd wʊkt ˈɪntu ə ˈmuvi ˈonlɪ tu dɪˈskʌvɚ
ðət aɪ æd sin ðə pɪktʃɚ jɪrz əgo ʌndɚ əˈsʌmhwʌt dɪfɚnt nem ænd
wɪð ə dɪfɚnt kæst. ˈdʊrɪŋ ˈnaɪnˌtin ˈsikstin ˈsɛvənˌtin aɪ wəz
wʌn əv maɪ faðɚz ˈsɛkrətɛrɪz. æz ˈmɛnɪ əv ju rɪˈmɛmbɚ, hi fɔt tə
ðə læst dɪtʃ tu pəvent ði ɪnˈvalvmənt əv ðə lænd hi lʌvd ɪn ðɪ
jʊrəˈpiən wɔr ʌv hɪz ˌdʒænəˈreʃən. ˈfɔrtʃənətlɪ fɔr maɪ ˌedʒu-
ˈkeʃən aɪ wəz klos tu ði hɪsˈtɔrɪk bætl̩ hwɪtʃ redʒd ɪn ˈwɔʃɪŋtən.
ɪts fʊl ˈtrædʒɪk ˈminɪŋ bɝnd ɪntu mi fɔr laɪf. æz aɪ sɪt ɪn ði
juˈnaɪted stets sɛnət təde ðə wɝdz ðət ar spokən ən ðə θɪŋz ðət
ar dʌn hɪr ɪn ˈwɔʃɪŋtən hæv ə ˈtrædʒɪk rɪŋ əv fəmɪlˈjɛrəti. sʌm
əv ðə wɝdz ən slogənz ar dɪfɚnt bət ɪn spaɪt əv nu ˈfrɛ́zɪz kʊkt

ʌp baɪ ðə bɛst ˌprʌpəˈgændɪsts ɪn ðə bɪznəs wi ɑr ˈgoɪŋ stɛp
baɪ stɛp daʊn ðæt sem rod wi tʊk ɪn ˈnaɪnˈtin ˈsɪkˌstin ˈnaɪn-
ˈtin ˈnaɪnˈtin ˈsɛvənˌtin. ju ənd aɪ lʌv ɑr ˈkʌntri. ðɪ ˌovə-
ˈhwɛlmɪŋ məˈdʒɑrəti ʌv əs wɔnt wɪð ˈɛvri faɪbɚ əv ɑr ˈbiɪŋ tə
du hwʌt ɪz bɛst fɚ ðɪs neʃən. wi sɛns wɪð ðæt tru ˈɪnˌstɪŋkt
hwɪtʃ gad hæz gɪvən tu pipəl ɪn taɪmz əv gret kraɪsəs ðæt ðə
dɪˈsiʒən wi mek wɪl bi ʌv wɚldˈʃekɪŋ ɪmˈpɔrtəns....]

HELEN GAHAGAN DOUGLAS, former senator from California:

[....wɛl. aɪ æm goɪŋ tə traɪ tə ænsɚ mɪstɚ dɚksən ɪn ðə haʊs
təmaro. mɪstɚ dɚksən lɛft səm ɪmˈpreʃənz ɔ traɪd tu kriˈjet səm
ɪmˈpreʃənz hwɪtʃ ɚ kənˈfjuzɪŋ tə se ðə lɪst tu ðoz əv ʌs hu ar
nat ˈɪntəmətlɪ kənetəd wɪð ðə fæks ɒn haʊzɪŋ...wɛl, mɪstɚ dɚksən
traɪd tʊ liv ði ɪmˈpreʃən ðæt ɪf wi dʒʌst liv ˈbɪldɪŋ tu praɪvət
ˈɪndəstrɪ əlon ðət ðɛ wəd bi haʊzəz fə ði əmɛrəkən pipl, ɔl ðə
haʊzəz ðət ðe nid ɔr kən juz æn ðət ˈɛniwe ðə nid ɪznt ˈvɛrɪ gret
ən ðət ju kant gɛt ˈɛnɪ tu əθarətɪz tu əgri ɒn hwʌt ðæt nid ˈæk-
tʃuli ɪz. ðə bɪgəst ˈhaʊzɪŋ prədʌkʃən wəz ɪn ðə ˈnaɪnˌtin ˈtwɛnt-
ɪz, mɪstɚ dɚksən sɛz, ænd ət ðæt taɪm ðə ˈbɪldɪŋ ˈɪndəstrɪ ən ðə
ril əstet bɔrdz wɚ lɛft əlon. ɪn ðə ˌnaɪnˌtin ˈθɚtɪz θə gʌvəmənt
ɪnvɛstəd ˈtwɛntɪ bɪ.ljən dalɜz ɪn ˈhaʊzɪŋ ən naʊ lʊk hwɛr wir æt,
mɪstɚ dɚksən sɛz. tə traɪ æn ʃo haʊ ˈɪnəfɛtɪv ðə gʌvəmənt ɪz,
mɪstə dɚksən meks fʌn əv ðə ˈwaɪət ˌproˈgræm æn sɛz ðæt ɪt wəz
ˈonlɪ æftɚ wi gat rɪd əv ðə waɪət ˌproˈgræm ðət wi gat e ril
ˈhaʊzɪŋ prədʌkʃən ˈprogræm ˈgowɪŋ ɪn ˈnaɪntin ˈfɔrtɪ sɛvən. ɪn
ʌðɚ wɜdz, mɪstə dɚksən traɪz tə liv ði ɪmˈpreʃən ðət ɪf wi pæs
ðə ti i dʌbljə ˈhaʊzɪŋ bɪl ju nat ˈonlɪ wont gɛt ˈɛnɪ ˈhaʊzɪŋ bʌt
ðæt ˈpæsɪdʒ ə ðə bɪl wɪl ɪnˈkris ɪnˈfleʃən....]

HARLEY KILGORE, then senator from West Virginia:

[əmɛrəkən ˈʃɪpɪŋ ɪz vaɪtəl tə ˈwɪnɪŋ ðə wɔr. ɪt kən brɪŋ ar
bɔɪz hom frəm ðə ˈbætlˌfrʌnt sunɚ ɪf ɪt əz betɚ ˈmobəlaːzd. aɪm
 n̄at karpɪŋ hwɛn aɪ se ðət ar ˈʃɪpɪŋ kæn bi ˈmobəlaɪzd betə. e
ˈkʌntri ət wɔr məst wɚk fɚ pɚfɛkʃən. wi mʌst ˈkanstəntlɪ tʃendʒ

ən tʃendʒ ən tʃendʒ ar ˈtæktɪks əntɪl wi hæv ðə bɛst mɛθəd tə
du ðə dʒab æn wi məst rɪˈmɛmbɚ ðət ðə dʒab ɪn ˈʃɪpɪŋ ɪz tə gɛt
ðə gretəst pasəbəl ˈtʌnɪdʒ əv wɔr məˈtɪrɪˌɪʒ tu ðə ˈfaɪtɪŋ fɔrsɛz
ət ðɪ ˈɝˈlɪəst ˈpasbḷ momənt. wi məst dil ɪn ˈmæksməmz; mɪnəməmz
ən ˈævrɪdʒəz hæv no plɛs ɪn ðə prasˈkjuʃən əv ə wɔˌɚ. ðɛə mʌs bi
no dɪˈvɝʒən əv ʃɪps ɔr ðə mɛn ðət sɛl ðɛm frəm wɔr ˈʃɪpɪŋ ænd
ðɛr mʌst bi no dəˈvɝʒən əv wɔr ˈʃɪpɪŋ frʌm ðə most əˈfɛktɪv jus
tu e lɛs əˈfɛktɪv jus....]

FRANKLIN D. ROOSEVELT, former president of the United States:
[maɪ ˈfɛlo əˈmɛrɪkənz: ðə sʌdn̩ krɪmənəl ətæks ˈpɚpətretɪd baɪ
ðə ˈdʒæpəˌniz ɪn ðə pəˈsɪfɪk prəvaɪd ðə ˈklaɪˌmæks ʌv ə ˈdɛˌked
əv ˌɪntəˈnæʃnəl ˌɪmɔˈrælətɪ. pauəfəl ən rɪˈsɔsfəl gæŋstəz əv ˈbæn-
dɪd təgəðʌ tə mek wɔːr əpən ðə hol hjumən res. ðɛə tʃælənʤz həz
nau bɪn flʌŋ æt ðɪ juˈnaɪtəd ˈstets əv əˈmɛrəkə. ðə ˈdʒæpəˌniz
həv ˈtretʃɚəslɪ ˈvaɪəletəd ðə ˌlɔŋ ˈstændɪŋ ˌpis bəˈtwin əs. mɛnɪ
əmɛrəkən ˈsoldʒəz ən ˈseləz həv bɪn ˌkɪld baɪ ˈɛnəmi ˈækʃən....]

ALFRED SMITH, former governor of New York:
[æt ði ˈautsɛt ə maɪ rəˈmaːks lɛt mi fɝst se ðət aɪ du nat
no əv ˈɛnɪbadɪ, aɪ ˈnevər ivən hɝd əv ˈɛnɪbadɪ ɪn ðɪ juˈnaɪtəd
stets əv əˈmɛrɪkə hu wɒnts ðɪs ˈkʌntrɪ tə go tə wɔə. sɝtnlɪ aɪ
du nat fər aɪ æv θri sʌnz əv ðə ˈfaɪtɪŋ edʒ. ði oldəst əv ðəm ɪz
ɔlˈrɛdɪ ɪn ðɪ aːmɪ æn wud bi əmʌŋ ðə fɝst tə liv ðɪs ˈkʌntrɪ ɪn
ðɪ əvent ðət ðɪ juˈnaɪtəd stets wəz brɔt ˈɪntu ðɪ ˌjurəˈpiən
ˈstrʌgḷ. so ðɛfɔɚ ðɪ ˈaːgjəmənt æz far əz aɪm kənˈsɝnd rɪˈzalvz
ətsɛlf ɪntə ðɪs: hwʌt ʃəd wi du ðæt ɪz bɛst ˈkælkjəletəd tə kip
ʌs autə wɔɚ? ɪn ðɪ dɪsˈkʌʃən əv ðɪs ðɛr ɪz no rum fɔ pɝsənælə-
tɪz, paːtɪz, klæsəz ɔ krɪdz. ɔl dɪfrənsəz mʌs bi waɪpt aut ɪn
ðɪs aur əv tʃælənʤ. pɝsənəl ɪntrəs mʌs bi səˈbɔdənetəd tu ðə
kamən gud. wi mʌs bi ˈsɛlfɪʃ nat fɔr auəˈsɛlvz bʌt fə ðə hol
neʃən. aɪ wəz brɔt ʌp ɪn ə tʌf pəˈlɪtɪkəl skul wɛr fæks kauntəd
fɔ mɔ ðən θɪrɪz. maɪ ˈtrenɪŋ hæz bɪn tu diˈstɪŋgwɪʃ bɪˈtwin haɪ

saʊndɪŋ prɪnsəbəlz ænd ˈæktʃuwəl riˈzʌlts. maɪ ɛkˈspɪrɪəns hæz
tɔt mi tʊ‾wæsk ʰɑt hæz ɪt ə ˈlɔftɪ pɝpəs bʌt tu dɪˈmænd ən ænsɚ
tʊ ðə kwɛstʃən dʌz ət wɝɪk. ðə prɛzənt nuˈtrælətɪ ækt dʌz nɑt
wɝɪk....]

GENERAL DOUGLAS MACARTHUR, then a commander of United
States forces in the Pacific:

[təde ðə ˌdʒæpəˈniz aːmd fɔːsɪz θruˈaʊt dʒəpæn kəmˈplitəd ðɛə
ˌdiˈmobəlzeʃən ænd sist tu ɪgˈzɪst æẓ sʌtʃ. ðɪz ˈfɔsɪz ar naʊ
kəmˈplitli əˈbaɪɪʃt. aɪ no əv no ˌdiˈmobələzeʃən ɪn ˈhɪstrɪ iðɚ
ɪn wɔr ɔr ɪn pis baɪ aʊr on ɔr baɪ ˈɛnɪ ʌðɚ ˈkʌntrɪ ðæt hæz bɪn
əˈkamplɪʃt so ˈræpədlɪ ɔr so ˈfrɪkʃənləslɪ. ˈɛvriθɪŋ ˈmɪlətərɪ,
nevəl ɔr ɛr ɪz fɔrˈbɪdn̩ tu dʒəpæn. ðɪs ɛndz ɪts ˈmɪlətərɪ maɪt,
ɪts ˈmɪlətərɪ ˈɪnfluwəns ɪn ɪntɚˈnæʃənəl əˈfɛrẓ. ɪt no lɔŋgɚ rɛ-
kənz æz ə wɝld paʊɚ iðɚ lardʒ ɔr smɔl. ɪts pæθ ɪn ðə fjutʃɚ ɪf
ɪt ɪz tu sɝˈvaɪv mʌst bi kənfaɪnd tə ðə wez əv pis....]

NORMAN THOMAS, author and lecturer:

[wi əmɛrəkənz hæv wʌn səprim ɪntrəst ɪn ðɪs wɔr. ɪt ɪz ðæt
ɪt ʃæl bi ˈfalod baɪ ə ˈlastɪŋ pis ˈdʊrɪŋ hwɪtʃ ɒl əv əs kæn
gɪv aʊr dɪˈvoʃən tʊ ðə ˌjunəˈvɝsəl ˈkankwɛst əv ˈpavɚtɪ baɪ ðə
sem marvələs ˌtɛknəˈladʒɪk skɪlz hwɪtʃ təde ar ˈwɝkɪŋ dɪsˈtrʌk-
ʃən bɪˈjand aʊr kəˈpæsətɪ tʊ ˌʌndɚˈstænd. ɪt ɪz ˈprabəblɪ ə
ˌmɝsɪ ðæt nʌn əv ʌs kæn ˌkamprɪˈhɛnd ðə harɚ ɪnˈdjʊrd baɪ ɑr
brʌðɚz æn sʌnz ɪn iwo ɔr əlɔŋ ðə raɪn ɔr baɪ ðə mɪljənz ʌv wɪmən
æn tʃɪldrən hu ˈpɛrɪʃt ɪn ðə totl̩ dɪˈstrʌkʃən ʌv gret ˈsɪtɪz.
jɛt wi no ənʌf tʊ no ðæt bæd əz ðɪs wɔr ɪz, ðə hɛks wɪl bi ˈɪn-
fənətlɪ wɝs. ðə nɛks taɪm wi əˈmɛrəkənz kænət əskep ðə ˌdɛvə-
ˈsteʃən hwɪtʃ nju ˈmɛθədz əv ˈwɔrˌfɛr mek pasəbəl, nɔr ʃæl wi
ˌɪnˈdɛfənətlɪ mənˈten ðɪ ɪnˈdʌstrɪəl səˌpɪrɪˈjɔrətɪ əpan hwɪtʃ
ar prɛzənt paʊr ovɚ far mɔr papjələs neʃənz ɪz best....]

NEVILLE MILLER, radio executive:

[ðiz ɑr nɒt nɔrməl taɪmz. ɔlˈrɛdi ən ʌnˈlɪmətɪd næʃnəl əˈmɝdʒənsi hæz bɪn diˈklɛrd baɪ ɑr prɛzədənt æn əˈmɛrəkɚ ɪz ˈgowɪŋ æt ful spid əhɛɫəd wɪθ ʌr dʒaɪˈgæntɪk næʃnəl dɪˈfɛns progrəm. wi no ðət ɑr ˈkʌntrɪʲ hæz ˈfɪzɪkəl æn məˈtɪrɪəl ˈrisɔrsəz səˈpæsɪŋ ðoz əv ˈɛnɪ neʃən ɪn ðə wɝl. wi no ðət ʃɪps æn ˈɛrplenz, gʌnz ən æmɪˈnɪʃən ɔr ˈpɔrɪŋ aut əv ɑr ˈfæktrɪz æn ˈʃɪpˌjɔrdz æn wi no ðət ɑr bɔɪz baɪ ðə ˈθauzənz ɑr ˈkraudɪŋ ɪntə ɔrmɪ kæɫmps æn ˈnevəl besəz. bət ˈmɛnɪʲ ʌv ʌs du nɒt æz jɛt ˈrɪəlaɪz ðət ðɛr ˈɪz e ples fɔr ɪtʃ əv ʌs ɪn ðɪs gret næʃnəl ɛfɚt. ðə. səksɛs əv ˈɛnɪ ˈɑrmi ʊr ˈnevɪʲ dɪˈpɛndz ɔn ðə spɪrət əv ɪts mɛn. nəˈpoljən ɪz ɔfən kwotəd æz sɛɪŋ ðət ən ˈɑrmi trævəlz ɔn ɪts stʌmək, bət i ˈɔlso sɛd ðɛᵣr ɑr ˈonlɪ tu pauɚz ɪn ðə wɝl,⁽ᵈ⁾ ðə spɪrət æn ðə sɔrd. ɪn ðə lɔŋ rʌn ðə sɔrd wïl ˈɔlwez bi ˈkaŋkɚd baɪ ðə spɪrət....]

GEORGE BENDER, then congressman from Ohio:

[ðiz ɑr moˈmɛntəs dez. wi ɚ ɪn ðɪ θroz əv ˈfɔrdʃɪŋ ə nu wɝld. wi ɚ ˈgræplɪŋ wɪð ˌdʒaɪˈgæntɪk ˈɝθ ˈʃekɪŋ ˈɪʃuz ðæt wɪl diˈtɝmən ðə ˈdɛstənɪʲ əv ˈdʒɛnəreʃənz nɒt jɛt bɔrn. ɪn ðə mɪdst əv ðɪs, sʌm ˈwɛl-ˈminɪŋ pipḷ æsk hwaɪ ɔl ðɪs fʌs əbaut ðə ˈpol ˌtæks; hwʌt ˈdɪfɚəns dʌz ɪt mek wɛðɚ ðə pol tæks ɪz riˈpild ɚ nɒt? ðiz ɚ ˈkwɛstʃənz ðət ɚ æskt ˈanɛstlɪj. tənaɪt aɪ ʃəl ətɛmpt⁻tu ænsɚ ðɛm wɪθikwəl anəstɪj. aɪ fɝst hɝd əbaut ðə pol tæks ˈmɛnɪ jɪrz əgo æz ə bɔɪ ˈgrowɪŋ ʌp ɪn oˈhaɪo. aɪ mʌst kənfɛs ðət maɪ fɝst ˌriˈækʃən waz wʌn əv ˌtriˈmɛndəs ʃʊk. aɪ faund ət ˈdɪfəkət tu bəliv ðət ə grup əv stets bɪˈlo ðə mesṇ dɪksṇ laɪn kʊd bi so ˈsɪnɪkəl əbaut əmɛrəkən ˌdiˈmakrəsi æz tʊ ples ə praɪs tæg ɔn ðə bæləт, kəmˈpɛlɪŋ ðɛr ˈsɪtəzənz tə pe ə tæks ·bɪˈfɔr əˈlauɪŋ ðɛm tə vot.sɪns aɪ əv bɪn ə mɛmbɚ əv kaŋgrəs aɪv bɪn ˈtraɪɪŋ țə waɪp aʊt ðɪs fjudəl rɛmənənt. aɪ du nɒt bəliv ðət ˌdiˈmakrəsi ɪz strɛŋθənd(h)wɛn tɛn mɪljən əmɛrəkən ˈsɪtəzənz--sɛvən mɪljən waɪt ən θri mɪljən.kʌlɚd pipḷ ɪn sɛvən sʌðɚn stets--ɑr kɛpt.vɔɪsləs æn votləs....]

Following are three interesting speech samples from the
radio program, Town Meeting of the Air. The dialects represented
are generally Eastern American (Mr. Denny), General.American (Mr.
Eastman) and Southern British (Mr. Laski):

GEORGE V. DENNY JR., president of Town Hall:

[gʊd ˈivnɪŋ ˈnebɔz. tə'naɪts ˈkwɛstʃən ɪz no lɔŋgə ˈbirŋ
dɪsˈkʌst dʒʌst ovə baːz ən bæk ˈfɛnsɪz. ɪt əz ɪndid bɪˈkʌm ə
grev ɪntəˈnæʃnəl prɑbləm. ðæts waɪ wɪə dɪsˈkʌsɪŋ ɪt hɪə tənaɪt
wɪð rɪsˈpɑnsəbəl əˈθɔrətɪz hu wɔnt tə du ˈɛvrɪθɪŋ ɪn ðɛə paʊə
tu əvɔɪd ənʌðə wɔː. əpɪnjənz dɪfɚ əz tə haʊ wi kən əten ðɪs
gol....]·

MAX EASTMAN, author:

[æz θɪŋz ar naʊ wi ar kwaɪt ˈɑbvɪəslɪ hedəd fɔr wɔr wɪð
rʌʃə. ðə kwɛstʃən ɪz hwɛðɚ wɪr goɪⁿn tə drɪft əhɛd ˈblaɪndlɪ
əlɔŋ ðə sem kɔrs əntɪɫ wi get ðɛr, əᵘnd ðɪ ænsɚ dɪˈpɛndz ɔn
hwɛðɚ aʊr fɔrən ˈpɑləsɪ ɪz tə bi best ɔn fækt ɔr ɔn ˈsɛntə-
ˈmɛntəl iˈmoʃən. sɪnts ˈnaɪnᵢtin ˈfɔrtɪ wʌn ɚ ˈpɑləsɪⁱ həz
bɪn best ɑn ˌɪrˈæʃnəl ˈfilɪŋz, ðə ˈfilɪŋ ðət bɪˈkɔz rʌʃə wəz
fɔrst ɪntə ðə wɔr ɔn aʊr saɪd ˈðɛrˈfɔr hɚ ˈgʌvəmənt mʌst hæv
sist tə bi ə toᵢtæləˈterɪən ˈtɪrənⁱ dʒʌst æ³z ˈæbsəᵢlut æ³z
hɪtlɚz. ˈsevənˈtin mʌns biˈfɔr hɪtlɚ ətækt rʌʃə ˈrozəvɛlt stetəd
ðə fækt fɔr ɔl əv ʌ³s. ðə ˈsavɪjet junjən, æz ˈɛvrɪbʌdɪ noz hu
hæz ðə ˈkɚdʒ tu fes ðə fækts--aɪ əm ˈkwotɪŋ hɪm vɚˈbetəm-- ɪz
e ˈdɪkᵢtetɚʃɪp æz ˈæbso³lut æz ɛnɪ ʌðɚ ˈdɪkᵢtetɚʃɪp ɪn ðə wɚld
...rʌʃəz ˈpɑləsɪ tɔrd ʌs ənd ʌðɚ ᵢdeməˈkrætɪk neʃənz kʊld ɪm-
ˈpɪrɪjələst stets ɪn ðə ˈbɔlʃəvɪk lɪŋgo ɪz ˈplɛnlɪ rɪtŋ daʊn
hwɛr ˈɛvrɪ mæn kən rid ɪt. hɚ ˈpɑləsɪ ɪz tə prəmot keas ɪn aʊr
ˈkʌntrɪ ᵢʌnˈtɪl ɪn ə kraɪsəs hɚ frfθ kaləm led baɪ ðə kamjənəst
ˈpartɪ ænd bækt baɪ hɚ ˈmɪləᵢterɪ paʊɚ wɪl ˈovɚˈθro aʊr gʌvən-
mənt ænd ᵢriˈples aʊr ᵢdeməˈkrætɪk ᵢɪnstəˈtuʃənz wɪθ ə ᵢtoᵢtælə-
ˈterɪən stet ˈkæpɪtəlɪst ˈdɪkᵢtetɚʃɪp. ðɪs kraɪsəs, ʃi bəlivz,
wɪl kʌm hwɪᶜn ðə wɚld ɪz æt wɔr. æn stælən ɪz ˈgetɪŋ redɪⁱ fɔr
ðæt wɔr....]

HAROLD J. LASKI, economist:

[mɪstə 'dɛnɪ , 'lɛdɪz ən 'dʒɛntəlmən: sɜtɪn θɪŋz ə boθ
klɪr ənd ˌɛlɪ'mɛntrɪ ənd aɪ hop lɛts θət maɪ ol frɛn mæks ɪst-
mən wɪl kʌm bæk tʊ ðəm. 'fɜst ð3 me bi pipəl ɪn grɛt brɪtən ɔr
ɪn ðɪ juˈnaɪtəd stets tu hum ə wɔ wɪð rʌʃə wəd bi wɛlkəm. ðɛr
ɪn ən ˌovəˈhwɛlmɪŋ maɪˈnɔrətɪ ɪn boθ !kʌntrɪz. 'sɛkəndlɪ, 'ɛnɪ
'rʌᵃʃən 'lidʒ wɪð 'ɛnɪ kamən sɛnts--ənd ðe 'mostlɪ hæv ə gʊd ̄dil
əv kamən sɛnts--noz ðət rʌʃɚ ɪz nʊt ɪn ə pɔzɪʃən tu ɪnˈgedʒ ɪn
ə wɔ: fəʃ ə vɛrɪ lɔŋ taɪm tə kʌᵃm, ænd θɜdlɪ^ɪ 'ɛnɪwʌᵈn u əz
wɔtʃt rʌᵃʃə 'kloslɪ, ənd ivən mɔr əz dɪsˈkʌᵈst ɪts prɔbləmz
wɪð 'kɔmjɛnɪst lidəz ət fɜst hænd noz haʊ raɪt mɪstə idən wɔz--
ən ə 'trɪbjut tə mɪstə idənz raɪtnəs frəm mɪj minz 'sʌmθɪŋ--
wɛn i ɪnˈsɪstɪd ðət ðə 'praɪmərɪ ˌmotɪˈveʃn ʊᵊv rʌᵃʃən 'pɔlɪsɪ
wəz sɪkˈjurətɪ. ɪn ðə laɪt əv ðɪ 'twɛntɪ jɪəz sɪnts ðɪ ɔkˈtobə
revəˈluʃən ðə rʌʃənz sɜtʃ fə sɪkˈjurətɪ iʲ z æᵃmplɪ 'dʒʌstɪ-
faɪd....]

Section 2--Other Dialects

WINSTON CHURCHILL, British statesman:

[ˈɪθɪʒ suˈprim əbˌdʒɛktɪvz hæv 'nat bin ˌlʊst. wi æv ˌgɪvən
ˌɑə kənˈsɜvətɪv səˈpɔɚt tə ðə 'mɛn 'prɪnsəpəlz av ðə ˌgʌvəmənts
!fɑrɪn 'pɔləsɪ so ˌhwaɪl ət ðə ˌsɛm taɪm wi əv dɪˈplɔɑd ðɪ
əˌstanɪʃɪŋ 'ɛrəz hwɪtʃ həv 'hæmpəd ɪts ˌæplɪˈkeʃən. ɪn ðɪ ˌɛnd
haʊˌɛvʌ ɪt ɪz ðə 'lɑ:ˌdʒɑə ɪsju ðət wɪl 'kaʊnt. 'bʌt, mɪstə
ˌtʃɛəmən, 'hwaɪl wi ɑɚ ˌso 'bɪzɪʲ wɪð ˌaːr ɪnˈtɜnəl 'pɑːtɪ ˌkan-
trəvɜsɪz wɪ məst ˌnɔt fəˈgɛᶻt ðə 'grævətɪ əv ə pəˈzɪʃən ɔr ɪn-
dɪd 'ðæt ʊv ðə 'hol wɜld...ʌ bænd əv mɛn 'gæðəd təˈgɛðʌ ɪn ðə
'krɛmlɪn hæz 'rɛzd ɪtˌsɛlf ˌəˈgɛnst ðə 'wɛstən dɪˈmakrəsɪz. ðe əv
'ædɪd tə ˌðɛə dəˈmɪnjənz ðə 'sætɪˌlaɪt 'stets əv 'jurəp, ðə ˌbɔl-
tɪk stets, 'poɫənd, 'tʃɛko sloˌvækjʌ̃, 'hʌŋgərɪ, bʌl'gɛrjʌ̃, ru-
'menjʌ--ən 'ɛmpaɪə n ɪtˌsɛlf. 'tito əv ˌjugoˈslavjʌ̃ hæz brokən
əˈwej; 'gris hæz bin 'rɛskjud ˌbaɪ ðɪ juˈnaɪtəd stets 'kærɪjɪŋ
aʊt æn 'kærɪjɪŋ 'an ðə tæsk hwɪtʃ ˌwi bɪ'gæn....]

ELY CULBERTSON, bridge expert:

[ɪt meˑ sɪm stɹendʒ tʊ ju, ledɪz ən dʒɛnəlmən, ðæt ə mæn
ʌv ə sɪstəm əv bɹɪdʒ ʃʊd biˈkʌm ˈɔlmost ovɚnaɪt æ mæn ʌ̃v ə
sɪstəm fɔr wɜld pis. æftə ɔl ɪt ɪz kwaɪt ə lip fɹəm ə sɪstəm
əv ˈfɪftɪ tu kɑːdz æn fɔə suts ɪntəwə sɪstəm əv tu bɪljən jumən
kɑːdz æn hʌndɹəts əv suts əy neʃənẕ. ðɪ ˌɛkspləˈneʃən ɪz sɪmpl̩,
ɔlðo aɪ dɪd nat go ɪntʊ ðɪ fild əv ˌɪntəˈnæʃənəl ˈpɑlətɪks frʌm
ˈkɑntræk bɹɪdʒ. aɪ əˈɹɪdʒənəlɪ wɛnt ɪntə ðə wɜld ʌv kɑrdz frʌm
maɪ ˈstʌdɪz ʌv səˈsaɪətɪz ænd ɪntəˈnæʃənəl rɪˈleʃənẕ. sɪnts maɪ
ɜlɪ juθ ɪn ˈrʊʃjə æn ˌɪnsəˈdɛntlɪ aɪm ðɪ ˈonlɪ ˈnetɪv əmerəkən
hu spiks rɑʃən wɪ̃ðˈaʊt æn ˈæksɛnt æn ˈɪŋḭɪʃ wɪ̃ð ən ˈæksɜnt aɪ
hɛv bɪ̈n ˈfæsənetəd wɪ̃ð ðɪ pəˈlɪtɪkəl ˈsɪstəm æn mas saɪˈkalə-
dʒɪ. bɹɪdʒ wɪl ˈɔlwɪz bi maɪ ˈhɑbɪ æn maɪ bret ən bʌtə bʌt ɪn
ðɪẕ trædʒɪk taɪmẕ aɪ wɔnt tə juz maɪ ˈlaɪf ˈlɔŋ ˌɪksˈpɪɹɪjənts
tʊ bɪld ə nu kaɪnd əv e bɹɪdʒ, ɛ bɹɪdʒ ɪntʊ ðə fjutʃɚ, æ̃kɜd ɪn
ɪn ðɪ riˈæˑlətɪz əv tuˈde ovə hwɪtʃ ðɪs wɔə tɔːn hjuˈmænɪtɪ
kəˣn krɔs ˈɪntu djurəbl̩ pis æn fridəm....]

HERBERT MORRISON, British statesman:

[....ˈʌnˌlaˆɪk ˈmeˣnɪ ˌdɛməˈkræˑtɪk ˌkɑˆntəˈnɛntəl ˈkʌntrɪz,
auə ˈkʌntrɪ ɪz trəˈdɪʃənəlɪ ə ˈkʌntrɪ ʌˣv tu ˈpɑːtɪz, ɒv ˈgʌvəmənt ænd ˌɑpəˈzɪʃən. næˣʊ ðɪs ˈprɜˣktɪs, ðɪs ˌkanstəˈtjuʃənəl
trəˈdɪˑʃən əv aˣʊəz ɒv hwɪtʃ ðɪ ɔθəz a ˈrɪəlɪ ðə ˈbrɪtɪʃ ˈpipəl
ðəmˈsɛlvz, ðɪs ˈpræktɪs brɪŋẕ gret ədˈvæntɪdʒəˣz ɪn ðə we əv ɪ
ˈvɪgɜ ænd ðə stəˈbɪlɪtɪ ɒˆv ə ˌpɑləˈmɛntrɪ ˌɪnstəˈtjuʃənz, ænd
meks ɪt ˈpɒsɪbəl fɔ ðɪ ɪˈlɛktɜz tu prəˈnaˣʊns fɛr ənd klɪə ˈdʒʌdʒmənt, ə mɔə fɛr ɔə klɪə ˈdʒʌdʒmənt, ðæn wəd ˌʌðəˈwaˆɪz bi ðə
kʌjs. ænd ˈɛnɪˈwe, mʌtʃ tu ðɪ ɛmˈbɛrəsmənt əv sʌm pipəl, ðɛr ar
ˈoˣnlɪ tu drɪˑˈvɪʒən ˈlɑbɪz ɪn ðə haˑʊs əv ˈkɑmənz. sʌm wʊd laˆɪk
θri. sʌm wʊd laˆɪk faˆɪv. sʌm wʊd laˆɪk fɔː. bət hwɪn ðə ˈspikɜ
pʊts ðə ˈkwe stʃən frəm ðə tʃɛə ðɛrɪz ˈonlɪ tu θɪŋz tə du, tə
vot fɔːə ɔr əˈgɛnst. bət ðɛr ɪz ə θɜd, ən ðæt ɪz nɒt tə vot ə
tɔˣl, ən d͡ðæt ɪz ˈsʌmˌtaɪmz dʌn. bət ðɛ a oˣnlɪ tu ˈlɑbɪz ɪn

ðə haˑʊs əv ˈkamənz, ən ʔaɪ θɪŋk ɪt ɪz ə gʊd θɪŋ ðət ɪn ɑ̃ə
ˈkʌntrɪ wi ʃʊd hæˑ⊥v tu ˈpɑːtɪz, ət ˈɛnɪ ret tu gret ˈpɑːtɪz,
ænd ðət ðɛ ʃʊd bi ˈgʌvəmənt ɪn·ˌapəˈzɪʃən——ðə ˈgʌvəmənt tə
gʌvən wɪð ði əsɛnt əv ðə haˑʊs əv kamənz ənd ɪts səpoɹət, ɪf
ɪt kən geˑt ɪt, hwɪtʃ əz ɪts ˈbɪznɪs. ɪf ɪt dʌznt ðɛn ðə pipəl
məst dɪˈsa͡ɪd....]

   JAN MASARYK, former president of Czecho-Slovakia:
[aɪ wʌndɜ weðə hwɛˈnɛvə ɾaɪ se hʌᵋ lo tu ju foks ɪt minᵹ
d͡ʒət d͡ʒɛɾ ɪz ə medᵹɜ ˈkɾaɪsɪs ɑn. aɪ wʊd het tu bi ə ˈd͡ʒonʌ,
bət əgeˑn·ɪt wʊd·naᵵ bi nàɪs əv mì tu riˈfjuz ə vɛɾɪ kaɪn(d)ˌɪn-
ˈvaɪt frʌm ðɪˑ, juˈnaɪtəd stets əv əˈmɛɾɪkʌ tʊ tel ju haʊ ɪt
fiɫz tu bì ɪˑnsaɪd ə vʌᵃ lgɜ ʌˈnedᵹuˌketəd ˈnå̃tsɪ̀ hwel. bɪˈliv
mi, ɪt ɪz ə ʃakɪŋ ɪkˈspiɾɪəns æn maɪ lɪtʃ ˈkʌntrɪ dɪˈzɜvz ɔl
ðə prez ðə disnt pipˌ ʌᵊv ðə wɜld ɑ ˈgɪvɪŋ hɜ. bət aɪ ɪnˈtɛn
tʊ traɪ ɛˈlɪmɪˑˌnetɪŋ ˈtʃɛko sloˈvakɪə frəm maɪ lɪtˌ tɔk æz
mʌtʃ əz pasəbl hæˑvɪŋ wʌnts əgən reᵏitəˌɾetəd maɪ ˌfʌndəˈmɛntəl
reˈfjuzəl tu ˌakˌsept ˈmjunɪk ɔr ˈɛnɪθɪŋ ˈfalowɪŋ ˈmjunɪk ʌp tu
det. aɪ əm ˈspikɪŋ frʌm ðə sem lʌndən frʌm hwɪˑtʃ ju hɜd mi
hwïn aɪ wəz ˈfaɪtɪŋ fɔr ˌɪntəˈnæʃənəl ˈdisənsɪ̀ ə jɪɾ əgo. tuˈde
aɪ m ˈfaɪtɪŋ fɔ ðə ˈvɛri sem ɪʃju bət nat æz ən əfɪʃəl pɜsən bət
æz wʌn əv ðə kauntləs mɪljənz əv əˈnanɪˑmʌs ˌrepɾɪˈzɛntətɪvz ʌv
ðə ˈgloɾɪjəs aɪdɪə əv ˈlɪbətɪˑ, fridəm æn raɪt ovə maɪt....]

APPENDIX C

These transcriptions are made with pause marks, in addition to the occasional modifiers previously used. Speech samples from public figures, professional readers and actors, and student speakers are presented.

Some samples were taken from broadcasts, most of which originated with the Columbia Broadcasting System and were heard in the Seattle, Washington, area over KIRO; others originated with KIRO. Electrical transcriptions of the broadcasts were presented to the University of Washington by KIRO for whatever scholarly use might be made of them, and they constitute a historical collection with the School of Communications. Speech samples from professional readers and actors were taken from commercial records and are used through the courtesy of Caedmon Publishers.

Section I--Public Figures (varying dialects)

JAMES F. BYRNES, American politician and jurist:

[bɪˈkɑẓ wi no ðət wi kən wɪn ðɪs wɔˀ| tu ˈmɪnɪ əv əs ɑɾ
ˈæktɪŋ| æz ɪf ðə wɔɾ ɪz ˌɒlˈrɛdɪ wʌn|| ɪt ɪz nɑ̂t|| ðə most
ˈkrɪtɪkəl ən ðə ˈblʌdɹəst ̄bætǀz əv ðə wɔɾˈ ɑɾ əhɛd əv ə̂s||
aʊe bɔɪz ət ðə frʌ̂nt ɑ nɒt ˈfaɪtɪŋ| æz ɪf ðə wɔɾ wɚ ɔlˈrɛdɪ
wɑ̂n|| ðe no| ðæt mʌtʃ ˈfaɪtɪŋ æn ˈdaɪːŋ məst kɒm| bɪˈfɔɾ ə
ˈvɪktəɾɪ brɪŋẓ pis|| ðe ɑ ˈfaɪtɪŋ hadɚ ðæn ɛvɚ|| wi ɒn ðə hom
frʌ̂nt mʌst ˈɔlso faɪt hadɚ ðæn ɛvə| tu wɪn ðə wɔɾ ən stɑp ðə
daɪːŋ|| tu wɪn ðə pis| ænd mek ɪt ˈlæstɪŋ|| wi əv kʌm ə lɒŋ we
sɪns pɚl ˈha:bə|| ṇstɛd əv ən ɑːmɪ əv wʌn mɪljən sɪks hʌ́ndəd ṇ
θɜtɪ faɪv θaʊzən| tude wi hæv ən ɑːmɪ əv sɛvən mɪljən θri hʌn-
drəd ən ˈnaɪntɪ θaʊzən|| ðæt ɑːmɪ ɪz.betɚ iˈkwɪpt| æn betɚ
trend ðɛ²n ˈɛnɪ ɑːmɪ ɪn ˈhɪstrɪ|| aʊr ˈprɑgrɪs ɪn prəˈdʌktʃən|
ɪz æz ɪnˈkɜɪdʒɪŋ tu ʌs| æz ɪt ɪz ˌdɪˈskɚᶦdʒɪŋ tu aʊr ˈɛnɪmɪz||
wi prədust læs,mʌnθ| ɔlmost əz ˈmɛnɪ ˈɛrplenz æz wi hæd ɪn aʊr
ɑːmɪ ɛr fɔrs| æt.ðə taɪm əv pɚl ha:bə....]

329

MADAME CHIANG KAI-SHEK, wife of the Chinese statesman:

['ledɪz æn 'dʒɛntəlmən:|| tu ɔI maɪ frɛnz ɪn ə'mɛrɪkʌ| ɪn-
'kludɪŋ ðgʊz ʌv ju hu hæv kʌm hɪə tu lɪsən tu mi ðɪs 'ivnɪŋ|
aɪ wɪʃ tʊ ɪk'sprɛs tʊᵊ jul maɪ 'haːt'fɛlt ə,prɪi'ʃjeʃən əv jʊə
kən'sɜn fə mi| ænd jɔə 'θɔtfɪnɪs fɔ raɪ ,wɛl 'biɪŋ| hwɪtʃ ju
hæv so 'dʒɛnrəsli 'dɛmənstreʇɪd ɪn 'vɛrɪjəs wez| 'djʊrɪŋ maɪ
'ɪlnɪs| ænd ,kʌnvə'lɛsəns|| aɪ 'wʌndʌ| weðə aɪ kən kən've tə
jul haʊ 'dipli tʌʇʃt aɪ æm| ðæt so 'mɛnɪ pipəl| frʌm 'ɛvrɪ sɛk-
ʃən əv ə'mɛrɪkʌ| hæv tekn̩ ðə taɪm æn trʌb| tʊ sɛnd mi 'mɛsɪdʒəz
ʌv əfɛkʃən ænd gʊd'wɪl|| aɪ wɪʃ aɪ kʊd ɪk'nɑlɪdʒ| 'ɛvrɪ wʌn| əv
ðə 'mɛnɪ θaʊzənz ʌv 'lɛtʌz| ænd 'tɛligræmz hwɪtʃ aɪ hæv rɪ'sivd||
bət sɪnts ðɪs ɪz ɪm'pɑsɪbəl| wɪl ju nɒt lɛt mi tek ðɪs əpə'tjun-
ɪti tu θæŋk jul wʌn ænd ɔl||| aɪ wɪʃ 'tul ðæt ɪt wə 'pɑsɪbəl fə
mi tʊ ɪk'sɛpt jɔr ɪnvə'teʃənz̩| tu 'vɪzɪt jɔə stets| 'sɪtɪz| 'kal-
ɪdʒəz| 'tʃɜtʃəz| ænd ʌðə ,ɔːgɪnə'zeʃənz||,....]

THOMAS E. DEWEY, former governor of New York:

[ɪn ðə sɪks jɪrz| frʌm 'naɪntin 'θɜtɪ'θri| tə ðɪs ɛnd ə(v)
'naɪntin 'θɜtɪj 'et| wi nidəd 'θɜtɪ sɪks 'brɪljən ,dɑləz| 'dʒʌst
tə rɪ,plɛs ænd tə ,stænd 'stɪl|| ðə græn(d) ,totəl əv 'ɔːl 'kæpə-
ətəl| ,pʊt 'ɪntʊᵊ ar prə'dʌktɪv ,plænt ɪn ðoz 'jɪrz wəz ,onlɪ
,twɛntɪ ,naɪn ,brɪljən 'dɑləz| nat 'ivən ə,nʌf tə ,mek ʌp fə
'wɛr æn 'tɛr|| 'sevən 'brɪljən 'dɑləz ̄,ʃɔrt 'ivən ʌv ,holdɪŋ aʊr
'on| ar prədʌktɪv 'plænt æn i'kwɪpmənt hæv bɪn ,rʌnɪŋ 'daʊn ət
ðə 'hil æᵊt ðɪ ,ævrɪdʒ ,ret əˆv ,mɔr ðən ə ,brɪljən ,dɒləz ə jɪr||
'ivən ɪf wi wɚ ,holdɪŋ ar on| 'ðæt ,wʊdnt bi ə'nʌf|| ɪn ðə 'læst
dɛk,ed 'aʊr ,pɑpjə'leʃən ɪn'krist| ,nɪrlɪ ʌᵊ 'mɪljən 'pipl ʌᵊ
'jɪr|| hæf ə ,mɪljən nu 'wɚkɚz ə ,jɪr ar ,kʌmɪŋ tə mə'tʃɚeti|
ðæts ,hæf ə ,mɪljən mɔr ðən rɪⁱ,taɪr ɔr 'daɪ 'ɛvrɪ 'sɪŋgəl
'jɪr|| ,wi nid tu ɪks'pænd ar plænt| 'ɛvrɪ jɪr| 'dʒʌst tə kip
'ʌp wɪð ar 'groɪŋ ,pɑpjə'leʃən| tə gɪv ðoz nju ,wɚkɚz 'dʒɑbz|
æn(d) 'ðɛn wi mʌᵊst mek ɪt ,lɑrdʒɚ 'jɛt ɪf wi ar ə'gɛn tə riⁱ-
'zum ðə ,stɛ̈dɪ ,raɪz ɪn 'aʊr ,stændəd əv ,lɪvɪŋ....]

QUEEN MOTHER ELIZABETH, of England:

[æz jɔə petrən| aɪ æⁱm 'vɛrɪ glæ⁺d ɪn'did tə bi hɪə| tə tek
paːt ɪn ðiz̝ ,sɛ⁺lɪ'breʃənz|| æ⁺nd| ɪt ɪz ən 'ædɪd pleʒɚ tə mi|

tə nʒʊ ðət maɪ wɜdz ɑː ˈbiɪŋ ˌriˈled‖ nɑtˤ ˈʒʊnˈlɪ tə ðə ˈfɜðɪst
pɑːts əv gret brɪtn‖ bət ˈɔlsɜʊ tʊ ˈmɛmbʌz ɔn ðɪ ʌðə saɪd əv ðɪ
ətˈlæntɪk‖ ˌhɜʊldɪŋ ˈsɪmɪlə^ˌseˤɪˈbreʃənz‖ ænd hu ɑ nʒʊ ˌlɪs-
nɪŋ‖ tu ɔˤl‖ ˈmɛmbɜz əv ðɪ əˌsosɪˈeʃən‖ ɪn wʌt ˈɛvə^pɑːtˤ ə
θə wɜːld ðe me biˈ aɪ send ˈgrɪtˤɪŋz frəm ðɪs hom‖ aɪ wəd laɪk
ˈɔˤlsɜʊ tə se ə speʃˈ wɜd əv əˈpriʃɪˤeʃən‖ tə mɛmbəz əv stɑf‖
ænd ˈklʌbˈlidʌz bɜʊθ hɪɹ ænd ˈɜʊvəˈsiz‖ jɔez ɪz ðə tɑsk əv
ˈfɪtˤɪŋ juθ fɔ ðɪ rɪsˌpɑnsəˈbɪlɪtɪ+z əv təˈmɑrɜʊ‖ fɔˤ ðɪs‖
ju hæv tə kip əbrɛst wɪθ mɑːdən θɔ+t‖ æ+nd‖ æt ðə sem taɪm‖
tə gɪv ðə jʌŋ‖ ðæ+t krɪstʃən pɜːpəs‖ æn dɪˈrɛkʃənəl laɪf wɪ-
ˈðaˤʊt hwɪtʃ‖ no rɛəl bətˤ əmɛnt ɪz ˈpasɪb‖‖ jɔə tɑsk ðɛˤn‖
ɪz bɜʊθ ə haɪ ˈprɪvɪlɪdʒ ænd ə ˌdɛdɪˈkeʃn....]

CORDELL HULL, former secretary of state:

[...aɪ æm əˈmenslɪ plizd‖ tə bi bæk ɪn ðɪz ˌlɛdʒəˈsletɪv
hɔlz‖ ænd tu mit‖ numəs frɛndz‖ old ænd̥ nu‖ pəˈtɪkjələlɪ‖ ðoz
fɔrmə ˈkɑligz ɪn ðə tu haʊzəz‖ fɔr its əv huᵛm‖ aɪ hæv lɔŋ
ˌentəˈtend ˈsentəments ʌv gretəst rɪˈspɛkt‖ ænd ðɪ most dʒɛn-
jəwən æˈfɛkʃən‖‖ aɪ ˈpriᴵʃet ˈdiplɪ‖ ðə ˈkʌmplɪmənt‖ əv biɪŋ
ɪnˈvaɪtəd tə mit wɪθ ju tədeˈ‖ bʌt aɪ ˈpriᴵʃjet ivən mɔˤə‖ ðə
fækt‖ ðæt‖ baɪ jʊr ɪnvəˈteʃən‖ ju hæv ˈɛmfəˌsaɪzd jʊr prəfə-
faʊnd ɪntrəst ɪn ðə ˈprɪnsəpəlz æn ˈpɑlɪsɪz‖ fɔ hwɪtʃ ðə ˈmʌs-
ˈkaʊ kɑnfrəns stʊd‖ ænd ɪn ðə progrəs med baɪ ðɪ pəˌtɪseˈpetɪŋ
gʌvəments ɪn ˈkerɪŋ ðɛm fəwəd‖‖ ɪn ðə maɪndz əv lc ʌv əs hɪə
prɛznt‖ ænd ʌv ðə mɪljənz əv ʌˈmerkənz lc ovə ðə ˈkʌntrɪ‖ ðer
ɪz‖ æn ðer kæn biˈ æt ðɪs momənt bʌt wʌn kənˈsumɪŋ θɔt‖ tu dəfit
ðɪ ˈɛnəmɪ æs̄ spidəlɪ əz pɑsəb‖....]

ALFRED M. LANDON, former governor of Kansas:

[hwʌt ar ðə fjutʃə ˈpɑləsɪz ʌv əˈmerəkə?‖ θæt ɪz θə gret
kwestʃən‖ ðət ðə wɜld ɪz ˈæskɪŋ tədeˈ‖ ænd sɪnts ðə læst əˈlɛk-
ʃn‖ hwɪtʃ gev ðɪ rɪˈpʌblɪkən ˈpartɪ‖ sʌtʃ e riˈsɜdʒəns ʌv
strɛŋθ‖ ðə wɜld hæz bɪn ˈæskɪŋ ɪtˈsɛlf‖ hwʌt ɪz ðə pəˈzɪʃən
əv ðɪ rɪˈpʌblɪkən ˈpartɪ‖ ænd hwʌt ar ˈɪts ˈpɑləsɪz?‖‖ ðə
ˈmerəkən pipˈl ar ˈvɪwɪz ˌɪntəˈested əv ˈkɔrs‖ ɪn ðə næʃnəl
ˈɪʃjuz kənˈfrʌntɪŋ ðəm‖ æn ivən ɪn taɪm əv wɔr‖ ðe ɪnˈsɪst ɔn
ˈbiɪŋ fri‖ tu dɪsˈkʌs ðɪz ˈpɑləsɪz‖ æn tə tek ʌp əˈpozɪŋ saɪdz‖

ɪf ðe du nat əgri‖ təde ðɛrz wʌn 'kwestʃən ɔn hwɪtʃ ðɛr ɪz
no dɪ'vɪʒən‖ ʌv ə'pɪnjən‖ ɪn ə'mɛrəkə‖ wi mʌst wɪn ðə wɔr‖
ar θats‖ ar 'ɛnədʒi‖ ar weɪθ‖ ar di'votəd tə ðæt ɛn(d)‖ ðɛr
ɪz 'skɛrslɪ e hom‖ ðæt hæz nat kən'trɪbjətəd‖ ɪðɚ ə sʌn‖ ar ə
dɑtɚ‖ tə ðə kɑz‖ əv ar bi'lʌvəd 'kʌntrɪ....]

MRS. ELEANOR ROOSEVELT, wife of the former president of
the United States, Franklin D. Roosevelt:

[aɪ ˌθɪⁱŋk ɪt 'saʊndəd ə lɪtḷ 'ɑːbəˌtrɛrɪ ɔn 'maɪ ˌpɑːt
ðət aɪd 'wɒntəˌdʒu tə ˌask 'kwestʃənz‖ bʌt ðə 'rizən aɪ‖ wəd‖
'laɪk tə hæv ˌpipḷ ask 'kwestʃənz‖ ɪz ðət 'frikwəntlɪj‖ hwɛⁱn
wi tɔk ə'baʊt ðɪ⊥ juˈnaɪtəd 'neʃənz‖ ðə vɛrɪ θɪŋz ðæt 'sʌmˌwʌn
ɪn ðɪ ˌɔdiəns wəd ˌlaɪk tə hɪr əˌbaʊt‖ ɑ ˌnɛvə 'mɛnʃənd‖ ænd
ˌso‖ aɪ ˌɔlwez ˌfil ðət ðə 'kwestʃən ˌpɪrɪəd 'ɔftən ˌbrɪŋz 'aʊt‖
ðə θɪŋz ðət ar əv pə'tɪkjələ 'ɪntrəst‖ tu ði 'ɛrɪə‖ hwɪtʃ ju me
bi 'ɪn‖ ənd aɪm 'kwaɪt ˌʃʊə ðət ˌhɪə 'ɪn ðə ˌnɔθˌwest‖ hwɛə ju
ɑ ˌdurɪŋ ə 'gret 'diəl‖ ˌfɔːə‖ ðɪⁱ juˌnaɪtəd ˌneʃənzɔ ɪn ˌjɔ
'skulz‖ ənd ɪn jɔə 'æktɪv ˌɔgənɪ'zeʃənz‖ ðɛ 'mʌst ˌbi ˌkwes-
tʃnz‖ ðæt 'ju wʊd 'laɪk tə hæv ˌænsəd‖ ˌɪf‖ ˌwi no ðɪj 'ansəz‖
ən əz ˌlɔŋzaɪ hæv mɪstə 'aɪkəlˌbɜgə tu‖ ˌansə hwɛn aɪ 'dont no
ðɪ ˌansɜ‖ aɪ fil ˌkwaɪt ˌsef ɪn sə'dʒestɪŋ ðət ju 'ask ðə
'kwestʃənz‖ ˌnaʊ‖ ˌaɪm tə tɔk əbaʊt ðɪⁱ juˌnaɪtəd ˌneʃənz ˌænd
'ju‖ ænd ˌðæt 'taɪtḷ əv ˌkɔəs ɪz ˌgɪvən‖ bə'kɔːz‖ ˌso 'menⁱ əv
ʌs 'fil ðət ði juˌnaɪtəd ˌneʃənz ɪz ˌsʌmpθɪŋ 'far ə'wej‖ frʌm
'ʌs əz ˌɪndə'vɪdʒwəlz‖ ˌoʊ 'jɛs əts 'hɛdˌkwɔtəz ɚɪn nu ˌjɔːk‖
ænd ə‖ wi ˌhɪr ə gʊd ˌdil əˌbaʊt 'ræŋglɪŋ ðət ˌgoz ˌɔn ɪn ðə
sɪˌkjʊrətɪ 'kaʊnsəl‖ ˌbʌt‖ 'wi lid aʊr ˌon 'laɪvz ənˌwi ˌdont
ˌsi ðət ðɪ juˌnaɪtəd ˌneʃənz 'riəlɪ əfɛks əs ˌvɛrɪ ˌmʌtʃ....]

WENDELL WILLKIE, American politician from Indiana:

[gʌvənɚ 'duwɪ‖ mædəm dʒɑŋ‖ (Madame Chiang) maɪ fɛlo əmær-
əkənz‖ aɪm diˣ'laɪtəd‖ tʊ ri'sɪprəˌket‖ æn ˌɪntɚ'dʌkʃən tu
ən ə'mærəkən ɔdjənts‖ əv mædəm dʒɑŋ‖ far ʃi‖ ɪnɚ'dʌst mi‖ tə
sɛvrəl tʃaɪ'niz 'ɔdɪjənsəz dʒʌst ə fju mʌns əgo‖ ɪt ɪz bɪn maɪ

ˈapɚˌtunətɪ| tu əv sin| æn t̬əv dɪˈskʌst| mæt̬ɚz| av ðə prɛzənt
de wɝld| wɪθ ðə lidɚz əv ˈmɛnɪ əv ðə ˈkʌntrɪz əv ðɪs wɝld| ɪn
ðə ˈtɛrəˌtɔrɪz ɪn wɪtʃ ðə ˈapərɛt| ənd aɪ θɪˈŋk aɪ kən ˈse ət|
wɪˌðaʊt ɛnɪ ˈɪnəˈprɔprɪət| kʌmˈpærəsənz| ðət ðə gɛst əv anɚ hɪr
ðɪs ˈivnɪŋ| ɪz ðə most ˈfæsənət̬ɪŋ ˌwʌn av ðɛm ˈɔl|| me aɪ ˈɔlso
ˈse ðæt ʃi ɪz ðə most ˈpɝsn̩lɪ biˈlʌvd| baɪ ðə ˈpipəl av hɚ ˈkʌn-
trɪ|| ɪt ɪz əv kɔrs ˈsupɚˈabvɪəs tə spik av ɚ wɪt| ənd ɚ tʃarm
æn ɚ gres ænd ɚ ˈbjutɪ| bʌtʃu mɪs ðə pɜpəs av ɚ laɪf ænd ɚ
ˈkærɪtɚ| ɪf ju ˈθɪŋk ʃi ɪz ˈdʒʌst ən endʒəl| ʃi me bi wʌn bʌt
ʃiz ən əˈvɛndʒɪŋ endʒəl|| fɔr ʃi muvz wɪð ə pɝpəs| æn ʃi muvz
wɪð ə maɪnd|| ɪt wəz tʃaɪnə| ðət nat əlon fɝst wɪθstud| ði
əsɔlt əv ði əgrɛsɚz| bʌt ɪt wəz tʃaɪnʌ ðət fɝst ʌndɚstud ðə
tru netʃɚ av ðɪs wɔr....]

MRS. ROBERT TAFT, wife of the former senator from Ohio:
[aɪ æm glæd tə hæv ə paːrt ɪn ðɪs ˈbrɔdˌkæst| an ðə ˈsʌb-
dʒɪkt əv ðə ˈples əv ðə ˈlig əv wɪmən votɚz| ɪn ðə pəˈlɪtɪkəl
ˈfild|| aɪ həv bɪn ə sɪnˈsɪr bəˈlivɚ ɪn ðə lig aɪˈdɪə| ɛvɚ
sɪns ðɪs ˌɔrgənəˈzeʃən wəz ˌlantʃt| sun æftɚ ˌwɪmɪn wɚ ˌgræntəd
ðə ˌraɪt əv ˈsʌfrɪdʒ|| ði aɪˈdɪə hwɪtʃ wəz rɪˈspansəbəl fɚ ðə
ˈfaʊndɪŋ əv ðə ˌlig əv ˌwɪmən ˈvotɚz| ˈwʌz ðət ɪn əˈkwaɪrɪŋ
ə vot| ˈwɪmɪn hæd ˌtekən ɪntə ðɛr ˌhændz| ə trɪˈmɛndəslɪ ˈpaʊə-
fəl ænd ɪmˌpɔrtn̩t ˌtuwəl| fɔr ˌbɛtɚ ɔr fɔr ˌwɝs| ænd ðət ðe
wɪʃt tə lɝn tə juz ɪt ˈwaɪzlɪ| ɪn ɔrdɚ tə prəmot ðə ˈdʒɛnərəl
ˈwɛlˌfɛr|| ˈðæt wəz e naˈivlɪ ˈnju aɪˈdɪə ɪn ðə pəˌlɪtɪkəl
ˌfild|| ˈno grup əv pipl̩| ˈɛb| tu əˈten ðə ˈprɪvəlɪdʒəz əv
ˌsɛlf ˈgʌvəmənt| hæd ˌɛvɚ biˈfɔr ˈdaʊtɪd ðɛr ˈon əˈbɪlətɪ t̬u
dɪsˈtʃardʒ ðɛr rɪˈspansəˌbɪlətɪ | æz ˌnjulɪ ˌflɛdʒd ˈrulɚz
ʌv ðɛr ˈon ˈlænd....]

EDDIE CANTOR, American actor:
[a ju ˈsɪt̬ɪŋ ˈkʌmftəblɪ ɪn jɚ ˌon hom əz jə ˌhɪə maɪ ˈvɔɪs?||
a ju ˌðɛə wɪð ju ˈfæməlɪ | ən dɪˈsaɪdəd tə tɝn an ðə ˈredɪo tu
ˌlɪsən tu wʌˌtɛvɚ ˈkʌmz?|| aɪ kænət ˈprɑməs tə prɪˌzɝv ðɪs mud

əv ˈkwaɪət ən wɛl ˈbiɪŋ‖ aɪ ˌwɒntˉtə mek ju ˈæŋgrɪ ‖ aɪ ˌwɒnt
tə mek jʊə ˈblʌd ˈbɔɪl‖ æn jʊə ˌhɑːt ˈek‖ aɪ wɒnt tʊ tɛl ju
əbaʊt ˈʌðə ˌhomz hwɛ ˈdeθ ɪz ə ˈkɒnstən(t) ˈgɛst‖ æn dɪˈspɛr ən
ˌsɛpəˈreʃən ɑ ðə ˌdelɪⁱ ˈpɒeʃən ə(v) ˌfaɪn ˈwɪmən laɪk jʊə ˈwaɪf
æn swit ˌtʃɪldrən laɪk jʊron ˈsʌnz‖ æn ˈdɒtəz‖‖ ju ˈɑr ən əˈmerⁱ-
ɪ⋆kən‖‖ æn ˈæz ən əˈmerɪ⋆kən ju ˌo ðə ˌʌndəˈstændɪŋ‖ jʊə ˈkaɪnd-
nəs‖ ænd jʊr əˈsɪstəns‖‖ ju ˌo ətˉtə ðəm fə ˈmenɪⁱ ˈrɪzənz‖‖ bət
ˈtʃɪflɪˣ bɪˌkɒẓ ju ˈɑr æn əˈmerɪkən huz ˈlaɪf ən gʌvəmənt ɑ
ˈmotəveȶəd ˌnɑt ˌonlɪⁱ baɪ ˌwɜdz laɪȿ dəˈmakrəsi æn ˈfridəm‖‖
bʌⁱt‖ baɪ ˌwɑt ðiz ˌwɜdz ˈmin‖‖ ju ˈowətˉtə ðəm fɔr jʊr ˌom
pəˈtɛkʃən əz ˈwɛl‖‖ fɔr ɪf ɪn ˌenɪ ˈstaɪflɪŋ ˈgetowl‖ ðer ɪgˌzɪst
ˈmĕn ˈwɪmən ən ˈtʃɪldrən hu ˌno ðæt ði ˈæks‖ æn ðə naɪf‖ æn
ðə ˈhæŋmənz ˈrop ɑ ði ˌonlɪⁱ ˈsɜtəntɪz ɪn ðə ˌbɪtə ˈlaɪf‖ ˈju‖
æn əˈmerəkən‖ ˈkænət rɛst ˌɪzɪjən jʊ ˈbɜd‖‖ ju ˈkænət ˌdu ˌðæt
bɪˌkɒs‖ ɪn̊ ə ˌwɜl(d) wɪtʃ pəˌmɪts ˌsʌtʃ‖ ˈharəz‖ ðə rɪˈzʌᵛlts
wɪl ˈsip ˈθru tʊ jʊrˌon ˈtʃɪldrən‖ jʊˌron ˌwaɪf‖ jʊrˌon ˈgrænt-
tʃɪldrən‖ ˈnaʊ‖ ɔə ˈletərˌan....‖

JOSEPH DAVIES, American diplomat:

[...wʌn wik frəm nɛkst ˈmʌndɪ‖ ðə prezədən(t) ənd ðə ˈvaɪs
prezdənt wɪl‖ æz wi se bæk hom‖ bi swɔrn ɪn‖‖ ɔlˈredɪj ɪn æn-
ˌtɪsəˈpeʃən əv ði: vɛnt‖ ˌgrænd stændz ɚ biɪŋ əˈrektəd ɪn frʌnt
əv ðə ˈhwaɪt ˌhaʊs‖ æt ˈvæntɪdʒ pɔɪnts əlɔŋ hɪsˈtɔrɪk pɛnsəl-
ˈvenjə ˈævənu‖ æn ɪn ðə plazə ɪn frʌnt əv ðə neʃənz kæpɪtl‖‖
hwer ðə prezdənt wɪl tek ðɪⁱ oθ əv ɔfɪs‖ æn dɪˈlɪvɚ hɪz ɪˈnɒg-
jərəl ədrɛs‖‖ æz ðə det əˈprotʃəz‖ ðə dʒɔɪnt kənˈgrɛʃnəl ɪˈnɒg-
(jə)ˈrəl kəˈmɪtɪ əv ðɪ juˈnaɪtəd stets sənət‖ ŋ ðə haʊs əv repre-
zentətɪvz‖ æn ðə prezdənts ɪnˈɔgjərəl kəˈmɪtɪ‖ wɪð ɪts ˈmenɪ
ˈsʌbˌkəmɪtɪz‖ ɑr prɪˈpeɪrɪŋ ði faɪnəl (ə)rɛndʒmənts‖ fɔr ðɪs
ˈmemrəbəl əkeʒən‖ æn prɪˈpeɪrɪŋ ɪts wɛlkəm‖ tu ðə θaʊzənz əv
ɑr ˈfɛlo sɪtəzənz hu plæn tu paˈtɪsəpet ɪn ðiz ˈserəmonɪz
hɪr‖‖ ði æktʃuəl ɪnˈdʌkʃən əv ðə prezdənt ən ði vaɪs prezdənt
ɪntu ɔfɪs‖ ɪz ˈverɪ sɪmpəl....‖

FRANK GANNETT, American publisher:

[aʊr fɜst ˈdutɪ tə ˌsɪvəlaɪˈzeʃən] ɪn ðɪs jɪr əv wɜld ˈkraɪsɪs] ɪz raɪt hɪr ɪn ðɪ juˈnaɪtəd ˈstets]] bətwin naʊ æn noˈvɛmbɚ fɪfθ] ænd ðɛr ɚ ˈonlɪ ˈhʌndrəd ən ˈnaɪntɪ ˈfaɪv dez biˈfɔr ɪˈlɛkʃən] wi mʌs drˈsaɪd ðə fjutʃɚ əv əˈmɛrɪkʌ]] hwɛðɚ wi ʃæl bi e fri pipəl] ɔr slevz ʌv ðə stet]] hwɛðɚ wi ʃæl ˈmɛnˈten aʊr sɪstəm əv ˌkɑnstəˈtuʃənəl ˈgʌvəmənt æn fri ˈɛntəpraɪz] Andɚ hwɪtʃ ðɪs neʃən æz gron ˈgret æn ˈstrɔŋ ɔr hwɛðɚ wi ʃæl go fɚðɚ] ˈɪntu næʃənəl ˈsoʃəlɪzəm] nu ˈdiəlɪzm] ˈfæʃɪzəm] ˈnætzɪˌɪzəm] ɔr ˈkʌmjənɪzəm]] tɔrd wʌn mæn rul] e ˈdɪktetɚʃɪp]] ˈrɪsəntlɪ ði pɔrts əv ˈnɔrwe wɚ opənd tʊ ðɪ ˈɛnəmɪ baɪ tretɚz. ˈɪnˌsaɪd ðə ˈkʌntrɪ]] wi ɚ rɪˈmaɪndəd əv ðə ˈstɔrɪ əv ðə wʊdn̩ hɔrs] æn ðə fɔl əv trɔɪ]] hwɛn ðə ˈtrɔdʒənz ædˈmɪtəd ðə wʊdn̩ hɑrs] kənˈsɪlɪŋ soldʒəz ʌv drˈstrʌkʃən] ðe wɚ ˈʌnəˌwɛrr əv hwʌt ðe wɚ ˈduwɪŋ]] ðə wɚst ˈɛnəmɪ əv ˈsɛlfˌgʌvəmənt] ɪz ˌʌnəˈwɛrnəs]] hɪtlɚ hwɚl ˈraɪzɪŋ tu paʊwɚ æn ˈfæsənɪŋ ʃækəlz əv ˈtɪrənɪ an ðə dʒɚmən pip!] ˈædɔlf ˈhɪtlɚ] sed]] ɪt gɪvz ʌs ˈnætzɪz speʃəl plɚ̌ɜ̌ɚ] tə si haʊ ðə ˈpipl əbaʊt ʌs ɑr ˈʌnəwɛr əv hwʌt ɪz ˈrɪəlɪ ˈhæpənɪŋ ˈtu ˌðɛm]] ɪzn̩t ðæt ðə sɪtʃəˈweʃən ɪn əˈmɛrəkə....]

H. STYLES BRIDGES, American politician from New Hampshire:

[æz wʌn əv jɔ ˌsɛnətəz ɪn ˈwɔʃɪŋtən] aɪ wɔntə ˈkʌm ɪntə jɔ ˈhom təˌnaɪt] ən dɪskʌs wɪð ju eˌgɛn ðæt grev ˈprɑbləm] wɪð hwɪtʃ wi ɑr ˌɔl kənˈsɜnd]] ˌnuˈtrælətɪ] n̩ ðə ˈpis əv aʊə ˌkʌntrɪ]] wɪˌðɪn ðə wik aɪ wəz ˌgɪvən ðə ˌprɪvɪldʒ əv ˈspikɪŋ tə ˌju ɔn ðɪs ˌsem ˌsʌbdʒɪkt]] ət ðæt taɪm a(ɪ) med ˌsɛvrəl ˈstetmənts] hwɪtʃ aɪ wəd laɪk tə rəˌpit eˈgɛn fɚ ˈɛmfəsɪs]] aɪ sed ˌðɛn] ən aɪ rəˌpit əˌgɛn] ðət ðə ˌgretɪst drˈzaɪɚ əv ˌaʊr pipl̩] ɪz tə rɪˌmen æt pis]] wɪð ðæt ˌstetmənt wi ɑr ˌɔl ɪn kəmˈplit əgˈrimənt]] ɜlɪ́ ðɪs wik aɪ ˌʌlso ˌstetɪd] ðæt ɪt wəz ˌklɪəlɪ ˈɛvədənt] ðət ðə gret ˌbʌlk əv ˈaʊr ˈpipəl] ˌsɪmpəˈθaɪzd wɪð wʌn saɪd] n̩ ðə prɛzənt ˌjʊrəˈpiən kɑnflɪkt....]

Section 2--Professional Actors and Readers

"Beauty," by Lord Byron as read by Tyrone Power:

[ʃi 'wɔks ɪn 'bjutɪ‖ lɑɪk ðə 'naɪt əv 'klaʊdləs 'klaɪmz
ænd ·'starɪ skaɪz‖ ænd ɔl ðəts bɛst əv 'dɑrk ænd 'braɪt mit ɪn
hɚ 'æspɛkt‖ ænd hɚ ͵aɪz‖ ðʌs 'mɛlod tə ðæt tɛndɚ laɪt‖ hwɪtʃ
'hɛvən tu 'gɔdɪ de di'naɪz‖ wʌn ʃed ðə mɔr‖ wʌn re ðə lɛs‖
ðæt hæf ɪm'pɛrd ðə 'nemləs gres wɪtʃ 'wevz ɪn 'ɛvrɪⁱ revən
trɛs‖ ɔr 'sɔftlɪ laɪtənz ɔr hɚ fes‖ hwɛr θɔts sə'rinlɪ swit‖
ɛk'sprɛs haʊ pjur haʊ dɪr ðɛr 'dwɛlɪŋ ples‖ æn an ðæt tʃik‖
ænd or ðæt braʊ soʊ sɔft‖ so kam jɛt ͵ɛloͣ'kwɛⁱnt‖ ðə smaɪlz
ðət wɪn‖ ðə tɪnts ðət gloʊ‖ bət tɛl əv dez ɪn gʊdnəs spɛnt‖
ə maɪnd æt pis wɪθ ɔl bi'lo‖ ə hart huz lʌv ɪz'ɪnoseͣnt....]

From "The Book of Job," as read by Herbert Marshall:

[lɛt ðə de 'pɛrɪʃ hwɛrɪn aɪ wəz bɔːn‖ ænd ðə naɪt hwɪtʃ
sɛd‖ ə mæn tʃaɪld ɪz kənsivd‖ lɛt ðæt de bi daːknəs‖ me gad
əbʌv nɔt sik ɪt‖ nͻə laɪt ʃaɪn əpɒn ɪt‖ lɛt glum æn dip
'daːknɪs klem ɪt‖ lɛt klaʊdz dwɛl əpan ɪt‖ lɛt ðə 'blæknɪs
əv ðə de 'tɛrɪ͵faɪ ɪt‖ ðæt naɪt‖ ðæt sɪk daːknəs siz ɪt‖
lɛt ɪt nɒt ri'dʒɔɪs əmʌŋ ðə dez əv ðə jɪͻ‖ lɛt ɪt nɒt kʌm
əntʊ ðə nʌmbər əv ðə mʌnθs‖ je‖ lɛt ðæt naɪt bi bærən‖ lɛt
no dʒɔɪfəl kraɪ bi hɜd ɪn ɪt‖ lɛt ðoz kɜs ɪt hu kɜs ðə de‖
hu a skɪld tu raʊz ʌp lɪ'vaɪəθən‖ lɛt ðə staːz əv ɪts dɔːn
bi daːk‖ lɛt ɪt hop fɔ laɪt̄bʌt hæv nʌn‖ nɔ si ðɪ 'aɪ͵dɪz
əv ðə mɔːnɪŋ‖ bɪ'kɔz ɪt dɪd nɒt ʃʌt ðə dɔːz əv maɪ mʌðəz wum‖
nɔ haɪd trʌbl frəm maɪ aɪz‖ hwaɪ dɪd aɪ nɒt daɪ æt bɜθ‖
'kʌm fɔθ frəm ðə wum ænd ɪk'spaɪə‖ hwaɪ du ðə niz rɪ'siv mi‖
ɔ hwaɪ ðə brɛsts ðət aɪ ʃʊd sʌk‖ fɔ ðɛn aɪ ʃʊd əv len daʊn
ən bin kwaɪət‖ aɪ ʃʊd hæv slɛpt‖ ðɛn aɪ ʃʊd hæv bɪn æt rɛst...]

From "Death," by John Donne as read by Frank Silvera:

[dɛθ| bi nɒt praʊd|| ðo sʌm hæv kɔld ði 'maɪtɪ ænd 'drɛdfʊl||
fɔ ðaʊ a nɒt so|| fɔ ðoz hum ðaʊ θɪŋkst ðaʊ dʌst ˌovəˈθro| daɪ
nɒt| pʊə dɛθ|| nɔ jɛt kænst ðaʊ kɪl mi|| frəm rɛst ænd slip
hwɪtʃ bʌt ðaɪ pɪktʃəz bi| mʌtʃ plɛʒʌ|| ðɛn frəm ði mʌtʃ mɔə
mʌst flo| ænd sʌnsɛt ɑə bɛst mɛn wɪð ði du go|| rɛst əv ðɛ
bonz| æn solz dɪˈlɪvərɪ|| ðaʊ aːt slev tʊ fet| tʃans| kɪŋ æn
dɛspərət mɛn| ænd dʌst wɪθ pɔɪzən wɔr ən 'sɪknɪs dwɛl|| æn
'papɪ ɔ tʃaːmz| kæn mek ʌs slip əz wɛl| ænd bɛtə ðən ðaɪ strok||
hwaɪ swɛlts ðaʊ ðɛn|| wʌn ʃɔːt slip past| wi wek iˈtɜnəlɪ|| æn
dɛθ ʃæl bi no mɔə|| dɛθ| ðaʊ ʃælt daɪ]

From "Sonnet XXX," by William Shakespeare as read by
Hurd Hatfield:

[hwɛn tʊ² ðə sɛʃənz əv swit saɪlənt θɔt| aɪ sʌmən ʌp rɪ-
ˈmɛmbrəns əv θɪŋz paᵉˈst| aɪ saɪ| ðə læk| ɑv 'mɛnɪ ə θɪŋ aɪ
sɔt|| ænd wɪð old woz| nju wel| maɪ dɪə taɪmz| wɛst|| ðɛn kæn
aɪ draʊn æn aɪ| ʌnˈjust tu flo| fɔ prɛʃəs frɛndz| hɪd| ɪn
dɛθs 'dɛtlɛs naɪt|| ænd wip əfrɛʃ| lavz lɔŋ sɪn(t)s kænsəld
wo| ænd mon ɔɪ ɪkˈspɛn(t)s əv 'mɛnɪ ə 'vænɪʃt saɪt|| ðɛn kæn
aɪ griv æt grivənsəz fɔˈɡɔn| ænd 'hɛvɪlɪ| frʌm wo tu wo| tɛl
ɔə ðə sæd əkaʊnt əy fɔbɪˈmonəd mon|| hwɪtʃ aɪ nju pe| æz ɪf
nat ped bəfɔ|| bʌt ɪf ðə hwaɪl|| aɪ θɪŋk an ði| dɪə frɛnd| ɔɪ
lɔsɪz a rɪˈstɔːd| ænd 'sɑroz| ɛnd]

From Annabel Lee," by Edgar Allan Poe as read by Basil
Rathbone:

[ɪt wəz 'mɛnɪ æn 'mɛnɪ ə jɪr əɡo|| ɪn ə kɪŋdəm baɪ ðə siː||
ðət ə medən ðɛ lɪvd hum ju me no baɪ ðə nem| əv ænəbɛl li||
ænd ðɪs medən ʃi lɪvd wɪð nó ʌðə θɔt| ðæn tu lʌv| æn bi lʌvd
baɪ mi|| aɪ wəz ə tʃaɪld ænd ʃi wəz ə tʃaɪld ɪn ðɪs kɪŋdəm baɪ
ðə si| bət wi lʌvd wɪθ ə lʌv ðət wəz mɔə ðən lʌv| aɪ æᵉn maɪ
ænəbɛl li|| wɪð ə lʌv ðət ðə wɪŋəd sɛrəfs əv hɛvn kʌvətəd hɜːr
ən mi|| ən ðɪs wəz ðə rizn ̣ðət lɔŋ əɡo ɪn ðɪs kɪŋdəm baɪ ðə

siǀ ə wɪnd blu aʊt ə ðə klaʊdǀ ˈtʃɪlɪŋ maɪ ˈbjutɪfəl ænəbelǀ
liǀ so ðət ə haɪ bɔːn kɪnzmən kem aʊt ən bɔ heɾ əwe frʌm miǀǀ tu
ʃʌt hɚ ʌp ɪn ə ˈsepəlkɝ ǀ ɪn ðɪs kɪŋdəm baɪ ðə siǀǀ ðɪ endʒəlzǀ
nɑt hæf so hæpɪ ɪn hevṇǀ went ˈenvɪɪŋ hɝ ən miǀǀ jɛsǀ ðæt wəz
ðə rizṇǀ əz ɔl men no ɪn ðɪs kɪŋdəm baɪ ðə siǀǀ ðət ðə wɪnd kem
aʊt əv ðə klaʊd baɪ naɪtǀ ˈtʃɪlɪŋ ən ˈkɪlɪŋ maɪ ænəbel liǀǀ ðə
lʌv əv ðoz hu wɝ oldə ðən wiǀ əv ˈmenɪ fɑ waɪzə ðən wiǀ ən
niðə ðɪ endʒəlz ɪn hevn əbʌvǀ nɔɾ ðə dimənz daʊn ʌndə ðə si
kən evə dɪˈsevə maɪ soǀ frəm ðə solǀ əv ðə ˈbjutɪfəl ænəbel liǀǀ
fɔɾ ðə mun nevə bimz wɪˈðaʊt ˈbrɪŋɪŋ mɪ drimz əv ðə ˈbjutɪfəl
ˈænəbel liǀǀ ænd ðə stɑːz nevə raɪz bət aɪ fil ðə braɪt aɪz əv
ðə ˈbjutɪfəl ˈænəbel liǀǀ ənd so ɔl ðə naɪt taɪdǀ aɪ laɪ daʊn
bə ðə saɪd əv maɪ dɑlɪŋ maɪ dɑlɪŋ maɪ laɪf ən maɪ braɪdǀǀ
ɪn ðə ˈsepəlkɝ ðɛɾ baɪ ðə siǀ ɪn hɝ tum baɪ ðə ˈsaʊndɪŋ si]

From "Father William," by Lewis Carroll as read by
Cyril Ritchard:

[ju a old faðə wɪljəm ðɪ jʌŋ mæn sedǀ æn jɔ he hæz bɪˈkʌm
ˈverɪ waɪtǀ ænd jɛt ju ɪnˈsɛsəntlɪ ˈstænd ɔn jʊ hedǀ dju
θɪŋk ət jɔ edʒ ɪt ɪz raɪt?ǀǀ ɪn maɪ juθǀ faðə wɪljəm rɪˈplaɪd tu
ɪz sʌnǀ aɪ fɪəd ɪt maɪt ɪndʒə ðə brenǀǀ bət naʊ ðət aɪm pɝfɪktlɪ
ʃʊɾ aɪ hæv nʌnǀǀ waɪ aɪ du ət əgeːn æn əgenǀǀ ju a old sed ðə
juθ æz aɪ menʃənd bɪˈfɔǀ ænd hæv gron most ʌnˈkamənlɪ fætǀ jɛt
ju tɝnd ə bæk ˈsʌməsɔlt ɪn æt ðə dɔɾǀ pre hwʌt ɪz ðə rizən əv
ðæt?ǀǀ ɪn maɪ juθ sed ðə sedʒǀ æz i ʃʊk ɪz gre lɒksǀǀ aɪ kept
ɔl mɪ lɪmz verɪ sʌpəl baɪ ðɪɾ jus əv ðɪs ɔɪntməntǀ wʌn ˈʃɪlɪŋ
ðə bɒksǀ əlaʊ mi tə sel ju ə kʌpəlǀǀ ju a old sed ðə juθ æn
jɔɾ dʒɔz ɑ tu wik fə ˈenɪθɪŋ tʌfə ðən ˈsjuɪtǀ jet ju ˈfɪnɪʃt
ðə gus wɪθ ðə bonz ænd ðə bikǀ pre haʊ dɪd ju ˈmænɪdʒ tə du
ɪt?ǀǀ ɪn maɪ juθǀ sed ɪz faðəǀ aɪ tʊk tu ðə lɔːǀ ænd agjud
ɪtʃ kes wɪθ mɪ waɪfǀǀ æn ðə ˈmʌskjulə strɛŋθ hwɪtʃ ɪt gev tə
mi dʒɔǀ həz lastəd ðə ɾest əv mi laɪfǀǀ ju a old sed ðɪə
juθǀ wʌn wəd hɑːdlɪ səpoz ðət jɔ aɪ wəz əz ˈstedɪ əz evəǀ

jɛt ju bælənst ən il ɔn ðə ɛndəv jɔ noz| hwʌt med ju so ɔ°flɪ
klɛvʌ|| aɪv ænsəd θri kwɛstʃənz æn ðæt ɪz ɪᵊnʌf| sɛd ɪz faðə|
dont gɪv jɔsɛlf ɛəz|| dju θɪŋk aɪ kən lɪsən ɔl de tʊᵊ sʌtʃ
stʌf|| bi ɔf| ɔr aɪl kɪk jə daʊn stɛəz]

        From "The Mad Gardener's Song," by Lewis Carroll as read
by Cyril Ritchard:
[hi 'θɔt i sɔ æn 'ɛlɪfənt| ðət 'præk͵tɪst ɔn ə faɪf|| hi
lʊkt əgɛn| ænd faʊnd ɪt wəz ə 'lɛtə frəm ɪz ͵waɪf|| ət ͵lɛŋθ
aɪ 'rɪəlaɪz| hi sɛd| ðə 'bɪtənəs əv laɪf|| hi θɔt hi| sɔ ə
'bʌfəloʊ əpɒn ðə 'tʃɪmnɪ ͵pɪs|| hi lʊkt əgɛn ən faʊn ət wəz
hɪz 'sɪstəz 'hʌzbəndz 'nɪs|| ʌn͵lɛs ju lɪv ðɪs 'haʊs| hi sɛd|
͵aɪl ͵sɛn fə ðə pə'lɪs|| hi ͵θɔt hi ͵sɔ ə 'rætl͵snek| ðət
kwɛstʃnd hɪm ɪn grik| hi lʊkt ə'gɛn ənd ͵faʊnd ət wəz ðə 'mɪdl|
əv ͵nɛkst wik|| ðə ͵wʌn θɪŋ aɪ rɪ'grɛt| hi ͵sɛd ɪz ͵ðæt ɪt
'kænɔt 'spik|| hi ͵θɔt hi sɔ ə 'bæŋkəz 'klak dɪ͵sɛndɪŋ frəm ðə
͵bʌs|| hi ͵lʊkt ə'gɛn æn ͵faʊnd ɪt ͵waz ə ͵hɪpə'patə͵mʌs|| ɪf
͵ðɪs ʃʊd ͵ste tʊ 'daɪn| hi ͵sɛd|| ðɛ 'wont bi 'mʌtʃ fər 'ʌs||
hi ͵θɔt hi ͵sɔ ə ͵kæŋgə'ru ðət ͵wɜkt ə 'kafɪ ͵mɪl||| hi ͵lʊkt
ə'gɛn| æn ͵faʊnd ɪt wəz ə 'vɛdʒətəbəl ͵pɪl|| wə aɪ tə ͵swalə
'ðɪs| hi ͵sɛd| aɪ ʃʊd bi 'vɛrɪ ͵ɪl|| hi ͵θɔt hi ͵sɔ ə ͵kotʃ
ən 'fɔə ðət ͵stʊd bi͵saɪd hɪz 'bɛd| hi ͵lʊkt ə'gɛn æn ͵faʊn
ɪt wʌz ə 'bɛə wɪ͵θaʊt ə 'hɛd|| ͵pʊə ͵θɪŋ| hi ͵sɛd| 'pʊə ͵sɪlɪ
͵θɪŋ| ɪts ͵wetɪŋ tʊ bi 'fɛd|| hi 'θɔt hi sɔ ən 'ælbətrɒs ðət
͵flʌtəd raʊnd ðə 'læmp| hi ͵lʊkt ə'gɛn| æn faʊnd ɪt wəz ə
͵pɛnɪ 'pɒstɪdʒ ͵stæmp|| jud ͵bɛst bi ͵gɛtɪŋ 'hom| hi sɛd| ðə
͵naɪts a 'vɛrɪ ͵dæmp|| hi ͵θɔt hi sɔ æn 'ɑːgjumənt| ðət
͵pruvd hi wəz ðə 'pop|| hi lʊkt ͵əgɛn| ən ͵faʊnd ɪt wəz ə
'bar əv ͵matld 'sop|| ə 'fækt ͵so 'drɛd| hi fentlɪ ͵sɛd|
ɛk'stɪŋgwɪʃɪz 'ɔːl ͵hop]

APPENDIX D

Following are some examples of transcription which is narrower than has previously been presented. Illustrations are given of the use of more detailed modifying symbols and of pitch notation. The speech samples are "generalized" as they might be spoken.

Section I--Narrower Transcriptions

A few lines from the Declaration of Independence in a very substandard style:

[wi hol iz truz də bɨr sʌlf ɛvə(d)n͜|| ət ɔmɛˣn ɚ krɛɪːd ikwə(l)|| ət ɛ̈rəndad bəð̆ɛr kretɚ| wɪ sɝn ɪnɛlnəbə raɪs|| ət əmʌŋ nizɚ laɪf| lɪbdɨ͜i| ənə pɚsut ə hæpənəs|| ät ə skjɚ ɪz̠ raɪs gʌm.əns rɪns·tud mʌŋ mɛ̈n| draɪvin ɛ̈r pɑrz frʌm ə kənsɛn ə ð̆ə gʌvɚn(d)|| æt wənvɚ ɛ̃ɪ form ə gʌmən bɪkʌm:strʌktɪv ə dö̆iz ɛ̃nz̠ ɪzə raɪð̆ə pipḷ taldɚ tə balɨ̈ʃt]

A portion of "the seven ages of man" from "As You Like It," by William Shakespeare: (colloquial GA pronunciation)

[ˈʔɒl ð̆ə ˌwɝl(d)z ə ˈstɛjdʒ| ən ˌɒḷə ˌmɛn: n̩ ˈwï̈mən ˌmɪrlɪ˦ ˈp ˈleᴛrz|| ˌð̆ɛj hæ˦y ð̆ɚ ˈɛksəts| ʔən ð̆ɚ ˈɛ̈nt ̂ r̃ænsz|| æ̃n ˈwʌᴛn ˈmæ̃n: hï̈z tᶜʌɪm| plɛ̈ɪz̠ ˌmɛ̈nɨ ˈpɑrts|| hï̈z ˌæks bɹ̩ɪŋ ˌsɛ̈vn- ˈeᴛdʒəz̠|| ʌt ̄ fɝs t̪̩θ̩ɪː nfã̈nt ̄| ˈmjulɪˈn ən ˈpjuk ᶜɪ˦ŋ ɪn(d)ð̆ə ˌnɝsz̠ ˈɑrmz|| æn ˌd̪ð̆ɛˣn d̪ð̆ə ˈ(h)wʌɪnɪŋ ˈskuwəl ˌbɔɪ| wï̈ð̆əz ˌsæ˦tʃəl| n̩ ˌʃʌɪnɪn ˌmɔrnɪŋ ˈfejs| ˈkᶜrijpɪˈŋ lʌɪk ˈsnejəl ʌn ˌwï̈lɪˈŋlɪ tə ˌskuᵛl|| ʔæn ˌd̪ð̆ɛn d̪ð̆ə ˈlʌᴛvɚ|| ˈsajɪŋ laɪk ˈfɝnəˣs| wï̈ð̆ə ˌwowf| ˌbæː ləd ̄| mejd ̄təwï̈z ˌmï̈strəˣs: ˈɑ̈ɪ- ˌbrʌw|| ð̆enə ˈsɒɪldʒɚ| ˌfü̈l əy ˌstrɛjndʒ ˈowð̆z|| æn ˌbɪrdəd lʌɪk ə ˈpᶜɒrd| ˈdʒʌləs ə ˌnɑnɚ ˈsʌdn̩n ˌkwɔː rəl|| ˌsijkᶜɪˈŋ ð̆ə ˌbʌbḷ reᴛpjəˈtᶜeʃən| ivə nɪn d̪ð̆ə ˈkæ˦nəˣnz̩ ˈmaɱ̈θ]

340

From the writings of James Boswell:

[ɪ̃n 'barbərəs‾səsaɪ̯ɫətɪ| sə,pɪrɪ̯⁺jɔ⁺rət̞ɪ' əv 'parts ɪz
əv 'rijəl 'kãnsaɪ̯ᵡ‿kwẽn(t)s|| ‿greɪt strẽŋ(k)θ| ᵓᵃr ‿greɪt
'wɪ̃sdəm| ɪz ə mãtʃ væᶠljə tˢuw ən 'ĩndəᵡ'vɪdʒəwəl̞|| bə'dĩn
‿mᵓᵒr 'paɫ̟ĭʃt‾tᶜãɪmz| ðɛr a:(r) ‿pɪjp| tə duw 'ɛvrɪ̩θrĩŋ fɚ
‿mʌnɪ⁺|| ən d̟ʒ̃ɛn ðɛr ‿ar ə 'nʌmbə rʌv 'ʌ̃ðɚ sə‿pĭ̃rɪ'jɔᵒrət̞ɪzs:|
sʌtʃ əz ‿ðoz ə(v) 'bɝθ ən 'fᵓᵒrtʃən| ən 'rã̃ŋk| ð̟ə 'dɪsə‿peɪ?
mẽ̃z ə'tẽ̞ᵡn(t)ʃən| ã̃n ‿lɪjv́ ‿ŋʌ̃ɤ ‿ɛkstrə'ᵓrdnẽri 'ʃɛr əv
rɪ̃'spɛkt fɚ pɚsn̩| ã̃n(d) ‿ɪnt̞!'ɛkʃəwəl sə‿pɪrə'jɔᵒrət̞ɪᵡ||
ðɪsz waɪ̯zlɪ' 'ɔᵒrdəd‾baɪ 'prɒvədəᵡn̩(t)s| tə prɪ‿zɝv̥ 'sʌm
ɪkᶜ‿walətᶜɪ' ə‿mã̃ŋ ‿mæ̃n'kã̃ɪnd]

Section 2--Pitch Marks

From the writings of Daniel Defoe:

[²ðɛr ⁴a:r ³sʌm ²pip| 'ɪn ðə ²wɝld↗ || ³hu‿→| ³naʊ̯ ²ðeɪ ɚ
'ʌn²pɚtʃt↗| 'ən rɪ²dust:u 'ən ɪ²kwɔlətɪ wɪð ³ʌðɚ 'pip|²↗|
²ænd ʌndɚ ³strɔ:ŋ 'ən ³vɛ²rɪ dʒʌ:st æp'rɪ³hɛn'ʃənz əv ²biɪŋ
³fɝ²ðɚ trited əz ðeɪ dɪ³zɝ:v↗|| 'bɪgɪ³↗ |²wɪð ³i·sa·ps ka:k→|
'tə ³pri·tʃ ʌp:is ²ən ³jun 'jən↗| ²æn ðə ³krɪstʃən ²du·tɪ əv
³ma·də²reɪ'ʃən↘|| 'fɔr ⁴gɛ·'tɪŋ ðət hwən ⁴ðeɪ ³hæd ²ðə 'paʊ²ɚ
ɪn³ ðɛr 'hændz↗ | ³ðɒ̯z greɪsəz 'wɚ ³strɛn²dʒɚz ɪn ðɛr gets↘]

From the writings of Percy Bysshe Shelley:

[²aɪ mɛt ə ³træv²lɚ 'frəm ən ³æntik ²lænd→| hu sɛd→||
³tu: ²væst'n ²trãŋkləs lɛgzə 'stɒn↗| ²stænd ĩn ðə ³dẽzət'↘ ||
³nɪr 'ðɛm↗| ²ɒn 'ðə ²sãnd'↗| ³hæf ²sʌŋk↗|| '·ə ⁴sæt²əd
³vɪ²ɝ̃ɪdʒ laɪz↘| huz fraʊn 'ən²rɪŋk|d lɪp↗| ²ænd ⁴snɪr 'əv
⁴ko:ld 'kəm²ænd↗| tɛl ðət ɪts:kʌlptɚ² wɛl ²ðoz pæsənz rɛd→|
'hwɪtʃ ²jɛt sɝvaɪv→| ³stæmpt ²an ðiz ³laɪfləs' ²θɪŋ·z↘||
'ðə ³hænd 'ðət³ ma·kt² ðɛm↘| 'ænd ðə ³hɑrt' ðət ³fɛd↘||² ænd
³an 'ðə ³pɛd'əstəl↗| ³ði:z²wɝ·dz əprɪr'↘|| ³maɪ nɛm² ɪz
²a·zə³mæn²diəs↘| ²kɪŋ 'əv ³kɪŋz↘|| ²luk əpɒn maɪ wɝks '·ji
maɪ²tɪ↗| 'ən³dɪspɛr²↘|| ²nʌθɪŋ bɪsaɪd rɪmɛnz'↘]

INDEX OF SPEAKERS TRANSCRIBED

INDEX OF SELECTIONS TRANSCRIBED
BY AUTHOR

SUBJECT INDEX

[ɑ], 94–98, 277, 278
  (*See also* Back vowels)
[a], 59, 77, 95
  (*See also* Back vowels)
Abduction, 29
  (*See also* Anatomy)
Abutting consonants, 251
  (*See also* Juncture)
Accent (*see* Dialect; Stress)
Acoustic variables of speech, 259–273
  (*See also* Vocal variety)
Acoustics of speech, 24, 26, 31, 32, 260,
    261, 266–271
  complexity, 266–268
  consonants, 26
  duration, 270, 271
  frequency, 260, 261
  intensity, 269
  vowels, 24, 31–32
Adduction, 29
  (*See also* Anatomy)
[æ], 57–62
  (*See also* Front vowels)
Affricates, 172, 173, 176
  affrication of consonants, 176
  alternate symbols for, 173
  nature of, 172, 173
  (*See also* Stops and affricates)
After-glides, 27
  (*See also* Glides)
Age factors and pitch, 263
  (*See also* Pitch)
[aɪ], 125–128
  (*See also* Diphthongs)
Allophones, 19, 20
  allophonic variations, 20

Allophones, influence of phonetic context
    on, 20
  (*See also* Assimilation)
Alveolar sounds, 34
  (*See also* Articulation)
American dialects, 5–7, 274–278, 286,
    287
Analogy, errors from, 279
Anaptyxis, 283
Anatomy of articulatory mechanism,
    29–41
  abduction, 29
  adduction, 29
  alveolar ridge, 34
  bicuspid, 37
  bony (hard) palate, 34, 36, 37
  canine, 34
  cord tone, 29
  diagram, 30
  glottis, 29
  incisor, 34
  larynx, 29
  lingual structures, 34
  lip formation, 32, 33
  lips, 34, 35
  maxilla, 36
  molar, 34
  nasal passages, 36
  nasopharynx, 36
  palate areas, 37
  palate mechanism, 34
  pharyngeal muscles, 35, 36
  pharynx, 30
  phonation action, 29, 30
  place of articulation, 37–39
  premolar, 34

345

PHONEMES OF AMERICAN SPEECH

Vowels

Front vowels

SYMBOL	KEY	SYMBOL	KEY
[i]	heed [hid]	[u]	who'd [hud]
[ɪ]	hid [hɪd]	[ʊ]	hood [hʊd]
[e]	hayed [hed]	[o]	hoed [hod]
[ɛ]	head [hɛd]	[ɔ]	hawed [hɔd]
[æ]	had [hæd]	[ɑ]	hod [hɑd]

Back vowels

(Back vowels header spans the right two columns above.)

Central vowels

SYMBOL	KEY
[ɝ-ɜ]*	hurt [hɝt]
[ʌ]	hut [hʌt]
[ɚ-ə]*	under [ʌndɚ]
[ə]	about [əbaʊt]

Diphthongs†

SYMBOL	KEY
[aɪ]	file [faɪl]
[aʊ]	fowl [faʊl]
[ɔɪ]	foil [fɔɪl]
[ju]	fuel [fjul]

Consonants

Stops

[p]	pen	[pɛn]
[b]	Ben	[bɛn]
[t]	ten	[tɛn]
[d]	den	[dɛn]
[k]	Kay	[ke]
[g]	gay	[ge]
[tʃ]	chew	[tʃu]
[dʒ]	Jew	[dʒu]

Fricatives

[f]	few	[fju]
[v]	view	[vju]
[θ]	thigh	[θaɪ]
[ð]	thy	[ðaɪ]
[h]	hay	[he]
[s]	say	[se]
[ʃ]	shay	[ʃe]
[z]	bays	[bez]
[ʒ]	beige	[beʒ]

Nasals and lateral

[m]	some	[sʌm]
[n]	sun	[sʌn]
[ŋ]	sung	[sʌŋ]
[l]	lay	[le]

Glides

[w]	way	[we]
[hw]	whey	[hwe]
[j]	yea	[je]
[r]	ray	[re]

* [ɝ] and [ɚ] are the "r-colored" vowels. [ɜ] and [ə] are the pronunciations typical of r vowels in Eastern, Southern, and English speech.

† Does not include the "nondistinctive" and centering diphthongs.